Software Engineering Fundamentals

Software Engineering Fundamentals

ALI BEHFOROOZ

FREDERICK J. HUDSON

Towson State University

New York   Oxford
Oxford University Press
1996

Oxford University Press

Oxford   New York
Athens   Auckland   Bangkok   Bombay
Calcutta   Cape Town   Dar es Salaam   Delhi
Florence   Hong Kong   Istanbul   Karachi
Kuala Lumpur   Madras   Madrid   Melbourne
Mexico City   Nairobi   Paris   Singapore
Taipei   Tokyo   Toronto

and associated companies in

Berlin   Ibadan

Published by Oxford University Press, Inc.,
198 Madison Avenue, New York, New York, 10016-4314

Library of Congress Cataloging-in-Publication Data

Behforooz, Ali, 1942-
    Software engineering fundamentals / Ali Behforooz, Frederick J.
Hudson.
        p.   cm.
    Includes bibliographic references and index.
    ISBN 0-19-510539-7 (cloth)
    1. Software engineering.   I. Hudson, Frederick J.   II. Title.
QA76.758.B44   1996
005.1—dc20   95-35796
                                                             CIP

ISBN: 0-19-510539-7 (cl)

Printing (last digit): 9 8 7 6 5 4 3 2 1

Printed in the United States of America
on acid-free paper

Preface

Software development currently suffers from three major deficiencies: (1) software engineering principles and practices, which should be the backbone of the software development life cycle, are not fully accepted and followed by academia or industry; (2) straightforward, well-established, and universally accepted design standards are lacking for the software development process and for representation of both process and product; and (3) the software development process is empirical in nature and not yet predicated on easily quantified and confirmed mathematical models. The effect of these and other deficiencies has been amplified by the rapid growth in the volume of software being produced and the almost exponential increase in the complexity of the problems now being solved with software. In spite of the need for a strongly structured approach to software development, in many organizations software development is still basically a freestyle event.

There are other deficiencies in the software development process that many may feel are more important than those just cited. We feel strongly that the three we have cited are the root cause of many failed software developments. We do not offer another "silver bullet." We do, however, offer the reader, interested in entering the software development field, a realistic preparation for the new software engineering environment. The purpose of this book is to prepare the entry-level software engineer with a comprehensive picture of the roles and responsibilities of a software engineer in a variety of software development settings.

Specifically, we offer the following: (1) recognition that software development is usually embedded in a system development and as a consequence expands a software engineer's responsibilities beyond the software product; (2) recognition that a software engineer must behave more like a system engineer than a hardware engineer; (3) provision of a simple, comprehensive, and understandable model of the system and software development process; (4) provision of models, templates, outlines, tables of contents, and other guidelines extracted from DOD,* NASA,* IEEE,* and various corporate sources to assist the beginning software engineer in understanding what is expected in each of the software engineer's products and why it is needed; (5) a mental image of a successful development process and how application of software engineering principles and practices contribute to that success; and (6) an emphasis on the importance of planning and the software engineer's responsibility in preparing the software development plan and participating in the development of other plans. Our treatment of items 1, 2, 3, and 6 are quite different from the treatment found in current software engineering textbooks.

The overall objective of this book is to give the reader a sense of the flow of events in an integrated system and software development effort, and appreciation for and understanding of the software engineer's role in the system development process, and a comprehensive preparation for assuming the responsibilities of a software engineer. We have also defined the following five fundamental objectives for our book: (1) motivating readers with limited application experience by using realistic examples from recent experience and examining future directions for the discipline; (2) organizing and presenting material in such a way that the experienced practitioner will find it an accurate portrayal of the real-world of software development; (3) developing a bridge from theory to practice in specific topics of interest to software engineers; (4) providing an algorithmic approach to each task or process carried out by a software engineer; and (5) providing a firm foundation upon which the reader can build.

The central theme in this book is that software development when reduced to its essential elements can be explained in simple terms, the product characterized quantitatively, and the development carried out using standard engineering principles and practices based on the scientific method. The better we understand the system development life cycle, software development life cycle, and software engineering, the more likely that software development will become a predictable process and progress can be made toward eliminating many of its current ills.

We have written this book as much for ourselves as for our students. Drafts of this book have been our handbook for teaching, consulting, and research. Many of our students are themselves experienced software engineers and have influenced the material we present in this book. To them we owe a debt.

The majority of students graduating from a computer science program will be involved in software development in one form or another. Some will enter development environments where software is "hacked out." Others will join organizations that follow a rigid software development discipline. The former group will not, at first, notice an appreciable difference between school and work environments; both involve small projects characterized by emphasis on get it finished, get it working, and get on to the next assignment. For these persons the book will help in understanding an alternate lifestyle, and perhaps some of the ideas expressed herein will be useful. For the latter group the book is an excellent introduction and primer in the relatively new field of software engineering.

....
* DOD = Department of Defense; NASA = National Aeronautics and Space Administration; IEEE = The Institute of Electrical and Electronics Engineers.

ORGANIZATION OF THE BOOK ■

The book is organized into five units and a set of four appendices. The five units are the following: Introduction, Analysis and Design, Implementation and Maintenance, Software Metrics or Attributes, and Special Topics. This organization coincides with the natural progression in a software development process.

Unit 1 (Introduction) consists of chapters 1, 2, and 3. Chapter 1 describes systems, particularly large information systems, in a way that is useful to software engineers. This utility stems from (1) the need for a software engineer to know and understand external (to the software) interfaces and (2) the fact that a software engineer is often expected to be an active participant in a system development before software requirements have even been identified. Chapter 1 also describes system and software development life cycles; shows the relationship between a system development life cycle and a software development life cycle; and describes the activities and responsibilities of system engineers, system analysts, and software engineers within the framework of a system/software development environment.

Chapter 2 provides a description in narrative form of how two different information system projects originated and got underway. The reader can easily appreciate what is expected of a software engineer in these two projects. Chapter 2 also conveys a sense of how major information system developments are organized and a general appreciation of how the request-for-proposal process works.

Chapter 3 addresses the technical planning associated with developing a software product. A software development plan (SDP) outline similar in many respects to the IEEE, ANSI,* and DOD standards is employed as the model. Three significant ideas are introduced in this chapter. The first idea suggests a team or workshop approach to the planning task. The second idea suggests the use of the product of the planning effort, the SDP, as an agenda for regularly scheduled software development team meetings. The third idea is that a software development plan represents a corporate and team commitment.

Unit 2 (Analysis and Design) consists of chapters 4, 5, 6, 7, and 8. Chapter 4 provides full discussion of a table of contents for an SRS and works out two illustrative examples. Chapter 5 describes a few of the available tools that can assist in both requirement and design specification.

Chapter 6 describes software development environment and platform and CASE tools. Software development environments could be viewed as the machine tools of software production. In many instances these tools also support the development and test of software specifications.

Chapter 7 discusses the software design process independent of any specific design methodology or tool. A generic design process is described in some detail and specific, systematic, step-by-step guidance is offered for developing a software design.

Chapter 8 is devoted to a discussion of object-oriented analysis and design tools and methodology that have recently captured the attention of software developers. Object-oriented analysis and design methodology attempts to capture both software requirements specification and software design specification.

Unit 3 (Implementation and Maintenance) consists of chapters 9, 10, 11, 12, and 13.

....
* ANSI = American National Standards Institute.

Chapter 9 classifies and describes programming languages from a software engineering point of view and defines some of the important terminology. The specific features of programming languages that are essential aids to the coder or programmer are described. Criteria for selecting a programming language for a specific application are considered. Programming style is discussed and 28 simple rules whose application will lead to developing a good programming style are presented. Although coding is only a small part of the software development life cycle, the quality of the code can exert a strong influence on its testing, debugging, maintenance, and maintainability.

Chapter 10 treats testing in the broadest context. The purpose is to show the complete setting within which software is ultimately tested for acceptance. This test environment will typically include all elements of the operational environment, hardware, software, people, operational timelines, etc. The chapter emphasizes the importance of planning in the test process and describes how a test plan is constructed.

Chapter 11 addresses the module level test process. The chapter considers static and dynamic testing, white and black box testing, and cyclomatic complexity as important tools in effective module testing. An approach that uses cyclomatic complexity and basis paths to find the minimum number of independent paths through a module and then uses black box testing techniques to complete white box tests is described in chapter 11. Formal testing methods are also discussed in chapter 11 and several examples are worked out.

Chapter 12 discusses a systematic procedure for isolating, identifying, and confirming the fault that caused the failure during module test, system test, or during field operation. Chapter 13 addresses software maintenance and maintainability issues. A great deal of a software engineer's time is spent either maintaining an existing software product or developing a software product so that it may be easily maintained in its operational phase.

Unit 4 (Software Metrics or Attributes) consists of chapters 14, 15, 16, 17, and 18. Chapter 14 categorizes and describes a number of software attributes and offers suggestions as to how they might be quantified and measured. Unfortunately there is no National Institute of Standards and Technology to whom we may appeal for the precise definition of key terms used in estimating and evaluating software attributes.

Chapter 15 suggests that perhaps the reason that many software products have taken so much longer and have cost so much more than originally estimated is not entirely due to poor control and management of the software development process but due, at least in part, to inability to estimate software product size accurately and forecast resources and time required to develop the software product. Chapter 15 provides a simple procedure for estimating the resources and time required to completely develop a software product.

Chapter 16 describes a flexible methodology for estimating software development risk and establishing a risk containment plan. A major component of the risk containment plan is the periodic measurement and evaluation of certain software attributes. The generic term for this process is *technical performance measurements*. Technical performance measurements are the means by which certain software attributes are used as indicators to recognize impending development problems.

Chapter 17 is devoted to the discussion of software reliability and availability. A software reliability model chosen from among many available ones is described in this chapter. It has been shown that the reliability model can be used effectively in testing and maintainability planning, performance evaluation, and, in conjunction with hardware reliability, to estimate overall system reliability for a given operating period. Design rules that, if followed, will lead to more reliable software products are discussed in this chapter.

Chapter 18 is devoted to software quality and quality assurance. It has been clearly established that software quality assurance measures, when properly carried out, significantly increase software quality.

Unit 5 (Special Topics) addresses two topics that are of increasing concern in software engineering, real-time software design (chapter 19) and human factors in software engineering (chapter 20). Chapter 19 identifies a key concern in the development of real-time software, the schedulability of tasks. In software products designed to meet real-time requirements, tasks must be scheduled to execute within specific time windows. This requirement, of course, implies that task execution times are known. Chapter 19 also offers some guidance as to how to estimate task execution times.

Chapter 20 discusses human factors in software engineering. The chapter first provides some background as prelude to discussion of the human computer interface (HCI). Throughout the book there has been an emphasis on the fact that the operator is an important component of any system. The fact that nearly half of the source lines of code in a typical software product are devoted to the human-to-computer interface certainly bears that out.

Appendix A emphasizes planning as a critical step in improving one's communication skills. A useful planning tool, the storyboard, is described. Some hints as to how to make better oral presentations are provided. Effectiveness in participating in or conducting meetings is discussed. The importance and utility of maintaining a software engineer's notebook is considered. Participating in design reviews, often a major activity in a software engineer's career, is discussed. Finally, listening skills are discussed, and it is emphasized that listening is part of the communication process. Appendix B provides a brief overview of how a cost-benefit analysis is conducted. An example is provided to convey the important points. Appendix C describes a simple trade-off study approach whose main value lies in its simplicity and its self-documenting features. The central theme in Appendix C is that every important decision should be made using an objective decision-making procedure, and the rationale for the decision reached should be documented. Appendix D describes the variety of reviews that are conducted during a software development and describes the roles of the participants.

THE EXPECTED READERSHIP PREPARATION   ■

In our view, it is very helpful, but not mandatory, that the readers of this book have the following preparation: (1) extensive experience at the undergraduate level with problem solving and algorithm development; (2) some understanding of the business and technical management problems and issues (the key management concepts needed by software engineers are discussed in the book); (3) at least one year of college mathematics and some familiarity with the fundamentals of mathematics and logic, in particular, the deductive and inductive proof process; and (4) an understanding of the fundamental ideas in probability and statistics.

HOW TO USE THIS BOOK ■

The authors have used this book for one-semester undergraduate courses, for two-semester graduate courses, and for professional development courses. We believe our book may be used in any one of the following settings:

1. For a one-semester overview course at the undergraduate or first-year graduate level. For this audience we recommend that chapters 1 through 14 be covered in some detail. A semester long team project may be assigned to perform a requirements analysis on an SRS and develop an SDS for a moderately complex software product (a component of one of the case studies described in chapter 2, for example).

2. For a one-semester course at the undergraduate level with a programming language as adjunct to the course. That is, for courses like ''Software Engineering Using XXX.'' For this audience we would recommend covering chapters 1 through 7 and chapters 13 and 14 in some detail. Topics in chapters 8, 9, 10, 11, and 12 may be covered within the context of the programming language XXX. We have successfully used a draft of chapters 1–7, 13, and 14 of the book and the Ada language for just such a course. However, we do not recommend that a course in software engineering be coupled to a specific language.

3. For a two-semester in-depth course in software engineering. For this audience the entire book should be covered and a team project assigned. The project should include estimation of software parameters as well as planning, scheduling, designing, testing, reviewing, and maintenance issues for development of a specific software product.

ACKNOWLEDGEMENT ■

We would like to acknowledge the implicit contributions to this book of those colleagues who pioneered along with us in applying an engineering approach to specifying, designing, coding and testing high performance software products in the late 1950s and early 1960s. Especially we would like to recognize the contributions of Bob Orrange, Ed Smythe, Bob Wasek, Nancy LaRue, Bob Poupard, Jerry Donovan, Jim Medlock, Bill Carson, Bill Budurka and Keith Schonrock of the old IBM Federal Systems Division. We also thank our students, staff and fellow faculty at Towson State University for their patience, persistence, and good humor.

It is a rare event indeed when a practitioner of system and software engineering with 35 years of field experience; and an accomplished academician from the field of computer science form an alliance and write a book that attempts to capture the essentials of software engineering from both a practitioner's standpoint and a theoretical viewpoint. Moreover, we have made it our first priority in our software engineering courses to prepare our students for their interviews and for their first job assignment. While we felt confident that our approaches were sound, we needed confirmation. We gratefully acknowledge those graduates who took the time to return to campus and tell us what worked and what didn't work and to discuss their interview and work experiences with the next generation of students. We also acknowledge the contributions of the many practitioners whom we consulted for advice. Also, we are indebted to those professors who took time to review the manuscript and provide us with feedback: David Rine, James Cross, and a host of anonymous reviewers.

A. Behforooz
F. Hudson
January 1996

Contents

UNIT 1

Introduction

1
Overview of System and Software Development Life
Cycles . . . 5

3

Technical Planning . . . 76

UNIT 2

Analysis and Design

4

Software Specifications and Requirements Analysis . . . 107

5
Software Specification Tools . . . 147

6
Software Development Environment . . . 185

7
Software Design . . . 204

8
Object-Oriented Analysis and Design . . . 231

UNIT **3**

Implementation and Maintenance

9

Fundamentals of Coding . . . 266

10

Software System Test and Integration . . . 298

11

Module Level Testing . . . 324

UNIT **4**

Software Metrics or Attributes

16

Software Development Risk Assessment and
Containment . . . 467

17

Reliability . . . 487

18
Software Quality and Quality Assurance . . . 537

UNIT 5

Special Topics

19
Real-Time Software . . . 559

20
Human Factors in Software Engineering . . . 584

Appendixes

A
Communication Skills . . . 601

B
Cost-Benefit Analysis . . . 618

C
Decisions and Trade-Offs . . . 626

D
Reviews . . . 637

Software Engineering Fundamentals

U N I T

Introduction

New arrivals (particularly computer science graduates) to a software development team are often not fully aware that a software product is a component of what is usually a complex system of hardware, people, software, and procedures. Many of these new-comers are also a little vague on just what constitutes an integrated system and software development process. Almost all of us have a blind spot when it comes to planning. Software engineers, as well as most others, feel that planning is something that someone else, management probably, does. The purpose of Unit 1 is to provide an overview of system development and its many interfaces with software development. A general description of the software development process and how a software product development might be initiated is provided in Unit 1 as well as a description of the software development planning activity.

Chapter 1 describes systems, in particular large information systems, in a way that is useful to software engineers. This utility stems from (1) the need for a software engineer to understand interfaces that are external to the software and (2) the fact that a software engineer is often expected to be an active participant in a system development before software requirements have even been identified. Chapter 1 also describes system and software development life cycles; shows the relationship between a system development life cycle and a software development life cycle; and describes the activities and responsibilities of system engineers, system analysts, and software engineers within the framework of a system/software development environment.

Readers who have completed a course in system analysis and design will find chapter 1 a comprehensive overview of that course material. Practitioners will also identify with much of the material covered in the first chapter. As a note to instructors, even if chapter 1 is not covered in detail, it is strongly recommended that chapter 1 be assigned as supplemental reading. It is important that the student be exposed to this point of view before moving on to other material.

Chapter 2 provides a description in narrative form of how two different information system projects originated and got underway. The reader can easily appreciate what is expected of a software engineer in these two projects. Chapter 2 also conveys a sense of how major information system developments are organized and a general apprecia- tion of how the request-for-proposal process works. Chapter 2 provides material for many exercises and examples throughout the remainder of the book. Also, segments of the case studies in chapter 2 may be used for semester-long team projects.

Chapter 3 addresses the technical planning associated with developing a software product. A software development plan (SDP) outline similar in many respects to the IEEE, ANSI, and DOD standards is employed as the model. Three significant ideas are introduced in this chapter. The first idea suggests a team or workshop approach to the planning task. The second idea suggests the use of the product of the planning effort, the SDP, as an agenda for regularly scheduled software development team meetings. The third idea is that a software development plan represents a corporate and team commitment. The discussion of planning is valuable on two counts. The first as an illustration of what a software engineer does during the software development cycle and the second as a catalogue of the tasks that constitute a software development pro- cess.

Overview of System and Software Development Life Cycles

1.0 OBJECTIVES ■

Chapter 1 has four primary objectives. The first is to demonstrate that the software development process, and for that matter, software engineering is part of a larger and more comprehensive activity called system development. To regard software engineering as an independent process is inappropriate and misleading. The second is to substantiate the need for a software engineer to transcend the traditional programmer role and participate, willingly and strongly, in both the technical and planning activities that precede development of software requirements. The third is to depict the setting, a system development, in which software acquisition and development (and, of course, hardware acquisition and development) is typically embedded. The fourth is to acquaint the reader with the essential features of the software engineering process.

1.1   INTRODUCTION ■

System development is an iterative team-oriented process beginning with the definition of system needs and ending with a product that is supposed to perform specific tasks to a predefined degree of precision and accuracy for a predefined length of time. Systems of interest to this book all have a major component that we call the *software subsystem*. In this chapter, a general overview of the system development life cycle is given. The software development life cycle is presented within that setting. Some of the terminology commonly used in system analysis and design are defined in this chapter.

Software development is not a disjoint activity in the system development process. A key factor in the success of any system development team is the involvement and the cooperation of system analysts and software engineers throughout the development life cycle. There is no point in the system development life cycle where the job of the system analyst is finished and the job of the software engineer begins. On the contrary, software development is embedded within the system development process. Software engineers and system analysts must be fully involved in every phase of the system development life cycle. This approach has been the mark of successful system and software developments.

1.2   SYSTEMS: DEFINITION AND DISCUSSION ■

A useful definition for *system* may be derived from the following: ''A system is a collection of related, interacting subsystems combined or organized in such a fashion as to be responsive to external stimuli and the influences and constraints of its environment, to accomplish a general or specific purpose.''

This definition covers biological, financial, manufacturing, medical, legal, government, and other systems. However, Figure 1.1 schematically illustrates the kind of systems considered in this book. Systems of this kind accept their inputs from an external point called a *source*, perform operations that transform inputs into outputs, and send their outputs to an external destination called a *sink*. The hardware/software subsystem most often consists of the following: sensors, S, with which input data are collected; a processing element, P, that processes data obtained from sensors into information; and actuators, A, that are controlled or driven by information distilled from inputs. Other components of the system include people, training, documentation, and maintenance. Every system discussed in this book fits this narrower definition. Systems shown in Figure 1.1 are called information systems.

1.2.1   System Characteristics

Synergism

There is an enhancement to function and performance capability of a system that transcends contributions of the individual subsystems that makes up the system. This effect is sometimes referred to as *synergism*. For example, consider a personal transportation system used for transporting a specified number of individuals and their luggage from point A to point B. This system might include such subsystems as vehicles, road networks, service stations, and

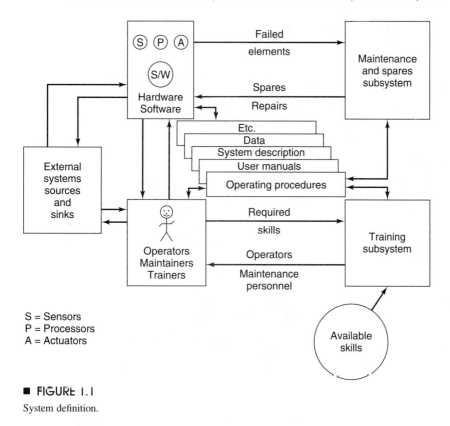

■ FIGURE 1.1

System definition.

traffic management control. No individual subsystem of this set could by itself provide the capability to transport people and their luggage from point A to point B as specified. The synergism comes from the manner in which the system is structured. The interactions and relationships among the subsystems create the synergism.

Adaptability

Systems are dynamic; that is, they grow and change. Many of the systems considered in this book have a 20-to-30-year lifetime during which the system will change dramatically due to changing technology, environment, and functional needs. An important property of a system is its ability to adapt or be adapted to these changes. The more specialized the system, the less adaptable it is to changing circumstances and environment. The larger the system, the more of its own resources must be devoted to its everyday maintenance.

Compromise

A system design is a compromise among many frequently conflicting requirements and desires. A system may not, in general, be an optimum solution for satisfaction of all requirements.

1.2.2 Recurring Problems and Suggested Solutions in Large System Developments

The importance to the software engineer of understanding systems and system development are many. Virtually any software product is a subsystem of a larger system. Software itself can be thought of as a system; software development, the software engineer's domain, is an integral part of some system development. Software engineering has much in common with system engineering, more so than with hardware engineering. The reason is that many system requirements are met directly through software. Many of the problems and concerns associated with the development of systems have their counterpart in software development. Finally, software is intrinsic to the satisfaction of user interfaces requirements.

Software engineers have implicit as well as explicit responsibilities that transcend software development issues and problems. They are responsible for providing software sizing, cost, schedule, and risk estimates, all of which are part of a larger system picture. The software development and system development processes should be carefully coordinated. The software engineer must always integrate his or her efforts with those of the system analyst and system engineer.

Major Problems in System Development

A list of some problems and concerns that are frequently associated with the development of large systems follows:

1. Development Time Problem: Some large systems take so long to develop that the technology (computers, software, and other hardware components) goes through a generation change between the time the system is first conceptualized and the time it is ready for delivery to the user. In some cases, system needs change so drastically during the course of system development that the problem the system was originally designed to solve no longer exists or has changed so fundamentally that the system design is no longer germane. This situation can lead to a very exciting and dynamic system development process or, in the worst case, delivery of a system designed to meet outdated needs.

2. System User Interface Problem: The system user interface (or as it is sometimes called, the man-machine interface) and associated operational procedures are frequently neglected during initial system design efforts. The impact on the system development process is the discovery, late in the development process, that a large number of new displays and controls must be added. These additions frequently require additional hardware as well as software.

3. Test and Integration Problem: In the hectic system design activity, we often find that insufficient thought is given to how the system will be integrated, tested at all levels, and finally sold off to the customer or client.

4. Maintenance Problem: System maintenance concerns frequently get short shrift during the system design phase. This problem is not surprising since the pressure, at this point in the development, is on achieving short-term goals, and the operation/maintenance phase is far down the road. However, most large systems will be in their operation/maintenance phase for a much longer time than they are in the development phase: they will experience many technology changes, many changes in functional and performance requirements, and many generations of users.

5. Lack of Common Purpose Problem: Last and certainly not the least of problems with large systems is the fact that the contractor, the builder of the system, does not always share mutual goals with the procuring agency, and the procuring agency is often not the operator or user of the system.

Suggested Solutions

The following are offered as possible solutions for the problems and concerns that are commonly associated with the development of large systems:

1. Development Time Solution: This problem can be overcome to some extent by postponing technology decisions for as long as possible or by shortening the system development cycle in some way. Unfortunately the system development "culture" often demands that commitment to detail designs be made early in the system development cycle. Those making the financial decisions frequently insist on detailed insights into the design and detail cost estimates based on those designs, which in turn may require immediate technology decisions. Technology decisions usually turn on maturity issues. For example, a project manager is reluctant to risk his or her career pioneering a new untried technology. This conservatism can lead to delivery of technologically obsolete systems. Of course, using existing hardware and software, wherever possible, can reduce development time. Major stumbling blocks to using off-the-shelf software and hardware are the lack of truly uniform standards for both software and hardware functions, interfaces, and performance. Phased development is yet another approach. In phased development, the system is specified, designed, developed, and installed in segments. This approach has proven effective in certain business information systems.

2. System User Interface Solution: Problems can be prevented by taking into account, through operational timelines,* how users and operators will actually use the system and make the operator/user community an intrinsic part of the requirements formulation and initial design process.

3. Test and Integration Solution: Problems can be avoided by assigning a member of the system team, preferably someone with testing experience, responsibility for defining a comprehensive test program, especially acceptance testing, as soon as an initial conceptual design is in place. Obtaining agreements with the client as to what constitutes acceptance of the new system is a critically important part of this effort.

4. Maintenance Solution: Problems may be resolved by designing a system to accommodate these expected changes. Such design circumvents problems in replacement parts, additional computing capacity, and adding faster and more accurate hardware components. When these concerns can be factored into system design, the system has a better chance of performing effectively throughout its life cycle.

5. Lack of Common Purpose Solution: Robert Orrange [8] once described the system engineer's main responsibility as being the client's and user's advocate in the contractor's plant and the contractor's advocate while in the client's plant. This is not a bad personal guideline or code of conduct for a system analyst/designer or system (or software) engineer. The system engineer can frequently use his or her credibility with both parties to coach them

---

* Ordered sequence of steps required to execute a specific system function.

into recognizing that there is a mutual benefit that derives from cooperatively putting an effective system on line.

1.2.3   System Engineering

The word *engineer* is defined in *Webster's New World Dictionary* as "to arrange, manage or carry through by skillful or artful contrivance," and *engineering* as "the art or science of making practical application of the knowledge of pure sciences such as physics, chemistry, biology, etc."

System engineering is the application of engineering to the design and development of systems. A system engineer or system analyst typically performs the following technical tasks:

1. Thoroughly analyzes the problem to arrive at a set of established needs.
2. Develops an architecture or a structure and a conceptual design for the system from a set of firmly established needs.
3. Specifies system boundaries and constraints and develops a detailed description of system's inputs, outputs, and/or interfaces.
4. Defines functions to be performed by the system and parameters by which system performance can be measured.
5. Establishes a range of system performance values from optimum to unacceptable. These performance measures will then find their way into various specifications and acceptance tests and will provide performance goals for subsystem designers. Optimum performance may never be achieved by the design team, but knowing and understanding what optimum performance is can be valuable information in making design decisions.
6. Defines the internal structure of the system, identifies what can and cannot change, and determines the system-dependent and independent variables, especially performance-critical variables.
7. Develops mathematical models to support objective evaluations of system performance. These models are then used in simulations to aid in evaluating alternate designs and devising design strategies for achieving functional and performance requirements.
8. Makes objective technical decisions based on firmly established and weighted evaluation criteria and also a fair assessment of all viable alternatives.
9. Decomposes or partitions the system into logical, integrable elements or subsystems.
10. Participates in the process whereby the system is developed, built, tested, integrated, verified, delivered, and installed.
11. Uses physical performance results as they become available throughout the process to modify system and subsystem models and simulations to achieve higher levels of system understanding.

There are other equally important technical tasks performed by the system engineer that are associated with planning and development aspects of a project. These include (1) preparing the project plan with the help of a number of others, including a scheduling specialist; (2) identifying risks and developing contingency plans; (3) determining required system reliability and availability; and (4) preparing system development cost estimates and performing cost-benefit analyses.

A system engineer or system analyst must recognize the importance of the following to the success of a system development:

1. The level of detail and the accuracy of the interface description are critically important in establishing clear boundaries and constraints and developing both baseline designs* and system acceptance criteria. Contractual agreements frequently include specific interface details as well as function and performance requirements.
2. Throughout the system design process, emphasis should be on objective decision making. The best design solutions are selected by means of objective comparisons made using models, prototypes, and analyses and based on predetermined performance and decision criteria.
3. Partitioning criteria should lead to independent (cohesive) elements with a low degree of coupling among the elements. Moreover, these elements should be easily reassembled during integration and system testing.

A system function and performance specification (or requirements) should be partitioned and allocated by the system engineer to individual subsystems in such a way that system functions and performance requirements can be easily traced to subsystem implementations.

1.2.4   System Analysis

The *Webster New World Dictionary* defines *analysis* as "the breaking up of any whole so as to find out their nature, function, etc. A statement of these findings." It defines *design* as "to make preliminary sketches of; to sketch a pattern or outline for; plan. To plan and carry out especially by artistic arrangement or in a skillful way." Paul Licker [6] characterizes system analysis and design (and his description applies equally well to system engineering) as a set of techniques and processes, a community of interest, a culture, and an intellectual orientation.

The tasks performed by system engineers (for more technical systems) and by system analysts (for more business-oriented systems) are similar and include the following: (1) understanding the application, (2) planning, (3) scheduling, (4) developing candidate solutions, (5) performing trade studies, (6) performing cost-benefit analysis, (7) recommending alternative solutions, (8) writing requirement specifications, (9) selling off the system, (10) supervising installation, and (11) maintaining the system. The main differences, aside from the nature of the application areas, are usually in project size, number and formality of reviews, and documentation volume. This view is consistent with that of current system analysis and design literature [9, 10].

Some of the tasks performed by the system analyst/designer are the same as those performed by the software engineer. The distinction between the role of the system analyst/designer and the software engineer is not always perfectly clear. There is some overlap in responsibility that must be resolved on a case-by-case basis.

System analysis involves the study of an application area to fully understand the problem being posed. This study includes interviews, observations, hands-on experience, consultations, and many other forms of data gathering. Activities are focused on developing a comprehensive knowledge of the existing system, its strengths and its weaknesses, and the underlying reasons for the need to restructure, replace, or automate the existing system. The analyst produces a problem statement as a result of this activity.

....

* Baseline design is a current approved design configuration as represented by an appropriate, to the design methodology, depiction in graphic and text.

Subsequently, a system analyst develops candidate solutions to the problem. This activity may require developing system-level architecture and implementation-free design and conceptually partitioning the solution into separate components. While implementation-free designs may seem a contradiction, the analyst must at first focus on characterizing solutions in terms of what functions are to be performed rather than how a function is to be implemented. Realistically, however, an analyst does need to develop a physical design to verify that specified functions can be implemented. For example, specifying response times or computations that cannot be implemented is counterproductive. By preparing a physical implementation, the analyst can confirm that there exists at least one solution to the specification. Functions are expected to be partitioned and allocated without implementation implications. However, allocating function among hardware, software, and personnel would, on the surface, seem to dictate an architecture or form of implementation. The system analyst produces feasibility studies showing operational and technical feasibility along with an economic feasibility (a summary of cost-benefit analysis results). Risk assessments and perhaps risk containment plans, cost estimation, schedules, and plans for the remainder of the development are results usually prepared by the system analyst as a by-product of system analysis.

1.2.5 System Architecture and Design

A preliminary step in system design involves the development of a structure or architecture for the system. This initial step in the system design process establishes, usually from several options, the underlying structure of the system. A simple example might be selecting, after extensive study and trade-off analysis, a decentralized architecture for a spare-parts distribution system instead of a centralized architecture.

The dictionary definition of the word *design* would lead one to believe that design is an ongoing process that began at project inception. However, conventional use of the word *design* in system and software development means that system design begins when attention shifts from what is to be built to how it is to be built.

The active involvement of software engineers during the system design phase is essential to the success of the system. Such active involvement begins with attending meetings with users, reading preliminary documentation, and participating in system level reviews and walkthroughs. This approach helps the software engineer develop a deeper understanding of the system, the operators, the users, and other team members. The software engineer can be involved in prototyping efforts, if prototyping is needed. The prototyping referred to here is the development of a physical model of a critical portion of the system to confirm that a particular requirement, usually a performance critical requirement, can be met.

If the software engineer is well versed in the application area, he or she might become a member of the team writing the software function and performance specifications. Before that task, the software engineer might be involved in the allocation of system function and performance requirements to various subsystems. In addition, the software engineer may participate in system architecture development and in studies leading to system design decisions. The most significant contributions, however, can lie in the questions asked, issues raised, and problems identified while the software function and performance specification is being written. As an example, detail questions regarding the characteristics of input parameters that are important to software design, such as rates, protocols, message structures, verifications, and security, can often force system engineers and analysts to penetrate to a deeper level of understanding and consequently produce a *better overall design*.

In summary, the system design process is complete when (1) a system architecture is in place, (2) all system functions are defined, (3) performance parameters are established, and (4) function and performance are allocated to hardware, software, and operator personnel. Hardware, software, and operator allocations are further partitioned to be consistent with system architecture and conceptual designs. For example, a radar subsystem allocated the functions to search, locate, and track might suballocate the function to a transmitter, a receiver, a computer/software subsystem, and an operator. A software subsystem suballocation might be to an operating system and several application packages, each of which might be regarded as a separate software subsystem.

1.3   SYSTEM-LEVEL PROJECT PLANNING   ■

Whenever a system development project is initiated, there is an associated planning effort. The quality of this planning effort often plays an important role in the success or failure of the project. There are different types of project planning methods. One project planning method that has been tried successfully in many situations is the *workshop planning approach.* This approach is related to the concurrent engineering concept [4, 10]. The idea behind the workshop planning approach is to call together representatives of various organizations that will, at some point, participate in the project development process and have them jointly prepare the project or program plan. In large system and software projects, a wide range of specialists would be expected to participate in the project planning. There might be one or more specialists involved from each of the following areas: application, operations, software engineering, human factors, reliability, testing, finance, configuration control, and the project management office.

Table 1.1 presents a table of contents for a system-level development plan. The reader will note that virtually every section of the system-level project plan either requires help from the software engineer to write or contains valuable information that dictates controls and constraints on software development.

Specific questions to be answered by the project plan are as follows: (1) What is to be produced for delivery? (2) What tasks must be accomplished? (3) When must these tasks be started and completed? (4) What is the order in which these tasks must be accomplished? (5) What are the task dependencies? (6) What are the criteria for acceptance of the end product? (7) Who will perform the tasks that are required to produce the deliverable items? and (8) How, specifically, will these tasks be performed? These are not easy questions even for a simple project and they can be very difficult questions to answer if resources and schedules are limited.

A major advantage in using the workshop approach to planning is that all participants in the project are represented at the initial planning phase and may contribute to the plan. Other advantages of using the workshop method are (1) establishing good communication links and personal contacts, (2) drawing from a greater pool of experience, and (3) creating a sense of ownership, once the plan is in place. When the workshop approach is used, there is a much greater sense of commitment to the plan than if it had been prepared by a small cadre and then imposed on development team members. In many highly structured system developments, one finds among the deliverable items a project plan, a management plan, a hardware development plan, a software development plan, and a safety plan. These subordinate plans

■ TABLE 1.1   **Contents of System-Level Development Plan**

I. Document scope
II. System description
  Describe system, super system, and interfaces
  Itemize deliverable products
III. Contract description
  Description of contractual commitments
  Essential features of contract
IV. Project organization
  Performing organizations and their responsibilities
V. Work breakdown structure
  Related to project organization
  Related to product
VI. Resource profile
  Supporting information by organizational unit
VII. Schedules
  Schedule for each deliverable product
  Schedule for each major task
VIII. Technical reviews (walk-throughs, audits)
  Schedule for all associated products
  Pass/fail criteria
IX. Risk management
  Technical performance parameters identified
  Scheduled reviews
  Technical performance reviews
X. Action assignment and management
  Assignment, tracking, and closure method
XI. Management
  Identification of control board structure
  Rules and regulations
XII. Standards, procedures, and processes to be used on this project

are simply refinements or extensions to the system project plan. Much effort can be saved if all these plans are well coordinated and make reference to each other where appropriate. This task is, of course, much easier if the project plan has been developed in a workshop environment.

Some disadvantages of the workshop approach are as follows: (1) more people must be brought up the project learning curve faster, (2) key people are required to dedicate a significant amount of time to a planning activity, and (3) there is naturally more likely to be debate and discussion with a large planning team over plan specifics. It is important to understand that a software engineer should be an active participant in the planning activities and a major contributor to every decision regarding the software development process.

Regardless of the planning method used, a good development plan should begin with an overview of the total project and list deliverable products with references for additional information. This overview should be followed by a comprehensive description of each product including tools and facilities required for the development. The system-level planning workshop should establish schedule constraints on software products that are needed to support hardware development, training, and testing plans as well as software product delivery.

1.3.1   System Development Plan

One often hears the question, ''Why should we plan while things are continuously changing?'' Change is precisely why we must plan. To think that there won't or shouldn't be any changes is absurd. A good system (or software) development plan must successfully accommodate change. The effort that goes into planning should enable a project to get a good start. To keep the plan current and at the same time gain maximum benefit from the planning effort, the system development plan should be an agenda item for system development team meetings. By reviewing each element of the plan regularly for changes, progress, and problems, the team can modify the plan to reflect project dynamics. Like all other aspects of system or software development efforts, planning is an iterative activity. Unexpected problems will arise, and external changes will occur that call for plan revisions.

Planning is a critically important step in any successful venture, particularly for system and software development. Moreover, planning is something that most of us do not like to do. Patience, discipline, and hard work are required to plan out a system or software development to the level of detail needed to assure success. Once implemented, dedication, courage, and discipline are necessary in following the plan, particularly in the face of adversity.

System engineers (or system analysts) cannot be expected to be technical experts in every field. However, they should have a good grasp of the important fundamental principles in many technical areas. The system engineer must identify and recognize specific technical problems and bring the appropriate expertise to bear on them at the appropriate time. The most important time to employ these technical consultants is during the planning phase when formal project plans are first being developed.

Representatives from the software development world should be brought into the project at its inception. In many instances, the experience and wisdom of the software development world can be focused effectively on system level problems. Valuable advice and counsel as to what functions might logically be allocated to software could be provided by a person knowledgeable in software. Identification of specific risk areas in software, developing software sizing estimates, software cost estimates, software reliability estimates, and software development schedule estimates are clearly software-oriented tasks that are best performed by someone with software-related knowledge. This information is needed during system-level project planning activities.

The basis for sections IV, V, VI, and VII of the system development plan is a set of task descriptions. Task descriptions are described in the paragraphs that follow.

Task Description

Each task description should identify required inputs, their sources, and due dates. Output or task results should be identified and described as to where each result goes, who gets it, and when it will be available. In some large projects, forms or templates are often made up to assure that each task is consistently described in this fashion. Table 1.2 provides an example of such a form.

Figure 1.2 illustrates how each task description of Table 1.2 can be further partitioned into subtasks; each subtask is then described in a Table 1.2 format and scheduled. If task resource

■ TABLE 1.2   **Task Description Format**

1. Task identifier
2. General description
3. Input required to initiate the task
    Date needed
    Source of input (who provides the input)
4. Output of task
    Date completed
    Sink (who gets the output)
5. Reviews planned
    Dates
    Participants
    Agenda, pass/fail criteria
6. How to accomplish the task
7. Resources required
    People
    Hardware and software
    Other
8. Gantt chart or PERT chart

estimates are available, they can be allocated to subtasks as shown. The approach in Table 1.2 may be applied to each subtask in a stepwise refinement process. How far the refinement process is carried is a function of project standards. PERT charts or bubble charts* can be used to convey the same schedule information as the Gantt charts.

Identifying each task with a specific delivered product is a good practice. This approach offers a number of advantages. The two most important ones are as follows: (1) the team is forced to focus on only those tasks that are absolutely required in production of a deliverable item, and (2) it helps for future resource estimation to associate development cost with individual products and their characteristics. Another advantage of the workshop approach, aside from task description consistency, is that task dependencies can be identified and task schedule inconsistencies recognized and treated during the planning effort when representatives of the entire performance team are together.

Resource and Schedule Estimation

A complete set of task descriptions and task schedules can form the basis for a so-called bottom-up resource or cost estimate based on task descriptions. Most well-run projects will estimate system development cost using two independent methods to increase confidence in the cost estimates presented to management and client. If funds have already been allocated in a lump sum for development (design to cost projects, for example), then the task descriptions become the basis for allocation of funds among system development tasks.

Staffing

When tasks are defined and schedules are estimated, the planning effort has sufficient information to begin staffing plans and organizing a team into units to address the development

....
* A graphic means employed to portray task schedule and task interdependence.

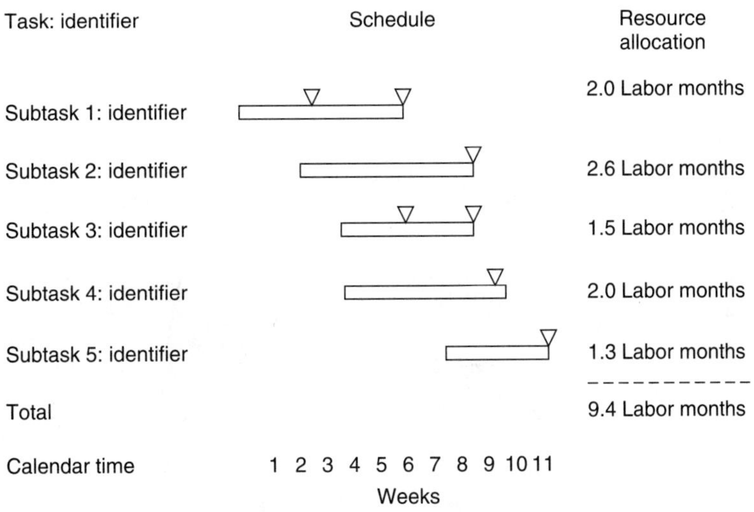

Task: identifier	Schedule	Resource allocation
Subtask 1: identifier		2.0 Labor months
Subtask 2: identifier		2.6 Labor months
Subtask 3: identifier		1.5 Labor months
Subtask 4: identifier		2.0 Labor months
Subtask 5: identifier		1.3 Labor months
Total		9.4 Labor months
Calendar time	1 2 3 4 5 6 7 8 9 10 11 Weeks	

Triangles at the top of the timelines indicate either deliveries, milestones, or checkpoints.

■ **FIGURE 1.2**

Task partitioning.

problem. Figure 1.3 illustrates how top-level staffing plans for a system development project might be presented in summary form in a system development plan. Staffing plans and organization charts are part of the plan. A comprehensive staffing plan identifies the required skills and schedules the right people to be brought onto the project at appropriate times and released from the project when their tasks are completed. Figure 1.4 shows a project organization chart as it might appear in a system development project plan.

Technical Reviews

One frequently overlooked area in planning is technical reviews and inspections. A technical review requires substantial preparation on the part of the presenters. Documents must be published and distributed and presentation material organized and made into slides or overheads. Practice sessions are conducted by presenters with an audience of critics to prepare for the review. The reviewers must read the material, attend the presentations, and write reports. On large projects with many reviews and walk-throughs involving many participants, a substantial number of labor hours can be consumed analyzing documents, attending meetings, and writing reports. For example, a system design review for one module or unit can require 150 labor hours. When overlooked, this labor can result in a very large error in resource and schedule estimation.

Risk Management

Many projects include risk assessment and risk management as a key part of the planning process and expect the plan to identify specific risk areas. The plan is expected to quantify

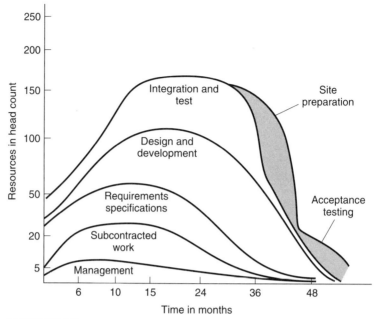

■ FIGURE 1.3

Project staffing profile.

both probability of failure and consequences of failure and to describe what will be done to contain development risk.

Change Control

All large development projects experience changes during their lifetime. A good system development plan will also describe how these changes are to be handled. The plan that describes this process is called the configuration control plan. There are a number of questions to be answered regarding control of changes to specifications, hardware and software designs, and other system elements. The first is, to what extent is the system development organization free to deal with system changes? How large a cost and schedule impact will the system development team handle internally before the change must be escalated? There is the question of how to inform development team members regarding the nature of the change so that they may assess change impact on their part of the system development process. Figure 1.5 shows a formal configuration control board designed to deal with monitoring, coordinating, and controlling change activity during the system development process. Before the presence of the formal configuration control board, someone, preferably the system engineering manager in conjunction with the software engineering manager, is responsible for maintaining an informal control board.

Managing the inevitable change activity on a major project is critically important. Recognizing and accounting for change activity, particularly during planning and cost estimation, is very important. One of the principal objectives is to assure that a consistent system and subsystem configuration is maintained during project planning and all early phases of system design. Each change to the system or any of its subsystems must be thoroughly assessed for technical, cost, and schedule effects on all subsystems.

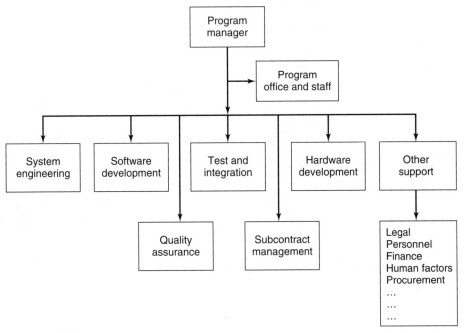

■ FIGURE 1.4

Project organization chart.

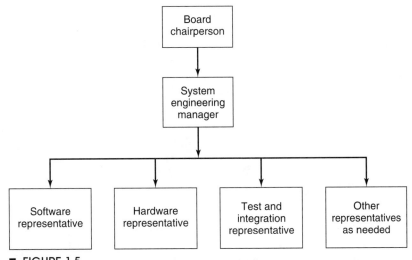

■ FIGURE 1.5

Formal configuration control board organization.

■ TABLE 1.3   **Summarized Table of Contents for Software Development Plan**

I. Introduction
II. Resource and Schedule Estimates
III. Organization and Staffing
IV. Work Breakdown Structures, Work Packages, and Cost Accounts
V. Technical Management and Control
VI. Standards and Procedures
VII. Reviews, Audits, and Walk-throughs
VIII. The Development Environment
IX. Technical Performance Measurements
X. Documentation
XI. Verification and Validation
XII. Maintenance
XIII. Human Factors
XIV. Delivery, Installation, and Acceptance
XV. Appendices and References

Appendices and References

Appendices or references can be employed to cover other items that are unique to specific projects. For example, specific company or organization procedures used in the development can be referenced or modified and published in an appendix as can specific documents describing development methodologies, project-unique standards and conventions, and data item descriptions (DIDs) characterizing document content.

1.3.2 Software Development Plan

In most systems of interest to readers of this book and to the authors, the software subsystem is a primary component of the system. Having discussed the overall system development plan, the next step is to focus on the software development plan. Chapter 3 is devoted to a discussion of technical planning for software development. In this section, for the sake of the completion of the discussion, we present the table of contents for a typical software development plan (Table 1.3).

1.4 SYSTEM DEVELOPMENT LIFE CYCLE DEFINITION AND OVERVIEW   ■

A *system development life cycle* (SDLC) is a framework composed of a sequence of distinct steps or phases in the development of a system [1]. The Department of Defense (DOD) [3], National Aeronautics and Space Administration (NASA) [1], and many companies engaged in the development of large-scale systems have a well-developed SDLC. The required activities in each step of the process are described in formal documentation. The documentation products of each step (including reviews) are usually well described. Documentation contents (the products) of the SDLC process are described in what are called data item descriptions or DIDs. The DIDs give a detailed account of the contents expected or required in each document (a specification). An important part of documentation development is the review process. Reviews permit users and operators as well as managers, peers, and consultants to influence problem formulation and system design and test.

Various organizations have sought to establish and standardize an SDLC process within their organizations. This standardization makes it possible to improve program management and technical training, make personnel more readily able to move from project to project, reduce the learning curve for outside reviewers, and permit the technical and management team to concentrate on system design and development issues rather than on the SDLC process design. Not all organizations have the same needs or the same infrastructure. Therefore, unique internal policies and procedures can dictate slightly different SDLCs for different organizations. In many instances, development of certain unusual systems can call for the tailoring of a ''standard'' SDLC to satisfy special features of the system being developed.

1.4.1   System Development Life Cycle Models

System development life cycle models are attempts to ascribe an ordered structure to the system development process. Virtually all system development life cycle models are variations of what is called the *waterfall model*. The waterfall model takes its name from figures used to depict the process. These figures usually show the process as a chronological sequence of development events flowing from left to right and descending. Although figures and attendant descriptions would lead one to believe that the process is sequential, it is in fact highly parallel and also highly iterative. While system-level concept development and preliminary system design (allocation of functions to subsystems) is largely sequential, specification of subsystem function and performance, subsystem design, development, and test are concurrent development activities. System integration and system test are of necessity more nearly sequential as is acceptance testing.

Life cycle models are characterized by strategically placed reviews and documentation with well-defined contents. In some cases the process is driven by the documentation while in others scheduled reviews are the driving force. The two approaches simply reflect a difference in emphasis rather than a fundamental difference in the models.

Efforts to modify or change the basic system development life cycle have focused on introducing more concurrency into the process, improving document and review content and quality, and improving overall process quality. Concurrent engineering [4, 11] was developed to improve the system development process and reduce system development schedule length. In the following sections, two slightly different system development life cycle models are described.

1.4.2   DOD System Development Life Cycle

During the past 35 years, the Department of Defense (DOD) has been very active in system and software development. Figure 1.6 depicts one of several possible DOD system devel-

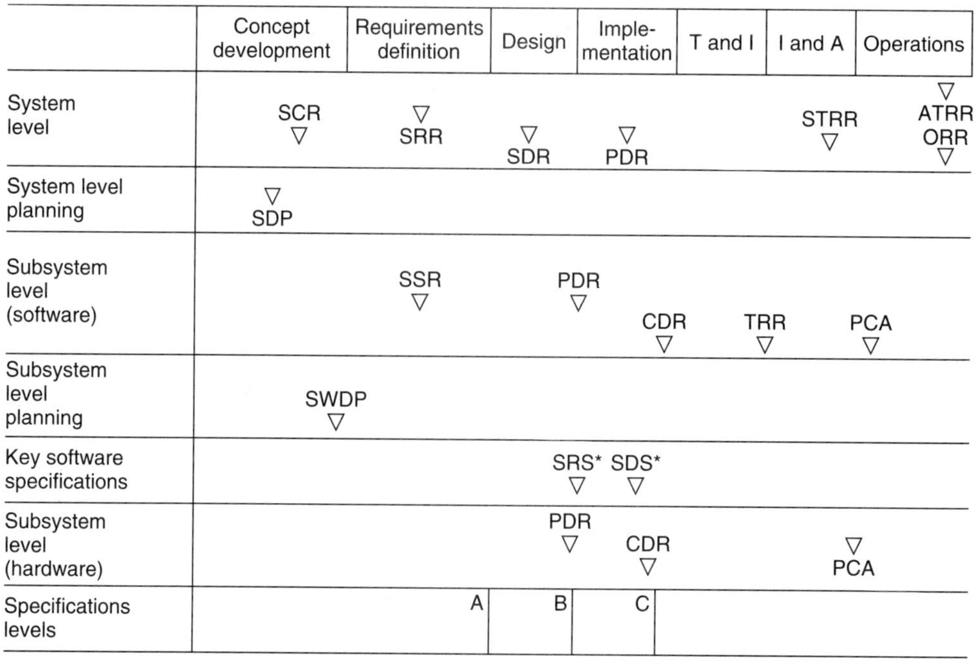

	Concept development	Requirements definition	Design	Imple-mentation	T and I	I and A	Operations
System level	SCR ▽	▽ SRR	▽ SDR	▽ PDR		STRR ▽	▽ ATRR ORR ▽
System level planning	▽ SDP						
Subsystem level (software)		SSR ▽	PDR ▽	CDR ▽	TRR ▽	PCA ▽	
Subsystem level planning	SWDP ▽						
Key software specifications			SRS* ▽	SDS* ▽			
Subsystem level (hardware)			PDR ▽	CDR ▽		▽ PCA	
Specifications levels		A	B	C			

*Key documents: SRS = Software requirements specification
             SDS = Software design specification

See Table 1.4 for a description of other acronyms used in this figure.

■ FIGURE 1.6

DOD system development life cycle.

opment life cycle models [1, 3]. Table 1.4 lists important reviews that mark major milestones in the development process and explains some of the milestones of Figure 1.6.

In the concept development phase, the system team develops the rationale justifying the need for the system and explores a variety of conceptual designs to assure that a reasonable solution exists. A system concept review, SCR, marks the end of the concept definition phase. In this phase a number of formal documents are produced and reviewed. The main goal, however, is to receive an approval to move on to the next phase, which requires technical, programmatic, operational, and economic justification.

In the requirements definition phase, there are several subphases in which system requirements are first defined, documented, reviewed, and approved. Then in a stepwise refinement manner, individual subsystem requirements are defined (after being allocated from system requirements), documented, reviewed, and approved concurrently.

In the design phase hardware and software designs are produced, documented, reviewed, and approved concurrently. In the implementation phase hardware is built or purchased, software is coded, purchased, or modified, and preparation for user training is initiated.

In the test and integration (T and I) phase, the system is assembled from its subsystem components after individual components have been tested. The assembled system is then tested to assure that system requirements have been fully met. Also, in this phase user training is initiated, sites are prepared, and peripheral elements of the system are completed.

The installation and acceptance (I and A) phase includes delivery and installation of the

■ TABLE 1.4   **Important Reviews**

ATRR	Acceptance Test Readiness Review
BDR	Build Design Review (Subsystems)
CDR	Critical Design Review (Subsystem/s)
	(Review of subsystem design specification.)
FCA	Functional Configuration Audit
ORR	Operational Readiness Review
PCA	Physical Configuration Audit
PDR	Preliminary Design Review
	(Review of subsystem function and performance specification.)
SCA	System Configuration Audit
SCR	System Concept Review
SDP	System Development Plan
SDR	System Design Review (Subsystems)
SRR	System Requirements Review
SSR	System Specification Review
STRR	System Test Readiness Review
SWDP	Software Development Plan
TRR	Test Readiness Review

....

Specification levels:
   A: refers to function and performance at system level
   B: refers to function and performance at subsystem level
   C: refers to design at subsystem level

full system. The final tasks of this phase are the completion of the full system acceptance test, the placement of the system into service, and the initiation of the system maintenance phase.

The key characteristics of this SDLC are as follows: (1) each phase has definable products; (2) these products include plans that describe how the development process proceeds and specifications that describe the hardware, software, and operating procedures that will be developed; (3) each phase has a formal ''public'' review with an approval sign-off that provides assurance that all reviewers (including operators and users) agree on what is to be built; (4) each phase has a clearly defined end; (5) all major problems and issues have been satisfactorily closed out; and (6) there is mutual agreement on what constitutes acceptance of all end products. In a well-structured system development environment, a software engineer is frequently assigned to support the effort in the early phases of an SDLC. It is, therefore, important for the software engineer to understand the SDLC process and its goals.

1.4.3 MIS-Oriented System Development Life Cycle*

In the previous section a very brief description of an SDLC for a DOD system development was provided. NASA, DOD, other government agencies, and some aerospace companies

....

* Management Information System (MIS) is the collection of hardware, software, and procedures that a business uses to create, collect, manage, and disseminate its information.

■ TABLE 1.5   **A Generic MIS-Oriented SDLC**

Phase 1:	Survey the situation
Phase 2:	Study the current system
Phase 3:	Define new system requirements
Phase 4:	Develop logical (functional) design (Design-to specification)
Phase 5:	Develop physical design (Build-to specification)
Phase 6:	Construct new system
Phase 7:	Install or deliver new system
Phase 8:	Maintain system and audit performance

embrace this type of SDLC. It has been found to be effective in developing weapon systems and aerospace-oriented systems and should apply to any large, complex system and especially to embedded systems and command and control systems.

This section addresses a generic SDLC, Table 1.5, that is more typical of development of a large business information system. System analysis and design textbooks are usually centered around an SDLC associated with business information system applications [6, 9, 12]. There is a strong similarity between the two processes. Although the SDLC described in this section is often associated with information system maintenance actions, our discussion is centered around application of this paradigm to the development of large, complex business information systems. This particular SDLC is described in more detail because of the need to characterize at least one system development environment as background.

Phase 1: Survey the Situation

This phase begins with meeting the client/operator. The first meeting is usually with a manager or executive who provides an overview of the organization's charter and history and an organization chart. Members are identified in the organization who will be the primary interface for the system analysis and design team. The manager or executive will also provide a description of constraints and limitations and his or her own perception of the problem. For the analyst to hear from the client a very definitive solution to the problem at this time is not unusual.

Two major observations to be made in the first contact are the client's perception of the problem and the establishment of credibility. The term *perception of the problem* has been chosen carefully. The client/operator rarely has a comprehensive appreciation of the true problem. Without understanding the problem it is doubtful that a viable solution can be formulated. As the survey continues, the analyst will gradually come to understand the true nature of the problem. More often than not it will be different from the initial description he or she will get from the client/operator. The diplomatic analyst will have to find a way to develop a problem description and postpone consideration of a problem solution until the problem is completely understood without offending the client/operator. The first contact is, for the system analyst, an opportunity to establish credibility and win the confidence of the client/operator.

The main goals for phase one, not necessarily in this order, are as follows:

1. Understand the given organization's charter and mission.
2. Understand the true organization chart and who is really in control.
3. Identify system users, operators, maintainers, managers, and others served by the system.
4. Develop a written description of the step-by-step operation of the current system. This description is sometimes called *operational timelines, operational concepts*, or *operational scenario.*
5. Establish system boundaries, inputs, outputs, and interfaces. A simple checklist for inputs and outputs should include the following:

Inputs	Outputs
■ Manual/operator originated	■ Soft/hard/electronic
■ Source data automated	■ Number of distinct outputs
■ Number of distinct inputs	■ Rates
■ Rate	■ Word length
■ Word length	■ Accuracy/validity
■ Accuracy/validity	■ Coding/encryption
■ Coding/encryption	■ Structure
■ Protocols	■ Protocol
■ Calibration	
■ Structure	

6. Develop a brief and accurate problem statement.
7. Probe limits and constraints for accuracy, consistency, and ranking.
8. Collect and document relevant data and information.
9. Make recommendation to management.

At the completion of phase 1, the analysis team members should be relatively confident that they have identified the real problem(s), at least to a superficial level, and that they have a plan to perform the next phase. The plan should include identification of additional resources required to perform the next phase. The plan should also, as a minimum, contain a list of specific well-described tasks with identified end products, a schedule for each task, and assignee(s) to each task. At this juncture a strong recommendation should be made regarding continuation into the next phase. However, at the first briefing questions may arise that the analysis team is not yet prepared to answer. The hard part of this phase of the SDLC is deciding how to answer the client/operator questions and what recommendations to make. Some obvious questions that will be asked of the analysis team are as follows: (1) What is the problem as you see it? (2) Are there any viable solutions? (3) How much will these solutions cost and how long will they take to implement? (4) What is the cost and schedule to continue through the next phase?

After only a cursory look at the problem, it is premature for analysts to present solution alternatives. However, three generic solutions do exist for most systems. These generic solutions are as follows:

1. Retain existing system, revise and improve some subsystems and operational procedures. Expand capacity.
2. Add some additional automation, revise and improve existing subsystems, and revise operational procedures to accommodate the new automation. Expand capacity.

3. Major change anticipated. Transition to a fully automated system is recommended. New subsystems and a new work force makeup may be required.

The system analyst could use one or all of these three generic approaches in conjunction with the problem statement to produce a response to questions regarding solutions to the stated problem. The analysis team should avoid jumping to any conclusion and if possible restrain others from doing so. Many system projects get off to a poor start by producing implementation answers before the problem is fully and deeply understood.

Phase 2: Study the Current System

The second phase is, to a great extent, a repeat of the first phase at a deeper level of detail. Generally, there are questions raised during reviews and briefings associated with the first phase for which no acceptable answers have been given. These questions can be an initial focus or action for the second SDLC phase. Nothing improves credibility and demonstrates professionalism more than crisp, written answers to questions left unanswered or poorly answered during briefings and reviews at the end of the first phase. Aside from answering open questions, the main objectives of the second phase are to do the following:

Develop a comprehensive implementation-free abstract description of the current system.
Develop a comprehensive set of operational timelines as described in phase 1.
Initiate a data dictionary to include interface definitions and system level terminology.
Relate a description of the current system to the problem statement as understood in phase 1.
Develop a preliminary design for both a logical model and a physical model.
Develop a set of requirements for the new system.

Table 1.6 shows an outline for a review briefing that might be given to close out phase 2 of the SDLC. Most of what appears in Table 1.6 has been discussed. Identification and description of performance parameters refer to establishing a means to measure quantitatively the improvement in new system performance over the system being replaced. The briefing probably is best concluded with a summary statement of the requirements as currently understood, followed by a description of alternate design solutions in just enough detail to show how system requirements are met and to justify technical and operational feasibility. When solutions are presented, questions are to be expected. But the analysis team should have anticipated most of them and have a prepared answer or position for each.

Phase 3: Define New System Requirements

The information obtained in phases 1 and 2 is the basis for the formal products of the next three phases (3, 4, and 5). The new system requirements spring from the problem statement and draw from several other sources. The initial problem statement tends to focus on what's wrong with the current system and does not always reflect a comprehensive view of how the new system will deal with the future environment. The job of the analyst is to address such issues as fixing what is wrong, growth, additional functions, accuracy, ease of use, flexibility, automation, and overall throughput. She or he must also factor responses to these questions into requirements.

Some helpful ground rules for requirements development and documentation include the following: (1) each requirement should be treated on the basis of input/process/output, (2)

■ TABLE 1.6   **Report Presentation Template**

Client organization description
    Organization chart with functions, names, products added
    Interface definitions/client calls required by management
    Identified organization issues that could affect development
    Who will make key client decisions in this development?
    Identify open questions
Description of current system operations
    Step-by-step description of each system function service
    Support by DFD/EC/HIPO*/....
    Avoid implementations, focus on logical description
    Define system boundaries and interface descriptions
    Use input/process/output/retained data format
    Include personnel via operational timelines
    Identify open questions/issues
Characterize available resources in current system
    People/hardware/software
    Identify open questions
Describe customer's perception of problem
    Collect other views and present
    Give your views, support with hard data
    Identify open questions/issues
Identify and describe performance parameters that will be used to evaluate new system
Explain how improved performance/problem solution will be measured
Identify potential solutions/approaches
Show economic feasibility of potential solutions
    Return on investment
    Payback period
    Present value analysis
Show technical/operational feasibility of potential solutions
Identify tangible/intangible benefits
Present cost-benefit analysis results and expect other questions
Recommendations

....
* DFD = Data flow diagrams
FC = Functional configuration
HIPO = Hierarchical input/process/output

for each requirement there should be a precisely defined method for assuring that the require-ment has been satisfied, (3) functional requirements, wherever possible, should contain quan-tifiable performance attributes, and (4) all requirements should include consideration of all aspects of the system. With the advent of object-oriented methodologies in the design and development of software, there is mounting pressure to employ object-oriented methods in the preparation of system requirements. However, system requirements are often stated in functional form and developed in an hierarchical manner following the top-down stepwise refinement approach.

    Requirements specifications (logical model) are distinguished in the following way: *design-to* requirements or specifications include implementation-free requirement descriptions or specifications describing (1) what functions a system or subsystem must perform and to what performance level; (2) inputs and outputs at a level consistent with functional and performance requirements; (3) data access and retrieval requirements, both local and global; and (4) a description of tests to be applied to confirm successful implementation. *Build-to* requirements or specifications (physical model) include requirements or specifications for building or producing systems or subsystems that implement the design-to specification. There may be a variety of different terms that are employed to describe these two levels of specification.

Phase 3 of the SDLC is concerned with developing a specification for requirements at the subsystem level. At the close of phase 2, the system requirements specification was nearing completion and with the possible exception of a few open issues represented an accurate assessment of the design requirements for the new or revised system. These requirements are typically stated in an implementation-free format and are devoted exclusively to functions and performance parameters. Table 1.7 is a typical table of contents for such a document.

■ TABLE 1.7   **System Level Specification**

SECTION 1. Scope
SECTION 2. Applicable documents and references
SECTION 3. Requirements
      3.1 System definitions
      3.1.1 General description partition (See 3.7)
      3.1.2 Missions
      3.1.3 Threat
      3.1.4 System diagrams
      3.1.5 Interface diagrams/tables
      3.1.6 Operational concepts/scenarios
      3.1.7 Characteristics
      3.2 Performance characteristics
      3.2.1 Physical characteristics
      3.2.2 Reliability
      3.2.3 Maintainability
      3.2.4 Availability
      3.2.5 Environment description
      3.3 Design and construction
      3.3.1 Human factors
      3.3.2 Safety
      3.3.3 Interoperability
      3.3.4 Materials processes and parts
      3.3.5 Workmanship
      3.4 Documentation
      3.5 Logistics
      3.5.1 Maintenance
      3.5.2 Facilities
      3.6 Personnel and training
      3.7 Description of each partition from 3.1.1
SECTION 4. Quality assurance
      4.1 General discussion
      4.1.1 Test responsibility
      4.1.2 Special tests
      4.2 Inspections

The requirements phase of the SDLC is associated with capturing the system design-to requirements in a format consistent with the methodology being used. A major task in this phase is the partitioning and allocation of individual function and performance requirements to hardware and software subsystems or to operators. At this point, the analysis team initiates development of a system architecture and allocates implementation-free system functions among the various possible implementations in hardware, computer/software, and personnel. Even though system architecture design is initiated during phase 2 of the SDLC, the entire architecture design process is now revisited and reworked.

Writing a good subsystem functional and performance specification is a difficult task. It requires a wide range of skills and a good imagination. Table 1.8 summarizes a few major points that can serve as guidance to the system analyst. Since this document will be a major interface between the system analyst and the software engineer, both parties must understand its significance and reach agreement on details that are not already reflected in the data item descriptions.

At the close of phase 3, system requirements are complete, including allocations to subsystems and a system architecture. The credibility of the system architecture and design is supported by a logical, physical, and operational baseline.

■ TABLE 1.8   **Individual Function and Performance Specification Structure**

Input

Characterize completely
Quantify completely
Projected growth

Output

Characterize completely
Quantify completely
Projected function growth

Process

*Describe functions and operations performed on inputs to produce outputs
Quantify performance requirements
Projected growth
Define retained data
Define changes to data store and data retained locally and globally
Quantify data requirements
Define testing required

*Specification for the Functional Performance Specification
1. Shall be expressed in a form that can be understood by users/system analysts/testers
2. Shall be expressed in a form that can be effectively communicated to individuals with widely differing backgrounds
3. Shall not dictate design/implementation decisions
4. Shall be free of ambiguities
5. Shall be testable

Phase 4: Develop Logical Design

During the logical design phase, allocated subsystem function and performance requirements are elaborated and developed into subsystem function and performance requirements. The products of phase 4 of the SDLC are to produce implementation-free design-to specifications for each system element. At the close of this phase, the system analysis and design team have completed their main tasks. The design-to specifications are the interfacing point with hardware development and software development. It is the responsibility of each development group to develop build-to specifications for their respective subsystems. The system analysis group can then be assigned to writing operational procedures or position description handbooks. At this point, database requirements should be clearly understood, and, if appropriate, design efforts to produce build-to specifications for database development should be initiated.

Each of the subsystem requirement reviews is accompanied by a short review of the preliminary physical design implementing the functional and performance requirements specification for each subsystem consistent in level of detail with the design-to specification. Another review of operational timelines is conducted at this time. For systems with complex operator interfaces, it is often useful to have an operator step through one of the more critical timelines. Completion of logical design marks the conclusion of the system design phase. However, production of the design-to document by no means should be considered the completion of the system analyst's responsibility in the system development life cycle.

Phase 5: Develop Physical Design

Phase 5 is primarily the domain of the hardware and the software engineer. Drawings, pseudocode, and other formal and informal documentation required to build hardware and software are produced, reviewed and approved during this phase. Each subsystem goes through this process. Table 1.9 is an example of a table of contents for a software build-to specification. A detailed discussion of physical design process is presented in Chapter 7.

■ TABLE 1.9   **Build-to Specification Table of Contents Software Product**

1. Scope
2. Applicable documents
3. Requirements
    3.1 Function allocation/rationale
    3.2 Function description
        3.2.1 Interface description
    3.3 Storage allocation
    3.4 Computer program functional flow
        3.4.1 Program interrupts
        3.4.2 Logic of subproduct reference
        3.4.3 Special control features
    3.5 Trace to higher level
    3.6 Test matrix (test for each requirement)
    3.7 Expansion of 3.1 (input/output/process and data)
    3.8 Pseudocode or equivalent
    3.9 Listing for delivered product

Phase 6: Construct New System

Phase 6, construction of the new system, involves manufacture of hardware and software coding. As individual subsystems are completed, tested, and delivered to the test and integration team, the full system begins to take form. As more subsystems are completed and added to the system configuration, the tests become more sophisticated and comprehensive. After a series of dress rehearsals, the system is ready for installation and acceptance.

During the construction phase, the remaining members of the analysis team will be involved in various reviews, resolution of issues that arise in implementing requirements, acceptance criteria, and other related problems.

Phase 7: Install or Deliver New System

During system test and installation and delivery of the new system, phase 7, the remaining members of the analysis team will again find themselves in demand. The most knowledgeable people in system folklore will be the system analysis team. They will be busy bringing users, system, and testers together on issues related to function, performance, operation, and acceptance criteria.

Phase 8: Maintain System and Audit Performance

Typically a small cadre of system analysts and perhaps some hardware and software specialists will remain during the operational phase, phase 8, to implement change requests that have accumulated during the SDLC. In addition, this small team will probably collect performance data and establish the environment to effect changes, maintain the system, train new operators or maintainers, and in general make the system effective.

The foregoing has been an overview of one SDLC. No two system developments are alike. The challenges are many and varied. It is important that software engineers understand this process on two levels. The first level is that the software development life cycle (SWDLC) is a proper subset of the SDLC. Hence, the process and products are very similar and in many instances the software engineer is a main contributor as a member of the system analysis team. The second level is to understand what should be contained in a software specification document and where it should come from. Moreover, the software engineer should understand the iterative nature of the software development process. Also, it should be understood that the software engineer has the responsibility to raise the appropriate questions, issues, and problems early in the process and participate in their resolution.

1.5 SOFTWARE DEVELOPMENT LIFE CYCLE: BRIEF OVERVIEW ■

A software development life cycle (SWDLC), an abstract representation of how software is developed, consists of a series of sequential or concurrent steps or phases in the software development process. Each phase consists of a set of related activities usually culminating in a product (document and/or review) that contributes to the completion of the software product.

The phases of a generic software development life cycle are described below. The term *generic* is used to emphasize that regardless of the SWDLC model being used, in a software development environment, the process will go through these phases.

Phase 1: Requirements Analysis

Input: The explicit software requirements specification (SRS document) and the implicit requirements specification, which may be obtained by studying the problem domain, operational timelines, and the operational environment. The SRS developed by the system analyst may include hardware and software requirements. The requirement analysis phase will clearly separate software requirements and hardware requirements.

Output: A set of verified and validated software requirements along with the results of a system/software architecture review. Also, the final draft of the software development plan should be considered an output of this phase. System acceptance test criteria will also be developed in this phase.

The IEEE* Standard 729 defines *requirement* as follows: ''(1) A condition or capability needed by a user to solve a problem or achieve an objective. (2) A condition or capability that must be met or possessed by a system . . . to satisfy a contract, standard, specification or other formally imposed document.''

The software requirements specification document is the interface or contract between system engineers/analysts and software engineers. This implementation-free specification is the basis for the software engineer's requirements analysis efforts and the software engineer's development of specifications to programmers or coders implementing the design of the software. Table 1.10 provides a table of contents that meets one of the ANSI† and IEEE standards for a software requirements specification [5]. An important addition to this outline is a section devoted to testing. This section should include acceptance criteria for tests planned to demonstrate that the software meets its stated criteria. When requirements are being written, it is important to know if they are testable and to know how they are to be tested. It is equally important that the client agree with the conditions of acceptance.

It is highly recommended, if not required, to have a software engineer involved in the system analysis effort. The system engineer or system analyst will be helped by an individual who understands the software development process, limitations and capabilities of software, and software implementations. A software engineer who can also comment constructively on function allocations and support sizing and cost studies is indeed useful. For the software engineer involved in the system analysis effort, there is an opportunity to learn about the application area, to understand the rationale behind many of the decisions, and to have some influence on those decisions that the software engineer will have to live with during the software development life cycle. Also, involvement of a software engineer in analysis-related activities helps the software engineer to identify development facilities required, acquire insight, and gain lead time to address unique software development problems.

Although many other system analysis products are valuable to the software developer, they are an adjunct to the formal software requirements specification. In some development cultures the SRS is called the B-5 specification and in others, the software function and performance specification. The contents of this document should include detailed interface description, functions to be performed, quantifiable performance and test requirements, and how software function and performance will be confirmed. Generally, the software requirements specification is the formulation of the software design problem.

Informal studies tracing errors uncovered during test and integration indicate that more than 50 percent of all failures can be traced back to faults in the software function and

---

* Institute of Electrical and Electronics Engineers

† American National Standards Institute

■ TABLE 1.10 **IEEE/ANSI Software Requirements Specification**

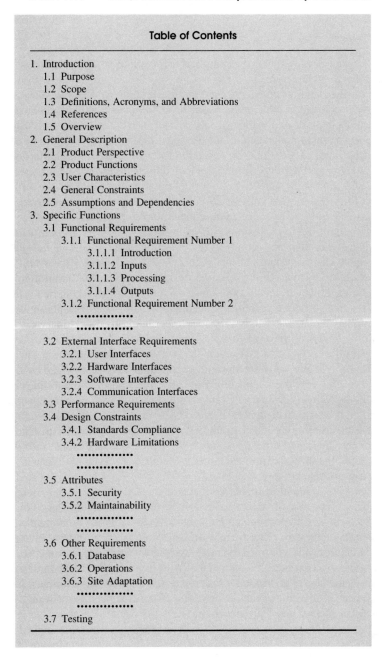

Table of Contents

1. Introduction
   1.1 Purpose
   1.2 Scope
   1.3 Definitions, Acronyms, and Abbreviations
   1.4 References
   1.5 Overview
2. General Description
   2.1 Product Perspective
   2.2 Product Functions
   2.3 User Characteristics
   2.4 General Constraints
   2.5 Assumptions and Dependencies
3. Specific Functions
   3.1 Functional Requirements
       3.1.1 Functional Requirement Number 1
             3.1.1.1 Introduction
             3.1.1.2 Inputs
             3.1.1.3 Processing
             3.1.1.4 Outputs
       3.1.2 Functional Requirement Number 2
             ● ● ● ● ● ● ● ● ● ● ● ● ● ●
             ● ● ● ● ● ● ● ● ● ● ● ●

   3.2 External Interface Requirements
       3.2.1 User Interfaces
       3.2.2 Hardware Interfaces
       3.2.3 Software Interfaces
       3.2.4 Communication Interfaces
   3.3 Performance Requirements
   3.4 Design Constraints
       3.4.1 Standards Compliance
       3.4.2 Hardware Limitations
             ● ● ● ● ● ● ● ● ● ● ● ● ● ●
             ● ● ● ● ● ● ● ● ● ● ● ●

   3.5 Attributes
       3.5.1 Security
       3.5.2 Maintainability
             ● ● ● ● ● ● ● ● ● ● ● ● ● ●
             ● ● ● ● ● ● ● ● ● ● ● ●

   3.6 Other Requirements
       3.6.1 Database
       3.6.2 Operations
       3.6.3 Site Adaptation
             ● ● ● ● ● ● ● ● ● ● ● ● ● ●
             ● ● ● ● ● ● ● ● ● ● ● ●

   3.7 Testing

performance specification [7]. Clearly, a more accurate SRS document will reduce the number of software failures during test and integration as well as during operation.

Phase 2: Design Specification

Input: Software development plan, implicit and explicit software requirements specification, and software architecture.

Output: Verified and accepted software architecture along with the verified and tested software design specification at the pseudocode level. Output should also include algorithms, data structures, database design, database access, user interfaces, unit test criteria, etc.

With full and complete understanding of the requirements specification in hand, the software engineer initiates and continues to refine the software design, usually in orderly stages, with appropriately placed reviews (sometimes called *inspections* or *walkthroughs*). Typically the last stage of design is documented in a formal program design language, pseudocode, or structure chart form. The design phase is a multistep process with the objective of converting software functional and performance requirements into implementable designs in a format that can be communicated to programmers, system analysts, reviewers, and users.

The word *design* is rather ambiguous in the present context. One could argue effectively that design begins when a system concept is formulated, and every step in every phase of a system, hardware, or software life cycle is a design refinement to the original conceptual design. Convention, however, breaks out a single SDLC or SWDLC phase and calls it design. Figure 1.7 discussed in detail later in this chapter, shows the design phase as a two-level process, preliminary and detail. This approach is implicitly indicated by the two reviews (PDR and CDR). Some SWDLCs have as many as four separate design levels. In that case, each of the four design levels has a formal review and a separate documentation set.

The development of the software design specification (SDS), or as we call it, build-to specification, is exclusively the responsibility of software engineers. Ideally the design process should result in the following: (1) a software architecture that is a layered sequence of logical partitions and refinements with increasing levels of detail at each new layer, (2) a clear exposition of data structures, control structures, algorithms, and interfaces, (3) a realization in software of the goals and objectives carefully spelled out in the software requirements specification, and (4) a design expressed in terms that reviewers (including users) with varied backgrounds can understand.

Software designs can manifest themselves in two ways, internal and external. The internal design is prepared, represented, and described by a variety of existing design methodologies all leading to a form of pseudocode at a language level suitable for directing the coding step in a clear, unambiguous way. The internal design also deals with internal interfaces, algorithms, data structures, and control structures associated with implementation of the stated requirements. The external design is associated with user interfaces, other software product interfaces, hardware (sensor and actuator) interfaces, global data structures, and global control structures. Both internal and external designs should together constitute a unified depiction of the product. Chapters 7 and 8 are devoted to a discussion of this phase.

Phase 3: Coding and Unit Testing

Input: Software design specification document, software architecture, unit test criteria, and system test criteria.

Output: Tested, documented, and certified (formally accepted) program modules.

The code and unit test phase entails converting the design language into program code and, most important, designing and carrying out tests of the individual units. Once individual modules or units have been tested and accepted, the integration and test phase begins.

Phase 4: Test and Integration

Input: Individual modules as developed, tested, and certified in phase 3; acceptance test criteria for each module and system acceptance test criteria.

Output: Certified collections of program modules and eventually the complete, integrated system ready for acceptance test.

In this phase individual modules or units are assembled and tested as subsets of the software end product. These tests frequently require that system hardware elements and operators be used to exercise the software. At other times tests can be made using software to model missing system elements. Sometimes testing requires a combination of the two approaches. The end goal is to prove that the software meets its functional and performance requirements in the operational environment and that the system containing the software subsystem meets its requirements.

Many software development organizations separate software development from software system level testing. Once unit or module testing is complete, the unit or module is turned over to an independent test group for system level testing. The objective is to subject the software to a set of tests designed to show that the software won't meet its specifications. By employing a separate group to design and perform system level software tests, it is expected that the software will be exercised more thoroughly and rigorously. System test and integration is discussed in chapter 10.

Phase 5: Acceptance Test

Input: Tested and integrated software and the acceptance test criteria as it has matured during the development process.

Output: A decision to accept or reject the system along with a document describing every acceptance test case and the results produced by the system. This document must be well written and well supported by data. In the case of rejection, this document may end up in the hands of lawyers.

The system level acceptance test is likely to be a systematic test or demonstration of all system functions and modes with operators and users in place and with realistically scripted operational timelines. Software unit and perhaps even software product tests are the responsibility of the software development organization whereas system level testing in many cases is the domain of a separate integration and test organization. Acceptance testing is one of the responsibilities of the integration and test organization.

As far as the software development organization is concerned, when a unit, module, or product is accepted as complete by the integration and test organization, that unit, module, or product is in its maintenance phase. In the maintenance phase, errors found in the software are corrected, and software changes brought about by either changes in the operating environment or new system needs are implemented. Both system and software operational performance is observed and recorded. The approach to correcting errors (or adding new functions) is to follow the software development life cycle pattern. That is, corrections are functionally defined and reviewed, a fix is designed and reviewed, the change is implemented, and then the entire system is put through regression tests to assure that the fix or change did not cause any other problems or perturb system performance in an undesirable way. System performance, in particular failure data and operator/user comments, is analyzed to improve reliability models, identify specific failure sources, improve the software development process, and evaluate the use of new development technologies.

System and Software Maintenance

Some authors include system maintenance as the last phase of the SDLC and software maintenance as the last phase of the SWDLC. Others treat maintenance activities as separate from development activities mainly because when the system/software is delivered and accepted, the maintenance team will take over the operation of the system. Exclusion of maintenance activities from the development phase will in no way reduce the importance of maintenance-related decisions that must be made throughout the development process. Some maintenance-related decisions are made as early as the first phase of the development or even during requirement specification. Chapter 13 is devoted to the discussion of software maintenance and maintainability.

1.6   SWDLC MODELS ■

Most SWDLC models encountered in practice are variations of the waterfall model. The DOD model, documented in DOD-STD-2167A, and the NASA information system life cycle model [11] fall into this category. Other formal models in this category include rapid throwaway prototyping, incremental development, and evolutionary prototyping. These three models employ repeated applications of the waterfall model for each of the individual steps. The spiral model, introduced by Boehm [2], combines the prototyping model with that of the waterfall model and inserts a risk analysis step and a proceed or halt decision in each phase. Chapter 16 discusses a risk analysis approach that supports the spiral model.

1.6.1   Generic Waterfall Model

The generic waterfall model, depicted by Figure 1.7, is an abstraction that is far removed from practice. While it is true that a set of clearly stated requirements is needed before designing, a design is needed before coding, and coded software is needed before testing, it is not generally true that a software development proceeds sequentially as depicted in the waterfall model. It is more likely that the software product requirements will be partitioned into smaller units using the well-known techniques of top-down design and structured programming. These units will be scheduled for design, coding, and unit testing to support a master test and integration schedule or perhaps to make efficient use of available resources. A given software product will then be developed concurrently in small increments. In addition, each independently developed module of the product will often be itself developed iteratively. That is, design activity will result in a revisit to the requirement specification phase

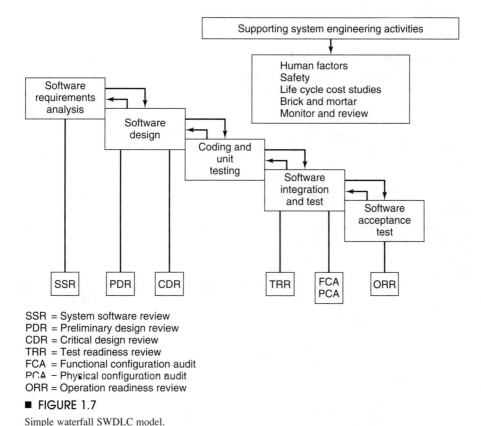

SSR = System software review
PDR = Preliminary design review
CDR = Critical design review
TRR = Test readiness review
FCA = Functional configuration audit
PCA = Physical configuration audit
ORR = Operation readiness review

■ FIGURE 1.7

Simple waterfall SWDLC model.

and coding will often result in a revisit to the design phase and requirement specification phase.

Exercising operational timelines during various reviews will also result in a reexamination of requirements and designs. Software development is both a concurrent and an iterative process, which the waterfall abstraction does not make clear. During a software development process, a formal document or review is often employed to establish the end of one phase and the beginning of the next phase. For example, a review and a document could be regarded as the formal termination of the analysis phase (phase 1). The document produced at this phase is called the software requirements specification (SRS), and the review is called the primary design review (PDR). The design phase begins at this point and ends with the software design specification (SDS) and a review process called the critical design review (CDR). Coding and unit testing begin at this point and end when units or modules are delivered to the test and integration phase of the development cycle. The documentation includes pseudocode or equivalent, listings, test cases, and test case results. The test and integration phase really begins at project inception and overlaps with analysis, design, coding, and unit testing. Planning for test and integration, especially acceptance testing, is performed concurrently with development of the software requirements specification. Chapter 10 describes this process in more detail.

The net effect of the reviews and documents at strategic points in the SWDLC gives the appearance of a waterfall-like process to an SWDLC model.

1.6.2 DOD Model

The DOD model, which is considered a classic waterfall structure, is shown in Figure 1.8. In comparison with the simple waterfall model, the DOD model (1) includes the system design as the first phase of the software development life cycle model, (2) divides the software design phase into preliminary and detailed design phases, and (3) divides the test and integration phase into two separate phases, software integration and test and system integration and test.

In the DOD model, software requirements originate in the system design phase where function and performance are allocated to the major system components (hardware, operators, and software.) A system design review (SDR) is the process whereby the allocation of requirements to the software component of the system is initially presented. The software system review (SSR) is a separate formal confirmation and acceptance of the allocation of requirements to the software subsystem. The software requirements phase ends with the completion of the SRS document. The PDR is the process by which the SRS document is formally reviewed and approved and a preliminary design is presented for approval. At the termination of the detail design phase, a software design specification document (SDS) is produced and reviewed in a formal review process called the critical design review (CDR).

As suggested earlier, formal documents and reviews tend to bring the concurrent and iterative development activities to a common point in the process for a public examination and approval. The initiation of the software integration and test phase is keyed by a test

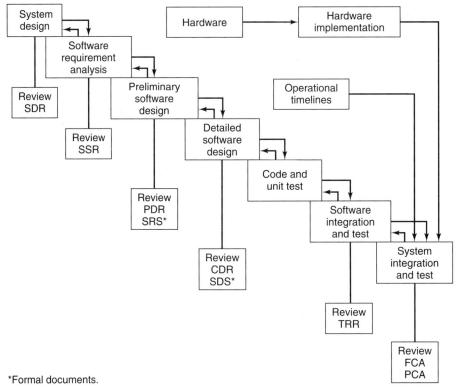

*Formal documents.

■ FIGURE 1.8

DOD SWDLC model.

readiness review (TRR). There are a number of documents and reviews of test plans and procedures, test cases, test scripts, etc., leading up to the TRR. The purpose of the TRR is to ensure that all the plans and documents required for performance of the testing are complete and sufficient for the test phase.

The advantages of the DOD SWDLC model and the simple waterfall SWDLC model are as follows: (1) the process is well documented; (2) the document content and review criteria are well defined; (3) the process, including reviews and documents, can be tailored to meet the unique needs of a particular project or product; (4) there is substantial experience with the process; and (5) standardization applies. The disadvantages associated with these models are as follows: (1) the paradigm often fails to recognize the concurrent and iterative nature of the process, (2) the process is often not effectively tailored to the application, (3) the process is thought to be incompatible with the use of Ada Language, (4) the process is thought to be incompatible with expert system development, (5) the process does not formally involve the users and operators, and (6) the process is thought to be expensive.

1.6.3 Spiral Model

The spiral model for SWDLC has been developed in response to the criticism that traditional SWDLC models discourage or at least do not encourage the use of prototyping and software reuse [2]. The spiral model is a risk-driven approach to software development that encompasses the best features of both classic life cycles and prototyping. Figure 1.9 depicts the spiral model of the software development process. In the A quadrant different levels of planning are performed. In the B quadrant a thorough risk analysis (see chapter 16) is done and an appropriate prototype is initiated. In the C quadrant various software development products (feasibility studies, design concepts, specifications, designs, etc.) are sequentially completed.

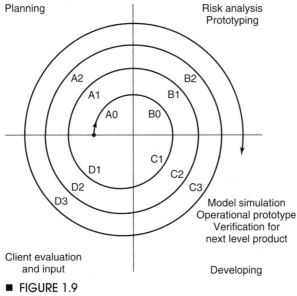

■ FIGURE 1.9

SPIRAL SWDLC model.

In the D quadrant client and management evaluate these products and provide permission to continue to the next level of the spiral.

The spiral goes from A to B, from B to C, from C to D and from D back to A (of course at a different level of detail) until the complete system is developed and accepted. As the spiral moves to its next level, cost and schedule estimates are adjusted to reflect the present status of the development.

Some of the advantages of the spiral model are that (1) it could be used as effectively for system enhancement as for system development, (2) most life cycle models can be considered as a special case of the spiral model, and (3) the embedded risk analysis built into the model avoids many of the difficulties that arise in other models. Boehm [2] gives an example, using the spiral model to develop the TRW software productivity system. The reader is encouraged to read reference 2 for a more in-depth discussion of the spiral SWDLC model.

1.6.4   NASA Model

The NASA software development life cycle is also a waterfall structure and except for a slightly different naming convention is identical to the DOD SWDLC model. In the NASA SWDLC model, the SWDLC is called the software acquisition life cycle, the coding phase is called the implementation phase, the function configuration audit is performed earlier in the development process, and system integration and testing is called acceptance testing.

1.6.5   Rapid Throwaway Prototype Model

To counter certain problems that usually arise in the waterfall approach to the software development process, the rapid throwaway prototype approach was developed. Problems often arise in obtaining correct, complete, and unambiguous software function and performance specifications. A fair question to ask in these cases is: If you don't know what you want, how will you know when you get it? Errors of omission and commission often remain concealed until the acceptance test when errors are most expensive to fix. Effective communication between operator and both system and software developer is frequently lacking.

The rapid throwaway prototype is used as a means to elicit, from operators and users during the requirements phase, a better picture of true software requirements. As part of the requirements generation process, a so-called quick and dirty implementation of a design that responds to a best estimate of the true requirements is effected. Feedback from users and operators engaged in using the prototype is used to converge to the correct software requirements. The process can be repeated, sequentially building a series of prototypes and discarding them as a better understanding of requirements emerges. In this case, prototypes converge to the finished software product. It should be pointed out that the prototypes are usually built using a waterfall model process.

1.6.6   Incremental Development Model

Incremental development refers to the process of developing to completion only a part of the requirements at a time. By selectively developing part of the requirements, designing, coding, and testing software that meets these required functions, the software product may be built up incrementally to its final configuration. This approach has been used successfully for business information systems. Developing a large, complex software product using this approach may tend to reduce the schedule and make each increment more manageable than taking on the complete product development at one time. Each increment is developed using a waterfall development process.

1.6.7   Evolutionary Prototype Model

Taking the incremental development approach to its limit leads to the evolutionary prototype approach. In this method, the development proceeds in a series of implementations, each of which meets those requirements that are recognized and understood at the time of implementation. User observations and experience are fed back to influence the next implementation. Each prototype is developed using a waterfall model to produce the prototype.

1.6.8   Reuse and Automated Development Models

Software reuse and automated software synthesis are two concepts that have been employed to reduce development costs. Both of these methods follow the waterfall model in development but take advantage of either software products already developed and used or tools that automate many of the waterfall SWDLC steps.

Software reuse, while on the surface sounds like an idea that would lead to substantial cost savings, should be approached skeptically. A software product or element already written, tested, and used cannot be plugged directly into a new application without some analysis to assure that the product meets all of the actual requirements. Some effort to document requirements and document the reused software product is needed, new interfaces must be confirmed, and the reused product must be tested in its new configuration and in its new operational environment. Reused software does have a cost associated with it (often 60 to 80% of newly developed software).

Automated software synthesis seeks to automate the software development process to the extent that formal requirement statements may, through use of automated tools, become direct prototypes for the required software. This concept is an extension to the idea of using very high level languages (VHLL) to implement business applications. The process was originally designed to permit users to develop their own unique business applications. Automated software synthesis is an area of current research. The idea is to make formal requirement statements rather than their implementation in code the maintained product. The major challenges are to transform informal specifications to formal specifications automatically and to convert formal specifications into a software product (code).

1.6.9   Resource- and Schedule-Driven Model

An interesting SWDLC paradigm was suggested by J. Thompson and K. Schonrock of IN-TERGRAPH [private communication]. The initial software product is developed using the simple waterfall approach but with very little formality. The main driver is schedule. The product is then passed through a series of formal software certification tests where a great deal of requirement reanalysis and product redesign takes place. Immediately upon product release, requirements that were tabled for lack of time or resources, as well as newly surfaced requirements from users, are incorporated into the next release of the product. Faults uncovered during field operation are fixed and funneled into the next release of the product. New releases can come as frequently as every six months. The most important step or phase in the model is the certification test. Certification testing features aggressive tests that thoroughly exercise the software product over operating environment extremes.

1.6.10   Cleanroom Approach

As an alternative to the more conventional SDLC models, Mills, Dyer, and Linger [7] have developed a clean room concept that depends on the following: application of statistical quality control techniques, a structured architecture, a specification language based on a mathematical approach to specifying functional requirements, elimination of unit or module testing, and emphasis on usage testing over coverage testing.

   The cleanroom approach attacks the problem of specifying correctly and precisely functional and performance requirements by employing the precision of mathematics. Having specified requirements mathematically, confirming or verifying correctness of design solutions by analysis is suggested as an option to testing, at least at the module level. The cleanroom approach also employs a structured architecture and design methodology based on objects. The cleanroom testing technique integrates untested modules into software system elements and employs a test plan that is based on ultimate product use. This testing approach surfaces the software faults that cause the most failures under operational conditions. The net result, it is claimed, is an efficient way to develop high reliability software.

1.6.11   Comments on SWDLC Models

In summary, the activities or functions that constitute all of these models are in principle quite simple: understand the problem, design a solution, and test the solution in the operational environment. There is a wealth of information on how to perform each of these functions. The difficulty lies in deciding the following: (1) how to define and organize each of the functions chronologically to suit project, personnel and client idiosyncrasies; (2) how to implement the iterative nature of the development process; (3) how to place reviews and associated documents effectively; (4) how to control the truly concurrent nature of what has been traditionally viewed as a sequential process; and (5) how to get the right product to the client at the right time.

   If each SWDLC model is regarded in terms of what new insights it offers, what better depiction of the process, or what clarification it offers, then we can benefit greatly by examining each one in detail. The practitioner, however, must accept the given paradigm, confront the sequence of activities and tasks that make up the software development process, and locate the sources she or he may use to help accomplish them.

   In the end, project success or failure depends more on how well each of the individual tasks or functions within the framework of the SWDLC is executed than on the nature of the SWDLC. The task execution depends strongly on the quality of the people involved.

From the forgoing summary of the SWDLC models, one can conclude that the software engineer and the software engineering process are key in creating and delivering a software product or subsystem. Hence, this section is concluded by giving a short description of the software engineering process and the responsibilities of a software engineer.

1.6.12 Best Practice

A recent initiative by the DOD seeks to phase out many of the existing and current military standards and specifications for software development and shift to standard commercial practices, standards of the Institute of Electrical and Electronics Institute (IEEE) or American National Standard Institute (ANSI), for example. The thrust of this effort is to permit software development contractors to substitute applicable commercial standards or best practice for DOD standards; the initiative is called *best practice*. The objective of the best practice approach is to reduce cost of software development by reducing the documentation and bureaucracy implicit in following current DOD standards. This goal may be achieved through substituting commercial standards that provide equivalent benefits in structure, discipline, and control for applicable DOD standards. The main areas that are addressed by this initiative are risk management, requirements, and inspections.

This approach is a logical extension to the DOD software development option that permitted contractors to employ their own standards and practices when it could be demonstrated, to the satisfaction of a contracting officer, that the contractor's standards and practices were equivalent to the applicable military standards and using the option would result in a lower overall cost to the Government.

1.7 SOFTWARE ENGINEERING PROCESS   ■

Software engineering is the application of the definition of engineering to software development. Recall that *engineer* and *engineering* are defined as ''to arrange, manage or carry through by skillful or artful contrivance. The art or science of making practical application of the knowledge of pure sciences such as physics, chemistry, biology, etc.'' Software engineering is the application of this definition to the development of software. In addition, software engineering can be regarded as a set of orderly procedures by which a software product is described, formally specified, designed, tested, and delivered to a client/user.

Until recently it was an accepted practice for most software engineering tasks to be performed by an experienced programmer. These experienced programmers usually had an interest in more than just designing and coding. In particular they had an appreciation for the full scope of software development, including application area knowledge, requirement sources, and programmatic issues. When programmers with these capabilities and interests were not available, a software-knowledgeable system engineer or system analyst took on the more technical roles of the software engineer. In today's software development environment, the expectation is that the technical tasks of the software engineering process will be assigned to a software engineer. Unfortunately, software engineers are in short supply and many critical software engineering tasks are still either performed by system engineers/analysts or managers or not at all.

There are two major components to software engineering. The first component is the timely and appropriate blending of efforts from disciplines such as reliability, safety, quality assurance, logistics, and human factors to assure a positive influence on design and development. The second component is translation of a software requirements specification into a software design specification and subsequent performance of verification and validation testing at all levels.

There are a few interesting points to be made regarding the lack of software engineering.

1. A good many of the problems one sees in software development are due in part to very poor or very little software engineering.
2. There is a very large backlog of software development projects to be addressed over the next decade.
3. Problems exist because real software engineers, good or bad, are in short supply.
4. Yet, in spite of the negative image projected by many critics, the United States is at the forefront of software development technology. To hold that edge in the face of increasing competition, the need is to expand the base of competent, well-trained software engineers.

The software engineer is expected to represent the software development team both technically and programmatically when dealing with system engineers or system analysts. The software engineer is expected to act with competence, integrity, and honesty so that realistic assessments and evaluations can be presented to senior management. The software engineer is expected to provide software-related expertise in (1) planning; (2) decisions involving software, size estimates, and cost and schedule estimates; and (3) making function and performance allocations. The software engineer is also expected to solicit and filter questions and issues from the software development team and present the questions and issues to appropriate members of the system team for clarification and resolution. At the same time, the software engineer must represent the system team to the software development team by explaining the rationale behind technical and economic decisions. The software engineer must keep the software development team generally informed and make them aware that there is more to the system than software. Clearly, the software engineer is expected to be a good communicator. Members of the software development team look to the software engineer as the technical leader, that is, a person who can help resolve knotty design problems and solve specification issues for them.

1.8 GENERAL OBSERVATIONS ON SDLC AND SWDLC   ■

Presented thus far is a very general overview of what happens in a system development life cycle and in a software development life cycle. This section provides a relatively simple model of both the system and software development life cycles to retain as you learn more detail regarding this topic. There are several points to remember from this chapter.

Software (even a word processor product) is always a subsystem, and the software development team members are always part of a larger system development effort. There is no such thing as a successful software development within a failed system development. It is important for the software development team to familiarize themselves with the application area. There are instances where project management has spent in excess of $200,000 to train the software development team in the technical aspects of a given application area and at the conclusion of the project, regarded the cost as an excellent investment.

A system development needs the software viewpoint and software expertise at the initiation of the system development life cycle. This support is required long before software requirements are formulated. The software viewpoint or expertise is needed to contribute to system documents that are required to obtain approvals to continue the system development. Some specific examples include the following: risk analysis and risk assessment studies, reliability estimates and/or reliability allocations, architecture studies, cost-benefit studies, schedule development, software development facility identification and sizing, computer system sizing, support to the hardware development team, software sizing, software development cost estimation, function allocation, allocation of project responsibility, and other planning activities that are conducted early in the system development process. Subsequently, software-cognizant personnel familiar with the application area can assist in preparing function and performance specifications, or in some cases, take full responsibility for writing the specification.

Experience teaches that even with extensive exposure to a wide variety of SDLC models and SWDLC models, a few hours must be devoted to understanding the specific phases, their products, and terminology. Once this information has been absorbed, there are very few intrinsic differences that separate one life cycle from another. The key point is that one must have an orderly, well thought out process or plan for the software and system development. There should be adequate formal documentation describing the process and defining intermediate products. There also should be detailed descriptions of document contents and pass/ fail criteria for reviews. All participants must understand the process, and more important, commit to following the procedures. All participants should be encouraged to keep a personal project notebook to document and date ideas, designs, test results, questions, problems, technical data sources, meeting attendees, meeting decisions, information disseminated at meetings, directions given, and any other pertinent project information. Such a notebook is useful in tracing the history of technical issues and problems, but even more important, to provide a database or reference for developing required documentation.

One must keep in mind that both system and software development life cycles are in a general sense iterative and converging processes. The SDLC provides the framework for an iterative design process with stepwise refinements occurring at each phase and subphase.

The user must be involved at each phase and step of the process for both system and software. The ultimate test for the system involves satisfying the user at acceptance test. The user brings operational realities to the process. An interesting operational reality was brought home to one of the authors when, during a test of an automated turnstile, a component in a subway fare collection system, one of the testers, to the astonishment of the designer, produced a pint of whiskey from his pocket and poured it into a slot in the turnstile that accepted fare cards. A little reflection will reveal that in a subway environment, this problem is certainly an operational reality and must be somehow accommodated in the design requirements and, in turn, in the design.

Operational timelines or scenarios, in the authors' view, are one of the most important tools that can be used to reduce design flaws and recognize oversights in requirements. An operational scenario is developed in conjunction with users to characterize in step-by-step detail, the manner in which the new system will be used in the operational phase. These scenarios should consider modes, operators, environments, and system/software. Early in the development cycle operational scenarios are primarily conceptual and rely largely on the imagination of both user and system/software engineer. As the development progresses and understanding of the system and the operational personnel and environment matures, operational scenarios will become more accurate portrayals of the operational environment. Some specific requirements that might surface as a result of working through operational scenarios include the following: (1) identification of the fact that more menus and more display panels will be required; (2) recognition of additional system modes of operation that must be provided; (3) discovery of new system threats that were overlooked early in the project when focus was on other more esoteric problems; (4) identification of inputs not accounted for in either hardware or software required to carry out a system function; and (5) additional reports not recognized until the operational scenario was developed and exercised in conjunction with the user. It is rare when a review of an operational timeline with users does not surface new requirements or clarify an existing requirement.

Effective planning is an important ingredient for success. The technical planning for system and software development is a major responsibility for both system and software engineer. Software metrics (discussed in chapter 14) developed during technical planning will help to manage and control the various phases of the SWDLC.

1.9 CHAPTER SUMMARY ■

Software development is almost always part of a larger activity called system development. Software engineers should not lose sight of the fact that the system is the primary product.

Software engineers have a lot in common with system engineers. The software engineer should assume responsibility for more than just the parochial design and development of a software product. The software engineer should use the system engineer as a role model in approaching tasks and responsibilities.

The software requirements specification (SRS) should be regarded as the joint responsibility of the system and software engineers. The efficacy of this document is of singular importance to an effective software development process.

The definition, quantification, and use of software attributes are important in planning system and software development. These attributes are useful in hardware and software sizing, making cost and schedule estimates for planning and controlling purposes, identifying areas of high risk, setting quality and reliability goals, and measuring important properties and characteristics of the software product. Developing software attribute measurement techniques and applying them is an essential part of applying the scientific method to software development.

It should be kept in mind that the SDLC, SWDLC, or any associated processes are not in and of themselves as important to the success of a development as is execution of individual tasks and activities that fall within the life cycle framework and its attendant processes. Just as in American football, the play, however well conceived and designed, will not be successful unless its objectives are thoroughly understood and successfully executed by the team.

A system or software engineer must understand what constitutes a successful system and software development. With a model in mind of just what is required for performance of a successful system and software development, the system and software engineer knows how to prioritize tasks, specifically what each task should produce and how to measure progress against plan. The following chapters are designed to aid in developing the model, prioritizing and performing the software engineering tasks, defining key products (documents), specifying their contents, and providing measurement parameters to assist in planning and controlling software development.

1.10 EXERCISES   ■

1. Why is it important for a designer to know what constitutes optimum performance?
2. Why do you think that software engineering is more like system engineering than hardware engineering? Relate a software engineer's tasks to those of a system engineer.
3. (A team-oriented problem) Give a full description of a typical university information system. List all interfaces and databases. Itemize deliverable products.
4. List the advantages and disadvantages of involving a software engineer throughout the entire system planning process.
5. In your view, should software engineers be selected from among experienced programmers? If your answer is yes, list the disadvantages of this approach.
6. In what ways would the following two software development projects differ?
   Project A: Approximately 670,000 source lines of Ada code for a new software product.
   Project B: Approximately 5,500 source lines of Ada code added to an existing software product.
7. In your view, what is a system-level architecture?
8. In your view, what are the main differences between a system analyst and a system engineer with regard to preparation and background?
9. Do you think a successful system analyst must be an experienced programmer? Give reasons for your answer.
10. Write a task description following the format of Table 1.2 for one of your recent programming assignments.
11. List three specific areas of risk in developing a software product.
12. Explain how change control boards can control project cost.
13. Develop a detailed step-by-step operational timeline for signing on to a system, reading electronic mail, responding to electronic mail, and signing off.
14. List any major differences you find between DOD, SDLC, and MIS SDLC.
15. In an MIS-oriented SDLC, show what phases could be performed in parallel because of time pressure.
   a. What phases would you combine and why?
   b. What phases would you eliminate and why?
   c. What phases would you do in parallel and why?
16. List all the advantages and disadvantages that you can think of for having a separate group perform software system-level testing.
17. Describe the task that might be performed by a software engineer assigned to an independent software system test group.
18. List the advantages and the disadvantages of having a separate test and integration organization perform the system test and integration task.
19. Using Figure 1.1 as guidance, draw a block diagram model of a complete word processing system and explain each block.
20. Specify the function and performance requirements for a software product that will be used by school children to learn the multiplication tables for the natural numbers 1–10.
21. What are the specific questions to be answered by:
   a. a Software Development plan
   b. a Systems Development plan
22. List major problems and suggested solutions which may arise during development of large information systems.

23. Describe the workshop approach to planning. List the advantages and disadvantages of this approach.
24. Explain tasks performed by a system engineer/analyst.
25. List qualifications required for a person to work as a system engineer and be successful in his or her job. Justify your list of qualifications.
26. Describe the generic waterfall model.
27. Define the characteristics of the DOD SDLC model.
28. Describe the MIS-oriented SDLC model. Explain the major differences between the DOD model and the MIS-oriented model.
29. What are the 3 generic solutions presented to the client at the completion of Phase 1 of an MIS-oriented SDLC.
30. What are the main objectives of the second phase of the MIS-oriented SDLC.
31. Give a brief description of the SWDLC.
32. Discuss, from a comparative point of view, the waterfall and spiral SWDLC models. Explain the contribution of spiral model to risk assessment.
33. Redo problem 20 assuming that others will design, code, and test the product, and the only communication you will have with them is the specification document. This problem is designed to illustrate how difficult it is to write a requirement specification without direct contact with the implementer.
34. Develop an operational timeline for the product of problem 20. Consider the user's background and experience in developing the timeline. List menus, prompts, etc., that would be required to interface children and teachers to the product. Did preparation of the timeline change your view of functional and performance requirements of problem 20?
35. Describe how you would prepare an estimate for the number of SLOC (single lines of code) required to implement the requirements of problems 20.
36. Design a standard form for dealing with identifying problems and issues, assigning actions, tracking efforts, resolving problems or issues, and changing an SRS document after it has been approved.
37. Estimate the size of a personal computer operating system with approximately the same functional capabilities and performance as MS-DOS. Explain how you arrived at your estimate. (You will repeat this problem at the end of chapter 3 and once again at the end of chapter 15.)

References

1. C. Anderson and M. Dorfman, eds. *Aerospace Software Engineering*, AIAA, Washington D.C., 1991.
2. B. W. Boehm, "A Spiral Model of Software Development and Enhancement," *IEEE Comp.* 21(5), pages 61–72 (1988).
3. Defense Systems Management College, *System Engineering Management Guide*, U.S. Government Printing Office, Washington, D.C., 1986.
4. *IEEE Comp.* 26(1), (1993). This issue is devoted mostly to computer support for concurrent engineering.
5. IEEE, *Standards Collection, Software Engineering*, IEEE, New York, 1994.
6. P. S. Licker, *Fundamentals of System Analysis with Application Design*, Boyd and Fraser, Boston, 1987.
7. H. D. Mills, M. Dyer, and R. C. Linger, "Cleanroom Software Engineering," *IEEE Software* 4(5), pages 19–25 (1987).
8. R. Orrange, "Direction to System Engineering," in *System Engineering Manager*, IBM, White Plains, New York, 1961.

9. J. C. Wethebe and N. P. Vitalani, *System Analysis and Design: Best Approach*, Ed. 4, West, St. Paul, 1994.

10. J. L. Whitten, L. D. Bently, and V. M. Barlow, *Systems Analysis and Design Methods*, Ed. 3, Irwin, Homewood, Ill., 1994.

11. R. Winner, J. Pennell, H. Bertrand, and M. Slusarczuk, *The Role of Concurrent Engineering in Weapon System Acquisition*, IDA Report, R-338, Alexandria, Va., 1988.

12. E. Yourdon, *Modern Structured Analysis*, Prentice-Hall, Upper Saddle River, N.J., 1989.

Case Studies

2.0 OBJECTIVES

The objectives of this chapter are as follows: (1) to describe two system development projects that have a strong software content for use as a source for illustrative examples and exercises throughout the book; (2) to recognize that large projects are not initially well defined and well thought out, requirements are not always reasonable and rational, there are often conflicting opinions as to what should or shouldn't be done, and senior management doesn't always know instinctively what is right; (3) to describe some of the many ways in which a major system and software development project can originate and get underway; and (4) to provide a wealth of small problems and large projects that an instructor can use to support lecture material, extend ideas, or provide examples of typical system and software engineering tasks.

2.1 INTRODUCTION

The two projects described in the following pages are system development projects with high software content. The XYZ Corporation, a multiproduct manufacturing enterprise, has a notion that by automating and integrating the infrastructure that supports corporate facilities, operating cost can be reduced and a better overall performance may be forthcoming. Several incidents have made senior management feel a vague sense of urgency regarding the need for an improvement. A small fire in one of the buildings went undetected until it became a serious threat to the building. The security organization was unable to tell who was in the building at the time of the fire or determine if all employees and visitors had safely exited the building. A second incident involved accidental discovery that in one building the air conditioning system was removing heat while in another part of the same building a heating system was adding heat. While not an unusual HVAC situation for a large building, when presented along with concerns about energy costs and environmental concerns, it was just another prompt for senior management to "fix" something. There is, among senior management, an uneasy feeling that no one is really in charge of the facilities infrastructure. Senior management would like better visibility than is currently available to them. Eventually the XYZ management will come to realize that the functions associated with the facilities infrastructure plus a few others need to be collected into a single organizational unit, placed under a vice president, and given a charter and appropriate resources to support the charter.

The ABC Corporation, a large mail-order company, has reached a performance limit with their existing "system" (people, procedures, and piecemeal automation). The temptation to buy a quick, short-term solution to their problems has been resisted. Senior management has looked down the road and anticipates significant change to the business environment. Specifically, they expect that home shopping via two-way cable television links may be the wave of the future for the mail-order business. They realize that the capital investment they make now in a new system can have enormous future benefits if the new system is properly designed.

2.2   CASE STUDY PROBLEM STATEMENTS   ■

In the following two case studies, we will develop scenarios as close to real-world situations as possible. The reader may, therefore, assume that the XYZ or ABC companies are real-world corporations and the process they are following to solve their information system problems is one of many that are typical of real-world cases. In the real world, system development projects are initiated by an urgent desire to deal with expansion needs, a need for better performance, and a need for more cost-effective operation, etc. Sometimes a number of these needs may suggest the initiation of a major system analysis and design activity. It is with this approach in mind that we begin the problem statements associated with the XYZ and ABC corporations.

2.2.1   XYZ Project: Problem Statement

The XYZ Corporation, after completing several general engineering studies, has decided to develop an integrated information system to assist initially in handling its energy management, security, and transportation needs. The XYZ corporation has 18 multistory buildings scattered over a 100-acre campus. The preliminary studies have indicated that employing an integrated information system through automation of energy management, security, and intercampus transportation can result in improved performance and substantial cost savings. Moreover, the studies have also suggested that such an information system, once developed, might be a marketable product. The XYZ management intends to issue a request for proposal (RFP) to one of the several qualified companies who responded to a recent letter soliciting interest in submitting a proposal.

The XYZ Corporation has currently assigned a small team of their own system engineers to develop a set of requirements for the system. This material is now expected to form the basis for a statement of work (SOW) to be included in the RFP. Within the corporation there is a lingering conflict over whether internal (XYZ) resources should be employed to design and develop the new system or whether a contractor should be used. The system engineers who did the original studies have strong feelings about the project and would like very much to build the system themselves. Senior management feels that in-house development of the system will require a substantial increase in staff.

At a heated day-long session, senior management concluded that they will use an outside contractor to design and develop the system and that an RFP should be issued as soon as possible. Further, they decided to allow the contractor to develop the requirements and implement them completely, constituting a turnkey project. A two-phased procurement is envisioned in which the first phase is devoted to requirements definition, a preliminary design, and an associated cost estimation for implementation. The second phase will implement the approved design.

To appease their own system engineering group, management assigns responsibility for technical direction of the contract to the team that performed the original studies. Other organizations within the XYZ corporation are directed to begin preparation of the RFP. The procurement group has a standard procedure that must be tailored to meet the unique aspects of this procurement. The legal department must review the final version of the RFP. The financial organization will want to be involved in setting up a financial reporting scheme for both contractor and XYZ people who will work on the project that is consistent with the corporation financial reporting system.

A program manager is appointed to run the procurement. The first order of business is to develop a procurement package and to establish a criteria for evaluating proposals and selecting a contractor.

The major functions the system is required to perform and some implementation ideas as identified by the system engineering studies are as follows:

1. Control all heating, ventilation, and air conditioning equipment to minimize energy use. Consider the use of fuzzy-logic HVAC control systems.
2. Recognize, diagnose, and "repair" all failures in heating, ventilation, and air conditioning equipment. Consider the use of expert systems. Repair should be interpreted as issuing a maintenance order.
3. Control and manage all lighting systems providing lighted offices, walkways, and parking lots to minimize energy use.
4. Recognize, diagnose, and "repair" all failures in the lighting system.
5. Schedule automatic interbuilding shuttles and automatically maintain accurate schedules in each building and in each office. Shuttle vehicles have onboard telephones.
6. Schedule and track all company vehicles in the motor pool. Each vehicle contains a telephone.
7. Schedule all vehicle preventive maintenance. Maintain fleet maintenance records.
8. Maintain a dynamic list of all employees and visitors on campus including time of entry and departure and location. Location will include parking lots.
9. Maintain a paperless telephone directory with a one-hour lag time between number assignment and appearance in the directory.
10. Control access to all buildings and secure areas. Limit free access to authorized employees only.
11. Sense and report attempted entry, fires, and off-nominal events in all buildings.

The system engineering team developed some additional requirements and implementation ideas as a result of their brief studies. The main objective of this system is thought to be to consolidate and automate all energy management, security, and transportation functions to improve overall operation and at the same time reduce operating cost. The reader will recognize that in many ways these requirements are generally similar to command and control system requirements.

According to Figure 1.1 in chapter 1, the system as envisioned is expected to require a number of sensors located in offices, hallways, utility rooms, and entrances throughout the building. The sensors will detect temperature, pressure, humidity, current, voltage, smoke, gas, light, valve positions, and door positions; they include various security scanners and sensors. Actuators will include motorized switches controlling heating units, blowers, lights, air conditioning units, humidifiers, dehumidifiers, valves, and door locks. Monitors, printers, telephones, control consoles, and displays will also be driven by outputs from the processor(s).

Several control consoles are envisioned located strategically around the campus. Redundancy has been mentioned frequently because of the need for the system to be on line a high percentage of the time. Some of the existing equipment will have to be modified to permit automatic control, and some existing equipment will have to be fitted with sensors to measure performance or recognize malfunctions as they occur.

Clearly a substantial maintenance function will be required to keep all subsystems including the information system operating. A complete maintenance library stored on a special maintenance computer has been suggested as a way to keep all maintenance documentation current.

Expert systems for maintenance and operation of heating, ventilation, and air conditioning subsystems have been suggested. The use of weather forecasts in controlling heating, ventilation, and air conditioning has been discussed. The question of central versus distributed control has been discussed with no resolution. The availability of various subsystems, including software to implement functions, has been mentioned, but serious considerations have been set aside until there is a better understanding of functional and performance requirements.

It has been recognized that a corporation-wide training program will be required to acquaint everyone with how the new system will work and why the new system is beneficial to both employees and the XYZ Corporation. Operators and maintenance personnel will need specialized courses. The security force will need specialized training. There will be a need to prepare courses and course material.

A quick look at documentation needs indicated a possible requirement for a document describing the system in its entirety. Manuals for operator consoles in general and one for each position at the main console should be considered. A document describing the data processing subsystem hardware and software in general terms is expected. The XYZ corporation will ask that the two main software specification documents be delivered formally. Test results and other pertinent documentation will be made part of the RFP. The system engineering team plans to ask that the contractor provide all project-originated documentation on an informal basis. Delivery schedules, document content, and other details have not been worked out. It is expected by the XYZ corporation that contractors will have concerns about protecting their proprietary information.

Initial results from earlier studies and designs have indicated that software will most likely include a small operating system for remote processors and a set of standard application packages for control and monitor functions, self test, equipment diagnostics, equipment performance analysis functions, redundancy management functions, and network interfaces. Either a mainframe or a workstation will be used to support special-purpose control consoles. In either case, application packages will be required for the following: (1) scheduling functions; (2) tracking vehicles, workers, and visitors; (3) establishing global equipment control policies; (4) implementing access and security functions; (5) maintaining operator interfaces; and (6) generating reports.

2.2.2   ABC Project: Problem Statement

The ABC Company is a family-owned mail-order business that has experienced a tremendous growth over the last 10 years. Corporate management at ABC has long recognized that they need to revamp their mostly manual information systems. The current system has been developed in piecemeal fashion. Each organization has automated independently as the need arose. Continued business success is now straining the ability of even the most loyal and dedicated employees and their systems to meet the information management needs of the business.

The information system problem came into sharp focus recently at a weekly management review when two separate presentations given by managers from two different organizations cited sales figures for the same period that differed markedly. Moreover, the differences could not be explained at the meeting.

Senior management took action the following day, assigning responsibility to one of their executives to take the necessary steps to develop an information system ''second to none in the mail-order business'' that will automate as much as possible of the data and information handling of the company. Further, the new information system will be viewed as a major capital investment and will be treated by senior management as such. They also charged the executive with developing a system that would handle projected growth and accommodate technology improvements. They cautioned the executive to be sensitive to employee concerns and feelings. Senior management wanted especially to assure employees that their jobs were not in jeopardy and that they were not being blamed for falling behind in this area of the business.

The executive begins the assignment by developing a list of the main functions the new system will have to perform. In the executive's view, system functional requirements should include the following:

1) Orders may be accepted by phone by an on-line order-entry operator or recorded message or may go directly to the computer by Touch-Tone phone. Faxed or mail-in orders can be accepted by either optical scanners or order-entry operators. The system must also be able to accept computer-to-computer order entry and must not preclude interface to a television-based home shopping system.

2) Each order-entry station must have full and complete access to inventory (number on hand and price), mailing information (postage, delivery date, and tax), and customer records including correspondence. This requirement is to assure that each operator can handle any customer situation that arises without handing the customer off to anyone except a supervisor or manager.

3) The new system must be able to accept orders originating from an interactive, two-way cable TV shopping system. Current thoughts are that when the projected interactive cable TV system (the electronic highway) has sufficient subscribers, ABC will enter the home shopping business. Customers will be able electronically to browse through catalogue offerings; examine merchandise via home television; order replacement parts; view operating, assembly, or maintenance instructions; ask questions; and place orders via the home shopping system.

4) The system must support a complete tracking system that will allow operators to locate an order placement and follow it through the process to merchandise delivery if required. Order-entry operators must be able to open new customer accounts and confirm charge cards on line. It is recognized that charge card confirmation will require an additional external interface.

5) The order-entry function must interface with accounts receivable, inventory management, customer lists, warehouses, and delivery carriers. The order-entry function will also provide means for monitoring order entries for quality control purposes and transaction histories for yet-to-be-determined purposes.

6) The publications function should include preparation of catalogues and flyers. Capability for an on-line catalogue is to be provided so that the catalogue can be accessed by computer. Catalogue and inventory must be consistent. Inventory is geographically distributed over several shipping centers.

7) The system must be on-line 24 hours a day. The availability of the system will be such that downtime will be less than four hours per year. The objective is never to have to use computer outage as an excuse to a customer.

8) The warehouse function should include an automatic picking system triggered by an input message from the order-entry function. Product codes in the message are employed to identify product. Labels are printed based on the name and address portion of the message. A complete order tracking system must be provided.

9) Automatic accounts receivable processing is required with reasonableness tests to prevent things like bills for $999,999.99 or $0.00 being sent.

10) Automatic inventory decrementing and automatic stock reordering are requirements

11) Ability to relate product purchases to specific area codes is required.

12) Ability to relate complaints, refunds, and replacements to product identifiers is required.

13) There are many reports required to satisfy all users of the system. At present, it is hard to identify all that will be needed.

14) An on-line customer service function should be available to deal with questions regarding product assembly, repair, spare parts, and product performance as well as other related subjects.

The list of the hardware required for this system includes appropriate computing power, sensors, and actuators. Sensors include telephones, keyboards, bar code scanners, magnetic ink character recognition (MICR), optical scanners, etc. Actuators include automatic picking systems (mechanical conveyor systems that locates products in a warehouse and delivers them to a mailing station), monitors, printers, disks, tape units, etc.

In addition to the hardware listed, software will be required to support the following functions:

order entry (including computer-to-computer)
accounts receivable
accounts payable
inventory management
automatic ordering
order picking
shipping and receiving
order tracking
report generation

purchasing
quality control
facilities
personnel
marketing and sales
publications
home shopping (growth)
customer service

In addition to the list of software and hardware, the young executive realizes that there are many other necessary decisions to be made. The system architecture is an open issue. Maintenance of the entire system will be an important consideration. Training and documentation will be important. Training current employees in using the new system is a high priority. In busy seasons ABC hires many temporary employees, and appropriate formal training and self-study documents are essential to maintaining the quality of order taking as well as other business activities.

2.3   XYZ PROJECT: ANALYSIS   ■

The XYZ program manager very quickly recognized the lack of real system development experience in the system engineering team and took immediate steps to recruit (hire or transfer) an experienced system engineering manager to lead the development of a technically sound procurement package. As more questions were raised, it became apparent that a great deal more technical work was required before a meaningful request for proposal (RFP) could be released. A promising candidate for the system engineering manager position was found and brought into the organization to lead procurement package development.

The recently recruited system engineering manager immediately began a series of meetings with the XYZ system engineers who had been involved in the original studies. They were found to be very knowledgeable people in their own areas of expertise but to be somewhat lacking in their ability to grasp the "big picture." It was also found that questions that called for a quantitative answer too frequently went unanswered. There was, in fact, a lack of hard data throughout all of the previous work.

Several meetings with senior management revealed that they, too, were somewhat naive regarding expectations for the new information system. The new system engineering manager realized that a cost-benefit analysis would be essential in justifying the commitment of resources to develop the new capital equipment (the new information system). Furthermore, support from the board of directors will be required to carry out the development. At his urging, a presentation to the XYZ Board of Directors, to discuss the proposed system, was scheduled. A cost-benefit analysis of the new system was performed and presented along with a description of the planned system.

Senior management continued to refer to the development of the procurement package as designing the new system and continued to offer detail design ideas at every opportunity.

The system engineering manager's first step forward was to circulate a short memorandum outlining system requirements in the broadest of terms and issuing technical direction to the engineering team. The list of the requirements included the following:

1. A 25 to 30 year lifetime with growth provision for hardware upgrades and new applications.
2. Maximum automation consistent with technical performance and cost-benefit analysis. This included ideas regarding control systems using fuzzy logic, expert systems, and neural nets.
3. Simple interfaces with existing systems such as personnel, security, HVAC, transportation, the campus LAN, and the corporate telecommunication system.
4. A payback period of less than 5 years.
5. Use fuzzy and expert systems only where cost effectiveness can be shown. Don't, however, preclude growth to use of these systems in the future.
6. Employ existing data processing (DP) equipment (hardware and software) wherever possible. Justify any unique and new development by cost-benefit studies.
7. Minimize impact on operations, personnel, vendors, and customers.
8. Reduce amount of paper used in current system.

The memorandum closed with direction to the engineering team to group all functional requirements identified thus far into six separate groups: security, transportation, HVAC, maintenance, data gathering, and other. The category ''other'' was to contain functional requirements not associated with the first five functions. Minimum coupling and maximum cohesion were to be the criteria used in the allocation process.

The engineering team was also directed to gather hard performance data to support functional requirements. In particular, there was a need to project growth for the next 25 to 30 years and to quantify volumes, rates, traffic, etc. For the most part these requests only formalized questions that had been left unanswered in prior meetings.

Component-responsible analysts and engineers were assigned to become intimately familiar with the present personnel, HVAC, security, and transportation systems. Each engineer was charged with the responsibility for becoming an authority on his or her assigned system (people, procedures, hardware, software, interfaces, and folklore). A system architecture team was assigned to develop candidate system architectures based on original system studies and information being developed by task teams and requirement grouping efforts.

The engineering manager scheduled a short daily team coordination meeting to ensure good communication and keep everyone focused on the right problems. The agenda was usually confined to (1) problem discussion, identification of actions that needed to be taken and assignment of the problem to an individual, and (2) reports from those who had completed their assigned actions.

2.3.1 XYZ Project: System Architecture

Under the direction of the system engineering manager, meetings were crisply run and usually finished on time. At the third meeting the architecture team reported that they had identified two viable architecture candidates (Figures 2.1 and 2.2) and circulated for review and comment a six-page technical note describing them. They also asked that a software engineer be assigned to their team to begin looking at software architectures and to assist them in system architecture studies.

The engineering manager assigned one of the senior engineers to establish criteria for evaluating the two architectures. At the next meeting the senior engineer circulated the first

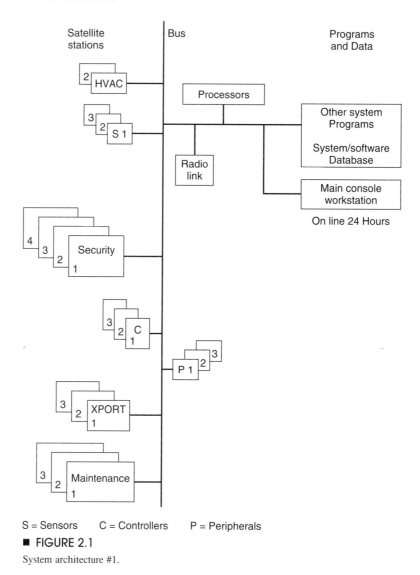

S = Sensors   C = Controllers   P = Peripherals

■ **FIGURE 2.1**

System architecture #1.

cut at criteria, criteria weighting, and the rationale for picking the criteria for review and comment. The criteria and weighting are as follows:

Weighting	Criteria
10	Cost (life cycle cost)
9	Growth accommodation (new function and change)
8	Operator training requirements
7	Security (potential for outside penetration)
6	Use of existing systems (without modification)
5	Robustness (resistance to failure and recovery from failures)

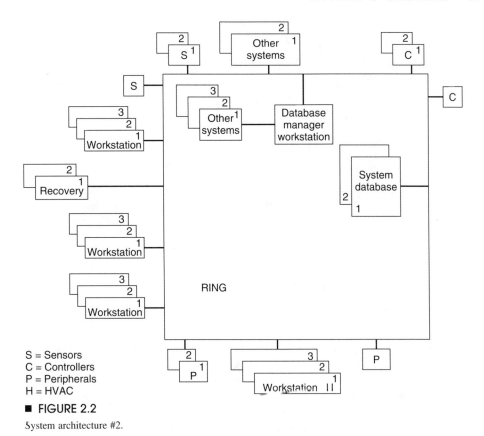

■ FIGURE 2.2

System architecture #2.

At the following meeting the newly assigned software engineer presented his idea for a software architecture that corresponds to the requirements outlined in the engineering manager's memorandum. It was also noted that there was a need for a longer look at some of the software requirements that were implicit in the top-level requirements. The first suggestion for a software architecture is shown in Figure 2.3. The platform interface would be designed as a flexible interface that could be adapted to changing hardware and operating environments. Thus the inevitable hardware and software changes can be accommodated by modification to the interface without disturbing the applications. Similarly, the application interface can adapt to new or changing applications by simply changing the application interface. The trend toward standardization was thought to be a positive factor in support of this particular software architecture.

Architecture 1, as illustrated in Figure 2.1, consists of a bus network with a dual redundant main console as the controlling node. Network control is via a polling method. A centralized control over all buildings and resources on campus is effected by this configuration. The satellite stations can access the system to pass information to the central console, to obtain status and performance information, or under some circumstances, to take direct control of a specific function. All scheduling is handled by the main console. The on-line telephone directory is also maintained at the central control console. Data gathering and database management are monitored by operators at the central console. The bus is redundant with cross-

Application 1	2	3	4	Growth

Application interface

Platform interface

Hardware, system software, networks etc.

■ FIGURE 2.3

Software system architecture.

strapping at each node. That is, each node is connected to both primary and backup bus and each redundant node is connected to both networks. Figure 2.4 illustrates the approach.

This architecture will have an impact on the existing organization and the responsibilities allocated to each operating unit. This fact is now clearly recognized and more interest is demonstrated in the architecture studies.

Proponents of architecture 1 argue that central control protects resources better. They also state that decisions made with architecture 1 will be better because they are made with the entire campus in mind. They also claim better performance visibility because operators have access to campuswide data as basis for actions.

Architecture 2, as illustrated in Figure 2.2, is based on a token ring network configuration using the international standard network protocol (seven-layer). Any workstation on the network can be configured to handle any function by simply using the appropriate identifications and passwords. Programs and data can then be downloaded to the workstation. Encryption/decryption software will be used for all network traffic. Portable workstations can be linked via radio and bridges to the network. The operating system will have a real-time component to support certain sensor and controller processing and peak traffic periods. The network will be redundant and routed over different paths to prevent one incident from physically inter-

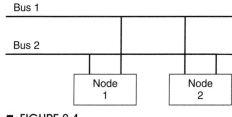

■ FIGURE 2.4

Redundant bus arrangement.

rupting both networks. Sensors will be redundant as will the system database. The database manager workstation will be responsible for the data gathering application and maintenance of the system database. Other workstations will access the database directly to perform their particular function. Access to the system is controlled by access codes and passwords.

The existence of two architectures implies a trade-off study to decide which architecture should be used. The results of the trade-off study are shown in Figure 2.5. The architecture trade-off study forced the engineering team to dig deeper into function allocation and begin to develop a feeling for the software architecture. After several tries, the function allocations originally spelled out in the system engineering manager's memorandum seemed to emerge as shown in Figure 2.6.

The new system engineering manager has suggested that the procurement package contain a draft system specification and draft function and performance specifications for each subsystem. The contractor will be required to complete the specifications to the satisfaction of the XYZ Corporation before going forward with implementation. The system engineering manager explains that these specifications will enable the XYZ Corporation to get their ideas on paper and will help bidders to understand better the problems they are expected to solve. With better understanding of the problem, bidders can be expected to provide better cost and schedule estimates. In addition, the ideas and problem solutions derived from a wider experience base may result in an improved system design. Although there is concern about increased analysis cost and schedule stretch-out, the idea goes over well and is accepted. Several qualified companies, some of which had expressed an interest in bidding, are contacted again, updated on status, and assessed for continued interest in bidding on the project.

The overall system and software architecture is beginning to take form, The token ring network and the distributed approach to implementing functions has some appealing features. Training costs are expected to be lower because it will not be necessary to cross-train operators for a central control console to control and manage all subsystems. Although the database management function is on every subsystem's critical path, development of individual subsystems is almost entirely decoupled and can proceed concurrently and independently. Another interesting feature of architecture 2 is that application programs can reside on workstations along with certain application-related data. Software changes or workstation failures can be overcome by downloading new or replacement programs and data from the redundant network server.

		Architecture 1			Architecture 2	
	Weight	Score	Total		Score	Total
Cost	10	10	100		8	80
Growth	9	8	72		10	90
Training	8	9	72		10	80
Security	7	10	70		9	63
Existing equipment	6	9	54		10	60
Robust	5	8	40		10	50
Total			408			423

■ FIGURE 2.5

Trade-off study results.

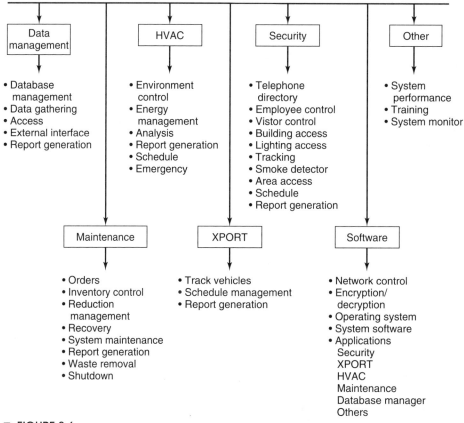

■ FIGURE 2.6

Function allocation chart.

Each functional area has a significant software component. Figure 2.6 breaks out software functions separately. However, in developing specifications for each functional area, an important consideration is allocation of functions to operators, software, and hardware. An engineer is assigned to each functional area to expand the functional requirements into more detail; allocate functions among hardware, software, and operator procedures; and to quantify performance requirements. Because each functional area is responsible for its own sensors and actuators, a software engineer is assigned to the data management function. This functional area is most likely to be implemented in software and operator procedures. Other functional areas will be implemented by a mix of software, hardware, and operator procedures.

For example, the HVAC function in its normal mode of operation will obtain HVAC sensor measurements from files located on the network server (memory). An expert system (software) will decide, based on certain rules, what actuators (hardware) must be turned on or off and issue appropriate commands. No functions will be performed by the operator. It is a fully automatic function. In case an off-nominal event occurs requiring operator intervention, the intervention function then is assigned to an operator and intervention procedures must be defined. These procedures will undoubtedly need software support. The elaboration of the HVAC functional area will result in hardware and software function and performance specifications, very closely related, and a set of operating procedures. By working through a series of operational timelines exercising all possible combinations of events, a comprehensive specification for the three implementation possibilities (hardware, software, operator) will be developed.

Since each subsystem is responsible for its own sensors and actuators, the software engineer assigned to the data management function is dealing almost exclusively with software requirements. The first step in developing the software requirements specification for this functional area is to expand on the allocated functions. He or she begins by breaking the data management function into separate subfunctions and listing, for each of the major subfunctions, all related functions, as follows.

Database Management

1. Maintain current copy of all sensor readings as defined by each subsystem. Note: sensors include those that report equipment failures.
2. Update backup memory at rate dictated by each subsystem.
3. Switch memory on error indication (define error).
4. Encrypt outgoing data to network.
5. Decrypt incoming data from network, excluding sensors and maintenance messages.
6. Maintain sensor history (measurements) as defined by each subsystem.
7. Resolve access conflicts.
8. Control access via passwords and keys.
9. Notify operator, via high priority message, of sensor or actuator anomalies.

Data Gathering

1. Read subsystem sensors at rate dictated by each subsystem.
2. Process redundant sensors.
3. Perform reasonableness tests.
4. Check for sensor failure indication.
5. Calibrate and convert raw sensor readings.
6. Store in database (pass to database management).
7. Save sensor history data as required by subsystem.
8. Check for subsystem failure indication via maintenance messages.

Similar data gathering activities must be done for other data management functions, interface management, and report generation. There has been some confusion regarding *data* and *database management*. Terminology is becoming a problem in other areas as well. The solution is, of course, to initiate data dictionary development and rename data management to data control to eliminate confusion.

A review of the allocation study results is scheduled, and a two-day meeting produces some changes and identifies several new functions. Data control picks up responsibility for (1) logging all accesses to the database and (2) archiving critical data on an off-line mass storage unit. Each subsystem engineer has the opportunity to present a more detailed picture of the functional requirements allocated to his or her subsystem. Unanswered questions and issues are documented and assigned for resolution at the end of the review.

A first cut, shown in Figure 2.7, as a top-level block diagram is circulated. This diagram will grow and change over the next few weeks as system design progresses. Each subsystem engineer is directed to expand his or her subsystem requirements in more detail. A standard

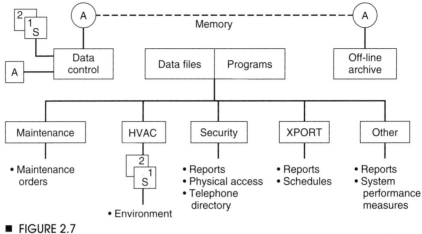

■ **FIGURE 2.7**

System diagram.

format is suggested for describing functional requirements. For each function there must be explicit input, output, and process requirements specifications. For example, for functional requirement 1, "Read subsystem sensors at rate dictated by each subsystem," explicit input, output, and process requirements may be summarized as follows.

Explicit Input Requirements

1. Inputs are normally automatically entered. They are operator originated for off-nominal or unusual modes.
2. The number of distinct inputs depends on the number of current sensors plus projected growth and the number of current maintenance messages plus projected growth.
3. Sample rates are determined by each subsystem.
4. Message structure is determined by each subsystem.
5. Parameter characteristics including units, range, etc., are determined by each subsystem.
6. Time samples are required to accompany each sensor sample. That is, each measurement has associated with it the time at which the sample was taken.

Explicit Output Requirements

1. Outputs are normally electronic and are passed to the data management subfunction.
2. Off-nominal cases will require, at operator direction, hard or soft copy for any sensor either directly from the sensor (raw measurement or processed measurement) or from the database dynamically or as a single value.

Explicit Process Requirements

1. Reasonableness tests on raw sensor measurements are determined by subsystem.
2. Polynomials for scaling, calibration, and conversion are provided by subsystems.
3. Structure input message for database management.
4. Sensor-related maintenance message processing is determined by subsystem.

5. Structure all messages for archival file.
6. Update check file.

The software engineer decides that to pin down input specifics, a questionnaire can be circulated to each subsystem manager to collect detailed information. The questionnaire may ask that, for each sensor, the following information be provided:

1. sensor identifier (identifiers if redundant)
2. sensor's physical characteristics (brief description)
3. frequency of samples
4. number of bytes
5. location of sign and high order bit/byte in message
6. other items, if any, in sensor message
7. sensor read command
8. range of valid sensor readings
9. sensor-related maintenance message
10. sensor accuracy
11. all conversion algorithms
12. redundancy management algorithms if any exist
13. time dependency (relation of sample to sample time)
14. sensor failure modes

As questionnaires are returned and compiled, the software engineer begins to see that a standard sensor processing function may be a possible implementation. At worst, separate processing functions for each sensor type would be an implementation solution. No sampling now or projected for the future requires a high rate (greater than one sample per second).

Maintenance messages are a relatively new idea. Each subsystem component is allocated a 32-bit maintenance message. The objective is to allow subsystem hardware components to input 32 binary indications as to operational health of the component. For example, the power supply for an HVAC controller provides an up level in one of the maintenance message bits whenever power is being supplied. If power is lost or turned off, a down level occurs in that maintenance message bit. In this way failures can be recognized and repaired as they occur. But more important, chronic failures can be identified and addressed by redesigning subsystem components or replacing subsystem components. The maintenance message can also be used to indicate switch or valve positions in a subsystem.

The data gathering function passes processed maintenance messages to the database management function in the following format:

Identifier	32 bits
Message	32 bits
Time of sample	Hours, minutes, seconds, milliseconds elapsed since midnight
Time of day	Hours, minutes, seconds, milliseconds in military time

The operational timeline associated with the data gathering subfunction is relatively straightforward. The normal mode will have the function entirely automated. Sensors are read and processed, and results are passed to the data control function, which makes sensor readings available for access by other subsystems. Maintenance messages are extracted, processed, and also passed to the data control function. In the event of a sensor failure or a critical failure indication in a maintenance message, an alarm condition will be established. Under these circumstances there may be a need for operator intervention. Operator intervention will include the following:

- troubleshooting the sensor
- resetting sensor processing parameters upon sensor replacement
- restarting automatic sensor processing
- reading and displaying selected sensor sets (40 per screen limit)

Similar activity in other subsystem areas results in development of system diagrams and a much deeper understanding of the functions allocated to each subsystem. Some migration of function takes place to improve coupling and cohesiveness. As a conceptual view of the system takes form, the system engineering manager and the program manager begin to focus on the project or program plan and on cost and schedule estimates. While cost information will not be shared with bidders, it is important for the client to have an idea of what to expect in terms of project cost.

Meanwhile, there have been meetings with prospective bidders designed to help them understand what the client wants. Over the few months that client and prospective bidders have been working together, some prospective bidders have dropped out and new prospective bidders have entered the competition.

Gradually the request for proposal (RFP), the procurement package, comes together and is released. The RFP in this procurement includes a schedule, a list of deliverable products, a statement of work describing what the contractor is to do in formal language suitable for inclusion in a contract, a model contract, financial reporting requirements, and references to applicable standards and practices. For this procurement the client has included in a separate document the system description, which is offered as a straw man design that contractors can use as a baseline for developing their own design or as guidance in preparing a cost proposal. The intent is to allow bidders to offer designs and ideas of their own to solve the client's problems. The procurement is in two phases. The first phase ends with a critical design review (CDR). The second phase is the implementation of the results of the CDR and ends with delivery of the new system. The program schedule in the RFP calls for completion of phase 1 in 6 months and completion of phase 2 14 months later. The bidders are asked to propose alternate schedules if reductions in project cost will result.

The list of deliverables specified in the RFP includes the following: the network with all required bridges and gateways, a radio link, and a network operating system; twelve workstations with operating system; two secondary memory units and a primary memory unit; eight printers; sensors and actuators; electrical and mechanical labor to retrofit existing hardware with new equipment; six software products; and twenty-six formal documents. A work breakdown structure and a financial reporting requirement are also described in the RFP. The bidders are given 45 days to respond.

2.4 BIDDER'S PERSPECTIVE   ■

Initiation of a system and/or software development can occur in any number of different ways. A company may employ its own resources to develop a needed system. A client company may choose to contract directly with a contractor company for development of their system. A third possibility is for a client company to issue a request for proposal (RFP) to several interested and qualified contractors, evaluate competitive proposals or bids subsequently submitted by prospective contractors, and award the contract to the best proposal. In the latter approach, the prospective contractor engages in intense planning and technical activity during the proposal writing phase. A great deal of energy is expended in defining and sizing both system and software and in estimating schedules, development cost, and risk. We have elected to describe the proposal path to project initiation. In proposal preparation the software engineer has a responsibility to assist in many of the system-level technical and planning efforts as well as taking a principal role in software-oriented technical and planning activities. The following narrative traces the efforts of the software engineer through proposal preparation completion.

2.4.1 The Proposal

A software engineer may be first introduced to the new project by accompanying a cadre of the potential project team to a briefing given by the potential client. The briefing is given for the benefit of a number of potential contractors who will compete for the project in the near future. The client, the XYZ Corporation, wants to be sure that each competitor has an equal chance and that each competitor fully understands what will be required. The software engineer will have done his or her homework before the briefing to maximize information obtained at the briefing and to develop a list of key questions that need to be answered. The client will also benefit from these questions, possibly modifying the formal procurement documentation as a result.

After these briefings the client will release what is called a request for proposal (RFP). The RFP contains directions for the bidders or contractors who will prepare a competitive proposal to perform the project. Proposal preparation time may be short, a few months perhaps. These months are a very intense period characterized by long hours, much soul-searching, hard decisions, and high visibility. For many organizations this is the main source for new projects. Therefore, senior management is very much interested in all aspects of what is happening. For the ambitious software engineer, it is an opportunity for exposure to senior management, an opportunity to demonstrate technical abilities, judgment, performance in stressful situations, leadership, dedication, and communication skills.

The proposal process itself is fast-paced, very dynamic, and very exciting. The software engineer's parent organization is competing with other organizations to win a major system procurement project by exhibiting better designs or approaches to the project, more creative ways to perform project tasks, lower cost, deeper understanding of the problem, and better project technical and management plans. The specific criteria by which the contractor proposals will be evaluated is usually spelled out in the RFP by the client. Since only a few months are allowed to assemble the proposal, the proposal team that has trained the hardest, learns the quickest, and responds with the best all-round proposal usually wins. The rate at which team members learn their craft is high in a proposal environment and the understanding they develop as to how their company really works is also accelerated in proposal environments. Obviously, most successful companies will use their very best people on proposals.

The RFP usually contains, in addition to instructions to the bidders, a statement of work defining what specifically the project is to accomplish, directions for how the bidders are to describe their management plan for this project, and directions for how to prepare and submit the cost for the proposed work. The client's RFP often contains a work breakdown structure that the client would like bidders to use.

Even though the software engineer's organization has been preparing for this proposal effort for many months, receipt of the RFP triggers a flurry of intense activity. The software engineer is assigned to read selected sections of the RFP. The objective is to surface any questions that remain unanswered and to look for any unusual requirements or problems not already identified during preproposal activity. It is often said that if you must learn about the project through the RFP, you will more than likely lose the competition. There is, therefore, an emphasis on doing your homework before the RFP is released, which includes making calls on the client as permitted, finding out as much as possible about the client and about the problem the client wants solved. After release of the RFP, there will be a great many demands on the software engineers' time. There will be meetings to attend and support to other organizations that need software wisdom to assist in sorting through the RFP.

As quickly as possible after receipt of the RFP, the proposal manager will call a meeting and reveal the plan (which includes a schedule) for proposal preparation. At that time the proposal team will be expanded by adding additional people. Assignments will be given and critical questions resolved or scheduled for resolution. The proposal effort is now fully underway.

A mainstream assignment for a software engineer would be preparation of the software segment of the project plan. This effort entails developing a thorough understanding of the software needs for the entire project. If the master schedule calls for a hardware delivery and the hardware needs software to complete the delivery, then we have an interlocked schedule that must be worked carefully and jointly with other interested organizations. This situation occurs frequently for most modern projects of the size this book considers. Some obvious areas that need software engineers' support are as follows: embedded systems and embedded software (that will rely on the software development team to provide the software), early delivery of software elements to support hardware testing, modeling software, support to computer sizing, special demonstration software, and support to system prototyping efforts.

Preparation of a software development plan involves the following: (1) identification of all software products (deliverable and nondeliverable), (2) an estimate of the size of each product using some software attribute value such as function points or SLOC, (3) an estimate of the required quality using some software attribute value such as fault density (faults per source line of code), and (4) a brief description of each product in terms of its inputs, outputs, and functions. Other elements of the software deliverables might include formal documentation and development tools that must accompany the deliverables. The descriptions are stepwise partitioned into smaller elements, and the process of estimating size, quality, and documentation requirements is repeated. The level of detail is limited by the time available and the depth or extent of the understanding of the software product. The next step in the planning effort is to schedule the software product elements to be consistent with main schedules and hardware schedules.

With product descriptions, schedules, and the estimated parameter values for each software product in hand, the software engineer can go to his or her software development organization and obtain cost and schedule estimates. This brief description of the schedule and cost planning is a simplification of what is a complex and extremely important task. We will revisit this task when we discuss cost and schedule estimation in chapter 15.

The software engineer will usually make use of one of the top-down methods (algorithms) for estimating software development cost as a cross-check on results obtained from the bottom-up estimate provided by the software development organization.

As in most cases, this process is an iterative one designed to obtain the most accurate assessment possible of what must be done and when it must be done, how much it will cost, how it will be done, and who will do it. It is important that the entire software development team be part of the process and agree with the result. Often software bids are based on what it takes to win rather than results of a cost estimation process. This situation does not relieve the software engineer of the responsibility for developing the best possible cost estimate. Management needs to know what the magnitude of the risk is and establish a plan for dealing with the problem.

The question of how the software development will be accomplished is often answered by the RFP. The client may have strong ideas, not only on the SWDLC paradigm, but may also dictate design methodology to be used and the programming language to be used. Proposal writers have learned to give the client what he asks for. If the contractor would like to see changes made in the SWDLC, design methodology, language, etc., to be used, the changes should be suggested immediately after contract award. In general, it is not a good idea to waste proposal effort in selling the client on a different software development course. It may indicate to the client that you don't understand the project or the client.

If a good rationale for using another SWDLC paradigm exists (for example, a cost saving of some significance substantiated with hard data), then this topic might be good to address at one of the first client/contractor meetings immediately after award of the contract. One good reason for a software engineer to remain open-minded about software development life cycles, design methodologies, and programming languages is that most times he or she has little to do with the choice for a given project. A language or a design methodology may be chosen simply because more people on the project are familiar and comfortable with it. It is better to understand the objectives behind the SWDLC, the intent of the design methodology, and the purpose of a programming language in implementing designs rather than developing a bias toward one or another language, SWDLC paradigm, or work breakdown structure.

Figure 2.8 shows a generic organization chart for a software development project. Many large organizations employ a matrix organization approach to staffing a project. The matrix organization performs project tasks but does not form a separate project team expressly for performance of one project. The matrix organization commits to performing the project tasks without committing specific individuals to the tasks. If a matrix organization is employed, task descriptions take on an additional importance. Good task descriptions assure that a clear understanding exists between the project manager and the matrix organization managers as to task content, cost, and schedule.

Figure 2.9 shows a matrix organization that might perform project tasks. The staffing plan and organization chart for the matrix organization or the software development team is structured from cost and schedule information. Cost information will be cast into the format required by the client. It is at this point that writing assignments for the proposal are given.

An important task for the software engineer during a proposal is identification of risk in the software area. When senior management reviews the proposal before submission to the client, the areas of keenest interest will be cost estimations and risk assessments. Many managers have learned to be wary of software cost and schedule estimates and will almost always want to have a thorough risk assessment performed. They want to see contingency plans for areas of greatest risk, which are frequently some aspect of software development.

Technical effort during a proposal is usually limited to developing a thorough understanding of what the client needs or wants in enough detail to identify end products clearly; confirm technical approaches; and support accurate cost, schedule, and risk estimates. Writing skills are an important prerequisite for anyone working on proposals.

In meeting these objectives it is often necessary to prototype software for better product visibility, increased confidence in software technical performance, cost and schedule estimates, and risk assessments, and to provide help to prototyping efforts used to confirm hardware and system-level technical performance, cost, schedule, and risk estimates. The proposal

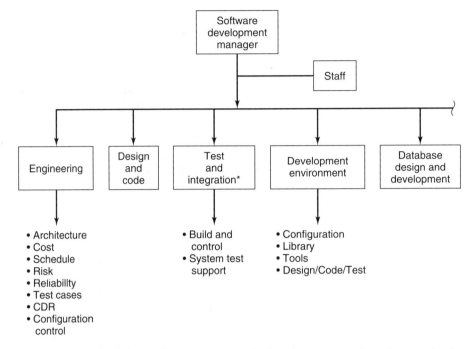

*Test and integration is frequently a separate organization whose manager is on the same level
as the software development manager.

■ FIGURE 2.8

Software development project organization.

technical activities are usually conducted with short deadlines and under considerable pressure. The process usually resembles a very creative yet chaotic environment. The results are
often pivotal in winning and performing successfully. For many companies a major system
procurement proposal represents a significant investment of resources, people, and dollars.

2.4.2   We Win

A few months after proposal submission, one contractor will be selected to perform the
project. In the months while the proposals are being evaluated, most members of the proposal
team will return to other assignments. A small nucleus will remain to continue to refine plans,
revisit estimates, and record new questions. Frequently, the client will ask for more information and clarification of parts of the proposal. Following an award notification, the team
immediately begins work on the project.

The first activity, after the victory party, involves a thorough review and revision of the
important material (project plan) prepared for the proposal—in particular, product definitions,
sizing estimates, schedules, and task descriptions. This time these tasks are performed with
help from the client organization. During the proposal period, the team has been constrained
from direct communication with the client. The software development plan will be updated

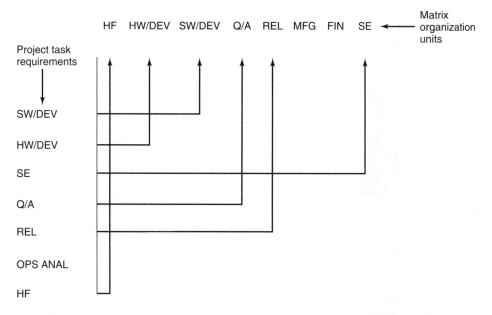

HF   HW/DEV   SW/DEV   Q/A   REL   MFG   FIN   SE ◄──── Matrix organization units

Project task requirements

SW/DEV

HW/DEV

SE

Q/A

REL

OPS ANAL

HF

Abbreviations

HF: Human factors
HW: Hardware
DEV: Development
SW; Software
Q/A: Quality assurance
REL: Reliability
OPS ANAL: Operations analysis
MFG: Manufacturing
FIN: Financial
COM SER: Com
SE: Software engineering

Advantages

Cost-efficient;
utilizes best talent,
develops people
technically

Disadvantages

Project loyalty,
team spirit,
project understanding,
client interface
are lacking

The column labels represent independent organizations and the new labels represent the activities during the project development process.

■ **FIGURE 2.9**

Matrix organization.

and worked to another level of detail. Key members of the software development team, software engineers, will be assigned to work with the system development team where software experience would be helpful.

Agreements as to the contents of the software requirements specifications will be negotiated with system analysts. These content agreements are for items not covered in data item descriptions (DIDs) or at a level of detail below that of the DID. Negotiations with other organizations with which the software development team will interface are conducted to establish what will be done, when, by whom, how, what products will be exchanged, and other related topics. Figure 2.10 shows other organizations that are part of the system development effort and for which an interface to the software development team is required.

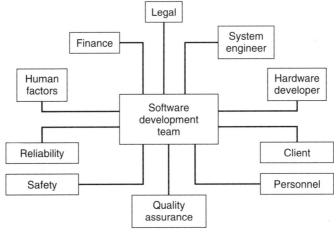

■ FIGURE 2.10

Software development team interface.

Throughout the life of the project there will be other people and other organizations that will interface with the software development organization. The success of the project will depend on how well these interfaces are managed and maintained. The following paragraph lists organizations and specialists that might interface with a software development team and their contributions to the end software product.

Human factors can provide display standards or guidance for design of soft copy and hard copy output. *Operations and system engineers* provide operational scenarios for various system modes, define operator functions that must be supported by software, and develop user and operator documentation. The *reliability organization* provides allocations of reliability requirements to software and analysis and modeling support for software reliability. *Quality assurance* provides people to select and impose standards and review products for conformance to standards. *Publications* provides editors and other support to produce contract documents. *System engineers* provide specifications and auditors for reviews. The *test organizations* provide reviewers, acceptance criteria, and schedules for intermediate software product deliveries. The *program office* provides guidance as to formal configuration control, schedules, communication with the client, and all product deliveries. The *finance organization* tracks costs and makes sure resources are being expended as planned and perhaps makes formal reports to the client as to how his money is being spent. The *legal department* provides answers to questions involving, for example, copyright laws and site licenses. The *personnel organization* provides recruiting support. The *contracts organization* resolves issues associated with specifics of the contract. The *procurement organization* makes purchases of equipment, software, and labor. *Subcontract management* assists in managing subcontractor activities.

All these interfaces must be understood and used as appropriate. In the life of a project, a software engineer may have occasions to consult every one of these organizations in carrying out his or her responsibilities. Each company defines slightly different roles for these organizations. It is important for the software engineer to understand, within his or her own company, what responsibilities these organizations are charged with and what they expect of the software development organization. The software development team, as we have seen, can draw on a wide range of people and organizations to help in the development of the software subsystem.

After the preparation of the software development plan, the next purely software development responsibility is an in-depth review of the SRS document to assure that (1) all functional and performance requirements are fully understood; (2) all external interfaces (input/output), both physical and functional, are quantified and communication protocols clearly described; (3) every allocated software requirement can be traced to a system level requirement; (4) every requirement is a testable requirement; (5) every constraint is clearly stated and can be defended as a real constraint; (6) each functional requirement is described in an input/process/output format; (7) both global and local databases are defined completely; (8) all internal interfaces are defined and consistent; (9) all sources for hidden requirements have been examined; and (10) algorithms needed for the design have been appropriately documented.

In large system development projects with a significant software component, there might be twenty to thirty or more individual software requirements specifications, each of which describes a major system function allocated to a separate software product. For example, a system-level architecture might allocate all automated communication functions to a single software element, all orbit determination functions to another, and all tracking functions to yet another. Each of these software elements might require 25,000 to 50,000 SLOC to implement. Each of these products would require its own separate software requirements specification.

Software requirements analysis focuses on the functional and performance aspects of the software product as well as external interfaces and data structures. In parallel a software design or architecture is being established using project design methodology, which in most cases involves a process of partitioning a major product or application package into major subfunctions following good practices regarding modularity, cohesion, and coupling. Each step in the requirements partitioning is accompanied by a physical implementation to confirm that at least one implementation does exist. If an object-oriented methodology were employed, we would establish subclasses, message characteristics, and subsequent elaborations. Documentation and reviews are performed at each level defined by the methodology. The target for partitioning is a level that has modules of a few hundred lines of code that perform a single function with a single entry point and single exit point, a simple input/output structure, and no local data storage required. The target for the final build-to specification is pseudocode or structured English so written that any entry-level person with no knowledge of the application can translate the pseudocode into the object language with minimum difficulty. For each module, the designer must provide a comprehensive set of test cases that will confirm correct execution of the module. Any special test driver software will be specified in pseudocode in the same manner as the prime software is specified.

The test and integration team is frequently made organizationally independent of the software development team and elevated in stature to foster a tougher, more objective test environment. If the test and integration organization is to perform its test function effectively, it is better to make a separate organization just to perform testing and integration of the software, operational timelines, and hardware into a system. The developers, it is felt, will not try to "break" their own product, whereas testing should try to find ways to "break" the product under test. The software development team sells its products to the test and integration team according to established formal acceptance criteria. Insofar as those modules are concerned, they now belong to the test and integration team. Once modules and strings are accepted, the software development team is in the maintenance phase for the delivered modules. We shall revisit the notion of a separate organization to conduct software testing and the idea of ''ownership'' again in the chapter on testing. Working in conjunction with the test and integration team, a software engineer will develop a detail plan for step-by-step assembly of the tested modules into a series of strings of modules. Each string should implement at least one major system function. Test case results and, if required, software drivers are developed for this purpose.

2.5   CHAPTER SUMMARY

The XYZ Corporation is now deep into the problem of developing, with the help of a knowledgeable contractor, a solution to the problems posed in section 2.2 and subsequent. The system that evolves will be somewhat different from the one originally envisioned during early engineering studies. The XYZ Corporation will change in many ways as the new system comes on line. In many ways the new system will reflect the XYZ Corporation's character. In the following chapters we will address many of the problems encountered in the development of XYZ Corporation's new system.

In a similar fashion, the ABC Corporation will establish functional and performance requirements, an architecture, and a system design. The ABC Corporation is more likely to call in and rely on a contractor or consultant to analyze the problem, establish requirements, and procure or build the system. The ABC Corporation's experience will also provide us with many examples of tasks and problems that a software engineer will encounter in his or her career.

2.6   EXERCISES

1. Using Figure 1.1 as guidance, sketch out a block diagram of a system that will meet the XYZ Corporation's requirements.
2. List as many of the deliverable products for the XYZ project as you can.
3. Discuss centralized, decentralized, and distributed approaches to a system architecture for the XYZ Corporation's problem. Will differing system architectures influence software design?
4. Using Figure 1.1 as guidance, sketch out a block diagram of a system that you think will meet the needs of the ABC Corporation.
5. Identify as many of the individual products that must be procured or built to satisfy ABC's needs.
6. For the ABC Corporation, make a technical argument for or against encrypting all electronic communication.
7. Develop a set of requirements for a disaster recovery subsystem (hardware/software/procedures) for the ABC Corporation.
8. List all the functional requirements you can think of associated with the ABC Corporation's projected cable television home shopping subsystem. Identify key interfaces. In what ways will these requirements differ from other order-entry subsystems?
9. Do you think four hours of downtime per year for ABC Corporation's system is achievable without redundancy?

10. Make an allocation of ABC Corporation's functional requirements to at least six subsystems. Use coupling and cohesion as the criteria. Explain your allocation rationale.
11. Develop the system architectures 1 and 2 (proposed for the XYZ project) into a more detailed architecture and develop a new trade-off study based on different criteria.
12. Describe what data encryption and decryption mean in terms of cost and implementation problems and issues.

Technical Planning

3.0 OBJECTIVES

We have already alluded to the importance of planning to the success of any venture. The more complex the venture, the more people involved, the more organizations participating, the more the need for effective planning. This chapter is about planning a software development venture. The main objective is to provide guidelines for building a software development plan. The guidelines discussed here are general enough to be applied to any software development.

3.1 INTRODUCTION

System and software development planning is an iterative process with periodic stepwise refinements. A system-level project plan needs information from the software organization as input to its planning effort. Similarly the software development planning effort requires inputs from the project plan. Orchestration of the planning process requires good coordination skills. Frequently project or software development planning takes place in an environment where there are a great many demands on the time of those best qualified to perform planning functions. In particular, the best qualified people are usually involved in establishing essential client contacts, initiating project tasks associated with short-term deliveries, recruiting and staffing, supporting or contributing to project level plans, and working on administrative issues associated with cost accounting, task authorizations, and subcontractors.

What is often not fully appreciated is that a software development plan is an implied commitment to perform specific tasks and deliver certain products on a specified schedule. Failure to carry out the plan is a commitment not met. Such a failure results in an erosion of personal and corporate credibility. Planning is also finding credible ways to produce results with limited resources and limited schedule flexibility. Planning is negotiating compromises in completion dates and resource allocations. Planning is identifying and accommodating the unforseen. Planning is blending the efforts of many people to produce a timely product, system or software, that satisfies client needs.

It sometimes takes a little encouragement to get management and staff to focus on planning when there are so many other important and more interesting tasks to pursue. By emphasizing the importance of planning and devoting the appropriate resources to producing a complete and viable plan, management can set a positive theme for a project. This theme is, "For every task, we will plan our work, work our plan, and deliver the product on the schedule we committed to."

Even with the best of planning there will be instances where subtask schedules cannot be met due to conditions not recognized or problems not anticipated in the plan. With good planning and clear project visibility, such delays may be identified early enough for "work-arounds" to be developed. Schedule delays may then be communicated projectwide so that dependent and related tasks can be adjusted and cost and schedule impacts assessed. This approach will prevent situations in which, a few months before scheduled delivery, the software project manager suddenly announces a 6-to-12 month delay in product delivery.

The software development plan should serve as a guide, a constant companion and a prompter to the software development staff throughout the entire project development process. The plan should describe in detail each deliverable product, its delivery schedule, the responsible organizations, the resources required to carry out the plan (including support from other external organizations), applicable standards and procedures to be employed in the development process, the technical and management control structure, and a risk assessment and containment subplan. The plan need not be contained in one document, but the critical elements of the plan need to be formalized in documents that are given formal review, revised based on the review results, and distributed to development team members.

If the software engineer leading the planning effort has already participated in or is concurrently participating in system-level project planning, visibility into overall project planning is implicit. If access to system-level planning is not directly available, it must be obtained in a timely manner to assure consistency between software development plans and other project plans. For example, if the hardware development plan calls for a software product delivery at a particular point in its plan, the software development plan must show a delivery of the product on or before that date.

The material presented in this chapter is designed to provide guidance and justification in the preparation of a software development plan. Initially, a strong recommendation is made for use of a workshoplike approach to plan development. The need to define the products of the development process thoroughly using well-defined, quantifiable attributes is strongly emphasized. A means for tracing changes in attribute values throughout the development to ensure visibility and improve future estimating is discussed. The preparation of work packages from the work breakdown structure, cost accounts, and task descriptions is discussed. Means to deal with change activity in a formal way is described in terms of the development plan. Questions such as (1) how to treat reviews, walkthroughs, and inspections; (2) how to treat formal and informal software documentation; (3) how to manage problem resolution; (4) how to manage and control the software development plan itself as it is being executed; and (5) how to manage and control interfaces with other performing organizations are all important considerations in planning a software development and are addressed in this chapter.

The software development plan, if well written and kept up to date, can be an effective tool for the education of newcomers to the software development team. The SDP will be the most important source of information to show what tasks have been completed and what tasks are left. It also identifies the people involved with each part of the project.

3.2 SOFTWARE DEVELOPMENT PLANNING ■

The software development planning effort is most effectively accomplished in a workshoplike environment. All the major participants in the software development should be assembled in one location for the planning activity. A dedicated room where participants in the planning activity can meet, and where schedules, organization charts, and other planning materials can be posted on walls, should be obtained for the duration of the planning. It is also helpful for the planning effort to be formally initiated by senior management to convey a sense of how important management views the planning activity and to disseminate planning ground rules to the planning team. Of course there must be a plan for developing the plan. This plan is also presented at the initial planning meeting.

Participants in the software development planning effort should include software engineers and test engineers from all test levels. Each major software product should have a software engineer responsible for the planning associated with that product. For example, in a large development effort for a software subsystem comprised of an operating system, system software, and ten application products, we might find two or three software engineers planning for the operating system, one or perhaps two for the system software, and one assigned to each application product. Additional help from the project manager's staff is needed to document schedules, assure consistency in applying planning ground rules, and facilitate the use of some of the automated program management tools adopted by the project.

Other members of the software development planning team are drawn from outside the software development world. Their presence will not be required on a full-time basis during the project performance phase. However, they are needed during planning to negotiate schedules, define their contributions to the software development, and determine allocation of human resources during the development process. A short list of these members would include system engineers, reliability engineers, quality assurance representatives, safety engineers, hardware engineers, test engineers, computer center representatives, major software subcontractors, configuration management representatives, human factors engineers, and operations representatives. Each of these participants should appreciate the importance of planning and should have the authority to commit their parent organization. Each of these individuals would attend meetings, participate in discussions and negotiations, and return to their home organization to seek advice before making major cost and schedule commitments.

In short, planning for a major software development involves a company-wide commitment of resources and reputation. Moreover, the planning process is a description of how an organization develops software and at the same time describes what a software engineer does. The final product of the software development planning team is a document called the software development plan (SDP). Table 3.1 is a table of contents for a typical SDP document. The remainder of this section is devoted to a discussion of the topics included in the SDP document, as shown in Table 3.1 Sections 3.2.1 through 3.2.15 correspond, respectively, to items I through XV in Table 3.1.

■ TABLE 3.1   **Table of Contents Software Development Plan**

I. Introduction
    A. Summary of contents of SDP document
    B. Scope and purpose of SDP document
    C. System-level project description
        1. System description (summary-level)
        2. Contract summary
        3. Technical performance management issues/constraints/challenges
        4. Software architecture/configuration
    D. Software subsystem description
        1. Deliverable software products and their description
        2. Nondeliverable tools and development facilities
II. Resource and Schedule estimates
    A. Resource profiles
        1. Summary
        2. Detailed allocation by products
    B. Schedules
        1. Summary schedules
        2. Detailed schedules by products
III. Organization and staffing
    A. Responsibilities defined
    B. Linked to cost account
IV. Work Breakdown structure, work packages, and cost accounts
V. Technical management and control
    A. Change management
    B. Risk containment
    C. Cost and schedule control
    D. Issue resolution
VI. Standards and procedures
    A. Development methodologies
VII. Reviews, audits, and walk-throughs
    A. Schedules
    B. Procedures/criteria
    C. Responsibilities
VIII. Development environment
IX. Technical Performance Measurements
X. Documentation
XI. Verification and validation
XII. Maintenance
XIII. Human factors
XIV. Delivery, installation, and acceptance
XV. Appendices and references

3.2.1 Introduction

Subsections A and B of the introductory section describe the contents, scope, and purpose of the software development plan. In addition to summarizing the contents of the SDP document, these sections describe the use of this document as an effective management tool.

Subsection C should contain an overview of the project within which the software development takes place. A few sketches or figures borrowed from system-level documents and augmented with top-level software diagrams along with a brief narrative will serve as a sufficient summary. The purpose is to indicate how and where the software products fit into the overall project/system and how the software products support the overall project/system goals.

Contract and adjunct project documentation should be read carefully to glean every reference that could impact software development. Each relevant reference should be copied and retained in the project library as a basis or justification for various elements of the plan. In similar fashion, organization standards and procedures should be researched, and copies of those applicable to the software project should be obtained for the project library.

Many system developments offer unique challenges to technical managers, carry special constraints, or present unusual issues. These challenges might include cost and schedule constraints, certain unusual risks, difficult system performance requirements, use of new or leading-edge technology, public safety, etc. These special areas of concern should be identified and documented in this section of the SDP. Recognition and treatment of these special areas is important to every member of the development team. Oftentimes these areas of concern are within the purview of the software product development environment and should be examined periodically by software development managers and engineers to see how well the development process is dealing with them. In many instances, particular quantifiable attributes are chosen as a measure of how well the development process is handling these special challenges. Section IX of the SDP should contain a detailed description of these attributes and explain how each attribute is measured and reported; it should also describe a contingency plan in the event the measured value of an attribute gets out of its acceptable range. The purpose of this SDP section is to highlight potential problem areas so that the development team can focus its resources on the critical problems. Other problem areas will be identified as the development progresses. This section of the SDP should be updated to reflect each newly identified problem area and the attributes that will be used to measure how well the problem is being contained.

Large software subsystems may consist of many individual software products. As an example, let us consider a command and control system that consists of an operating system, twenty to thirty separate application software products, a hardware subsystem, and ten to twenty operators. Each software product has its individual specifications and development cycle schedule. These individual software products must interface with each other and provide a synergism that results in satisfaction of system-level command and control requirements. To effect this synergism, there must be a structure or architecture associated with both system and software. The architecture of both system and software must be clearly understood by the development team. System and software architecture can often have a subtle influence on detailed design decisions. It is important for the development team to have an overview of system and software structure readily available. This section of the SDP documents the architecture or configuration and references sources where more information can be found.

An awareness of the overall structure of the system and its basic modes of operation serves as a guide to a better understanding of the role of each product in the system and can lead to a better appreciation of function and performance requirements. In general, preparation of this section of the SDP contributes to a better understanding of the application area, modes of operation, and the framework of the system. The software structure must support the system architecture and at the same time be consistent with the principles of modularization, information hiding, and abstraction. Software product control structure, database structure, and functional partitioning flow naturally in situations where the overall architecture is clearly understood. It is also helpful to provide a brief rationale for the selected architecture in this section of the SDP.

Subsection D should contain a comprehensive definition of all software products deliverable to the client or other organizations within the system development team. The descriptions should include software development facilities and deliverable documents. The software descriptions should describe the product in terms of function and performance using, wherever possible, software attribute measures as descriptors. The media for delivery and the criteria for acceptance should also be described in subsection D.

The importance of a thorough understanding of the software product cannot be overstated. While lists and narratives make good software product descriptors, well-designed diagrams can impart a wealth of information in a small space. A sense of the operational dynamics and interrelationships among system and software elements can be conveyed effectively using graphics.

3.2.2 Resource and Schedule Estimates

Estimation of the resources needed to effect a successful product development and the calendar time required to complete the development process implies the need for a software engineer first to quantify product size in some form. Subsequently, software size can be used to determine labor in terms of quantities and skills as well as development environment resources and calendar time required for the development process. Chapter 14 describes three approaches to size estimation, and Chapter 15 describes two resource and schedule estimation approaches in detail and provides some specific examples.

The results of resource and schedule estimates are presented in this section of the SDP in summary form and also by software product. Results of the analysis and rationale that led to these estimates should be either documented separately and made part of the project file or placed in the SDP appendix. These estimates should be reworked periodically and this section of the SDP revised accordingly so that the plan reflects current status. Estimates will become more accurate as the development progresses. Many development projects monitor product or module size, resource expenditure, and progress versus schedule on a periodic basis to confirm that the project is proceeding as planned.

Figure 3.1, A, shows the top-level software development schedule as it would appear in the system development plan. At this point there may be one or two lines in the master schedule to describe the software schedule. Figure, 3.1 B and C, show how the schedule might appear in the SDP. The software development plan would show a more detailed top-level schedule, Figure 3.1, B, with perhaps one or two lines for each major software product. The next level of schedule in the software development plan would show detail schedules, Figure 3.1, C, for each individual software product including software requirement specifications, the interface control document (ICD), software design specifications, test plan, reviews, coding, testing, etc. This hierarchical schedule structure will provide a graphic picture of the important interactions, dependencies, and critical milestones.

3.2.3 Organization and Staffing

A number of planning activities are driven by the results of sizing studies and resource estimates. The first is a staffing plan. Knowing what resources are required for development of each software product and having a schedule for each software product enables the planner

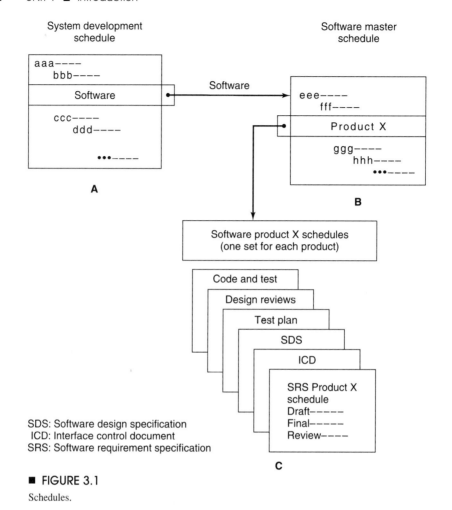

■ FIGURE 3.1

Schedules.

to assemble an organization to perform the development. Typically, there are many constraints on staffing a software development project. Ideally, we would like to assign complete product responsibility to an organizational unit. However, there are usually well-defined, company-established limits on organization unit sizes.

The schedules for software products are frequently staggered for integration and testing purposes, further complicating the scheduling picture. Availability of lead software engineers and design personnel to match the schedule is yet another factor. An ideal organizational unit for software development is an experienced software engineer with management responsibility to lead a ten-person team. Two experienced software engineers, each to provide technical leadership for four designers/coders, rounds out the unit. Separate organizational units supply library support, documentation support, etc. If more than seven or eight such units are required, it is time to think about a second tier of managers. The right numbers for unit size and number of units for each second-line manager are dictated by project characteristics and policies of the performing organization. One can say, however, that at each upper level the manager should be technically oriented and have at least one technical staff assistant.

Once the ideal organization structure is designed and put into place, available personnel can be penciled into the various slots. Commonly only the lead people are identified, and the recruiting of the remaining staff is left to those who have been identified to manage them. This process is frequently a delicate activity best conducted behind closed doors by management sensitive to personnel issues and problems.

For the software engineer who has had some experience in planning, it is enough to structure an ideal staffing plan by characterizing key individuals in terms of required skills rather than specific names. The software engineer is frequently asked for specific names to fill open slots or to give more specifics regarding experience and skills of the people required to fill key positions in the staffing plan. Software engineering career paths often lead into technical management. Staffing plans and associated issues regarding personnel go with the territory.

Selection of individuals to fill positions in the staffing plan is a very important step. Errors in staffing can lead to cost increases and schedule slips just as readily as errors in requirements, designs, or coding. Good leadership qualities and communication skills are important attributes to look for in recruiting software engineers for a project.

In many large projects, a separate organizational unit is charged with the responsibility for software architecture. This unit is responsible for making sure software architecture is consistent with system-level architecture and planned operational modes. The architecture group also maintains consistency within the software architecture by reviewing partitions and designs and by maintaining intrasoftware interfaces.

An organizational unit to treat database problems and issues is frequently a separate part of the project organization. This unit is responsible for collecting and publishing all data definitions and establishing common values for global constants and data items. For some data-intensive applications, this activity can be a major task.

The details of the staffing plan should also contain a schedule for when people are needed on the project and when they may be released from the project. Likewise, for each review and each task performed by an external organization, an indication of when the support will be required and when the task is to be completed must be provided. These tasks and associated schedules are the result of negotiations with the performing organization. For example, a design review will require help from several organizations to review documents, attend presentations, and write up results. The performing organizations need to know that they will have to provide this support, what skills are required, and when they will be needed. Similarly, if help from the software reliability engineering organization is needed, the time of the need and the exact nature and amount of help must be communicated to the reliability engineering organization so it can be incorporated into their planned efforts.

A project organization will change over the project lifetime. A staffing plan can reflect this view by showing the major phases with a separate organization chart and staffing plan for each phase. One frequently hears from the inexperienced software engineer that staffing plans and organization charts are the domain of management. While approval and implementation of these plans are certainly the work of management, the raw material for the staffing plan should be provided by the software engineer.

3.2.4 Work Breakdown Structure, Work Packages, and Cost Accounts

A means for managing the resources allocated to software development must be incorporated into the plan. The usual approach is to establish individual resource allocation (cost accounts) for each major software product. Based on standard practices of the contractor company or at the direction of the client, each product-level cost account is further partitioned into smaller cost accounts. Each of these smaller cost accounts is associated with a given task description and is assigned to a software development organizational unit.

The hierarchical structure of tasks is called the work breakdown structure (WBS). Figure 3.2 is an example of a WBS for a software subsystem. The individual cost accounts plus the associated task descriptions and schedules are called work packages. The work packages are assigned to the performing organization. Project management can use the task descriptions, schedules, and cost accounts to measure project progress at the task level and to sense schedule slip and technical difficulties before they become serious problems. Management asks for progress reports in terms of task technical progress and expenditure of resources allocated to the task. A properly designed WBS is an important tool in the technical management of a software development. Task descriptions are frequently prepared as part of the cost estimation process.

The development of a WBS is sometimes constrained by the client to follow a structure of his or her own choosing. There may be many reasons for this approach. A contractor's internal company policies for financial management and reporting can also apply constraints. The project's organizational structure can influence the shape of a work breakdown structure. In some projects two separate work breakdown structures for the same work may be maintained to satisfy all project financial reporting requirements and to provide project management with the desired visibility and control.

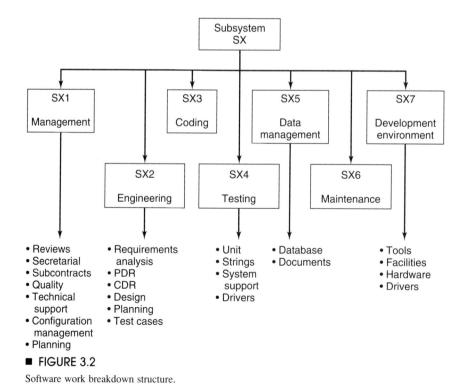

■ **FIGURE 3.2**

Software work breakdown structure.

The main interest in a software development work breakdown structure for a software engineer is to organize the structure to accumulate cost at an individual product level. The goal is to bring the lowest cost account reporting level to a point where performance, cost, and schedule problems will become visible almost immediately, and at the same time reduce cost account reporting and cost account maintenance overhead to the minimum possible. As in many other instances, if the software engineer does not take an active interest in the development of the software work breakdown structure, someone else will get the assignment by default. The resulting work breakdown structure may be clumsy and not as good a management and control tool as it might have been if the software engineer had influenced its development.

At some level, all work packages that are associated with a product should accumulate all the costs associated with that product. This approach helps to identify individual product costs and to design work packages for implementation by a single development organization. Under these conditions, the cost account, task description, and task schedule can then form a minicontract with the performing development organization.

Another visibility and control point that is intrinsic to the WBS cost accounts and task descriptions is the ability of management to turn a task on or off. Authorization to initiate a task allows the controlling authority to permit tasks to be started only if all inputs are available and all required resources are ready. The same authority can also stop tasks that are out of control or out of step with project direction or schedule.

With software development there are tasks that are part of software development but performed by other organizations. Work performed by system analysts related to software development are part of software development costs, although in many instances not performed by the software development organization. Similarly, if there is an independent test and integration organization (separate from the software development organization), some software development tasks may be performed by that organization. The point is that a product-oriented WBS and associated cost accounting process will help immeasurably in determining the actual software development costs. Failure to recognize all costs associated with development of a software product has often led to inaccurate estimations for software development and maintenance.

3.2.5   Technical Management and Control

There are four important functions that are intrinsic to the technical management of a software development. These functions are change management, risk containment, cost and schedule control, and issue resolution. The success or failure of a software development can often be directly related to how well these four functions are handled by the development team and its management.

Change Management

Change is an inevitable event in any software development. Changes to the SDP, requirement specifications (to correct errors of commission and omission), designs, test plans, schedules, and resources are unavoidable in any software development environment. When a project has a formal means for identifying a change and determining the impact of the change on cost and schedule estimates as well as on other development organizations, and there exists a timely and systematic way of escalating the change information to an appropriate level of management for decision and action, then we can say that changes will be effectively managed.

For example, changes can often be grouped into blocks of changes to effect a more efficient update and reduce the amount of regression testing. Changes can sometimes be tabled until the next release or the next major test step. The important idea is that the development team take control of the change activity and not find themselves controlled by the change activity.

To control change activity, the software development manager must have a clear understanding of why the change is needed, what part of the software or other subsystems is impacted, what the effect is of not implementing the change, and what is at stake in terms of cost, schedule, and performance. To be in possession of this information requires a formal process with appropriate reviews. This section in the SDP provides a place to document the procedure. There is usually a system-level configuration or change control board charged with the responsibility for dealing with system change activity. The software change control process must be integrated into the system change control process. How that interface will be accomplished should be documented in this section.

Risk Containment

In the course of performing the risk analysis, described in chapter 16, a set of critical software attributes will be identified that can be used to gauge how well the development is progressing. These attributes can provide an early warning that anticipated problems identified in the risk analysis are indeed about to become real problems. This section of the SDP documents the attributes, the acceptable range for the attributes, a schedule for measuring the attributes, and a procedure for reporting the values. In addition, this section should describe the actions that will be taken if any of the attributes should get out of the acceptable range. For example, the size in function points or source lines of code might be selected as a technical performance measurement for a particular real-time software element. The element has an execution time requirement. Risk analysis has revealed that if the size of the element increases beyond a certain point, the execution time requirement would be in jeopardy. By closely monitoring this attribute on a regular basis, one could recognize trends that indicate that a possible problem was becoming a real problem and that it is time to initiate the contingency plan prepared as part of the risk assessment and containment planning. In some SWDLCs this procedure is standard and well documented.

Cost and Schedule Control

This section of the SDP should spell out how often and at what level of detail actual cost and progress against schedule will be reported and how often the cost and schedule will be reestimated. As the project nears completion, estimates become more accurate. Watching these values is extremely important because they are indicators of project health. Monitoring cost and schedule (actual expenditure versus planned and progress against plan) is simply another way to measure potential problems. If each task description has a tangible product (and each task should be designed to produce a tangible product), a cost account (resources allocated), and a schedule, it is relatively easy to identify situations in which a task has used up most of its allocated resources and there is no visible evidence that a product will be forthcoming. If cost accounts and task descriptions reflect a small enough project increment, there may be enough time to shift resources, rearrange schedules, or develop alternate plans. Chapters 14 and 15 provide more details with regard to the use of cost and schedule as control metrics for project management.

Issue Resolution

During the course of a software development, many profound questions, problems, and issues will surface. These problems and issues must be addressed in a timely manner to assure that the development process will not be slowed or halted waiting for the resolution of a technical or administrative issue. A plan for identifying these issues, allocating resources to address the issue, and formally resolving the issue should appear in this section of the SDP. These issues usually arise in the course of technical reviews and cannot be directly answered at that time. A form to record the question, identify the responsible system analyst or software engineer, and provide for a formal answer is usually included in this section. The manner in which this form is handled (logged in, tracked, and reported) and how quickly and how thoroughly the issue is formally and satisfactorily closed is important to the success of a software development.

In one specific example, a 90,000-SLOC software product generated approximately 1000 questions or issues during the design phase. To resolve these issues and satisfactorily close out the forms required an average of eight labor hours (analysts and software engineers) per issue. Many of the closures required changes to requirements documents, design documents, test plans, etc. The cost of the technical work to effect documentation changes is included in the 8-hour average, but the publication costs are not. Since the product had not been released for coding, no physical changes were required. The product, a very complex one with real-time requirements, proceeded through code, unit test, system integration and test and acceptance test with very little difficulty.

This section should also answer such questions as the following: (1) how the SDP will be kept current, (2) how the project will be managed, (3) how progress will be measured, (4) how schedules will be tracked, (5) how cost accounts will be monitored, (6) how new cost and schedule projections will be prepared, (7) what specific methodology is chosen for software development and why, (8) how configurations will be managed and controlled, (9) how verification and validation will be conducted, (10) how safety and software quality assurance will be handled, (11) what specific policies, practices, and standards will be employed, (12) what the formal review/audit plans are, and (13) any other management-related questions. Many of these items will be addressed at a general policy/philosophy level with a reference given for specifics. The manager of the software development organization may write this section or assign a staff software engineer to write it.

3.2.6 Standards and Procedures

Many practitioners have felt that standardization can be an effective means for improving the quality of system and software development efforts. Table 3.2 lists a few of the sources for standards and some of the areas where standards have been applied with success. In general, standardization is helpful in hardware and software interfacing and subsystem development and integration. It also provides more options to the designer and reduces hardware and software upgrade issues. There are, of course, additional benefits to be realized in training, maintenance, and logistics by using products that conform to standards. On the other hand,

■ TABLE 3.2   **Standard Sources**

International: IEEE/ISO
National: ANSI, Military
Industry: ASME
Intracompany: As developed by individual companies
Typically covered by standards:
    Interfaces
    Structure and architecture
    Process and procedures
    Symbols and codes

it can impose artificial architectural constraints and force design solutions to be built around a particular standard to the detriment of the overall system. The use of standards should be evaluated carefully to ensure that there is a value added and that a more effective overall design and consequently a better overall product will result.

Military standards offer a number of procedure and process standards. These standards have been developed using information and data gathered from a large experience base. Many system and software developments use versions of these standards tailored to suit the unique needs of a given project. Table 3.3 contains a partial list of standards applicable to system and software development. For those intending to make system or software engineering a career, the listed standards can offer valuable guidance and a source of ideas and checklists even though these standards may not be mandated for use on the project. A recent government initiative seeks to permit replacement of the standards cited in Table 3.3 with equivalent commercial practices.

Section VI lists all application development standards and provides guidelines to resolve conflicts if they should arise. For example, a particular IEEE standard might be employed unless it is in conflict with a company standard, in which case the company standard would apply.

■ TABLE 3.3   **Military Standards**

490	Specification practices
499A	Engineering management
1521B	Technical review and audits
483	Configuration management
46855B,	Human engineering requirement
2167A	Software development
2168	Software engineering
1679	Weapon system software
7935	ADS* documentation standards

....
* Automated data system.

3.2.7   Reviews, Audits, and Walkthroughs

Scattered throughout most software development schedules are a number of formal and informal reviews. Three key formal reviews are the software requirement review (SRR), the preliminary design review (PDR), and the critical design review (CDR). The SRR reviews the allocation of functions to the software subsystem. The PDR reviews the software function and performance specifications and a preliminary software design. The CDR reviews the software design before release for coding. An SWDLC must include the substance of these three reviews even if the nomenclature is different. There are many other reviews, sometimes called audits or walkthroughs, that are essential to an effective development process.

The first requirement for an SDP with regard to reviews is to identify each review, each scheduled audit, each scheduled walkthrough, and to estimate the expected number of unplanned or unscheduled reviews, walkthroughs, and audits. The reasons for identifying and scheduling these events are as follows: review events may require projectwide participation, there is a substantial effort associated with each event, and many of these events are either major project milestones (decision points) or associated with major project milestones.

When a review event requires projectwide participation, the data must be made public so that all participants can plan for participation. Participation may require reading documents, research, travel, and writing reports. A participant may have to study many pages of documentation, prepare written questions, travel a great distance to attend the review, sit through many hours of presentation, write or contribute to a report on the review, and make decisions based on what has been heard and read. This effort must be planned in advance. Many of these reviews are critical milestones and reflect points in the development where major decisions are made. A great deal of preparation may be required involving substantial project resources. Even informal walkthroughs require significant effort. It is not uncommon for a module design walkthrough to consume a total of 100 hours of labor to produce and read documents, attend the actual walkthrough, and prepare summary reports.

A second requirement for an SDP with regard to review events is to define entrance and exit criteria for each review, that is, to establish for each review event the conditions that must exist before the review can be conducted and to establish the criteria that must be satisfied before the review item is declared acceptable. For example, before reviewing a software module design, project standards may require that all documentation be complete, all inputs and outputs defined and entered into the data dictionary, all global variables identified, a requirement to implementation trace completed, pseudocode completed, and desk checked, etc. To exit a review successfully, project standards might require that all review issues raised at the review must be resolved to the satisfaction of the review team.

The entrance and exit criteria should be established, at least in general terms, as part of the planning effort. In many software development organizations there exist standards and procedures for the conduct of review events. Many SWDLCs are driven by documentation and associated document reviews. A software development plan should recognize the importance of both. The plan should define the documentation content thoroughly and schedule its release. Likewise review entrance and exit criteria should be thoroughly defined.

3.2.8   Development Environment

Another important section of the SDP document is a description of the software development environment. The description should include the development environment configuration and its specifications either directly, if a simple configuration, or by reference to a separate document, if the configuration is complex. The physical location and the schedule for development of the environment as well as development environment test plans should be included in the plan directly or by reference to another document. Other important aspects of the development environment include security, access details, computers, and responsibility for collecting and maintaining performance measurements.

During the planning it is prudent to devote ample time for sizing and conceptual design of the software development facility or environment. For large projects involving tens and perhaps hundreds of software developers, the importance of the development environment cannot be overstated.

The SDP should contain a detailed configuration of the development facility for each phase of the SWDLC. The plan should also show schedules for development or acquisition of hardware and software and identify the specifiers, procurers, testers, and maintainers. A comprehensive, top-level test schedule should be included as part of the planning information.

Many times special software must be written and hardware constructed to implement a software development environment. Since the development environment is a major tool in the development of the delivered product and indeed in some cases may be delivered along with the software product to support maintenance, it deserves the same level of attention as is given to the operational software product.

The development environment also includes computer-aided software engineering (CASE) tools and other software to support debugging, configuration control, cost-tracking, etc. It is important that these items also appear in the plan along with references and a description of how they are to be used.

3.2.9 Technical Performance Measurements

A number of software attributes along with their use are defined, in quantifiable terms, in chapter 14. A list of such attributes includes the following: size, schedule, costs, resources, development environment, labor, quality, performance, complexity, and reliability. A subset of these attributes is often monitored on a regular basis to enable the development team to identify problems as early as possible so that some corrective action may be taken. Chapter 18, software quality and quality assurance, presents a more detailed discussion of performance measurement as a management and quality control tool.

Section IX of the SDP document should list these attributes, describe how and when they will be measured, and define acceptable ranges for these attributes. This section should also establish review schedules and identify the software engineers responsible for monitoring these attributes. Some of these software attributes may also be monitored as part of the system risk containment plan. Risk assessment and containment is discussed in chapter 16.

The importance of defining, quantifying, and monitoring certain software attributes can be appreciated by noticing the number of places that these attributes appear in the SDP. Section IX of the SDP is probably the most volatile and will require frequent change to keep the SDP current. For example, software product memory and CPU requirements may be an important attribute to monitor because getting a bigger computer may not be an option; or monitoring software size may be important because development resources are constrained or schedule is critical. Carefully monitoring these attributes on a regular basis is a way to maintain visibility and perhaps catch problems in time to prevent them from becoming disasters.

3.2.10 Documentation

Documentation is an important product in software development. It is the only manifestation of the product that is visible. Documentation is the vehicle by which the software configuration is managed and controlled. In some cases the SWDLC is document driven. That is, the entire SWDLC process structure consists of a set of formal documents with formal reviews of each document. In addition to interim software development documentation (products that are direct fallout of the software development effort), there are user's manuals, general software descriptions, a position description handbook (operating procedures), and system operator's manuals. Appendix A provides some general communication guidelines that could be used in developing usable and understandable documents for every aspect of the software development process.

Good maintenance requires a base of good up-to-date documentation, well maintained. In addition to current listings, the design and test documentation should reflect current configurations. This means that maintenance actions should be formalized so that all documentation impacted by a maintenance-driven change is revised when the change is implemented and tested. One of the stated advantages of CASE tools is the value to field maintenance of the documentation they produce. This feature is enough of an advantage that developers are often willing to pay for the additional cost of training, tool acquisition, and additional development cost just to reap the benefits of better documentation for the operation and the maintenance phase.

Evans, Piazza, and Dolkas [3] claim that a good software development organization should be able to provide instant answers to the following four challenges during development:

1. Show me a copy of the current xyz document and a list of all changes that have been approved since the last time it was officially published.
2. Show me a copy of the latest version of the executable system with a list of all outstanding problems and a list of features not yet implemented.
3. Show me a source listing for module A, version n.
4. When was (a specific change) made to the new document, who approved it, and why was it implemented?

Instant answers to these questions is a stern test of software development documentation and configuration control.

One could, of course, add to this list of questions, but the thrust of these questions is that project documentation is responsible not only for describing the product but also for describing very important development information. Traceability, the ability to trace from an implementation through change actions and other documentation back to source requirements, is important to keeping a product under control during the operation and maintenance phase.

Documents that are delivered with the software product should be treated as another deliverable item. Quality reviews, specifications, configuration control, and formal standards should apply to these products as well.

Documentation is a vital element of the system. Poor documentation can give a good system or a good software product a bad reputation. Once a product has established a bad reputation, it is extremely difficult to change people's thinking about the product. Frequently, documentation errors can manifest themselves as serious operational errors. The point is that documentation should not be an afterthought. It needs to have the same attention as other products of the development process.

Many large development efforts with significant documentation requirements will provide a staff of technical writers to help in producing better documentation. This approach does not absolve the software engineer from responsibility for technical accuracy. An in-depth review for accuracy of the final product by the document's authors is an essential requirement.

Writing skills can and must be acquired by the software engineer. The software engineer cannot afford the luxury of not learning to write well. Communication skills are also important attributes of a good software engineer. The software engineer will be called upon frequently to communicate via the written word.

In addition to listing all of the documents, both formal and informal, a software development plan should provide an outline or table of contents for each document that will be produced. The outline or table of contents should spell out the contents of each section and subsection in enough detail to support an accurate estimate of the effort required to produce the final document. Often the client references certain standard documents whose table of contents is already spelled out in a data item description that is very specific as to expected contents and level of detail. Internal standards and practices could also provide the same guidance. This level of detail provides direction as to the technical effort required to provide the information needed to complete the document and some insight as to the total cost of producing the document.

3.2.11   Verification and Validation

A separate plan is usually prepared for test and integration in large software development enterprises. In fact, test and integration is frequently performed by a separate organization outside the confines of the software development organization. For these very large development efforts, the software development organization delivers completed and tested modules, units, or elements to the test and integration team for integration into the system and testing at the system level.

This section of the SDP contains an overview of the process by which it will be (1) verified that the product was designed and developed in accordance with requirement specifications and development standards and (2) validated that requirements (and resulting product) satisfy client or customer needs.

The contents of this section should indicate in general terms what will be done, when it will be done, and by whom. The section would also describe the contents of the test sections in specifications, describe overall test policy and philosophy, identify responsibility for test case generation, and list ground rules for acceptance of modules, units, or elements.

This section of the plan frequently forms the interface between the software development organization and the test and integration organization. Liberal use of references to other project documents, especially test and integration plans, is appropriate for this section. Chapters 10 and 11 discuss test and integration planning in detail.

3.2.12   Maintenance

Planning for maintenance early in the process is frequently required by some clients. Projects that require life cycle cost analysis are concerned with maintenance cost. Estimating required maintenance early in a project or at the beginning of a project includes answering such questions as the following:

1. Will a software development environment/facility be required to support maintenance?
2. What is the expected change activity?
3. How large a staff will be required to support the maintenance activity?
4. Can the software development environment/facility be used for both training and maintenance?
5. Where can we obtain touchstones for our answers to these and other questions?

The operation and maintenance phase is so far into the future at initial planning that it is difficult to focus on planning for maintenance of the system and software product while we are struggling to define its basic characteristics. It is worthwhile to reflect on the fact that the system, including the software product, may be in its operational and maintenance phase for perhaps 20 to 30 years. It is, therefore, important that software developers try to visualize the system in its operational and maintenance phase throughout the SWDLC.

Predicting the number of software failures that will occur per unit time in a released product is relatively straightforward if we know the mean time to failure at product release and have confirmed or at least increased confidence through testing that the reliability requirements have been met. Even if a relatively high reliability or low error density has been predicted, a large project can still expect to deal with many maintenance actions. For example, if an error density of one fault per 500 SLOC is predicted (a very reliable software product), for a 1,000,000-SLOC product we might expect 2000 faults to trigger as many as 2500 failures over product lifetime. Reliability models help to predict the rates at which these failures would occur. This information would enable planners to decide on maintenance needs in terms of development environments and human resources. If the client is not software-knowledgeable, discovering that he or she is taking delivery of a product with as many as 2000 faults would not be very well received. It probably wouldn't help much to explain to the client that the average American automobile may have as many as 150 defects when it is delivered to a customer. At best this subject is a touchy one. However, if it is ignored it will become even more difficult to deal with later. Chapter 13 is devoted to discussion of software maintenance.

This section of the SDP should describe how the product will be maintained after delivery. The description should include tools, environments, resources, and documentation required to carry out the maintenance plan.

3.2.13 Human Factors

In most large systems there is a substantial human element; the operators, the maintainers, the trainers all constitute an important element of an operational system. Human factors is a generic name for the treatment of the interaction between man and machine and the quantitative performance of humans in both dynamic and static situations. It is a very large discipline encompassing many facets of human performance. During project planning, the role of the human factors specialist should be well defined. The human factors specialist can give advice as to what can be expected of an operator in terms of response time, the amount of information that can be digested in a given period of time, the length of time required to process information and produce a response, the proper physical environment for operators, standards for screen designs, etc. These human factors efforts must be blended into the SDP in conjunction with representatives from the human factors organization.

Another area where joint efforts are required is in formulating training plans. The human factors, software engineering, and training organizations must jointly configure a plan for establishing required skill levels for operator positions and developing training programs including training instructors, developing lesson plans, preparing student materials and training facilities, which as mentioned previously, may require use of the software or system development facility.

There are other areas of potential application that must be addressed in planning a software development project. Many of these areas require a specialist for advice and perhaps a contribution. For example, client requirements involving system security or integrity, separate start-up and shut-down subsystems, interoperability with other related systems, and disaster recovery may require consultants, vendors, or in-house specialists for support. Each of these is identified during project planning, and a plan for the required help formulated jointly. Chapter 20 is devoted to the discussion of human factors.

Section XIII should describe how tasks and responsibilities associated with the operator-to-system interface will be treated. This description should include what would be done, how it will be done, and when it will be done.

3.2.14 Delivery, Installation, and Acceptance

The last step in the plan is to develop and document the procedure for delivering the system. In some large system projects, complete delivery of the system may take some months to complete. After installation, a training period may take place followed by a transition to the new system. The transition may take one of several forms, all of which require some time to implement. This phase of the development should also be thought through during development planning. We will revisit many of the issues that arise during delivery, installation, and acceptance in subsequent chapters, especially chapter 10.

3.2.15 Appendices and References

Appendices and references should be employed to cover items that are unique to specific projects. Specific company procedures to be followed during the development process, project-unique standards and conventions, and data item descriptions characterizing the content of the SDP document are examples of items that could go to appendices. Specific documents describing techniques, formulas, algorithms, and development methodologies mentioned in SDP are examples of items to be included in references.

3.3 USE OF SDP AS TECHNICAL MANAGEMENT TOOL ■

Much effort will go into planning. This effort should enable the software development team to get off to a good start. A useful way to accommodate the inevitable plan changes, keep the plan current, keep team members fully informed, and gain maximum benefit from the effort expended in planning is to use the SDP as an agenda for the regular software development team meetings. These meetings should be conducted weekly or at least bimonthly depending on product size and development phase.

As in other aspects of a development project, there will be unexpected problems, external changes, etc., that will call for changes to the SDP. By using the SDP as the agenda for the software development team meeting, these changes can be identified, researched, and systematically incorporated into the development plan. In addition, this approach will keep the team focused on the plan and prevent unauthorized, unapproved, and disruptive departures from the plan.

This use of the SDP as a management tool should be described in the Technical Management and Control section. The following describes how this approach works.

At each weekly or bimonthly development team meeting, the SDP is reviewed section-by-section for changes or deficiencies and revised or expanded as required. Revisions will be effected by page replacements with old copies of the pages retained in the project file for reference. As an example, section I.A or I.B of the software development plan in Table 3.1. If there have been any changes since the last meeting that would alter this section or its references, after a brief discussion to confirm that changes will be needed, a project member will be assigned to prepare a revision to that section of the plan to reflect identified changes. After the changes have been made and approved, change pages will be delivered to each official holder of the document at the next meeting.

Official holders of the document are formally invited attendees (mandatory attendance) at these meetings. They include a representative from system engineering, a representative from test and integration, a representative from every major software product, and a representative from the software development environment. Other attendees may be identified and invited. These invitees would also be regarded as official holders of the planning document. It should be noted that attendees may vary through project phases, and for short periods new attendees will be invited for specific purposes. Current copies of the SDP should also be distributed to key project managers.

If there are any description changes to be made or more detail required to expand on the current system descriptions, after a brief discussion, an assignment would be given to update these pages. In similar fashion, descriptions of software product, resource, schedules, organization, budgets, tasks, etc., are reviewed, and changes are identified to make the plan more current. A review of the status of unresolved issues that are being addressed should be made part of the agenda as well. Arrivals to and departures from the project of key personnel will be noted. Changes in responsibility assignments will be factored into the updated plan also via change pages. Each section of the plan will be reviewed and revised as necessary in this fashion.

One of the most important items addressed during any regularly scheduled development team meeting is a review of all software attributes, especially a set of software-related attributes, that have been identified for risk-tracking purposes. These attributes are called technical performance measurements. These technical performance measurement attributes are to provide assistance in containing software development risks. During the planning stages a strong effort is made to develop accurate estimates of software attributes. These attributes include SLOC or function points, expected productivity rates, development schedules, resource requirements, expected errors per SLOC, CPU utilization, and memory needs. A regular review of these estimates is essential to the health of the software development. As better project understanding is developed, better software product estimates are expected. The need to stay current with these estimates is obvious. Project leadership can shift resources, elevate major problems, or obtain additional technical help if given better visibility as to estimated size, schedule, and resource requirements. The central idea is that early recognition of problems allows more time to develop solutions. Figure 3.3 shows that the earlier a problem is identified, the lower the solution cost. For example, fixing an error found during acceptance test costs about twice as much as fixing the same error found during the test and integration phase.

Typically, attention will shift from one software product to another during the course of software development as focus moves from one product to the next one on the schedule. Each time a problem arises in one product, those responsible for other products will be encouraged to look for symptoms of the same problem in their product. The result is an increased sensitivity to early problem recognition.

Reviewing the software attribute estimates at the development team meeting is only the tip of the iceberg. In preparation for the software development project meeting, the software engineer responsible for the product should revisit the entire estimation process to assure that all assumptions are still valid, no new requirements or information has emerged, and there have been no requirement clarifications that will change estimates. This process should be a continuing one. Software attribute estimates are important tools in developing schedules, sizing computer resources, sizing human resource needs, and in the recognition of symptoms of deeper trouble. Eventually estimates will be replaced with actual attribute values. Comparisons between estimated software attributes and actual values should provide calibration for future estimations.

In summary, using the SDP as the agenda for regularly scheduled software development team meetings makes maximum use of the effort expended on planning and accommodates change. Experience has shown that a well-formulated plan will experience a flurry of plan change activity as the project understanding matures. Subsequently, plan change activity will stabilize and be relatively light. Each meeting is a reaffirmation of team commitment to the plan and a prompt for team members to follow the plan or change it. If the project remains on track and no significant cost, technical, or schedule difficulties arise, the meeting will move

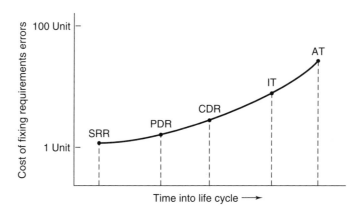

SRR: Software requirement review
PDR: Preliminary design review
CDR: Critical design review
  IT: Integration test
  AT: Acceptance test

■ FIGURE 3.3

Early recognition of problems versus leverage in cost control.

swiftly to conclusion. The meeting chairperson must establish discipline and confine discussion to problem identification, leaving solutions for outside the confines of the meeting. The approach described has been used successfully on proposals for which time constraints are rigid and on very complex projects with tight budget and schedule constraints.

3.4   ATTRIBUTE (METRICS) ESTIMATIONS   ■

It is very difficult to plan the construction of a building if the number of floors, dimensions of rooms, number of doors, number of bathrooms, materials to be used, etc., are not known. To complete the SDP document we must have access to the estimated values of a number of key software attributes. Therefore, a major activity for the software engineer during software development planning is to provide an estimate for the key software attributes. These attribute values will drive the planning effort.

The objective of estimating software attributes is to provide a means of quantitatively describing a software product while it is still an abstract concept. This approach is not a new idea. The aircraft industry uses the estimated weight of a new aircraft design to develop project plans and estimate cost. An electronic box development cost estimate can be determined by estimating the number of circuit boards and connectors required to implement the specification. In a similar fashion, software engineers have used SLOC or, less frequently, function and feature points to size computer resources and develop cost and schedule estimates.

For example, to estimate the cost of developing an electronic box, one should estimate the cost of designing and building the enclosure, then translate the function and performance requirements specification into the estimated number of circuit boards and plugs or connectors. This aspect is where estimator experience comes into play. By partitioning functions into small pieces, the estimator can either relate each subfunction to a previous implementation or estimate how many components will be required to implement the function. In this fashion, by knowing how to lay out parts on a circuit board, the estimator can arrive at the number of circuit boards required. The development cost for individual circuit boards can be obtained from project archives. Surprisingly good electronic box development cost estimates can be derived in this fashion.

Similar methods can be employed by the software engineer to obtain sizing information and to make cost estimates. If the software engineer examines the function and performance requirements carefully, a function partitioning can lead to identification of recognizable subfunctions similar to software that has already been developed elsewhere. Knowing the number of SLOC or function points used in the previous implementation provides guidance in sizing the new function.

Memory sizing is a direct fallout of the SLOC or function point estimation process. Primary and secondary memory allocations can be made based on operational characteristics. Table sizes and file sizes can be estimated from application considerations. Growth and contingency can also be factored into memory estimates. The rationale should be thoroughly documented and circulated for comment to individuals who are experienced in preparing such estimates. Revisions, if any, to assumptions, estimates, and rationale should then be included in the document released for general use by the project.

The most important product of any estimate is the documented rationale. A repeatable process with clearly stated assumptions permits the next estimation to start from a defined base and provides a trail of estimates for review each time a new estimate is made. The foregoing has given some simple examples of what can be done to get the sizing estimation process started.

While estimation of SLOC (or function point) attributes is underway, each function should be evaluated for its importance in terms of performance criticality. Some functions are more important than others. It is certainly more important to meet a critical real-time deadline than to spell a word correctly in an output report.

While the sizing analysis is under way it is a good idea to begin thinking of weighting each software element and subelement in terms of its value to system performance. A simple rating system may be adequate at this point. Each software element that is involved in the implementation of a major system requirement should be given a 1 rating. Each software requirement associated with the direct implementation of a real-time requirement should be given a 1 rating. Software for new or unusual applications and any embedded software or software directly associated with embedded systems should be given a 1 rating. Software indirectly or peripherally associated with the previous software should be given a 2 rating. All other software should be given a 3 rating. These ratings should be part of the general characterization of the software in terms of software attributes.

In addition to sizing estimates, the software engineer must provide an appropriate estimation for risk, costs, resources, labor, schedules, reliability, and availability associated with the software product. Because of the important role played by these estimates in the development of the SDP and in the management of a software product, we have devoted several chapters to the definition and estimation of software attributes. In particular, chapter 17 discusses reliability and availability attributes and provides models for their estimation, chapter 16 discusses software risk assessment and containment, and chapter 15 discusses cost and schedule estimation.

3.5   AUTOMATED PLANNING TOOLS   ■

There are many automated tools available that can be employed in the software development planning process. For example, schedules can be automatically examined for conflicts, dependencies, and critical paths by a scheduling tool. Project WBS cost and task descriptions can be linked to the schedule to automate changes to the software development plan. For large software developments, the volume of information and data that must be created, managed, and disseminated is enormous. The availability of automated tools that support the creation of the original SDP and its maintenance through the development cycle provides managers with the visibility required to track task progress, expenditures versus plan, schedule conflicts, and progress along critical paths. The advantage in using these tools is a substantial reduction in the program manager's staff; reduction in the time required to recognize schedule, technical, and cost problems; and a more efficient and effective change management process. The self-documentation feature of these tools is an added benefit.

Standard office automation tools such as word processors, spreadsheets, database managers, electronic mail, voice mail, fax, etc., are important in improving team productivity. These tools are also effective in specification preparation and dissemination of information in preparation for reviews, inspections, etc.; creation and management of all project documentation; and in maintaining a project history. In order to ensure that the productivity improvement implicit in these tools is actually obtained, some thought must be given to explicitly how tools will be used, standardization of tools (with the client as well as among team members), and maintenance of tools.

At another level, there are automated tools that support software cost estimation and management, decision making, design graphics, prototyping, etc. CASE tools provide support to the entire software design process in various methodologies. There are tools that support the measurement of software complexity at both design and implementation levels.

These tools are intrinsic to the software development environment. The SDP would not be complete without a full description of the tools that will be used, how they will be used, and how they will be maintained.

3.6 MANAGEMENT, METHODOLOGY, AND
METRICS   ■

The key to a successful software development process is the appropriate mix of the three Ms: management, methodology, and metrics (or as we call them, attributes). In simple terms, the software development manager plans the work and then works the plan. The plan involves identifying and sizing the tasks that must be performed, scheduling the tasks, allocating resources to the tasks, and determining how the tasks will be performed. Working the plan involves making sure the task starts and finishes on time, using only those resources that were allocated to the task and following established procedures.

With a perfect plan, perfect visibility, and perfect procedures, software development management would be very easy. Unfortunately, the plan is imperfect. We often do not really understand the problem, overlook major tasks, are too optimistic, etc. Moreover, the environment changes, or we didn't really understand it in the first place. Often our procedures and practices are immature, not followed, or lacking entirely. Under these circumstances software development management is an exacting and challenging problem.

In order to control the software development process and converge to a successful outcome, a software development manager must begin with the best possible plan given the particular circumstances. Contained within that plan must be a mature development methodology. The methodology must be understood and fully accepted by the development team and client. The plan should also identify project and product attributes or metrics that will be used to measure progress against plan. It is easy to visualize how management can regularly monitor project expenditures to see if the cost component of the plan is being followed. What is not easy to see are the subtle technical indications that the project is going off track. For example, a software requirements specification that appears to be on course in terms of cost and schedule may be riddled with errors of omission and commission. This fact may not be visible to management until late in the development cycle, at which point the design task that depends upon this particular requirement specification will be affected. The subsequent ripple effect can be devastating to the SDP. A metric or attribute that measures the technical progress of the software requirements specification is needed by management to manage effectively. In this case reviews, inspections, walk-throughs, etc., at strategic points in the software requirements specification task can be used to provide technical visibility regarding progress against plan. The number of comments, actions, errors, etc., uncovered by these reviews can be used as a quantifiable measure of progress. In this fashion a manager can use various quantifiable software attributes to measure technical progress against the plan.

How effectively the three Ms are applied to a software development depends upon the experience and maturity of the software development organization. W. S. Humphrey [5] describes a software maturity model for software development organizations. There are five maturity levels in the model. Each maturity level is described in terms of the degree of planning, process, and procedure sophistication exhibited by the organization.

The software maturity model allows a development organization to make an assessment of its level of maturity and set a course to improve its software development capability. Reference [5] is a highly recommended reading for software engineers. This book, *A Discipline for Software Engineering*, fully supports the maturity model concept and provides, for the software engineer, a clear view of a mature software development process. Four other references [1–4] are also highly recommended.

3.7   CHAPTER SUMMARY ■

The activities associated with software development planning span all of the tasks and interfaces that a software engineer must confront and deal with in the course of a software development. Chapter 3 has ranged over the full spectrum of planning tasks. To understand and appreciate the contents of the software development plan is to understand software engineering. Many of the topics introduced in chapter 3 will be revisited in subsequent chapters. Chapter 3 emphasizes that a comprehensive and accurate characterization of all deliverable software products, documents, tools, and facilities is central to the preparation of the SDP. Chapter 3 stresses the point that a good plan not followed is no plan. Working the plan is an essential component for success in software (or system) development. Working the plan means not only following the plan but keeping the plan current by revising, expanding, and correcting the plan to reflect changes in environment and project dynamics. The plan should identify risks and provide a vehicle for watching these risk areas carefully. A plan should be regarded as a commitment and should be viewed as such by all concerned parties.

While it is unlikely that an entry-level software engineer would be assigned complete responsibility for an SDP preparation, it is not unreasonable to expect that an entry-level software engineer would be asked to contribute to an SDP preparation effort. Knowing what constitutes a good SDP is important. For small software developments, the planning discipline described in chapter 3 is very effective in producing good results. In large developments it is an absolutely essential factor in determining success.

An SDP that grows and changes with the project can also be a source of project information to help people joining the project move up the learning curve more rapidly.

3.8   UNIT ONE SUMMARY ■

This long introduction to and overview of the field of software engineering was intended to give the reader a sense of the structure and flow of the software development process. By now the reader should have a grasp of the big picture, in particular, the natural surroundings of a software development, a system development, the major responsibilities of a software engineer, and the elements of a software development plan. The remainder of the book contains the details. Some additional comments are, however, appropriate before moving on.

There is a recurring theme in these first three chapters. That theme is as follows: for each system or software development activity there should be a repeatable, documented procedure or guideline for performing that activity. In the absence of any other guidelines, this book provides them.

For a successful development effort, all participants should commit to following the development procedure. The results of following each of these procedures and the rationale implicit in the results should be documented. Many formalized system and software development life cycles require this approach.

Every software development task or activity is iterative. One of the jobs of software or system engineers is to guide the iterative process to convergence. Each iteration should be built upon the preceding iteration. That is why it is important to document results.

Software and system engineers should strive to take advantage of all available experience by circulating results and/or convening reviews and resolving conflicting opinions in order to fill any information or knowledge voids pointed out in these reviews and audits. The software or system engineer should maintain a professional attitude and an active concern for his or her own credibility as well as the development organization's credibility.

The system development life cycle and software development life cycle's descriptions or paradigms are somewhat akin to the reports submitted by the village blind men concerning the nature of the elephant. They are in a sense all correct and yet not really complete in their descriptions.

There are strong similarities between a good software engineer and a good craftsman. They both know the materials with which they work. Even though some craftsmen favor a large collection of tools while others use only a few different tools, all know their tools, use them effectively, and keep them sharp. Good craftsmen plan and organize their work for best results. Watching a craftsman beginning a job often leaves one wondering if he will ever get to the heart of the task. Once the preparation is complete, however, the job proceeds smoothly and quickly to completion. The preparation, planning, setting up the work process, trying the process on waste material to assure everything is ready, and taking into account what might go wrong makes the major task for which the craftsman was hired seem routine. So it should be with the software engineer. Preparation is an important ingredient of a successful development.

Software attributes are useful in building an experience database for use in future projects. The attributes can also be used for the project on which they were collected, providing the development cycle is long enough and the development of individual software elements is staggered in time. Of considerable importance is selecting and defining the attributes of concern for the project and establishing a means of collecting, editing, and reducing the raw data and providing written rationale and description as required. Often a single independent organization can be assigned to perform this task for all ongoing developments within a development organization. This repository of historical information can provide a means for objectively comparing development methodologies, new technologies and tools, and approaches to software development.

Recorded software attributes can be used in the following endeavors: (1) cost and schedule estimates, (2) software product reliability predictions, (3) staffing for maintenance, (4) managing the development process (status and progress measurements), (5) tracking risk (6) assigning and evaluating risk, (7) enforcing project standards, (8) personnel assignments, and (9) personnel evaluation. A relatively inexperienced software engineer can find, in such a repository, guidance in estimating software attributes for a new project or in using one of the estimation models. A well-kept repository can also assist in designing a software development plan. The design of a software development facility and selection of development tools can also be influenced by the information contained in the repository.

It is hard to imagine how an effective software development project can be conducted without quantifying and using at least some critical attributes. Moreover, it is difficult to envision a successful software development organization that does not carefully collect and analyze software metrics and maintain an historical file of these attributes and carefully select certain software attributes for use in guiding and controlling developments and collectively learning from experience.

Finally, there are no silver bullets or magic formulas that will always give the right answers or do the work for us. Each new development has its own unique problems and character. The challenge is to take what we have learned collectively and apply that, in conjunction with common sense and logic, to each new situation. That is what can keep a software engineer interested and excited for a full career.

To paraphrase the late Vince Lombardi, everyone wants to have a successful software development and produce a first-rate software product, but not everyone is willing to accept the discipline and make the effort and sacrifice to assure that success.

3.9 EXERCISES ■

1. Describe the workshop-like software planning environment. List the advantages and disadvantages of this kind of planning process.
2. Describe the use of the SDP document as an effective management tool.
3. What are the unique challenges that a software technical manager faces during the SWDLC?
4. Resource and schedule estimation during requirement analysis is proven to be inaccurate and the management knows this fact. Explain why it is still advantageous to include in the SDP documents a section on resource and schedule estimation.
5. Describe the effects of early organization and staffing on the SWDLC.
6. Suppose you are the Software Engineer in charge of technical management of a medium size project (75,000 to 128,000 SLDC). Give your ideal staffing plan for this project.
7. A software project organization will change through its lifetime. How would you, as a technical manager, cope with this phenomenon.
8. One of the software subsystems for an office automation system is the accounting subsystem. Give a detailed WBS for this subsystem.
9. One of the software subsystems used by many retailers is the employee schedule subsystem. Give a detailed WBS for this subsystem.
10. The technical manager of a software project has the authority to turn on or off development work. As a technical manager, explain what criteria you will use to turn off the work on a subsystem and when you will initiate or reinitiate the work on a subsystem.
11. As a technical manager, list all the activities in a SWDLC whose cost should be charged to the cost of the software product.
12. Explain the four most important functions that are intrinsic to the technical management of a software product. Explain how these functions may be used as control measures.
13. One of the major tasks confronting a technical manager is to resolve issues and answer design-related questions. What are the common issues and questions which may arise during the design process?
14. Technical performance measurements are discussed in chapter 14. At this point, as a

technical manager, explain several measurements that you would use as software performance measurements without referring to Chapter 14.

15. As a technical manager, you are to state four questions that measure the accuracy and the currency of the system documentations. What are those four questions?

16. Describe SRS verification and validation. Give an example of a requirement that is verified but not validated.

17. State several factors that will directly affect the cost of maintenance of a software product.

18. Explain how the SDP document could be used as a tool for technical management.

19. What complications might arise when you plan for a five-member team working on a semester-long project. Assume that you will all share a common grade on the project. Is a common grade fair?

20. List six quantifiable software attributes that you think would completely characterize a software product.

21. List five quantifiable software attributes that describe the maintainability of a software product. Could these attributes be used to compare one software product with another?

22. How can a software development organization's ability to develop software be quantified?

Some of the following exercises are team-oriented. Therefore, when appropriate, it is assumed that a team of three to five persons will work on each problem and discuss their results.

23. Assume that XYZ project will prepare separate subplans for each application. Write a draft of section I (Table 3.1) for the data gathering function. Modify the outline it you feel it will improve the plan. Refer to chapter 2 for a description of the data gathering function.

24. You are given an estimate of the resources required to implement the data gathering application (131 labor months and 17 calendar months). Prepare a detailed schedule for the development of this application package. List all the questions you would ask before beginning the scheduling task. List assumptions you have made in order to proceed with the scheduling.

25. For exercise 24 describe and schedule all major reviews associated with the development of the data gathering application product.

26. Discuss the need to integrate XYZ project system software plans and schedules with each application product. Lay out a top-level schedule indicating specific dependencies.

27. Describe the software development environment required for the XYZ project. Draw a block diagram and describe the components.

28. Describe the assistance that might be needed from the human factors organization for the XYZ project, in particular, for the data gathering function.

29. Develop Table 3.1 into a more detailed software development plan table of contents covering the XYZ project's entire software development effort.

30. The computer science department at your university wants to design a software system to reduce the amount of paperwork and reduce access to the university database. The main objectives of this software system are to maintain the following:
    a. records of student advising
    b. on-line student transcripts
    c. student graduation records including catalog year, general university requirements, and major requirements

  d. on-line student enrollment
  e. student follow-up records
  f. three specific mailing lists: active, inactive, and graduated/transferred student lists

The assignment is to discuss the details of this project with the department chairperson and design a plan and develop the SDP for this project. Note that it is your job to understand the detailed requirements of this project through an iteration process. In your planning, you may delay cost and schedule estimation until you have studied the chapter on cost and schedule estimation.

31. Repeat problem 37 of chapter 1. Use both function point and SLOC to estimate the project size.

References

1. M. W. Evans, *Productive Software Test Management*, Wiley, New York, 1984.
2. ———*Software Quality Assurance and Management*, Wiley, New York, 1987.
3. M. W. Evans, P. Piazza, and J. B. Dolkas, *Principles of Productive Software Management*, Wiley, New York, 1983.
4. W. S. Humphrey, *Managing the Software Process*, Addison-Wesley, Reading, Mass., 1990.
5. ———*A Discipline for Software Engineering*, Addison-Wesley, Reading, Mass., 1995.

UNIT 2

Analysis and Design

Unit 2 is concerned with specifications related to the software product and some of the tools that are helpful in producing specifications. The two most significant steps in developing a software product are the determination of (1) precisely what the software product must do and (2) how, specifically, the software product will accomplish its task. The results of these two steps are manifested in two critically important specifications: the software requirements specification (SRS) and the software design specification (SDS). These specifications have a number of aliases and sometimes appear in different formats. The SRS has been called the part 1 specification, the ''B'' specification, the design-to specification, the software function and performance specification, and the software design and performance specification. The SDS has been called the software design document (IEEE), the part 2 specification, the ''C'' specification, and the build-to specification.

A thorough understanding of what the software product must do is an essential prerequisite for a successful design. At least half of the operational failures and much of the dissatisfaction with a software product can be traced to the allocation and specification of function and performance requirements: what the product must do. One common characteristic of successful software developments is the implicit or explicit sharing of responsibility for the development of a complete, accurate, and understandable SRS by software engineers and system analysts/engineers.

Chapter 4 provides full discussion of a table of contents for an SRS and works out two SRS examples. Chapter 4 also identifies and describes some of the important attributes intrinsic to any specification and discusses requirement analysis.

Chapter 5 describes a few of the available tools that can assist in both requirement and design specification. We have an objective for selecting each of these tools from among the many tools available. The data dictionary is selected because it provides for a structured and easy-to-follow definition of the terminology used in the specific software development environment. In a software development process many important decisions must be made. Decision support tools help the software engineer to make such decisions in an objective manner. Data flow diagrams are used extensively in both requirement analysis and design phases. The use of data flow diagrams as design tools is deeply rooted in the function and performance viewpoint of software development. Finite state machines, Petri nets, mathematical logic, and predicate calculus are mathematical tools (models) to express complex requirements and designs with minimum use of natural (ambiguous) languages.

Chapter 6 describes software development platforms, environments and CASE tools. Software development platforms and environments could be viewed as the machine tools of software production. In many instances these tools also support the development and test of software specifications. Because of their importance to the software development process, these tools should be specified, designed, and controlled at least as well as the delivered software product. CASE tools are used to support the preparation of both the SRS and the SDS as well as postdelivery maintenance.

Chapter 7 discusses the software design process independent of any specific design methodology or tool. A generic design process is described in some detail, and specific, systematic, step-by-step guidance is offered for developing a software design. The contents for a universally acceptable SDS to document the results of the described design process are worked out as an example.

Chapter 8 is devoted to a discussion of object-oriented analysis, design tools, and methodology. Object-oriented analysis and design methodology attempts to capture both software requirements specification and software design specification.

4

Software Specifications and Requirements Analysis

4.0   OBJECTIVES

Software specification documents in general and the software requirements specification in particular are the blueprints for a software system. The most important objective for this chapter is to justify the need for high-quality specifications and the important role played by the requirement specifications at all levels of the software system development process. Other objectives for this chapter are as follows: (1) to discuss the different levels of specifications; (2) to present a table of contents for the software requirement specification document; (3) to discuss a set of attributes for a good specification document; and (4) to present examples of a software requirements specifications document.

4.1   INTRODUCTION

In this chapter, we will consider software specifications, not as a single document, but as a series of documents developed by different people for different purposes and from different points of view. Eventually, a collection of specification documents will describe the entire software system from the standpoint of clients, users, operators, system analysts, system engineers, software engineers, test and integration engineers, human factors engineers, and management. The bulk of the chapter is devoted to a discussion of the software requirements specification.

The success of a software development is directly related to the following:

1. Level of detail in which team activities are recorded
2. Quality of the software specification
3. Integrity of the software specification
4. Accuracy of the software specification
5. Established development processes
6. Rigor with which the established process is followed
7. Quality and number of reviews and audits
8. Accuracy of the models that have been used to estimate software attributes
9. Effectiveness of the test and integration plan, specification, and test data
10. Level of preparation for system maintenance

Seven of the ten items are directly related to specifications.

Specification preparation for a software system begins when the client/user recognizes the need for a new system or decides to modify an existing system. For example, in the XYZ project, as soon as the company recognized the need for an automated maintenance/control system, someone or a committee consisting of a few key people were given the task of defining system requirements. In the case of the ABC project, they already have a smaller limited system and now want to develop a much larger system with more automation, a system that has the capability to grow as the company grows. The ABC company will, therefore, develop a short document, sometimes referred to as the problem statement, to list their requirements, identifying their current needs, their needs for the near future, and their needs for the next twenty to twenty-five years. When the company becomes more serious about investigating the development of a system, they will call in a specialist to review the project, allocate certain requirements to the software component of the system, and begin preparation of a software requirements specification (SRS) document.

The starting point in writing the SRS is typically at the client/user/contractor interface. Writing the SRS is no different from any other activity in the system development process; it is an iterative process. The client/user provides the initial system requirements, and the contractor's analysts/software engineers translate system requirements into specific hardware, software and operator requirements. The SRS is prepared from the requirements allocated to software. The SRS, along with a top-level design, is delivered to the client for review and verification. When the review is satisfactorily completed, the SRS and the top-level design become the basis for a second level of software specification called the software design specification (SDS). In some development environments the SDS is developed in a single step or a single level. In other environments it is a two-step or two-level process. In any event both the SRS and the SDS are given to clients, implementers, maintainers, testers and integrators, and operators. They must be able and willing to understand, discuss, and review the SRS and SDS documents until they are satisfied with their content. If a major change should be necessary, it must be approved by the committee that oversees not only the development of the software product but the entire system. This committee should have client representatives as well as management as members. Once the level 2 design is completed, documented in a software design specification, and passes its review, it goes to production.

It is extremely important to understand that the document(s) that specify a software system must be well written, must contain no conflicts or contradictions, and must be precise. In addition, these documents should (1) identify a point of contact to handle questions regarding the document, (2) have a means for logging changes, (3) have a complete table of contents, and (4) be readily accessible. Note that the different software specification documents may be collected into one volume or several volumes with different names. The important point is that each specification document should be easily identified and properly prepared. A brief discussion of the potential audience for software specifications follows.

4.2 PEOPLE INVOLVED IN SOFTWARE DEVELOPMENT PROCESS

■

In discussing the software development process and SWDLC, we come to realize that there are several groups of people involved in this process.

1. Operators/Users: These are people who will operate and use the final products of the software system. Users are also the ones who may initiate the discussion leading to the birth of a new system. In a healthy environment, the operators/users are also involved in writing/ verifying some of the specification documents. Note that a system, no matter how expensive or how intelligent, won't be successful if the operators/users do not use it at its designed level of performance. Therefore, it is beneficial to both the client and the system development team that the operator/user be involved and be educated as the system is being developed.

2. Client: This term refers to the person or company for whom we are building the system. The client is the one who makes financial decisions, who presents the system development team with the first draft of the perceived system requirements, who signs all the relevant contracts and checks, and who must approve any changes to the system suggested by either the operators/users or the developers.

3. System analysts/system engineers: These are people who usually make the initial technical contact with the client, analyze the problem as it is seen by the client, obtain client requirements, and write the requirements specification.

4. Software engineers: Software engineers work with system engineers/analysts to understand the software requirements and to help develop the software requirements specification. During software development, software engineers will work with other groups involved with software to assure that they also understand and follow development procedures and the software design specifications.

5. Programmers: These are the people who receive the software design specifications (SDS), write the code for each module, and test each individual module against its specifications. Programmers must be knowledgeable of the programming language(s) being used to implement the software. They also must be knowledgeable of the operational environment for which the software is being developed.

6. Test and integration group: These are people who receive each tested module of the software system, assemble the modules, and test the assembled modules until the complete software system is fully integrated and tested.

7. Maintenance group: These are people in charge of monitoring software system performance during operation and modifying it to match the current stated requirements. The trend in software development indicates that by the turn of the century, over 80 percent of all the efforts in the software development industry may be spent on maintenance, reengineering, revision, and upgrading of existing systems [8].

8. Technical support: These are people maintained by the developer, possibly as consultants, for verification or description of highly technical aspects of the software system. For instance, information on algorithms and equations used in the design of a software module should be available from the technical support group. A help desk would be regarded as technical support.

9. Staff and clerical help: These are people who have been assigned to the project to perform many of the important tasks including word processing, data entry, program entry, document entry, etc. Without a very good clerical staff, it is hard to imagine producing software on time with all the appropriate documentation. Also, one of the important jobs of the clerical staff is to facilitate communications between different teams involved in the development process.

In addition to these separate groups of people involved in the SWDLC, there is often a steering committee that oversees all of the review/audit processes; investigates, approves, and documents any changes to the product; and, more important, makes sure that the development process agreed to is rigorously followed. This committee makes sure every meeting is documented and every document pertaining to SWDLC is readily available. This committee should have members or representatives from all of the nine groups just discussed. Without such an active committee, the continuity and integrity of the software development process is in jeopardy. Current practice is to assign many of these responsibilities to the quality assurance and configuration management organizations.

It is, therefore, important that specification documents be readable by the intended audience. These groups are, in effect, users of the specifications.

4.3   SOFTWARE REQUIREMENTS SPECIFICATION (SRS)   ■

Every engineered and manufactured product must be specified in some fashion. As a product becomes more complicated, it will require more detailed specification. For example, if a product is a kind of cereal the specification may include (1) texture, (2) color, (3) taste, (4) precise amount of each ingredient, (5) vitamin content, (6) the packaging shape and size, and so on. On the other hand, if the product is a space shuttle, specifications will be much more detailed and specialized. These specifications are needed to describe the requirements and design of each component of the shuttle, operational timelines, acceptance and performance standards, and many other detailed requirement and design specifications.

A given product may be specified in terms of its behavior and performance. Such specifications are called operational specifications. A product may also be described by its effect on its environment and by its properties. Such specifications are called descriptive specifications. Descriptive specifications tend to define a product in terms of its output whereas operational specifications tend to describe a product by its operational performance [4]. Both of these specifications are used in describing what software products must do.

The SRS document, when completed, serves as a contract between client and developer. The more attention given to the SRS document, the more accurate and precise the SRS document, the better the quality of the final product. While the possibility of developing a new system or, as often is the case, modifying an existing system is being discussed, a team of analysts (system engineers) are called into the process. Often this team may consist of one or two independent consultants or they may be from a prospective development organization. This team, in cooperation with the operator/user group, produces the initial system requirement specification that often, upon its final approval, will be published as part of a request for bid. The development organization selected by the client organization will revise/rewrite the original system requirements specifications into several subordinate specification documents, one of which is called the software requirements specification.

Table 4.1 gives the table of contents of a generic SRS as suggested by IEEE software engineering standards [5]. This table of contents is divided into three parts. The first two parts contain general information about the users, environment, operation, constraints surrounding the system as a whole, and the software product as it relates to the entire system. Section 3 provides specific requirements for every function.

4.3.1 Introductory Section of SRS (Section 1)

Section 1 of the SRS includes general information about the software product, its objectives and its scope. In particular, it does the following:

a. Gives a full description of the main objectives of the SRS document.

b. Lists key people involved in developing the document. Identifies the contributions and responsibilities of each person.

■ TABLE 4.1*   **Software Requirements Specification Outline**

Table of Contents

1. Introduction
    1.1 Purpose
    1.2 Scope
    1.3 Definition, Acronyms, or Abbreviations
    1.4 References
    1.5 Overview
2. General Description
    2.1 Product Perspective
    2.2 Product Functions
    2.3 User Characteristics
    2.4 General Constraints
    2.5 Assumptions
3. Specific Requirements
(This section appears in Table 4.2.)

....

* The reference for Table 4.1 is IEEE Std. 830-1993, ''Recommended Practice for Software Requirements Specifications,'' *Standards Collection on Software Engineering*, IEEE Press, New York, 1994.

c. Identifies the software products to be developed by name and function. Lists product limitations, if any, and highlights any distinct feature in each product.

d. Describes and lists the benefits of the software product as clearly and precisely as possible. Does not use vague terms or unsubstantiated claims such as ''the system implemented will increase productivity by 20 percent.'' In this section, each subproduct of the software product is described along with the tasks it must perform, its limitations, its quantified performance parameters, and its expected advantages over the previous product. The description must be consistent with regard to higher-level specification documents such as the system requirements specification.

e. Defines all acronyms and abbreviations in a common location and whenever used for the first time. A collection of acronym definitions serves as a glossary. One approach is to locate definitions in an appendix called Acronyms and Abbreviations Definition. The existence and the use of terms that mean different things to different people in the SRS document is a common source of problems related to misunderstandings and misinterpretations.

f. Includes both internal and external references for every specification listed. Internal references are those within the SRS document, and external references are those referring to documents outside the SRS document. When listing an external document, include the full identification of the document, the publication date and publishing organization, the ownership of the document, and a source to obtain the document. This collection of references may appear in a separate appendix.

g. In the overview for the introductory part of the SRS, a short description of how the rest of the SRS is organized and what can be found in the rest of the document is given.

4.3.2 General Description Section of SRS (Section 2)

Section 2 of the SRS document (Table 4.1) should include general information regarding the factors that affect the final product and its requirements. The information to be included in section 2 of the SRS document includes the following:

a. Placement of the product in proper perspective within the overall system; if an independent product, a description of its relationship to other independent products; if a part of a larger product, identification of the interface of this product with other products; identification of the product's external interfaces with its environment; a description of use of any existing hardware by this product; and evaluation of any extra loads caused by the introduction of this product into the overall software product; a detailed explanation of hardware requirements, if this product requires new hardware.

b. A short description of the functions performed by the software. The description that is helpful at this point may already exist in the overall system specification. Functional specifications must be in a form understandable to users, operators, and client. The specific requirement specifications are left for a later point in the SRS document. In any event, we must stay away from hints as to how to implement certain functional requirements. Whenever possible, quantified performance requirements should be included along with function requirements.

c. Description of any user behavior characteristics that may be required in the use of the software. During the operational life of a system a variety of people will interact with the system. They are users, operators, auditors, and maintenance people. It is important to list some of the critical characteristics of the system's human interfaces. A number of systems have failed in the operational mode, not because of errors or incompleteness, but because they had not recognized and incorporated user and operator characteristics in the design of the system.

d. Factors other than user and operator needs that may impose constraints on a software product. Such factors may impose physical limits on the design and development of the software product. These constraints and limitations must also be specified in the SRS document at this point. Examples of such limitations and constraints may come from the following: hardware limitations, government policies, communication policies, interfaces to other application software, networks, pipelining, parallel operation, audit functions, control functions, etc.

e. Any assumptions made in the SRS or implicit dependencies must be clearly stated to identify any assumptions made before the design and coding of the software. For instance, software products are released that work only with certain operating systems or with a particular network environment. When a developer is asked to design a software package for the MS-DOS environment, an implicit assumption is that the software is to be implemented under the MS-DOS operating system. If we change this assumption, some of the detailed implementation specifications of the system may also change.

4.3.3 Specific Requirements Section of SRS (Section 3)

Section 3 of the SRS (Table 4.1) must contain all of the technical information and data needed to design the software. In practice, the software engineer uses this part of the SRS to create a new document that is called software design specification (SDS), or as defined in the IEEE Software Engineering Standards 1016-1987 and 1016.1-1993 [5], software design description (SDD). There are several IEEE standards that apply to writing specific requirements for a software product. However, all of these standards are function and performance oriented. Specific software requirements are usually developed by people who are knowledgeable in the application area. For instance, if the software is developed for a satellite tracking system, requirements specification is usually written by communication and electrical engineers. For a banking system the SRS is probably developed by a person familiar with the banking business.

Table 4.2 [5] includes four separate tables of contents for section 3 of the SRS referred to in the IEEE software engineering standards [5] as ''specific requirements.'' Whatever this section is called, it must contain a detailed description of each functional requirement imposed on the software system. A functional requirement is usually centered on an action. Regardless of what format is being used, one must include specific information about each functional requirement. A functional requirement normally refers to an independent portion of the software system. Such functional requirements may eventually be decomposed and translated to pseudocode and from there to a computer program or a program module. In the material that follows, we briefly describe what should be included in the specification for each functional requirement imposed on the software product.

1. Describe the purpose of each functional requirement. Any special algorithms, formulas, or techniques that must be used or observed in order to achieve the objectives of the function should be specified here. Quantifiable performance requirements or goals should appear in the description.

2. Describe the input to the function. Specifically, what inputs must be accepted, in what form or format inputs will arrive, from what sources inputs are derived, and the legal domains

■ TABLE 4.2   **Table of Contents for Section 3 of SRS**

First Recommendation	**Second Recommendation**
3. Specific Requirements	3. Specific Requirements
3.1 Functional Requirements	3.1 Functional Requirements
3.1.1 Functional Requirement 1	3.1.1 Functional Requirements 1
3.1.1.1 Introduction	3.1.1.1 Specification
3.1.1.2 Inputs	3.1.1.1.1 Introduction
3.1.1.3 Processing	3.1.1.1.2 Inputs
3.1.1.4 Outputs	3.1.1.1.3 Processing
3.1.2 Functional Requirement 2	3.1.1.1.4 Outputs
⋮	3.1.1.2 External Interfaces
3.1. *n* Functional Requirement *n*	3.1.1.2.1. User Interfaces
3.2 External Interface Requirements	3.1.1.2.2 Hardware Interfaces
3.2.1 User Interfaces	3.1.1.2.3 Software Interfaces
3.2.2 Hardware Interfaces	3.1.1.2.4 Communication Interfaces
3.2.3 Software Interfaces	3.1.2 Functional Requirement 2
3.2.4 Communications Interfaces	⋮
3.3 Performance Requirements	3.1. *n* Functional Requirement *n*
3.4 Design Constraints	3.2 Performance Requirements
3.4.1 Standards Compliance	3.3 Design Constraints
3.4.2 Hardware Limitations	3.4 Attributes
⋮	3.4.1 Security
3.5 Attributes	3.4.2 Maintainability
3.5.1 Security	⋮
3.5.2 Maintainability	3.5 Other Requirements
⋮	3.5.1 Database
3.6 Other Requirements	3.5.2 Operations
3.6.1 Database	3.5.3 Site Adaptation
3.6.2 Operations	⋮
3.6.3 Site Adaptation	
⋮	

....

* The reference for Table 4.2 is IEEE Std. 830-1993, Recommended Practice for Software Requirements Specifications, *Standards Collection on Software Engineering*, IEEE Press, New York, 1994.

Continued on the following page.

of each input element are just a few of the input characteristics that must be described in this section.

3. Describe in unambiguous and precise language the process that the function must perform on the input data it receives. This process must be described from the outcome point of view, not from the implementation point of view. For example, we may state a requirement for an HVAC control function as follows: if the temperature reading at a given point is more than 80°, open windows. If it is less than 65°, close any open window and turn on the heat. If the temperature is more than 85°, close all the windows and turn on the air conditioner. As you see, these are all action-oriented processing descriptions. How a window should be

■ TABLE 4.2   **Continued**

Third Recommendation	**Fourth Recommendation**

Third Recommendation

3. Specific Requirements
  3.1 Functional Requirements
    3.1.1 Functional Requirements 1
      3.1.1.1   Introduction
      3.1.1.2   Inputs
      3.1.1.3   Processing
      3.1.1.4   Outputs
      3.1.1.5   Performance Requirements
      3.1.1.6   Design Constraints
      3.1.1.6.1 Standards Compliance
      3.1.1.6.2 Hardware Limitations
        ⋮
      3.1.1.7   Attributes
      3.1.1.7.1 Security
      3.1.1.7.2 Maintainability
        ⋮
      3.1.1.8   Other Requirements
      3.1.1.8.1 Database
      3.1.1.8.2 Operations
      3.1.1.8.3 Site Adaptation
      ⋮
    3.1.2 Functional Requirement 2
    ⋮
    3.1. n Functional Requirement n
  3.2 External Interface Requirements
    3.2.1 User Interfaces
      3.2.1.1   Performance Requirements
      3.2.1.2   Design Constraints
      3.2.1.2.1 Standards Compliance
      3.2.1.2.2 Hardware Limitations
        ⋮
      3.2.1.3   Attributes
      3.2.1.3.1 Security
      3.2.1.3.2 Maintainability
        ⋮
      3.2.1.3   Attributes
      3.2.1.3.1 Security

      3.2.1.3.2 Maintainability
        ⋮
      3.2.1.4   Other Requirements
      3.2.1.4.1 Database
      3.2.1.4.2 Operations
      3.2.1.4.3 Site Adaptation
        ⋮
    3.2.2 Hardware Interfaces
    3.2.3 Software Interfaces
    3.2.4 Communications Interfaces

Fourth Recommendation

3. Specific Requirements
  3.1 Functional Requirement 1
    3.1.1 Introduction
    3.1.2 Inputs
    3.1.3 Processing
    3.1.4 Outputs
    3.1.5 External Interfaces
      3.1.5.1   User Interfaces
      3.1.5.2   Hardware Interfaces
      3.1.5.3   Software Interfaces
      3.1.5.4   Communication Interfaces
    3.1.6 Performance Requirements
    3.1.7 Design Constraints
    3.1.8 Attributes
      3.1.8.1   Security
      3.1.8.2   Maintainability
      ⋮
    3.1.9 Other Requirements
      3.1.9.1   Database
      3.1.9.2   Operations
      3.1.9.3   Site Adaptation
    ⋮
  3.2 Functional Requirement 2
  ⋮
  3.n Functional Requirement n

opened or closed or how a heating unit is turned on or off should not be described here. In this section we must also specify (1) any form of validity check of the data, (2) the exact timing of each operation (if such a requirement is needed), and (3) the frequency and sequence of the handling of any form of unexpected and abnormal situations, such as data overflow, communications failure, and run-time errors. Any list of substitutions for any specific formula or algorithm should be specified here. Also, the accepted range or the domain of any processed data should be specified, and there should be specification given for what to do in case a value falls outside a specified range.

4. Describe the output desired from the function. This description should include the following: the form and the shape of the output, the destination for the output, the volume of output (if appropriate), output timing, the range of parameters in the output, the unit measure of the output, the process by which the output is stored or destroyed, and the process for handling error messages produced as output. If there is an interface between the output produced by this function and any other function or segment of the software system, references must be specified appropriately.

In describing the input, process, and output sections of the functional specification, as well as any other part of the specification, nothing should be taken for granted or assumed. For instance, the example in (3) did not specify that heat must be turned off before starting the air conditioner because it was taken for granted that if conditions tell you to turn on the air conditioner, you would not run the heat at the same time. Remember that the SRS is the blueprint for the software being produced. Any missing details, such as turning off the heat before turning on the air conditioner, may cause major problems (if not detected soon) in the development of the system. For example, the pseudocode for the specification in (3) will be as follows:

If temp $< 65°$ then set the heater on;
If $80° <$ temp $< 85°$ and windows are closed then open them;
If temp $> 85°$ then close windows and turn air conditioner on.

Now suppose at a given point the temperature goes below 65°; then the heater is turned on, and the temperature starts going up until it reaches 80°. At this point the windows are opened while the heater is working. A bit later, the temperature goes over 85°, the windows are closed, and the air conditioner is turned on. Now both the heater and the air conditioner are working. We needed to add one more line to the description:

If $65° ≤$ temp $≤ 80°$ then heater should be off, air conditioner should be off, and windows should be closed.

Now the control function based on the room temperature measurements will work properly.

In addition to describing the objectives, input, process, and output for each functional requirement, we must specify any form of external interfaces required for the function to become fully operational. Also, it is desirable to specify the performance requirement, the design constraints, and the system attributes for each functional requirement.

External Interface Requirements

This section should specify all of the external interface requirements needed to make the software product a successfully operational product. Some of such external interface requirements are as follows: (1) operators/users interface characteristics from the human factors point of view required to optimize system performance with respect to the human users and operators; (2) hardware interface to describe all of the characteristics required to interface the software product with each of the hardware components; (3) interfaces with other software components or products including other systems, utility software, databases, and operating systems; (4) communication interfaces specifying various interfaces between the software product and networks, the communication link, and the protocols; (5) database requirements specifying any database to be used by this software product and giving the specifications regarding the frequency of the use, the accounting procedure, file and data description, static/dynamic nature of its use, and data retention requirements; (6) operational modes specifying various modes of operation including backup and disaster recovery plans; and (7) site adaptation requirements specifying data, initialization, and other features that are specific to the operational site.

Performance Requirements

This section should include any form of static or dynamic requirements specified by exact measurement. Such requirements may include the number of connections to the system, number of simultaneous users, response time, number of files, size of files and tables, number of open files, number of records, number of transactions per interval, amount of data to be processed within a time unit, database access per time unit, and similar specific performance requirements. These numbers must be defined in terms of an acceptable range. Note that within each functional requirement, we may have similar numeric specifications regarding the performance of a single function. In this case, requirements are specified as part of the process definition of the function, or in some cases as input and output description of the function. In some cases, we employ a separate subsection called attributes to describe numerical attributes of the function.

Overall Design Constraints

Any form of design constraint caused by environmental limitations, hardware limitations, audit and tracing requirements, accounting procedures, and compliance with standards would be specified here. Constraints may be listed in the introductory part of the functional requirement specification.

Attributes

In this section, most of the attributes required of the software product would be specified. A short list of such attributes would include the following: (1) detailed security requirements, (2) software product availability requirement, (3) product maintainability requirement, (4) mobility requirement, and (5) reliability requirements. These attributes must be specified in a quantifiable way such that they can be accurately measured in the end product.

Any of the suggestions given in Table 4.2 may be used to develop section 3 of the SRS. It is important to understand what must be included in the SRS. In what form it should appear and how it should be organized for fastest access is a decision to be made by the individual software development team. Each company may have its own specific table of contents and standards for the SRS document. However, the difference in format must not alter the essential information that should be included in the SRS document.

4.3.4 Software Requirements Classification

When software product requirements are assembled, especially performance, operation, and maintenance requirements, we may think that the harder and the more rigorous the requirements, the better the final product. In many cases this belief may be true, but we must also pay attention to the cost of each requirement specified. We must be aware that some requirements are not only costly, but will substantially delay the delivery of the final product. For every specific requirement residing in SRS documents, or in any other specification document, there should be a classification code to identify the requirement as being essential, highly desired, desired, short-term improvement, and long-term improvement.

Essential requirements are those without which the system will not be fully operational and will not be accepted by the client, regardless of the cost or time associated with such requirements. Highly desired requirements are those requirements that are viewed by the client as very important requirements, but the client is willing to listen to a convincing argument against implementation of such requirements. In other words, the client may revise or reconsider highly desired requirements based on the recommendation of the system development team. It may be argued with the client that it is more cost-efficient to move the implementation of a highly desired requirement to the maintenance phase or to a future release.

Desired requirements are those whose implementation requires a minimal cost increase and does not delay product delivery; these should be implemented. Otherwise, a cost-benefit analysis for implementing desired requirements should be proposed. The client may then decide to move a desired requirement to a lower classification, a higher classification, or remove it completely based on the results of the cost-benefit analysis. Short-term and long-term improvement requirements must be considered within the framework of system maintenance.

To appreciate the benefit of classifying requirements, we may consider the following example. A common requirement in software product performance is overall response time. When a client company classifies this requirement as essential and finds that meeting this requirement is costly, it may reconsider carefully before insisting on a one-second response time, for example. Therefore, the client identifies a one-second response time essential only when it has been proven to be an absolute necessity. However, without classifying requirements, one may always be tempted to ask for a faster system thinking that the faster the system is, the better it performs. For instance, in an inquiry system that a person telephones to acquire information about his or her account, a response time of one second may not be necessary. Even a 15-second response might be considered satisfactory. On the other hand, for aircraft flight control software, a 0.05-second versus a 0.5-second response time may mean the difference between stability and instability.

4.3.5   Software Requirements Analysis

Software requirements analysis is a two-step process. The first step is usually conducted at a system level where system-level requirements are analyzed and allocated among major system elements (hardware, software, and operators). It is often helpful to have software engineers participate in this activity because of the insight that an experienced software engineer can bring to the analysis and allocation task.

The second step in software requirements analysis begins when the SRS is in its final form. A clear understanding of precisely what the software must do is the foundation for successful development of a software product. Requirements analysis assures that such a level of understanding exists not only for the software development team but for the system engineer or analyst and clients as well.

The requirements analysis task involves a thorough examination of the SRS and related documentation. There are many discussions conducted with clients, system engineers, analysts, operators, etc. These meetings focus on resolving such issues as ill-defined requirements, internal (to the SRS) contractual requirements, requirement statements that dictate design, missing requirements, missing performance requirements, etc. These meetings are often volatile because the expectation by all is that the SRS is or should be correct, complete, etc. Of course it is not, and much additional requirement analysis work is required to make it correct, complete, etc.

The best approach to the requirements analysis task is a formal one. That is, every legitimate issue or problem should be documented (a standard form is usually employed) and assigned to an individual, usually an analyst or system engineer, for resolution. A date is assigned for closure. In order to bring structure and discipline to this approach, there must be someone empowered to decide what is a legitimate SRS issue or problem and decide when an issue or problem is satisfactorily closed. This role is often assigned to a senior technical manager.

Structured Approach to Requirements Analysis

The structured approach to requirements analysis consists of two main steps, system level requirements analysis and software level requirements analysis.

System-Level Requirements Analysis

Study system requirements specification and other relevant documents, including the contract, to understand clearly, identify, and confirm the following:

a. All software-relevant issues, problems, questions, and concerns
b. All areas that need clarification
c. All apparent contradictions in requirements (performance and functional)
d. All missing requirements
e. All requirements that will drive designs

While performing these tasks, do the following:

a. Build a file for each individual problem or issue identified to include copies of relevant pages from existing documents, notes taken in related meetings, etc.
b. If a formal change control board has been established, follow the established procedures. If not, then bring files to the attention of a responsible manager.
c. If necessary, develop operational timelines or prototype designs to illustrate points of concern.

Item e, identification of design drivers, is useful in establishing which requirements are most critical to the design. For example, a requirement whose implementation will consume large quantities of system resources over an extended period may not be an important requirement. Knowing which requirements will have an important influence on design is of value to client, contractor, and user, especially during trade-off studies when the client can decide whether to implement a requirement based on how critical that requirement is to design.

When a problem file is brought to the change control board, it is either assigned to an investigator for resolution or rejected. When the investigation is completed and a satisfactory resolution is presented, the issue is closed. Closure may include introduction of change pages to the specification or preparation of a white paper to assist designers in interpreting requirements. The file becomes part of the project documentation.

Software-Level Requirements Analysis

The only difference between system-level requirements analysis and software-level requirements analysis is in the object specification. For instance, item e for software-level requirements analysis would involve looking for software requirements (functional and performance) that stress IO, CPU, and memory resources; have real time implications; rely on human intervention, etc. These requirements will drive the architecture and design and should be made visible to designers.

Conclusion

The perfect specification will probably never be written. All specifications will contain (1) errors of omission and commission that must be corrected, (2) problems that must be solved, (3) issues that need to be resolved, (4) contradictions that must be clarified, and (5) requirements that must be changed because of cost or other relevant concerns. The important consideration is how objectively and effectively these issues are identified, resolved, and closed out.

A very successful software product of approximately 50,000 SLOC was developed from a specification that had nearly 1000 separate files documenting issues and problems. Average time to close out a file was 8 labor hours. On a productivity basis, five percent of the cost of a SLOC was due to closing out software requirements issues, after the release of the SRS.

The structured requirements analysis process just described will lead to a far better foundation for both system and software design. It will also lead to a deeper and clearer understanding of the application area, the basis for requirements found in specifications, and the requirements that are driving the architecture and design.

4.4 EXAMPLES OF SRS PREPARATION ■

Example 4.4.1 ABC Project

To illustrate the approach to developing an SRS, let us return to chapter 2 and the ABC Corporation's mail-order system. The system analysts assigned to the ABC project have developed a system-level architecture and design (hardware, software, and procedures) around a set of operational timelines developed jointly with users, operators, a set of volunteer customers, and others who must interface with the system. Through a series of design exercises, trade-off studies, and reviews, a system architecture and a system operational concept was developed. Figure 4.1 is a block diagram of the system design. The system consists of a network of dedicated workstations, servers, and a network controller. Access to data files is through built-in software control in each application software product. Growth is accommodated by adding more workstations. The fibre optic network has abundant traffic capacity. The network controller stations monitor system health, control network traffic, and support major revisions to network servers.

Other subsystems not shown on the diagram include personnel, customer service, facilities, and accounts payable. Inventory control is maintained centrally over several geographically distributed shipping centers. A major component of the system is a set of operating procedures and position description handbooks. A training subsystem will be used for supervised training of new employees and cross-training operators. The system design is documented in a system specification and a system design description document. A data dictionary has been initiated and much of the database has been defined by the analysis team assigned to database development.

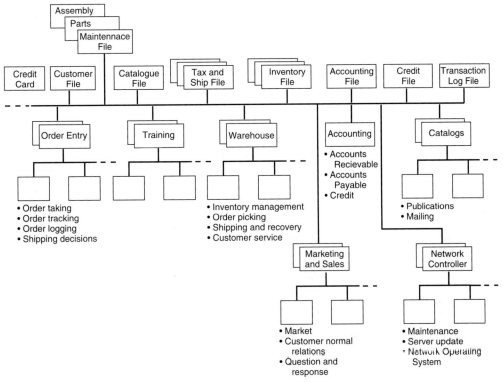

■ **Figure 4.1**

Block diagram of ABC system design.

Requirements

Among the separate subsystems identified in the system specification and system description is a software product that supports order-entry workstations. An operator with a headset sits at each workstation and interfaces directly with a customer, usually via telephone. The list of functions allocated to the order-entry subsystem by the system analysts includes the following 15 functions:

1. Accept orders (customer ID or in case of new customer, name, address, telephone number, credit card information, and product ID) from any source. Sources include direct telephone, telephone handoff from a salesperson/customer or service/customer relations, home shopping terminal, mail, direct verbal, or employee.
2. Accept shipping mode request/quote options (filtered for product size and shape).
3. Confirm product availability and location on line (inventory).
4. Check for sales/discounts (catalogues and flyers).
5. Confirm price: base price, tax, shipping cost (inventory).
6. Confirm customer status (accounting).
7. Confirm credit card status (external interface).
8. Confirm/commit delivery date (shipping mode).
9. Assign customer ID if new customer (accounting).

10. Respond to questions (customer correspondence file access)
11. Decrement inventory
12. Pass completed order to warehouse
    a. shipping label data
    b. shipping mode
    c. product ID
    d. date and time
    e. operator ID
13. Pass billing data to accounting
    a. customer ID (customer data if new customer)
    b. product ID
    c. total cost of product
    d. date and time
    e. operator ID
14. Mail demographic questionnaire to new customer (customer relations)
    a. name, address, telephone number
    b. product purchased
    c. date and time
    d. operator ID
15. Log transaction data (transaction file)

Requirements Analysis

The analysis team in conjunction with timing studies and input from experienced operators has established 180 seconds as the objective for an average transaction. The initial decision is not to make this timing a requirement, but an objective. Tests are being defined to determine if 180 seconds is an achievable objective. Senior management, however, does not want operators to feel rushed; and they certainly do not want customers to feel rushed. Many times additional products are ordered as an afterthought just before termination of a transaction. They are concerned that operators will subliminally communicate this desire to meet a 180-second deadline to customers. Finally it is decided to drop any mention of transaction times and concentrate on just reducing hardware and software response delays to less than one second.

The allocation of functions to the order-entry subsystem, several operational timelines, and a list of the order-entry interfaces is enough to get started on the order-entry software requirements specification. A reasonable first step might be to group or organize allocated functions into several components emphasizing coupling and cohesion as criteria. Lacking any better idea, the analyst might consider an input, process, output grouping. That is, collect all functions associated with making an order decision or transaction into one group. There are two components to the order placement: (1) the customer must make the decision to buy and decide how the item is to be shipped, and (2) the order entry clerk must decide if the customer is financially qualified and which center will ship the product; then he or she will place the order. The customer's decision may include sizes, colors, etc., which may require an on-line access, by the operator, to the catalogue. The order-entry clerk must consider the customer's credit status, account balance, warnings in the customer file, credit card status, and availability of product. All of these functions might be allocated to one component called input.

The process component might include software support to making the final order decision, preparing the output information, answering customer questions, and gently suggesting other items that might be considered for purchase. The output component might include changing the inventory file, passing shipping information to the warehouse, passing billing information to accounting, passing information to the mailing function, and logging the transaction. Figure 4.2 shows the architecture of the order-entry subsystem.

Additional requirements dealing with the physical characteristics of the information shown on the screen to operators, such as rate of change, amount, location, size, and error indications, have been imposed by human factors specialists. A standard screen or panel has also been developed by human factors specialists, and all displays (soft copy) must conform. The need to minimize operator key strokes and at the same time provide as many operator aids as possible to reduce or eliminate operator errors is an implicit requirement. A requirement for an on-line help menu to guide new operators or operators with unusual problems is now emerging from system analysts.

There is also a requirement to summarize for each operator the number of transactions, average transaction time, total dollar volume, and any noteworthy events at the end of each shift and at the end of each operator pay period. This requirement is for self-evaluation as well as management review.

For many steps in the process, a help screen will be required to assist an operator in dealing with specific problems. For example, in the event that a credit card check results in a problem, the operator will call a decision table to the screen that provides guidance in handling the problem. System analysts are developing the details for each of these tables. It will be required that these tables be accessible for revision because many of these decisions are based on policies that are dynamic. This requirement is to become part of a single component called the help function.

Continuing activity in developing and refining requirements, refining operational timelines into order-entry operating procedures, and synthesizing realizations in a form consistent with the design tools being employed will result in a complete characterization of the function and performance requirements for the order-entry subsystem and a sense that operators feel comfortable with operational procedures. It should be noted that many of the requirements are strongly rooted in the manner in which the ABC Corporation does business. In short, much of the ABC corporate culture is embedded in the software requirements.

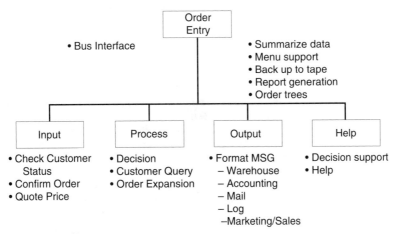

■ Figure 4.2

Architecture of order entry subsystem.

The next step is to document the order-entry function and performance requirements in the format depicted in Table 4.1, the SRS table of contents.

The most important function of the SRS is to convey to software designers an unambiguous and complete description of function and performance requirements. Following the format of Table 4.1, the order-entry SRS would probably have the following contents. Note that section references and names are just for the purpose of the example and are not related to the sections and names used in this book. Here we follow sections 1 and 2 of Table 4.1 for an introduction and a general description of the order-entry subsystem and section 3 of Table 4.2, first recommendation, to give the design-to specifications for the subsystem. The rest of this section is a sample of an SRS document developed for the order-entry subsystem of the ABC project.

Actual SRS Document

The following is the actual text that may appear in the SRS for the ABC project. We have selected a different margin and a different font size to separate the SRS text from the book content.

1. Introduction

This SRS describes the function and performance requirements allocated to the order-entry subsystem. The order-entry subsystem is a component of the ABC Corporation's automated mail-order system. The automated mail-order system is described in a document entitled Automated Mail-Order System Design Description Release 4 October 1996. The requirements specified in this document have been allocated from the automated mail-order system system specification approved on September 12, 1995. Section 3.8 of this specification traces requirements and requirement testing to the ABC automated mail-order system system specification.

Scope: This specification is intended to form the basis for design of a software product that will support up to 100 special-purpose order-entry workstations manned by trained operators.

Definitions, Acronyms, and Abbreviations: See data dictionary reference 24.

References: A list of all directly applicable references along with their release number, date, and source for obtaining copies.

Reference 1

Reference 2

•

•

•

2. General Description

Product Perspective: The order-entry subsystem interfaces with the order-entry operator's keyboard. The keyboard is unique with special function keys that are made available to reduce the number of keystrokes that are required to effect common steps in order-entry transactions. The special key functions are described in reference 31. The special-purpose keyboard is adjunct to the standard QWERTY keyboard provided with the workstation. For more detail refer to system diagram of the ABC Corporation's automated mail-order system.

Product Functions: The order-entry software product is expected to provide support to the order-entry operator or clerk in the following tasks: (1) accepting customer orders correctly, (2) quoting product price correctly (including tax and mailing), (3) confirming customer credit status and credit card validity, (4) passing order details to shipping department, (5) passing billing information to accounts receivable, (6) updating customer files, (7) opening new customer files, (8) adding customer to mailing list, (9) logging each transaction, and (10) writing to tape a log of each transaction.

The order-entry software product is also expected to provide a help function to enable operators to deal with unusual situations.

A principal objective of the order-entry software product shall be to minimize information entry required by operators and to automate as much as possible of the order-entry operating procedures. Order-entry timelines are documented in references 7 and 51.

Information displayed to operators or clerks shall conform to the automated mail-order system human factor's guidelines, May 19, 1995 (reference 9).

User Characteristics: The order-entry operators typically have the following personal characteristics:

■ High school graduate frequently with one to two years additional academic training.
■ Selected for ability to deal successfully with public and comfortable with telephone communication.
■ Highly motivated and conscientious.
■ Computer-literate with minimum one 40-hour week hands-on training on workstation.
■ Operators are not computer professionals.
■ System-to-operator interface design standards are described in reference 9.

General Constraints: The order-entry software product shall* execute under release 4 of the Zebra 7 Operating System (references 11 and 12). The network operating system is GIRAFE-12 release 3 (reference 8). The order-entry software product code shall be written in C++ (references 19 and 20). The order-entry workstations shall be UNIGRAPH, model A-3 (references 25 to 27). A special-purpose keyboard is associated with each workstation. This keyboard is used as adjunct to the standard QWERTY keyboard (reference 31). Order-entry subsystem shall be designed to interface with the following data files:

■ Customer (read and write)
■ Inventory (read and write)
■ Tax and shipping charges (read only)
■ Catalogue (read only)
■ Credit validation (read only)
■ Credit card validation (read only)
■ Accounting (AR) (read only)
■ Transaction log (write only)

The order-entry subsystem shall interface with the following subsystems:

■ Warehouse (write only)
■ Accounting (write only)
■ Marketing and sales (write only)
■ Catalogue (write only)
■ Network control (read and write)

Four order-entry workstations shall be designated as manager stations. Manager stations shall have additional functions associated with management of subordinate workstations. These are as follows:

1. ability to take over a transaction in progress
2. ability to view any transaction in progress
3. direct access to all transaction logs

....
* Shall is used to express mandatory or binding requirements.

4. ability to transmit messages to any workstation to be displayed on workstation message line
5. control access to the network

The order-entry workstation is a key subsystem. Each operating workstation shall be on line 16 hours per day. Order-entry workstations shall have an availability of 99.9%. Availability includes operating system, application software product, and workstation hardware.

Order-entry product software is allocated the responsibility for ensuring that only authorized order-entry operators, clerks, and managers can access the order-entry workstation software and access files and other subsystems through the order-entry workstation's order-entry application software. Similarly, other subsystems shall be prevented from accessing and activating order-entry functions or manipulating files via the order-entry subsystem.

3.0   Design-to or Specific Requirements

Notes:
a. These requirements are binding in that the software design realization is expected to respond fully and completely to the specifications documented in this section.
b. Subsections 3.7 and 3.8 have been added to the ANSI/IEEE recommended format (Table 4.2, first recommendation). It has been found that a test subsection and a traceability subsection have the effect of screening requirements in terms of testability (it makes little sense to specify a requirement that cannot be tested) and in assuring that all requirements allocated from the system-level specification have been considered by showing a system specification paragraph to SRS paragraph mapping.
c. In discussing specific requirements, we have retained the paragraph numbering scheme shown in Table 4.2.

3.1   Functional Requirements (overall description)

The order-entry function consists of the four components depicted in Figure 4.2. The first component, order-entry input, performs the following functions.

3.1.1   Order-Entry Input Function

3.1.1.1   Introduction

This function gathers and displays all essential data required to effect a buy (by the customer) and sell (by the operator) decision. The function accesses databases on a read-only basis and presents information to the operator that is to be relayed to the customer via telephone. An implicit requirement is that the transaction be effected as quickly as possible without appearing to hurry the customer.

3.1.1.2   Input

Standard inputs to the order-entry input function shall be customer identification number (CID) and product identification number (PID). The CID shall be a 6 character alphanumeric value. The PID shall be a 12-character alphanumeric value (reference data dictionary).

A second input type (new customer code) shall be accepted by the order-entry input function. This input identifies a new customer without an assigned CID. A new-customer transaction shall be identified by the operator with a single keystroke. A menu shall be provided by the order-entry input function to accept customer name, address, and telephone number. This information shall be retained in local memory until transaction completion.

The order-entry input function shall accept credit card type, number, and expiration date. The operator shall enter a single keystroke command to activate the credit card validate menu. The menu shall list acceptable credit card types. A single operator-generated keystroke shall be provided to select credit card type. Credit card number and expiration date shall be entered via keyboard. Credit card type and number are fields in a customer record.

A single function key shall be provided to bring up a catalogue menu with the following options:

a. Catalogue—season, year (12 characters)
b. Flyer—season, month, year, number (18 characters)
c. Home shopping—week, month (10 characters)
d. Other

A submenu shall be provided for a, b, and c with the following options:

a. PID (6 characters)
b. Product key words (50 characters)
c. Page number (6 characters)
d. Other

3.1.1.3 Processing

The order-entry input shall use the PID as a key field to download catalogue text and images for a specific product or family of products to the workstation. The order-entry input shall download a complete customer record using the CID as the key field.

The complete download of both records shall be accomplished in less than 1 second. Download time shall be measured from keystroke entry of PID or CID to on-screen appearance of the subject record.

Credit card information for new customers is normally entered at this point. The order-entry input function shall format a message containing credit card information (type, number, expiration date, operator ID, station ID, date, and time). The message shall be forwarded to the credit card validation file within 1 second. The reply shall be displayed within 2 seconds. The reply shall be unambiguous and clearly readable by the operator.

3.1.1.4 Output

The order-entry output function shall format and transmit over the network the following messages to files and subsystems:

To accounting subsystem, a single record with the following fields: CID, PID, price, tax, shipping cost, date, time, operator ID, (reference data dictionary).

- •
- •
- •

3.1.1.5 Error Handling

The order-entry input function shall recognize the following data entry errors and respond with appropriate error messages (reference 40):

- ■ Too many characters
- ■ Too few characters
- ■ Invalid characters
- •
- •
- •

3.1.2 Order Entry Process Function

3.1.2.1 Introduction

- •
- •
- •

3.1.2.2   Input
-
-
-

3.1.2.3   Processing
-
-
-

3.1.2.4   Output
-
-
-

3.1.2.5   Error Handling
-
-
-

3.1.3   Order Entry Output Function

3.1.3.1   Introduction
-
-
-

3.1.3.2   Input
-
-
-

3.1.3.3   Processing
-
-
-

3.1.3.4   Output
-
-
-

3.1.3.5   Error Handling
-
-
-

3.1.3.6   Order Entry Help Function

3.1.4.1   Introduction
-
-
-

3.1.4.2   Input
-
-
-

3.1.4.3   Processing
-
-
-

3.1.4.4   Output
-
-
-

3.1.4.5   Error handling
-
-
-

3.2   External Interfaces

3.2.1   Users/Operators (reference 9 applies)

3.2.2   Hardware Interfaces (references 5, 25–27, 31 apply)

3.2.3   Software Interfaces (references 11, 12, 18–20 apply)

3.2.4   Communication Interfaces (Not applicable)

3.3   Performance Requirements

General 1-second requirement on all database accesses, unless otherwise specified.

3.4   Design Constraints

3.4.1   Standards Compliance

Design and development shall conform to ANSI/IEEE Standard 1016-1987, and ABC corporate standards for software development. In the event of conflict, ABC Corporation's software development standards shall apply.

3.4.2   Hardware Limitations

UNIGRAPH model A-3 characteristics and limitations are as described in references 25 to 27.

3.5   Attributes

3.5.1   Security (reference 41 Security provisions for ABC automated mail-order system and reference 44 design guidelines for workstations, section 1.2.2)

3.5.2   Maintainability

Design documentation shall include a complete listing for the order-entry input application product and a complete SDS per ANSI/IEEE Standard 1016-1987. Testing documentation shall include test plan, test cases, and test case results.

3.6   Other Requirements

3.6.1   Database (Not applicable)

3.6.2   Operations (See reference 2)

3.6.3   Site Adaptation (Not applicable)

3.7   Testing (For test plan and test cases, see test and integration specification document.)

3.8   Traceability (For traceability matrix and test vs. requirement matrix, see test and integration specification document.)

Example 4.4.1 may be a little sketchy in some places, but the essential idea of how an SRS is prepared and what is to be expected in terms of content has been accurately portrayed.

Example 4.4.2   Truck and Driver Incident Report Project

Problem Statement

An independent trucking company wants to track and record its driver driving habits. For this purpose, the company has rented an 800 phone number and has printed the number on the front, back, and sides of all trucks owned by the company. Next to the 800 number a message is written: ''Please report any driver or truck problem by calling this number.'' The trucking company wants you to develop a system that (1) collects information from callers about driver performance and behavior as well as truck conditions; (2) generates daily and monthly reports for each driver and management; (3) reports problems that require immediate action to an on-duty manager.

Clarification of Problem Statement

This problem statement is passed on to a system analyst who is assigned to develop a solution to the stated problem. The first step is to obtain more information and enlarge on the problem statement. After obtaining an organization chart; learning in detail how the current system operates (understanding the application area); and establishing system boundaries, interfaces, and constraints the analyst begins to develop a comprehensive requirements database in preparation for writing an SRS for the software component of the system. Additional information sought by the analyst and the answers to the questions and concerns are as follows:

1. What is the number of vehicles involved and what is the projected growth, in number, over the next 10 years?
    Vehicles involved total 5000 with growth to 7000.
2. Will calls be processed manually or automatically?
    Manual initially.
3. Will an operator be on duty 24 hours per day?
    Yes. Voice mail, fax to be worked in as a growth item.
4. Describe the existing database.
    Schedule file, maintenance file, personnel file, security file, and route file. The analyst obtained a detailed description of the record structure for each file and a detailed descrip-

tion of how the files were updated and maintained and what security measures were required.

5. Will on-line, experienced (in the firm's operation) operators accept calls and enter callers' data directly into the new system?

   A prompt-driven template will be used to capture data. Calls will be recorded by a separate recording subsystem.

6. Will the truck license number be used as the key identifier for both vehicle and driver?

   Yes.

7. Will caller identification be an optional entry?

   Yes. Some callers may prefer anonymity. The two important pieces of information generated by the call are driver incidents, which may include both positive as well as negative comments, and certain hazardous truck conditions.

8. Why not fully automate the process with voice mail?

   Management wants a personal touch and the ability to respond to critical incidents immediately.

9. What are operator criteria for passing driver behavior reports and hazardous condition reports immediately to manager on duty?

   Operators will have an on-screen decision support system to assist in making decisions.

10. What is the structure of weekly and monthly reports to drivers, supervisors, and executives?

    Samples will be provided.

11. What is the structure of complete emergency report?

    Samples will be provided.

12. How many reports will be generated each day, each week, each month?

    Estimate is that 350 individual driver reports will be produced per day and one management report per day. Also, about fifty emergency reports are expected in each 24-hour period.

13. Will drivers be expected to reply to report?

    Yes. Provide space in driver's report to reply to each incident.

14. Will all calls be recorded?

    Yes, initially on audio tape system, eventually as voice mail. System will be updated to include a digitally recorded call as part of the incident record.

15. What communication equipment does the driver have onboard the truck?

    Many trucks are equipped with cellular phones, fax, and GPS (global positioning system) receivers. The plan is to equip all long-distance trucks with these features.

16. What is the platform (hardware and software) on which this software package will execute?

    Will be provided.

In this example, the analyst found that an SRS based on three major functions—data gathering, build incident file, and generate reports—would make for a good organization. For this example, we only show section 3 of the SRS document.

Section 3 of SRS Document

Just as in the previous example, we have selected a different font size and a different margin to separate the text of the SRS from the text of the chapter.

3.0 Specific Requirements

3.1 Functional Requirements

The function and performance specification for the truck and driver incident report software product is divided into three major functions: data gathering, build incident file, and generate reports.

3.1.1 Data Gathering (DG) Function

All of the data and information required to construct an incident report record is collected, assembled, and validated by this function. The system-to-operator interface is also effected through this function. An interface with a recording device is maintained through the data gathering function. The DG function also provides an interface to an authorized manager for the development of reports in both hard and soft form. A completed incident record is the output product of this function. A second interface to an authorized manager is provided to permit an update to the decision matrix.

3.1.1.1 Introduction

The DG function provides a menu interface to the operator when the truck and driver incident reporting system is loaded. One selection results in a form being presented to the operator and a series of operator prompts designed to assure that the operator captures and validates all of the critical data and information. A second selection results in a discrete command being sent to a recording device along with a date and time stamp. Completion of the DG function will result in a discrete command being sent to the recording device to terminate the recording and affix a time stamp. The completed incident report record is passed automatically to the build incident file function. The last entry in the record is a subjective evaluation of the incident. The operator decides, based on prepared criteria, if management intervention is needed. This decision is made while the caller is on-line.

3.1.1.2 Input

The DG function shall accept keyboard inputs that select one of three menu options. The three menu options shall include Caller On-line, Incident Evaluation, and Reports.

Provision for growth to six menu options shall be incorporated into the design. Only Caller On-line and Incident Evaluation options shall be made available to an authorized operator. Authorized operators shall be identified by an access code entered during the loading process. The DG shall accept and verify access codes for authorized operators and managers. The DG shall accept changes to decision matrix cells from authorized managers only via keyboard entry. Changes shall be recorded in a transaction log along with the access code of the manager making the change.

3.1.1.3 Process

The selection of the Caller On-line option shall result in the on-screen presentation of an incident call report form. Caller On-line shall be selected by an operator-initiated keyboard command whenever a call is received. The incident report record shall contain the following fields:

Operator ID code	6 Characters
Truck license number	10 Characters
Incident description	600 Characters
Incident location	100 Characters
Other vehicles Y/N	4 Characters
Other people Y/N	4 Characters
Explanations/References	200 Characters
Tape ID #	4 Characters

Incident report status	4 Characters
Emergency status	4 Characters
Caller name, address Tel. # (optional)	100 Characters

A discrete command shall be sent to the call recording device to initiate a recording of the call. The DG function shall issue a time and date message to the recorder. TBD* memory addresses shall be used as destination for both the discrete command and the date and time stamp. The date and time stamp shall be in the format DD/MM/YYYY_HH:MM. Hours and minutes shall be in military time. The operator shall be restrained from returning to the main menu until every input entry is complete. For those entries where no input is appropriate, the operator shall enter NA.

The operator shall not terminate the call before making the last entry on the incident report record, emergency status. Before making an emergency status determination, the operator shall return to the main menu and select the emergency evaluation option. The DG function shall download a 20 × 20 decision matrix as decision support. The operator shall decide, based on the decision criteria presented in the matrix, if an emergency condition exists. An emergency condition shall be indicated by a TBD keyboard entry. The decision matrix shall be changed only by authorized management personnel. The emergency status entry shall signal completion of the incident report record. The operator shall terminate the call after making the emergency condition decision. The DG function shall automatically return to the main menu. The data gathering process shall automatically transfer the incident report record to the build incident file process. The DG function shall issue a time stamp for the recording device to mark the termination of the call and a discrete command to halt the recorder.

The DG function shall confirm that every field of the incident record has at least a two-character entry. The operator shall be notified of any fields that have not had at least a two-character entry. The operator shall be notified that the incident report record has been accepted if, and only if, every field contains at least two characters. The DG function shall interactively prompt the operator through the data-entry process. The record structure and screen prompt design shall not preclude growth in number and size of fields. The DG function shall automatically affix a case number to each record. The case number shall be a six-character value.

3.1.1.4   Output

The DG function shall output a completed incident report form. The DG function shall issue on/off commands to the recording device. The DG function shall issue a time and date stamp indicating when the recorder was turned on and when it was turned off. The DG function shall display a menu to the operator.

3.1.2   Build Incident File (BIF) Function

The BIF function accesses, for each incident record, an existing relational database and builds a comprehensive record containing all pertinent information related to the reported incident. The BIF is the source for incident emergency report generation and both driver and management incident reports. An incident file record will be retained on-line for 6 months. After expiration of 6 months, the record will be archived on tape for 3 years, after which it will be destroyed. The BIF process is activated as soon as an incident record is validated. The BIF process accesses six files, personnel, cargo, security, incident, maintenance, and routing. The output of the process is a single comprehensive record for the incident file. A transaction log is maintained to correlate all file access times with incident record times. Access to all files is read only. The BIF is also a read-only file. Access to the BIF is limited to employees with special access codes. A transaction log will record all accesses or attempted accesses to the BIF.

....

* To be defined.

3.1.2.1 Introduction

The BIF process develops an incident record for each incident call. The inputs are obtained from the incident report and the five files. The process does not alter existing fields or records of files employed in building the incident file. The incident file is the source for three standard reports and is accessible only to authorized personnel. Incident records may be displayed on screen or printed in hard copy. The user will be able to (1) select fields to be printed or displayed and (2) produce reports based on common field characteristics.

3.1.2.2 Input

The BIF shall accept validated incident reports from the data gathering function. The BIF shall accept data and information from the following five sources: personnel file, routing file, maintenance file, security file, and cargo file. The BIF shall not alter the contents of these files in any way. A transaction file shall be maintained by the BIF process identifying the time of access to each of the five files.

3.1.2.3 Process

The BIF shall build an incident record with the following fields. The number of characters in each field are shown in parentheses.

Incident ID (6)	Incident text (600)	Cargo (20)
Date (10)	Recording ID (5)	Weight (6)
Time (8)	Driver ID (8)	Volume (6)
Location (100)	Medical code (10)	Route plan (200)
Caller ID (60)	Marital status (1)	Checkpoints (120)
Emergency status (4)	Age (2)	Security, 3 fields (20 characters each field)
Operator ID (8)	Prior incidents (60)	Maintenance history, 6 fields (8,10,8,10,8,10)
Truck ID (10)	Date employed (10)	Disposition (1000): to be left blank
Incident type (3)	Training code (12)	

The number of fields and the number of characters in each field shall be modifiable.

The appearance of an emergency code in the incident record shall result in the immediate transfer of a completed copy of the incident record to the active workstation assigned to the manager on duty. An alarm signal shall be transmitted to alert the on-duty manager's workstation that an emergency incident has occurred. A duplicate copy of the recording associated with the incident shall also be forwarded immediately to the on-duty manager's workstation.

3.1.2.4 Output

The BIF process shall produce and store a record of each incident. Records shall remain on-line for a period of 6 months. Records whose incident date is older than 6 months shall be archived on tape. The BIF shall provide access for authorized on-line queries and for generation of three reports: the emergency, driver, and management reports.

3.1.3 Report Generation (RG) Function

The RG function provides a capability for producing a driver report, an emergency report, and a management report. Some fields in the incident record will be suppressed for the individual driver's reports, and some fields will be suppressed for the management summary report. The driver's report will contain one or more incident reports associated with the driver receiving the report. The driver will be provided space for a written reply on the report. The management report will include all incidents reported in the last 24 hours. The emergency report will contain all fields of the incident record as well as the recorded conversation with the operator. Selected fields from the emergency report may be produced in hard copy to be faxed to the driver. The disposition field will be completed by the manager on duty. Most trucks are equipped with a cellular phone, a fax machine, and a GPS receiver. Emergency incident report priorities will be established by the on-duty manager.

3.1.3.1   Introduction

The RG function provides a means for producing a series of reports for use by management and drivers. A summary report of all incidents occurring within the last 24 hours will be prepared for management review at 8:00 A.M. each morning including Saturday and Sunday. The reports will include location, emergency status, type of incident, driver involved, and actions taken if any (to be entered by the on-duty manager). Driver reports will not include the caller identification.

3.1.3.2   Input

The RG function shall accept as input records from the incident file. The RG function shall accept alarm signals from the data gathering function. The RG function shall accept keyboard queries from authorized management personnel. The RG function shall accept a disposition input (1000-character limit) from an authorized manager.

3.1.3.3   Process

The RG function shall provide capability through keyboard commands to browse the incident file. The RG function shall provide capability through keyboard commands to produce reports with all or a subset of selected fields from records that meet a relational criterion ($=$, $>$, $<$) on any field in the record. The RG function shall permit the authorized on-duty manager the capability to add fields or inhibit fields for both the driver report and the management report.

3.1.3.4   Output

The emergency report shall contain all fields of the incident report record. The driver report shall contain as a minimum the following:

Incident ID (6)
Date (10)
Time (8)
Emergency status (4)
Operator ID (8)
Truck ID (10)
Incident type (3)
Incident text (2000)
Driver ID (8)
Prior incidents (60)
Route plan (220)
Checkpoints (120)
Driver reply (2000) Left blank

The management report shall contain as a minimum the following:

Total number of incidents in last 24 hours (4)
Location of each incident (100)
Time of each incident (8)
Driver(s) involved in each incident (8)
Tape ID for each incident (4)

Total emergency incidents (4)
On-duty manager comments (2000)

3.2   External Interfaces

External interfaces shall be maintained with telephone-based reports as interpreted and entered by the operator. An external interface shall be maintained with the Philco RR model 3561 recording system. A read-only interface shall be maintained with the five files described in paragraph 3.1.2.2. Hard- and soft-copy reports shall be the only output maintained. These outputs shall be controlled by authorized management personnel.

3.3   Performance

All operator requests shall be responded to within one second. Response shall be measured from the last entry keystroke to the appearance of an on-screen reply.

3.4   Design Constraints

3.4.1   The following design standards shall apply (list of all applicable standards).

3.4.2   The hardware and software platforms shall be ...

Hardware description (all items)
Software description
Network description
Monitor description
Printer description

3.5   Attributes

3.5.1   Security

Security of all files shall be a major design requirement. Only authorized operators shall be permitted access to a designated operator terminal or workstation. Access codes shall be assigned only by authorized management personnel with dual access codes. Only authorized on-duty managers shall be permitted access to the report generation function.

Three unsuccessful access attempts shall be recorded in the transaction log, and access shall be denied after the third unsuccessful attempt. Access denial shall require a reinitialization of the workstation and issuance of new access codes.

3.5.2   Maintainability

Software product documentation shall include a design specification as described in IEEE 830-1992, a commented listing (one comment line per three executable lines), and a set of executable test cases with appropriate results. A user's manual shall be provided in a reproducible form.

3.6   Others

3.6.1   Database

Any requirements for maintenance of the database will appear here.

3.6.2   Operational Timelines

Specification of operational timelines will appear here.

3.6.3   Site Preparation

If any site preparation is needed, it will appear here.

Requirements Analysis:

The SRS draft was circulated to several interested individuals including Holly, the software engineer assigned to the project. After a three-day review of related materials and a thorough review of the draft SRS, Holly asked for a meeting with the system analyst. Holly began the meeting by saying that the SRS looked pretty good, but there were some problems that needed to be discussed and some design ideas that she wanted to try out. Holly handed the analyst the following list of concerns and questions.

Data Gathering Function

User Interface: Design Question and Requirement Confirmation.
  I suggest a Windows-based GUI*. Does this sound OK?
  Will a password file and appropriate security be needed?
I would propose three main menu options:
  1. Caller On-line:
      A form for the operator to capture and validate all critical data should pop up and an automatic command sent to start recording device. A time and date stamp will be included with this command.
  2. Incident Evaluation:
      Operator evaluation of incident based on management decision matrix.
  3. Reports:
      This will be the entry to the report generation function.
Problem: Design question
  There is a need for management to make changes to the decision matrix. However, SRS has not specified how or where this is to be done.
My suggested design:
  Additional main menu option called administration:
  Provides capability of changing the decision matrix. User must be verified as an authorized manager.
SRS problem: Contradiction in requirements
      To fill out emergency status field of incident report form, user must exit to the main menu to call up the Incident Evaluation menu option. This procedure cannot be done if the user is not allowed to exit to the main menu until the entire form is completed.
Suggested solution:
      When the user selects the emergency status field, the decision matrix should automatically pop up. The operator shall choose a cell from the matrix. This action will automatically place the contents of the selected cell into the emergency status field, following which a message window will pop up that needs to be responded to with OK or Cancel. The message shall inform the operator that this session is about to end, and a stop signal with a time and date stamp will be sent to the recording device.
      If this approach is taken, the Incident Evaluation menu option can be eliminated. What do you think?
Build Incident File Function (BIF):
  Question:
      The BIF is supposed to provide access for authorized on-line queries and for the generation of three reports: emergency, driver, and management reports. If this is the case, then what does the report generation function do? Shouldn't the capability of generating reports be left up to the report generation function? Why not let the BIF simply build the incident file?

....
* Graphic User Interface.

Report Generation Function: Incorrect and incomplete requirements

1. The RG function shall accept alarm signals from the BIF, not from the DG function.
2. Should the manager on duty fill out the disposition field for all reports or just the emergency report?
3. Are the summary reports to be prepared automatically or by an operator?
4. Are driver, manager, and emergency reports automatically generated?
5. For the manager to add or inhibit fields for the driver or management report, does the system need to force the report to have the minimum criteria established in the SRS and allow the manager to build a report from the minimum?

General:

1. There are several inconsistencies in the field definitions, primarily in the number of characters.
2. Field types have not been defined: character, numeric, etc.

Each of these topics was discussed and views were exchanged on changes that needed to be made to the SRS. Also, some ideas were offered for design approaches.

If the SRS had been formalized by a sign-off, requirement problems and issues presented by Holly would have been formalized by documenting each problem on a separate form. These problems would then be resolved by the system analyst and formally closed out. Closure would result in changes to the SRS, a white paper expanding on a requirement or design question, or withdrawal of the issue or problem. Since this is a draft SRS, these issues can be resolved and included in the next version of the SRS.

The reader is invited to update the SRS to respond to Holly's problems. Be careful that only issues involving the "whats" are addressed in the SRS. The "hows" are issues that should be addressed in the design document.

4.5   OTHER SOFTWARE SPECIFICATION DOCUMENTS   ■

The SRS document is the first official document produced purely to define software requirements. There are other documents that are developed before the software system is completed. Some of these documents are listed below.

Software Design Specification (SDS)

The design-to specification document is used by software engineers to produce the software design specification (SDS) document, which IEEE standard refers to as the SDD (software design description). The SDS is at the level of detail that can be given to the programming team to start coding the software. The development of the SDS document is discussed in both chapters 7 and 8.

Test and Integration Specification

One of the important reasons for this document is to specify tests and test cases for each module as well as for the integrated system. The acceptance criteria must be specified in this document and must be constantly updated as changes are imposed on the software system. More detailed description of this document is presented in chapter 10.

Software Performance Specification

This document may be part of the SRS document (in this case it should be in a single independent section) or, for convenience, it might be published as a separate document. In this document, a clear specification is given for all of the quantifiable performance requirements for the software system. Performance requirements include the following:

1. Reliability: The probability that the system and its allocated software products will perform their required functions under specified conditions for a given period of time. This requirement may become part of the acceptance criteria, and a demonstration may be required at acceptance test.
2. Availability: The probability that the system is operating as required under specific conditions at a given time. A demonstration may be required as part of the acceptance test criteria.
3. Response time: Acceptable time to respond over a predefined set of operations and transactions. Again, response time may be carefully monitored during the acceptance test.
4. Backup facility: What form of backup system is required, how often the backup system may become operational and under what conditions.
5. Recovery procedures: How the system will recover from unforeseen shutdown and the length of time before the system must become minimally operational after a crash.
6. Initialization procedures: How the operator can reinitialize the system in case of a crash or a normal shutdown.

The data provided in performance requirements are used to arrive at decisions regarding the following:

- Off-the-shelf software acquisition
- Hardware acquisition
- Algorithm selection to help response time and efficiency
- Data structure selection to help optimum memory utilization
- If appropriate, programming language selection
- If appropriate, operating environment selection

It is, therefore, important to specify formally any operational requirement that is truly needed. It should be understood that hard requirements will cost money and development time. For example, designing a system in which one failure occurrence for every 100 hours of operation is much less costly than designing a system that may have only one failure for every 10,000 hours of operation. However, it would take a cost-benefit analysis to arrive at a decision to specify the number of acceptable errors per hour of operation. A decision like this should not be made simply because having one error every 10,000 hours of operation sounds better than having one error every 100 hours of operation.

Maintenance Requirement Specification

This document should include all of the detailed agreements regarding the maintenance of the software during the operational phase by the system developer or, as in many cases, by a third party. One of the important elements in this document is the approach to a revision release—that is, how often a new software product will be released and to what extent the system will be modified before a new release. Maintenance requirements also influence documentation requirements. We will discuss the content of this document in more detail when software maintenance is presented in chapter 13.

4.6   SOFTWARE SPECIFICATION ATTRIBUTES ■

Some of the desired attributes for software specifications in general and the SRS in particular are listed in this section. The following SRS attributes apply to almost any form of software-related specifications. These attributes may be used to quantify the quality of the SRS document.

The SRS Must Be Correct

An SRS is said to be correct if it specifies every true requirement for the system being built known at the time of SRS preparation. An incorrect requirement specification can also mean stating a requirement that is not needed to make the system work. For example, the SRS document might state that a message delay time of 10 milliseconds is required (to prevent system jams), but in the operational environment the actual delay time requirement is 100 milliseconds. This is a case of incorrect specification.

The SRS Must Be Precise

The SRS document is the blueprint for developing the SDS document, which is eventually going to be coded into a computer program. It is not possible to design software from requirement specifications such as the following:

- An appropriate time delay between signals is required.
- If the temperature is cold, the system should start the second generator.
- When the air pressure is below standard level, the system should automatically open the valves.

Appropriate, cold, and *below standard level* are examples of imprecise requirement specifications.

The SRS Must Be Unambiguous

Every stated requirement must have only one interpretation. When there is more than one interpretation of a given requirement, the implementor is forced to implement only one interpretation. If this interpretation is incorrect, the system has a known fault. One way to prevent ambiguity is to use some form of formal language to write the specification. There is far less chance of being ambiguous in a formal language than there is in using English as a tool for specification. Here is an example.

The system shall send alert messages to any aircraft that is hostile (assume there is a definition given for *hostile*) and has an undefined mission or the potential to enter the prohibited airspace within the next 5 minutes. The system shall fire after the third alert and before the aircraft enters the prohibited airspace.

In order to formalize this specification, we define the following terms:

A = Aircraft
HA = Hostile aircraft
UM = Undefined mission
TC = Too close to enter the prohibited air space (5 minutes or less)
AL = Alert message
F = Fire

Conditions for sending alert messages are as follows:

1. (HA and UM) or (HA and TC)
2. (HA and UM) or (TC)

These two conditions for sending alert messages are different, but both are correct interpretations of the English specification. The first condition means that the hostile nature of the aircraft is a necessary condition for sending alert messages to the aircraft. The second condition states that alert messages must be sent to an aircraft that is within 5 minutes of the prohibited airspace regardless of whether the aircraft is hostile or not. As can be seen, depending on how we interpret the SRS, there are two entirely different actions to follow.

The SRS Must Be Complete

An SRS is said to be complete if it specifies everything that the software must do and it includes proper responses to all possible classes of input within every possible environment. In addition, there are two important attributes for completeness: (1) the document must have a table of contents, page numbers, figure numbers, table numbers, etc; and (2) there must be no section or subsection marked TBD (to be defined).

For example, consider the following specification from an SRS document.

"If an electronic message is sent to party A and party A is not on-line, the message shall be stored on the electronic mailbox."

A software engineer develops the software using the following design specification:

1. Message arrives for A.
2. If A is on-line write the message on A's screen.
3. If A is not on-line write the message on the mailboxes not currently on-line.

The test engineer tests the program as specified and it works. The system is delivered and causes chaos. Why? Because party A is on vacation and everyone on the network is getting his E-mail. The specification was incomplete on two counts: (1) it did not specify what to do if party A was connected to the system; (2) it did not specify that the message should be written to party A's electronic mailbox and no other mailboxes. This kind of error is very hard to detect during testing. Because the SRS review missed the error, the tester tests to the requirements as stated in the SRS.

The SRS Must Be Verifiable

An SRS is said to be verifiable if every requirement stated within the document is verifiable. A single requirement specification is verifiable if we can check the software built against the SRS. Certainly, imprecise and ambiguous requirements are not easily verified. A nonverifiable requirement is always cause for misunderstanding, miscommunication, and sometimes can become a contract issue between client and developer.

The SRS Must Be Consistent

An SRS that includes conflicting terms, conflicting characteristics, and contradictory specifications is said to be an inconsistent SRS. For example, in the hostile aircraft problem it is stated, ''The system shall fire after the third alert and before the aircraft enters the prohibited airspace.'' Since we have not specified any time delay between messages, if we wait for the third message, the hostile aircraft may enter the prohibited airspace. In that case, should we fire at the aircraft even if it is in the prohibited airspace? The description says *no*; the logic says *yes*. As can be seen, there is an inconsistency in the SRS.

The SRS Must Be Understandable

This characteristic is one of the more controversial characteristics. There are those who believe that to have an unambiguous, verifiable, complete, and consistent SRS, one must use a formal mathematical specification [2, 6]. This approach raises the question, understanding by whom? Resorting to complete formal specifications makes the SRS document understandable to only a few software engineers. It would be necessary to provide an automated translation from specifications written in a formal language to an SRS in an informal language so that practitioners can understand and implement the SRS. There are those who support this approach [1], and there are those who think that since the desired end product is an SRS written in an informal language, why not write the specification in an informal language to begin with [3]? Ravn, Rischel, and Hansen [7] give a complete, formal, and verifiable specification for a real-time system (a gas burner). Clearly the SRS document must be understandable by everyone directly involved in the development process including reviewers, operators, users, clients, system engineers, software engineers, test and integration engineers, human factor engineers, and managers.

The SRS Must Be Modifiable

The IEEE standards [5] define modifiability as follows: ''An SRS is modifiable if its structure and style are such that any necessary changes to the requirements can be made easily, completely, and consistently.'' A large number of new systems may be considered as modification to an existing system. New versions of a software system are marketed before the old version is completely understood by users.

In order for the SRS document to be modifiable, a clear and precise table of contents, a cross reference, and an index are needed. In addition, a glossary is helpful. The original SRS must be designed with the least amount of interdependency among the modules and segments so a modification can always be considered, either as a small change to an existing functional module or as an addition of a new functional module. This attribute is especially useful in maintaining software products that go through a series of releases over product lifetime.

The SRS Must Be Traceable

One other important characteristic that helps to make the SRS modifiable and verifiable is traceability. The IEEE standard [4] defines traceability as follows: "An SRS is traceable if the origin of each of its requirements is clear and if it facilitates the referencing of each requirement in future development or enhancement documentation."

During the design period, we may run into a specification that is hard, impossible, or very costly to implement. We would like to know the source of the requirement and the reason for its existence so that we can see if it can be modified. Therefore, in an SRS, we should be able to trace forward from the requirement source to implementation and backward from implementation to source. We also should be able to trace a top-level requirement to the various components of the system in which it is implemented. This approach helps to determine the impact of requirement changes on all components associated with the changed requirement.

We need to be able to go back into the documents that logically, as well as physically, precede the SRS document to find the original source of a specific requirement. Also, we must be able to go forward to all documents that logically and physically succeed the SRS document and evaluate the effect of any changes within the SRS document.

Here is an example. You are using an SRS developed for a manufacturing facility to monitor the operation of assembly lines, the movement of raw materials between inventory and assembly line, and to monitor the flow of the finished product from the assembly line to a shipping and handling location. You encounter a specification stating that "the acceptable response time is 4 seconds or less for any operation." The system is developed and integrated. The integrated system consistently shows a response time of 6 to 15 seconds. Now, we either have to rewrite a good portion of the software using more efficient algorithms to bring the response time down to its acceptable level, or the system may be rejected. If there exists an easily traced path, we may find the source of this requirement and the overall impact of changes in this requirement. The result of such a process may be as follows:

1. We find out that 4 seconds was just an estimate and there is no hard evidence to support a response time of 6 to 15 seconds. In such case, we may accept the system without any change or modification regarding the response time.

2. We may find that the 4-second response time is well documented, and valid reasons are given that there will be a serious breakdown in the system if the response time exceeds 4 seconds. In this case, we must redo as much of the system as needed to achieve the required response time of 4 seconds or less. The trace will show what components are affected by the change.

There are different methods to support this kind of traceability in the SRS document. A good cross-reference document along with detailed index may be sufficient, or we may develop a requirement traceability flow graph or a requirement traceability matrix to help us to trace back and forth between requirements at design and testing times. There are also automated tools that can support traceability.

The SRS Must Separate Whats from Hows

A specification, by the nature of the definition of the word *specification*, means to describe what is desired rather than how the desired characteristic is to be realized. This objective is best realized by considering the SRS to define input and output of the software product and assume that the input enters a black box and the output comes out of the same black box. The SRS must leave the definition of the black box interior to the designer.

The SRS Must Encompass the Entire System

The software product is generally a part of a much larger and more complicated system. The SRS document must be developed with this characteristic in mind. For example, developing software for an aircraft monitoring system that produces output signals that are not detectable (readable) by the actuators is the same as not having the software at all.

The SRS Must Encompass Its Operational Environment

The SRS document must specify the environment in which the system is to operate and with which it is going to interact both physical and operational. We must understand that the environment itself is a system composed of many interacting objects. The SRS must precisely portray the operational environment of the system as it is viewed by the users, and in as much detail as is required by test and integration engineers.

The SRS Must Describe the System as Seen by Users

The terms used to specify the software system must be the terms used by the user community. When such terms are inconsistent with the development environment, we should develop aliases to make their meaning clear to the software engineers and allow users to define and use their own terminology.

The SRS Must Be Tolerant of Incompleteness, Ambiguities, and Inconsistencies

We have already emphasized that an SRS document must be complete, consistent, and un-ambiguous. However, achieving these goals using informal or even semiformal specification languages is not an easy task. Therefore, in cases where incompleteness arises, the SRS must be written in a way that can tolerate such incompleteness with minimum impact on development cost and schedule. When ambiguous statements and constraints do occur and when inconsistency or contradiction arise, correction must be easily achievable.

The SRS Must Be Localized

Localization is a necessary condition for an SRS document to be tolerant of unavoidable inconsistencies and incompleteness. An SRS document that is localized with a minimum degree of coupling will result in a software system that is modulized, which will make test and integration flow more easily. A localized SRS makes it easy to modify, change, or correct specifications. When an inconsistency is surfaced, it is much easier to locate and remove or change it in a localized SRS than in a heavily coupled SRS.

4.7 CHAPTER SUMMARY ■

Developing the "right" specification is the most important activity in the software development process. Following the planning, a set of well-written specification documents is the first step toward the successful completion of a software product. Among the software specification documents, the SRS is the most critical one. The SRS document plays the role of the blueprint for the software product as well as the role of the legal contract among client, software engineer, and developer organization.

Categorization of the requirements will be helpful during the development process, especially when there is a strong correlation between a specific requirement and development cost or schedule. Categorizing requirements may help clients to prioritize requirements in light of cost and schedule implications.

A set of fifteen attributes were listed for the SRS, as well as other specification documents. It is very important to observe these attributes as we develop the SRS document. Many software disasters have been traced back to inconsistency and ambiguity in the SRS. Especially in a large software system, keeping track of the changes, documenting the changes, and tracing the requirements to their origin are some of the most difficult tasks to do. A well-written SRS makes these difficult tasks much easier.

4.8 EXERCISES ■

1. In section 4.2 we listed a group of people involved in the development of a software system. State, in your view:
   a. the responsibility of each group,
   b. the required qualification for each group, and
   c. the contribution of each group.
2. Table 4.2 gives suggestions for the table of contents for section 3 of an SRS document. Compare these four recommendations and present your results in terms of advantages and disadvantages for each recommendation.
3. Develop a table of contents for the acceptance test and system delivery (software part) document.
4. Develop a table of contents for the test and integration specification document.
5. Develop a table of contents for the system (software part) performance specification document.
6. Develop a table of contents for the maintenance requirement specification document.
7. Identify people, and their roles, involved in a software development process.
8. Explain advantages and disadvantages of the use of requirement classification as described in this chapter.

Exercises 9 to 13 refer to the SRS document developed for Example 4.4.1 discussed in section 4.4.

9. Write a draft of the functional requirements for section 3.1 of the order-entry function.
10. List the information you would expect to find in references 2, 9, and 51.
11. In what ways would users' characteristics aid in design of a software product?

12. Write the specification paragraph for logging each transaction. Assume these paragraphs are the only communication you will have with the software designers and coders.
13. List the information you would expect to find in references 11, 12, and 40.

Exercises 14 to 17 refer to Example 4.4.2 discussed in section 4.4.

14. Separate the points raised by the software engineer (Holly) into two groups: ''whats'' and ''hows.'' Answer all the ''whats'' questions/points.
15. Write sections 1 and 2 of the SRS for the problem in example 4.4.2.
16. Incorporate the results of the requirement analysis meetings and efforts to develop a second draft of the SRS, including sections 1 and 2.
17. Perform a requirement analysis on section 3 (specific requirements) of the SRS for example 4.4.2, without considering the analysis done by Holly. Compare your results with those of Holly.

References

1. R. Balzer, ''Operational Specifications as the Basis for Rapid Prototyping,'' *ACM Software Engrg. Notes* 7(5): 3–16, (1982).
2. V. Berzins and Luqi, *Software Engineering with Abstraction*, Addison-Wesley, Reading, Mass., 1991.
3. A. M. Davis, *Software Requirements Analysis and Specification*, Prentice-Hall, Upper Saddle River, N.J. 1990.
4. C. Ghezzi, M. Jazayeri and D. Mondrioli, *Fundamentals of Software Engineering*, Prentice-Hall, Upper Saddle River, N.J. 1991.
5. IEEE, *Standards Collection on Software Engineering*, IEEE Press, New York, 1994.
6. B. Liskove and J. Guttag, *Abstraction and Specification in Program Development*, The MIT Press, Cambridge, Mass., 1986.
7. A. P. Ravan, H. Rischel, and K. M. Hansen, *Specifying and Verifying Requirements of a Real-Time System*, IEEE Trans. Software Engrg. 19(1): 41–55 (1993).
8. K. Schonrock and J. Thompson from Intergraph Corp.; G. Kennedy and J. Rymer from IBM Corp.; and R. Mital and D. Denzler from CSC. Private conversations and meetings.

Software
Specification Tools

5.0 OBJECTIVES ∎

There are a variety of tools and techniques used in developing and representing software specifications. Most of these tools and techniques have been used at one time or another by practitioners, some with great success. The main objective of this chapter is to introduce a number of tools that are more commonly used in developing the software requirements specification, the software design specification, and other related specifications. Another objective of this chapter is to emphasize that tools, although they may have an effect, by themselves are not enough to develop a successful software product. It is the process in which the tools are embedded and the people who use the tools that are essential to the completion of a successful software product.

5.1 INTRODUCTION ∎

As previously noted, several software specification documents are developed, some in sequence and some concurrently, for each software product. In this chapter we will discuss tools that, over many years, have been successfully employed by system analysts, system engineers, and most recently, by software engineers to produce various software specification documents. Examples of such documents produced by system and software engineers and system analysts are the SRS and the SDS documents. Some of these tools have been so closely associated with the software development that they have been thought of as complete software development methodologies [4]. However, it should be emphasized that what are described in this chapter are only tools, or notations.

In the same way that a carpenter is not limited to the use of a single tool to build a table, a software engineer should not be limited to the use of a single tool to produce software specification documents. Since a software system is complex and contains many components, it may be wise to choose different tools for different parts of the system. That is, for a single software system, we may use data flow diagrams, data dictionaries, Coad object diagrams [2, 3], finite state machines, decision tables, etc., to develop SRS and SDS documents. It is a mistake to think that only one specific tool should be used to arrive at the SRS or SDS document for a large software system. Some tools tend to be better suited to express and explain real-time system requirements. Other tools may be better suited to explain the requirements of non-real-time systems. System analysts and software engineers must analyze each subproblem using the tool best suited to that subproblem. This is the primary reason for introducing specification tools (as we have named them) separate from the specification and requirements development process. For project consistency, a team decision about the use of tools should be made and recorded along with the rationale for the decision.

5.2   DATA DICTIONARY   ■

An important tool in the software development process is the data dictionary. The data dictionary, as the name implies, is a comprehensive definition of all of the data (and control) elements in a given software system. The data dictionary has, in many software system developments, evolved into the only repository for project-unique jargon and terminology. In a data dictionary one should find a clear and complete definition of each data item and its synonyms. The data dictionary often becomes a source document for specification and design of input processing, files, and data structures, processing algorithms, and output processing. Typically data dictionary development begins very early in the development process and expands as the software development process continues and more detail becomes available.

The information required to design a module to process inputs, for example, must include descriptions of protocols, scaling, encryption, rates (maximum, minimum, and average), calibration, timing, and related characteristics of input data. The design of files and records requires a detailed knowledge of both static and dynamic data elements. Computer-aided software engineering (CASE) tools will usually implement a set of templates that drive, through a series of prompts, development of a data dictionary concurrently with analysis and design activity. Production of structure charts, data flow diagrams, and process specifications are also major parts of this activity.

There are a number of approaches to capturing information about data items. In some development methods, information about data items is embedded in requirements, design, and interface specifications rather than in a central repository like a data dictionary. In other development methods, data item information resides in a separate document called the data dictionary. For each item in the dictionary the following information is collected:

Description:
Name: Formal name of the data or control item
Alias: Other names or acronyms used
Use: Which processes or modules use the data or control item and how or when
                   it is used

Description: Standard format for representing data or control item
Additional: Other information such as initial value, limitations, defaults, etc.

The description format is frequently given a highly structured form. For a data item internal to the software system, Table 5.1 shows one such notation convention.

As an example, using the convention of Table 5.1, a telephone number might appear in a data dictionary as follows:

Telephone number	=	[Local extension∧outside number]
Local extension	=	[2001|2002| . . . 2999]
Outside number	=	9 + [Local number|long-distance number]
Local number	=	Prefix + access number
Long-distance number	=	(1) + Area code + local number
Prefix	=	[345|346|347|348]
Access number	=	*Any four-digit string*
Area code	=	[001|002| . . |999]

With this description there should be no doubt in anyone's mind about what is meant by the data item called telephone number.

In the case of a data or control item coming from an external source, there is substantially more information required. In these instances, the format for data or control item data dictionary content should include the following:

Protocol: Bit-by-bit or byte-by-byte structure of the data or control item.
Rate: The rate at which data or control item may appear at the input device. There should be three rates given: maximum, average, and minimum.
Encryption: If data or control item is encrypted, and source for information regarding keys, etc.
Scaling: Required scaling, if any.
Calibration: Required calibration and scaling format.
Tests: Reasonableness tests.

As an example, consider a sensor that is sampled at a rate of ten samples per second. The sensor message or data item contains four bytes. Let us say that one byte is for the address,

---

■ TABLE 5.1   **Symbols and Their Definitions**

Symbol	Definition
=	is composed of
+	and
[ ]	either/or
{ }^{n}	n repetitions of
( )	optional data
* *	delimits comments

one for the sensor value, one for sensor status, and one for a calibration and scaling code. The convention of Table 5.1 describes the sensor data item. The extended description is needed to specify the message structure in terms of high-order bit location and position of each byte in the message. This information can be important in processing the message. Rate is specified in this case as either zero when the system is off or ten per second when the system is operating. If the signal were encrypted, some information would be required to direct the designer to the appropriate sources to find out how or where to encrypt and decrypt messages. Scaling and calibration is frequently performed in a single operation, usually in the form of a polynomial where bit level representation of the sensor value is converted to a binary number representing the value of the physical quantity.

Often there is a reasonableness test applied to input data to assure that only "reasonable" sensor values are allowed into the system. These reasonableness tests can be comparisons with a table of limits, comparisons with preceding values, or other tests. The tests would be described in the data dictionary.

The data dictionary is a tool that can aid in standardizing terminology, describing the characteristics of data and control items, and identifying change impact. In addition, the data dictionary makes it easier for managers, clients, operators, and new members of the development team to understand requirements and designs.

Questions that may be answered using the information in a data dictionary include the following:

1. Names by which a data item is known
   Standard names
   Colloquial names
   Machine-readable names
   Name as it might appear in reports
2. Formal definition and use for each data item and control item
3. Characteristics (technical details)
4. Originator
5. Location where data or control item is known to exist
6. Rules by which item is created, validated, and maintained
7. Who uses the item and how

Specific uses for a data dictionary include the following:

1. As summary documentation for maintainers, operators, and during development to assist employees new to the project in learning the system and the software.
2. As a tool to reduce or eliminate data redundancy.
3. As a basis for input/output design.
4. As a means to focus responsibility for data structure integrity and maintenance of data values. For example, responsibility for development and maintenance of the data dictionary can be assigned to an individual or an organization.
5. As a control point for assigning official naming conventions.

The data dictionary is also a major repository for design information. For a more extensive treatment of this important tool, the reader may refer to reference [7].

5.3 DECISION SUPPORT TOOLS   ■

A software engineer is frequently confronted with important decisions involving selection of one alternative from several possible alternatives. Ideally, the software engineer would like to make an objective decision based on all of the information and wisdom available at the time the decision is required. It is worthwhile to note that decisions should be made when they are needed, not before. The longer a decision can be postponed without adverse effect on morale, cost, or schedule, the greater the opportunity to develop information that can be brought to bear on the decision. It should be noted that the quality of a decision is time dependent. A good decision in January may turn out to be a poor decision in July. The importance of recording the decision rationale is obvious. Moreover, the software engineer's management would like the rationale for the decision reviewed, documented, and retained in project files. The decision process itself should make visible why one alternative is better than others, reveal ways in which the quality of the decision can be improved, and indicate means for making the decision turn out to be the correct decision.

A tool or template that can assist in making objective decisions is the trade-off matrix. The trade-off matrix captures the decision criteria, the relative importance of each decision criterion, and the comparison of each alternative in quantifiable terms. The trade-off matrix can also show the quality or strength of a decision and point out ways to reduce development risk and ensure that decisions are robust.

Important decisions should always be made in terms of objective decision criteria. Most decisions involve several criteria. For example, in selecting one software architecture from several alternative software architectures, the cost of implementation, use of CPU and memory resources, ease of performing test and integration, and ease of maintaining the software and accommodating changes during operation are criteria that might be used to select the best alternative from among competing candidates. That is, the alternative selected would be the one that best satisfied the selected decision criteria.

The criteria chosen for the decision process may not be of equal importance. For example, the ability to accommodate change and to maintain the software during the operational phase may be very important criteria, whereas use of CPU and memory resources may be less important. This difference leads to ranking the decision criteria in order of importance to the decision being made. There are several ways to implement relative ranking. A very simple and effective ranking can be assigning a 10 to the most important criterion and assigning a 9 to the next most important criterion. The next in importance is assigned an eight, and so on. Other criteria ranking schemes involve quantifying the ranking more precisely. For example, if cost is far and away the overriding criterion, cost might be assigned a weighting of 10 while the next criterion in the ranking might receive a 7.

Clearly selection and ranking of appropriate criteria is a critical step in the decision process. In many instances the trade-off matrix or template is filled in with decision criteria and weighting or relative importance and reviewed with interested parties or consultants. Some of the questions that can be resolved by this step are (1) Are these the right criteria? (2) Are there any others? (3) Do we have the appropriate weighting? (4) By what rules will we quantify how well each alternative satisfies the criteria? By getting feedback before evaluating each alternative, effort associated with rework and revision can be reduced substantially.

The rules for evaluation of each alternative or candidate with respect to each criterion are important in establishing the climate for an objective comparison. A very straightforward way is to simply rank each candidate in terms of relative satisfaction of the specific criterion. In this approach 10 is awarded to the best candidate, 9 to the next best, and so on. It might be

■ TABLE 5.2   **Comparison of Alternatives**

		Alternative 1		Alternative 2		Alternative 3	
Criteria	Weight	Relative Score	Weighted Value	Relative Score	Weighted Value	Relative Score	Weighted Value
SLOC	10	8.6	86	10	100	7.1	71
Maintainability	9	8	72	9	81	10	90
Resource Use	6	9	54	10	60	7	42
Testing	7	6	42	7	49	10	70
Management Control	8	10	80	8	64	9	72
Total Value			334		354		345
Cost			4.4		3.5		4.8
Ratio of Value/Cost			75.91		101.14		70.41

argued that a more precise approach would attempt to quantify each candidate's performance more exactly in satisfying a given criterion. For example, if candidate A costs twice as much as candidate B, then candidate B is awarded ten points and candidate A is awarded five points (one-half of candidate B's points), whereas in the simple ranking, candidate B would be awarded ten points and candidate A nine points.

Establishing rules for applying each criterion to an alternative should be carefully thought through, reviewed, revised if necessary, documented, and made part of the project files.

Table 5.2 is a trade-off matrix established to evaluate three candidate architectures for a software product. For this example the most important criteria is size, in terms of source lines of codes (SLOC). The evaluation rule established for this example is to estimate the source lines of code required for each alternative and award relative scores based on SLOC ratios. That is, the lowest number of estimated source lines of code gets a score of 10. Subsequent point awards to other candidates are based on the ratio of the lowest number of source lines of code to the number of source lines of code required for the next candidate times 10. Table 5.3 shows how this evaluation is performed. Relative scores for other criteria (Maintainability, Resource Use, Testing and Management Control) are computed in a similar way. A full discussion of trade-off study is presented in Appendix C.

It is impossible to eliminate subjectivity completely from the decision process. For example, the criteria of maintainability and management control require subjective judgments by experienced practitioners. Some of the subjectivity can be removed by establishing a means for quantifying differences in the alternatives. For instance, the degree of cohesion and coupling at the structure level can be used as a measure of relative maintainability. The implicit assumption, of course, is that better modularity leads to better maintainability. Cyclomatic complexity at the structure or architecture level can also be employed along with technical judgment born of experience as a measure of relative maintainability. Using other software attributes related to maintainable software and better management control as means to quantify

■ TABLE 5.3   **Cost Criteria**

Alternatives	SLOC	Ratio	Relative Score
1	42,000	36000/42000	$0.86 \times 10 = 8.6$
2	36,000	36000/36000	$1.0 \times 10 = 10.0$
3	51,000	36000/51000	$0.71 \times 10 = 7.1$

differences in alternatives can also reduce subjectivity. By a similar process, each criterion can be applied to each candidate, and the remainder of the matrix can be filled out. When the matrix has been filled out and reviewed, the relative scores are multiplied by the weighting factor to obtain a weighted value. Weighted values are then totaled and divided by an estimated dollar value for implementation cost. The ratio of total weighted value to cost can be used as a single-parameter summary of the relative worth of each alternative.

There are two approaches to filling out the trade-off matrix. In the first approach, the analyst performs the following steps: (1) establishes the criteria and the weighting, (2) documents a description of viable alternatives, and (3) establishes and documents the rules for evaluating each alternative in terms of each decision criterion. Then the blank trade-off matrix is circulated among consultants and experienced software developers to make the evaluations and compute relative scores. The results are collected, major differences are resolved, and the decision is made and documented. The trade-off results are then formally reviewed and made part of the project database.

In the second approach, the trade-off matrix is filled in completely by the analyst and then circulated among experienced software engineers and consultants for review and comments. If required, changes are made and the results are used to make the decision. Only the associated documentation becomes part of the project record.

By careful examination of Table 5.3, we can see that by improving alternative 2's performance in the testing criterion, a more robust decision can be forthcoming. That is, alternative 2's score can be improved, making the decision even more convincing, by increasing the total weighted value. There may be ways in which alternative 2 can be improved in the testing criterion without compromising relative scores received in other criteria. In situations involving many criteria and several alternatives, the visibility afforded by the trade-off matrix can lead to deeper understanding of the solution alternatives and perhaps to an improved decision process.

A low score in any of the criterion can be an indication of risk. For example, alternative 2 scored well in all but the testing and management control criteria; if there is to be substantial subcontracting of development work, the trade-off matrix points toward potential risk areas. The prudent software engineer will look more deeply into these concerns and search for ways to reduce risk in these areas.

In summary, the decision support tool can, if properly applied, introduce a quantification to the decision process, involve more people in the decision process, help to get wider commitment to decisions, and show where to focus effort to improve the quality of decisions. A few simple rules regarding alternative candidates in a trade-off study are as follows: (1) all candidates should meet the basic requirements to qualify for the trade-off study, (2) the candidate evaluations in terms of each criterion should be fair and unbiased, (3) rules for evaluations should be documented, and (4) sensitivity analysis should be performed to assure that small changes in scoring do not result in a major change in the decision.

5.4 DATA FLOW DIAGRAMS (DFD) ■

Data flow diagrams are a widely used modeling technique derived from a functional view of the problem domain. DFDs are employed to describe both requirement and design structures. The DFD graphic depicts (1) data flowing through a network of processes, each of which operates on a data item to produce some transformation in the form or substance of the data; and (2) storage elements, which may be viewed as simply time-delayed data paths.

The first step in the general DFD approach is to model a system or software product in terms of function and performance requirements as well as the flow of data among the various functions and required storage elements. This step accomplishes two tasks: (1) it decomposes or partitions a general functional requirement into subfunctions following the tenets of low coupling and strong cohesion; and (2) it develops an architecture or structure for the model, which often carries over to the detail software design. The second step in the DFD approach is to develop further the description of function and performance requirements into a level of detail that can be directly translated into program design language (PDL) or perhaps directly to programming language statements.

Data flow diagrams and their close relatives have been used to model the flow of data and control in business-oriented information systems. However, a DFD may be used to represent the flow of data and control in any type of system, manual or automated. A DFD may represent a single module within a software product, a complete computer system, a library information system, or any combination of systems. The basic symbols used in a data flow diagram are shown in Figure 5.1. The edges or arrows in a data flow diagram represent the flow of data from one node to another. There are four types of nodes: function node, input or source node, output or destination node, and static/stored data node.

Data flow diagrams are hierarchically structured. The top-level diagram is referred to as the context chart, fundamental system model, or the level zero design. The purpose of the context chart is to define thoroughly external (to the system) interfaces and identify system boundaries. The system (or software product) of interest is usually contained in a single function or process bubble.

Subsequent DFD levels will show increasing system detail with increasing DFD levels. Each DFD symbol should be numbered to identify the symbol with its level. It is important to label clearly, with meaningful names, all of the DFD symbols. However, to prevent cluttering the diagram with text, a data dictionary can be used to provide additional detail information about all data items. DFDs can often be directly reduced to program design language statements when developed in sufficient detail. DFDs can also serve as the basis for requirement descriptions as well as for design descriptions. A DFD is also referred to as a bubble chart or data flow graph.

Figure 5.2 shows a three-level DFD for a simple process called controller. Level zero shows the interface with external (to the system of interest) sources and destinations, level 1 expands the controller process bubble, and level 2 expands the second validation bubble (VAL2). The controller system accepts two data items, a and b, from external origin #1 and c from external origin #2. The outputs from the controller system go to external destinations #1 and #2. The

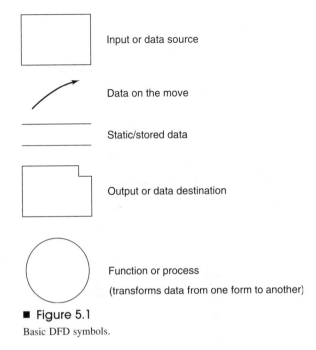

Input or data source

Data on the move

Static/stored data

Output or data destination

Function or process

(transforms data from one form to another)

■ **Figure 5.1**

Basic DFD symbols.

data dictionary should contain the required detail information (cast in the data dictionary format, of course) regarding the structure of a and b and other data items and symbols. For example, the data dictionary might describe the symbol a as a 16-bit, scaled value of the boiler temperature measurement; the high-order bit is the sign bit, and conversion and scaling is obtained by a fifth-degree polynomial, etc. Similarly, b, c, and other symbols may be described in the data dictionary. In such cases, for instance, level zero DFD could show characters a and b as boiler temperature and boiler pressure, respectively.

On the other hand, if a and b are transaction records called invoice and bill of lading and r is a summary report, then the zero level diagram would show a as invoice, r as summary report, and b as bill of lading. The data dictionary would provide a detailed description of each field in the record or the summary report content. The main criterion is that enough information to produce a complete design specification must be contained in the data dictionary for each data item to make the DFD a complete requirements and design instrument.

The level 1 DFD expands the level zero process bubble into five bubbles and two storage symbols. The external inputs and outputs remain the same. The expansion process should not create any new system inputs or outputs, although the need for additional system inputs may be identified as the DFD is expanded and developed. In level 1 we see that the inputs, a and b, are validated to make sure they are within acceptable or specified limits and perhaps to confirm that record-to-record changes are also within specified limits. Validated a and b inputs, a' and b', are input to a conversion process called CONV1. A validated c input, c', is input to a computation process called COMP. COMP also accepts the processed a' and b' inputs, a'' and b''. The output of COMP, z', is input to a process called CONV2. The output of CONV2, z, is passed back to the external environment.

An additional level (level 2) expanding each bubble in level 1 might be needed to provide

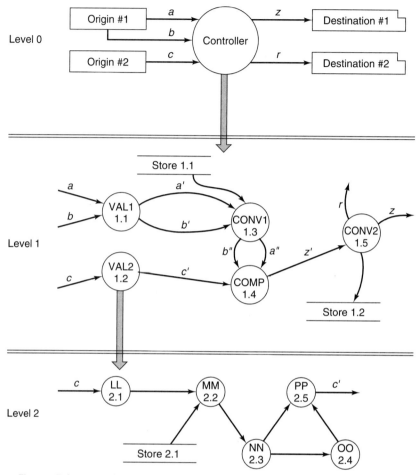

■ Figure 5.2

Three-level data flow diagram.

enough detail to describe fully system or software requirements and design. Figure 5.2 shows an expansion of one of the bubbles from level 1. In general, not all the bubbles of level n must be expanded in level $n+1$. For example, the COMP bubble of Figure 5.2 need not be expanded any further. We could, as the software architecture is being laid out, decide to make the COMP process bubble an independent module. Specification of COMP requirements might take this form:

The COMP module shall accept a'', b'' as inputs (a'' and b'' are as defined in the data dictionary). The COMP module shall produce for each a'' and b'' input pair and c' an output z'. The value of z' shall be obtained from the following algorithm: $z' = k[c' - (a''/2 + b''/2)]$. The value of k shall range between 100 and 200. The quantity z' shall be accurate to 1 part in 1000.

Note that this specification is function oriented. The bubble specification uses verbs like produce, accept, obtain, etc., to establish transformation requirements. Each module (process bubble) would be specified in a similar fashion. The next step is to produce pseudocode or PDL from module requirements.

From this relatively simple illustration, we can see how the hierarchical data flow diagram depicts the flow of data through a system in increasing levels of detail. We can see that the structure of the design is also revealed in the DFD graphic. When an appropriate level of detail has been reached, each bubble or group of bubbles can be identified with a module and a specification written in an input/process/output format. The assembly of module specifications then forms the basis for section 3 of the SRS. Conversion of the SRS to an SDS becomes a straightforward task. That is, simply continue the decomposition or expansion process until the level of detail is such that transforming to PDL or directly to programming language statements is obvious.

The requirement and design process are integrated to some extent as the DFD graphic represents a design structure. It should be clear from the example in Figure 5.2 that a good knowledge and understanding of the application area is essential in producing complete and accurate DFDs and data dictionary.

The example presented in Figure 5.2 shows how, in a transaction-driven system, data flows from process step to process step. The DFD implies that each occurrence of a, b, and c results in producing a value for z and r. The basic DFD symbols and the few simple rules for their use provide an adequate representation tool for systems whose inputs arrive synchronously from external sources. These inputs are transaction records, source documents, variable values, or other data aggregates defined at discrete points in time. Each different input type is accepted by a separate process. The process transforms the input into a composite output that serves as input to another process or output to an external destination. The processors are connected by data storage elements that are often regarded as time-delayed data paths, which permit outputs to be conditioned by the results of previous processing. The model is most effective when inputs, outputs, and storage structure are fully understood in an input/process/output format. Three implicit assumptions are made in using the simple DFD model: (1) processes are executed in zero time, (2) data storage capacity is not limited, and (3) inputs arriving simultaneously are accepted sequentially but in random order.

The example in Figure 5.2 does not, however, show the control function (what controls the behavior of the controller process), process sequence (although bubble numbering schemes could be used to show a required processing sequence), and process continuity (the fact that processes are cyclic). In fact, if *a*, *b*, and *c* are continuous inputs or, in the case of digital inputs, continuous signals sampled at regular intervals, and the output *z* is also a sampled value, then our DFD model won't be an adequate abstraction of the system (software).

The DFD symbols, as defined in Figure 5.1, are simple but limited. Over time people have tried to overcome some of the deficiencies by introducing new symbols and rules for their use and modified usage rules for the basic set of symbols. In particular, there has been a concerted effort to do the following:

1. Augment the DFD model by introducing new symbols and usage rules to depict elements not included in the basic DFD symbol set.
2. Revise the DFD model symbols and usage rules to make it as formal as possible.

Some of the extensions or augmentations may be reviewed in the work of Ward [9], Hatley [5], Yourdon [12], and Woodman [10]. The extensions introduced by Ward [9] became the IEEE standard extension for DFD symbols. Ward's extension (Figure 5.3) allows for control

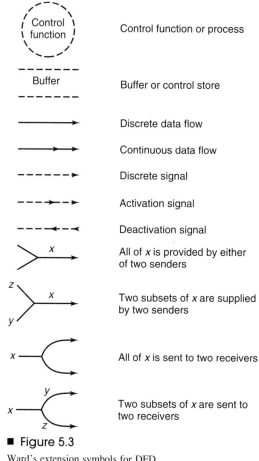

Control function or process

Buffer or control store

Discrete data flow

Continuous data flow

Discrete signal

Activation signal

Deactivation signal

All of x is provided by either of two senders

Two subsets of x are supplied by two senders

All of x is sent to two receivers

Two subsets of x are sent to two receivers

■ **Figure 5.3**

Ward's extension symbols for DFD.

functions, buffers, discrete data flow, continuous data flow, activation signals, and deactivation signals.

Suppose the controller example of Figure 5.2 is to be modified to model a software product that periodically computes the difference between a desired value and an actual value of a parameter; it uses this difference to activate an external device that drives the actual value to equal the desired value, thereby reducing the difference to near zero. To represent such a control system we require additional DFD symbols to represent activation, deactivation, and process control actions. In this particular application, the processing sequence is important, and the controller is executed cyclically. When the difference is very near zero the activation command is turned off, and when the difference reaches a predefined threshold the activation command is turned on.

To illustrate the use of the extended DFD symbols, let us assume that a, b, and c represent continuous inputs (a continuous variable sampled at regular intervals), z represents a continuous output, and r is a record of each transaction. Figure 5.4 shows an integrated DFD and control flow diagram (CFD) for level 1 of Figure 5.2. Figure 5.4 employs the symbols described in Figure 5.3. The timer control function initiates the process at specified intervals by

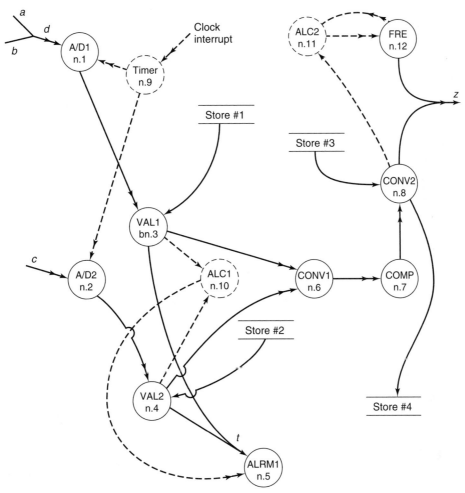

■ **Figure 5.4**

Integrated data and control flow.

triggering sampling of a, b, and c. A more complete and accurate depiction of the validate and timer function will require additional bubbles to indicate an analog signal to digital signal conversion if a, b, and c entered the system as continuous signals. Figure 5.4 shows the three additional bubbles and uses some of the newly introduced symbols. VAL1 or VAL2 functions activate a process that produces alarm signals if a, b, or c is not validated by comparison with values found in Store 1 and Store 2. Similarly, if z is not within a range found in Store 3, a control signal will result in freezing the value of z at its last value.

Figure 5.5 shows an example of direct conversion of a DFD bubble to PDL. The figure also shows both data transformation and control function bubbles being converted into PDL syntax. The CHK_TEMP process accesses a data store symbol to obtain upper and lower temperature limits. An arrow going from the data store symbol to the process symbol indicates a nondestructive readout of the data. An arrow going from the process symbol to the data store symbol indicates that data is being written or modified. If the sensed temperature is

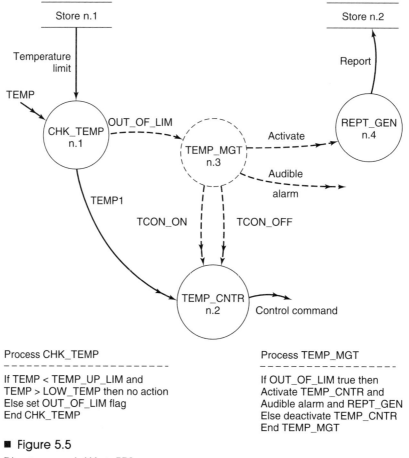

Store n.1

Store n.2

Temperature limit

Report

TEMP

CHK_TEMP
n.1

OUT_OF_LIM

TEMP_MGT
n.3

Activate

REPT_GEN
n.4

Audible
alarm

TEMP1

TCON_ON

TCON_OFF

TEMP_CNTR
n.2

Control command

Process CHK_TEMP
- -
If TEMP < TEMP_UP_LIM and
TEMP > LOW_TEMP then no action
Else set OUT_OF_LIM flag
End CHK_TEMP

Process TEMP_MGT
- - - - - - - - - - - - - - - - - - -
If OUT_OF_LIM true then
Activate TEMP_CNTR and
Audible alarm and REPT_GEN
Else deactivate TEMP_CNTR
End TEMP_MGT

■ Figure 5.5

Discrete process bubble to PDL.

outside the range defined by the upper and lower bounds, an OUT_OF_LIM temperature signal is sent to the dashed process symbol called TEMP_MGT. This signal causes TEMP_CNTR to change state and go into an active temperature control mode. The TEMP_MGT process issues a TCON_ON activation command as a result of the OUT_OF_LIM temperature signal. The TEMP_MGT process also activates a report generation process and issues an activation command to an audible alarm. If the temperature is within limits, the TEMP_CNTR issues a deactivation command.

In some applications, notably certain real-time applications, the control flow and process sequencing are as important and complex as the flow of data. In these cases it is often useful to draw two independent diagrams, one for data flow and one for control flow. Both diagrams will be identical in process symbols but will differ in other respects. The data flow diagram will show only the flow of data, and the control flow diagram (CFD) will show only the control flow. The data flow diagram will show activation interfaces and data condition interfaces to the CFD. Those same interfaces will also appear in the CFD. Control requirements will be derived from CFD process bubbles and, along with DFD process bubbles, form the basis for the SRS. This approach, developed by Hatley [11], also introduces some new symbols and rules.

State transition diagrams and decision tables or process activation tables are useful in identifying states, processing conditions, etc., for developing the CFD and preparing the SRS and SDS. State transition diagrams are covered in section 5.5. However, in creating a state transition chart, the software engineer or system analyst will need to do the following:

1. Identify all possible finite states the system may occupy.
2. Identify all activities and conditions that cause a transition from one state to another.

A process activation table (PAT) identifies input events or conditions, the processes activated for each of the events or conditions, and associated outputs. A process activation table is closely related to a decision table with its conditions, rules, and actions.

Table 5.4 shows an example of a process activation chart associated with the DFD fragment of Figure 5.5. The upper portion of the table shows all internal and external system events that trigger process activity. These events are usually identified during concurrent development of the DFD and the state transition diagram. The middle portion of the table is reserved for system output as a result of event occurrence. The lower portion of the table lists each process or transform bubble and shows which are activated by certain input events. Each column of the table represents a complete condition/action set or, as it is called in decision tables, a rule. The 0s represent the absence of an event, output, or process; the 1s represent their presence.

The first column of the table indicates that the on-off switch is in the on position and temperature is normal. Under these conditions only the CHK_TEMP process is activated. The second column indicates that an over temperature event has occurred and the on-off switch is in the on position. For this set of input events, all three system outputs are produced

■ TABLE 5.4   **Process Activation Chart**

	Input Events					
Over temperature	0	1	0	0	0	1
Under temperature	0	0	1	0	1	0
Switch on	1	1	1	0	0	0
Switch off	0	0	0	1	1	1
Normal temperature	1	0	0	1	0	0
	Output					
Temperature control command	0	1	1	0	1	1
Alarm command	0	1	1	0	1	1
Event report	0	1	1	0	1	1
	Process Activation					
CHK_TEMP	1	1	1	0	1	1
REPT_GEN	0	1	1	0	1	1
TEMP_CNTR	0	1	1	0	1	1
Audible alarm	0	1	1	0	1	1
TEMP_MGT	0	1	1	0	1	1

and all five process bubbles are activated. In the construction of the process activation table, the software engineer might raise a question as to turning the system off when the temperature is outside its defined limits. The answer is that the system can be turned off only when temperatures are within defined limits. The last two columns of the table show that the switch-off event can result in system shutdown only if the temperature is within its defined limits. This discovery would lead to a revision to the DFD. The point of the example is to emphasize the value of the PAT and the iterative nature of the requirement determination and design process.

In creating a control flow diagram the analyst or software engineer should look for events, data conditions, timing requirements, etc., that are instrumental in controlling the flow of data through a system or a software product. A checklist is useful in identifying potential control processes and control data. The following is a CFD checklist:

- Sensor processing conditions (time or event)
- Interrupts (initiating conditions)
- Discrete keyboard entries by operators
- Internal data conditions triggering an activity
- System or software states and transition conditions
- Activation of external entities (discrete and continuous)

The development of a software product, including SRS and SDS, will most certainly involve both CFDs and DFDs, data dictionary, state transition diagrams, decision tables, operational timelines, and a database definition. The purpose of these tools is to communicate to those involved in the development process as clear a picture of the planned product as possible.

Some general observations regarding use of DFDs, CFDs, and their close relatives are as follows: (1) no set of symbols and usage rules will satisfy every possible situation; (2) the DFD/CFD symbols and usage rules should be tailored and perhaps augmented for specific situations, especially where complex methodology will generate symbol and usage issues that will divert attention from product design efforts; (3) for each application, symbol and usage rules should be standardized and documented; (4) operators, users, reviewers, clients, and developers should be trained in recognizing symbols and understanding usage rules; (5) correct symbol and rule usage should be made entry and exit criteria for reviews; and (6), the symbols and usage rules depict only an abstraction of the creative design process—they have no other intrinsic value.

5.5 FINITE STATE MACHINES (FSM) ■

A finite state machine is a model for describing an entity that is characterized by its operation and behavior. In software product design we often deal with software elements that are best described by their operation and behavior. Finite state machines can be used to express the requirements and design specifications of such elements. In general, we may place systems and software specifications in two groups, operational and descriptive. Operational specifications present or describe a product by its behavior and performance, whereas descriptive specifications present or describe a product by its properties or by its output. Many software products are best described by their performance. Finite state machines are appropriate tools to present the requirements and design specification of such software products. In this section the main objective is to introduce the reader to the basics of the finite state machine as a model for representing operational specification of a subsystem or a software product.

Definition 5.5.1   A finite state machine (FSM) consists of a finite set of input symbols, Σ, a finite set of states, Γ, a specific state, S, called the starting state, and a transition function, δ, from {input $\times$ state} to {state}.

$$\delta: \text{Input} \times \text{State} \to \text{State}$$

or

$$\delta: \Sigma \times \Gamma \to \Gamma$$

We may represent a finite state machine by a diagram or by a transition table. In the diagram representation of an FSM, the states are represented by circles; the transition from state A to state B is represented by a directed line, called a transition line, from state A to state B; the input symbol used in each transition is written on the transition line; and the starting state is marked by an arrow into it from no other state.

Example 5.5.1   The following is the description of an FSM:

$$\Sigma = \{a,b\} \qquad \text{input set}$$

$$\Gamma = \{S,A,B\} \qquad \text{state set}$$

$$S = \text{starting state}$$

$$\delta\,(S,a) = A$$

$$\delta\,(S,b) = B$$

$$\delta\,(A,a) = B$$

$$\delta\,(B,b) = A$$

All other transitions are undefined.

This FSM may be represented by the diagram in Figure 5.6. The FSM in Figure 5.6 describes the processing of character strings consisting of as and bs. The class of character strings that is processible by this machine consists of a single a followed by as many pairs of ab as there are or a single b followed by as many pairs of ba as there are.

For an FSM to be an effective tool in requirements specification, we need to extend its definition to include the following:

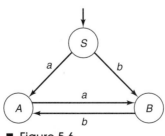

■ Figure 5.6

Finite state machine.

1. The input set includes a special symbol, $, to indicate the end of input.
2. At any point during processing of an input string or when the entire input is processed, it should be possible to decide whether the input has been accepted or rejected.

For example, suppose we want to design an FSM to process a group of words that start with letter R, say, {Read, Rest, Right, Revise}. If the first letter of input is anything other than R, the FSM must reject the input and must report an error. On the other hand, if the input string is *Rests*, the FSM should stop processing after the second s is read and should report an input error. In order for an FSM to provide this kind of representation and processing capability, we must extend the definition of FSMs.

   Definition 5.5.2   To extend the definition of FSMs, we add the following to definition 5.5.1:

1. Add a termination symbol, $, to the set of input symbols to indicate the end of input.
2. Add two termination states to the set of states to indicate rejection and acceptance states.

A rejection state indicates that there has been a problem with the input and the input has been rejected. A transition to the rejection state occurs when there is no other transition specified. The acceptance state indicates that the input has been completely processed and no error has occurred. The transition to accepting state is usually with the end-of-input marker, $.

   When an extended FSM is processing a string of input, one of the following three possibilities may occur:

1. Before we reach the end of input, the FSM transits to the rejection state. In this case the input is rejected because it did not meet the requirement of the FSM.
2. The end of input is reached, the end-of-input symbol just processed, and the FSM is currently in the acceptance state. In this case the input has been accepted. That is, the input has followed the specification of the FSM.
3. The end-of-input marker has been reached, but there is no transition to the acceptance state from the current state. In this case the input has been rejected after it has been completely processed.

The extended FSM, with acceptance and rejection states, is called a finite state acceptor or a finite state automaton (FSA). In an FSA, since there are many transitions to the rejection state, we may set the following default rule: If at a given state a transition is not defined, a transition to the rejection state is assumed.

   In the presence of the default transition rule, we can eliminate the rejection state along with all the transitions to this state. The transition to the accepting state may occur only under the end-of-input marker. In a given FSA those states that have a transition to the acceptance state are called the final states. All the states for which a transition under the end-of-input symbol is not defined are called nonfinal states. Therefore, an FSA with a default rejection state is defined as follows:

$$M = \{\Sigma, \Gamma, S, \mathcal{F}, \delta, A, \$\}$$

Where Σ is a finite set of input symbols, Γ is a finite set of states, S is the starting state, $\mathcal{F}$ is the collection of final states, δ is the transition function, A is the accepting state, and $ is the end-of-input symbol. In diagram representation of an FSA, we show the nonfinal states by a circle, the final states by a double circle, the accepting state by a flashing circle, and, if present, the rejection state by a square.

Example 5.5.2   The FSA in Figure 5.7 recognizes the set of words

{Read, Rest, Revise, Right, Revisit}

In this example $ is used to indicate the end of input. All nonspecified transitions are transitions to the rejection state.

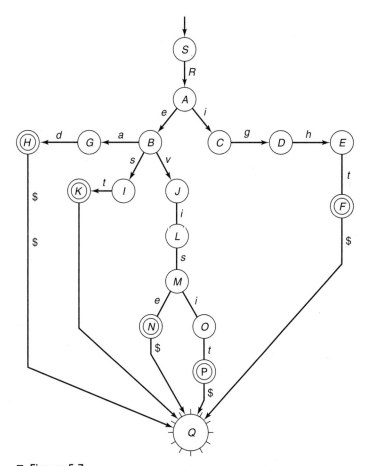

■ Figure 5.7

Finite state acceptor.

Example 5.5.3   As a third example, we are going to use FSA to give the specification of numeric constants as accepted by the Pascal programming language (and many other programming languages). The purpose of this example is to show that not only can we specify some requirements using FSA or FSM, but we can read and understand the requirements represented by a finite state machine. For this reason, we first present the machine (Figure 5.8) and then read the specification from the machine. In this example, the input symbols are as follows:

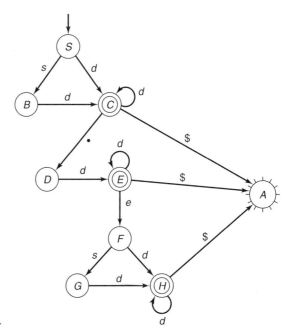

■ **Figure 5.8**

Requirement specification for numeric constants.

$$\Sigma = \{+, -, ., 0, 1, 2, 3, 4, 5, 6, 7, 8, 9, e, \$\}$$

We may define $s = \{+,-\}$ and $d = \{0, 1, 2, 3, 4, 5, 6, 7, 8, 9\}$; then

$$\Sigma = \{s, ., e, d, \$\}.$$

In Figure 5.8, starting from state S, we may process a plus sign, a minus sign, or a digit. Anything else at this state causes the input string to be rejected. At state B, we have seen a plus sign or a minus sign and we must next process a digit. Any other input at state B is an error. At state C, we can see as many digits as there are until either the end of input is encountered or a period (.) is seen. If the end-of-input symbol is encountered, we have processed a signed or unsigned integer (whole) number. If a period (.) is encountered, we are beginning to process a real number. At state D, the only processible input is a digit. At state E, we may process as many digits as there are and then see the end-of-input signal, which in this case a real number in its decimal representation has been processed. If at state E we see letter e (or E) as input, then we begin to process a real number in its exponential form. At state F, we may process a plus or minus sign or a digit. A plus sign or a minus sign takes us to state G, which can process only a digit. A digit in state F takes us to state H. At state H we can process as many digits as there are.

This is a short description of the model shown in Figure 5.8. However, the FSA in Figure 5.8 precisely defines what a numeric constant consists of. To specify a numeric constant in English language, we might write a full page. Figure 5.8 shows all twelve possibilities for a numeric constant. In an English language description, each possibility would be described separately.

Finite state machines may be used to represent specification of a large variety of requirements. However, it cannot describe requirements for all problems encountered in system and

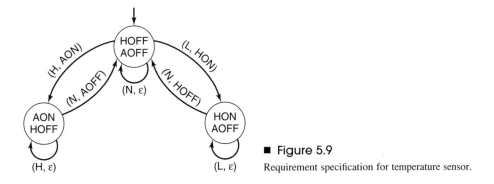

■ Figure 5.9

Requirement specification for temperature sensor.

software specifications. An example of a specification that may not be best described by an FSA is the specification of nested loops in a programming language like Ada.

Definition 5.5.3   Let us define a finite set of symbols, Ψ, as output symbols. To each transition of an FSA, associate zero or more symbols from Ψ as the output symbols produced by that transition. The resulting machine is an FSA with output, commonly called a finite state translator (FST). Each edge of the graph representing the FST is labeled by an ordered pair (input, output). When there is no output associated with a transition, the output may be shown by symbol ϵ or just a blank space.

Example 5.5.3   Suppose in one of the chemical storage facilities of the XYZ project there are three types of sensors: (1) a sensor to measure the air temperature, (2) a sensor to measure the air pressure, and (3) a sensor to measure the air humidity. Each of these measuring devices will continuously send out one of three signals: High, Normal, or Low. For the type 1 sensor, if the temperature signal is High, then the air conditioner is turned on; and if it is Low, the heater is turned on. Both the air conditioner and the heater are turned off when the temperature signal is Normal. For the type 2 sensor, the pressure actuator is set to Compress if the pressure signal is Low and is set to Decompress if the pressure signal is High. The pressure controller device is set to Off if the pressure signal is Normal. Similarly, for the type 3 sensor, the humidity control switch is set to Humidify if the signal is Low, to Dehumidify if the signal is High, and to Off if the signal is Normal. Figures 5.9, 5.10 and 5.11 show FST's representing the specification for each of the three types of sensor devices. Note that in order to go from a High signal to a Low signal or vice versa, the device must first issue a Normal

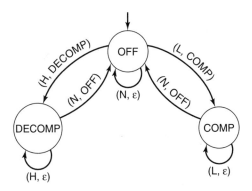

■ Figure 5.10

Requirement specification for air pressure sensor.

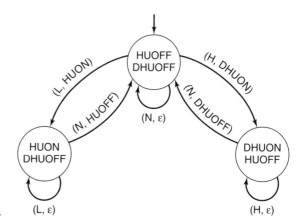

■ **Figure 5.11**

Requirement specification for humidity sensor.

signal. Initially both the heater and the air conditioning units are off, as is the air pressure actuator.

In the case of air temperature (and humidity) control, we have assumed the heater (humidifier) and air conditioner (dehumidifier) are two separate units with separate on/off switches. In the case of air pressure, we have assumed that there is a single machine with a three-way switch, Compress, Off, and Decompress. The names of the states are selected to represent the positions of the switches involved. The signals produced by the sensors are represented by L (Low), N (Normal), and H (High); the state of switches is as follows:

HOFF (heater off), HON (heater on)
AOFF (air condition off), AON (air condition on)
DECOMP (decompress), COMP (compress)
HUON (humidifier on), HUOFF (humidifier off)
DHUON (dehumidifier on), DHUOFF (dehumidifier off)

The three FSTs of Figures 5.9, 5.10, and 5.11 may be put together via a single master switch that turns on each of the three sensors. See exercise 5 in the next section.

5.6   PETRI NETS   ■

The Petri net's primary application is in modeling systems. A model is a representation, often in mathematical and/or notational form, of the behavior and features of a system. Today, there is not a single field of study in which modeling is not being used. Examples of the use of modeling in research, development, and application include aerospace research and technology, astronomy, nuclear physics, biomedical research, genetic engineering, human social behavior, economic systems, transportation systems, worldwide communication networks, worldwide financial networks, and, last but not least, information systems.

Modeling and manipulation of a representation of a real-word system will help researchers and engineers in many ways, including the following:

1. By studying a model of a system we learn more about the system itself.
2. The deficiencies of a system may be detected much more easily through the study of an accurate model of the system.
3. Mistakes that are made during modeling of the system may be corrected much faster and more cheaply than those made during actual creation of the system.
4. Complete comprehension of a large system is difficult, if not impossible. However, a representative model of the system could be understood and comprehended much more easily.

Regardless of the diversity of the systems we want to model, there are fundamental properties that are shared by all the systems. Common characteristics include the following:

1. Each system consists of many separate and interactive subsystems or components.
2. Each component of a system is itself a system.
3. On one hand, each component of a system has its own identity and characteristics. On the other hand, each component must fit into the system just as a piece of a puzzle must.
4. Some of the components of a system require concurrent processing.
5. Each component of a system, including the system itself, has always a current state, a background state, and a future state.

The concept of *state* with regard to a system is an important concept. For example, a software module at any point in its processing may be in one of the following three states: execution, waiting, or idle. Waiting state is often the consequence of concurrency and may be required for synchronization.

Petri nets are tools, designed for modeling systems with interacting concurrent components. A software system definitely has all these characteristics. Therefore Petri nets may be used to model a software product. The requirement and design specifications of a software product play the role of a model for a software system. Hence, a Petri net may be a helpful tool in developing the requirement and design specifications of a software product.

Definition 5.6.1   A Petri net C is composed of four parts shown by the 4-tuple

$$C = \{P,T,I,O\}$$

Where P is a finite set of places, T is a finite set of transitions, I is an input function, and O is an output function.

The input function I maps a transition (t_j) to a collection of places shown by $I(t_j)$. These places are called the input places for transition (t_j). Similarly the output function O maps a transition (t_j) to a set of output places shown by $O(t_j)$. These places are called the output places for transition t_j. Note that the word *collection* was used for $I(t_j)$ and $O(t_j)$ for a reason. We did not say $I(t_j)$ or $O(t_j)$ is a set of places because they may contain multiple instances of the same place P_i. Sets that allow multiple elements are called bags. The number of times a given element x is in a bag B is shown by $\#(x,B)$. Therefore, a bag B is called a set if and only if

$$\text{For every } x, \#(x,B) = 0 \text{ or } 1$$

Definition 5.6.2   For the input function I the multiplicity of an input place P_i for a transition t_j is the number of appearances of P_i in $I(t_j)$. Similarly, the multiplicity of an output place P_i for transition t_j is the number of appearances of P_i in $O(t_j)$.

We may extend the definition of I and O to include the reverse mapping. That is, a transition

t_j is an input of a place P_i if P_i is an output of t_j and vice versa. Therefore, we may have the following equations for every place P_i and every transition t_j:

$$\# (t_j, I(P_i)) = \# (P_i, O(t_j))$$

$$\# (t_j, O(P_i)) = \# (P_i, I(t_j))$$

where $I(P_i)$ and $O(P_i)$ are the extended input and output function, respectively.

Example 5.6.1 Suppose we have

$$P = \{P_1, P_2, P_3, P_4, P_5, P_6\}$$

$$T = \{t_1, t_2, t_3, t_4, t_5\}$$

and

Input Function	Output Function
$I: T \rightarrow P$	$O: T \rightarrow P$
$I(t_1) = \{P_1, P_4\}$	$O(t_1) = \{P_2, P_3\}$
$I(t_2) = \{P_3\}$	$O(t_2) = \{P_2, P_5, P_5\}$
$I(t_3) = \{P_2, P_3\}$	$O(t_3) = \{P_4\}$
$I(t_4) = \{P_4, P_5, P_5\}$	$O(t_4) = \{P_5\}$
$I(t_5) = \{P_2\}$	$O(t_5) = \{P_4, P_6\}$

Extended Input Function	Extended Output Function
$I: P \rightarrow T$	$O: P \rightarrow T$
$I(P_1) = \{ \}$	$O(P_1) = \{t_1\}$
$I(P_2) = \{t_1, t_2\}$	$O(P_2) = \{t_3, t_5\}$
$I(P_3) = \{t_1\}$	$O(P_3) = \{t_2, t_3\}$
$I(P_4) = \{t_3, t_5\}$	$O(P_4) = \{t_1, t_4\}$
$I(P_5) = \{t_2, t_2, t_4\}$	$O(P_5) = \{t_4, t_4\}$
$I(P_6) = \{t_5\}$	$O(P_6) = \{ \}$

The reader can verify the equations:

$$\#(t_j, I(P_i)) = \# (P_i, O(t_j))$$

and

$$\#(t_j, O(P_i)) = \# (P_i, O(t_j))$$

for every pair of (t_j, P_i). For instance, we have:

$$\#(P_5, I(t_4)) = 2 \text{ and } \# (t_4, O(P_5)) = 2$$

or

$$\#(t_1, O(P_3)) = 0 \text{ and } \# (P_3, I(t_1)) = 0$$

For application purposes and ease of visibility, we use a graph to represent a Petri net. Graphs that represent Petri nets are called Petri net graphs.

A Petri net graph, G, is a directed bipartite graph, $G = (V, E)$, for which the set of vertices, V, is $V = P \cup T$ and the bag of directed edges, E, consists of two groups of edges:

1. (P_i, t_j), which is an edge from place P_i to transition t_j or
2. (t_j, P_i), which is an edge from transition t_j to place P_i.

These edges are such that

$$\# ((P_i,t_j),E) = \# (P_i,I(t_j))$$

and

$$\# ((t_j,P_i),E) = \# (P_i,O(t_j))$$

We denote the vertices that are representing places by circles and those that are representing transitions by bar lines. With this notation, Figure 5.12 represents the Petri net defined in example 5.6.1.

Definition 5.6.3   The dual of a Petri net $C = (P,T,I,O)$ is another Petri net resulted from C by changing place to transition and transition to place.

Petri Net Markings   We may mark the places (not the transitions) of a Petri net by one or more tokens or symbols. The marking is shown by function μ:

$$\mu = (\mu1, \mu2, \mu3, \ldots \mu n)$$

where n is the number of distinct places in the Petri net and μi is a nonnegative integer. Such a Petri net is called a marked Petri net (MPN) and is shown by

$$M = (P,T,I,O,\mu)$$

where $P,T,I,$ and O are as we defined for the Petri net and μ is the marking function.

Usually when a Petri net is represented by a graph, we represent the marking of the places by a darker dot in circles representing places. Figure 5.13 shows a marked Petri net graph. For this graph the marking function is as follows:

$$\mu = (0, 1, 2, 2, 3)$$

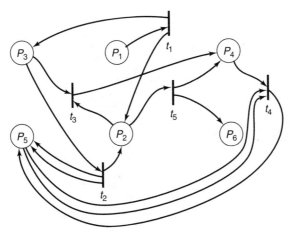

■ **Figure 5.12**

Sample Petri net.

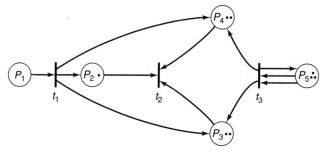

■ **Figure 5.13**

Sample marked Petri net.

Definition 5.6.4 A transition t_j in a marked Petri net (P,T,I,O,μ) is enabled if for all P_i's in P EP we have the following:

$$\mu(P_i) \geq; \# (P_i, I(t_j))$$

Definition 5.6.5 If a transition t_j removes $(P_i, I(t_j))$ of its enabling tokens from its input place and deposits one token in each of its output places, we say the transition t_j has fired. Note that token may be duplicated for different output places.

Definition 5.6.6 A transition t_j in a marked Petri net may fire whenever it is enabled. Firing an enabled transition t_j changes the marking of the place P_i as follows:

$$\mu'(P_i) = \mu(P_i) - \# (P_i, I(t_j)) + \# (P_i, O(t_j))$$

Definition 5.6.7 A marked Petri net is executable if at least one of its transitions is enabled. The execution of an MPN happens when one of its enabled transitions fires.

In Figure 5.13 transition t_1 cannot fire, but all other transitions can fire. For example, if transition t_3 in Figure 5.13 fires, it will deposit a token in each of the three places P_3, P_4, and P_5. However, the firing of t_3 will also remove 2 tokens from P_5. Therefore, the number of marks in P_5 will reduce by 1.

5.6.1 Petri Net State Space

For a marked Petri net (P,T,I,O,μ), let us define function δ as follows:

$$\delta(\mu,t_j) = \begin{cases} \text{undefined} & \text{If } t_j \text{ is not enabled} \\ \\ \mu' & \text{If } t_j \text{ is enabled} \end{cases}$$

where μ' is the marking that resulted from firing t_j. Function δ is called the next state function. The number of possible next states for an MPN with n places is the set of all possible markings, which is equal to N^n. Therefore, δ may be defined as follows:

$$\delta: N^n \times T \rightarrow N^n$$

For a marked Petri net, function δ is defined if and only if

$$\mu(P_i) \geq \# [P_i, I(t_j)] \text{ for all } P_i \in P$$

If $\delta(\mu, t_j)$ is defined then

$$\mu'(P_i) = \mu(P_i) - \# [P_i, I(t_j)] + \# [P_i, O(t_j)]$$

for all $P_i \in P$.

Assume at the initial state a marked Petri net has the marking function μ^0. When a transition is fired, the MPN is in the next state; the marking of this state is denoted by μ^1 where

$$\mu^1 = (\mu^0, t_j).$$

In general, if we are at a state with marking μ^k and we fire the enabled transition t_q, we will arrive at marking state

$$\mu^{k+1} = \delta(\mu^k, t_q).$$

The firing of a transition is called the execution of a marked Petri net. Each execution of a marked Petri net results in two sequences:

$$(\mu^0, \mu^1, \mu^2, \ldots)$$

and

$$(t_{j1}, t_{j2}, t_{j3}, \ldots)$$

where

$$\delta(\mu^k, t_j) = \mu^{k+1} \text{ for } k = 0, 1, 2, \ldots$$

Suppose in an MPN we have been at state X, a transition has been fired, and we are now at state Y; the question is, "Can we go back to state X?" That is, if the marking of X has been μ^x and the marking of Y, μ^y, is there a transition t_j such that, if fired, $\delta(\mu^y, t_j) = \mu^x$? The answer is, "Not always." However, if there is such a transition, then we say there is a backfire for state X.

5.6.2   Using Petri Net To Model System

In a system we have a set of events and a set of conditions that are observed before or after an event takes place. The state of a system may be described as a set of conditions. These conditions may be true, in which case we say the condition holds, or they may be false (condition does not hold). In order for an event to occur, the system must be in a certain state. The occurrence of an event may change the state of a system. This new state of the system is a direct consequence of the event that has just occurred. The conditions that hold before event e occurs are called the preconditions for event e. When event e occurs it may cause certain conditions to become true. The conditions that hold after event e occurs are called the post-conditions for event e.

To represent a system with a Petri net, we represent conditions by places and events by transitions. The preconditions for each event are shown by edges coming to the event. The postconditions for an event are shown by the edges going out of the event.

Example 5.6.2   Let us consider a one-person automobile body shop with the following set of events:

t_1: A car arrives for body work
t_2: The worker gets busy
t_3: The body work on the car is done
t_4: The car is washed and waxed

The states of this body shop may be defined by the following conditions:

P_1: Body shop is ready to accept a new order
P_2: A car arrives for body work
P_3: The worker is working on the car
P_4: The worker is done working on the car

The preconditions and postconditions for each of the four events are as follows:

Event	Precondition	Postcondition
t_1	None	P_2
t_2	P_1, P_2	P_3
t_3	P_3	P_4, P_1
t_4	P_4	None

Figure 5.14 shows the Petri net representation of this simple automobile body shop.

Example 5.6.3   For a more complicated example let us consider a body shop that is more elaborate than the one we just discussed. Let us assume a car entering this body shop goes through the first three of the following jobs:

M_1: Smoothing
M_2: Undercoat preparation
M_3: Painting and final touches
M_4: Washing and waxing

Some cars go through service M_4 before being delivered to the customer and some cars do not go through M_4.

There are three people working in this body shop:

Person W_1: Can work only on smoothing job, M_1
Person W_2: Can work on jobs M_1 and M_2
Person W_3: Can work on jobs M_3 and M_4

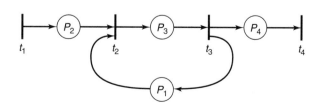

■ Figure 5.14

Petri net representation of bodyshop in
Example 5.6.2.

The conditions or the states of the system are as follows:

P_1 : A car has arrived and is waiting for M_1
P_2 : A car is done at M_1 and is ready for M_2
P_3 : A car is done at M_2 and is ready for M_3
P_4 : A car is done at M_3 and is ready to go out (order done)
P_5 : A car is done at M_3 and is ready for M_4
P_6 : A car is done at M_4 and is ready to go out (order done)
P_7 : Station M_1 is idle
P_8 : Station M_2 is idle
P_9 : Station M_3 is idle
P_{10}: Station M_4 is idle
P_{11}: Worker W_1 is idle
P_{12}: Worker W_2 is idle
P_{13}: Worker W_3 is idle
P_{14}: Worker W_1 is working at M_1
P_{15}: Worker W_2 is working at M_1
P_{16}: Worker W_2 is working at M_2
P_{17}: Worker W_3 is working at M_3
P_{18}: Worker W_3 is working at M_4

The following events may occur at this body shop:

t_1 : A car arrives
t_2 : Worker W_1 starts to work at M_1
t_3 : Worker W_2 starts to work at M_1
t_4 : Worker W_2 starts to work at M_2
t_5 : Worker W_3 starts to work at M_3
t_6 : Worker W_3 starts to work at M_4
t_7 : Worker W_1 finishes working at M_1
t_8 : Worker W_2 finishes working at M_1
t_9 : Worker W_2 finishes working at M_2
t_{10}: Worker W_3 finishes working at M_3
t_{11}: Worker W_3 finishes working at M_4

Events	Preconditions	Postconditions
t_1	None	P_1
t_2	P_1, P_7, P_{11}	P_{14}
t_3	P_1, P_7, P_{12}	P_{15}
t_4	P_2, P_8, P_{12}	P_{16}
t_5	P_3, P_9, P_{13}	P_{17}
t_6	P_5, P_{10}, P_{13}	P_{18}
t_7	P_{14}	P_7, P_{11}, P_2
t_8	P_{15}	P_7, P_{12}, P_2
t_9	P_{16}	P_3, P_8, P_{12}
t_{10}	P_{17}	P_4, P_5, P_9, P_{13}
t_{11}	P_{18}	P_6, P_{10}, P_{13}

In Petri net graph representation of this example, the places that correspond to a station or a worker being available are marked by a single token. When a transaction is enabled, the Petri net is executed; otherwise, it is not executed. That is, in our example, if station M_1 finishes the smoothing work for a car but station M_2 is busy, this car must wait until M_2 becomes available.

If we decide to use the Petri net as a tool for system and software specifications, we may need to expand our knowledge about Petri nets beyond this discussion. We especially need to learn about concurrency, parallelism, and self-ordering characteristics of Petri nets. Reference [8] may be used for further study of Petri nets.

5.7 MATHEMATICAL LOGIC   ■

During the past 20 years there has been continuous but slow progress toward the use of formal specification in software development. The main objective of formal specification is to enable software engineers to specify, develop, and verify software by employing a formal specification language. In formal specification methods the objective of producing consistent, complete, and correct specifications is achieved through mathematically provable statements. While some progress has been made and there have been reported successes, the use of formal specification languages in software design specification will require training a new generation of system and software engineers.

A software specification is called a formal specification if it is written entirely in a language with precisely defined semantics and syntax, which sounds like coding and is, to an extent. The semantics and syntax of a formal specification language are very much like any high-level programming language. However, a formal specification language provides for automatic logic verification. A formal specification may be checked for inconsistencies and contradictions before being coded in a programming language.

The advantages of a formal specification are as follows: (1) it can be studied mathematically, (2) correctness of modules can be proved, (3) equivalency can be shown, (4) incomplete definitions and inconsistencies can be detected, and (5) in some cases, it may be produced automatically from requirement statements. The main disadvantage of formal specification is the level of training required to prepare software developers. Those who develop formal specifications as well as those who must code from formal specifications must have a good mathematical/logical understanding and maturity. A partial solution for this problem is to create interpreters to convert formal specifications directly to computer programs using a given programming language. The list of formal specification languages designed for this purpose includes the following: PAISLEY [14], SPEC [1] and Z [11]. These formal specification languages are based on mathematical logic. In fact, all attempts at developing formal specification languages have used logic and predicate calculus as their base [6, 13].

Unfortunately, the feeling among practitioners is that formal specification is a good subject for research. Among practitioners the prevailing sentiment is that formal specification in its present form is not practical. We may disagree with this assessment of formal specification, but as long as the practitioner does not support the approach, formal specification will remain an interesting research topic.

A marriage between formal and informal specification may be a workable compromise. This approach allows a gradual migration from fully informal specification practice to a highly formal specification practice. This approach also allows those not favorably inclined toward formal specification to become acquainted with the methodology and to appreciate its advantages. In addition this approach provides for a smooth transition from informal specification practice to a fully formal specification practice. Meanwhile, research must be continued to smooth the rough edges in this transition process.

First-order logic is the basic block for presenting most of the descriptive specifications. The following is a list of mathematical symbols and their meaning as they are often used in first-order logic.

Symbol	Meaning
$\forall$	For all (a qualifier)
$\exists$	There exists (a qualifier)
$P \equiv Q$	P is logically equivalent to Q
$\sim p$	not p
$p \wedge q$	p and q
$p \vee q$	p or q
$p \rightarrow q$	if p then q
$p \Rightarrow q$	p implies q
$p \leftrightarrow q$	p if and only if q
$\ni$	such that
$p \nRightarrow q$	p does not imply q

Examples Using Logic Symbols. In the following examples assume x, y, and z are numeric values and p and q are logical values. The objective is to interpret each of the following lines.

1. $\forall\ x,y,z\ x > y \wedge y > z \Rightarrow x > z$
2. $\exists\ x \ni x > 10 \vee x + y < 100$
3. $\forall\ x,y \in N \rightarrow x + y \in N$
4. $\exists\ x,y \in \{1,2,3,4\} \ni x + y \in \{1,2,3,4\}$
5. $\forall\ x,y \in \{1,2,3,4\}\ x > y \Rightarrow x - y \in \{1,2,3,4\}$
6. $\sim (p \wedge q) \equiv \sim p \vee \sim q$
7. $x > y \leftrightarrow x - y > 0$
8. $x + y > 0 \nRightarrow x > 0 \wedge y > 0$

Line 1 means that for all numeric values x, y, and z for which x is larger than y and y is larger than z, x is larger than z.

Line 2 means that there exists a numeric value x such that either x is greater than 10 or for some value y the sum of x and y is less than 100.

Line 3 means that if numeric values x and y are elements of the set of integers, then $x + y$ is also an integer.

Line 4 means that there exist x and y in the set $\{1,2,3,4\}$ such that the sum of x and y is also a member of the set $\{1,2,3,4\}$.

Line 5 means that for all values x and y from the set $\{1,2,3,4\}$ if x is greater than y, then the difference between x and y $(x - y)$ is also an element of the set $\{1,2,3,4\}$.

Line 6 means that the complement of two logical values that are joined by an and operation is the same as joining the complement of each logical value by an or operation.

Line 7 means that numeric value x is greater than y if and only if the difference $x - y$ is positive.

Line 8 means that if the sum of two numbers is positive it cannot be concluded that both of the numbers are positive.

The following is a list of definitions often used in the application of first order logic. These definitions are especially used in problem specification using mathematical logic.

Definition 5.7.1 A variable in a formula is called a free variable if no qualifier is used with that variable. A variable that is used with a qualifier is called a bound variable.

Definition 5.7.2 Suppose $P(x_1, x_2, \ldots, x_n)$ is a formula. The closure of this formula is obtained by qualifying all of its free variables by the $\forall$ qualifier.

Definition 5.7.3 A formula $P(x_1, x_2, \ldots, x_n)$ is closed if all of its variables are bound variables.

Definition 5.7.4 If the formula $P(x_1, x_2, \ldots, x_n)$ is always true, then $p(x_1, x_2, \ldots, x_n)$ is called a tautology. If $P(x_1, x_2, \ldots, x_n)$ is always false, then it is called a contradiction.

Definition 5.7.5 A formula may have a set of constraints associated with it. Such constraints are called assertions.

5.7.1 Problem Specification Using Logic

Assertions are used to express preconditions and post-conditions for a given task. The preconditions are normally constraints placed on the input to a given formula (task), and postconditions are constraints placed on the output or results of the formula (task). The general format for specifying a functional task using formal specification is to define preconditions, the process, and the postconditions for the task within the syntax and semantics of the formal language being used. When logic is used as the formal language, we must follow the rules of logic in expressing our specifications. For more detail regarding formal specification in software development, reference [6] may be used. Here are three very simple examples of formal specifications using preconditions and postconditions as assertions.

Example 5.7.1 Suppose $M, N,$ and q are integer values. The task is to compute N/M only if N is divisible by M. The definition for this task may be written as follows:

$$\{\exists \, q \, \ni N = q \times M\} \qquad \text{precondition}$$

$$\text{Program to compute } N/M$$

$$\{\text{Output } q = N/M\} \qquad \text{postcondition}$$

These equations mean that if for integer values N and M there exists an integer value q such that N is equal to q times M, then the output of the program should be the quotient of N divided by M.

Example 5.7.2 The following is a specification for a function that must read two numbers and report the larger of the two numbers:

$$\{\text{true}\} \qquad \qquad \text{precondition}$$

$$\text{Program to read } x \text{ and } y$$

$$\{(\text{output} = x) \wedge (x > y) \vee (\text{output} = y) \wedge (y > x)\} \qquad \text{postcondition}$$

For this problem, as you can see, there is no precondition. That is, the program should work for any pair of ordered values. The postcondition defines the output to be x if $x > y$ or to be y if $y > x$.

Example 5.7.3 The following are the precondition and the post-condition for a function that is meant to sort an array of positive integers.

$$\{n > 0, \forall i \ (0 < i \leq n) \Rightarrow a \ [i] > 0\} \quad \text{precondition}$$

$$\text{Program to sort array } a[1 \ .. \ n]$$

$$\{\forall i \ (0 < i < n) \Rightarrow a[i] \leq a[i + 1]\}$$

This equations mean that before the task is performed we have an array of positive integers, after the task is performed we have the same array of positive integers, and the content of the array is in ascending order. Note that the postcondition expressed here will not guarantee that the sort program preserves the content of array a [inn].

The concept of defining a task being performed via a set of predicates (preconditions and postconditions) may be expanded to cover a wide range of complex problems. The ideal goal is to use logic and predicate calculus to state the specification for any given problem. As mentioned at the beginning of this section, verification and the correctness proof of the SDS developed in this fashion become much more effective. However, one of the major problems facing practitioners is that those who are most qualified to write SRS and SDS are not trained in using mathematical logic as their choice for a tool. Interested readers may consult reference [6] for more information about the use of logic in problem specification and reference [12] for more information about logic-based computer programming.

5.8 OPERATIONAL TIMELINES   ■

We have made frequent reference to operational timelines and their synonyms—operational scenarios, operational procedures, and operational flows—and emphasized the importance of developing a detailed operational description for a system (and especially its software product). Most systems accomplish their required functions by means of a sequence of steps involving hardware, software, and people operating in concert according to a set of operational rules. The software product is used to interface with operators and sensors to produce an output according to some algorithm, commands, reports, displays, etc.

The most effective time to formulate these operational timelines is during the development of software (and system) requirements. By going through a proposed operational timeline step-by-step and identifying the role of hardware, software, and operator in effecting required system functions, many new software requirements are uncovered that were originally overlooked, misunderstood, not explicitly stated, or are derived from existing requirements. The operational timeline is an extremely effective tool to support the timely development of requirement and design specifications.

Preparation of operational timelines involves an understanding of the operational environment, knowledge of the entire system, imagination, and the assistance of system operators. The most significant products of the effort required to develop operational timelines are as follows: (1) the definition of all of the display panels required to effect control and management of the system; and (2) a fully developed set of operational timelines that forms the basis for developing documents such as operator manuals, training materials, position description handbooks, and acceptance test scenarios and scripts.

5.8.1   Development of Operational Timeline

The first step in developing an operational timeline is to identify all unique modes of system operation and the active system components associated with each mode. Typical modes of operation include the following:

a. System turned off
b. Initialization and warm-up
c. File maintenance
d. Failure modes
e. Normal shutdown/Emergency shutdown
f. Recovery from failure mode
g. System function 1
h. System function 2

   •   •.
   •   •.
   •   •.

   system function n

There is a strong connection between state transition diagrams (STD) and system operational modes. It is appropriate to use the STD (if one exists) in the identification of system operational modes and the manner of transition from one mode to another. Mode descriptions should include mode entrance and exit criteria and other related system conditions as well as any operator actions and corresponding system actions.

Some other side benefits of producing these operational timelines are direct operator involvement in the requirement development process, a better understanding and appreciation of the operational environment and its realities, insights as to potential acceptance test scripts and a baseline for important user documentation.

5.8.2   Moving From Mode To Mode

In defining the manner in which the system undergoes transition from one mode to another, it is important to identify specific operator actions (response to system displays), system actions (system's response to operator actions, especially what is displayed), and the content of each display. An understanding of the role of both operator and system in effecting a mode transition can lead to confirmation that adequate software requirements are in place to support system operational mode transitions. It is highly likely that this step will lead to the discovery of new display panels or screens, new functions, and new commands.

It is often appropriate, especially for large information systems, formally to review system modes and mode transitions from an operational point of view before development of detailed operational timelines for each individual mode.

5.8.3   Operational Procedures For Each System Mode

On a mode-by-mode basis, a detailed step-by-step operating procedure is laid out in the following way:

1. The first step in developing a function timeline is identification of entrance criteria. That is, under what conditions would the system enter this particular mode of operation? What action (if any) must the operator take to enter the mode? What is displayed to the operator? How is the operator's action implemented in software?

2. The second step is to partition the system function into a sequence of operator, hardware, and software activities to effect the given function. The approach is to treat the operator as a system component having certain performance limitations and capabilities. For the operator as system component, the inputs are displays, prompts, audible signals, etc., and the outputs are set/reset of a device and keystrokes. A simple pattern of display to the operator, operator response, and system response (with particular emphasis on display to the operator) is followed for each step employed in carrying out the complete function timeline.

3. Upon completion of the function's timeline, the exit criteria and associated operational timeline for exit are developed in the same way as entrance and function timelines. After completion of the function the system may transit to another mode or remain in the current mode waiting for the next transaction.

4. Document new requirements identified in the preparation of operational timelines. Experience has demonstrated over and over that development and review of operational timelines results in new requirements and/or changes to designs.

As information system functions are mapped out in detailed operational timelines and the roles of software, hardware, and operator are clearly defined, the SRS becomes much better guidance for software design. More details are available, dynamics of operation are better understood, human-to-computer interface is better appreciated, and the specification is more complete.

A review with operators is essential to the development of operational timelines. There are certain operational realities that only operators are aware of. Exposure of these operational realities early in the development process is an effective way to assure that the software product (and system) will meet client needs. The review process is accomplished by presenting each display panel in an operational procedure in its normal operational sequence and describing operator actions and system actions (hardware and software) associated with each display panel.

There are strong similarities between developing operational timelines and performing certain kinds of prototyping. The operational timeline is usually more comprehensive and covers all system operational modes. Operational procedures are also essential inputs to human-computer interface design.

Example 5.8.1

An operator selects a particular operational mode from a menu as entrance to a particular system function. In order to enter the function certain system components must be active, certain external conditions must prevail, and certain software products must be resident in memory. These features would be listed as conditions for entrance into this operational mode. The system responds by activating certain system components and displaying another function level menu. If the system does not respond as expected, a failure mode is entered. This failure mode is treated separately and requires another unique timeline.

If the menu appears as expected, the operator selects one of the menu entries and enters a code(s) or command(s) at the on-screen prompt that appears. The prompt is one of the system responses to the menu item selection. Other hardware and software responses are identified. Each keystroke, command, or data item entered should be carefully described in a data dictionary format. Many of these data items will be documented in the data dictionary, and the detail descriptions will be useful in software design. As discussed in chapter 20, there are standards associated with how the human-to-computer interface should be effected. These standards are imposed on the display descriptions.

Each step of the function's operational procedure is described in terms of operator actions, system actions, and displays presented. For each step in the operational procedure, there is usually a related software requirement. A function that fits curves to data, for example, would have an opening menu identifying a selection of different curve-fitting techniques as required by the software requirements specification. Certain system conditions would have to be met, for example, regarding presence of a file with the data needed for the curve-fitting process. This might require action by the operator to identify the data source or load data from a disk. A variety of data editing options may be presented in the next menu. Selection of a data editing option may also require some action by the operator to access a set of data editing rules and display them in a window. An operator command would be required to indicate the end of the editing phase. A question might arise here as to retention of the edited data. Operator commands and actions required to retain edited data and link it to the curve produced may require yet another menu and additional action on the part of both system and operator.

Execution of the selected curve-fitting process may require intervention by the operator. Each intervention will require displays to the operator, attendant operator action, and system action.

5.9 CHAPTER SUMMARY ■

There are a variety of tools and techniques used to arrive at requirements and design specifications for a software product. We discussed just a few of these tools in this chapter. Students and practitioners should not be limited to the use of just these tools. We may use any single tool/method or combination of tools/methods that we like. The main objective is to arrive at a well-written requirement specification and a well-organized design specification.

We discussed the tools without attaching any judgmental ranking to them because we believe the software engineer or the development team must decide what tool to use. However, we would like to suggest that the selection of tools be based on the expertise of the team members and not on any other factor. If there is a new tool that is proven to be effective and there is a desire in the development environment to use this new tool, the first step is to educate the team members about the use and effectiveness of the new tool. In the software development environment, it is a serious mistake to try to learn about a tool while you are using it to develop a deliverable software product.

5.10 EXERCISE ■

1. Develop the data items for a data dictionary associated with the ABC project of Example 4.4.1 using the format of Figure 5.1.
2. What additional information would you need to process a record containing name, address, telephone number, and credit status to get a yes/no answer on a request for credit?

3. Explain why accuracy is an important attribute for a data dictionary.
4. Specifically, how can a data dictionary help a new member of the development team? A reviewer? An operator? A manager?
5. Develop a complete trade-off matrix—criteria, weighting, and alternatives—for the purchase of a transportation device. Automobile, truck, motorcycle, RV, and van are the alternatives. Explain and justify your criteria and weighting.
6. For problem 5, develop a set of rules for evaluating and scoring each alternative with respect to each criteria.
7. Apply your rules developed in problem 6 to fill in the trade-off matrix. Total your scores and declare a winner.
8. Now that you have arrived at a decision, is the decision what you expected? Can the decision be changed with a minor change in points awarded? Are there any unexpected results? Could you use this matrix to convince anyone that your decision is a sound one?
9. Use an FSA to give the specifications for the reserved words in Pascal (or a programming language of your choice). You should design an FSA to recognize all the reserved words of the language and reject any other English word.
10. Design an FSM (with output if needed) to represent the operation of the order-entry function of the ABC project.
11. Design an FST to recognize any binary string that has at least a sequence of three 1's in it and translate all 1's to a and all 0's to b.
12. Design an FSA to define and recognize identifiers that are accepted by the programming language Ada (or a programming language with which you are familiar).
13. With the help of a new starting state, MS, and a new input signal, on, combine the three FSTs of Figures 5.9, 5.10, and 5.11
14. Design an FSA that recognizes strings of 1's and 0's with an even (odd) number of 1's.
15. Describe the following problem using an FSM. A farmer must carry a fox, a hen, and an open can of worms across the river using a boat that can carry only the farmer and two of the three creatures. At no time can the farmer leave the fox and the hen or the hen and the worms alone. Note that the farmer is willing to take as many trips as needed. Also, note that you are describing the problem, not its solution.
16. Use any of the tools or a combination of the tools discussed in this chapter to present the specification for a complete banking system with electronic banking and mortgage services.
17. Use a DFD to characterize a complete credit card processing system. Give the specification for the customer service part of the system using any of the tools discussed in this chapter.
18. Do problem 17 for a car rental company.
19. Do problem 16 for the order entry segment of the ABC project; see example 4.4.1.
20. Use DFD and/on CFD to summarize the basic data and control flow for the problem discussed in example 4.4.1. Expand your diagrams to at least 3 levels.
21. Do exercise 20 for the problem discussed in example 4.4.2.
22. Suggest 2 separate data structures for storing a data dictionary. Create a trade-off matrix to evaluate the two structures. The evaluation criteria and their associate weight values are:

data retrieval efficiency	10
storage efficiency (in memory)	7
update operations efficiency	5
mobility	2

23. Describe 3 to 5 usages of a data dictionary.

24. List 5 to 10 questions, in the context of software engineering, that may be answered using data stored in a data dictionary.
25. Develop a marked Petri net for the body shop with three workers as discussed in section 5.6.2.
26. Represent the specification for adding two floating point numbers using a Petri net.
27. Represent the specification (algorithm) to multiply two numbers expressed in exponent form using a Petri net.
28. Give the specification and operation of a barbershop with a single barber and three waiting chairs, using a petri net.
29. Define preconditions and postconditions for a function that is to read a set of N ($N >=$ 0) numbers and compute the average of the numbers read. Note that when $N = 0$, the average is undefined.
30. Give the full specification for a function "is-prime (N)" which determines whether positive integer N is a prime number.
31. Give the full specification for a procedure that adds two polynomials. Define the input format, data structure, and output format.

References

1. V. Berzins and Luqi, *Software Engineering with Abstraction*, Addison-Wesley, Reading, Mass., 1991.
2. P. Coad, "OOA—Object-Oriented Analysis", in *COMPSAC 89, Washington, D.C.*, Computer Society Press of IEEE, New York, 1989.
3. P. Coad and E. Yourdon, *Object-Oriented Analysis*, Ed. 2, Prentice-Hall, Upper Saddle River, N.J., 1991.
4. A. M. Davis, *Software Requirements Analysis and Specification*, Prentice-Hall, Upper Saddle River, N.J., 1990.
5. D. Hatley and I. Pribhai, *Strategies for Real-Time System Specification*, Dorset House, New York, 1987.
6. B. Liskove and J. Guttage, *Abstraction and Specification in Program Development*, The MIT Press, Cambridge, Mass., 1986.
7. Rom Narayan, *Data Dictionary Implementation, Use and Maintenance*, Prentice-Hall Mainframe Software Series, Upper Saddle River, N.J., 1988.
8. J. L. Peterson, *Petri Net Theory and the Modeling of Systems*, Prentice-Hall, Upper Saddle River, N.J., 1981.
9. P. Ward, *The Transformation Schema: An Extension of the Data Flow Diagram to Represent Control and Timing*, IEEE Trans. Software Engrg. 12(2): pages 198–210, (1986).
10. M. Woodman, *Yourdon Data Flow Diagrams: A Tool for Disciplined Requirement Analysis*, Inf. Software Tech. 30(9): (1988).
11. J. B. Wordsworth, *Software Development with Z: A Practical Approach to Formal Methods in Software Engineering*, Addison-Wesley, Reading, Mass., 1994.
12. E. Yourdon, *Modern Structured Analysis*, Yourdon Press Computing Series, Prentice-Hall, Upper Saddle River, N.J., 1989.
13. M. Zohar and R. Waldinger, *The Deductive Foundation of Computer Programming*, Addison-Wesley, Reading, Mass., 1993.
14. P. Zare, "An Insider's View of PAISLEY," IEEE Trans. on Software Engrg., 17(3), pages 212–225, 1991.

6

Software Development Environment

6.0 OBJECTIVES ■

The environment in which a software system is developed includes, in addition to people, the following: computers; software; programming languages; compilers; utility programs; system library; and tools for software development, test data generation, cost and schedule estimation, verification and validation, management, etc. The main objectives of this chapter are to (1) describe three typical software development configurations and (2) discuss the effects and benefits of software development tools. The tools are categorized as essential, very useful, and useful.

6.1 INTRODUCTION ■

Many activities are involved in developing a software system, including requirement specification, requirement analysis, requirement verification and validation, design specification, design validation, coding, unit testing, test and integration, acceptance testing, and delivery. A number of automated tools have been developed to assist the software engineer in each step of the software development process. Some of these tools are used only to facilitate or in some cases automate the process. For example, the work of system analysts and engineers during requirement specification and the work of software engineers, coders, and testers during other phases of the development process may be expedited by using automated development tools.

To focus our study of software development tools, we may categorize them into essential, very useful, and useful. Compilers, operating systems, assemblers, and programming languages are essential tools. Computer system utilities, editors, libraries, and the library of reused code are very useful tools. Finally, computer-aided software engineering (CASE) tools are among the group of useful software development tools.

A software product can not be developed without the use of essential tools such as programming languages, compilers, assemblers, linkers, and loaders. Developing a software product without tools such as editors, system library, and system utilities, although possible, is very difficult and time consuming. However, CASE tools are often considered an added value to the software development environment. CASE tools, properly selected and used with expertise in a tightly controlled environment, can automate some parts of the software development process and assure adequate documentation.

Historically speaking, a software development environment originally consisted of computer system, a limited operating system (single user, single program), a compiler, a limited input device (card reader), and a printer. At the time, the term *software system* was not widely used, and software products were called programs. By the late sixties, we had a much more advanced software development environment. The environment was time-shared with on-line disk storage; tape backups; a variety of compilers and programming languages; and multiuser, multiprogram operating systems. In the early seventies we had interactive on-line editors that provided direct program and data entry and editing. Features that in the early seventies were considered a great luxury are now considered minimum essential features.

Later we recognized that program statements are different from text and therefore, programs may benefit from a different type of text editor, one that can check the validity of a line as it is being entered. This advance led to the development of syntax-directed editors. We have now gone beyond this approach by developing predefined templates that can be used to simplify further the program entry process.

Today we have added so many other features and tools to the software development environment that it is hard to keep track of them. For example, a few of the many recent features are program verification tools to allow on-line debugging using program-defined identifiers instead of memory dumps; linkers to facilitate modularization of large programs; and interactive graphic tools that provide automated support for the early phases of an SWDLC.

As more development tools came to the market, the need for tool integration increased until the idea of an integrated project support environment (IPSE) took hold. IPSE is a collection of tools integrated into a single package to help a software engineer throughout the entire SWDLC. Although we have made great progress, we don't yet have a comprehensive integrated tool set that supports the entire SWDLC. The completion of such an integrated tool set is an important step in achieving rapid progress in improving software development schedules. Software systems are becoming so large and so complex that even with today's tools, it takes two to three years or longer to complete a major software system. By then many of the original requirements may be obsolete or changed. This factor alone extends completion time and delivery schedule.

In this chapter we will present a brief discussion of software development environment configurations and summarize a typical software development platform along with its three categories of tools—essential, very useful, and useful. A discussion of CASE tools and their applications in different phases of SWDLC is presented and is followed by the description of an ideal software development platform.

6.2 SOFTWARE DEVELOPMENT ENVIRONMENT CONFIGURATION   ■

A software development environment (SDE) can be configured in many different ways. The SDE often serves as the basis for a test and integration facility by modeling and simulating the operational environment or by directly connecting system sensors, actuators, and operator workstations into the software development environment. A simulated or actual operational environment is a necessary adjunct to an effective test and integration facility. Software can be developed on a computer that is different from the computer that will be used in the operational environment. This feature is required particularly in the development of embedded software systems. It is not unusual for software and the so-called target machine to be developed concurrently. In this case an interpretive computer emulator (ICE) is employed.

Figure 6.1 illustrates three different configurations. The first configuration, Figure 6.1(**A**), involves use of the actual system configuration as a development environment. Many problems surface in such an environment, not the least of which is scheduling time for all environment users. The actual system configuration does have the advantage of realism, but limits the use of certain software development tools. A great deal of control must be exerted to maintain a current configuration of the software product. The second configuration, Figure 6.1(**B**), permits off-line development of modules and products and downloading of finished products to the development configuration. In addition to more sophisticated debugging tools, an interpretive computer emulation of the target machine is usually employed in the software development environment. The third configuration, Figure 6.1(**C**), implies that the development environment computer system is separate but fully compatible with the computer subsystem embedded in the actual system configuration. There are many variations on development environments. Each project has unique requirements.

No matter what the development configuration, the key questions to be asked regarding the physical development environment are as follows: (1) Are there enough computer resources available to meet the needs of the system development team? (2) Are there enough computer resources to meet the needs of the software development team? (3) Are there enough computer resources available to meet the needs of the test and integration team? Any development project starved for development resources is a development project heading for trouble. It is important to identify potential users, size their resource needs, and determine their schedules. This issue transcends software development and should be fully explored during project planning.

A software development environment (hardware and software) that is developed in parallel with the delivered product presents several problems. First, there is a great dependency in the sense that changes or errors in the development system can ripple through much of the delivered product. After the fixes or changes are made to the development configuration, there are waves of regression testing that must be performed on the software product. Second, the two development schedules must be well synchronized to support the master schedule. It sometimes surprises the software development team to find that the highest priority for using the development configuration goes to another organization. The quality of the development configuration, including tools, models, and test drivers, must be at a level that is at least

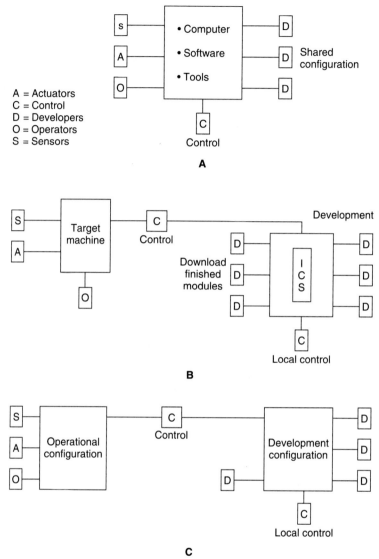

A = Actuators
C = Control
D = Developers
O = Operators
S = Sensors

■ Figure 6.1

Three software development environment configurations. A, Use of actual system configuration; B, Off-line development; C, Identical development and operational environment.

consistent with that of the delivered product. This requirement is sometimes forgotten in cost- and schedule-constrained projects.

Tools that make it possible to automate production of design documentation are intrinsic to the development environment. Maturity of the tool is an important factor in tool maintenance. Learning curves are associated with each tool, the development configuration, and the language. A number of parameters that directly influence software development are analyst capability, application experience, virtual machine capability, programming language experience, computer turnaround time, and virtual machine volatility. Quantification of these parameters is highly desirable. (A series of tables that enable the practitioner to select relative numerical values for development environment parameters is presented in chapters 14 and 15, Tables 14.11, 14.12, 14.13 and 15.2). The values of these parameters are used in models that predict resource and schedule requirements based on software development environment characteristics as one of their inputs.

The software development plan includes a description of the software development environment. The description should include the development environment configuration and its specifications either directly, for a simple configuration, or by reference to a separate document if the configuration is complex. The physical location and schedule for development of the environment as well as development environment test plans should be included in the plan either directly or by reference to another document. Other important aspects of the development environment include security, access details, computers, and responsibility for collecting and maintaining performance measurements.

During the planning it is prudent to devote ample time for sizing and conceptual design of the software development facility or environment. For large projects involving dozens and perhaps hundreds of software developers, the importance of the development environment cannot be overstated.

The plan should show a detailed configuration of the development facility for each phase. The plan should also show schedules for development or acquisition of hardware and software and identify the specifiers, procurers, testers, and maintainers. A comprehensive top-level test schedule should be included as part of the planning information.

Many times special software must be written and hardware constructed to implement a software development environment. Since the development environment is a major tool in the development of the delivered product and indeed in some cases may be delivered along with the software product to support maintenance, it deserves the same level of attention as is given to the operational software product.

The development environment also includes computer-aided software engineering tools (discussed in section 6.4) to support debugging, configuration control, cost tracking, documentation, test data generation, etc. It is important that these items also appear in the plan along with references and a description of how they are to be used.

6.3 SOFTWARE DEVELOPMENT PLATFORM (SDPF) ■

Software development platform is a term used to cover all of the tools that are used in the software development process. A software development platform includes a computer, an operating system, a number of programming languages, and an array of other system application programs such as file processing utilities, database management systems, system libraries, system utilities, editors, syntax-directed editors, compilers, interpreters, program generators, assemblers, linker-loaders, etc. Examples of SDPFs may be UNIX platform, X-Window platform, or object-oriented platform.

An SDPF must include both essential and very useful groups of development tools. Recall that essential tools cover elements such as programming languages, compilers, and operating systems; very useful tools include elements such as editors, debuggers, syntax-directed editors, and system libraries. Although it is not a must, most SDPFs include an array of CASE tools, which we categorized as useful tools. The very useful and useful tools may help to speed up productivity and reduce the cost of the software.

6.3.1 Essential Tools In SDPF

Often the operational environment of a software product dictates some of the characteristics of the development environment. However, there are many other development environment characteristics that may be selected by the software development organization. Among the set of essential tools, operating systems, programming languages, and compilers are most critical and should be selected with adequate knowledge.

Operating Systems

The attributes to look for in an operating system include the following: file processing capabilities, file structures and access methods, data integrity, database access facilities, concurrent programming, parallel programming, real-time features, and security. Not all of these features may be needed in a given software development, and not all of these features may have been equally emphasized in a given operating system. However, when there is a choice, the software engineer must be knowledgeable enough to choose or recommend the right operating system. Many software systems have failed not because they were developed with insufficient care and attention to details, but because the operating system in the operational environment had been less than adequate.

Programming Language(s)

Strictly speaking, the choice of a programming language should not affect software system performance. However, in the real world, the selection of programming language(s) used to code the software system can have a long-lasting effect on software system performance and maintenance. We discuss the selection of programming languages for two separate cases: when the language is specified and when it is left to the software engineering team to choose.

When the language is specified, the development team must study the language to verify that it is a good match for the project. If the study shows that the recommended language is not a good match for the project, hard data should be collected to convince the client that the recommended programming language is a bad choice. The client should be given a menu of appropriate languages from which to choose. There must be a strong and convincing argument to convince the client to select another language. Often by understanding the client's reason for recommending or requiring a given language, the software engineer can provide a list of alternative languages.

When the selection of the programming language is left to a later point in the SWDLC, the software development team must present alternatives to the client for selection or approval. While it is certainly true that object code is what executes, it is the source code that is maintained.

In selecting a programming language, the software engineer must consider the following general characteristics of programming languages:

Data structures provided within the language
Data structures easily manipulated
Modularity
Windows to other languages
File processing capabilities
Access to system libraries
Access to system utilities

Control structures provided by the language
Scoping
Real-time features
Concurrence features
Safety and security features
Efficient use of system resources
Features providing parallel processing

A more detailed discussion of the programming language selection process is presented in chapter 9, in which software coding is discussed. Appendix C describes a decision making process that may be employed in making language decisions.

Compilers

It was bad enough to have over 400 programming languages to select from without having a dozen or more compilers for each programming language. For some of the more popular programming languages such as Ada, C, C++, Fortran, and Pascal, there are many different compilers. Thus selecting a programming language, say Ada, for a project does not mean that the compiler has automatically been selected. There are a variety of Ada compilers that must be studied along with the language. To select a compiler, one must look for certain characteristics. Some of the more important characteristics of a compiler are the following:

Error handling and error recovery
Local optimization
Global optimization
Ease of modularization
Debugging support
Real-time constraint and considerations

6.3.2 Very Useful Tools

In this section we will discuss a small sample of the tools that are very useful in the development of a software system: editors, syntax-directed editors, linkers, debuggers, and interpreters.

Editors

Each development environment provides for one or more editors that are useful for program coding, data entry, and documentation. A number of CASE tools are also available to facilitate the document-writing process. The presence of an easy-to-use editor, with useful features, is best appreciated by the programming team, data-entry operators, and clerical assistants.

Syntax-Directed Editors

Some software development environments have special editors that have the capability to verify each program line entered to assure that it is syntactically correct, without delaying entry. This added-value facility may reduce the time needed to correct compiling errors; and speed up the compiling process. Syntax-directed editors may be designed to work with specific languages (monolingual) or they can be designed to work for any programming language (polylingual). In the latter case, the syntax rules of the language are fed to the editor before being used.

Linkers

A linker is utilized to combine object-code segments into a large software system. Linkers have broad implications in modularization of the software system as well as in the use of more than one programming language to code the software. More sophisticated linkers can perform name checking and binding across several modules in the software system.

Code or Program Generators

This element is not to be confused with the code generation that is performed by compilers. The software development process begins with the development of an SRS, then an SDS, then implementation in code. The implementation step refers to the translation of the SDS into a coded form that directly or indirectly is understood and executed by the computer. When we implement software using a programming language such as Ada, C, or Fortran, the compiler translates the program code into a machine-understandable code (assembly or machine language). However, there are other languages known as fourth generation languages or code generator languages that may be used for implementation. These languages don't usually have a compiler. The code created in those languages does not translate directly into machine-understandable code. Instead, these languages generate code written in COBOL, C, or other languages. Subsequently, a compiler is used to translate the code into machine-understandable object-level code. Code generators often shorten the length of the actual code generated by the programming team by a factor of 10 or more. This reduction in the actual lines of code written by programmers may help to speed up the coding process.

Debuggers

Debuggers are programs that behave as an interpreter. They execute the program in an environment controlled by the programmer. Debuggers give the programmer the capability to inspect the execution state of the program in a symbolic way. That is, they allow the user to refer to the symbolic name of the identifiers in the program and to their values during execution time, instead of referring to their absolute memory address. Debuggers allow the programmer to set the execution mode to be step-by-step, segment-by-segment, or by break points. Debuggers allow the insertion of output points without inserting code into the program. A good debugger can be used to monitor the dynamic nature of the program execution. This use will facilitate the understanding of programs written by other people and will help modification of existing programs.

Program Design Languages (PDL)

A PDL is often called the language of design specification. PDLs range from restricted English to pseudocode to very formal languages. There are PDLs that have automatic interpreters and code generators as extensions. However, the use of PDLs won't make writing design specifications an easier task. In fact, it is more difficult to use a formal PDL than pseudocode because one must learn another rigorous set of syntax and semantics. However, designs that are expressed in formal PDLs may be validated and verified by automatic verification programs.

6.3.3   Useful Tools

CASE tools (discussed in detail in the next section) are primarily programs written to facilitate any software development process. There are over 300 manufacturers of CASE tools, and each one claims their products are best. This situation makes the selection of a set of appropriate CASE tools a difficult task. Since there is no best CASE tool for a specific need, and since there are many CASE tools for any specific task [7], we present an overview of different activities in a SWDLC that are supported by CASE tools currently available in the market.

CASE tools may be categorized based on their functionality or by the phase of SWDLC they support. In addition to these two categories, there are specialized CASE tools to support software reuse, software reengineering, reverse engineering, etc. Generic CASE tools are available to perform the following functions:

Code generation
Configuration management
Debugging
Diagram and chart creating and editing
Data dictionary creation, verification, and editing
Document preparation and text editing
Modeling and simulation
Planning, estimation, and measurement
Program verification
Prototyping
Test data generation
User interface management

Each of these tools may support one or more phases of the SWDLC. Table 6.1 shows each category of tools and the phases or activities they support.

In addition to the tools listed in Table 6.1, there are CASE workbenches and integrated CASE tools. These tools are discussed in the paragraphs that follow.

Workbenches

Workbenches are semiintegrated CASE tools designed for extensive support to the activities associated with developing, analyzing, and documenting the SRS and the SDS for a given software system. CASE workbenches (CASEW) have improved steadily and have become more readily available. There are several components within a CASEW tool; the most important is the creation and editing of data flow diagrams, structure charts, entity-relation diagrams, code object diagrams, and many other graphic representation tools used in specification and design phases.

A CASEW tool accesses a central information repository and imports and exports information for use in other segments of the design and analysis activities. CASEWs provide great help in developing a data dictionary for the named entities and provide query processing

■ TABLE 6.1 **CASE Tools and Activities They Support**

FUNCTION	SRS	SDS	CODE	T&I
Code Generation			X	X
Configuratiuon management	X	X	X	X
Debugging			X	X
Diagram and chart creating and editing	X	X		
Data dictionary creation, verification, and editing	X	X		
Document preparation and text editing	X	X	X	X
Modeling and simulation	X			X
Planning, estimation, and measurement	X	X	X	X
Program verification			X	X
Prototyping	X			X
Test data generation				X
User interface management		X	X	

facilities to access the data dictionary. They also provide on-line error checking and alert the user to any form of anomaly that occurred during use of the CASEW tool. The editor and error-checking capabilities of the CASEW may be combined to check diagrams as they are being built.

Another function of the CASEW tool is to provide an array of different forms that must be completed and placed in the SRS, SDS, or other documents. The format for documentation pages may be produced by the CASEW.

Some future improvements to CASEWS are as follows:

1. Integrate the system with word processing and spreadsheet software.
2. Allow the user to override some of the internal rules of the CASEW system. This feature would make the CASEW tool much more adaptable to different types of application software.
3. Allow diagram generation and placement to be performed in the text mode. This feature will speed up the tedious task of diagram generation.

Integrated CASE Tools

The integration of CASE tools may be studied from two points of view. One is to integrate individual CASE tools designed for different phases and/or activities of the SWDLC. The most advantageous of this form of CASE integration is the creation of some sort of standards for symbols, charts, diagrams, etc., throughout the SWDLC. To some extent, this form of CASE tool integration has been done, and a number of integrated CASE (ICASE) tools are available.

The second form of CASE integration means the integration of CASE tools not only among themselves but with the rest of the development tools. Such integration creates an integrated software development environment or an integrated software development platform (ISDPF). This form of integration, on a large scale, has not yet been introduced. Also, there is no agreement among practitioners as to whether or not ISDPF is a useful and practical idea.

6.4 COMPUTER-AIDED SOFTWARE ENGINEERING TOOLS ■

Automated requirement analysis and design tools, mostly in the form of computer programs, to support various aspects of the system or software development process are called computer-aided system/software engineering tools or simply CASE tools. Software engineers believe CASE is an acronym for computer-aided software engineering. However, as Martin [6] points out, systems analysts/engineers use CASE as an acronym for computer-aided system engineering, and others use it to mean both system and software engineering [1]. The international workshop on CASE (IWCASE) defines CASE in the broadest terms, namely, "tools and methods to support an engineering approach to software development at all stages of the process." Forte and Norman [3] interpret the term *engineering approach* to mean "a well-defined coordinated and repeatable activity with widely accepted representations, design rules, and standards of quality."

Gane [4] states that "the distinguishing characteristic of a CASE tool is that it builds within itself a design database, at a higher level than code statements or physical data element definitions." This design database is what is called the repository, data dictionary, or encyclopedia. A common view of CASE tools architecture is represented in Figure 6.2. In this

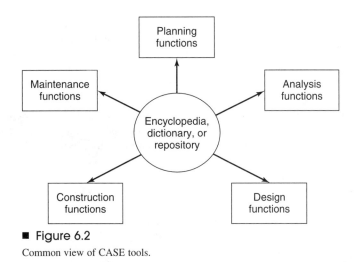

■ Figure 6.2

Common view of CASE tools.

view CASE tools are considered as a wheel with the various components in a circle around the hub, which is the repository. The repository stores facets related to the system.

The CASE manufacturers differentiate their products based upon how they support the software development life cycle stages. The front-end or upper CASE tools support the strategic planning and analysis phases of the life cycle, whereas the back-end or lower CASE tools support the design and construction phases of the life cycle. An integrated CASE (ICASE) product is one that adds such capabilities as reengineering, project support, or any other project management capabilities to the full life cycle.

The origin of CASE tools may be found in the development process of large commercial and research software systems developed during the early 1970s. The vision and functionality, as well as the problems of those early efforts, resulted in the design and development of the CASE tools of the 1990s.

The various CASE tools developed during the 1980s were not mature by today's standards. Yourdon [10] lists nine reasons why many system and software developers of that decade did not use CASE tools. The primary reasons were limited capabilities of the CASE tools themselves, such as graphics, repository, life cycle support, error checking, methodology support, single vendor platform, and flexibility for change.

Properly implemented with considerable prior preparation and planning, CASE tools can substantially reduce or even eliminate many of the analysis and design problems inherent in software projects of all sizes [3]. CASE allows the software engineer to focus on the architecture design rather than the details of implementation.

The ultimate goal of a CASE tool is to increase productivity. Martin [6] points out that the collection of automated aids (CASE along with application, code, and prototype generators) have four major goals:

1. Productivity: Software development productivity is difficult to measure because there are qualitative as well as quantitative factors. Many of these measures can be considered as part of the project management process, with such items as efficient personnel utilization, meeting cost constraints, staying within time constraints, timeliness of management reports, etc. However, CASE productivity will likely drop at the beginning of the endeavor, and it may take a year or longer to realize productivity gains. The drop in productivity is due to the learning curve.

2. Quality: To be effective, the software development life cycle must be highly organized and thoroughly planned. A well-orchestrated set of CASE deliverables that support and enhance the SWDLC will have the effect of greatly enhancing the quality of output. Such deliverables include graphic diagrams, data definitions, structure charts, and program code.

3. Standardization: Standardization has to be a critical goal for any set of automated aids. The basic parameters that must be measured are such things as time expended, utilization of people, number of defects, projected costs vs. actual costs, etc.

4. Communication and Documentation: Team communication is essential to a successful software development effort. A cohesive set of tools along with a set of standards should naturally evolve into (1) increased ease of communication among all members of the project team as well as end users and (2) a formalized set of documentation standards. Documentation must evolve as a natural by-product of CASE tool use and not as something that is added on as an afterthought.

CASE benefits do not occur quickly. Of course, the time and effort to achieve a reasonable level of competence in CASE usage will vary significantly from organization to organization. Wenig [9] says that typical times to reach acceptable levels of usage are as follows:

3–6 months to initiate the CASE process
6–12 months to learn the basics and work pilot projects
12–18 months to build expertise
18–24 months to build discipline

The international workshop on computer-aided software engineering (IWCASE) is a valuable source of up-to-date information about new development in the CASE industry. The fourth issue of *Communications of the ACM*, volume 35, April 1992, is devoted to the discussion of CASE tools. Articles in this issue discuss current trends, the future of CASE tools, industry assessment of case tools, use of CASE tools in producing reusable specifications, and evaluation of vendor CASE tool products [5,8].

The most significant value of CASE tools may lie in the operation and maintenance phase of the software life cycle where traditionally lack of adequate documentation impedes all three types of maintenance actions. The documentation discipline enforced (or at least demanded) during software development may result in improved maintenance.

6.4.1 CASE Tools Categorization

CASE tools can be categorized as integrated or functional. Integrated CASE tools cover the entire SWDLC from requirements definition through maintenance, and functional CASE tools are built for a specific phase of the SWDLC.

There are five seamlessly integrated toolsets to assist the entire software development process. These toolsets are the following:

1. Planning toolset: Produces deliverables targeted to top-level managers.
2. Analysis toolset: Produces deliverables expressed in end-users' terms.
3. Design toolset: Produces business system deliverables targeted to end-users and technical design deliverables targeted to trained data processing professionals.
4. Construction toolset: Produces deliverables that can be executed by computers.
5. Implementation toolset: Enables actual installation in the target environment.

The word *toolset* means that there are individual tools that will support, for example, the planning function.

6.4.2 Graphic Modeling

An easy way to use a CASE tool for the first time is to do some graphic modeling. Figure 6.3 shows a simple data flow diagram. Many CASE tools have powerful composition and symbol management facilities. Symbols can be selected from a template that appears on the screen, and once selected, the symbol can be placed anywhere on the drawing space. All actions are interactive, giving the user the ability to move the symbol to a predetermined location before "locking" it into place. Inserting text, arrows, and other symbols follows naturally.

Yourdon [10] summarizes several critical considerations to which the user should pay very close attention when creating and using graphic models. These considerations are as follows:

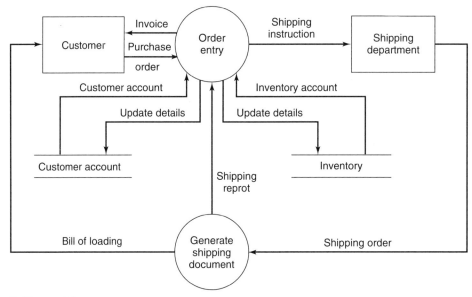

■ Figure 6.3

Simple data flow diagram generated by CASE tool.

(1) the efficiency of editing a diagram; (2) the ease of retrieving a diagram; (3) the number of objects that can be placed on a diagram; (4) the number of different diagrams that can be shown on the screen at the same time; (5) the capabilities for planning, zooming, etc; (6) the capabilities for free-form drawings or annotations on a formal diagram; (7) the ease of creating customized icons or modifying the standard ones; and (8) user control during and after error checking.

6.4.3 CASE Repositories

A key factor in the definition, design, and implementation of an information system is the collection and organization of all the relevant data associated with that system. As the new system starts to unfold during the systems development process, data elements are added, modified, changed, updated, deleted, etc. It is vital that everyone associated with the development of the new system be able to interact with some form of flexible repository. This repository must be kept current, especially when the system is in its maintenance phase, as the repository can be utilized to indicate the what, why, and how some piece of data was defined and used during the development process.

The repository should be an easily accessed library of descriptive information of all forms about all the various components of the information system. The repository should have identification fields containing fixed information or even free-form text that allows the users to define the contents in some reasonable manner. The repository should be able to store physical structures such as screen and report designs as well as system documentation and project documentation. In the broad sense, a repository contains metadata (data describing data) plus data describing processes, objects, or anything else vital to the continuing management of the project.

The repository is a large database containing prodigious amounts of descriptive and numerical information about the details of the project. However, the ultimate forms of usability are (1) the ease of locating individual items to edit, update, change, add to, or modify; (2) the ability to browse, move sequentially, search, match, etc; and (3) the ability to print or display the information that has been requested so that appropriate actions can be taken.

The repository or encyclopedia usually provides access to an extensive set of predefined reports such as the model content report, model cross-reference report, duplicate name report, model history report, user access report, and when changed report.

Since most repositories are implemented with a conventional relational database management system, it is possible to take advantage of the report generation and query facilities of that database management system. However, the successful use of CASE tools will ultimately depend on the successful implementation of the repository.

6.4.4   CASE Tools as Aid to Reengineering

A new kind of CASE tool has emerged that can be used to reengineer the existing body of source code into a more understandable and maintainable form. The idea is to allow the CASE tool to work backwards from the statement level (say COBOL) to the module and/or block level. The reengineering tool has the task of retaining knowledge about program branches, subroutine calls, and source code manipulations while generating new source code that is exactly equivalent in function to the old working application. As explained by Fisher [2], several of the common reengineering tool operations are as follows:

1. Identifying common subroutines and modules
2. Collapsing blocks of source code into single line statements for convenient reference and use
3. Generating subroutine calling hierarchies (topology)
4. Moving and restructuring entire blocks of code
5. Reordering and simplifying conditional branches and loops
6. Generating new compilable, working source code from the restructured original

A key component of any reengineering technique is the repository. The CASE tool must be able to consolidate all the various components into the repository.

The full reengineering cycle has not been completely automated, and therefore, the human element is still there with its associated communication and management problems. The business application to be reengineered must be synchronized with the organization's strategic goals. Also, the goal of the recreated application must be to optimize efficiency, minimize maintenance costs, and make the application more focused and ready for migration to more economical platforms and architectures.

6.4.5   Impact of Object-Oriented Methodology on CASE Tools

In order to focus clearly on object-oriented methods (OOM), it is desirable to revisit in somewhat more detail the two paradigms that preceded the OOM. First came the structured methods (SM), which appeared in the late 1960s with the introduction of structured programming. Structured design appeared in the mid-1970s, and structured analysis appeared in the late 1970s. The technological core of many CASE vendors today is structured methodology. Two of the most widely used graphic modeling tools of this methodology are data flow diagrams and structure charts. They emphasize what functions are performed by the system and the relationships among the various functions. Data stores are included, but in general, they play a secondary role. Structured methods tend to emphasize functions and processes and their interrelationships. Structured analysis, then, tends to be a function-oriented methodology.

Next came the information engineering methodologies (IEM), which reversed the emphasis from functions/processes toward a data-oriented methodology. The IEM was perceived to be a higher-level methodology primarily intended for modeling of the entire enterprise first, then modeling the individual components that are a part of it.

The next step in the evolution of methodologies is OOM. Object-oriented methodology refers to more than just object-oriented programming. It covers a whole philosophy of systems development that encompasses programming (OOP), analysis (OOA), design (OOD), as well as database management systems (OODBMS).

Even though the object-oriented methodology is, at present, highly fluid and research is somewhat erratic, a number of benefits are promised by proponents of OOM. Two of the key benefits are reusability and extensibility. That is, object-oriented systems are to be assembled from prewritten modules (with minimal effort), and this assembled system will be easy to extend without the need to modify its existing components.

The question now might be, where do CASE tools come in? In summary, there is no clear path from the CASE tools developed based on structured and information engineering methodologies to the object-oriented methodology. There are essentially two schools of transition. One is to build a bridge from the function world to the object world and the other is to start all over again. There are CASE tools that support both approaches. Also, the repository presents a problem. Companies must migrate from their function-based repositories to an object-based repository. Retraining the entire staff is one reason that the bridge approach should proceed slowly. It may be that the development life cycle itself will have to be changed to support an object world.

6.5   IDEAL SOFTWARE DEVELOPMENT PLATFORM   ■

An ideal software development platform, in addition to all essential and very useful tools, would include an integrated set of CASE tools that provides the following capabilities:

1. Supports every phase of the SWDLC. That is, there should be automated tools for planning, management, requirement analysis, verification, validation, design, coding, test and integration, documentation, and maintenance.

2. Supports formality throughout the entire process. The use of formal specification, verification, and validation must be incremental and dictated by the users of the CASE tools.

3. Supports the incremental build of every step of the development process. That is, CASE tools must be able to resolve inconsistencies and incrementally remove them as the system is being developed. In fact, the incremental nature of the tools may be applied to every aspect of the software development including the formal specifications.

4. Supports modularization. Modularization must be at the heart of any successful tool developed. Software systems of the future are going to be so large that without modularity throughout the entire development process, it would be impossible to comprehend the design of the software system.

In addition to the development of automated and integrated CASE tools that support these four characteristics, we must provide for a healthy and sound human interaction environment. The environment should be based on a set of sound and tested methods and standards. Planning, reviews, and audits must be taken seriously. Education must be provided to allow the development team to achieve its highest level of potential. The environment must provide for a natural human-computer interface. Hard-to-use tools will never be used.

Tools, standards, and methodologies must be supported by a software engineering infrastructure that facilitates progress and productivity for both environment administrator and environment users. The environment users are those who interact with the environment to develop a software system; environment administrators are those who control and manipulate the environment.

6.6 CHAPTER SUMMARY ■

A software development platform includes three categories of tools: essential, very useful, and useful. Essential tools include operating systems, programming languages, assemblers, and compilers. Very useful tools include editors, linkers, program generators, debuggers, and program definition languages. The primary tools classified as useful tools are known as CASE tools; two types are workbench or integrated CASE tools. Functional CASE tools are designed to assist software engineers in a specific phase of the SWDLC. Integrated CASE tools cover the entire SWDLC.

A CASE repository is a large database containing huge amounts of descriptive and numeric information about the details of the software product. The information kept in a CASE repository helps to build and verify the data dictionary for the software product. It also serves as a cross-reference between the data dictionary and other documents required by the software product.

The application of CASE tools and their effect on the SWDLC has yet to be documented. There is no hard evidence to support many cost- and schedule-saving claims made by CASE tool vendors and developers. One established benefit of CASE tools is to assure discipline and require predefined procedures in the software development process. This reason alone is sufficient to encourage and promote the use of CASE tools in software development.

6.7 EXERCISES ■

1. Business information systems quite often are developed by teams rather than by individuals. There is a need for a work-sharing environment. List several type of CASE tools that could provide this capability with a brief description of each one.
2. If you were a CASE tool designer, list several kinds of errors that your software would check for in a typical graphics diagram.

3. If you were employed by a manufacturing company and were asked by the chief information officer to list five important criteria that could be used to evaluate a CASE vendor, what five capabilities would you list, in decreasing order of importance?

4. You have just overheard one of your employees say, ''I am not sure why we are spending money on ICASE when applications can be jointly prototyped by a developer and a user.'' What would your response be?

5. One of your co-workers, an excellent programmer, has made the comment that she feels CASE will stifle her creativity. If you disagree, explain why.

6. Selecting the right CASE tool is just one of the steps in the strategic plan to acquire and deploy CASE technology. The risk of CASE failure is everpresent. List several possible reasons CASE could fail in an organization.

7. Object management systems (OMS) are software systems that facilitate communication between the CASE user and the operating system. List three major tasks performed by an OMS.

8. A CASE environment may be closed or open. In a closed environment, CASE tools are integrated with the environment infrastructure. In an open environment, CASE tools are not limited to what is available within the environment. That is, other tools may be introduced into the environment. Discuss the advantages and disadvantages of each of these two CASE environments.

9. Suppose you are to procure an ICASE tool for your company. What are the five most important functions/attributes you will require the ICASE tool to demonstrate before purchasing.

10. Describe data integration, user interface integration, and activity integration with regard to CASE tools.

11. Public tool interface (PTI) is the name given to a number of library routines that may be accessed by CASE tools. These interface-providing library programs should not be confused with the interface facilities provided by the CASE tool vendors. The very first such PTI was developed for an Ada programming support environment and was called kernel-APSE. Two more recent PTIs are PCTE and CAIS. Research the literature about these two PTIs and write a summary report for each one.

12. Discuss the role and the effect of the following on procurement of an integrated CASE tool or a CASE workbench:
    a. existing company standards and methods
    b. existing hardware and system software
    c. hardware and software near-future expansion plans
    d. the nature of the application software being developed
    e. classified top secret application software

13. Is the UNIX environment a software development environment? Why?

14. Any SDPF must provide consistent user interface. Explain why this feature is so important, especially from the CASE tools point of view.

15. What are the distinct characteristics of CASE workbenches? If you have access to a CASE workbench, develop the list of activities supported by that workbench.

References

1. J. G. Burch, *Systems Analysis, Design, and Implementation*, Boyd and Fraser, Boston, 1992.
2. A. S. Fisher, *CASE Using Software Development Tools*, Ed. 2, Wiley, New York, 1991.

3. G. Forte and R. J. Norman, ''A Self-Assessment of the Software Engineering Community,'' *Comm. ACM* 35(4): pages 28–32, (1992).

4. C. Gane, *Computer-Aided Software Engineering, the Methodologies, the Products, and the Future*, Prentice-Hall, Upper Saddle River, N.J., 1990.

5. C. G. Huff, ''Elements of a Realistic CASE Tool Adoption Budge,'' *Comm. ACM* 35(4): pages 45–54, (1992).

6. M. P. Martin, *Analysis and Design of Business Information Systems*, Macmillan, New York, 1991.

7. T. Shepard, S. Sibbald, and C. Wortly, ''A Visual Software Process,'' *Comm. ACM*, 35(4): pages 37–44, (1992).

8. I. Vessey, S. Jarvenpaa, and N. Tractinsky, ''Evaluation of Vendor Products: CASE Tools as Methodology Companion,'' *Comm. ACM* 35(4): pages 90–105, (1992).

9. R. P. Wenig, *Introduction to C.A.S.E. Technology Using Visible Analyst Workbench*, Macmillan, New York, 1991.

10. E. Yourdon, *Decline and Fall of the American Programmer*, Yourdon Press Computing Series, Prentice-Hall, Upper Saddle River, N.J., 1992.

7

Software Design

7.0 OBJECTIVES ■

The primary objective for this chapter is to expose the reader to some of the fundamental ideas associated with software design. Other specific objectives are (1) to describe the requirements for a good design process, (2) to define and characterize design levels, (3) to identify design objectives at each design level, (4) to describe the purpose and contents of a design database, (5) to explain the seven generic design steps, (6) to provide an annotated table of contents for a typical SDS, and (7) to illustrate the seven steps in a generic design process.

7.1 INTRODUCTION ■

Design, the first step in the development of an engineered product, is initiated only after a clear exposition of expected product function(s) becomes available. The design of a software system and its component parts should follow an orderly sequence of steps. Paradoxically, the creative process, which is the essence of design, should be permitted to operate unfettered. Even though the creative process itself is not always structured and predictable, the design framework that surrounds the creative process should be. That is, within the organized and scheduled design framework, the creative design process should be free to produce ideas and concepts and continually challenge the current design baseline. The challenge to product design leadership is to maintain this delicate balance. No amount of words or discussion can convey this point as well as the direct experience of participating in a design process.

The designer's goal is to develop a model or abstraction of the product based on experience, heuristics, formal synthesis and realization techniques, or by following some fundamental design principles. The model is then evaluated based on criteria derived from the original set of product requirements and the realities of the operating environment and economic environment. The design process continues by means of stepwise refinements through a series of abstraction levels until a physical realization replaces the abstraction.

Certain elements of design are intrinsic to any of the methodologies available to the practitioner. This chapter focuses on these fundamental design activities to afford some insights into the design process. The idea of top-down design and a stepwise refinement approach to design is implicit.

Recently we have witnessed an increased interest in object-oriented analysis and design. A major obstacle in applying object-based methods is that the SRS, particularly that prepared by system engineers, is typically cast in function and performance formats. That is, the problem space has already been analyzed and interpreted in terms of what functions the software must perform and to what performance level. To apply an object-oriented approach at this point, the designer may have to reinterpret the problem in an object-based format. However, once the problem has been reformulated in an object-based format, the original function-based SRS may lose some of its value. Traceability may be obscured, and system level testing involving software elements may be compromised. The originators of the SRS may lose some of their visibility in the reformulation process, making their role as design reviewers less effective as a consequence. The potential upside to this point of view is that the effort required to translate the function point of view to an object point of view may force a better overall understanding among specifiers and implementers of the application requirements.

Two chapters are devoted to discussion of the design process. Chapter 7 presents a generic design process based on function and performance specifications. Chapter 8 presents a discussion of an object-oriented analysis and design approach.

7.2   OVERVIEW OF SOFTWARE DESIGN PROCESS ■

Design is the application of the scientific method to selection and assembly of components to form an optimum realization that attains specified goals and objectives while being subject to given constraints or restrictions [5]. In the case of software design, goals, objectives, and constraints are extracted from the SRS document by a thorough analysis. The analysis, if correctly performed, provides a variety of perspectives on design requirements. In general, the separate perspectives reveal information in forms that will provide a firm basis for design. Certain constraints and restrictions are implicit in the information system configuration and its characteristics. Other restrictions and constraints are either explicitly stated in the SRS or derived through analysis of the SRS and the system within which the software must operate.

The scientific method in the design context consists of four steps. They are as follows: (1) collecting design data on observations of a particular problem space, (2) formulating a design hypothesis capable of predicting future behavior in the problem space, (3) testing the hypothesis to confirm the accuracy of predictions, and (4) revising and replacing the hypothesis if it proves to be an unsatisfactory model.

Software-critical data from the problem space are typically compiled in the SRS and in other system documents. Independent analysis by the software engineer is almost always required to confirm completeness of the requirement information and disclose software-related issues as early as possible in the design process. It is important to establish a controlled means for documenting SRS deficiencies, software-related issues, and technical questions and their subsequent resolutions. Many of these resolutions will result in formal changes to specification documents, particularly the SRS.

The hypothesis or hypotheses in the design case are candidate design structures or configurations to solve the problem posed in the SRS. Usually several possible solutions will fully solve the design problem. If design solutions are predicated on a thorough understanding of the entire problem space, relatively accurate performance predictions can be made.

Each candidate design solution can be evaluated using preselected criteria to obtain the best design solution for the given problem space. One of many available trade-off methods or tools can be employed to effect an objective selection process. The criteria for selecting the best design might include development cost, complexity, ease of testing, compatibility with design methodology to be used, consistence with the availability and skill level of design team personnel, and compatibility with system level architecture. The rationale for the decision, including trade-off data, should be documented and made part of the design database. It may become very important at a later date, when memories have faded and people have left the project, to know the reasons behind the design decisions. By circulating the trade-off document to other experienced designers, oversights and errors of commission can be identified and resolved before emotion, time, and effort have been committed to a particular design approach.

Design reviews can be used to bring additional expertise to bear on each important design decision. Formal design reviews at critical junctures in a design process are invaluable in detecting errors in specification interpretation and design logic. Design reviews can also provide quality assurance windows as well as opportunities for peers, managers, clients, and operators to have a positive influence on design details. There is a strong correlation between the quality and quantity of design reviews and the quality and reliability of the software product.

7.2.1   Design Requirements and Criteria

A design for a software product (or any other product) should answer the following general questions:

1. What is the designed product expected to accomplish (goals, objectives, performance criteria, etc.)?
2. What conditions will exist within the operational environment that are not under the designer's control?
3. What performance requirement criteria can be used to confirm the designed product's operational performance acceptability?

A design can also be regarded as a detailed plan for a solution to a problem. Design usually proceeds in levels following the tenets of top-down structure and modularity. The design process is rarely an orderly process.

The sequence of steps in a generic design process should follow a general pattern like that shown in Figure 7.1.

Step 1:   Collect and organize appropriate data and information and formulate the problem. Establish evaluation criteria to apply to physical realizations. Evaluation criteria are derived from software and system specifications.

Step 2:   Synthesize at least two realizations of the software unit that will satisfy the formulated problem.

Step 3:   Analyze, evaluate, and rank realization(s) in terms of the established criteria.

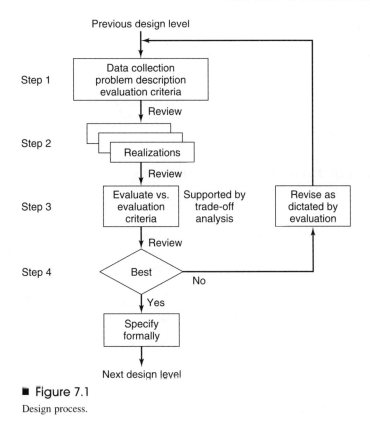

■ **Figure 7.1**

Design process.

Step 4:   Choose the best realization and specify to the next design level or continue to revise evaluation criteria, realizations, and/or problem definition until the best design emerges.

At the completion of each step, a review is planned. The purpose of the review is to verify the outcome of the step and, if necessary, make any necessary revisions before initiating the next step.

It is often said that a simple design approach is best. Certainly it has been demonstrated over and over that simplicity is at the heart of design elegance. Simple designs are easily understood, easily built, and easily tested; simplicity is the most important criterion of a design. Other design criteria include the following:

Documentation: A good design always comes with a set of well-written documents. An excellent design without good quality documentation becomes a poor design.

Testability: In a good design, *every* requirement is testable. A design that cannot be easily tested against its requirements is not an acceptable design.

Structure: A good design presents hierarchical structure that makes logical use of control policies among components.

Modularity: A good design is modular and exhibits the properties of high cohesiveness and low coupling. That is, inter-component communication is minimum (low coupling), and complete functions or subfunctions are allocated to individual components (high cohesiveness).

Discreteness: A good design separates data, procedures (functions), and timing considerations to the extent possible. Although separated, these three design considerations cannot be completely isolated.

Representation: A good design should be easily communicated to all interested parties through appropriate abstractions and representations.

Reusability: A good design should be repeatable or reusable. That is, given a similar set of conditions (SRS, design database, and environment) the design process should produce a relatively similar design realization.

7.2.2 Design Levels and Their Objectives

From a system perspective, design is seen to proceed in a series of discrete levels. As depicted in Figure 7.2 each design level begins with a set of requirements as input and produces some form of realization as its output. The output or realization for one design level is the input or

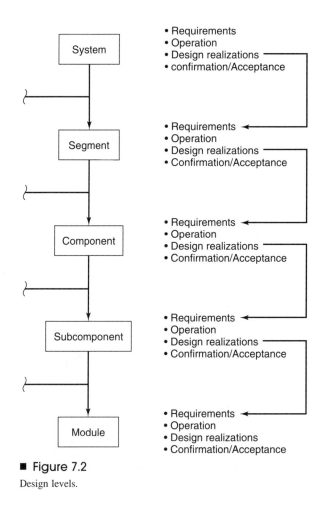

■ Figure 7.2

Design levels.

set of requirements for the next design level. Realization refers to the development of a solution to the problem posed in the requirements at each design level.

The design process continues until the next output or realization is in a physical form, that is, the design level produces results that are in the form of a specification for a specific physical realization in hardware or software. At each step in the process, there is an expansion of problem understanding, an increase in the detail of problem space descriptions, and a better appreciation of conditions limiting solution options.

As an example, consider for a moment a system-level design effort that results in allocating a subset of its requirements to a set of software products. The design realization at the system level is an architectural diagram showing the allocation of specific functions to a block called software. The next design level (software design) might result in a further allocation of software functions among several separate software products. The result at this design level would then be realization as a diagram showing a suballocation of functions to separate software products. The functions allocated to each software product would then be input as requirements to the next software design step.

The first design level, after analysis of input requirements, is a partition or decomposition of the stated requirements. Generally, this process leads to an architecture or structure for that design level. If the design has progressed top down, then at each design level the architecture is an extension of the top-level architecture. In virtually all cases, the top-level architecture is a system architecture. It is important to keep in mind that the software architecture is a detailed extension of the system architecture. Understanding the system architecture can provide important guidance in developing a supportive software structure.

An interesting quote from Eberhardt Rechtin [7, 8] bears repeating here because of its relevance to this discussion.

> Retrospectively, it is apparent that the success or failure of many defense, space and civil systems of the last half century has depended in large part on how they were structured. The most successful ones were conceived, built, tested, certified, and operated in a way that ensured their integrity and performance. They were based on a consistent set of principles and techniques that were maintained throughout all phases of the project. And their designs were resilient enough to bend to the inevitable changes brought about by time and circumstance. As civil architects would say, they had good bones; they also had fine architects who supervised their projects from beginning to end. The systems that have failed—whether technologically, politically or economically—lacked these essentials.

Some valuable insights can be extracted from this point of view: in particular, the emphasis on the importance of structure to successful design; the importance of continued monitoring by the software engineer throughout the specification, design, test and operation of the product; the importance of following a well-structured set of development methods and designing so that the product can accommodate changes.

At each design level, it is important to answer the three design questions posed at the beginning of section 7.2.1. Since each design level depends strongly on the products of the previous design level, the final physical realization can be affected by errors of omission or commission at each design level. The first question can be answered only by a thorough analysis of the requirements. The quality of analysis can be no better than the quality of the requirement statements, and the quality of the design can be no better than the quality of the analysis. Successfully answering question 1 can often entail probing deeply into requirement sources as well as adjunct information sources at every design level.

The answer to the second question requires a thorough understanding of system boundaries, operating environments, and the overall system development process. To develop the best possible design, designers must be able to distinguish between soft constraints and hard constraints. The designers must also understand what they can influence and control and what is not under their direct control.

Question 3 can be answered by carefully establishing criteria for confirming that each design step has met its obligations. System-level performance criteria are criteria for acceptance established jointly by developer and client. Each design level must answer question 3. That is, each design level has an implicit responsibility to contribute to meeting the system acceptance criteria.

At each design level there are several generic design products. These products can appear in many different forms and formats depending upon product, client, design methodology, tools used, and design standards employed. The essential products and their content are as follows:

1. Results of analyzing requirements that drive the specific design level
2. Operational perspectives including timelines and operator scripts
3. Design realization at a detail level consistent with the design level
4. A rationale for the design realization and a description of how confirmation of correctness will be accomplished for the specific design realization

Requirement analysis should result in an exhaustive description of all of important parameters associated with satisfying design level function and performance needs. At each level, requirement descriptions should be formalized, reviewed, and at least conditionally accepted by the group responsible for the next design level. Checklists are useful tools in assuring that all the needed information and descriptions are included.

Intellectually exercising the item under design in an operational setting is an extremely valuable source of new, unforeseen requirements and acts as a filter for design ideas. An operational setting includes all operational modes, especially nonstandard modes of operation such as start-up, shutdown, failure modes, etc.

The output of each design level should be prepared at a level of detail corresponding to the level of design. A top-level design need not specify too much detail, whereas a low-level design must present as much detail as needed to build an acceptable product. At each design level a means for documenting the design-level products is essential for the communication of critical information to the next level. Moreover, it is essential to provide a sound rationale for key design decisions and to document these decisions as justification or support for design information.

How design level products are to be confirmed as correct is an important question at each design level. Reviews, walk-throughs, audits, inspections, analyses, tests, and demonstrations are examples of tools or means for assuring that each design level product is correct.

7.2.3   Input/Process/Output (IPO) Approach

A convenient way of organizing one's thoughts in a design environment is to treat each design step as a single transfer function. That is, for each level or step in the design process, a definite input is required, some transformation of the input is needed, and a definite output is produced. There is also a feedback path within the currently active design effort and perhaps to previous design levels. By regarding each level and each step within each level as an input/process/output procedure, it is easier to concentrate on (1) what product is expected from the design activity, (2) what must be done with the inputs to the design activity to meet these expectations, and (3) what inputs are required by the design activity. The IPO process is depicted in Figure 7.3.

The purpose of establishing a clear beginning and a clear ending to each design level is to bring some temporary order to the chaotic design process at critical points in the process. These critical points permit clients, managers, operators, and peers to assess progress, confirm design correctness, coordinate with other design efforts, and identify problems.

7.2.4 Design Tools

A number of tools are available to the designer to support design activities. Table 7.1 lists some common tools employed as a means to facilitate the design (and analysis) process. Some design tools embody a structured sequence of design steps that include unique graphic notation and terminology to guide the designer through the design process and produce a documentation set that fully captures the subject design.

A second set of tools provides a means to organize information and accomplish some design task. Examples of the second set of tools are (1) a trade-off matrix to aid in decision making, (2) a decision table to aid in understanding how an operator or system deals with input conditions and subsequent actions, and (3) a template to guide a risk analysis.

A beneficial result of using these tools (in addition to guiding the designer through the design process) is good documentation to aid reviewers in understanding the design and to aid, at least initially, in maintenance of the design object after delivery. These design tools are often laced with useful checklists and caveats. Many of the available CASE tools are simply automated versions of design, specification, and documentation tools.

Some common problems with using currently available design tools are as follows: (1) the tool itself requires a substantial intellectual effort to learn and apply correctly, often to an extent that detracts from focus on the object design problem; (2) there are a number of design tools, each with its own unique terminology and graphic notation, making it difficult to thoroughly to prepare a student or practitioner to be proficient in even a few of them; and (3) although many design tools start out with simple terminology and only a few graphic symbols, augmentation to cover the full range of potential design problems introduces additional undesirable complexity.

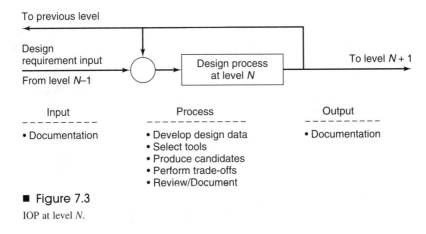

■ Figure 7.3

IOP at level *N*.

■ TABLE 7.1   **Software Design Tools**

**Data dictionary: Abstract descriptions of
problem space in terms of**

Function and performance
Timing diagrams (real-time)
Data and information flow
Control flow
Information models
Objects/attributes/operations
Flow diagrams
Structure charts
Hierarchical input-process-output (HIPO) charts
Block diagrams
Risk analysis charts
Operational timelines

Information compression tools

Decision tables
Test requirement matrix
Timing diagrams
Traceability matrix

Support rationale tools

Trade-off matrices
Operational timelines
Risk analysis charts

Realization tools

PDL/Pseudocode/Structured English
Flow diagrams
Warnier diagrams

7.3   SOFTWARE DESIGN ■

Ideally, for pedagogical reasons, it is desirable to have a generic software design process that is independent of any language or specific design tools and applies to the full range of software products. Several attempts have been made (Military Standard 2167A and Military Standard 490 [1, 2]) to establish just such a generic design process. The most recent attempt is the ANSI/IEEE std 1016.1-1993 *Recommended Practice for Software Design Descriptions* [4].

Conventionally, software design is what takes place between completion of the SRS and the completion of the software design specification (SDS). One can obtain a general idea of what this design process is by examining an annotated table of contents of the SRS and SDS documents. The formal contents of these two documents may differ from reference source to reference source but only in superficial ways. Any significant omission by one source usually means that the omission is documented separately. For example, a section on how the designed item is to be tested may be included in the SDS or it may be documented separately. In any event it should be clear that each legitimate requirement implemented in a design should be testable. Moreover, developing a plan for testing the design should be an intrinsic part of the design process no matter where documented.

Simply stated, the SRS should document specifically and precisely what functions the software product must perform and should quantify how well it must perform its assigned functions. The SDS must convey to coders very specific and precise directions about how basic control structures are to be organized and employed to respond to the SRS.

The software design process is the sequence of steps that systematically lead from function and performance requirements to pseudocode, Nassi-Shneiderman [6] diagrams, or any other form of PDL suitable for coding. There are four general approaches to developing a software design structure or architecture: normative, rational, argumentative and heuristic. The normative approach entails adapting an established architecture that has proved effective in prior similar situations and following policies, standards, and practices instituted by the company, client, or standards group. The rational approach is implicitly embodied in the scientific method already discussed. The argumentative approach makes use of techniques like brainstorming, concurrent design, or design teams along with extensive outside audits and reviews. The heuristic approach is based on applied common sense, rules of thumb, experience, and good engineering judgment. An effective design effort uses a blend of all four approaches.

There are only a limited number of established software architectures or structures. Adapting one of these general architectures, for example the transform structure [6], is an effective means for getting a design effort underway. Using a set of design standards, wherever possible, is also effective provided standard methods, products, techniques, protocols, and development approaches do not impose undue restrictions or constraints that will inhibit the designer.

The rational or scientific method with its trade-off charts, simulations, and performance analysis applied to design introduces objectivity to the process and attempts to obtain the best solution. There is no conflict in applying both the normative and the rational approaches to the same design problem.

The argumentative approach, by formally reviewing each step in the design process with peers and other interested parties, achieves a broad consensus and a teamwide commitment to the design. The combined experience and expertise of the full team and reviewers should result in a better product.

The heuristic approach brings experience to the design process, representing the collective wisdom of many practitioners in the form of rules of thumb and serving as a designer's checklist. For example, the notion of minimizing information flow among major subsystems is tested over and over in practice and found to be a good heuristic. There are many benefits in subcontracting, subsystem development, management, testing, and responsibility allocation that can be derived from following this heuristic. Other equally useful heuristics can also contribute to a design effort.

The central and most important point is that a good design effort should and will use all four approaches at various times to assure that the best software architecture is forthcoming.

7.3.1 Seven Generic Design Steps

A thorough evaluation of many different design approaches reveals that, regardless of the design approach used, there are seven steps that should be followed to obtain a good design. These steps are as follows: function decomposition, interface definition, operational timeline development, data definition, concurrency and real-time consideration, consolidation, and test procedure development.

Step 1: Function Decomposition

The first step in the design process involves an intelligent partitioning of the software product into components or design entities. There are several software development tools (both manual and automated) that support this step. Examples are block diagrams, structure charts, and tools that support modularization efforts. The objective is to partition software function requirements into smaller requirement packages, observing rules assuring that re-combining and reassembling the components when developed will lead to intelligent testing scenarios and assistance to management in maintaining control over the process. Some criteria and constraints for partitioning include the following:

a. unit testing improvement
b. system testing enhancement
c. modularity (cohesion and coupling)
d. managerial visibility and control
e. information hiding
f. contractual and organizational compatibility
g. data, time dependency, and function separation to extent possible

The partitioning step should be subjected to careful review, and the rationale for the selected partition should be documented.

The partitioning step is the realization of a structure or architecture for the software product. The components are the building blocks. In addition to concerns regarding component cohesion and coupling as partitioning criteria, product components or modules can have other characteristics that are considered architectural in nature. For example, a component can be reentrant and be used by more than one task simultaneously (multiprocessor) or concurrently (uniprocessor); it can be noninterruptable; it can be initiated via a call statement or invoked by an internally or externally generated interrupt. The degree to which information hiding is intrinsic to the architecture is another important architectural characteristic.

Step 2: Interface Definition

The second step in the design process is to identify and define all component-to-component and component-to-external interfaces. There are many tools that support this step. Examples of such tools are object diagrams, data flow diagrams, timing charts, and data dictionaries. The interface information includes everything a software designer, coder, and tester needs to know to use other design components that make up the software product.

Step 3: Operational Timeline Development

The third step in the design process involves developing realistic operational timelines or scenarios to exercise, at least intellectually, each design step. These timelines should include operator interactions with the system and especially the design component in question.

Step 4: Data Definition

The fourth step in the design process is associated with developing data structures, in particular, defining the files, records, fields, access methods, global and local data structures, and file maintenance procedures. Transactions are determined and file size estimates are made in this design step. Tools for this step include the data dictionary, information modeling, and entity-relation diagrams.

Step 5: Concurrencey and Real-time Considerations

The fifth step in the design process is associated with concurrence and real-time require-ments. It is highly desirable to decouple timing requirements and their design and correctness tests from function, performance, and data correctness. This step (if it is required) establishes the timing for the design component. Some tools that are useful in supporting timing designs are timeline extensions to data flow diagrams and McCabe's analysis approach [3, 9]. Real-time requirements and design are discussed in chapter 19.

Step 6: Consolidation

The sixth step in the design process requires consolidation and organization of the design information developed in steps one through five and a realization of the consolidated design information into direction to coders in the form of Nassi-Shneiderman diagrams, pseudocode, structured English, or any other form of PDL.

Step 7: Test Procedure Development

The seventh step in the design process examines ways in which the design can be tested as a design component and determines how the design component contributes to confirming a system-level acceptance criteria. This step also serves to verify that all requirements in the SRS are formally traced to implementation in the SDS. The reason is to confirm that (1) all requirements have been implemented and (2) only those requirements in the SRS have been implemented. A tool that assists in this step is the requirements verification test matrix.

Control hierarchy and data structures are also important aspects of the overall software product architecture. The control relationship among product components is sometimes referred to as *visibility*. The component has access to many other components and connectivity only to those components directly invoked by the given component. The data structure is a representation of the relationship among data items in a software product design. In particular, the design of a data structure describes the organization, access methods and controls, definitions, maintenance of the database, degree of association, and processing alternatives for the data. The important points in data structure design are that it (1) is consistent with overall architecture, (2) is developed in conjunction with the overall architecture, and (3) stays synchronized with control and procedure design throughout the design process. Formal design reviews may be inserted at appropriate junctures to assure that design efforts are fully coordinated, not only among individual design components but also among the individual steps for a given design component.

7.3.2 Component Design

The first step in software design process produces a decomposition of requirements into several software components (segments, products, modules, submodules, etc.). Each component is characterized by a set of attributes. The quality (completeness and accuracy) of these attributes is frequently a direct measure of the quality of the design. The collection of design attributes forms the basic design information required to drive the design effort. Once collected and confirmed, the design information can be organized and presented in a number of different ways.

The list of required design attributes to be specified for each design component should include the following:

Identification: This attribute provides a unique name for the component and its location in the system of components.

Type: This attribute categorizes the component. Examples of component types are subprogram, data file, control procedure, etc.

Purpose: This attribute provides function and performance requirements implemented by the design component including derived requirements. Derived requirements are not explicitly stated in the SRS. However, they are implied or adjunct to formally stated SRS requirements.

Function: This attribute should provide answers to questions such as the following: What does the component do? What is the transformation process? What specific inputs are processed? What algorithms are used? What outputs are produced? What data items are stored? What data items are modified?

Subordinates: This attribute provides answers to questions such as the following: What are the constituents of this component? What is its internal structure like? What is the relationship among the constituent parts of the component? Which functional requirement is satisfied by which part?

Dependencies: This attribute provides answers to questions such as the following: How is this component's function and performance related to other components? What are the uses of this component? What other components use this component? This attribute also provides specific details including timing; interaction conditions such as order of execution and data sharing; and creation, duplication, use, and storage or elimination of components.

Interfaces: This attribute provides detailed description of interfaces between this component and other components. External interface descriptions are explained in the data dictionary tool and can be referenced or copied. Internal interfaces include mechanisms for invoking or interrupting the component and for direct access to internal databases. This attribute also indicates mechanisms for communicating through parameters and common data areas or messages. The protocols governing the interaction include those used for communication, data formats (descriptions of electrical formats are also appropriate), range of values, and data item semantics. Error messages and error codes are also important to identify as part of this attribute. For certain types of software systems, screen formats and complete descriptions of the interactive language are part of this attribute.

Resources: This attribute provides a complete description of resources (hardware and software) external to the design object used or required by the component to carry out its function. These resources include the following:

- CPU execution time
- Memory—primary, secondary, and archival
- Buffers and input/output channels
- Plotters, printers, etc.
- Math libraries, access to interrupt structures, and hardware registers
- System services

Interaction rules and methods for using these resources are also part of this attribute. In addition, this attribute provides usage characteristics such as process time and sizing.

Processing: This attribute is an extension to the function attribute. A complete description of the algorithms used by the component to perform its operation or function is contained in this attribute. It is a good idea to use pseudocode to document algorithms, equations, and logic. The processing attribute should also include timing, event sequencing, prerequisites for process initiation, priority of events, processing level, actual processing steps, path conditions, and loop termination requirements. The handling of contingencies should describe the actions to be taken in case of anomalies or other validation failures.

Data: This attribute describes data internal to the component in terms of representation method, initial values, use, semantics, format, etc. The data dictionary is the tool employed to collect and record much of this information. Included in the data are such descriptions as static or dynamic, shared by other components, control data items, value only; and characteristics such as loop iteration counts, pointers, and link fields. A description of how the data item will be created, maintained, and validated is also included.

Any other attribute can be tested for inclusion by answering the following three questions in the affirmative:

1. Is the attribute common to all software products?
2. If the attribute is incorrect, will it result in a software fault?
3. Does the attribute convey only intrinsic design information? (Information related to the design process itself is not included.)

Collection and organization of data for the ten attributes listed above may, at first, seem like an overwhelming task. On reflection, however, it is clear that without this information it is virtually impossible to produce a design that responds effectively to the requirements explicitly spelled out or implicit in the SRS. The foregoing attributes provide a checklist for the designer or design team.

7.3.3   Preparing Software Design Specification (SDS)

Specific direction to coders is the critical output of the design process. A clear design realization in a design language, structured English, pseudocode, or any other form of PDL is the objective. The SDS captures this realization along with much of the supporting rationale and data that led to the design. Table 7.2 is one of many possible formats for an SDS Table of Contents. The format shown in Table 7.2 covers most of the important design information.

Section 1, the introduction, should contain a brief description of the purpose of the SDS document and its authority. The document scope contains the formal name of the software product and a brief summary of the document contents including an overview of the major functions performed by the software product and a description of its external interfaces. A list of the definitions, acronyms, and abbreviations used in the document would also be included in the introduction.

Section 2 should contain only those references that must be used in conjunction with the SDS to understand and use the document. In particular, as a minimum, it should reference the SRS and the PDL documents.

Section 3 describes the rationale for the partitioning of the software product and shows, perhaps by means of graphics, the allocation of specific SRS requirements among several software components that make up the software product. Each module is described in terms of the functions it performs and its interfaces to other components. External interfaces are, of course, also described in the SRS and in section 3. If all external interfaces have been allocated to one component of the software product, exhaustive interface details would appear in that component design description.

Section 4 is a detailed design description of each component in the following format:

Structure: Internal organization of the component including any suballocations occurring as a result of component decomposition into subcomponents.

Function: Specific functions allocated to the component with additional detail as required, including requirements derived by stepwise refinements of functions allocated to the component and secondary requirements spawned by top-level requirements.

Interfaces: Interface details including message structures, protocols, rates, etc.

Program Interrupts: Generated or invoked interrupt priorities and other related interrupt information.

■ TABLE 7.2 **SDS Table of Contents**

1.0 Introduction
1.1   Purpose
1.2   Scope
1.3   Definitions and Acronyms
2.0 References
3.0 Decomposition Description
3.1   Component or Module 1 Preliminary
    Description
      (Functional)
3.2   Component or Module 2 Preliminary
    Description
      (Functional)
      .
      .
      .
3.n Component or Module n Preliminary
    Description
      (Functional)
4.0 Component Detail Design Descriptions
4.1   Component or Module 1
    4.1.1 Structure
    4.1.2 Function
    4.1.3 Interfaces
    4.1.4 Program Interrupts
    4.1.5 Timing and Sequencing
    4.1.6 Sequential Control Feature
    4.1.7 Storage Allocation
    4.1.8 Application Data
    4.1.9 Detailed Design Descriptions
        (As Rationale)
4.2 Component or Module 2
    4.2.1 Structure
      . . . . .
      . . . . .
      . . . . .
    4.2.9 Detailed Design Descriptions
        (As Rationale)

4.3 Component or Module 3
    4.3.1 Structure
      . . . . .
      . . . . .
      . . . . .
    4.3.9 Detailed Design Descriptions
        (As Rationale)
4.4 . . . .
  .   . . . .
  .   . . . .
  .   . . . .
  .   . . . .
  .   . . . .
  .   . . . .
4.n Component or Module n
    4.n.1 Structure
      . . . . .
      . . . . .
      . . . . .
    4.n.9 Detailed Design Descriptions
        (As Rationale)
5.0 Quality Assurance
5.1   Test Plans and Procedures
5.2   Test Cases
5.3   Test Cross-Reference Matrix
6.0 Preparation for Delivery
7.0 Traceability
8.0 Appendices
8.1   The Complete Design expressed in a
    PDL
8.2   Software Parameter Estimation
    Update
8.3   Mathematical Formulas and
    Algorithms Not Documented in SRS
8.4   Program Listing (Source and Object
    Code after Acceptance test)

Timing and Sequencing: Repetition rates, deadlines, and other timing considerations and constraints are to appear in this section.

Sequential Control Features: Control details are covered in this section depicting the order of processing, precedence enforcement, etc.

Storage Allocations: Describes allocation of memory to components for both process and data.

Application Data: Data required to deploy the software product in the application area, including all the files, records, and fields needed for the application.

Detailed Design Description/Rationale: Design description including operational use and operator interactions for all modes of operation. The results of trade-off studies and a summary of audit/review items that influenced design decisions are also included as part of the rationale.

Section 5 covers quality assurance issues. The quality assurance provisions and measures to be applied to the given product are defined in this section in detail. The test plan for the individual components and for the software product as a whole are covered in section 5.1. Section 5.2 describes the specific test cases including expected results that will be used to exercise components and products. Section 5.3 describes, in a matrixlike format, how each requirement assigned to the software product will be tested.

Section 6 describes the acceptance test phase in detail. The scenario by which the software product will be installed and acceptance tested, along with specific acceptance criteria, is documented in this section.

Section 7 is also best presented in a matrixlike format showing where each SRS requirement is implemented in the design. As in the test cross-reference matrix, this matrix can serve as a checklist for quality assurance reviews.

Section 8 contains very important information. Section 8.1 is the realization of the design in pseudocode, program design language, flow charts, etc. This section is the principal input to the coding process. Ideally, it needs only to be converted into language statements. Some practitioners use special compilers to convert program design language directly into executable code, thereby bypassing the traditional coding step. Section 8.2 contains updates or revisions to estimates of software parameters made earlier in project history. Such parameters as size, complexity, and resource requirements (labor months, calendar time, CPU, primary and secondary memory) should be tracked through the project on a continuing basis. Section 8.3 should document those algorithms and equations implemented in the software product but not documented elsewhere. Section 8.4 should include the final program, after acceptance test, both in Source Code and Object Code form. Section 8 is often separately bound. Section 8 is, of course, initially left blank.

7.4   DESIGN EXAMPLE   ■

To discuss the seven design steps and the SDS more thoroughly, it is helpful to have a specific example. The SRS for the XYZ project's data management (renamed data control) described in chapter 2 will serve that purpose. We will assume that Figure 7.4 is a diagram that appeared in the database control SRS. The structure and the functional allocations shown in Figure 7.4 are the first steps in establishing an architecture for the software product called data control.

The architecture makes function allocation among three main components. Data gathering is assigned the function associated with collecting maintenance messages and sensor readings according to a schedule provided by an authorized operator. The sensor readings and maintenance messages are processed according to requirements spelled out in the SRS. An update message is prepared for the database. These two modules will run continuously, initiated by a scheduler in the data gathering component. Authorized operator access to these modules is through data gathering. Schedule changes for sampling maintenance messages and sensors, changes in processing algorithms for sensors and maintenance messages, emergency messages indicating failures or impending failures, and restart are also handled through the data gathering component.

The management component consists of functions associated with archiving, access control for the database, and the generation of several report types. Interfaces to external software products and systems are handled through the external interface component.

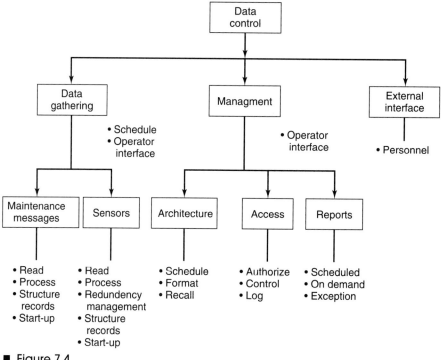

■ Figure 7.4

Functional allocation for database control component.

Internal interfaces among components and modules are important details that are part of the architecture. For example, the details of the read command for each sensor, the characteristics of the sensor message structure, and the characteristics of the update message are important design information. In the design example, it is found that a memory address is assigned to each sensor. Passing this address to the external interface component is all that is required. Sensor sampling has highest priority on the network. The sensor output (result of sampling) is placed in a sensor-unique memory location by the external interface component. Additional information for each individual sensor is needed before detail design can be completed. For example, we must know if the sensor value is contained in one byte or two, and the time of sensor sampling may need a constant bias to account for system delays. The specific formats for time and sensor IDs must be spelled out. Similarly, the update message produced by the data gathering component must be defined in detail.

7.4.1 Design Process

Selecting the Design Architecture

Let us assume that the architecture shown in Figure 7.4 has emerged as a result of a series of trade-off studies involving two viable architectures as shown in Table 7.3. The criteria—cost, skill and experience utilization, modularity, organizational compatibility, and unit test-

■ TABLE 7.3   **Architecture Trade-Off Study**

CRITERIA	WEIGHT	ARCHITECTURE 1	ARCHITECTURE 2
COST	10	10/100	9/90
SKILL AND EXPERIENCE UTILIZATION	9	8/72	10/90
MODULARITY	8	10/80	8/64
ORGANIZATIONAL COMPATIBILITY	7	10/70	9/63
TESTING (unit)	6	9/54	10/60
TOTAL		376	367

ing—were selected as the most important concerns in this example. The weighting shown in Table 7.3 indicates the relative importance of each criteria. Cost was determined by estimating the SLOC or function points and memory use required for each of the candidate architectures. Skill and experience utilization criteria recognize limits on available resources. That is, how well does each architecture make use of the team skills and experience, The modularity criterion refers to how the candidates compare relative to each other in terms of coupling and cohesion. Organization compatibility refers to how well each candidate fits into the existing organizational structure. That is, how well does each architecture respond to the desire to have one organizational unit be responsible for a complete component?

Table 7.3 shows that architecture 1 has a slight edge. On the other hand, architecture 2 has a slight edge in the unit testing criteria. The trade-off matrix of Table 7.3 is presented, reviewed, and discussed by team members as well as outside reviewers, and a consensus is reached on the fact that architecture 1 (Figure 7.4) is the better choice given the decision criteria. Team members would have had a hand in the decision, and the rationale for the decision would be visible to team members and made part of the design documentation. As part of the architecture development effort, the software design requirements have been allocated among the components shown in Figure 7.4. Our discussion is focused on the component called sensor processing with the knowledge that similar, closely coordinated activity would go on concurrently with other components. Next, we follow the seven generic design steps to arrive at a design document for the sensor processing module.

Design Steps

Step 1:   Function Decomposition

The sensor processing module is allocated the following functions directly traceable to the SRS document:

1. Sample each sensor at the rates specified in the SRS.
2. Process redundant sensors.
3. Convert each sensor sample into a value in units specified by the SRS.
4. Check for and report sensor failures.

5. Display each value or block of values in operator-requested units and quantities.
6. Confirm each sensor sample for reasonableness.
7. Create and maintain two global files, one for unprocessed samples and one for processed samples.
8. Retain latest sensor record in metric units.
9. At operator request produce hard copy of the contents of all three files in units requested.

   The detail structure of the database is now emerging from database design efforts. Sensor files have been defined and for each sensor record the following fields have been identified:

Sensor ID, description
Time of sample
Converted value, units
Redundant (Y or N)

   A second sensor data file will be maintained on-line for each sensor, containing the latest 100 records with the following fields:

Sensor ID, description, address
Time of last sample
Raw measurement value
Converted value, units
Redundant (Y or N)
Second sensor ID (redundant)
Time of last sample
Raw measurement value
Converted value, units

   A 100-record history file for each sensor is to be archived and retained for 30 days. Experience has shown that such information has many uses in system maintenance.
   The Check file contains the sensor information required to perform reasonableness tests and to process redundant sensors. This file also contains information that will help detect failed sensors. The Check file is a representation of the status of all sensors in the system. The record structure for this file is as follows:

Sensor ID: Description, date installed, type
Maximum reasonable value
Minimum reasonable value
Delta: Maximum reasonable sample-to-sample change
$a_0 \ldots a_4$: Polynomial calibration coefficients
ID for redundant companion sensor
Substitute value for failed sensor
Tolerance value
Message structure
Last sensor raw measurement value

   Requirements would be elaborated and expanded and additional detail added during initial partitioning of the SRS design requirements. Questions would be raised and answered as the design database is developed concurrently with the design.

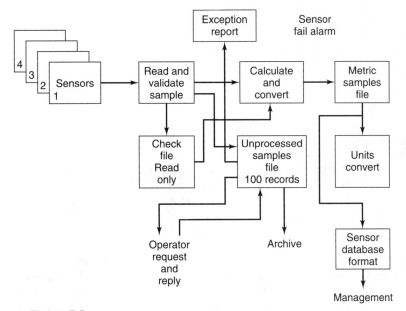

■ Figure 7.5

Partitioning of sensor procedure.

Another partitioning of sensor processing would lead to the block diagram shown in Figure 7.5. The stepwise refined partitioning in Figure 7.5 shows schematically the essential steps in sensor processing. Each functional block of Figure 7.5 is a small, self-contained module and could be assigned to an individual designer for detail design. With this partitioning, we have probably reached the right level of architectural modularity. Further partitioning would not be helpful. To press the design example further, the read and validate sample function accepts raw sensor data in 8-bit bytes, and validates the sensor reading by one of several methods defined by the subsystem owning the sensor. The output includes a request for a sensor reading, the validated raw sensor reading, exception reports (suspicious sensor readings or a failed sensor), and if appropriate, an alarm to system operators and to other components. Inputs are raw sensor samples, a binary representation of the measurement of a physical parameter such as temperature, pressure, humidity, etc. It has been agreed among subsystem designers and users that the sensor database will be maintained in metric units. However, for those operators unwilling or unable to work in metric units, a units conversion capability is provided. The metric sample file is formatted, and the entire sensor file is updated at the highest sensor sampling rate. Sensor file update is handled by the data management function.

We have deliberately refrained from using some of the familiar design tools to depict the partitioning so that just the design process is exposed. Taking each of the sensor processing requirements in turn, the designer can expand the detail via additional study or questions. For example, the specific algorithm for performing the reasonableness test and the settings for failure thresholds must be determined. The means for reporting unreasonable sensor readings and the action to be taken must be established. Much of the information required to build a comprehensive design database would be captured as design attributes described earlier.

Step 2: Interface Definition

Identification of all sensor processing interfaces is the next step in the design process. Each sensor interface must be thoroughly profiled as discussed in the data dictionary section in chapter 5. Interfaces to files and to display and control components, likewise, must be fully characterized. The obvious vehicle for documenting interface details is the data dictionary. Frequently a separate document called the interface requirements specification or interface control document is employed as a tool to capture all of the design-critical information associated with interfaces. The basic interface information is the same. The only difference is that it is collected into a special document.

Step 3:   Operational Timeline Development

In the third step, a series of operational timelines is created. Operational timelines explain how the component is used operationally and describe certain dependencies. What the system is supposed to do is documented in the SRS and in the design information compiled during the design study. For example, we might consider one of the simple sensor processing timelines shown in Table 7.4. By developing and reviewing all possible scenarios or timelines with operators, a strong sense of menu requirements and operator interactions can be obtained. The timelines can also serve as the framework for operator manuals. Table 7.4 shows the operational timeline for reinitializing the data gathering component and the system.

Step 4:   Data Definition

The fourth step involves development of the file structure. In this example, the first file is required to support sensor reasonableness tests. The SRS, the data dictionary, and the design database indicate that there is a range of reasonable values for each sensor. Moreover, there is also a value for the maximum change that can be expected between sensor samples. The SRS states that each sensor should be checked at each sample for reasonable values. The data needed for each sensor with fields for sensor ID, sensor type and description, maximum value, minimum value, maximum sample-to-sample change, date installed, and calibration coefficients is included in the Check file. In similar fashion the structure of the two sensor data files can be defined in the Check file.

· **Step 5:**   Concurrency and Real-time Consideration

The fifth step is concerned with timing requirements. The SRS states that there is a need to sample some of the sensors at different rates and there are deadlines that must be met. Pursuing timing concerns with the system engineers verifies this fact. In any event, we are

---

■ TABLE 7.4   **Operational Timeline**

Condition: System on   Action: Reinitialize files and return system to operational mode

1. Turn on system	4. Follow reinitialize prompts
Respond to menu prompt	5. Select item 3 on main menu (diagnostic)
Enter personal ID and operator password	If successful return to main menu
Enter time (military format)	else enter system maintenance mode (timeline 17)
Enter position code	6. Select item 4 on main menu
2. Select Restart from main menu	Run operational tests 1, 2, and 3
3. Select item 4 on main menu	If successful return to main menu
Add/delete sensors	else enter timeline 22
Update sensor calibration coefficients	7. Select item 6 on main menu
Alter check file	Let system run for 10 minutes
Reinitialize	Select item 5 on main menu
Return to main menu	8. Distribute reports (maintenance, first shift manager, second shift manager)

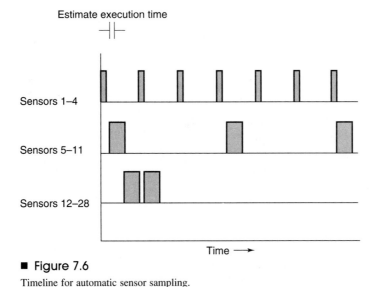

Estimate execution time

Sensors 1–4

Sensors 5–11

Sensors 12–28

Time ⟶

■ Figure 7.6

Timeline for automatic sensor sampling.

faced with another design concern in addition to function and performance concerns; there are now time constraints that must be observed. Figure 7.6 shows a timeline for sampling sensors and processing sensor readings. The execution times are not to scale.

Designs that respond to requirements based on sampling rates and deadlines must factor time as a new dimension into design consideration. The designer must, in these cases, rely heavily on the physical characteristics of the computer system and on features intrinsic to system software and the language. For example, a real-time operating system that provides direct access to the interrupt feature and the system clock, or a language that provides a capability to execute tasks periodically at prescribed rates, are some of the tools required to develop a design that meets requirements and avoids conflicts, missed deadlines, and deadlock.

In the case of sensor sampling, the design options might include using the system clock to set an interrupt that initiates sensor sampling and processing at the desired time. The last step in sensor processing would be to set the interrupt for the next sensor processing time. Another design approach might be to use a language feature that allows tasks to run independently and freely at a rate determined by a language statement. Another approach is to schedule all tasks deterministically using a time-based dispatcher task to control the sequencing of tasks. We will address real-time software design in a subsequent chapter. The important point for the designer to remember is the added time dimension in design considerations.

Step 6:   Consolidation

The sixth step involves pulling design materials together in a form that can be presented to coders. The objective is to provide clear, unambiguous direction to the team charged with the responsibility for converting pseudocode (or any form of PDL) into the selected language statements.

To express the design results for the sensor processing component shown in Figure 7.5, one could employ a variety of tools, many of which are described in chapter 5. For our example we will use a program design language (PDL). Table 7.5 shows the resulting PDL for the read and validate sample function. The processing of redundant sensors when the two

■ TABLE 7.5   **Structured English**

```
 1. Procedure Sensor_Read_and_Verify /* Procedure ID */
 2. Interface Sensor Check_File /* Sensor ID */
 3.           Sensor Address
 4.           Calculate_and_Confirm /* Sensor 1 */
 5.           Database_Mgr /* Sensor record */
 6.           Exception /* Sensor 1, sensor 2 */
 7.           Sensor Archive /* Sensor record */
 8.           Read Check_File /* Sensor ID */
 9. Issue Read Command /* Sensor 1 address */
10. Read Clock
11. If Sensor 1 Redundant Then Issue Read Command (sensor 2 address)
12. Read Clock
13. Interpret Sensor 1 /* 1 byte or 2 bytes */
14. If Sensor 1 Redundant Then Interpret Sensor 2
15. If (Sensor 1 redundant) and (Sensor 1 - Sensor 2) > Tolerance
        Then Exception (Sensor 1, Sensor 2)
           /* Redundant Sensor Processing */
16. If [Sensor 1(n) - Sensor 1 (n-1)] > Delta Then
        Exception (Sensor 1, Code A)
17. If (Min > Sensor 1) or (Sensor 1 > Max) Then
        Exception (Sensor 1, Code B)
18. Call Calculate_and_Confirm (Sensor 1)
19. Update Sensor Check_File
20. Update Sensor Archive
21. Call Database_Mgr (Sensor_record)
```

readings are not within prescribed tolerances is left as an exercise for the reader. The objective is to determine which sensor has failed, pass the correct sensor reading on to the calibration and conversion process, and report the failed sensor to the exception reporting function. The manner in which the sampling time is determined is not shown nor is the sampling structure. Only a few lines of PDL are shown to illustrate the process. Some points the designer must keep in mind are the following: (1) specifications for order and precedence are important, (2) every path must be closed off (no dangling if statements), (3) established constant and variable naming conventions must be followed, and (4) adherence to the basic control structures is important.

Step 7:   Test Procedure Development

The seventh generic design step addresses the question of testing. Unit tests are required to confirm that each module within the component has met design requirements, both those spelled out in the SRS and those that have been derived from requirements listed in the SRS through design studies. Many large software developments use an independent test organization to test software above the unit level.

Testing considerations for the read and validate sensor processing function would include demonstrating that all of the possible sensor events can be accommodated correctly (as required by the SRS). The designer should begin to think of ways to emulate sensor inputs for a wide range of expected environments and for a wide range of sensor failure types. Testing

■ TABLE 7.6 **Traceability To SRS**

REQMT.	SRS DOCUMENT	SDS DOCUMENT
1.	Sample sensor par xxx	Par yy line zz
2.	Manage redundant sensors par xxx	Par yy line zz
3.	Archive raw sensor reading par xxx	Par yy line zz
4.	Maintain sensor file par xxx	Par yy line zz
5.	Maintain most recent 100 records for each sensor par xxx	Par yy line zz
6.	Provide capability for unit conversion par xxx	Par yy line zz
7.	Provide for operator intervention par xxx	Par yy line zz
•		•
•		•
•		•

will require that the Check_File be filled with data. Specific test cases or scenarios with operator scripts must be devised and documented along with correct responses to the tests. Testing redundancy management and error detecting software is especially challenging. Installation of redundancy hardware and software usually means concern for reliability, which in turn means that software to manage the redundant equipment must be correct (highly reliable) to take advantage of the addition of redundant system elements.

Once test plans are complete and test cases defined, there is enough information to build the part of the test matrix associated with read and validate sensors. Tables 7.6 and 7.7 show parts of a traceability matrix and parts of a test matrix. The traceability matrix ties individual requirements listed in the SRS to specific paragraphs in the SDS and to specific lines in the pseudocode. Developing the traceability matrix can be assigned to an entry-level person or to a quality assurance engineer. The objective is to assure that all requirements listed in the SRS have been addressed in the design. A hierarchy of tests will determine if the requirements have been correctly addressed.

■ TABLE 7.7 **Test Matrix For Read and Validate Sensors**

REQMT.	COVERED BY MODULE TEST CASE	COVERED BY COMPONENT TEST CASE	COVERED BY PRODUCT TEST CASE
1	3–22	7–12	1–16
2	19–29	14–17	7–12
3	Component level	27–31	...
4	All cases	...	...
5	11–15	...	...
6	31–40	...	...
7	32–48	...	...

The test matrix matches specific module, component, and product test cases with specific requirements listed in the SRS. The quality of the test cases, the correctness of the criteria for passing the tests, and completeness of testing are technical judgments best administered through a review process.

When the design is complete, the design team should update estimates of all relevant software attributes. In particular, SLOC or function point sizing should be updated and memory and CPU utilization estimates revisited. The detail shown in Table 7.5 and Figure 7.6 should form the basis for an accurate estimate of the source lines of code required to implement the read and validate sensors function. More accurate estimates of CPU and memory use as well as bus traffic can also be made at this point.

7.5   CHAPTER SUMMARY   ■

Software design is what takes place between the completion of the SRS document and the completion of the SDS document. Software design is not different from any other design. Hence, a software engineer must understand the design product and its operational environment and must know its expected performance requirements. Simplicity is the most desired characteristic of a software design. Other attributes of a software design are testability, structure, modularity, reusability, robustness, discreteness, and documentation.

We believe that there are seven steps in the software design process that apply to any design methodology. These steps are: (1) partitioning the software product into design entities, (2) identifying and defining all interfaces, (3) developing operational timelines, (4) developing data structures and access methods, (5) identifying components with real-time requirements, (6) summarizing and representing the design in the form of a PDL understandable by programmers, and (7) testing the design component.

The designer is always searching for more and better information from analysts, application engineers, operators, clients, and people knowledgeable about the processing environment. In many instances assumptions must be made where solid information is not available. Judgments based on experience, common sense, or luck are often required to bridge over vague and uncertain requirements.

7.6   EXERCISES   ■

1. How can design reviews improve designs? How can design reviews help to educate operators, users, clients, analysts, engineers, coders, and testers? How can design reviews uncover deficiencies in the SRS?
2. Describe the three-perspective idea (function, operation, and physical realization) with regard to the design process. How can this approach reduce development time?
3. What did Eberhardt Rechtin mean by ''good bones''? How does this relate to software development?
4. How important do you think good software architecture is to good detail design? Explain.
5. Describe design levels in terms of designing an order-taking application package for the ABC Corporation. Identify levels, input, and output for each level and criteria for moving to the next design level.

6. Apply the input-process-output method to painting a table. List required input, outputs, and process.
7. Assume that a menu unit or design object is required that permits an operator to access and use five standard application products (a word processor, a spreadsheet, etc.). List the additional information a designer would need to know to proceed with the design.
8. With reference to Exercise 7, outline an approach to providing answers to the three general design questions discussed in section 7.2.1.
9. With respect to Exercise 7, discuss the five criteria for a good design. How can these criteria be used to help in developing a design? With respect to this design, what can be said about simplicity, testability, and documentation? Is documentation a design criterion?
10. Do you feel that the normative approach has been used in software architecture? Consider various word processing and spreadsheet products as examples.
11. Explain the seven criteria for evaluating a partitioning. Use the order-entry function in the ABC Corporation's software as an example.
12. Explain the seven design steps using the order-entry function as an example.
13. List the information you would need to continue with the order-entry design work.
14. Discuss the value of sections 5.0, 6.0, and 7.0 of the SDS to coders and testers (Table 7.2). Who else might benefit from these sections? Will the information in these sections be useful during the operation and maintenance phase?
15. Why is it important for the designer to specify, in program design language or equivalent, the complete design to coders. Use as an analogy a mechanical engineer specifying the dimensions, material, finish, and assembly of a part for a product.
16. How could the order-entry function (the ABC project) design be timelined and exercised operationally? If you were assigned the task, describe how you would proceed. What information would you need? What participation from others would be required?
17. Assume you are responsible for developing the SDS for the order-entry function design (the ABC project). List the specialists you would want to help prepare and to review the SDS.
18. A maximum sample-to-sample change for each sensor has been established and the range of each sensor has been determined. For dual redundant sensors, design a process that will determine which of the two sensors is most likely to be correct if the two redundant sensors provide different results when sampled. Assume that the sensor accuracy specification is also known.
19. Prepare PDL for the redundancy management process.
20. Prepare a test plan to confirm that the process will work. Describe the test cases you would use.
21. Using the PDL and any programming language you are familiar with, estimate the number of statements that will be needed to implement the PDL. How should comment statements (internal documentation) be treated? Can you think of any other statements that are not directly executable but require effort to document and check?
22. What additional (derived) requirements might be added to the process redundant sensors requirement in the SRS.
23. How would you answer the question ''How much CPU time is required to select the sensor most likely to have failed?'' Explain how you would obtain a good estimate.
24. How would you prepare for a design review for the process redundant sensor subcomponent. Outline your presentation to the review team. Would an input-process-output structure be useful?

References

1. DOD, *Military Standard Specification Practices*, DOD-STD-490 Oct. 30, 1968, U.S. Department of Defense, Washington, D.C., 1968.
2. DOD, *Draft Military Standard Defense System Software Development*, DOD-STD-2167A Oct. 27, 1987, U.S. Department of Defense, Washington, D.C., 1987.
3. IEEE, ''Structured Real Time Analysis and Design,'' in *COMPSAC-85* IEEE, New York, 1985.
4. IEEE, *IEEE Standards Collection Software Engineering*, IEEE, New York, 1994.
5. F. S. Merritt, ed., *Standard Handbook for Civil Engineers*, McGraw-Hill, New York, 1983.
6. I. Nassi and B. Shneiderman, ''Flow Chart Techniques for Structured Programming, *ACM SIGPLAN Notice* 8(8): pages 12–26, (1973).
7. E. Rechtin, *System Architecting: Creating and Building Complex Systems*, Prentice-Hall, Upper Saddle River, N.J., 1991.
8. E. Rechtin, ''The Art of Systems Architecting,'' *IEEE Spectrum*, Oct. (1992), pages 66–69.
9. P. T. Ward and S. J. Mellor, *Structured Development for Real-Time Systems*, Vols. 1, 2, and 3, Yourdon Press Computing Series, Prentice-Hall, Upper Saddle River, N.J., 1985.

8

Object-Oriented Analysis and Design

8.0 OBJECTIVES ■

Chapter 7 presented a generic approach to software design and discussed certain design topics that are independent of design methodology and design tools. The main objective of this chapter is to introduce object-oriented methodology in general and to discuss application of this methodology to the software design process.

8.1 INTRODUCTION ■

Since the early 1970s, three independent ideas have been introduced to facilitate the design, development, and implementation of software products. These three ideas have culminated in an object-oriented methodology that spans the complete software development life cycle. These ideas are: information hiding, reuse, and object-oriented view of the problem domain. Information hiding or encapsulation is a design strategy that promotes hiding as much implementation-related information as possible within the design envelope of a software component. This design approach was first introduced by David L. Parnas [4]. An information hiding strategy helps to minimize the side effects caused by execution of a component of a software product. Information hiding makes the design documentation more readable and creates a high level of cohesion within components and a very low level (zero in the case of object-oriented design) of coupling among components. Encapsulation helps to localize requirement and design volatility. This feature alone helps minimize the effect of changes made during design and modifications made during maintenance. Encapsulation helps to keep dependent design concepts together, which in turn reduces the amount of data traffic among software components. Hence a comprehensive grasp of the overall system becomes less difficult.

Another idea that has been around since the 1970s is the idea of reuse of existing designs and even of existing code. When design and development of software are compared to any other engineered product, the arguments lead to uniqueness of each software product versus duplications found in other engineered products. Those who believe each software product is unique also claim that each software product must be designed "from scratch." Thus, the same development mistakes are often repeated and the same development problems often arise. There are others who don't agree with this idea of software product uniqueness. They are firmly convinced that the designs of two different software products have as much or more in common as the design of a jet airplane and a sports car. We selected these two engineered products to point out that although software products are different, there are certain low-level components and design processes that are very similar for two software products designed for two completely different applications.

The airplane must (1) have seats, (2) be as light as possible, (3) be resistant to certain pressures, (4) provide easy access and exit, (5) have heat-resistant wheels, (6) use an engine that compresses air for its combustion process, (7) burn a petroleum product for its power, etc. If in the preceding sentence we substitute the words *sports car* for *airplane*, everything else can remain the same and the sentence will still make sense. In fact, it is a strong requirement statement for designing a sport car. Therefore, what we learn designing sport cars should be useful in designing a jet airplane. In fact, a lot of low-level component drawings may be used for either the jet airplane or the sports car.

The third and more promising idea that has persisted since the 1970s is the object-oriented view of the problem domain and the software development problem. Rumbaugh et al. [5] introduced the idea of object-oriented modeling techniques (OMT) as a superclass of object-oriented things. They related OMT to an object-oriented software development process, including object-oriented analysis (OOA), object-oriented design (OOD), and object-oriented programming (OOP).

This chapter is devoted to object-oriented methodology as it relates to the software development process. In this chapter we provide an overview of an object-oriented paradigm; introduce principle definitions and representation notations; introduce the basics of OOA and OOD; and discuss both the advantages and the difficulties associated with object-oriented design and development.

8.2   OBJECT-ORIENTED PARADIGM   ■

Object-oriented methods for analysis and design have gained in popularity during the 1980s and 1990s. Object-oriented analysis and design approaches and associated tools are intended to provide a means to extract from a real-world problem space, as defined by a problem statement or a software requirements specification, an abstract representation of only the essential features of the problem. The object-oriented analysis approach makes use of the following: (1) objects and classes to identify major components of the problem, (2) attributes (object or class characteristics or properties), and (3) operations (services or functions) to characterize object behavior (what they do within the framework of the system).

Conceptually, the object-oriented approach captures requirements, both functional and performance, and converts them into abstract representations that involve operations, controlled by messages, on objects that make up the system or problem space abstraction. To use this method effectively, the analyst must develop a point of view different from the functional partitioning concept embodied in the data flow approach and the structured design approach. The analyst must find objects and classes that jointly describe all of the important aspects of a system.

Object-oriented design methodology employs both information hiding (or encapsulation) and design reuse. The main characteristics of an object-oriented design methodology as applied to software development procedure are as follows:

1. Common data areas or global data definitions are eliminated.
2. Communication among object classes is through messages sent from one object class to another object class.
3. Object classes are independent entities within the software product.
4. The design is not necessarily sequential. Objects may be executed sequentially or concurrently.
5. There is no access to the internal information contained within a given object by any other object.

It is the collection of these characteristics of the object-oriented design that provides for both information hiding and design reuse. The first two characteristics provide for information hiding. The overall system coupling reduces to near zero, and the operation on any object class creates no side effect since there is no shared data area. Characteristics three and four provide for design reuse. An object class may be designed so that it operates differently based on the messages it receives. Therefore, an existing object may be used in a different component or even in a different software product with little or no change to the object definition. What has to be changed are the messages that produce operations on the object class. Finally, characteristic five provides for data and action integrity of the system.

The claimed advantages of object-oriented design methodology may be summarized as follows:

1. The maintenance of software products developed using object-oriented methodology is much easier than that of software products developed using the function-oriented and structured top-down design approach. This advantage is primarily because of the complete lack of dependency among the software product components in object-oriented design.

2. The three primary maintenance operations—corrective, adaptive, and perfective—are more efficient and less costly for a software product developed with object-oriented methodology.

3. Design and even code reuse is not only practical but encouraged by an object-oriented design and implementation process.

4. The understanding and comprehension of an object-oriented design is much easier, especially if there is a natural mapping between object classes used in the design and the real-world entities of the software product being designed.

One might say the collection of these advantages and the benefits associated with object-oriented design are enough to encourage everyone to use OOD methodology instead of any other design approach. This argument may sound convincing until we examine some of the disadvantages of the OOD methodology. The primary disadvantages of OOD are as follows:

1. Finding objects and object classes that naturally fit the problem domain is not an easy task. For certain software products, such as embedded software, finding appropriate objects may be so hard that the software engineer will give up on OOD altogether.

2. System engineers and system analysts who develop the SRS document for a software product often think and work in a function-oriented environment. Developing an OOD from an SRS that is function-oriented may not be an easy task. Often the SRS must be rewritten using the OOA approach before being used with an OOD methodology. There is, of course, an increased development cost associated with the rewrite effort. The risk of introducing errors in rewriting the SRS document is so high that many feel that rewriting of the SRS document is not advisable, especially for large software products.

3. CASE tools for implementing OOD are in their infancy. Programming languages, compilers, and system platforms are not yet fully available to handle OOD and development with the same degree of efficiency and understanding available for structured top-down design and implementation based approaches.

It is as important to recognize what an OO paradigm is as it is to know what it is not. OOD/OOA is a methodology derived from structured design and modular top-down design approaches with much attention given to data independence among the components of the software product. OOD is not a programming style/methodology, it is not C++, nor is it a programming language.

Object-oriented analysis and design is a different way of defining problems, designing solutions for problems, and implementing problem solutions. As can be seen, at no point is it necessary to talk about implementation tools. However, there should be no doubt that existence of appropriate tools, such as programming languages that are able directly to implement an OOD, will help the implementation process.

Object-oriented programming languages are developed to facilitate the implementation of certain characteristics of the OOD in a more direct way. In 1972 Pascal facilitated the implementation of record and set structure and provided for three forms of iteration structure instead of the one form available in Fortran; in the same way, Smalltalk, Ada 95, C++, Eiffel, and other object-oriented programming languages facilitate the implementation of object-oriented design solutions.

OOD should not be confused with OO programming. Most OO programming languages can be used to implement conventional data- and function-oriented designs as well as OO designs. On the other hand, one can also implement a fully object-oriented design using any high-level programming language such as Pascal, C, or Fortran. However, a programming language that provides specifically for implementation of OOD concepts such as objects, classes, inheritance, and encapsulation would be a much better choice for implementing an OOD.

In general, there are two groups of OO programming languages. One group includes those that are simply extensions to existing high-level procedural languages; Object Pascal, Objective C, and C++ are examples. This group, called hybrid object-oriented languages, may be used to implement both OO and traditional designs. The second group of OO programming languages comprises those that were designed specifically to implement OOD and are not extensions to existing languages. The oldest member of this category is Smalltalk. Smalltalk is not like other languages such as C++, Objective C, or Object Pascal, which can be used to implement conventional and function-oriented designs as easily or more easily than implementing OOD.

One of the reasons that Smalltalk did not become as popular as hybrid OO programming languages is that it is fully OO and it is difficult to implement a traditional structured data-oriented design using Smalltalk. Hybrid OO languages such as C++ allow for mixing OOD with data- and function-oriented design approaches at implementation time. As long as software engineers are not employing OOA and OOD on a 100% basis, languages such as C++, Ada, and Modula-2 are the best choice for implementation. When OOD becomes as practical and commonly used as conventional design approaches, then a programming language like Smalltalk is needed, which forces object-oriented implementation and does not allow other forms of implementation.

For the OO software development process to reach its highest potential, OOA/OOD methodology must be considered. The methodology must be independent of the implementation platform and programming language. Eventually, more efficient OO programming languages will facilitate and speed up the OOD and OO software development process.

Although there are several object-oriented design methodologies, there are no major differences among these methodologies. Differences, if any, are superficial and are due to the way designs are represented, not in how the designs were created. A few OOD methods are the Coad/Yourdon method [1, 2], the Booch Method [6], the Rumbaugh method [5], and the fusion method, which seems to be a combination of methods. The Coad/Yourdon method is more commonly used and promoted for use in the business environment. The Booch method is more adaptable to an Ada environment. The Rumbaugh method is based on modeling objects from the real world and then using these models to build language-independent designs.

Every design method has its own means of representation. Flow charts were among the first graphic tools used to represent designs for software products. Next came the structured programming approach, and with it came modified forms of flow charts called structure charts. OOD also has its own graphic representation. In fact some of the differences among OOD methodologies are nothing more than minor differences in graphic representation of the design.

We will use the graphic representation introduced by Coad and Yourdon in this chapter [1, 2]. The next section is devoted to the definition of basic concepts and presentation of the graphic representation of these concepts.

8.3 BASIC DEFINITIONS AND SYMBOLS   ■

This section is devoted to the definition of the basic vocabulary used in object-oriented methodology. The definitions are not, for the most part, mathematical; there is, therefore, a chance for different interpretations by different people. However, we will provide enough descriptive information for each definition so that different interpretations are covered. Along with the definition of each entity, a graphic representation for each entity will be shown.

8.3.1   Objects

Webster's New World Dictionary defines *object* as ''A thing that can be seen or touched; material thing; a person or thing to which action, thought or feeling is directed.'' In the OO domain an object is one of many things that together constitute the problem domain. An object may have a name, a set of attributes, and a set of actions or services. An object may stand alone or it may belong to a class of similar objects. Examples of objects that may stand alone are shown in Figure 8.1. Each object is represented by a round-cornered rectangle. The first item in the rectangle is the name of the object. The name of the object is separated from the object attributes by a straight line. An object may have zero or more attributes; each attribute has its own name, value, and specifications. The list of attributes is followed by a list of services (or actions). Each service has a name associated with it and eventually will be translated to executable program code. Services are separated from the list of attributes by a horizontal line.

8.3.2   Classes

Webster's New World Dictionary defines *class* as ''A number of people or things grouped together because of certain likenesses; kind; sort.'' This meaning is used to define a class in object-oriented analysis and design. A class has a class name, a set of attributes, and a set of actions or services. With this definition of classes, we assume there are two implicit service or action functions defined for each class. These functions are GET<attribute> and PUT<attribute>. The GET function will determine the value of the attribute associated with it, and the PUT function will assign the computed value of the attribute to the attribute's name.

   Figure 8.2 shows a class called Student with three instances: Joe Smith, Mary Lord, and David Boyed. Each instance is an object belonging to the class called Student. The services associated with this class are Store (write the student object to a file), Print (print out the object attributes), and Update (replace the value of one or more attributes with a new value). In this illustration, class name is Student each instance of Student is an object which has all of the attributes and services of Student class. For a matter of distinction we have used the class name to name each object for the same class. For instance, Joe Smith may be a member of the Student class as well as a member of Employee class. Naming each object of a class with the class name helps to associate an object to its class. Note that an object may be considered as a class with one member. Therefore, to distinguish an object from a class, we

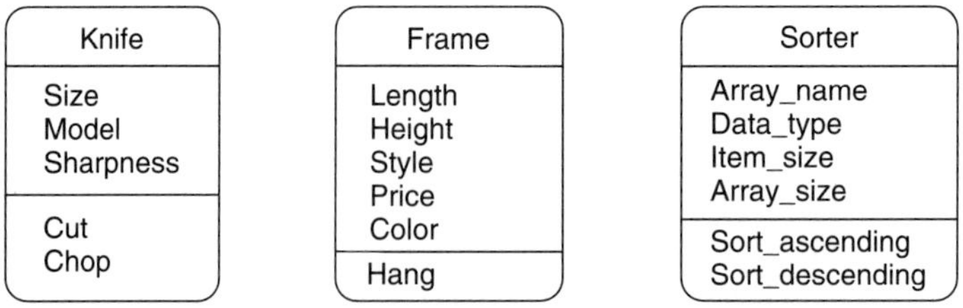

Knife		Frame		Sorter	
Size		Length		Array_name	
Model		Height		Data_type	
Sharpness		Style		Item_size	
		Price		Array_size	
Cut		Color		Sort_ascending	
Chop		Hang		Sort_descending	

■ Figure 8.1

Objects.

Object class

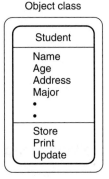

Student-1	Student-2	Student-3
Joe Smith 24 PO Box 12 Math • •	Mary Lord 22 PO Box 102 Comp. Sci. • •	David Boyed 31 PO Box 21 Physics • •
Store Print Update	Store Print Update	Store Print Update

■ **Figure 8.2**
Object class and three examples.

may represent a class with a double-lined round corner rectangle and an object with a single-lined round corner rectangle. Double line may be interpreted as there are more than one object in the class.

A class defines a group of objects with similar attributes, common operations, a common relationship to other objects in the class, and common semantics. For example, Person, Student, House, and Car are all classes. Some authors call a class an *object class* or class object. We use the name *class* to mean a set of similar objects. Some implementations require that all objects be unique. Objects may be made unique by adding an extra attribute to the class of object, say SS# for a class called Employee. In some cases objects in a class may identify themselves uniquely through their attribute values. Even if all attributes of two objects are the same, we may still want to consider both objects in the system. This problem of object uniqueness will be left for implementation time.

The term *common semantics* in classifying objects is best described by an example. Consider two classes, Car and House.

```
Name: Car            Name: House
Attributes:          Attributes:
 Cost                 Cost
 Color                Color
 Model                Model
Services:            Services:
 Maintenance          Maintenance
```

These two classes have the same set of attributes and the same service functions. Questions such as ''Should both of these objects be considered of the same class?'' or ''Should they belong to different classes?'' may be answered by looking at the semantics of these two classes. If the underlying semantics is based on object usage, then the two classes should not be combined even if their attributes and services are the same. On the other hand, if the underlying semantics is based on the object's asset computation, then both House and Car belong to a class called Asset.

8.3.3   Relationship or Association among Objects

Binary Associations

Two objects, either of the same class or of a different class, or two classes may be associated with each other by a given relation. For example, in the class called Student we may define the association Same-major to associate particular objects of this class with each other. With this definition, we say two objects are associated if and only if their Major attributes have the same value. That is, two students of the same major are related to or associated with each other.

As another example consider the classes Person and Company. We define the relationship between objects of these two classes as Employed-by. Therefore, an object P from the class Person is related to an object C from the class Company if and only if person P is employed by company C.

An association among classes (or objects) may be a *one-to-one*, *one-to-many*, *many-to-one*, or *many-to-many* association. The graphic representation of association among objects is shown by a line connecting the associated classes or objects together. For associations that are not one-to-one, we may introduce a multiplicity number (or range of numbers), written below the association line, to indicate the association multiplicity number. When the name of the relationship is not clear from the context or when there is more than one association between objects, the name of the association may be written on the top of the relation line. For relations whose inverse have a different name, the two names may be written on either side of the association line. For example, the inverse of the relation Work-for between class Person and class Company becomes Employee-of.

As an example, consider the class Person and the relationships Parent-of, Married-to, Child-of, Sibling-of, and Landlord-of. The association Parent-of is a one-to-many association, Married-to is a one-to-one association, Child-of is a many-to-one association, Sibling-of is a many-to-many association, and Landlord-of is a (0 or more)-to-many association. Whenever the inclusion of zero with the word *many* is understood, instead of 0 or more we can say many.

Figure 8.3 illustrates the relationships or associations among classes, the association lines, association multiplicity numbers, and association names. In Figure 8.3(**A**), the relationship between Student and Course is called Enrolled and is a one-to-many association. That is, a student may be enrolled in 0 or more courses. In Figure 8.3(**B**), the association between Student and Advisor is called Advisee-of and is a many-to-one association. The association between Advisor and Student is called Advisor-of and is a one-to-many association. In Figure 8.3(**C**), the association between Student and Sport_Team is called Member-of and the association between Sport_team and Student is called Team. Both of these associations are many-to-many.

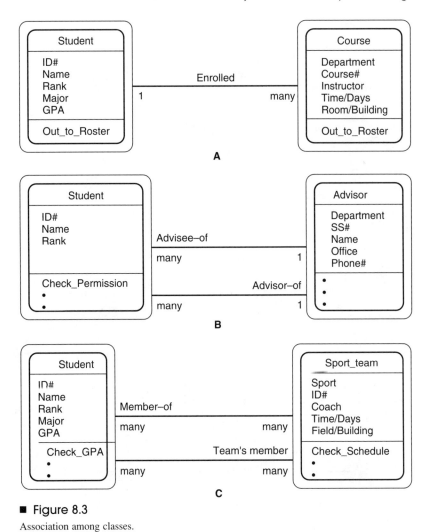

■ **Figure 8.3**

Association among classes.

n-ary Associations

Associations may not be binary, meaning that they take more than two classes to make an association. Such associations are called *n*-ary associations. One example of such association is the Whole_part association between an object and its parts, discussed in the next section. Generally, *n*-ary associations are harder to understand. Thus, *n*-ary associations are often subdivided into several binary associations before they can be fully understood.

8.3.4 Structures, Inheritance, and Generalization

Consider the following classes: Person, Student, Employee, Graduate, Undergraduate, Administrator, Staff, and Faculty. Graduate and Undergraduate are each a subclass of Student

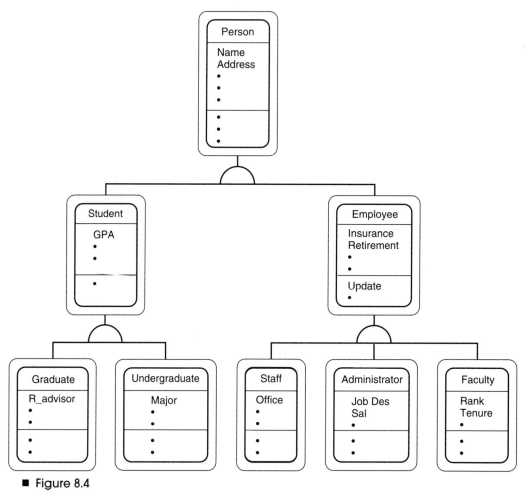

■ Figure 8.4

Superclass and subclass structure.

class; Faculty, Staff, and Administrator are each a subclass of Employee class; and Student and Employee are each a subclass of Person class. On the other hand, Person class is a superclass for Student and Employee classes; Employee is a superclass for Faculty, Administrator, and Staff classes; and Student class is a superclass for Graduate and Undergraduate classes. *Generalization* is the relationship between a superclass and its subclasses. *Inheritance* is copying the attributes of the superclass into all of its subclasses.

Figure 8.4 illustrates the superclass and subclass relationship among classes. Person is a superclass for Student class and Employee class. Student is a subclass of Person but a superclass for Undergraduate and Graduate classes. Employee is a subclass of Person but a superclass for Staff, Administrator, and Faculty classes.

8.3.5 Assembly Structure (or Whole-Part Structure)

An assembly relationship is used to identify the parts of an object or a class. Figure 8.5 illustrates the assembly structure for an object called Mg-Desk. Based on the diagram in Figure 8.5, a desk has several parts: a top; three sides (two sides and a back panel); five drawers; and zero, 4, 6, or 8 wheels. For the Whole-part relationship, as for a general relationship, we can write the multiplicity of the parts needed next to the association lines.

Association lines between a superclass and its subclasses all originate from a half circle that is connected to the superclass, as shown in Figure 8.4. The association lines between the Whole and Part each have a triangle, as shown in Figure 8.5. This convention distinguishes structural relationships (subclass-superclass and whole-part) from other relationships among objects and classes.

8.3.6 Combined Structures

There may be situations in which an object or a class is a subclass of another class and also has an assembly relationship with its own parts. For example, Figure 8.6 shows a superclass called Furniture, which has subclasses Chair, Sofa, and Desk, etc. As we saw in Figure 8.5, subclass Desk has an assembly relationship with its parts, Top, Side, Drawer, and Wheel. As

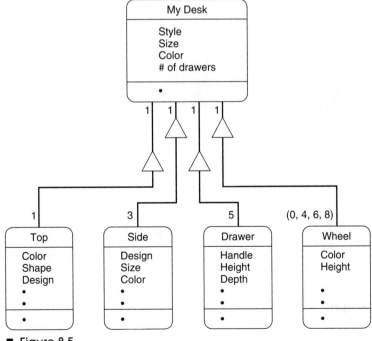

■ **Figure 8.5**

Assembly relation between desk and its parts.

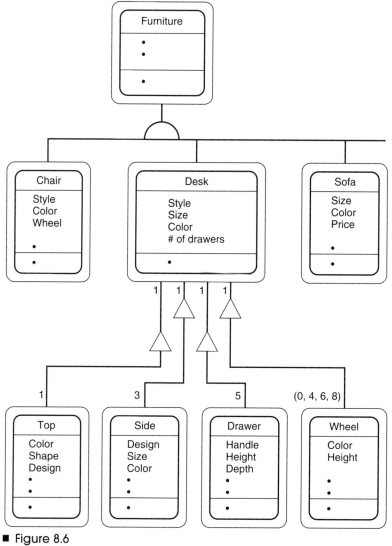

■ **Figure 8.6**

Combined structures (superclass-subclass and whole-part).

is shown in Figure 8.6, we may combine the two relationships Superclass-subclass and Whole-part on the same diagram.

8.3.7 Comments on Structures

Note that in the superclass-subclass relationship, a subclass could be replaced by an attribute added to the superclass without loss of any information. For example, a class roster may have three parts: Instructor, Students, and Building/Room. The instructor teaching the course may be a full-time or a part-time instructor. Therefore, Instructor could be a superclass with two subclasses, Part-time and Full-time. Students, on the other hand, may be freshman, sophomore, junior, senior, or graduate. Thus, Student could be a superclass with five subclasses. However, if the only distinguishing feature of the separate classes Part-time and Full-time is the identification of the instructor as being part-time or full-time, the same effect can be achieved by adding an attribute, say Employment-Status, to the class Instructor. Similarly, if classes Freshman, Sophomore, Junior, Senior, and Graduate are used only to identify a student's rank, the same effect can be achieved by adding a new attribute called Rank to the Student class. Similarly, with regard to whole-part relationships, when a part is used to identify only a single element (with no attribute or function) within the assembly relationship, we can add this single item as an attribute of the Whole class.

On the other hand, there are cases where a given attribute, XXX, of an object has a Does Not Apply value associated with it. Assume that one or more of the actions defined for this object are completely different when the value of attribute XXX is Does Not Apply. In such

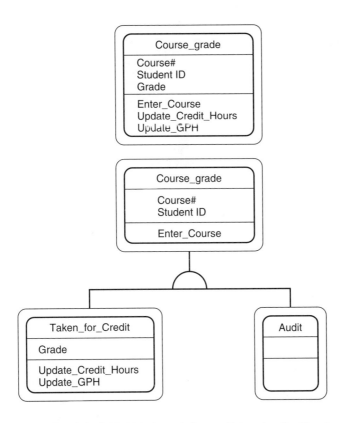

Note that the course_grade is divided into two subclasses, Taken_for_Credit and Audit. The attributes for Audit subclass are inherited from Course_grade class. We have not shown attributes Course# and Student ID in the subclasses. Also service function Enter_Course is inherited from the object Course_grade and it is not shown in the subclasses.

■ Figure 8.7

Creating subclass.

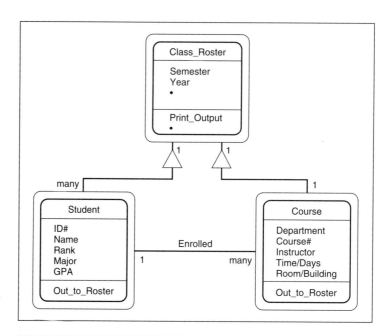

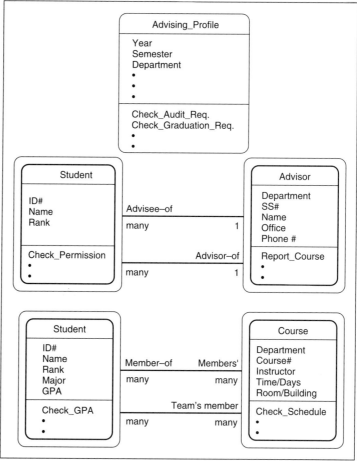

■ Figure 8.8

Subjects.

cases, it is advisable to break the class into two subclasses, one corresponding to the case where attribute XXX has a Does Not Apply value and the other class for all other cases. For example, suppose "Course_Grade" is an object with two attributes (Student_ID and Grade) and three service functions (Enter_Grade, Update_Credit_Hours, and Update_GPA). For a student who is auditing the course, the value for attribute Grade is Does Not Apply. When a course is audited, the functions Update_Credit_Hours and Update_GPA need not be performed. In this case we may divide Course_Grade into two subclasses, Taken-for-Credit and Audit. This example is illustrated in Figure 8.7.

The highest order of abstraction in object-oriented methodology is the definition of *subjects*. To those familiar with the structured analysis approach, a subject in OOA plays the same role as a module in the structured analysis approach. A subject contains objects, classes, associations, structures, etc. The main purpose of defining a subject is to facilitate comprehension and understanding of the entire system. Proper definition and identification of subjects provides the following advantages:

1. Facilitates communication by avoiding information overload. That is, a reader needs to understand, remember, and comprehend only what is included in the subject.
2. Helps to guide the reader through a large system architecture one subject at a time.
3. Helps to maximize the abstraction level.
4. Helps to visualize the system architecture. By placing the graphic for each subject on a single page, we can help the reader to visualize the entire subject in one glance.

Figure 8.8 illustrates some examples of subjects. Each subject is placed entirely within a rectangle. In general, the structure of subjects, classes, objects, relationships, etc., for a given problem domain is dictated by the specific requirements imposed on the system by the stated needs of users and operators.

8.4 OBJECT-ORIENTED ANALYSIS ■

The main goal of object-oriented analysis (OOA) is directly to establish a software structure or architecture in terms of problem domain objects and classes. The association between objects and classes and the attributes and operations associated with each object are simply further elaborations on the abstraction of the problem space. Messages represent the control (including the required parameters) exercised over each object by other objects. Object-oriented design employs the same notation to refine and elaborate further on the initial object-oriented depiction and ultimately to realize, in pseudocode, an implementation of the object-oriented design.

At present, most software requirement specifications are developed not by software engineers but by analysts and/or system engineers deeply familiar with the application area. A radar tracking system, an energy management system, an air traffic control system, a reservation system, a credit card processing system, and an electronic switching system are a few examples of cases for which the SRS would probably be prepared by an engineer or analyst, perhaps with the help of a software engineer. Typically, the SRS requirements are expressed in terms of functional decompositions or partitions of higher-level requirements. These decompositions or partitions are based on required actions to be performed by the system and allocated to software. The emphasis is on the verbs or actions found in the higher level specifications. The requirements are stated as follows: shall track . . .; shall search . . .; shall control . . .; shall respond . . .; shall accept . . .; etc.

Restating the SRS in the context of an OO vocabulary and producing an OO SDS document from a data- and function-oriented SRS document has its own disadvantages and advantages. On one hand, the abrupt transition from function to object can result in increased cost, a longer development cycle, and a loss of technical and management visibility. On the other hand, it is also possible to take advantage of the dual view offered by using both object and function perspectives to improve intrinsic understanding of the problem space and overall system requirements.

Some object-oriented analysis methods employ operational scenarios or timelines to support development of software requirements and extract objects from functional requirements that are implicit in the operational timelines. There are two advantages to this approach: (1) the users or operators are involved in the development of requirements, so human factors problems are surfaced early in the design process; and (2) operational scenarios can form the basis for operating manuals and other user documents.

Given a problem statement, an object-oriented analysis requires the satisfactory completion of the following steps: (1) developing a set of classes that fully represent the problem domain, (2) identifying instance and structural association among classes, (3) identifying the set of attributes for each class, and (4) checking the access path for each class. Note that the identification of the services associated with each class and the messages communicated between objects are deliberately left out. These will be treated in section 8.4.4 and again in a discussion of the object-oriented design process.

It must be realized that there is no unique way to perform any of the steps defined earlier. Therefore, it is useful at the end of each step to look back at achieved results and verify their appropriateness. Also, results should be improved through an iterative process. The exact meaning of improvement depends on the step being performed. For example, if we are identifying classes, the improvement is to find whether any crucial class is missing or whether any redundant class is among the identified classes. When we are identifying the associations among objects, the improvement is to make sure the associations found are truly representative of the real-world associations and no crucial relationship among objects is missing.

8.4.1   Finding Objects and Classes

Recall that a class is just a group of similar objects with common attributes and service functions. Therefore what we discuss about objects will apply to classes and vise-versa. The identification of objects can be aided by realizing that an object may be any of the following:

External entities: Systems, people, sensors that interface with the system in question.

Things: Displays, reports, signals within, or output from, the system.

Events: Caused by the system or suffered by the system.

Roles: Managers, operators, maintainers of the system.

Organizational units: Related to system operation.

Places: Locations that have relevance to the operation of a system.

Structures: Classes of objects with certain commonality attributes and/or operation.

To identify candidate objects or classes in a problem space, one can look at the nouns in the SRS or in the problem description. Applying the preceding guidance and the following tests will enable the analyst to settle on a particular set of objects that completely characterize an abstraction of the problem space.

Object and class definition as well as most other activities in OOA are iterative processes. Thus the first group of objects and classes identified may be neither complete nor minimum. We must revisit every object and every class to assure that each object/class meets the following criteria:

1. The object/class derives from the SRS and/or problem domain.
2. The object/class is needed for a complete representation and definition of the system being built.
3. The object/class is not redundant.
4. The object/class cannot be combined with other objects through the use of additional attributes.
5. The object/class is adequately defined.
6. The information presented by the object class is unique.

A semialgorithmic way to confirm these criteria is to apply the following six test questions to each individual class of objects:

1. Must information about the object be retained or remembered for the system to function properly?
2. Does the object perform an operation that changes another object's attributes?
3. Does the object have more than one attribute?
4. Does the object have an attribute set that does not change as attribute values change or for other occurrences of the object? An object can occur many times in a system. For example, a record may be an object and there may be many records in a problem space.
5. Do object operations change for other instances of the object? (An instance of an object is a specific manifestation of the abstract object.)
6. Does the external entity object produce or consume information essential to the system operation?

Note that these test questions should be applied repeatedly as objects and classes are defined (Table 8.1, discussed later, gives a template for defining an object). As we progress in completing the object template for each object, we should go through the following steps on an iterative basis:

Step 1:   Study objects and classes initially created; remove the redundant and irrelevant ones and keep the good ones. Redundant classes should be removed and only the one with the most descriptive name should be kept. For example, in an airline reservation system we may have three classes called Customer, Client, and Passenger. It is apparent that these three classes are redundant. The one that should be kept is the one with the most descriptive name, that is, Passenger.

Step 2:   Identify vaguely defined classes in the set of classes and break them down into meaningful classes. Then identify the relevance of the classes to the problem domain and remove those classes that are not relevant to the problem being solved.

Step 3:   Reexamine object and class names to see whether they are better defined as an attribute of another class. Also, study the names of attributes to see whether they should be defined as separate objects. Study the names of objects to see whether they play a significant role or they are, in fact, objects. The names that play a role should be identified as relationship or association among objects. For example, names such as Owner, Operator, Part, etc., may be best defined as a relationship between two classes and not as an object. Note that associations often have their own attributes. Therefore, a name with attributes does not mean that since the name has attributes it should be identified as an object. It may still be identified as a relationship or an association with attributes.

   Step 4:   Eliminate noun phrases that are related to a later stage in the development process from the list of viable class names. Examples of such noun phrases are Efficiency, Response time, Complexity, Interrupt, etc. When combining classes, be sure to study the problem statement and its requirements. Sometimes, depending on the problem statement and its requirement, classes such as Person and Employee should not be combined to create one class. For example, if a person works at two or more places, this person is a taxpayer with two or more separate incomes and is also an employee at each of the places he or she works.

   Objects and classes that are good candidates to be studied for possible elimination fall into one or more of the following categories:

1. Objects or classes that have a single attribute.
2. Classes with only one object in the entire class.
3. Objects or classes with no applicable service associated with them. An applicable service is a service that, when performed, will produce external output.
4. Objects or classes whose attributes and services hold or produce information that is not required to create a design.
5. Objects or classes with attributes that have or require no value.
6. Classes that provide no contribution to the SRS. There are noun phrases in the SRS that when manifested as objects classes have no meaning in regard to system design. These noun phrases are usually associated with system testing and implementation characteristics. We should not create objects corresponding to such noun phrases; if created, we should eliminate them. Examples of such noun phrases are response time, storage, batch processing, distributed data processing, etc.
7. Objects or classes that are associated with noun phrases such as vendor address, client age, patient insurance company, etc. These noun phrases are good candidates for object attributes.

8.4.2   Determining Attributes of Each Object/Class

Attributes of an object or a class are a further abstraction of the characteristics of the problem space. Given an object name, only those attributes that are essential to the operation of the system being designed are included in the object. For example, in a problem space involving control of an automobile engine's speed, an object called Auto_Speed_Control does not require attributes such as color, body style, etc.

   Table 8.1 shows a template for defining an object or a class. A combination of graphic representation and data dictionary may provide an ideal tool to represent an object or a class. The problem statement can be searched for adjectives and these adjectives used as the starting point for establishing object attributes. The graphic representation includes the name of the attributes, and the data dictionary stores the description and specification of the attribute.

   The main goal of attributes of an object is to define that object to the outside world as it relates to the problem domain and the system being built. Note that it is very important to understand the phrase "as it relates to the problem domain and the system being built." For

■ TABLE 8.1   **Object (Class) Specification Template**

1. OBJECT/CLASS NAME
2. ATTRIBUTE DESCRIPTIONS (*n* REPETITIONS)
   (For each attribute we may include a name, content, data type, data structure, limits, and constraint, if any.)
   ATTRIBUTE NAME
   ATTRIBUTE CONTENT
   ATTRIBUTE DATA TYPE
   ATTRIBUTE DATA STRUCTURE
   ATTRIBUTE VALUE LIMITS
   ATTRIBUTE CONSTRAINTS
   2.1 EXTERNAL INPUT TO OBJECT
       (Identify by name each external input and its associated attribute.)
   2.2 EXTERNAL OUTPUT FROM OBJECT
       (Identify by name each external output and its associated identifier. Each external output sends the value of an attribute.)
3. SERVICES (OPERATIONS or FUNCTIONS) (*n* REPETITIONS)
   (For each service there should be a name, an interface with external inputs and attributes, a process defined in the form of program code, the expected performance of the service, and the list of constraints, if any.)
   SERVICE NAME
   SERVICE INTERFACE
   SERVICE PROCESS
   SERVICE PERFORMANCE
   SERVICE CONSTRAINTS
4. INSTANCES AND STRUCTURAL CONNECTIONS
   (This is part of the graphic representation of objects and classes. However, it is a good habit to list such structural and instance connections within the object or class itself.)
5. MESSAGE CONNECTIONS
   (For each message we include message identification, values to be transferred to the receiving object, values to be received by the sending object, and services to be executed by the message.)

example, an object called Truck has a different set of attributes for each of the following problem domains: motor vehicle administration, highway transportation department, maintenance, and company asset evaluation. The selection of attributes has its root in the problem definition and the SRS document.

In general, object or class attributes do the following: (1) identify the class, (2) define the special characteristics of the class, (3) define the state of the class, (4) retain certain information about the class, and (5) identify the behavior of the object. When attributes are selected and their presence in an object is verified, then each attribute must be specified. To specify an attribute we must define the following for that attribute: (1) value limits, (2) measurement unit, (3) expected accuracy, (4) individual value, (5) default value, (6) initial value, (7) tracing chain, (8) Put and Get function constraints, and (9) constraints caused by other attributes of the object or class.

External inputs to objects and external outputs from objects may be fully described in the data dictionary. If desired, we may associate an attribute name with each external input and output element. However, attributes associated with external input and output values should be used only for input values and output values, respectively. A better approach is to separate external inputs to the object and external outputs from the object from the list of object attributes, as shown in Table 8.1.

8.4.3 Defining/Identifying Services for Each Object/Class

Operations or services performed by objects or classes can be found by examining the problem statement for verbs associated with each object. Guidance as to what operations to look for can be found by considering the following three categories of operations: (1) manipulation of data and control items, (2) computational operations, and (3) monitoring operations for periodic events.

Services are listed by name in each class. The service interface to the class and external interfaces are listed in the class and described in the data dictionary. The service process is what eventually will be translated to pseudocode or a programming language. Detailed design and definition of services and messages are the main responsibility of the design phase. In this section we present the identification of services and messages only as they relate to the OOA phase.

In order to define services for an object or a class, we must be able to identify the state of the object. An object state refers to a set of values for the attributes of the object. When one or more attributes of the object change values, we say the object has changed its state. Therefore, at any given time, an object is in a given state identified by the value of its attributes.

For example, the object representing sensor controller for a device required to control air temperature, humidity, and pressure will have three attributes: Air_Temperature, Air_Pressure, and Air_Humidity. Each of these variables has three values: Normal, Low, and High. Based on the values of these attributes, the object is in a given state. One state may be defined by (Normal, Normal, Normal), another state may be defined by (High, Normal, Low) and so on. Depending on the state of the object, different services may be performed. For instance, when Air_Temperature is High, the service is to set the air conditioner to On; or when the Air_Humidity becomes Normal, the service is to set the humidifier to Off.

The next step is to identify required services for each object or class and give an operational specification for each defined service. Services may be grouped into three categories: simple, moderate, and complex. Simple services are routine computations that are simple to perform and are of a control nature. Such services are equivalent to what is called utility functions in a conventional programming environment. Examples of such services are Create(Object), Connect(Object_i, Object_j), Access(Object), etc. Moderate services may require some form of computation and validation of input/output data. For instance, a function like Compute(Attribute) is used to compute the value of an attribute from the list of all attributes included with the service name. Complex services require a high level of algorithmic computation with a fine level of precision. Often the results of such services are used to control the behavior of the object. Examples of such services are security verification, data encoding, data decoding, and access validation.

8.4.4 Defining Messages for each Object/Class

A message in OO programming language is similar to a command line in conventional languages. A message is sent from an object or class (Sender) to another object or class (Receiver) to perform certain services. A message may carry with it the external input needed to execute services required for the message sender. It also may return some of the external outputs from the receiver object to the sender object. One of the objectives of messages is to create communication among objects and classes without creating side effects. This communication is provided through the execution of services named within messages. When a message is sent from one object to another object, (or from one class to another class) in general, four things can happen [3]:

1. The message brings to the object the value of external variables, if any, needed to execute the service requested by the message.
2. Each message calls for one or more of the services of the receiving object to be executed.
3. The state of the receiving object may be changed by the execution of a message. Recall that the state of an object is identified by the value of its attributes. The execution of a message may change the value of one or more attributes of the object.
4. Similarly, the state of the sending object may be changed after the completion of the message by means of the values returned by the message.

A message connector line may be considered as a relationship between two objects or classes. That is, there may be more than one message line between two objects or a message line from an object may split and go to several objects, each requiring a different service to be performed. For example, an Update_Personnel_Record message may be sent from the Personnel class to three different objects. One object is Employee_Department, which identifies employees working in a given department; the second object is Employee_Payroll, which updates any changes in employee salary and tax status; and Employee_Profile updates employee address and related data.

In order to identify the message connection lines needed for each object or class, we must study the object/class to determine the following:

1. Services defined in object *A* that are used by other objects. These objects are prime candidates to send messages to object *A*.
2. Services in object *A* where execution requires data from other objects. Object *A* is connected to these other objects to acquire needed data to perform the services defined in the object.

Sometimes a message may not be completed by the services in a given object or class. In such cases we must follow the message from the sending object to as many levels of receiving object as required for the message to be completely executed. For instance, message *M* is sent from object *A* to object *B*. However, the service requested by message *M* won't be executed unless message *M'* from object *B* to object *C* is processed first. We must make sure that message *M'* is specified from object *B* to object *C*. The specification for message *M'* becomes part of the completion of message *M*.

A message line may be named and its input/output may be identified and written on the message line. This, however, clutters the graphic representation of the OOA document. One way to prevent this clutter is to identify a message with the sender object, the receiver object, and a numeric value. Then in the data dictionary, for each message identification include the list of attribute values needed by the message, the list of services requested by the message, and the list of external outputs returned by the execution of the message.

All the instance relationships and structural relationships as well as message lines may be represented graphically, as shown in section 8.3. However, there are CASE tools that may automatically create an OO diagram from the information provided in the data dictionary. In such cases, we may need to identify structural and instance relationships and messages in the data dictionary. Such identification, if appropriate, must follow a certain format dictated by the CASE tools being used.

The detailed design of each service is to be discussed in the OOD phase. During OOA, however, a first-level design will be to determine messages and external input and output for an object or a class. During the design of each service we may discover details of operations performed by the service and the results obtained. The external inputs and outputs and the redundancy of certain services may also become apparent during the design phase.

8.4.5 Time-Dependency Considerations

The time-dependent behavior of objects and classes should be studied by looking for events that are time dependent within the model represented by the collection of objects, classes, messages, and services. In a time-dependent environment the correctness of a function or task depends on its sequence, its rate of execution, and its time of completion. In preparing the OOA for time-dependent systems, we must do the following:

1. Prepare several operational timelines that fully reflect the time dependency of the system. This step should help in creating messages and connections among objects that recognize time dependencies.
2. Identify user interface format and sequence. Control the sequence of user interfaces to allow for meaningful time-related commands being issued in a logical sequence and executed in the required time interval.
3. Identify external events and their logical sequence. An event may be an input event, an output event, or both input and output events. If necessary, show an event flow diagram, similar to the data flow diagram, to show events happening between classes without regard for the sequence of events.
4. For each object or class with some form of dynamic behavior, develop a state transition diagram to define the dynamic nature of the object or class.

The results of these four steps should add significantly to the design database. This process should lead to the design of messages and services that guarantee task execution in the necessary order. For real-time process design, chapter 19 should be consulted.

8.4.6 Finding Association among Objects

There are three common forms of association or relationship among objects, superclass-subclass, whole-part, and instance relationships. To identify superclass-subclass relationships, we investigate objects whose name indicates they may be a subclass of or superclass for other objects. Then we examine the attributes and other entities of each object to see whether they can be identified as subclass of another object. Similarly, objects may be studied, based on the original naming, as being a superclass for certain numbers of objects. Sometimes looking at inheritance may help to identify subclasses of objects.

The second form of association among objects is the assembly or whole-part association. One way to find this relationship among objects is to look at the structure and behavior of each object. The structure of each object may identify its parts. Also, the behavior of an object can help to identify the parts necessary for the behavior needed. A second way to identify a whole-part relationship is to decompose an object to its parts and then try to find the object parts in the list of objects. This method will also help to create new objects, in case of such a need.

The third form of association is called instance association. Relationships among objects as discussed in section 8.3.3 are simply categorized as instance relationships. Examples of instance relationship are Parent-of, Employee-of, Employed-by, and Student-of. For instance, if Student and University are two classes, the relationship Student-of associates one or more students with one university.

In general, instance association identifies one or more objects of a class needed for an object *A* to perform its duty. The instance association is shown as a line connecting two objects or classes. The multiplicity of the association is written on the association line next to the object or class. For example, the relation between Owner and Car is a many-to-many relation, which is an instance association. When objects of the same class are related to each other by an instance relation, we draw a looplike line from the class back to itself.

8.4.7   Checking Access Paths through Classes

Checking access paths is of primary concern in the design phase. Access paths among objects are established via association lines and message lines. To verify the existence of proper access paths among the objects, we must trace through association lines and service connection lines to verify the following:

1. The access path through the entire OO diagram provides useful design information.
2. When there must be a unique path producing a unique result, such unique path and the uniqueness of the result is guaranteed.
3. For many-to-many associations, there should be a way to produce a unique result, if one is needed.
4. There should be no important and relevant questions that the OO diagram (in conjunction with the data dictionary) cannot answer.
5. If the OO diagram seems much more complex than the real world, there should be a review and revision of the OO diagram.

The access paths among objects and classes are to assure the availability of the services defined in the objects whenever and wherever needed. Therefore, the design process must assure that there are proper access paths throughout the entire object diagram.

8.4.8   Complete OOA Document

A complete OOA document includes the following items in the order that they have been generated:

1. Specification of Classes and Objects   The object/class template of Table 8.1 is used to identify each object and class. The attributes, services, external inputs, external outputs, message communication definitions, etc., are all defined in the OOA document.

2. Relationship among Objects and Classes   Structural and nonstructural relationships among objects and classes are defined and graphically represented in the OOA document, especially the subclasses, superclasses, and the whole_part relationships.

3. Subjects   Subjects are identified, defined, and graphically represented in the OOA document.

4. External Documents   Several supplemental documents are also developed as adjunct to the OOA document. The most useful one is the data dictionary. There may be documents (including data flow diagrams) that define the first-level design of the services specified for each object.

8.4.9   Final Clean-up before Design Phase

Things that may go wrong during an OOA process may include the following: (1) too many objects or classes are defined, (2) too few objects or classes are defined, (3) irrelevant attributes are defined for a class, (4) the list of defined attributes for a given class is not complete, (5) irrelevant associations are defined, (6) unnecessary associations are defined, and (7) association lines are placed incorrectly.

For each of these anomalies, there are specific signs that may alert the software engineer to their presence [5]. Also, there are ways to resolve each of them. Next we list the signs and the possible cures for each.

Too Many Classes   Signs of too many classes include the following: (1) lack of attributes for some classes, (2) lack of services for some classes, and (3) lack of association among classes. When any or all of these signs are present for a class, perhaps the class is not needed.

Too Few Classes   Signs of missing classes include the following:

1. It is not easy to generalize a group of objects into a superclass. Perhaps the definition of the class is not clear or the class combines too many characteristics. The answer is to split the class into two or more classes.
2. Association among classes is asymmetric (A relates to B, but B does not relate to A). A new class should be defined.
3. Attributes defined for a class won't, semantically, fit the rest of the attributes of that class. The class should be divided into two classes.
4. Operations defined on a class are disparate. The class should be divided into two coherent classes.
5. It is difficult to generalize classes into superclasses. Perhaps a given class plays more than one role. Splitting such classes into two or more classes may solve the problem.
6. There are operations with no defined target classes. We should add classes to contain these operations.
7. There are duplicate associations with the same name among classes. We should generalize the associations to create a superclass that can unite the duplicate associations.
8. There are associations that shape the semantics of a class. It is possible that such associations should be converted to a separate class.

Irrelevant Attributes   When an attribute is not used in services defined for the class, does not define a necessary characteristic of the class, and/or is not used as an external input/ output place holder, probably the attribute is not needed.

Incomplete Set of Attributes   Signs of an incomplete set of attributes for a class include the following: (1) services defined for the class cannot be computed, (2) external input values are needed to compute services, and such external input values are not defined within the class, and (3) external output values produced by the service functions of the class are not associated with any attribute. We should define new and semantically appropriate attributes to resolve any or all of these problems.

Unnecessary Associations   When redundant information is produced by an association or an association is not used by any of the services defined in the class, perhaps the association is not needed. Remove such association from the object diagram.

Missing Associations   When the operations or services defined in a class have no access path to classes providing data needed to complete such operations, perhaps an association line is missing. Create association lines capable of bringing proper data to the class.

Incorrect Placement of Association Lines   Incorrect placement usually happens when an association line is drawn at an incorrect hierarchy level of classes. When an association name is too broad or too specific for the classes that are joined by that association line, the line must be moved in the hierarchy of classes so that the role of the association becomes meaningful.

Irrelevant Structural Association Lines   The signs of irrelevant whole-part and super-class-subclass include the following: (1) some superclasses and subclasses don't make sense, (2) there is only one subclass of a superclass, (3) the whole and part objects do not relate to each other, and (4) there are not enough part objects to make the whole object. Remove these association lines.

An important observation is that the OOA process is not a sequential process as defined in this chapter. In a real-world environment the process is parallel, and normally all four steps defined here are combined and performed iteratively until we produce an appropriate OO diagram and its associated data dictionary for the system being designed. In other words, when we identify an object we concurrently assign attributes, make associations with other objects, define services performed by the object and messages that may invoke the object, and develop operational flows. During the OOD phase we may reevaluate the OOA outcomes and, if needed, revise them.

8.5   OBJECT-ORIENTED DESIGN

It should be noted that in an object-oriented development environment, regardless of the SWDLC being used, the object-oriented approach distinguishes four overlapping phases: analysis, design, coding, and test and integration. One of the advantages of object-oriented development is that there is no distinct separation between analysis and design activities. During the object-oriented analysis phase the system analyst, system engineer, or software engineer is primarily concerned with the problem domain, the user domain, and the system function and performance domain. During the object-oriented design phase the software engineer is concerned with moving the logical specification of the system into a physical realization, that is, showing how each requirement of the system is to be satisfied.

The primary benefits of OOD following an OOA include the following [1, 2]:

1. OOD requires a deeper understanding of the problem domain. This benefit by itself helps to improve communications among problem domain experts (system engineers and/or system analysts and client), design experts (software engineers), and implementation experts (programmers, test and integration engineers, data acquisition engineers, and quality assurance engineers).
2. The use of consistent symbols and terminology for the OOA/OOD forces consistency across analysis, design, and implementation phases.
3. OOD helps to minimize redundancies via interaction of common attributes and services.
4. OOD helps to develop a system that is resilient to changes during both the development and the maintenance phases by proper use of procedural and data abstractions.
5. OOD provides for reuse at all levels, especially at analysis and design levels, by proper use of classes, superclasses, attributes, services, and encapsulations.
6. When a well-equipped OO programming language is used, the consistency among the notations and methods applied from OOA to OOD and to coding provides for a smooth transition from requirements specification to design and to implementation.
7. OOD forces many intermediate and informal reviews and walk-throughs during analysis and design phases before coding begins due to the continuing search for redundant/missing objects, classes, attributes, services, associations, and messages.
8. OOD provides for clearer and more constructive human interfaces through communication among classes using messages.
9. OOD may be applied to any form of SWDLC including waterfall, spiral, or incremental because the same notations, vocabularies, and representation tools are used across the life cycle phases.

The OOD process consists of two major parts for the design of software products. The first part consists of the specific functions and procedures that perform specific tasks to satisfy the system requirements. This part is already logically defined in the OOA document and is presented mostly as services defined within classes/objects, as special tasks defined, as an independent object, and as communication and command messages. During the design phase we must develop detailed implementation steps for each service defined in each object or class. This step is the physical realization of the services described during the OOA phase.

The second part consists of those design components that are not necessarily directly defined in the SRS document and therefore are not specified as services or special objects. Although such components are not directly specified, they are needed for the overall operation of the software product. The major system components that fit this description may be put into four categories: (1) problem domain, (2) human interface, (3) task management, and (4) data acquisition and management.

8.5.1 Problem Domain

Problem domain components primarily arise from the changes to the OOA document surfaced during the design phase. A second reason for the problem domain component is the improvement to the OOA document realized during the design phase.

Changes to the initial OOA may be due to changes found in the system's operational environment, changes in the marketplace, technological advancements, misunderstanding of requirements, misinterpretation of requirements, change in requirements forced by the client, etc. Changes are neither always bad nor always costly. Therefore changes, after being reviewed and approved through the change management process, should be incorporated into the OOA results and become part of the problem domain.

Improvements and additions to the OOA results may be made during the OOD phase, especially those changes resulting from a better understanding of the problem domain, its characteristics, and the implementation environment, including the programming language being used. Some of the improvements and additions made during the design phase are (1) enhancing the reuse of the OOA results and (2) adjusting the OOA results to take full advantage of the programming language features, including design support for the data management component of the system.

The following are guidelines for implementing changes and improvement within the problem domain component:

1. Look for reusable results in the OOA as well as off-the-shelf software components. If what you find (including software products) is not part of the OOA and OOD, place it in a class by itself. Then minimize the number of unused operations within that class and use structural associations to connect the reuse component (design or code) to the OOD of the problem.
2. If the implementation language does not support the proper level of inheritance, lower the hierarchy of class structures so that they will be supported by the language. On the other hand, if the language supports a higher level of inheritance, add generalized superclass structures to the OOA results to take full advantage of the level of inheritance provided by the implementation language.
3. Check the OOA results for data management support. Add necessary OOD elements to provide full support for the data management component of the system. This step may be done by adding a ''save'' service to some of the classes and adding certain attributes to fully identify an object.
4. Add a new superclass to include most of the classes defined in the problem space. This addition will prove helpful in system integration.
5. During OOA we may create classes and objects that are very similar. At OOD time we can introduce a generalized class to facilitate prototyping such similar classes.

8.5.2 Human Interfaces

The OOA results include all the information needed to identify both users and user interfaces. During the design phase we should review operational timelines to establish a better understanding of the command hierarchy and details of all interfaces.

Different users with different needs and levels of expertise will use the software product or information system being developed. We must study and classify users before designing interfaces to be used by them. What may be a wonderful interface design for one class of users may turn out to be disastrous for another class of users. Therefore, it is wise to create user interfaces for specific classes of users. A user may be categorized by level of experience, organizational level, service needs, and job definition (staff, vendor, customer, manager, etc.) Within each user category we may have to establish three levels of experience: novice, experienced, and expert.

As can be seen in today's environment, a software product or an information system that has only a single window to the outside world will not be successful. In addition, if a software product is developed for the general public we must consider safety, health, and disability issues in designing human-to-computer interfaces.

When designing the command hierarchy, the main objective is to present to the user what is available in and provided by the information system. In addition to the specific design issues applicable to individual problem domains, some general guidelines should be followed in the design of system command hierarchy. These are as follows: (1) minimize space to present the command, (2) minimize key strokes to get to a command, (3) minimize any damage done by user error, (4) provide for some form of retrace of commands, (5) if possible, provide for reverse command operation, and (6) whatever design you choose, prototype it, refine it, test it with human users, improve it, and go through this process until no more improvement is needed.

The other major objective in the design of command hierarchy is to focus on human interface concerns. We should design command hierarchy in a way that (1) minimizes the time and the process for obtaining meaningful results, (2) is always consistent, (3) is always in touch with the user, (4) provides an undo option, (5) does not require the user to memorize, (6) groups the commands into meaningful classes and superclasses, and (7) uses the capability provided by graphic user interface to create a design that best fits the software product's operational environment.

8.5.3   Task Management

An information system at each state of its operation may require the performance of certain tasks that, although not directly a part of the system, without their proper execution the system will not be operational. As a simple example, consider reading a block of data from a disk. The application program is concerned only with issuing the correct read statement at the correct place in the program. For the read statement to produce the correct results, however, several tasks—checking the disk for readiness for reading, locating the block of data to be read from the disk, transferring the data into an initialized input buffer, etc.—must be performed before the read statement produces the correct results. These tasks and many more like them are assigned to the input/output manager of the operating system, and the application program need not be concerned with them. The answer is definitely no. Depending on the information system being developed, there may be requirements whose implementation requires development of tasks that are not directly named in the SRS document but are needed to satisfy the requirements that are stated in the SRS document. These requirements are usually called derived requirements.

Tasks may be categorized as critical, noncritical, priority-oriented, event-oriented, independent, and dependent. Independent tasks may be performed concurrently or sequentially. Dependent tasks must be performed in an order that satisfies the dependency relationship between tasks and optimizes performance. Sometimes dependency is caused by one task requiring the output of another task to operate; sometimes two tasks may be dependent because they must share the same resources.

When there is a set of independent tasks, there is a need for a new task called the coordinator task. The design of the task management component for a system needs to: (1) study the OOA results and identify all the tasks that may be needed, (2) define each task using a template similar to that of an object, and (3) state the nature of the task as being time driven, event driven, prioritized, resource sharing, independent, dependent, etc.

In defining each task we must provide the following within the body of the task: task name, description, priority, services, messages or communication lines, and coordinator task. Specifically, the means by which a task is coordinated with the rest of the system should be explained. Also, the input/output for the tasks including the source for the input and the sink for the output should be identified through the communication definition.

Each defined task must be challenged to ensure that it is really needed. In other words, each task should be considered as a candidate for deletion until its inclusion is clearly shown to be a necessity. This approach should identify tasks that could be eliminated without creating any side effect in the overall performance of the system. We should not attempt to eliminate coordinator tasks. It is true that a coordinator task will add complexity and overhead to the software product, but it will provide another layer of abstraction. That is, all task communications are conducted through the task coordinator.

8.5.4 Data Management

Each information system will require access to one or more databases for data acquisition and possibly data store operations. The main objective of the data management component is to provide the infrastructure for the storage and retrieval of objects. Any of the following design approaches may prove effective: individual file management systems, relational database systems, or object-oriented database systems.

The individual file management system or as it is called by Coad and Yourdon, the flat file system, is a design of the past. However, it does provide simple sequential access to files and allows for individual files to be sorted if such ordering is beneficial.

Relational database systems store object classes in the form of named tables. Each row of the table may be considered as an individual object and a table may be a class of objects. Tables may be related to each other by the structural relationship defined between object classes. Each database management system (DBMS) provides access to the database in a variety of ways that may be adjusted to access objects stored in a relational database. Operations are provided to facilitate cut and paste of columns in the tables or among the tables. Other operations allow the reorganization of columns in a table for redundancy purposes.

The main concern in storing objects using a relational data model is the redundancy problem. In a relational data model there are five levels of data redundancy known as normal forms. The first normal form is the lowest level of data redundancy, and the fifth normal form is the highest level of data redundancy. The first normal form requires that the fields in the records (attributes in each row) be atomic data, that is, having a single value and no structure. In the second normal form, in addition to the conditions stated for the first normal form, each nonkey attribute must describe something uniquely identified by the key attribute. In the third normal form, in addition to the conditions set for the second normal form, each nonkey attribute depends only on the key attribute and is not a description of a nonkey attribute. The fourth and fifth normal forms become more and more restrictive to the extent that no relational database system has yet attempted fully to adopt fourth and fifth normal forms.

Object-oriented database systems are beginning to appear in the commercial market. They provide certain facilities that simplify storage and access of objects. The combination of object-oriented programming languages and object-oriented database management systems suggests a separate platform for data management in OOD.

8.5.5 Designing Services

In OOD there are, practically speaking, n levels (where n is typically 4) of design. Level 1, and in some cases part of the level 2 design, is the direct result of the OOA process. Other levels of design start from definition of services, identification of messages, and evolution of message communications to the actual pseudocode design for each service, message communication, task, etc. Different designers may divide the distance between the results in the OOA document and detailed pseudocode into different formal refinement levels. Also, a service or a task may dictate, based on its complexity, the number of levels of refinement required by that service or task. A common number of design levels is four, with an understanding that not all the services must go through four levels of design. There may be services and tasks that require more than four levels of design as well as those that may require two or three design levels.

Services are at the heart of an OOA/OOD process. The attributes of an object are the data to be processed by the services defined in the object. Therefore without the services, data are not actually processed but rather, moved around. In order to design services for an object we must first identify the states of the objects and then decide what services are required to arrive at the next logical state of the object. We must also design communication messages to facilitate communications among objects.

Services may be categorized as simple or complex. Examples of simple services are Create (Object), Connect (Object_i, Object_j), Access (Object), Store (Object), and Free (Object). Each of these services may be included in a given object. They must simply verify the existence of the necessary environment for the service to be performed. For example, in order to create a new object, Employee, we must check the Employee file for a new employee name, then gather values for each attribute needed for the employee object. If all the values are proper, we then create a new object, Employee, and place it in its own class.

Algorithmically complex services perform complex computations and also perform monitoring of external and internal devices. Often control services are among the most computationally complex services. Some task management services and task control and monitor services are also algorithmically complex.

The reader is encouraged to read the summary of OOA and OOD strategies presented in Appendices B and C of reference [3]. A number of guidelines and suggestions are given in this reference that can be appreciated only when read in context.

8.6 CHAPTER SUMMARY ■

This chapter has presented a complete object-oriented paradigm for software requirement analysis, design, and design implementation. The chapter began with a discussion of how the problem domain, whose initial abstractions are most often rooted in function and performance terminology, can be translated into object-oriented terminology and graphic symbols. The object-oriented terminology of Coad and Yourdon was selected as representative and defined along with its associated graphic symbols.

Some important guidance was provided to help in recognizing objects, classes, and subjects in the problem space; establishing class and object attributes and associations; developing relevant hierarchies and structures; and defining services and messages. Time-dependent requirements (essentially the behavior of objects and classes in the time domain) were treated in terms of their effect on messages and services. It should be noted that chapter 19 addresses real-time processes in a broader and more comprehensive manner. The importance of the operational timeline in object-oriented analysis, design, and implementation was emphasized. In fact, operational timeline development is an essential step in any analysis and design paradigm. The value of developing these timelines as early as possible in the analysis phase was emphasized.

Object-oriented design was addressed in section 8.5. Change management and control issues, human-to-computer interfaces (more fully discussed in chapter 20), task management, data management, and service design issues were discussed.

The chapter emphasizes the potential advantages intrinsic to an object-oriented approach to system analysis and design and software product specification and design. There is, however, an underlying recognition that object-oriented methodology is not a "silver bullet." There is as yet no hard evidence that the object-oriented approach is significantly better than any other approach. Moreover, unless the process and discipline of software engineering are applied in concert with an object-oriented methodology, the object-oriented approach may indeed be significantly worse.

8.7 EXERCISES   ■

1. Prepare an object-oriented model representing each of the following machines:
    a. An electronic typewriter with spell-checker.
    b. A telephone answering machine.
    c. A cruise control for a car.
    d. A change machine capable of changing quarters, half-dollar coins, dollar coins, dollar bills, 5-dollar bills, and 10-dollar bills. The rule for change is to produce the minimum number of coins with maximum variety. For example, for a ten-dollar bill the machine produces one 5-dollar bill, one 2-dollar bill, 2 one-dollar bills, 3 quarters, two dimes, and a nickel.
    e. An automatic teller machine.
    f. A stamp machine.
    g. A soft-drink machine.
2. Create an object diagram for the following problems:
    a. A system to transfer data between two computers over a data communication line.
    b. A system for distributing electronic mail over a local area network. Each user should be able to send e-mail from any number of accounts and should be able to receive e-mail on only one account.
3. Suppose you are asked to prepare a software product for a specific sport tournament. There are N teams in the tournament. Each team has M members and A alternates. There are S playing sites. Each team must play S games, one game at each of the S sites. After a team has played at all S sites once, at any time during the tournament that the team loses more than it wins, the team is dropped from the tournament. Develop an object-oriented diagram representing this tournament.
4. Consider the following function-oriented requirement specification:

   The software shall establish an absolute time base to an accuracy of ± 1 millisecond. The software shall sample the X, Y, and Z sensors 20 times per second. The time between the X,

Y, Z samples shall be less than 2 milliseconds. The time between individual sensor samples shall be 50 milliseconds ±5 milliseconds. Sensor samples shall be tested for reasonable values using a stored table. Sensor samples shall be tested for reasonable changes between consecutive sensor readings.

Design an object-oriented model representing these requirements.

5. Define objects, messages, attributes, and associations for the following requirement specification:

The software shall download a complete customer record. The key field shall be customer identification number. The software shall use credit card number and type to confirm customer credit status. Credit card number and type shall be encrypted and forwarded by the software to the credit check software product. The software shall decrypt and display to the operator results returned from the credit check software product.

Make whatever reasonable assumptions are needed to work the problem.

6. Give an object-oriented analysis of the order processing organization of the ABC mail-order company as discussed in chapter 2.

7. Give an OOA for an automated teller machine (ATM). Each ATM is connected to a main computer that reroutes transactions to one of many banks connected to the ATM. Each bank has many customers who are issued an ATM card and are expected to use their cards in any ATM station. Discuss the needs of such a system and include the essential needs in your design.

8. Many conventional data structures may be defined as objects or classes. Define a complete object diagram to represent each of the following data structures: arrays, stacks, queues, lists, linked lists, binary trees, sets, disjoint sets, and binary search trees. List attributes, services, and message lines for each of the structures.

9. Define the cover page of a typical newspaper as an object diagram. Expand your definition to define the Sunday *New York Times* using object diagrams.

10. Give an OOA and OOD for a solitaire game.

11. Design an object-oriented solution for a tournament scoring system. The objects of such systems are season, meet, event, judge, league, team, etc.

12. Define a plastic money system in which each person has only a single plastic card. Real money or cash has no meaning in this system. What would be the role of banks in such a system? Would only one bank be enough? Define the objects and classes for this system. Investigate the services, communications, and message connections for each object or class in this system.

13. One of the main concerns in many information systems is the development of a method of storing data that is not volatile in case of power failure or hardware crash. Some answers may be as follows: reset everything anytime the system is turned on, never turn the power off, keep continuous back-up copies, use special battery-powered memory, or use data communication lines to send data outside the processing environment.
   a. Give a few suggestions of your own.
   b. Compare the solutions based on reliability, low cost, ease of implementation, maintenance, and retrieval and storage speed.

14. Use object-oriented specification tools and techniques and data dictionary (as needed) to prepare an OOA for the following problems:
   a. A vending machine that sells hot coffee, hot tea, and hot chocolate. Coffee may be decaffeinated or regular, with or without sugar, with or without cream, and strong or

normal. Tea may be decaffeinated or regular and with or without sugar. Hot chocolate may be regular or diet.

b. The game of bridge.

c. An automobile cruise control system.

d. A complete voice mail system.

e. A complete e-mail system.

15. a. Prepare a function-oriented SRS for an automated teller machine.

b. Apply OOA techniques and tools to arrive at an OOA document.

c. Prepare the first- and second-level OOD for this problem. Assume the detailed pseudocode is achieved at the fourth level of OOD.

16. Do problem 15 for a cigarette vending machine that reads a magnetized ID card for age verification. Develop the OOA document in two ways as described in problem 15 or directly from the statement of the problem. Compare the results for accuracy, time, cost, understandability, and reusability.

17. Create an object diagram for each of the following problems:

a. A spell-check system.

b. A system that transfers data between two computers over the telecommunication lines. Data shall not be lost under any circumstances. All exchanges of data must be acknowledged; the absence of data exchange must also be indicated.

c. A system that records the sales of lottery tickets. The system shall compute the jackpot on a continuous basis.

18. Consider the SRS developed in exercise 4.4.2 of chapter 4. Using the function-oriented SRS, develop an OOA document for the same problem.

References

1. P. Coad and E. Yourdon, *Object-Oriented Analysis*, Ed. 2, Prentice-Hall, Upper Saddle River, N.J., 1991.

2. ———. *Object-Oriented Design*, Prentice-Hall, Upper Saddle River, N.J., 1991.

3. P. Coad and J. Nicola, *Object-Oriented Programming*, Yourdon Press Computing Series, Prentice-Hall, Upper Saddle River, N.J., 1993.

4. D. L. Parnas, "On the Criteria to be Used in Decomposing Systems into Modules," *Comm. ACM* 15(12), pages 1053–1058, 1972.

5. J. Rumbaugh, M. Blaha, W. Premerlani, F. Eddy and W. Lorensen, *Object-Oriented Modeling and Design*, Prentice-Hall, Upper Saddle River, N.J., 1991.

Additional Reading

6. G. Booch, *Object-Oriented Design*, Ed. 2, Benjamin-Cummings, Redwood City, Calif., 1994.

7. Anton Eliens, *Principles of Object-Oriented Software Development*, Addison-Wesley, Reading, Mass., 1995.

8. Ian Graham, *Migrating to Object Technology*, Addison-Wesley, Reading, Mass., 1995.

9. M. Lorenz, *Object-Oriented Software Design: A Practical Guide*, Prentice-Hall, Upper Saddle River, N.J., 1993.

10. M. Lorenz and J. Kidd, *Object-Oriented Software Metrics*, Prentice-Hall, Upper Saddle River, N.J., 1995.

Implementation and Maintenance

Once we have come to understand thoroughly *what* the software product must do in terms of a requirement specification and have established *how* the software product will do it in terms of a design specification (PDL for example), then the software product design abstraction must be implemented or realized in the selected language statements (coded), tested comprehensively, revised as needed, and finally, maintained during its operational lifetime. Unit 3 focuses on the implementation phase of the software development life cycle. The unit begins with a chapter (9) on coding fundamentals. This chapter is followed by a chapter (10) on testing at the software product level and system level. We feel that the reader will be better served by having a sense of what testing in the large is all about before considering software module-level testing in chapter 11. We have leaned heavily on proven IEEE and DOD standards as well as on our own experience in structuring the testing chapters (10 and 11). A separate chapter (12) is devoted to debugging. Chapter 13 is devoted to maintenance and maintainability. The maintenance phase of a software development life cycle (SWDLC) is often characterized (with justification) as a microcosm of the complete SWDLC.

Chapter 9 classifies and describes programming languages from a software engineering point of view and defines some of the important terminology. The specific features of programming languages that are essential aids to the coder or programmer are described. Criteria for selecting a programming language for a specific application are considered. The chapter discusses programming style and presents 27 simple rules whose application will lead to developing a good programming style. Internal documentation or comment statements, often a major factor in the maintainability of a software product and a component of programming style, are discussed and guidance in their effective use is provided. Quality attributes associated with or intrinsic to the coding phase are discussed and means for quantifying or evaluating the programming or coding quality of a software product is described. The main theme expressed in chapter 9 is that although coding is only a small component of the software development life cycle, how a software product is coded can exert a strong influence on its testing, debugging, maintenance, and maintainability.

Chapter 10 treats testing in the broadest context. The purpose is to show the complete setting within which software is ultimately tested for acceptance. This test environment will typically include all elements of the operational environment—hardware, software, people, operational timelines, etc. The chapter emphasizes the importance of planning in the test process and describes how a test plan is constructed. Software test and integration is conducted at the end of the software development life cycle when schedule slack has been used up and contingency funds have been spent. In this environment it is tempting to cut corners and skip tests. The message of the chapter is that testing discipline must not be compromised if the software product is to meet its requirements. Software integration and testing is a documentation-driven process. A description of the documentation structure and document content is a convenient way to describe the process. The documentation descriptions provide enough guidance and required content detail to enable an entry-level software engineer to develop a credible first draft of each of the documents.

Chapter 11 addresses the module-level test process. The chapter considers static and dynamic testing, white and black box testing, and cyclomatic complexity as important tools in effective module testing. An approach that uses cyclomatic complexity and basis paths to find the minimum number of paths through a module and then uses black box testing techniques to complete white box tests is described in chapter 11. Formal testing methods are also discussed in chapter 11 and several examples are worked out. The chapter concludes with a description of specifically how test cases are executed, how test logs are maintained, how anomalies and incidents that occur during testing are documented, and how each sequence of module tests is summarized.

Chapter 12 discusses a systematic procedure for isolating, identifying, and confirming the fault that caused the failure during module test, system test, or field operation. Regression testing is discussed and an extensive practical example is worked out to illustrate an application of the debugging process to a real problem.

Chapter 13 addresses software maintenance and maintainability issues. A great deal of a software engineer's time is spent either maintaining an existing software product or developing a software product so that it may be easily maintained in its operational phase. Three different types of maintenance actions are described. The chapter depicts a generic maintenance process and identifies those activities and tasks during software development that directly influence the maintainability of a software product. A method for estimating maintenance costs for a software product is discussed. Reverse engineering and reengineering as related to software products are also discussed.

Unit 3 is a comprehensive discussion of the problem of converting a software design specification (program design language) into a fully tested software product and maintaining the product during its operational lifetime. The unit also links those development activities and software attributes that most strongly influence software product testability, debugging, and maintainability. The central theme is that what happens during requirement specification, design specification, and coding dictates what will happen in testing and ultimately how the quality of the software will be perceived.

9

Fundamentals of Coding

9.0 OBJECTIVES ◼

Programming, or as it is commonly called, coding, means translating the detailed design of a software product, developed during the design phase, into a sequence of statements that can be executed by a computer. The program statements are sometimes called code, and the programmers are often called coders. The main goal of coding or programming is to translate the design specification of a software element into programming language statements. The main objective of this chapter is to provide guidelines that will enable a programmer to produce an executable program from a given design so that less time is spent in testing and maintaining the end product. In other words, the main objective of this chapter is to illustrate how a software product design can be most effectively realized in code. Other objectives are (1) to discuss the selection criteria for the implementation language, (2) to present style rules that will assist in producing good quality code, and (3) to discuss program quality and cite one way that program quality can be measured. We believe that the nature of programming is as much a craft as it is a science. Its craft is mastered by years of practice and its underlying scientific nature requires a mature, logical thought process.

9.1 INTRODUCTION ◼

A software product will spend only a small fraction of its total development time in the coding phase. The time spent in testing and integration of a large software product is as much as four times greater than the time spent in coding the product. Readable, well-structured code can reduce test and integration time as well as improve maintainability of a software product. It should be clear that during the coding phase the programming team should not try to reduce coding resources, reduce scheduled coding time, reduce module size (SLOC), or create multipurpose subprograms through extensive argument lists at the expense of code simplicity and quality. Attempts to achieve any of these goals may have an adverse effect on later phases. Instead, the programming team should attempt to reduce the cost of subsequent phases by producing better structured, more readable code.

The coding phase of a software development cycle represents only about 10% to 15% of the total software cost. A 20% increase in the cost of coding represents only 2% to 3% of the total development cost. If this additional effort results in a better-structured, better-commented, and more readable code, the benefits that accrue during test and integration and during the operational phase will more than make up for any additional costs incurred during coding.

Several evaluation criteria are used in judging the quality of a program. These criteria include size (in SLOC), memory utilization, readability, execution time, cyclomatic complexity, and algorithmic complexity. If certain software design information was given to several different people, each of whom was given different evaluation criteria for coding the design, the result would be drastically different programs. For instance, the person asked to develop the fastest program would have a different program from the person asked to write the shortest (fewest SLOC) program.

The use of various reviews, inspections, and walk-throughs in today's software development environment has a leveling effect on the code produced. The tendency is to impose a group style on the code. In addition, the SRS often imposes requirements that implicitly influence programming style. In summary, readability, ease of understanding and comprehension are important criteria in judging the quality of a software product.

9.2   PROGRAMMING LANGUAGES   ■

Over 250 commercial programming languages are in use today. A commercial programming language is defined as a recognized language that is available for purchase and is supported (maintained). Also, a commercial programming language is supported by standard compilers, input/output access, utilities, documentation, library, etc. Programming languages can be categorized in many different ways. Some of the categories are as follows: procedural, nonprocedural, imperative, declarative, functional, logic, object-oriented, fourth generation, and fifth generation [3]. Some of these categories overlap, and some languages belong to more than one category. It is not our goal to discuss detailed characteristics of each of these categories. Moreover, it is not clear that such distinct characteristics exist. However, it is beneficial to give an overview of each of these categories of programming languages.

Procedural Languages

A procedural programming language provides the means for a programmer to define precisely each step in the performance of a task. That is, the programmer knows what is to be accomplished by a program and provides, through the language, step-by-step instructions on how the task is to be done. Using a procedural language, the programmer specifies language statements to perform a sequence of algorithmic steps. For example, if the task is to compute the average of three numbers, a procedural language will direct the computer through language statements to add the three numbers by adding the first two, then adding the third one to the result, and then dividing the sum of the three numbers by 3 to obtain the average of the three numbers. Examples of procedural languages are Ada, Algol68, BASIC, C, C++, CLU, COBOL, Fortran, Forth, Modula-2, and Pascal.

Nonprocedural Languages

In a nonprocedural language the programmer tells the computer, through the language, what must be done, but leaves the details of how to perform the task to the language itself. For example, given the problem of computing the average of three numbers, a nonprocedural language would require the programmer to state: Compute the average of X, Y, Z. Examples of nonprocedural languages are SQL, dBase, ADS, and Paradox. Note that fourth-generation languages are all considered nonprocedural.

Imperative Languages

In an imperative language, expressions are computed and results are stored as variables. Language control structures direct the computer to execute an exact sequence of statements. Most procedural languages, especially the ones we know as high-level languages, are imperative languages. Examples of some of the imperative languages are COBOL, Fortran, Basic, Pascal, Modula-2, C, C++, and Ada.

Declarative Languages

The semantic definitions in declarative languages are called declarative semantics. In an imperative language, say Ada, the programmer is required to keep track of many elements that may be distributed throughout the program. These elements include type definitions, data structure definitions, and scoping. In contrast, in a declarative semantic the meaning of an expression is contained within the expression itself [5]. Most logic programming languages are considered declarative languages.

Functional Languages

As the name implies, the basic difference between this family of languages and imperative languages is that in functional languages every entity is a function. A function in functional languages has the same meaning as a function in mathematics. In mathematics a function has a name and one or more arguments. So it is with a functional programming language. Problem solving for implementation in functional programming languages requires a fundamentally different approach. One cannot design a solution in an imperative language such as Pascal and then code the design in a pure functional language. In a pure functional language functions are all that is available. Lisp is the oldest and most widely used functional programming language. There are different dialects of Lisp available, and some versions are modified to have the characteristics of imperative languages, such as control structures. However, pure Lisp is fully functional. Examples of some other functional programming languages are FP, Miranda, ML, Hope, and FQL. Both functional and imperative languages are mainly procedural languages.

Logic Languages

As the name indicates, these languages are designed around mathematical logic, predicate calculus, and lambda calculus. The objective of the design of logic programming languages is to use mathematical propositions to define objects and operations on objects. Languages used for logic programming are usually declarative languages. As Slonneger and Kurtz [6] state, ''Logic programming allows a programmer to describe the logical structure of a problem rather than prescribe how a computer is to go about solving it.'' Prolog is a widely used logic programming language. Other logic programming languages are SASL, HASL, LOGLISP, and FUNLOG [5]. Logic programming languages, with the exception of Prolog and all of its variations, are not yet fully practical.

Object-Oriented Languages

Recently the term *object-oriented* has become a buzzword in the computing industry. The first truly object-oriented programming language was Smalltalk. In the view of some programmers and users Smalltalk is still the only truly object-oriented language. Smalltalk was originally designed as an object-oriented programming language, whereas many other object-oriented languages are modifications or addendums to existing languages. Examples of such object-oriented languages are Objective C, C++, and Object Pascal. Three main characteristics separate a procedural language from an object-oriented language. Object-oriented languages define and use classes, inheritance, and polymorphism. The DOD, FAA, and NASA have designated Ada 95 as their standard object-oriented programming language. You may be surprised to learn that Ada 95 is the first object-oriented language to be standardized by ISO and ANSI.

Visual Languages

The rapid development in Graphic User Interface (GUI) environment and its acceptance in the user community has encouraged the introduction of a series of languages called visual languages. Example of such languages are Visual Basic, Visual C++, Visual Foxpro and Visual Pascal. As the name of these languages indicates, they are the implementation of the existing languages in GUI environment. The main characteristic of these languages is their graphic interactive communications with the user. The visual languages are gaining popularity in application development environments. For small application programs, visual languages may prove to be very effective. The contribution of visual languages to the field of software engineering remains to be seen.

Fourth-Generation Languages (4GL)

During the 1970s and early 1980s many languages were developed whose main goal was to be nonprocedural and very easy to learn and use. These languages were put into a new category called fourth-generation languages. The original goal was to give users the capability to define, design, and develop application software that normally would have required the services of a system analyst/designer and a professional programmer. This approach to satisfying the information system needs of the user community has been a successful strategy.

The combination of 4GLs and databases created powerful database management systems. Examples of 4GLs are ADF, ADS, APL, Application Factory, DMS, Focus, Intellect, Natural,

Ramis II, SQL, System W, and Use-It. Many of these languages are available, and some are implemented for PC platforms [3].

Fifth-Generation Languages (5GL)

In the view of many authors and researchers we do not have, as yet, a fifth-generation language. The 5GLs are supposed to make communication with computers as easy as communication with another person and possibly with the same tools—voice and vision.

9.2.1 Specific Programming Language Features

Each programming language must provide a means for implementing certain essential features, such as sequential structures, selection structures, and iteration structures. Other features are specific to one language and not available in another. For instance, data abstraction is directly available in some languages such as CLU or Ada and not available as a fully complete feature in other languages such as COBOL or BASIC. In this section we list some of the more popular and useful features found in programming languages. Not all of the listed features are useful or needed in all applications. The software engineer and the programmer must study the design details of the software and list the features they consider to be (1) essential, (2) good to have, and (3) not important. The list can be used as guidance in selecting a language for the application.

Preprocessor

There are programming languages that provide some form of preprocessor. Some of the tasks performed by a preprocessor are indentation, line numbering, level numbering, printing each subprogram on a separate page, and creating structure charts for flow of control among subprograms. Some preprocessors can, with a single key stroke or a combination of two keys, type specific key words of the language. Some preprocessors attempt to add internal documentation to the program. An Ada preprocessor prompts the programmer, with a series of menus, to follow a prescribed structure.

Naming Constraints

The lexical rules applied in naming an entity in a program are referred to as identifier definition or naming. The more flexible the identifier definition rules are, the more specific and meaningful the identifier can be. Most languages allow the use of letters and digits in naming a program entity. Some languages limit the size of a name (the number of letters and digits) to use in the program to a small number, for example, 6 in Fortran 77. Other languages have a high size limit, say 30, and others may have no limit on the size of names.

Named Constants

Some programming languages allow the programmer to define named constants in the program. Some even allow the programmer to define named constant expressions. There is no difference between a constant name and a variable name except that a constant name may not be redefined during execution. The advantage of being able to define named constants in a program is that the value of these named constants will be assigned at compile time and won't take any execution time. Also, definition of named constants provides some help in modification of a program and may also help in program readability.

User-Defined Data Type

This added feature allows programmers to define data types other than the basic types provided by the language itself. The use of this feature can effect the readability of a program and its structure. For example, suppose we wish to define an array to store the population of each state in the United States, broken down by sex and race for all fifty states. One such declaration might be a three dimensional array (one dimension for States, one for Sex and one for Race) as follows:

Population: Array of [1 . . . 50,1 . . . 2,1 . . . 4] of integer;

Suppose the content of Population [1, 2, 2] is found to be 78,980. Without reading program comment statements or understanding what is represented by each index of the array, it is impossible to know that 78,980, for example, is the number of black females in the state of Alabama. This program would be regarded as having poor readability because it places a burden on comment statements for explanation. Now consider the following user-defined type declaration:

State = (Alabama, Alaska, Arizona, . . . ,Wyoming);
{note that . . . must be replaced by names of all 46 states arranged alphabetically between Arizona and Wyoming.}
Sex = (Male, Female);
Race = (White, Black, Native_American, Asian);
State_Index = Alabama . . . Wyoming;
Sex_Index = Male . . . Female;
Race_Index = White . . . Asian;

Next we define Population using the user-defined types State_Index, Sex_Index, and Race_Index.

Population : Array[State_Index, Sex_Index, Race_Index] of integer;

With this new declaration, instead of writing

Population [1, 2, 2] := 78,980

We can write

Population [Alabama, Female, Black] := 78,980

Subprograms

This feature allows a programmer to split a program into smaller programs called functions, procedures, or other generic subprogram names. This feature is available in most commercial programming languages and provides help in structuring a program.

Most programming languages provide for two forms of subprograms. One form of subprogram is to compute a value and return the computed value. We call this kind of subprogram a function subprogram or just a function. The second form of subprograms is to perform a simple task. We call this kind of subprogram a procedure subprogram or just a procedure. Many languages use function and procedure as defined here. There are other programming languages that associate a procedure with a function that does not return a value. Our use of function and procedure should not be identified with the syntax of the words "function" and "procedure" in a programming language like Pascal.

Recursive Subprograms

A programming language that allows a subprogram to call itself directly or through intermediate calls is said to have a recursive programming feature. Recursive programming simplifies certain algorithms, and it is an advantage to have this feature available. Excessive and unwise use of the recursive feature in a programming language may, on the other hand, slow the execution of a program and waste memory. Therefore it is advisable to use this feature carefully.

Scoping

This term refers to how data can be moved or shared between the main program and its subprograms as well as among subprograms. In a program we may have global definitions, local definitions, and parameters or arguments that are defined in a subprogram declaration statement. Each language has its own method of passing information among subprograms and creating data communication paths between the main program and its subprograms.

Available Operations

Most programming languages provide basic arithmetic, relational, and logical operations. These operations are addition, subtraction, multiplication, division, less than, greater than, equal, not equal, less than or equal, greater than or equal, and, complement, and or. Other operations are available in some languages and not in others. Examples of such operations are raising integers and real numbers to a power, modulo division, integer division, set operations (union, intersection, subtraction, belong to, included in, and includes), and Boolean operations (Nand and Nor). A given application may use some of the nonregular operations. For these applications, in general it is advantageous to select an implementation language that provides those operations.

Variety of Control Structures

Control structures are statements or structures that control the flow of execution in a program. Iteration and selection structures are often called control structures. There are different ways to implement an iteration structure or a selection structure. For instance, condition-controlled and counter-controlled iterations are two forms of iteration structures. The condition-control structure itself divides into two groups: condition checked first (while condition do) and condition checked last (repeat . . . until condition). There are also a variety of selection structures: two-way selection, *m*-way selection, and case structure. A programming language may support certain structures directly and certain other structures indirectly. The direct availability of a given structure helps to create more readable programs.

Data Structure Support

Most programming languages provide for arrays, random access data structures, of one or more dimensions (or subscripts). Some languages provide for other data structures such as records, sets, stacks, queues, and heaps along with their appropriate operations. When the application being programmed is data structure–sensitive, it is advisable to look for a programming language that has an easy implementation of the structure(s) most needed in the application being programmed.

Data Abstraction and Information Hiding

Recently developed programming languages include facilities for data abstraction within their development environment. If the application requires information hiding (we think that the majority of applications will benefit from its use), we should look at languages that have information hiding and data abstraction features.

Memory Allocation

At program execution level the part(s) of the program being executed and the data being used must be loaded into the memory. Two general ways to assign memory to a block of code or to new data structures are called dynamic and static memory assignment. Some languages implement only static memory assignment, some languages provide only dynamic memory assignment, and some provide both types. If the application requires a large amount of memory to run, then the dynamic memory allocation may be advantageous.

File Handling Utilities

Most programming languages provide a window to the operating system for input and output handling. The use of a text file (file of characters) is common in almost any programming language. However, there are many other file organizations and access methods that a large software product may need to implement. Examples of such file structures are indexed-sequential files, direct files, hashed files, ring files, tree-structured files, hierarchically structured files, and distributed files. A programmer can create any of these files directly using her or his own programming knowledge. However, if a language has a predefined structure for some of these file organizations, the programmer can create the file structure by adding a few additional lines of code to the program.

Access to Other System Utilities

Every system environment has a library of prewritten and compiled programs that perform certain tasks. These programs are usually called utility programs. Examples of utility programs are text editors, sorters, searchers, graphic interfaces, file handlers, and data communication facilitators. Utility programs may be used independently while in the system environment. Some programming languages have the capability to transfer from program execution, use one or more utility programs and return to the transfer point. For example, in COBOL the sort utility may be called using a single command line inside the program. An example of such a program line would be as follows:

SORT Student-File ON ASCENDING KEY Student-Name, Phone

USING Scratch-File GIVING Sorted-Student-File.

where words in upper case letters are COBOL key words. Availability of utility programs within the programming language is often very helpful. Sometimes novice programmers attribute the availability of utility programs within a programming language to the power of the programming language.

Compilers

Compilers, in addition to translating a high-level language to object code executable by the host computer, perform some other tasks. Examples of such tasks are code optimization, code motion, memory management, ''garbage'' collection, and vectorization. Some compilers provide numerous on/off switches to be set at program compile time. These switches trigger certain activities within the compiler. Examples of such switches are out-of-range error switch, time-limit switch, optimization switches (there are multiple switches for optimization), and error switches.

Debuggers

A debugger is a software support tool that helps the programmer to walk through the program at his or her own speed while the program is being executed. Today, compilers with visual debuggers have become available. These compilers are capable of placing the execution path of the program on the screen and showing the content of each selected variable on the screen as the program is being executed. Debuggers may discourage an inexperienced programmer, but they are powerful tools for performing dynamic desk checking of programs while the program is being executed.

Programming Language Library

Each programming language has a library of functions and procedures of its own. The more extensive the library, the more services are provided by the language. Unfortunately, the library must be linked with the compiled program, which is somewhat similar to adding the size of the entire library to the program during table linkage. There are other implementation disadvantages that limit the addition of large libraries to a language. However, a large and powerful library would prove very useful to a large software project.

Exception Handling

Some languages have no capability to recover from a run-time error or any other exceptions that occur. Programs written using these languages will be likely to experience problems in both application and operational environments. Each of us has had the experience, at one time or another, of being left with a blank screen in the middle of a program execution with no alternative other than to reboot the system. Exception handling means that in exceptional situations the program communicates with the operator instead of crashing, or even better, allows the programmer to predefine what is to be done for each run-time error and exception. Many languages have a feature equivalent to the ON ERROR clause in COBOL. However, exception handling requires more. There are many different forms of run-time error and exceptions that require special attention. For example, there are several run-time errors associated with input/output operations such as record length too high, incompatible record format, overflow, key does not exist, duplicate keys, improper file status, improper access clearance, file does not exist, etc. Exception handling should be able to recover from any of these and other situations; the language should provide the programmer with the ability to recover from each of the exception cases.

Real-Time Considerations

Real-time applications have many special compiler needs that are applicable only to real-time software products. If there are concerns about such needs, we must be sure that the language and its environment provides help for those needs. For example, if certain tasks must be completed in a specific time interval or certain events must be responded to within a given time, the language must have the capability to account accurately for real time with the appropriate resolution. Ada 95 (and to a lesser degree Ada 84) contain features that provide support to real-time requirements.

Concurrency Considerations

Some languages provide facilities for concurrent execution of programs or tasks. Language constructs that support concurrent task execution provide support for applications in which many events occur concurrently. Examples of such applications are operating systems, database systems, and certain real-time systems. Concurrent programming, in addition to facilitating the execution of concurrent events, can help speed up execution of the program. Some of the programming languages that support concurrent programming are Concurrent C, Concurrent Pascal, Ada, Modula-2, and Concurrent Euclid. If an application calls for heavy use of the concurrency features of a programming language, it is better to select a programming language that provides such features directly.

Parallelism Considerations

Taking full advantage of parallel architecture requires the cooperative efforts of both hardware and software. Having a parallel machine and programming it as if it were a serial machine will not produce the desired performance gains. Therefore, if an application requires high computation speeds, software engineers and programmers must assure themselves that the design and coding approach make full use of the resource before coding the software.

9.2.2 Selecting a Programming Language

The programming language to be used for the software product may have already been defined in the SRS document. In this case, the software engineers and the programming team must carefully evaluate project needs against the specified programming language. If the language meets or almost meets all the requirements of the software product, the implementation should use the specified language. On the other hand, if the language specified is not an optimum choice, then the development team must prepare a strong case to convince the client that the recommended language is not a good choice. A convincing argument must be backed up by facts to show the effect of the recommended or required language on the cost and schedule. Appendix C describes a process for preparing such an argument.

The decision criteria include, in addition to the technical requirements imposed by the nature of the application and software design, the following:

Compiler Status How well documented is the compiler? How well maintained is the compiler? Is the compiler certified? Standardized?

Programming Team Familiarity and Experience At least half of the members of the programming team should have extensive background and experience in the programming language used for coding. Those with less experience in the specific programming language should be assigned simpler modules to code until they gain more experience in the language.

Availability of Training The language maintainer should provide for audio and video tapes, professional development courses, etc., as part of the training package.

Language Library The language should have a strong library, relative to the application being coded.

For each development situation, individual decision criteria should be expanded into more detail, and a means should be found for quantifying each language in terms of the criteria. The decision criteria should be weighted and the trade-off matrix filled in as described in Appendix C.

9.3 PROGRAMMING STYLE AND PROGRAM QUALITY

■

One definition for the word *style* is, "A manner of expression or speaking, characteristic manner of expression, execution or design, . . ." As applied to programming, style dictates the manner in which the program is expressed in the language syntax and semantic.

Design reviews, inspections, code walk-throughs, and desk checking tend to impose a group or standard style on the software produced by a software development team. Often the language itself exerts an influence on programming style, which is probably desirable because consistency in style leads to improved readability and understandability. A program developed using a good programming style would be readable, understandable, structured, robust, efficient, and at least partially reusable.

9.3.1 Simple Style Rules

The following are some rules and guidelines that will lead to a better programming style:

1. Make identifier names as meaningful as possible. Never use names and identifiers that need to be explained, using comment statements.
2. Avoid using identifiers such as SUB1, SUB2, TOTAL_1, TOTAL_2, etc. It is common, for instance, to mistype SUB2 for SUB1. This kind of typographical error won't be diagnosed by the compiler and may cause program logic errors.
3. Never use the same name to mean two different things in two different places. For example, having a global variable called NUM and a local variable with the same name and with a different purpose may cause confusion at debugging time.
4. Use local definitions, data types, and identifiers for local purposes. The overuse of global definitions may save a few lines of code but it will probably cost hours of debugging and frustration.

5. If the programming language being used does not support some desired feature, do not try to create the feature in an artificial manner. Simplicity is the key element in the successful completion of a program. Shortcuts, tricky code, and complicated algorithms will conceal errors and reduce readability.

6. If your programming language provides for function subprograms (functions that return a value) and procedure subprograms (functions that return no value), use them appropriately. Use a function subprogram (functions that return a value) as it is used in mathematics. A function in mathematics has one or more arguments and produces one value. The arguments of a function are used to arrive at a single value called the result of the evaluation of the function. A mathematical function does not redefine or change the value of its arguments during a computation. Function arguments should not be used to return values to the calling program. In summary, a function should be simple and should compute one value. Use a function subprogram only in this manner.

7. Even if the programming language being used allows for a function without an argument, avoid using that feature. A function with no argument is easily confused with a single variable name.

8. A procedure (function that returns no value) is used to perform a simple task that may require multilayered computations. A procedure is task oriented and a function is value oriented. Use a procedure subprogram only to perform a simple task.

9. At the beginning of each subprogram, define arguments and their initial values. Also, for those arguments that return values to the calling program, define the value they must return. If the subprogram redefines any global variable, name the variable and give the nature of its modified value. For a function subprogram, define the value computed and returned by the function.

10. For control structures, the program control pointer must enter the structure at its entry point and leave the structure at its exit point. Do not create a conditional jump from the middle of a control structure to a point outside the structure. This shortcut may save execution time but it may also result in loss of readability, understandability, and comprehension.

11. If it is necessary to use nested control structures, limit the direct nesting to no more than three levels. Nested loops and if-then-else statements reduce the readability of the program. Too many nested subprograms make it extremely difficult to follow the logic of the program.

12. Use a GOTO, a BREAK or EXIT statement if and only if it can clarify a control structure or divide a long control structure in half. Limit use of GOTO statements to only these kinds of situations.

13. If the programming language being used provides for abstraction and information hiding, use this feature extensively. The less detail in evidence in a program, the clearer it looks. Extensive use and proper definition of abstract structures makes it easier for program segments to be reused.

14. To the extent possible, avoid defining subprograms whose execution will create side effects. Whenever there is a side effect, it should be clearly described.

15. Limit the number of formal arguments used in a subprogram to no more than five. Too many arguments reduces clarity and readability.

16. The better of two programs may not be the shorter of the two. The better program is simpler, clearer, easier to understand, and easier to maintain. Also, the fastest program is not necessarily the shortest program. Therefore, when developing a program avoid using difficult and tricky statements to shorten your program.

17. Adherence to structured programming principles will lead to a readable and easy-to-follow program.
18. Select data structures that are most appropriate from an efficiency point of view to implement the application being programmed.
19. Use abstraction in the design and coding of programs only to the extent that program readability is preserved. The use of abstraction helps to create reusable code.
20. Use those features of the programming language(s) that you know best. Misuse of a feature is much worse than not using that feature at all.
21. To the extent possible, avoid defining a function or procedure within a function definition.
22. You may define simple local functions or even procedures within another procedure, but only when doing so enhances program understanding.
23. Functions and procedures that act as utility subprograms should be defined at the start of the program. Such a subprogram should be identified as a utility subprogram. Examples of utility subprograms are Swap (X,Y) to swap the content of X and Y, or Sort (A, n) to sort the contents of array A $[1 \ldots n]$.
24. Consistent use of indentation makes your program easier to read.
25. Note that extensive use of system utilities makes the software less portable. Therefore, when portability is a requirement of the software product, the use of system utilities should be minimized.
26. For software products that are resident in only one operational environment, the use of system utilities can reduce the size of the software product and perhaps make it more efficient.
27. Effective use of comment statements strategically located in the code can enhance program understanding greatly. The use of informative comment statements has proven to be very helpful in maintaining software products.

The use of comment statements is mandatory in many software development environments. We devote the next section to a discussion of comment statements. In general, comment statements are used to extend the internal documentation of a program. Certain descriptive information and a sense of structure are implicit in the language statements themselves. Comment statements enlarge and expand on this information.

9.3.2 Comment Statements

We have already seen that some languages contain provisions for internal documentation as part of the syntax. Use of these features as well as additional comment statements can improve the maintainability of a program greatly. In spite of our best efforts to follow structured programming principles, correct use of the language's data description features, and good design practices, the understandability and comprehension of a program can be vastly improved by the addition of comment statements.

Comment statements fall into two categories: prologue and explanatory [2]. Prologue statements appear at the beginning of a program, subprogram, or block of executable statements. Some of the things that a prologue comment statement can do are as follows:

1. Describe briefly what the program, subprogram, or group of statements accomplishes
2. Provide a list of the important variables together with a one-line explanation of each variable
3. Provide a list of all data structures together with a brief description of their use

4. Provide a detailed list of all input data required
5. Provide a list of all output produced by the subprograms, program segments, and the entire program
6. List any special instructions needed to correctly execute subprograms and program modules
7. Identify the author, date of completion, company or institution, and related administrative information
8. List any subprograms contained within the program element and describe their individual task
9. Provide a summary description (or references) of any special methods or procedures used in the program element
10. Explain any special operating system and other system software instructions and operational needs
11. Describe any special cases that the program element cannot process
12. List all data and problem formulation and limitations intrinsic to the program element

Explanatory comments are used to clarify any program logic or structure that may, in the view of the programmer, be difficult for a reader to follow. We don't recommend extensive use of explanatory comments. Explanatory comments should not be used to compensate for poorly written code. The programmer should strive to develop code that requires little or no explanatory comment.

It is good programming style to clearly separate comment from executable statements by either inserting a blank line between comments and executable statements or by some easily distinguished feature such as indentation or asterisks. It is also important that comments be placed so that there is no confusion about what code the comment refers to. Good programming style should result in code that is easily read, understood, and comprehended even by the casual reader.

9.3.3 Program Quality

In this section the word *program* will be used to mean a software element ranging from a module to an entire software product. Although programming or coding consumes a small fraction (about 10% to 15%) of the entire software development cost and schedule, poorly written code can have a devastating effect. A badly written program prolongs testing and complicates maintenance. A poorly coded or programmed software product can quadruple life cycle cost.

A good program has certain measurable attributes. It should be noted at this point that many of these attributes can be specified in the SRS and tested during the test and integration phase. These attributes, when quantified, can also become quality assurance parameters to be followed by the quality assurance team. These attributes include the following:

Readability, Understandability, and Comprehensibility (RUC)

RUC refers to how easy it is to read the program, follow its logic and its structure, and understand and comprehend its logic. This is the most important feature of any program. These three attributes assist in debugging and maintenance. Most of the other program attributes discussed here will have a direct or indirect effect on the readability, understandability, and comprehensibility of the program. As we shall see, any experienced programmer can assign a value to the RUC attributes of a program or a module.

Logical Structure

This term refers to the logical way the program has been designed and implemented. A badly designed or unstructured program, among other things, has a high level of coupling and a low level of cohesion among its subprograms and may allow multiple entry and exit points in subprograms. It may also include many other ill-advised constructs. Application of structured programming rules will help create programs that are logically and structurally sound.

Physical Layout

Physical layout refers to the actual listing of the source code of a program. Good use of indentation, spacing, separation of key words from identifier, use of meaningful identifiers, extensive use of prologue comment statements, minimum use of explanatory comment statements, matching each "Begin" of a block with its "End," and clear separation of the comment statements from the program listing are among practices that can help to produce a good physical layout.

Robustness

Robustness refers to how well the program can handle incorrect input data. It is true that each software product has a user manual, and the user manual specifies how each input must be prepared and what the acceptable range is for each input. A software product must be protected against misuse and be designed to deal with bad input data. An application program that "dies," won't accept anymore input, or won't respond to any command after a bad input or other misuse is not considered robust. This attribute is often specified in the SRS and can be tested and measured during module and system testing.

CPU Efficiency (Speed of Execution)

This attribute refers to how fast the program executes. The speed of a program depends on two major factors, the hardware and the program itself. To be CPU efficient, a program must use fast and efficient algorithms, must make use of the available hardware capabilities, and must employ appropriate file and data structures and access methods. This attribute is often specified in terms of response time in the SRS document. Response time requirements will be extensively tested and measured during module and system testing. CPU utilization will also be measured during acceptance test.

Memory Efficiency

A program needs memory resources to operate. Memory is often a scarce resource in certain applications. If memory resources are indeed scarce, then a program should be designed to minimize use of computer memory. In general, programming should make efficient use of the memory resource without making memory efficiency a driving requirement. This attribute is often specified in the SRS and will be measured during module, system, and acceptance testing.

Complexity

This term accounts for both algorithmic complexity and cyclomatic or structural complexity (discussed in chapter 11). The less complex the algorithms used in implementing the program, the easier it is to understand the program. The less structural complexity, the fewer branches there are to follow and, hence, the easier it is to understand the program. The upper limit on cyclomatic complexity is often specified in the SRS and can be measured at any point during the development and testing process.

Human Factors

Ergonomics and human-to-computer interfaces play an important role in the success of a software product. Chapter 20 is devoted to designing for the human-to-computer interface. For instance, an input screen that is hard to read, has more fields than a person can easily comprehend, is not laid out properly, and is not robust with regard to human error will be rejected by users. The effect will be an economic failure for the software product. Human factors attributes should be and will be measured throughout the development cycle by real operators and users of the software product.

System Interfaces

This term refers to the interface between the system and the external environment. Many system interfaces are implemented in software. Over 50% of a software product's code is used to effect interfaces to users. Other interfaces to communication subsystems, actuators, and sensors are implemented at least partially through software.

Reusable Code

The cost of software development and the urgency in getting the software product to market in the shortest possible time have forced people to write segments of code that could be reused in different parts of the same product or even in a different software product. Hence, the reusability attribute of a program segment could be a measure of segment quality [4].

The preceding list does not include correctness. Correctness is the domain of testing. Testing is discussed in the next three chapters.

Each of the ten program or code attributes may be stated as an explicit or derived requirement in the SRS. For example, the SRS may contain the following requirement: ''All programs produced as a response to this specification shall follow the structured design and structured programming practices as specified in reference XXX.'' A formal requirement such as this would be a candidate for a quality measurement.

9.3.4 Quantifying Program Quality

Each of the ten program quality attributes just discussed may be assigned a weight of 0 to 10 and a raw score of 1 to 100. The weighting assigned to each attribute depends on the importance of each attribute to the software product and its operational environment and in meeting the SRS. The more important the attribute, the higher the weighting. The default weight value for each of the ten attributes is 1. The score assigned to each attribute is subjective and experience dependent. An independent team examines the program listing, its performance, its effectiveness in the user environment, its adherence to the standards and practices imposed by the SRS, and its proper use of the style guidelines to assign a score of 1 to 100 to the program for each of the ten quality attributes listed in Table 9.1.

The raw scores assigned to each attribute for a given program are independent of the program application area. However, the weight factors assigned to these ten attributes are application dependent and are fixed for a given module or even the entire software product. The weighted average of the ten weighted scores in Table 9.1 is called the composite measure of program quality [1].

In general, a program that is regarded as having met the style guidelines, is well commented, meets the standards and practices imposed by specifications, and responds favorably to the quality attributes would achieve a score of 90 or above. Programs that fall a little short of this goal would achieve a score between 80 and 90. Programs that are average would achieve a score between 70 and 80. A program that achieves a score below 70 points should be recoded and, if necessary, redesigned.

A simple method for quantifying the quality of the program code associated with a software product is outlined in this section. Chapter 18 addresses the topic of software quality and

■ TABLE 9.1 **Range for Quality Measure**

CHARACTERISTICS	RAW SCORE	WEIGHT	WEIGHTED SCORE
Readability, understandability, comprehensibility	80	10	800
Logical structure	75	8	600
Physical layout	80	5	400
Robustness	85	6	510
CPU Efficiency	85	3	255
Memory efficiency	80	6	480
Complexity	90	4	360
Human factors	80	8	640
System interfaces	80	8	640
Reusable code	60	2	120
Total		60	4805

....

Composite quality score = 4805/60 = 80.08

software quality assurance in a more general way. Program code as measured by the method described in this section is a candidate for a software quality attribute.

Table 9.1 is completed for a hypothetical example. The program in this example achieves a composite quality measure of 80.08. The composite quality measures of different modules of a software system are relative scores and can be effective comparisons among software modules in a development environment. If the quality assessment of the code is performed by an independent group with experience, scores may be more meaningful on an absolute basis.

The quality factors stated in Table 9.1 are not independent. In fact, some of them are very much dependent on each other. For instance, a program with a low score for its physical layout and its complexity cannot get a high score for readability and understandability. Therefore, in order to achieve a meaningful quality measure for a program, the quality evaluation team must be consistent in awarding scores.

Simply stated, in a competitive market a bad program is often much worse than no program at all. A bad program cannot be maintained effectively and will create a bad reputation for the developer that may be difficult to overcome.

The main purpose of a good coding or programming style is to produce a program that is of high quality. Programming style is best learned by practice. Sections 9.3.1 and 9.3.2 provide basic guidelines for producing a high-quality program.

9.4 Complete Programming Example

During the system planning phase of the XYZ project several software products were identified and requirements were allocated to each. This process resulted in the production of several separate SRS documents. During the final stages of SRS development and preliminary design of the software products, it became obvious that a simple line editor would be a required element in satisfying the SRS. For example, the following requirements appeared in several places:

Authorized operators shall be provided with the capability to enter system transactions via any workstation keyboard. A capability to execute these transactions individually immediately upon entry shall be provided. A capability to store a sequence of transactions for subsequent execution shall also be provided. The capability shall be provided for authorized operators to edit an existing transaction file. Authorized operators shall be able to view any lines in the transaction file, insert new line(s) any place in the transaction file, and delete one or more transactions from the transaction file.

A decision was made to establish a utility software product that would include a security module, a transaction interpreter module, and a simple line editor module. For each of these modules a new and separate SRS was developed from the requirements that were suballocated from other SRS documents. The new SRS for the line editor module also contained a description of the expected environment. In particular, the following requirements were stated:

Programming language:	Pascal, Ada 95, or C/C++
System environment:	VMS, Windows, or UNIX
Library:	Standard system library
Utilities:	Standard system utilities
PDL:	Pseudocode

Continued on the following page.

This example is concerned only with the design and implementation of the simple line editor module. We will assume that the SRS is already developed.

9.4.1 Top-Level Design Specifications

As a result of preliminary design efforts, the line editor requirements were allocated to a module called SIMPLE_LINE_EDITOR. The assigned software engineer developed a detailed description of the module interfaces and used an existing line editor as guidance for design of the SIMPLE_LINE_EDITOR. While the SRS was being completed, the preliminary design team met several times and formulated a first version of a design. The results of these meetings were documented as design guidelines and ground rules. The material developed as a result of these meetings will form the basis for the SDS document. A summary of the design guidelines and ground rules follows.

1. The name of the transaction file shall be provided by the operator, and the file that contains the edited transactions ready for execution shall be called Batch.Exe.
2. Whenever file Batch.Com is in use by the operator for possible editing, new batch transactions issued by users shall be written into the Batch.Tmp file.
3. When the operator has completed editing Batch.Com, one of the following shall be accomplished:
   a. The edited file is written into the Batch.Exe file to be executed under system control.
   b. The original copy of Batch.Com without any of the editing actions is retained and no file is submitted for execution.
4. Before the termination of the edit session, if the operator submits the edited file for execution, the transactions in the Batch.Com file shall be deleted, the transactions in the Batch.Tmp file shall be moved to the Batch.Com file, and the editing session shall be terminated.
5. If the operator decides not to submit the Batch.Com file for execution, no editing shall be performed on the Batch.Com file and the Batch.Tmp file shall be appended to the end of the Batch.Com file before terminating the editing session.
6. The name of the file being edited shall be specified. The software shall read the name of the file being edited from the keyboard. Similarly, the name of the file to append to Batch.Com shall be read from the keyboard. However, the file that receives the edited Batch.Com file is always called Batch.Exe.
7. The line editor shall perform the line commands described in Table 9.2 on the transaction file being edited. The first command shall always be the EDIT command, otherwise there will be no transaction file to edit. Also, the internal structure of the transaction file is a circular one. That is, if the current line is the last line and the command is FORWARD then the current line becomes the first line of the transaction file.
8. A command line for the editor shall have zero or more arguments. If an edit command is wrong, there shall be a message indicating so. If the line numbers of the commands are incorrect, they shall be corrected as follows:
   a. If a line number is less than 1, it shall be set to 1.
   b. If a line number is larger than the total number of lines in the file, it shall be set to the total number of lines in the file.
9. In the EDIT command the default file name is always Batch.Com. However, the program

■ TABLE 9.2   **Commands**

LONG	SHORT	ARGUMENTS	DESCRIPTION
EDIT	E	none	Reads the file into memory for editing.
PRINT	P	none	Prints the current line.
PRINT	P	n	Prints line n.
PRINT	P	-n	Prints from line 1 to line n.
PRINT	P	m-n	Prints from line m to line n.
			In each of the above PRINT commands line n becomes the current line.
PRINT	P	n-	Prints from line n to the end, first line becomes the current line.
DELETE	D	none	Deletes the current line. Next line becomes the current line.
DELETE	D	n	Deletes line n.
DELETE	D	-n	Deletes from line 1 to line n.
DELETE	D	m-n	Deletes from line m to line n.
			In each of the above DELETE commands line $n + 1$ becomes the current line.
DELETE	D	n-	Deletes from line n to the end. First line becomes the current line.
MOVE	M	n	Line n becomes the current line.
INSERT	I		Inserts as many lines as follow this command terminated by character @ on a line. Inserted lines go after the current line.
FORWARD	F		Current line becomes the next line.
BACKWARD	B		Current line becomes the previous line.
CLOSE	C		Save the edited file in Bacth.Exe file. Copy Batch.Tmp to the file being edited.
QUIT	Q		Do not submit the edited file for execution. Keep the file as it was before editing and append Batch.Tmp file to the end of it.

shall give the user a chance to enter the name of the file being edited if it is different from Batch.Com. If an invalid file name is provided or no file name is provided, the default file name must be used.

10. A variable called Current shall always identify the current line in the file unless the file is empty. When the transaction file is read into memory, the current line shall be the first line of the file. When the current line is the first line of the file, the BACKWARD command shall be ignored and a message shall be issued. When the current line is the last line of the file, the FORWARD command shall be ignored and a message shall be issued. When deleting a line, the next line shall become the current line. If more than one line is deleted, the line next to the last line deleted shall become the current line. When printing lines, the last line printed shall become the current line.

11. The length of a line in the transaction file shall always be less than or equal to 80 characters.

12. No matter what is entered as an editing command, the line editor shall provide either an error message or perform the command. No input condition shall cause the program or module to terminate in an error state.

13. To protect the program from being misused, if an authorized user enters a command line incorrectly three consecutive times, the program shall be terminated and a message issued.

14. When the transaction file in memory is empty, the only editing allowed shall be INSERT. Therefore, when the file is empty no other command shall be processed.
15. A command shall be given in a long form (the full word) or in a short form (the first letter of the command word). In either case a command word shall be separated from its possible arguments by one or more blank spaces.
16. Command words and their arguments are not case sensitive.

9.4.2 Analysis of Preliminary Design

A subsequent review of the top-level design notes and other related information revealed several problems. These problems were assigned to individuals for resolution. The problems and their resolution follow.

Problem I   Paragraph 7 and paragraph 10 are inconsistent. Paragraph 7 says the internal structure of the transaction file is circular and paragraph 10 says it is not circular. On the other hand, the DELETE command requires that when the last line of the file is deleted, the current line becomes the first line of the file.

Resolution   Paragraph 10 remains as stated and the last sentence of paragraph 7 is deleted. However we must set the current line to be the first line of the text when DELETE deletes the last line of the text.

Problem II   Paragraph 13 may be interpreted in several different ways: (1) only three errors are allowed, (2) only three errors per command are allowed, (3) only three consecutive errors are allowed, and (4) only three consecutive errors per command are allowed. Which of these interpretations should be implemented?

Resolution   Ignore paragraph 13 and let the user make as many errors as he wishes. That is, every time an error is made in entering a command line, the program shall issue an error message and continue. Note that, in general, this resolution is not acceptable because there is an implicit security problem associated with patterns of incorrect inputs. For example, when someone wants to break into a system, the first thing he or she does is provide random strings for password to the system. Therefore, in a security sensitive application we should not tolerate more than three consecutive errors at each point of input entry. However, the line editor is not a security-sensitive application, so the resolution suggested is an acceptable solution.

The design team recommended that Table 9.2 be included in the SRS and be incorporated into some of the acceptance tests. They argued that these are functional requirements imposed on the SIMPLE_LINE_EDITOR.

9.4.3 Main Data Structures

The design team continued to refine the design, producing data flow diagrams or equivalent graphic abstractions and a main data structure. Normally the data structure would be shown in pseudocode but because of its simplicity, it was decided that English statements are adequate.

1. A dynamic double-linked list shall be used to store the transaction file being edited in the memory. The pointer to (or address of) the first record of the file shall be stored in a dummy node called Head. Let us assume ListPtr is the pointer to the linked list structure used to store the text file in the memory. Each record of this structure has three fields: Blink (for backward linking), Flink (for forward linking), and Line (an array of at most 80 characters to store a line of text). To access the data in each of the fields we use the notations ListPtr^.Flink, ListPtr^.Blink, and ListPtr^.Line.

2. An array shall be used to store long command words for correctness checking. This array shall be initialized to the list of nine possible command words. The longest command word shall be eight characters. Assume Command_List is an array of nine elements, each of which stores one of the command words.

9.4.4   High-Level Program Structure

The high-level structure of the line editor module is defined as follows. Note that in the design of a module or program, when a statement or a block of statements needs additional description, we start the description with /* and end it with *\. Such descriptions are called comment statements.

```
    Begin SIMPLE_LINE_EDITOR
            Initialize all variables and data structures;
            Repeat
                    Perform Read_Command routine
            Until Command is EDIT
            Read the transaction file (Batch.Com) into memory
            While editing is not done perform the following
                    Read next command line
                    If transaction file is empty and Command is not INSERT then
                            tell the user that file is empty and only
                            INSERT may be performed at this point
                    Else
                            If command is PRINT          perform print routine
                            If command is DELETE         perform delete routine
                            If command is CLOSE          perform close routine
                            If command is FORWARD        perform forward routine
                            If command is BACKWARD       perform backward routine
                            If command is QUIT           perform quit routine
                            If command is INSERT         perform insert routine
                            If command is MOVE           perform move routine
                            If command is EDIT      -    give a message
                    End_else
            End_while
    End    SIMPLE_LINE_EDITOR
```

9.4.5   Detailed Design Description

Based on this high-level design structure, there are nine subprograms that perform each of the nine commands defined in Table 9.2. A tenth subprogram is needed to read each command line as it is entered by the operator. In addition to these ten subprograms, four utility subprograms are needed. These four utility subprograms are described first. Subsequently the detailed design for each of the ten subprograms is described.

Utility Subprograms

The four utility subprograms needed by the line editor module are as follows: Initialize, Insert_a_Line(Line,Position), Locate(M,Position), and Delete_a_Line(Position).

Subprogram Initialize is used to initialize variables, data structures, arrays, files, etc. The initialization process and the initial values for each of these elements are defined during the design phase.

Subprogram Insert_a_Line(Line,Position) is used to insert a line after the line pointed to by Position. Every time this subprogram inserts a line, the inserted line becomes the current line. The side effect of this subprogram is the change in the current line and the incrementing of the total lines in the file. No value is returned by this subprogram.

Subprogram Locate(M,Position) is used to find the position of line M in the transaction file. Parameter Position will contain the pointer to line M. The value of Position is the only value returned by this subprogram.

Subprogram Delete_a_Line(Position) is used to delete the line pointed to by Position, dispose of the deleted line, decrement Total_lines, and define current line to be the line after the line being deleted. No value is returned by this subprogram. All changes are performed on the global variables and structures.

The detailed designs of these subprograms are implementation dependent. Note that, when developing the detailed design for a software product, it is advantageous to leave the detailed design of implementation dependent subprograms for the programming team.

Subprogram Read_Command to Read Command Lines

Subprogram Read_Command has three arguments. The first argument returns the first letter of the command word, the second argument returns zero or the value of integer M, as defined in Table 9.2, and the third argument returns zero or the value of integer N. Read_Command uses subprogram Read_Command_Line to read the command line into an array, Command_Line, and ignore blank spaces. It then splits the data in array Command_Line into Command, First_Argument, and Second_Argument. Note that a Command may have no argument, it may have one argument, or it may have two arguments. Therefore, First_Argument and/or Second_Argument may not exist in the array, Command_Line.

According to Table 9.2 the arguments of a command are as follows: an unsigned integer, a dash followed by an unsigned integer, two integers separated by a dash, an integer followed by a dash, or nothing at all. Since the entire command line is read as character data, Read_Command calls subprogram Convert to convert the remainder of Command_Line to possible numeric values for M and N. The main function of the Read_Command subprogram is to accept input from the keyboard and (1) return the command read along with its possible arguments or (2) produce an error message in case of a flawed command. When a command has an argument, it must be entered on the same line as the command itself.

The Read_Command subprogram must perform three tasks. It must (1) read the command line from the keyboard into array Command_Line while skipping blank spaces, (2) detect and verify the command word, and (3) compute the command line arguments, if any. Subprogram Read_Command_Line(Command_Length) performs task 1, subprogram

Convert(M,N,Index) performs task 3, and task 2 is performed within the Read_Command itself. The argument Command_Length in Read_Command_Line returns a 1 for command words that are in short form. The detailed design of Read_Command_Line is as follows:

```
Subprogram Read_Command_Line (Command_Length)
Local Declarations
Begin Read_Command_Line
      Set Command_Length to 1 /* for short command *\
      Set Index to 1
      Skip the leading blank spaces
      While not end-of-line of input do
            Read(Next_character)
            If Next_character is not blank space then
                  Set Command_Line[Index] to Next_character
                  Increment Index
            End_if
            Else
                  If this is the first blank then
                        Set Command_Length to Max(Index and 1)
                        Set Index to 9
                         /* Longest command word is 8 characters;
                        therefore, the first 8 spaces in array
                        Command_Line are reserved for a command
                        word. *\
            End_else
      End_while
      Place "$" as the last character in Command_Line
      Return (Command_Length)
End Read_Command_Line
```

Subprogram Convert (M, N, Index) has three arguments: M, which must return the value of the first integer found in array Command_Line; N, which must return the second integer found in array Command_Line; and Index, which is 9 at the entry to this procedure and is the index of the last character of Command_Line, "$", at the return time. The detailed design is as follows:

```
Subprogram Convert (M,N,Index)
Local Declarations
Begin Convert
      Set Index to 9
      If Command_Line[Index] is '-' then
            Set M to 1
            Increment Index
      /* Convert the remaining of Command_Line to become N. *\
            Set N to 0
            While Command_Line[Index] is a digit do
                  Set N to N * 10 + the value of this digit
                  Increment Index
            End_while
      End_if
      Else
            /* Compute M *\
            Set M to 0
```

```
            While Command_Line[Index] is a digit do
                    Set M to M * 10 + the value of this digit
                    Increment Index
            End_while
    End_else
            /* If the next character in Command_Line is '-'
            then there is an N to be read. Therefore,
            next lines are to read such N, if any. *\
    If Command_Line[Index] is '−' then
            Set Temp to 0
            Increment Index
            While Command_Line[Index] is a digit do
                    Set Temp to Temp * 10 + the value of this digit
                    Increment Index
            End_while
    End_if
            If Temp is zero then
                    Set N to total number of lines in the file
            Else
                    Set N to Temp
    Return (M,N,Index)
End Convert
```

Subprogram Read_Command calls Read_Command_Line; if the command word is not a short word, it verifies the command word; and if array Command_Line indicates that there may be one or two arguments in array Command_Line, it calls Convert to compute M and N. The detailed design is as follows:

```
Subprogram Read_Command (Command,First_Argument,Second_Argument)
Local Declarations
Begin Read_Command
        Read_Command_Line(Command_Length)
        If Command_Length is 1 then
                Command is short and is Command_Line[1]
        Else
                The first 8 characters of Command_Line is Command
                Search for Command in Command_List
                If find it then
                    Set Command to Temp_Command[1]
                Else
                    Write a message indicating command word is bad
                If Command_Line[9] is not "$" then
                    Set Index to 9
                    Call procedure Convert(First_Argument,Second_Argument,Index)
                Else
                If no error in the command line then
                    Return (Command,First_Argument,Second_Argument)
End   Read_Command
```

Subprogram Read_File to Read the File To Be Edited

Subprogram Read_File should be invoked only once to read the transaction file from secondary storage into primary memory. The structure to store the file in memory is a double-linked list. As lines are read from the file, they are stored in this linked structure. The default name of the transaction file to be read is Batch.Com; however, the user may furnish another name if so desired. The edited transaction file is stored in secondary storage using the name Batch.Exe. When this procedure is completed, the current line is the first line of the file and Current_line_no is set to 1. The detailed design is as follows.

```
Subprogram Read_File
Local Declarations
Begin Read_File
        Set File_Name to default value
        Ask user to enter the file name, if other than default
        Open the file to be edited
                /* Since the name of the file may change from time to time, the
                generic name "Data_File" is assigned to the file being edited
                *\
        Prepare Data_File to be read
        While there are more lines to read do
                Set Line to Blank_Line
                /* to empty the container *\
                Read from Data_File a Line
                Call Insert_a_Line to place this line in linked-list
                Increment Total_line
        End_while
        Set Current line to the first line of the text
        Set Current_line_no to 1
End Read_File
```

Subprogram Print_Lines to Print Line(s) of the File Being Edited

There are four forms of PRINT command specified in Table 9.2. However, all four forms may be interpreted as to print from line M to line N, inclusively. When both M and N are zeros, the current line is printed; when M is not zero and N is zero, line M is printed. In any other case lines M through N are printed.

```
Subprogram Print_Lines(M,N)
Local Declarations
Begin Print_Lines
        If M and N both are zero then
                Print the current line
        If M is larger than 1 and N is zero then
                Locate line M
                Set Current line to line M
                Set Current-line-no to M
                Print line M
        End_if
        If M is 1 and N is larger than 1 then
                Locate line N
                Set Current line to line N
                Set Current-line-no to N
                Print from line 1 to line N
        End_if
        If M is less than N and M and N both are greater than 1 then
                Locate line M
                Locate line N
```

            Set Current line to line N
            Set Current-line-no to N
            Print from line M to line N
      End_if
End Print_Lines

Subprogram Delete_Lines to Delete Line(s) from the File Being Edited

The design of this subprogram is very similar to the design of Print_Lines. In the Delete_Lines, instead of printing a line, utility subprogram Delete_a_Line is invoked to delete a line.

Subprogram Close_File to Close the Editing Session

Subprogram Close_File must copy the content of the linked list storing the edited file to a file called Batch.Exe. Then it must copy the content of a file called Batch.Tmp into the empty Data_File. Note that Data_File is the generic name corresponding to the file being edited.

```
Subprogram Close_File
Local Declarations
Begin Close_File
        Prepare Batch.Exe file for output
        While it is not the last line in the linked list /+ Edited file in memory +/
                Set Line to the next line in the linked list
                Write Line into Batch.Exe
        End_while
        Prepare Data_File for output
        Prepare Batch.Tmp file for input
        While more lines on Batch.Tmp
                Read Line from Batch.Tmp file
                Write Line to Data_File
        End-while
End Close_File
```

Subprogram Append_File to Quit the Editing Session

Subprogram Append_File is called when the original copy of the Data_File must be preserved in its original form. This procedure should append the lines in the Batch.Tmp file to the end of Data_File.

```
Subprogram Append_File
Local Declarations
Begin Append_File
        Prepare a scratch file, called Temp_File, for output
        Prepare Data_File for input
        Prepare Batch.Tmp for output
        While it is not the end of Data_File do
                Read Line from Data_File
                Write Line into Temp_File
        End_while
        While it is not the end of Batch.Tmp file do
                Read Line for Batch.Tmp
                Write Line into Temp_File
```

```
            End_while
            Prepare Data_File for output
            Prepare Temp_File for input
            While it is not the end of Temp_File do
                    Read Line from Temp_File
                    Write Line into Data_File
                    End_while
                    Close all the files
    End Append_File
```

Subprogram Forward_Line to Move Forward a Line

Subprogram Forward_Line moves the current line to the next line. In the case where the current line is the last line of the file, the current line won't be changed.

```
    Subprogram Forward_Line
    Local Declarations
    Begin Forward_Line
            If Current line is not the last line then
                    Set Current line to the next line
                    Increment Current_line_no
                    Else
            Say the current line cannot move
    End Forward_Line
```

Subprogram Backward_Line to Move Backward a Line

Subprogram Backward_Line moves the current line to the previous line. In the case where the current line is the first line of the file, the current line won't be changed.

```
    Subprogram Backward_Line
    Local Declarations
    Begin Backward_Line
            If Current line is not the first line then
                    Set Current line to the previous line
                    Decrement Current_Line_no
            Else
                    Say the current line cannot move
        End Backward_Line
```

Subprogram Move_Line to Move to Line M

Subprogram Move_Line is used to set the current line from wherever it is to line M. First the position of line M with respect to the current line is determined. Then the current line is moved forward (or backward) to line M.

```
    Procedure Move_Line(M)
    Local Declarations
    Begin Move_Line
            Locate Line M with respect to the current line
            Set Current line to line M
            Set Current_line_no to M
    End Move_Line
```

Subprogram Insert_File to Insert New Lines into the File

Subprogram Insert_File reads one or more lines from the keyboard and inserts the line after the current line. The end of insertion is identified by character "@" at the end of the last line to be inserted.

```
Subprogram Insert_File
Local Declarations
Begin Insert_File
        While more lines to insert do
                Read Line
                Call Insert_a_Line(Line,Current)
                Increment Current_line_no
                Increment Total_lines
        End_while
End Insert_File
```

9.4.6 Program Development Process

The programming team uses detailed design in the SDS document (sketched out in general terms here), if necessary refers to the SRS document, and develops code for the line editor module. Since the most important procedure in the module is the procedure that reads a command line, the module test plan dictates that work on this procedure start first. In order to test program segments as they are developed, the team has created a test driver for the entire module. New procedures are sequentially developed, tested, and added to the module until the entire software product is developed and tested.

The testing and debugging performed by the programming team is different from the testing that will be done by the test and integration team. The programming team first tests each procedure or function to verify that it correctly performs its task as described in the module requirements and design specification. When all the procedures, functions, and program segments are developed and tested, the programming team assembles the entire module and again tests the module to verify that it works according to the specifications stated in the SRS and SDS documents. When the module has successfully passed all module-level tests, it is delivered to the test and integration team.

The test and integration team exercises the module in the system environment along with other modules. The testing objectives are to assure that all interfaces are correct and the module works in concert with other modules to satisfy system functional requirements correctly. Satisfaction of system functions usually requires hardware modules, software modules, operational procedures, and people all working together to satisfy a major system function.

When the test and integration team finds an error in a module, the error and all related evidence are carefully documented, and the module is returned to the development team for debugging. The test and integration team tests a module to find faults and errors, whereas the programming team tests a module to show that it works correctly. The test and integration team only reports the faults found in the module, whereas the programming team must isolate, confirm, and fix the errors. The goals and objectives of the programming team and test and integration team with regard to testing a module are somewhat different.

To avoid creating a lengthy chapter, the details of the code and unit test process, ending with the coded program, are not presented. One other reason, beside chapter length, for not including the source programs for this example in the book is that to give the message that software engineering is a discipline, whereas a programming language is one of the many tools used in this discipline. Including a large program in, for example, Ada or C++ may run the risk of promoting the language (Ada, C++, or any other language used) as the right tool for software engineers. The authors didn't want to take such a risk.

9.5 CHAPTER SUMMARY ■

There are more than 250 commercial programming languages, each having some unique features, and there are countless applications, each requiring certain unique features of a programming language. It is the responsibility of the software development team to study the special characteristics of the software product being developed and find a programming language that best responds to the needs of the software development project. Usually the needs of a large software development project are different for different segments of the software product. In such cases we may select more than a single programming language to code the software. The separation of programming languages into different categories such as functional, object-oriented, declarative, and imperative should help the software development team to choose the right language for implementation and coding.

The program quality of each module developed for a software product plays an important role in the maintenance of the product. When a module or a program segment does not pass the program quality test described in this chapter, it should be redesigned and rewritten. It costs a lot less to recode a poorly written program early in the development cycle than to fix it during the operational phase. In some cases, it may be necessary to redesign the entire program.

It is important that the quality of a program module be measured by someone outside the programming team. The weighting for each of the quality measures shown in Table 9.1 may be assigned by the development team. However, it is better to have an independent, experienced person assign the raw scores that are used to evaluate the quality of the program.

While only a small part of the software development cost and schedule is allocated to the coding process, coding can have a very strong influence on the maintainability of the product in the field. The use of the style guidelines cited in the chapter and well-thought-out comment statements strategically located can pay large dividends. The quality attributes described in the chapter are for the most part measurable and are often found in the SRS as explicit or implicit requirements.

It has been shown through experience that while a program is being coded, strict adherence to the programming style rules stated in this chapter will create a better quality program. Even when the programming team codes from a bad design, application of programming rules may help to expose design weaknesses.

9.6 EXERCISES ■

1. List major features for the following categories of programming languages:
   a. Imperative
   b. Object-oriented

    c. Functional
    d. Declarative
    e. Fourth generation
    f. Logic

2. Give three distinct features for each of the following programming languages. Choose only those languages with which you are familiar, or read about the language before answering.
    a. COBOL
    b. Fortran
    c. Ada
    d. CLU
    e. Modula-2
    f. Common Lisp
    g. Smalltalk
    h. C++
    i. Pascal
    j. Prolog

3. Which one(s) of the languages listed in problem 2 you would select for coding the ABC project? State your reasons. Note that, depending on the software operation environment, you may code a software product in more than one programming language.

4. Assume you are going to design a programming language for commercial application. List the features that you would include in your programming language.

5. List three more programming rules that may help to create a better program.

6. Suppose you are to develop an educational software product to be used by elementary school students and teachers and to be maintained by the development agency. Complete the weight values associated with Table 9.1. Give reasons for each of your weight assignments.

7. Discuss the effect of human factors on application software such as WordPerfect, Lotus, and Clipper.

8. Discuss the effect of system interface with regard to some moderate graphics application package.

9. Discuss the use and misuse of the GUI environment in the design of human computer interfaces.

10. Use Ada as the programming language of your choice to develop the complete program for the programming example discussed in section 9.4.

11. Do problem 10 using the C/C++ programming language.

12. Complete the weight values for Table 9.1 using the example discussed in section 9.4. Explain and justify the weight assigned to each of the nine quality measures.

13. Compute the program quality measure for the Ada program developed in exercise 10.

14. Compute the program quality measure for the C/C++ program developed in exercise 11.

15. Compute all possible branches for the subprogram Read_Command. Note that a call to a subprogram is counted as a branch by itself.

16. Code the Read_Command procedure using a programming language of your choice. Your main objective should be to create a more readable and understandable program segment.

17. Give an object-oriented analysis and design for the problem discussed in section 9.4.

18. Use object oriented C++, or any other OOP language, to code the design developed in exercise 17.

19. Develop a data flow diagram to represent the high-level design for the problem discussed in section 9.4.
20. Develop the complete data dictionary for the programming example of section 9.4.

References

1. A. Behforooz, *Software Quality Metrics: Defining and Measuring the Quality of a Computer Program*, Proceedings of the 13th Annual Conference of the Association of Management, Computer Science Group, Vancouver, British Columbia, Canada, August 1995.
2. A. Behforooz and M. Holoien, *Problem Solving and Structured Programming with Pascal*, Brooks/Cole, Pacific Grove, Calif., 1986.
3. J. Martin, *Fourth-Generation Languages*, Vols. 1, 2, and 3, Prentice-Hall, Upper Saddle River, N.J., 1986.
4. B. Meyer, *Reusable Software: The Base Object-Oriented Component Libraries*, Prentice-Hall, Upper Saddle River, N.J., 1995.
5. R. W. Sebesta, *Concepts of Programming Languages*, Ed. 2, Benjamin-Cummings, Redwood City, Calif., 1993.
6. K. Slonneger and B. L. Kurtz, *Formal Syntax and Semantics of Programming Languages: A Laboratory Based Approach*, Addison-Wesley, Reading, Mass., 1995.

Software System Test and Integration

10.0 OBJECTIVES ■

Testing is the most critical phase in the SWDLC. The test and integration phase is the final filter for all errors of omission and commission. All unresolved issues, postponed requirement decisions, undecided design issues, and lingering operator concerns must now be addressed and put to rest. Much happens in the test and integration phase, not all of which is visible even to those deeply involved in the development process. The objectives of this chapter are to (1) provide an overview of the dynamics of software test and integration as it manifests itself in a large information system development, (2) define the terminology and jargon used in software test and integration, (3) discuss some of the strategies, techniques, and tools that are used in software testing, (4) emphasize the importance of the test planning activity and its product, formal test plan documentation, and (5) identify the types of testing that make up the total test plan. In keeping with the approach taken in this book, software test and integration is described not as an independent event but as occurring within a system test and integration setting.

10.1   INTRODUCTION   ■

A wide range of testing goes on in a software development life cycle. Each review, inspection, audit, design walk-through, code walk-through, group code read, and desk check is in reality a form of test. The more effective we can make early static testing, the fewer problems that we will encounter in the dynamic stages of testing (execution of test cases). It has been shown again and again that the earlier a fault can be detected and removed, the lower the additional development cost associated with removing the error. The message in this chapter is that testing is not an afterthought. Preparation for testing should begin as soon as each software product is defined.

Several human factors studies have shown that the error rate exhibited by a human being performing certain repetitive tasks is about one percent. If we were to assume that the software development process followed the same error rate, there would be one error introduced for each 100 source lines of code written. If the three major steps in the SWDLC—production of SRS and SDS documents and the conversion from the SDS to code—each were to introduce errors in this proportion, we might expect to see as many as three errors per 100 SLOC in the finished product (as it is delivered to a system test environment). It is interesting that these figures compare closely with those cited by Yourdon [5] and RADC studies [4]. The point is that software is a labor-intensive activity and human errors that result in faults in the software product will always be with us.

It has been claimed by many, with some justification, that application of certain techniques such as group reading of code, specification reviews, audits, inspections, and walk-throughs can find as many as 80% of the errors that accumulate before a software product is ready for the test and integration phase. Without these "pre filters" we might experience an error density (errors per 100 SLOC) of three in code delivered to test. With the pre filters the error density might be reduced to 0.6 errors per 100 SLOC, which is certainly a significant improvement. But if the software product consists of 50,000 SLOC, the product will still arrive at the doors of the system test facility with approximately 300 faults in spite of our best efforts to filter them out beforehand.

Most students and entry-level software engineers, even those who have written many "toy" programs, have little experience in true software testing. Testing software is far more complex than exercising a program to see if it works.

This chapter begins with a presentation of basic concepts in testing, an overview of the entire software test process, and a description of the planning and documentation associated with testing a large software system. Verification and validation are defined, and the important role of reliability modeling in test planning and measuring progress in the test environment is also discussed. The chapter continues with a description of the test planning, documentation, and test strategies employed in integration of modules and testing of the threads in incremental system Builds that follow.

The material presented here describes a software test process as it exists for system developments where computers and software are a major part of the system. The model we describe is general and applies to cases where software is the dominant component (a word processing product or a management information system) as well as to cases for which software is an embedded element in a larger system. This chapter has been written with the notion that the description of the test documentation required by many formal software development life cycles provides the best overview of the test and integration phase of software development.

10.2 BASIC CONCEPTS IN TESTING ■

To an experienced software engineer, the difference between testing and debugging is clear. However, an inexperienced entry-level programmer often uses testing and debugging to mean the same thing. We debug a program when we know there is a fault in the program. We test a program to see whether it contains an error of omission or commission. When the existence of such an error is manifested as a failure in execution of test cases, the program must be debugged to locate and correct the error. A software module is delivered for testing only when there is a high level of confidence that there are no errors in the program module.

The main objective of testing is to prove (or when such proof is not possible, to show with a high level of confidence) that the software product as a minimum meets a set of preestablished acceptance criteria under a prescribed set of environmental circumstances. There are two components to this objective. The first component is to prove that the requirements specification from which the software was designed is correct. The second component is to prove that design and coding correctly respond to the requirements. Correctness means that function, performance, and timing requirements match acceptance criteria. No more, no less.

Software testing is further complicated by the fact that system acceptance criteria usually involves hardware, procedures, and operators so that acceptance tests involve more than just the software. Software tests are designed to force failures. In that regard software testing is intrinsically destructive.

What is also being tested during software testing are the documentation, operational time-lines, hardware-to-software interfaces, operator-to-system (software) interfaces, product maintainability, etc. The software engineer should be aware of this, and test cases and test procedures should recognize and account for it. What is also indirectly being tested is the development team, the engineers who allocated function to and specified the software requirements, the technical and administrative management, the development environment, tools, processes, procedures, etc. Even though attention is (and should be) focused on the software product, we cannot lose sight of the fact that there is more being tested than the software product.

10.2.1 Need for Planning

Successful enterprises require good planning. Software testing is not exempt from this adage. Software test planning begins before software design. The steps in test planning include, in this order, establishing acceptance criteria, developing an overall plan for integrating software modules, and testing them in an operational environment. The overall test and integration plan spawns two more detailed plans, one for tests at the module level and one for testing at a string or thread level. At this point we pause to define module, string (or thread), and incremental Build (or Build), terms we will use throughout this chapter.

Module A module, according to IEEE standards, is a program unit that is a discrete entity with respect to compiling, combining with other units, and loading. It is a logically separable part of a program. *Module, component,* and *unit* are often used interchangeably.

String or Thread A String or Thread is a collection of modules that together with support modules carry out one or more major system functions that can be exercised independently.

Build   An incremental Build or simply a Build is one step in the incremental build up of a system accomplished by assembling collections of threads in such a sequence that permits each Build to be tested independently.

The top-level module test plan is prepared by the software development team and describes the test philosophy, manner, and schedule to which modules will be tested. The schedule to which modules will be tested must, of course, be synchronized with the system test plan. Each module will have its own unique test plan consisting of a set of test cases and procedures for running module tests. The test case portfolio includes correct answers for each test. Test procedures may contain descriptions of certain software drivers or scaffolds required to carry out testing. A driver, in the context of testing, is a software module that invokes and perhaps controls and monitors the execution of one or more other modules. A scaffold or scaffold software is software including data files built to support software development and testing. Both drivers and scaffolds are often throwaway software, that is, software not delivered to the customer or reused. In spite of the fact that this software is often thrown away, it must be of the same quality as (or better than) the delivered software.

The top-level Build or Thread test plan describes the test flow, test objectives, schedules for the incremental Build, when each module will be delivered, and the acceptance criteria that each module must meet before it will be accepted for integration with other software units. Each incremental Build has its own test plan.

The establishment of acceptance criteria is extremely important. Common questions in the latter phases of testing are as follows: Have we tested enough? How good is the product? Is the product acceptable to the customer? If we have an agreed-to set of acceptance criteria carefully worked out with all involved parties, especially the customer, then we have a good chance to answer these questions.

Frequently, with software products having long development cycles, personnel changes and changes in the operational environment will result in many issues arising at final acceptance test. If acceptance criteria are well documented, these issues should be relatively minor. It is a good idea to revisit acceptance criteria from time to time to see if they are still applicable. Acceptance criteria should not be verbal agreements. As a young software engineer once put it, verbal agreements aren't worth the paper they are written on. With a knowledge of what constitutes acceptance criteria, we can begin to consider testing strategies and techniques and what kind of a test environment or test bed will be needed.

10.2.2 Need for Discipline and Control

The degree of discipline and formalism required in conducting tests is an important consideration. Software system testing is conducted at the end of the development cycle when schedules are compressed and resources are nearly exhausted. It is tempting sometimes to cut corners and skip steps in the testing process to save time and resources. These temptations should be resisted.

The test and integration phase of software development is very dynamic. Test cases are executed, failures are observed, debugging is performed, changes are made to the software product, and regression tests are performed, often in a multishift environment. There are many opportunities to lose control of the process and product. By losing control we mean that no one is sure exactly which changes have been made to the software or which tests have been run on which configurations.

The problem of keeping the test and integration team working on the same software configuration rather than different versions of the software suggests that some form of configuration control be established. In multishift testing where two teams are working on the same product, it is very easy to solve the same problem twice or lose control of the configuration. Strict discipline in using a common test laboratory notebook is helpful, as is overlapping shifts by an hour to allow for an exchange of testing information. Not maintaining tight control of the testing process will result in testers feeling as though they are trying to swim through a pool of molasses.

10.2.3   Software Verification and Validation

The terms *validation* and *verification* are used frequently in software development in general and in software testing in particular. We distinguish between these two terms and the activities associated with them by giving a simple definition of the activities associated with each term.

Software Validation: All actions taken at the end of the development cycle to confirm that the software product as built correctly reflects the SRS or its equivalent.

Software Verification: All actions taken at the end of a given development phase to confirm that the software product as being built correctly satisfies the conditions imposed at the start of the development phase.

At one point during the early days of software development when large system developments with significant software components were synonyms for disaster, the idea of independent verification and validation (V and V) surfaced. The idea was to have an organization that was financially, managerially, and technically independent of the software development organization (an independent contractor) perform validation and verification of the software product. Initially, it seemed like a good idea. In fact, it was employed on several major contracts.

The idea proved to be effective except that: (1) many software products were embedded in larger systems, often with significant hardware components, making test and integration lines of authority and responsibility difficult to identify, and (2) schedules were significantly affected and cost increased, sometimes by more than a factor of two, because testing activity really begins before the design activity. Thus the V and V contractor must work closely with the software development contractor almost from the start. Software development contractors were naturally not likely to share what they deemed as proprietary software development process information with potential competitors nor were they about to do anything to make potential competitors look good. Moreover, software development contractors were reluctant (refused) to take responsibility for products they were unable to test fully themselves. The consequence was increase in cost and delay in schedule.

The idea has evolved to the point where the test and integration function is organizationally separated from software development. This approach is a compromise between increased cost and increased independence in testing.

10.2.4   Using Reliability Models in Testing

Reliability models (discussed in chapter 17) can help in two ways in system/software test and integration. First, reliability models can provide a means to measure, in the test environment, whether or not a software product or component will meet an operational reliability or availability requirement if one appears in the SRS. Second, reliability models can help the test and integration team initially to plan the test process and subsequently to revise test plans to reflect what is actually being experienced in the test environment. That is, the reliability model can help to decide if a software product is ready for release to the next level of testing or delivery to the customer(s). It also can predict expected software failure rate, number of faults remaining in the software product, number of additional hours of testing required to achieve a particular failure rate, and number of failures that will occur in a given test period. Those test organizations using reliability models often use two different models and two independent teams to predict reliability attributes such as failure rates, residual faults, and required test time. Clearly reliability models offer considerable assistance in the testing environment. For example, when a reliability requirement or goal is given, the model can estimate the CPU hours (the number of hours the software product must be executed) and the number of failures that may be experienced to meet the reliability requirement or goal.

Having an estimate of the number of CPU hours required for testing the product can help a planner to establish a schedule and estimate the size of the staff required to perform the testing. The sizing estimates obtained early in the development cycle along with other software attributes will enable the software engineer to identify the software product type. These data can be used as an initial input to test planners. A combination of experience and reliability model results should improve planning significantly.

As an example, consider a software product of size 80,000 assembly language SLOC. Prior experience has shown that about 90% of the time when a failure occurs in testing, the fault that caused the failure is found. Furthermore, the processor that will execute these instructions in the test environment has an average instruction execution rate of 5.5 million per second. With this information as input, the reliability model described in chapter 17 provides an estimation of the following:

The initial failure rate at inception of system test in failures per CPU hour of execution
The total number of failures resident in the 80,000 SLOC software package
The CPU execution time required to reach a specified software failure rate
The number of failures that will be experienced during the test in order to meet the reliability
   specification

The information of particular value to test planners is the number of CPU hours required and the number of failures that will be experienced during test to reach a given reliability goal. Required CPU hours are converted into test hours and the number of failures that must be debugged, faults found, changes made, and retesting completed is then used to estimate required labor hours. This information is important for staffing the test phase.

Once testing begins and test data become available and are entered into reliability models, new predictions can be made and plans refined. When the software product enters system test and integration, actual measurements of software failure rates can replace estimates, and a curve-fitting scheme can be employed to estimate the probable initial failure rate and the resident faults in the software product. These kinds of data are useful feedback for a development team and certainly will enhance the team's collective memory of the project. The information derived can be used to improve estimating skills, the development process, and the effectiveness of new tools and procedures.

10.2.5 Software Engineers Find Careers in Testing

Many entry-level software engineers begin their careers in testing. In many organizations, software development and system test and integration are organizationally separated (section 10.2.3). This means that for the software development organization, software development activity terminates and maintenance begins once a module has passed acceptance test. The purpose of this organizational structure is to provide a semi-independent verification and validation of the software product. A career in testing for a software engineer requires acquiring a broader overall perspective and a better appreciation of the software development process.

Some software development managers favor this entry into a software development career for new employees. For the software engineer this entry path provides a glimpse of the good software and the bad software and an opportunity to examine the anatomy of many different failure types without going through the pain of being directly involved in the failure. It is also a good way to impress on beginning software engineers the importance of human factors and maintainability in software design.

10.3 OVERVIEW OF SYSTEM AND SOFTWARE TEST AND INTEGRATION   ■

In this section the system and software test and integration process is briefly discussed to remind the reader that the final product that must be tested and accepted is the system, which includes software as well as other components. A software system is composed of many smaller software components called modules. Chapter 11 discusses module level testing in detail.

An overview of the test process associated with a relatively large software system is shown in Figure 10.1. A mission definition or a set of mission requirements and interface definitions initiate the development process. In system design, system-level requirements are developed and passed to requirements allocation and specification where they are further developed and allocated to individual components in the system. The software requirements would appear in an SRS (there may be more than one). Following the right-hand path of Figure 10.1, software design, code, and module test would be accomplished as part of the development process. It should be noted that system modules or components are sometimes procured rather than designed and built.

The development produces a top-level module test plan that describes in general terms how module testing will be accomplished. Module acceptance tests are designed to confirm that each module has met its design goals. Once the module has been accepted, it is put under configuration control. That is, no changes can be made to the module without approval of a change control board.

As shown in Figure 10.1, while the development process is moving to completion, in parallel, the test team is (1) defining formal acceptance criteria and (2) preparing a system test and integration plan explaining how individual modules will be tested, assembled into

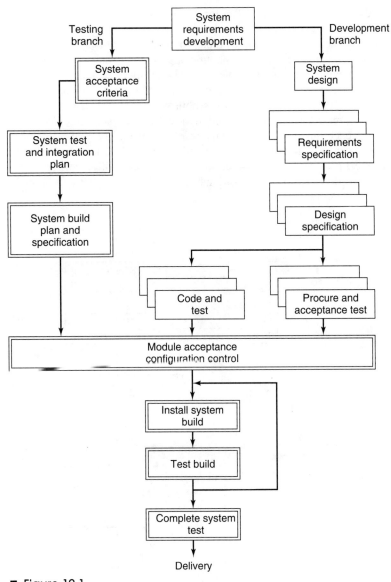

■ Figure 10.1

Software testing process embedded in SWDLC.

Builds, and Builds tested to confirm that system acceptance criteria have been met. The plan must, of course, be consistent with the schedule for module development. The plan also describes the test environment, test tools, personnel requirements, and schedules.

The test and integration activity is usually based on building the system in increments. Each incremental Build is designed to implement specific system functions. The approach is not only to build the system incrementally but also to execute incrementally system-level acceptance tests. The incremental Build process continues testing threads at each incremental

Build until the system is complete. The top-level Build plan describes the process. Several firsts are recorded in the system test and integration environment: (1) the first opportunity to comprehensively exercise and evaluate human-to-computer or machine interfaces, (2) the first opportunity to maintain the system, (3) the first opportunity to exercise operational time lines, and (4) the first opportunity to assess the value and utility of system documentation.

The documentation structure for all testing in a large system development process is presented by Figure 10.2. The diagram shows both system-level and module-level test documentation. A test matrix is usually included in the SRS. The test matrix identifies the required test method for each function and performance requirement. The SDS contains a similar test matrix, which identifies how each design requirement will be tested. At the module level, each module test plan design (module acceptance test plan) will have a set of test cases and a set of test procedures to follow. During module testing, a test log will be maintained doc-

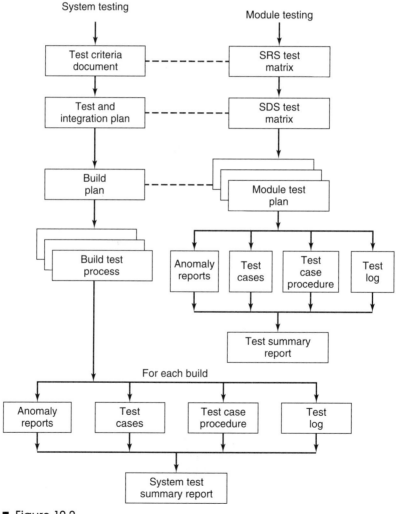

■ Figure 10.2

Test and integration documentation structure.

umenting what happened during the test. An unusual event or anomaly will be documented in the test anomaly report. The test anomaly report will be helpful during debugging. Finally, when the test is over, a summary report will be written. The structure and content of each of these documents is described in a module test plan. The module test plan design and its associated documents can be viewed as the operational plan for module test.

At the system level, a system acceptance test criteria document describes acceptance criteria. Ideally this document should be a contractual document and should be signed by both customer and contractor. The test and integration plan (a strategic plan) and the Build plan and specification (a tactical plan) are next in the sequence. Each incremental Build has its own individual plan, much like the module test plan. As in each module test, there are five individual documents associated with each incremental Build. The test case document and the test case procedure document are prepared before the actual test; three others—the test log, the anomaly report, and the test summary—report are prepared during and after the actual test. The contents and structure of each of these documents are described in subsequent sections of this chapter.

The foregoing description of the overall test and integration process conforms closely to ANSI, IEEE, DOD, and NASA standards, guidelines, and practices [1, 3]. Many software development organizations in the private sector have adopted similar approaches.

Many authors and practitioners believe that the testing phase of the software development process is the single most important phase. Michael Evans [2] has declared, ''The activities of the project should be focused from the outset on the most critical and complex stage of the project, software test and integration.''

The foregoing description has presented what looks like an enormously bureaucratic and documentation laden process. Experience has shown that the bureaucracy and documentation are required elements if the test and integration process is to be successful. However, documents in many instances are simply templates or forms to be filled in. Automated tools are available to ease the documentation burden. Other documents, if not delivered to the customer, can be relatively inexpensive to produce. It is difficult to convey how quickly a software test and integration activity can become a disaster when not rigidly controlled.

10.4 INCREMENTAL BUILD OF MODULES INTO SYSTEMS ■

Test and integration is defined as the testing phase that assembles qualified (certified) modules into logical subsets, each subset implementing some part of the overall system capability. The assembly or integration process is usually incremental and hierarchical. Testing of each subset of modules (incremental Build) includes confirmation that interfaces, data relationships, internal execution characteristics, performance benchmarks, etc., correctly implement requirements as interpreted by formal acceptance criteria; and that internal execution sequences and support characteristics are validated.

If we trace the left path of Figure 10.1 (the boxes with the double line borders), we will find the first stages of the testing activity. Software engineers in the testing organization and the customer begin to address the question of what the criteria are for acceptance of software products and, more important, what the criteria are for acceptance of the system itself. Software engineers will need to determine what software units are associated with specific system acceptance tests so that the role of software in the acceptance testing can be determined.

The test and integration team plays a significant part in the development of a software product. The responsibilities of the system test and integration team include the following: (1) providing an independent analysis of requirements and design, (2) developing an approach and plan to the test and integration of the system, (3) taking action to minimize the need for special test hardware, software, and databases, (4) providing a user's and operator's perception of the product, (5) showing how the software product will be operated, and (6) simulating a skeptical, knowledgeable, and hardnosed but fair customer.

The system test and integration team is also responsible for defining and negotiating the system acceptance criteria, producing the test and integration plan and the Build plan, determining which modules are included in each Build, deciding when they will be needed, and carrying out the plans. The system test and integration phase should not be a synonym for a software reengineering, redesigning, and recoding phase.

Figure 10.3 shows two possibilities for effecting integration of a system comprising many individual software (and perhaps hardware) modules that have been independently developed and successfully tested (certified). The first is to incrementally integrate all the tested modules in a series of well-orchestrated steps into a system and test at each incremental step for compliance with system acceptance criteria. The second is to assemble the entire system and begin system-level tests immediately. The second approach is called the ''big bang'' or all-up method. Incremental Builds can follow one of two different patterns: top down or bottom up. Top-down or bottom-up Builds can be accomplished in two ways: vertically (depth first) or horizontally (breadth first). Both approaches are driven by implementation of system capabilities such that, when a Build is successfully tested, it satisfies some system acceptance criteria. The decision as to which approach to use is usually dictated by the nature of the system and the software architecture. Attempts to use an all-up or big bang approach almost

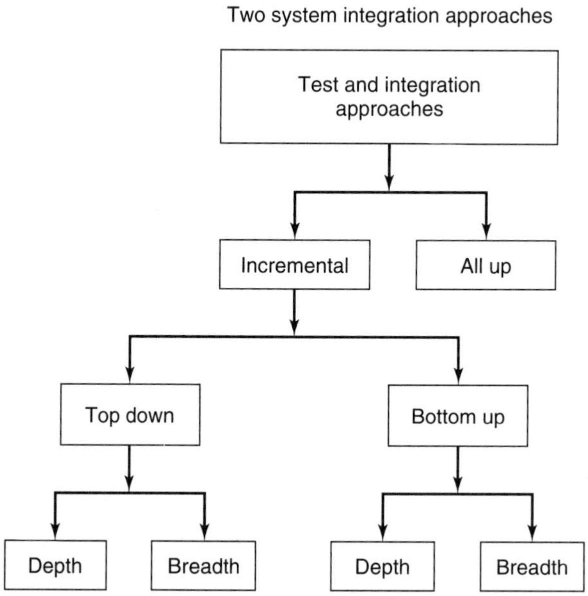

Two system integration approaches

■ Figure 10.3

Two system integration approaches.

always result in a very chaotic testing environment because there are just too many things that can go wrong and too many places for errors to hide. In the big bang approach, determination of faults is often very difficult because symptoms are often confusing. Several faults can conspire to produce misleading clues. Large system developments do not attempt the all-up system integration approach.

The incremental approach offers a more systematic attack in which only a limited quantity of unknown modules are being tested at any one time. Faults are easier to locate and fix when only small parts of the system are under test at any one time. Confidence is developed as the system is progressively assembled and tested with realistic operational timelines and operators.

A well-organized test plan can add modules in such a sequence that system functional capabilities can be tested on subsets of the modules that make up the total system. Sound software architecture, intelligent partitioning of software requirements into modules, and careful scheduling of module development can greatly benefit test and integration.

The top-down approach is based on establishing the top-level control structure first. Those modules that implement the top-level control structure are developed first and added to the system configuration. Interfaces are tested and basic control functions are exercised. Other modules that are unavailable but are called by control modules can be simulated or represented by stubs, module interfaces, and delays. Depending on the nature of the software architecture and other factors, modules may be added either by a uniform stepwise process (the horizontal approach) in which each layer of the architecture is filled and tested before moving to the next layer, sometimes referred to as breadth first testing, or a given function can be developed through all of its layers and tested. This vertical approach is sometimes called depth first testing. At each test step it is highly desirable to demonstrate compliance with system acceptance criteria. Top-down integration makes sense for systems in which control modules are the most critical to system performance and perhaps most error prone.

Bottom-up testing, as the name implies, begins with groups of modules at the lowest levels. In this approach drivers are used initially to provide interfaces, invoke calls, display or record results, and provide operator interfaces. As the system is built the need for drivers is reduced. Bottom-up test and integration makes sense when lower-level modules are most critical to system performance and perhaps are most error prone.

In some instances a hybrid of the top-down and bottom-up approaches can be effective in achieving test and integration goals and objectives. Either of the two approaches, top down or bottom up, can be effective if the following criteria are met:

1. Acceptance criteria are clearly defined at both module and system levels.
2. Module acceptance testing is thorough, rigorous, and based on comprehensive test cases.
3. The configuration is tightly controlled.
4. Each Build makes measurable progress toward satisfying system acceptance criteria.
5. Good test cases are used at each Build. A good test case is one that is designed to expose faults and weaknesses.
6. Human-to-computer interface interaction is an intrinsic part of the test plan.

The system test and integration plan and the Build plan and specification provide a desired schedule for units or modules required for executing each test scenario. System level tests are structured around operational timelines and operator scripts (sequence that the operator follows in carrying out an operational timeline). Even in a software-dominant system, operators are part of the testing. This desired schedule, developed by the test team, is driven by which software modules or units must be in place and fully tested in order to execute a string or thread test, a set of acceptance tests for a single system function. A single system function might be "start up the system," which would probably involve some operating system modules and a system startup software module. The development of these modules would have to be scheduled so that they were fully tested and ready when it was time to perform the thread test. Clearly there will be some negotiation between test sequence, organization of testing, and software product partitioning/structure to effect a consistent test schedule. We will focus on incremental Builds based on thread testing.

There will be an interdependence between architecture, partitioning, module development scheduling, and string or thread test scheduling. Even after this schedule is in place, we often find that schedules are revised on an almost daily basis when the integration tests begin. If a module is delivered late, rejected during acceptance test, or experiences serious problems in the integration environment, it may be necessary to reschedule a thread test. Thus the process of scheduling tests is dynamic and very challenging. Software engineers must be conditioned to work in this kind of environment.

In the system Build plan and specification block of Figure 10.1, we begin to expand upon the system test and integration plan with more detail. In particular, we expand by developing a set of acceptance criteria for each module delivered to the integration team and detailed test scenarios for each thread test.

At this point, we have reached the module acceptance and configuration control block in Figure 10.1. Here modules that are either procured or developed are acceptance tested (or certified) to acceptance criteria established jointly with the development team and the test team. The acceptance criteria may also include a review and or test of documentation.

Many organizations have adopted the following approach to the interface between the development organization and the test and integration organization. The interface is formalized to the extent that the software development team is responsible for the module or unit until it is accepted by the test team. Responsible means that any cost associated with testing, maintaining, changing, etc., is borne by the software development team. On the other hand, if the test team accepts the module, then the cost of testing, maintaining, changing, etc., is borne by the test team. In this approach, development cost and schedule pressure are expected to provide the motivation for test teams to perform complete acceptance tests and for development teams to perform comprehensive unit tests and get their software product, including documentation, accepted as soon as possible.

It is at this point that the products (units, modules) are put under configuration control. Configuration control means that software modules (listings) cannot be changed without a formal review and concurrence from all major development team participants. In this fashion, the control of the software is placed in the hands of the program manager. This approach may sound like elaborate bureaucracy but bitter experience has shown that even on small projects, if the configuration is not controlled, chaos will reign. When 200 people are involved in software development and another 300 are involved in hardware development, training, maintenance, testing, and system engineering, without configuration management and control, large systems would just never get off the ground. The inconvenience of the configuration control process is worth the investment. In fact, it can be implemented so that very little inconvenience results.

Once enough modules have been certified (successfully acceptance tested) and placed under configuration control, a collection (cluster) of modules needed to support a thread test is integrated and interfaces to hardware, software, and operator are confirmed by a series of tests. Each subsequent Build represents a larger collection of modules. Testing is performed on threads of modules that implement a set of system functions.

The major advantage of the incremental approach is that testing proceeds from the simple to the complex, with each test riding on the successful results of the previous one. A secondary advantage is that many CPU hours of successful operation of already tested modules can be accumulated, further bolstering confidence in the product.

The major disadvantage of the incremental approach is the slowdown in the testing process caused by rigid configuration control and the need to run regression tests for modules that fail and are repaired and returned to the test and integration team. This slowdown may get worse very rapidly when a few critical modules fail during the test process or are rejected at acceptance test.

The process of adding more modules to obtain a new Build and then testing the new Build continues as shown in the lower half of Figure 10.1 until the entire system is complete and running. Usually there is a comprehensive set of system level tests that completes the test and integration cycle. Once the complete system is accepted by the customer, it is put into service and enters the maintenance phase.

The foregoing describes the software test process as it exists for system developments in which computers and software are part of the system. The model is general and applies to cases where software is the dominant component. We can apply this model to the testing of a word processor product, a banking system, the FAA system, the space shuttle onboard data management system, etc. Figure 10.1 is representative of one of several approaches that can lead to success if carried out properly.

10.5 TEST AND INTEGRATION PLAN   ■

The test and integration process described in the overview in section 10.4 is structurally similar to those of ANSI, IEEE, DOD, NASA [1, 3] as well as many other software developers. A set of documents generally forms the backbone of the test process. A discussion of the contents of each of these documents should provide insight into the tasks that the test and integration team must perform to effect system testing. Figure 10.2 provides an overview of a typical documentation set related to the test and integration phase of the SWDLC.

Before or concurrent with establishing a test plan, however, the test and integration team must establish a system acceptance criteria with the client/customer. The importance of this task cannot be overstated. These criteria for acceptance will be used to judge whether the system meets the customer's needs. Acceptance test criteria are usually found in the system specification or mission statement. It is frequently a contractual agreement and often made part of the fee structure. That is, failure to comply with acceptance criteria can result in reduced profit or even in financial penalties.

In addition to function and performance criteria (a specific transaction must be performed a given number of times under specific conditions), there are acceptance criteria involving start-up and shutdown sequences of a system, recovery of the system from various types of failure, human factors criteria based on the interface between operator/user and the system (often through software), disaster recovery criteria, error message criteria, criteria based on how the system handles various overload conditions (stress testing), and criteria based on how well the system handles attempts by unauthorized users to penetrate the system, etc. Often system-level acceptance criteria are allocated almost entirely to computer, operator, and software. The validation of system requirements is the successful completion of all acceptance criteria agreed to by the contractor and client early in the system development cycle.

The acceptance test criteria established early in the program can influence system software as well as hardware architecture decisions. The acceptance test criteria can often be demonstrated by selected subsets of hardware modules, software modules, and operational timelines. An orderly sequence of incremental Builds can influence how we structure the software and how we schedule its development.

As system requirements are partitioned and allocated to hardware components, software components, and to operators, the acceptance criteria is implicitly allocated as well. For example, part of an acceptance criteria associated with a requirement for recognizing and handling an overload condition may be allocated to one of the software components. That software component now becomes part of the Build that tests for that acceptance criteria. The module implementing that requirement must be available and fully tested when that particular Build is to be prepared for testing.

The test and integration plan describes the tasks, schedules, approach, resources, and tools for integrating and testing software and other components of the system. The purpose of system testing is to detect differences between measured performance of a system and required performance (as described in the system requirements specifications) by exercising a sequence of test scenarios. Performance measurement should be conducted in an environment that matches, as closely as possible, the operational environment. Test scenarios should be as close as possible to operational timelines in every detail.

The test and integration plan contains a framework within which the software test plan fits. The system test and integration team and the software development team must come to a joint agreement on (1) how the software product will be partitioned into modules (the architecture) and (2) how these modules will be scheduled for development. This information is important to the test and integration team in developing the sequence in which the system is to be incrementally built and tested.

The test and integration plan is the top-level test document, describing the test and integration process from beginning to end. The plan describes the scope of the testing, the approach to be taken, resources required (including people, test beds, test drivers), test scaffolds, schedules, documentation requirements, test databases or files, etc. In systems in which the dominant element is software, the system test and integration plan has a somewhat stronger software flavor. A system test and integration plan answers questions such as: What is being tested? What are pass/fail criteria? When will each test occur? What kind of environment is needed to effect the testing? What features must be tested? What features will not be tested? What documentation is required? What are the responsibilities of individuals and organizations, etc.? Table 10.1 is a generic outline for a system test and integration plan.

Section 1 refers to any unique identifier assigned to project documentation. Section 2 summarizes the project and orients the reader to the extent the document can stand alone. Section 3 provides a general overview of the plan for testing the entire system and defines test objectives for all testing levels. This section should convey to the reader the guiding principles that will be used in test performance. This section is important in establishing policy for dealing with the inevitable conflicts that arise during the final stages of testing. Section 4 provides pertinent references such as development plans, quality assurance plans, configuration management plans, relevant policies, and applicable standards. Section 5 describes pass/fail criteria derived from or traced to acceptance criteria.

Section 6 describes the general approach to all levels of testing and integration of the system. It picks up from section 3 and provides detailed description of how test and integration will be effected. For each major group of software features, the approach that will guarantee that these features are adequately tested is specified. Major testing activities, techniques and tools used to test designated groups of features are also described. The approach is described

■ TABLE 10.1   **Test and Integration Plan Outline**

1. Test and Integration Plan Identification
2. Introduction
3. Test and Integration Description and Objectives
4. References
5. Criteria for Pass/Fail
6. Approach to Test and Integration
7. Criteria for Halting Tests and Resuming Tests
8. Tasks to be Performed
9. Schedule
10. Build Plan and Specification
11. Test Environment Description (diagrams, sketches)
12. Responsibilities, Staffing, Training
13. Risk Assessment and Containment

in enough detail to permit identification of major testing tasks and estimation of required resources and the schedule to perform the tasks. The minimum degree of coverage or comprehensiveness required is also described. Techniques used to judge the degree of comprehensiveness of the testing effort are specified (for example, determining which statements have been executed and how often). Additional completion criteria are described (for example, frequency of failure occurrence). Techniques for tracing requirements are specified. Significant constraints on testing are identified (for example, test item availability, testing resource availability, and testing deadlines).

Section 7 defines the criteria for halting or suspending all or portions of the testing activity and the criteria for resuming testing. The purpose is to reduce ''wheel spinning'' in the test process. It also defines criteria and ground rules for regression testing. Regression testing refers to tests executed after a fault is found and corrected. Section 8 describes the individual tasks that must be performed. These tasks should be developed from and be consistent with the project work breakdown structure. Section 8 is the basis for updating estimates for the time and labor required for testing.

Section 9 presents a top-level testing schedule identifying the major test milestones such as when acceptance test criteria are agreed to, beginning of module test, significant Build tests and demonstrations, delivery of all major system components for test, and development of the test environment. Section 10 describes in overview the Build test plan and specification. This document focuses on the specifics of the incremental integration of modules into Builds and the testing performed at each stage of the integration process. The outline of this document is similar to the test and integration plan outline. The major difference lies in the level of detail and its narrower focus.

Section 11 describes in detail the test environment including all test bed configurations, additional hardware and software requirements, tools, adjunct test software, floor space, operator terminals, training and maintenance requirements, etc. Section 12 identifies the test director and other participants in the test and integration process. It includes those individuals or groups responsible for managing, designing, preparing, executing, and witnessing tests, and for checking and resolving issues. The test director is responsible for conducting the test. Sources responsible for module delivery are also identified in this section. The groups may include developers, testers, operators, user representatives, technical support staff, data administration staff, and quality assurance support staff. Staffing and training needs are also included in this section.

Section 13 contains a risk assessment and containment plan for the test and integration phase. A likely occurrence is late delivery of a module or test tool. The risk assessment should identify those with a high likelihood of being late and develop work-arounds so that schedules can be maintained. Chapter 16 discusses risk assessment and containment.

A checklist for test and integration plan preparation would include confirming the following:

- Test scenarios match operational timelines exactly.
- All system and subsystem requirements are covered comprehensively.
- The test environment itself matches the operational environment.
- Plans for the test environment development or procurement are consistent with the system development schedule and the test and integration schedule.
- Both contractor and customer are in agreement with the testing approach and acceptance criteria.
- Adequate acceptance tests performed on modules that are certified for inclusion in a Build are fully planned.
- All efforts have been made to minimize regression testing by reducing, as much as possible, dependency of one Build on another.
- Provision has been made to assure that all test cases are completed and documented in time to execute the tests they were designed for.
- The test and integration plan calls for a systematic test in logical order of all module, subsystem, and system requirements against a well-defined set of test cases.
- The plan includes a method for documenting the performance of all tests in a test log; a method for identifying and reporting any events, anomalies, or discrepancies; and a procedure for tracking problems from symptom to closure.

10.6   BUILD TEST PLAN AND SPECIFICATION   ■

Build testing applies to both top-down and bottom-up approaches to testing and is based on testing only discrete subsets or clusters of the system's components at any one time. The concept is to gradually, through these separate Builds, incrementally assemble the system components, testing at each Build to assure that the Build meets specification, until finally the last Build is the complete system. It should be noted that only modules that have passed module-level acceptance tests to the satisfaction of the test and integration team are certified for inclusion in the Build. One way to accomplish this is to organize components for each Build so that each implements a set of testable system requirements and satisfies a set of system acceptance requirements.

For example, in a software-dominant system, the first Build might be installation of computer hardware and peripherals, loading a part of the operating system and a diagnostics software product, and running tests to confirm all interfaces, certain limited operating system functions, and the effectiveness of the diagnostic software product in recognizing a specific set of hardware and software problems. The second Build might add additional parts of the operating system and a few modules of the application software product to perform more tests to confirm that the system will meet a few more acceptance criteria. The process continues until the entire system is in place and all acceptance tests are completed.

In general, Build testing is characterized by an incremental test and integration of hardware, software, and operational timelines in a realistic test environment with operators at each system workstation. Functional and performance tests are performed on strings or threads of system functions. System acceptance criteria are the standard against which these tests are performed. Throughout the process the system configuration is rigorously controlled. That is, no changes can be made to specifications, timelines, designs, or implementations unless thoroughly reviewed and accepted by representatives of the entire development team. The purpose is to prevent individuals from making unilateral changes to the configuration that inadvertently have a negative impact on another part of the system. When large numbers of people are involved in a large system development, configuration control or management is absolutely essential.

The test environment also offers an opportunity to expose the test team to maintenance problems arising as hardware and software components fail during testing. This will be a time to see how easily the system can be maintained in the field. The test configuration can also serve to train operators and familiarize customers with the system.

The test configuration also permits hardware and software to accumulate many hours of operation. Hardware weaknesses usually manifest themselves early in the lifetime of a hardware component. The occurrence of software failures is a direct function of CPU time (execution time).

The Build test plan and specification document, which might be regarded as a tactical plan, is based on acceptance criteria, the system test and integration plan, the schedules for development of hardware and software modules, and test timelines for module testing. The purpose of the plan is to identify collections of components that make up strings that, together with supporting modules, implement system functions and to form them into individual Builds. The plan describes the configuration for each Build, identifies test objectives for each Build, specifies test cases and procedures for each Build, describes special test support required (hardware, software, personnel), and provides a Build schedule. Table 10.2 provides an outline for the Build test plan.

Sections 1 and 2 are self-explanatory. Section 3 provides a detailed description of each Build configuration and its test objectives. Specifically, this section discusses what system capabilities are implemented in each Build and what threads are to be tested in each Build. Section 4 includes a list of references needed for the Build being tested. Section 5 discusses the pass/fail criteria for each Build. In particular, this section contains test cases for each Build. If test cases are not included in this section, the paragraph should reference test case documents or folders where test cases can be found. Section 6 describes the approach that will be taken in performing the tests. The approach should include preconditions on beginning the assembly of each new Build, operator timelines or scripts that will be used, who will attend/witness tests, identification of the test conductor and his or her authority, and description of what will happen when discrepancies are encountered during testing. Section 7 provides procedures and criteria for deciding when to halt testing and under what conditions tests may be resumed. Implicit in these decisions are ground rules for regression tests. Section 8 includes a list of tasks to be performed, and section 9 provides the schedule for performing

■ TABLE 10.2   **Build Test Plan Outline**

1. Build Test Plan Identification
2. Introduction
3. Build Test Approach Description and Objectives
4. References
5. Criteria For Pass/Fail
6. Approach
7. Criteria for Halting/Continuing Testing
8. Tasks To Be Performed
9. Schedule
10. Test Products (documents)
    10.1 Test Design Specification Document
        10.1.1. Build Test Identifier
        10.1.2. Build Features To Be Tested
        10.1.3. Testing Approach To Be Employed
        10.1.4. Test Case List
        10.1.5. Thread Pass/Fail Criteria
    10.2. Build Test Case Specification Document (including expected results)
        10.2.1. Identifier
        10.2.2. Unit Description
        10.2.3. Input
        10.2.4. Output
        10.2.5. Environment
        10.2.6. Special Procedures
        10.2.7. Precedence and Dependencies
        10.2.8. References
    10.3. Build Test Case Procedure Document (including operator and test director scripts)
        10.3.1. Identifier
        10.3.2. Purpose
        10.3.3. Special Requirements
        10.3.4. Procedure
    10.4. Build Test Log Document
        10.4.1. Identifier
        10.4.2. Test Environment
        10.4.3. Tests Results
        10.4.4. References
    10.5. Build Anomaly Document
        10.5.1. Test Incident Identifier
        10.5.2. Summary of the Incident
        10.5.3. Incident Description
        10.5.4. Impact of the Incident on the Project
    10.6. Build Test Summary Document
        10.6.1. Test Summary Report Identifier
        10.6.2. Summary and Conclusions
        10.6.3. Variances
        10.6.4. Comprehensive Assessment
        10.6.5. Summary of Results
        10.6.6. Evaluation
        10.6.7. Summary of Activities
        10.6.8. Approvals
11. Test Environment Description
12. Responsibilities, Staffing, Training
13. Risk Assessment and Containment

these tasks. Section 10 describes the contents of each of the six test documents associated with each Build being tested. These documents are described in the paragraphs that follow.

Test Design Specification Document (Table 10.2, section 10.1)

The outline of this document includes the following sections:

1. Build Test Identifier
2. System Features To Be Tested
3. Testing Approach To Be Employed
4. Test Case List
5. Thread Pass/Fail Criteria

Section 1 identifies the Build and its location in the system structure and in the overall test plan schedule. References should be used where appropriate. Section 2 describes Build functions and combinations of system functions scheduled for test. System functions under test are traced to source requirements in requirement specifications or design specifications for confirmation.

Section 3 expands on the test and integration plan to the extent that it applies to a particular Build test. Included in this section are specific test strategies and techniques that will be employed; methods used to analyze results; rationale for choice of test cases; special conditions or environments needed to execute the test cases; and an explanation of the operational timelines if applicable.

Section 4 contains a list of all test cases and a brief description of each as well as a brief description of the procedure to be followed. Section 5 contains a detailed set of criteria that the Build must satisfy in order to pass acceptance test and the regression tests that must be performed.

Build Test Case Specification Document (Table 10.2, section 10.2)

This document defines each Build test case in detail. There will be one test case specification for each incremental Build. The outline of this document for a given Build includes the following sections:

1. Identifier
2. Unit Description
3. Input
4. Output
5. Environment
6. Special Procedures
7. Precedence and Dependencies
8. References

Section 1 links the test case specification to the applicable Build. Test cases may be used for more than one Build and more than one test. This link is important. Section 2 relates the Build, through references, to sections in the requirements specifications, design specifications, user's guide, operator's guide, and installation guide. Section 3 defines, for each test case, the inputs required to exercise the Build. Inputs should be specified in terms of ranges of rates and values, input protocols, and structure. All databases, files, and messages required to provide supporting inputs should also be spelled out in this section.

Section 4 specifies the correct output for the given test case inputs. Where possible, exact values for each output should be given so that test case analysis results in a simple pass or fail. Section 5 describes the hardware and software configuration needed to execute Build test cases. This section is used to document any other special test environment requirements such as specially trained personnel and recorders needed to support a particular test. Section 6 identifies unique procedural requirements such as special constraints and scripts for operators and testers. Section 7 describes the order in which test cases are run and any intercase dependencies. A short explanation regarding intercase dependencies is required. Section 8 includes the list of any pertinent references useful to the testing process.

Build Test Case Procedure Document (Table 10.2, section 10.3)

This document specifies the steps taken in executing a set of test cases or test timelines to exercise the Build and evaluate its function and performance. The outline of this document includes the following sections:

1. Identifier
2. Purpose
3. Special Requirements
4. Procedure

Section 1 provides a link to the Build and its other test documents. References to other documents by page and paragraph are the preferred means of coupling. Section 2 describes the purpose of the procedure and provides references to test cases that will be used. Section 3 identifies special requirements that are necessary for the execution of this procedure. These may include prerequisite procedures, special skills, or special environment requirements.

Section 4, the meat of the document, describes the manner in which test results will be accumulated, how each test will be recorded, and what constitutes an anomalous event. Section 4 also describes the sequence of steps necessary to initiate the module test, keep the test process going, measure results, shut down when anomalies occur, and action required to restart the test scenario and to stop in an orderly fashion on test completion. A major component of section 4 is the test director's scenario (each test has a test director) and operator's timelines for each position.

Build Test Log Document (Table 10.2, section 10.4)

This document provides an hour-by-hour, day-by-day account of the relevant details of a Build test. The Test log document is of primary interest to the development team. This document provides helpful information for debugging software failures. The outline of this document includes the following sections:

1. Identifier
2. Test Environment
3. Test Results
4. References

Section 1 includes test identifiers, references, and a descriptive paragraph that characterizes the Build in terms of revisions or version level and references. Section 2 identifies attributes of the test environment such as CPU model number, amount of memory used, other hardware or simulated hardware used, system software used, and other pertinent data or information that describes the characteristics of the test environment.

Section 3 includes results associated with the test execution and the occurrence of anomalous events (failures). For each test procedure execution, its identifier is recorded in this section along with attending personnel (test director, observers, witnesses, operators, and testers) and their role. Outputs recorded in this section may include visual results (error messages, aborts, requests for operator intervention, physical effects on hardware actuators, etc.), test results files (including physical location of files). The success or failure of the test execution is, of course, reported in this section. Also, any test environment conditions specific to the test execution not mentioned elsewhere should be recorded in this section. Occurrence of an unexpected event (usually a failure to execute a test case successfully) requires a record of all circumstances that surrounded the failure occurrence. All evidence is collected, and a unique identifier is assigned to each anomaly. Section 4 includes the list of any pertinent references helpful to the testing procedure.

Build Test Anomaly Document (Table 10.2, section 10.5)

This document contains a report corresponding to each test incident. A test incident report is prepared describing the incident in detail. This document will be used as the starting point for the incident investigation. Each test incident report contains the following sections, and there is one report for each test incident included in the test anomaly document.

1. Test Incident Identifier
2. Summary of the Incident
3. Incident Detailed Description
4. Impact of the Incident on the Project

The test log document contains most of the information required in sections 1 and 2. Frequently, copies of the appropriate pages of the test log document provide a good summary of the incident. Section 3 should include inputs to the Build being tested, expected results, actual results, date and time incident occurred, description of the environment at the time of the incident, what happened when attempts were made to repeat the test, and the names of personnel involved—any related observations or evidence that might help investigators to find the source of the incident. Section 4 should include a description of the impact of the incident on the Build test itself and on other tests scheduled.

Build Test Summary Document (Table 10.2, section 10.6)

The last document is the test summary report. This document summarizes the results of the Build testing activity and provides an evaluation based on these results. The outline of this document should include the following sections:

1. Test Summary Report Identifier
2. Summary and Conclusions
3. Variances
4. Comprehensive Assessment

5. Summary of Results
6. Evaluation
7. Summary of Activities
8. Approvals

Section 1 identifies the summary report. Section 2 identifies the unit being tested in terms of revision or version level; it indicates the environment and unit test references. Section 3 explains variances from any of the unit design or test specifications. Section 4 identifies specific areas or features that were not adequately tested. An explanation of why an area was not adequately tested is required. Section 5 summarizes results of the testing. All resolved incidents are summarized along with a brief description of the resolution. All unresolved incidents are listed and referenced.

Section 6 provides an overall evaluation of Build performance including any limitations based on its behavior in test executions and on pass/fail criteria. This section answers the question, "Should this Build test be declared a success?" Section 7 summarizes the test activity and records the hours required to perform the tests, resources used (CPU, memory), and CPU hours the Build actually executed. Section 8 certifies (accepts or approves) new modules via successful acceptance testing before incorporating them into the Build configuration.

10.7 PERSPECTIVES ON BUILD TESTING ■

During module acceptance testing, the software development team is the contractor and the test and integration team members emulate the customers. Some of the old Builds are augmented by new modules to form new Builds. The testing that follows should test all features of prior Builds and all new features planned for this Build. In addition, stress tests and tests in degraded modes of operation should be performed. The objective should be to perform test cases that will find ways to make the system fail. All discrepancies should be resolved and all problem reports should be closed out before the Build test is complete. The end objective is to show that the Build being tested satisfies users' and operators' needs and meets one or more specified acceptance criteria.

In closing, we present a few guidelines that have evolved from experience in Build planning and testing. They are as follows:

1. Minimize dependence on correct functioning of predecessor tests. That is, try to design Build tests so that failure to pass one test case will not preclude moving to the next test case while the problem surfaced in the first test case is being solved.
2. Test both modules and Builds at their performance limits and beyond and under stressful loads and conditions. Tests of this sort will expose instances where the system will fail catastrophically under combinations of extreme loads and operating conditions.
3. For each Build, performance characteristics should be measured. Throughput, accuracy, input and output capacities, and timing should be noted and recorded formally. It is far better to identify potential failures to meet performance requirements early in the test and integration process than when the system is ready for acceptance test.
4. Maintain an accurate and complete log book in the test environment. The log book often provides clues to help in debugging a failure. The intermittent problem that occurred a

few times during a test two weeks ago and written up in the log book may provide information that will lead to uncovering an elusive fault.

5. Do not try to solve all problems simultaneously. Follow the one-unknown-at-a-time principle. Several unrelated symptoms of a problem may occur during a test run. It is tempting to postulate an explanation or solution that will make all symptoms disappear. The best approach is to isolate one symptom and design a debugging procedure that finds the source for this one discrepancy or failure. A sure sign of an undisciplined test environment and poor testing is to begin making changes to components and timelines to see if it can be made to work. Each symptom or failure should be isolated and tests designed to locate the fault. The symptom or failure should be thoroughly understood before any attempt is made to fix it.

6. Lastly, an audit and critique should be conducted after testing for each Build is complete. The main objective of this audit should be a careful consideration of questions such as: What went right? What went wrong? How can we do the next one better? More detailed questions might arise as to adequacy of the physical test environment and personnel, system maintenance, quality of the product, test cases, and operators.

The same general approaches that are employed in designing module-level black box testing (discussed in the next chapter) are also used in Build testing. The Build tests require the presence of operators and a test director. Build tests are usually conducted by following a test script that simulates operational timelines.

Most Build tests involve substantially more than the software. It is important to realize that failures that occur in the system test environment may be the result of subtle combinations of failures in other system components such as hardware, operators, documentation, operational procedures, test configurations, and the software environment. Debugging is often a joint effort. The debugging approaches (chapter 12) are conceptually the same as those for a module failure.

Typical failure modes are interfaces (human-to-machine interfaces being the most common), unforseen consequences of successful operation of all modules that leads to a failure to meet an acceptance criteria, operational timelines that are not supported or are incorrectly supported by software design, and failures to handle combinations of peak traffic loads.

10.8 ALPHA AND BETA TESTING   ■

While not a direct test and integration approach, many software developers have had success with something called alpha and beta testing. Alpha and beta testing are test methods in which software products are tested in realistic environments and under realistic conditions with real operators. Alpha testing refers to tests in which a user/operator team from the customer/client community comes to the developer's environment and participates in the testing, sometimes on a separate system. The user/operator team frequently employs their own operational timelines and applications. The approach brings in additional test cases, new operators, and more operating time on the system. Failure occurrences are documented carefully and forwarded to the test team.

Beta testing involves delivery of one or more copies of the software or system to client/

customer site(s). Those sites that are given the status of a beta site must commit to reporting failures to the test team. Again with more users, with different operators, with more and different operational timelines, and with more CPU time on the system, more faults will be exposed.

10.9 CHAPTER SUMMARY ■

This chapter has described, in the context of a generally accepted testing model, a testing and integration approach for systems and software. A major point emphasized throughout is that software testing involves much more than running the software to see if it works. Software is almost always tested in an environment that includes hardware, operators, and other software not delivered as part of the product. Planning, management, and control are very important ingredients to successful software test and integration.

The various documents associated with the testing steps were described in terms of their tables of contents. It is thought that a knowledge of the contents of these documents will give the reader an insight into the tasks that must be performed to complete the documents and thereby the testing. There are many ways to capture and record the information contained in these documents automatically. The reader is cautioned not to be intimidated by what appears to be an overwhelming amount of documentation and bureaucracy.

When the software product is tested, implicitly all associated software development activity and the personnel involved in the development process are being tested as well as the process itself.

Software testing is without doubt the most important phase of the software development life cycle. Preparation and planning for the test phase should begin early in the development cycle and be a constant concern throughout the development process.

Software testing criteria appropriate for all levels of testing is summarized as follows:

Interface Integrity   Test for both internal and external interfaces. Use specifications and operational timelines as test case sources. Test at and beyond specification limits. Test with invalid or illegal inputs. Human-to-machine interfaces should be exercised with actual operators under all possible conditions with formal test cases.

Functional Validity   Test for conformance to specifications, particularly those embedded in acceptance criteria. Operational timelines are a good source for test case design. Algorithms should be exercised for input extremes and limiting conditions. Control structures associated with functions should be tested for all possible eventualities, even those that appear to be highly unlikely or nearly impossible occurrences.

Data Content   Local and global data structures, data protection features access protocols, integrity preservation features, and maintenance features should be thoroughly tested. Test cases should be designed to expose weaknesses.

Functional Performance   The performance requirements called out explicitly in the software function and performance specification and implicitly in system performance requirements and operational timelines should be tested exhaustively. Test cases should include those required to assure that the system (1) can be initialized and brought to operational readiness by operators, (2) can recover from catastrophic failures, (3) can shut down in an orderly fashion, (4) can be secure from threats as specified in the SRS, and (5) has been stressed to the breaking point in every possible dimension.

10.10 EXERCISES   ■

1. One of the positions open to a software engineer is working with the test and integration team. In your view, what are the advantages of placing a junior software engineer with the test and integration team, both from the company point of view and from the employee point of view?

2. Develop a test and integration plan for the ABC project of chapter 2. Use Table 10.1 as the table of contents of your plan. Make sure to provide entry for each of the thirteen elements in Table 10.1.

3. Do problem 2 for the XYZ project of chapter 2. The XYZ project is of an embedded nature and in that project software is a small portion of the entire system. Explain the effect of such an embedded system on the test plan.

4. If we categorize software products into three categories:
   i. A failure causes minor economic damage.
   ii. A failure causes major economic damage and delays.
   iii. A failure may cause loss of life, money, time, equipment, creditability, etc.

Give a modified version of the test and integration plan of Table 10.1 to identify with each of the above software categories.

References

1. Defense Systems Management College, *System Engineering Management Guide*, Ed. 2, U.S. Gov. Printing Office, Washington, D.C., 1986.
2. M. Evans, *Productive Software Test Management*, Wiley, New York, 1984.
3. IEEE, *Standards Collections on Software Engineering*, IEEE Press, New York, 1994.
4. Rome Air Development Center, *Methodology for Software Reliability Prediction—RADC-TR-87-171*, Air Force Systems Command, Griffis Air Force Base, N.Y., 1987.
5. E. Yourdon, *Modern Structured Analysis*, Yourdon Press Computing Series, Prentice-Hall, Upper Saddle River, N.J., 1987.

Additional Reading

6. B. Marick, *The Craft of Software Testing: Subsystem Testing Including Object-Based and Object-Oriented Testing*, Prentice-Hall, Upper Saddle River, N.J., 1995.
7. B. Meyer, *Reusable Software: The Base Object-Oriented Component Libraries*, Prentice-Hall, Upper Saddle River, N.J., 1995.

Module Level Testing

11.0 OBJECTIVES ■

Chapter 10 discussed the testing and integration process for a system in general and for a software product in particular. However, a software product is made up of a collection of software modules, each designed to meet certain allocated requirements. In an hierarchical testing process, it makes sense to test thoroughly at the module level. Hence, testing a software product begins with testing its individual modules. The main objective of this chapter is to demonstrate, with examples, some of the concepts, tools, and techniques employed in software testing, especially in testing a module. Other objectives of this chapter are as follows: (1) to describe the module test process in detail, (2) to describe the family of formal planning and test documents associated with most structured software development life cycles, (3) to discuss testing techniques that are employed in module testing, in particular white box testing, black box testing, and formal testing, (4) to provide some theoretical background to support discussions of cyclomatic complexity and formal testing, and (5) to show, through specific examples, application of testing approaches.

11.1 INTRODUCTION ■

A software module is exposed to testing both during its development phase and during its test and integration phase. During the development phase each function or procedure that is a part of a module is independently developed and thoroughly tested until the entire module is complete. The major difference between testing a module during its development phase and testing it during the test and integration phase is that, during the development phase, errors are fixed as they are found while during the test and integration phase failures, if any, are recorded and the failed module returned to the development team along with an explanation of the failures experienced (Test Anomaly Report).

Software module testing, while in practice tightly coupled, can be separated into four stages for discussion purposes. These stages are planning, static testing, dynamic testing, and debugging. The first three stages are discussed in this chapter, and debugging is discussed in chapter 12. Software module testing is the first in a series of testing steps leading to a complete and fully tested software product. A software product operates in a system involving other components such as computer hardware, system software, maintenance, human interfaces, training, and documentation that must be tested in one fashion or another. So there is really, even at the module level, no software-only testing. Module tests often involve more than just the software module.

The first component of a module test plan is a comprehensive set of test cases that fully exercise the module through its range of required functions at its specified performance limits and also exercise the module to assure that timing requirements and constraints, if any, are met. The second component of the plan is a detailed description of how each test is to be performed and what resources (drivers, scaffolds, system software, operators, etc.) are needed to support the test.

Static testing is an important adjunct to module testing. It has been claimed [2, 3, 5] that as much as 80% to 90% of software errors (perhaps we should call them human errors) or faults can be identified early in the development process by static testing techniques. Static testing includes reviews, inspections, walk-throughs, and desk checks, performed during requirements analysis, design, and code phases on nonexecutable products of the software development life cycle.

Dynamic testing involves actual execution of the test cases according to the test procedures, identification of failures, and resolution of module performance issues. In the case of a failure the test data, the module output, and the cause of the failure, if known, are recorded in a test log, and Test Anomaly Report.

The debugging stage is initiated whenever a failure occurs. The development team locates the cause of the failure(s), removes the error(s), and performs a complete retesting before returning the module to the test and integration team.

11.2   MODULE TEST PLANNING   ■

Software module test planning actually begins when function and performance requirements are allocated to each component of the system. The functions allocated to software components carry with them, implicitly, system acceptance requirements. For example, satisfactory compliance with a requirement stated as ''The software shall read and translate a bar code and perform four functions (access files, display, compute, output) within a 40 millisecond time window'' will be part of the system acceptance criteria.

11.2.1   Test Requirements Matrices

Each SRS contains a section devoted to explaining, through a matrix, how each requirement statement in the SRS will be tested. In fact, the guidelines for writing an effective requirement include a rule that says all requirements must be testable. Software module testing activity begins very early in the development cycle with the construction of the SRS test matrix. In analysis and formal reviews of the SRS, software engineers and others have an opportunity to review the test matrix, which may be viewed as the first stage of test planning.

The test requirements matrix, TRM, can take many different forms. In general, the contents are the same while the organization of the material may be different. Each specific requirement is assigned a requirement number. There are ten entries for each requirement: (1) requirement number, (2) requirement description, (3) specific variables associated with the requirement, (4) reference for the requirement, (5) means of testing (analysis, inspection, demonstration, testing), (6) range of variables associated with the requirement testing, (7) point of contact, (8) responsibility, (9) functions associated with the requirement, and (10) comments to explain any entry that needs explanation. The test requirement matrix, then, has ten columns and as many rows as there are requirements. It should be noted that the TRMs can be contained in a relational database. Table 11.1 is an example of a TRM with three requirements entered into the TRM.

■ TABLE 11.1 **A Sample TRM**

Fields	Entries		
Requirement Number	51	52	53
Requirement Description	Range Conversion	Coordinate Conversion	Heading Computation
Associated Variables	Altitude Speed Elevation	Altitude Elevation Rotation	Latitude Longitude
Reference	Section 3.2.1 SRS	Section 3.2.2 SRS	Section 3.2.2.1 SRS

Means of Testing
  Analysis
  Inspection
  Demonstration
  Test
	Demonstration
	Test
		Analysis
		Demonstration
		Test
			Analysis
			Demonstration
			Test

Value Limit	240–340 KM 2000–3000 KM 2.5–5.5 KM	240–340 KM 2.5–5.5 KM −180 to 180 Dg	−360 to 360 Dg
Point of Contact	E. L. Rogers X 3116	J. W. Luciani X1929	F. J. Shepherd X3955
Responsibility	G. W. Davis X3116	F. J. Shepherd X 3955	E. L. Rogers X3116
Functions Assoc. with Requirement	Navigation Control	Display Coordinates	Steering
Comments	None	None	See footnote SRS/ 3.2.2.1

A review of the functions allocated to software is performed twice: once when the initial allocations are made at the general software, hardware, operator allocation level; and once when the final allocations are made at the software product level with a preliminary software architecture and design in place. At this point, software product requirements are allocated to individual modules. One review criterion is confirmation of the existence of a comprehensive set of test requirements at each level. Many development processes require that each specification document contain a TRM. At the system level, this test requirements matrix would identify a means to test each requirement in the specification. At the software product level, the design specification would contain a TRM identifying a test for each design requirement. The TRMs are good candidates for static testing.

Module test requirements are derived from the TRM. The hierarchy of TRMs is a conduit for acceptance criteria flowing down to the individual unit (module or Build) level. The objectives of the TRM are to (1) establish a database to facilitate test planning and to control and track test activities, (2) form a bridge between SRS/SDS and test specifications, (3) link each requirement to a specific test, (4) provide references linking related specifications, (5) eliminate test redundancy, (6) establish test methodology, (7) identify testing responsibilities, (8) define test data and test activities, (9) establish the need for test configurations and environments, and (10) identify data analysis needs and pass/fail criteria. The TRM is one more way to keep requirements from falling through the cracks. It is easy to see how a specific system requirement (acceptance criteria) can flow down to a single module through a series of hierarchical TRMs.

11.2.2 Module Test Plan

Typically, a top-level module test plan is prepared to convey the test philosophy, provide a module test schedule, outline a general approach to module testing, and reference applicable standards, practices, and policies. The purpose is to set the tone for the test phase and establish broad guidelines for conducting module testing. A detailed module test plan is prepared for each module. Detailed module test plans are sometimes referred to as test design specifications.

Table 11.2 provides an outline for the top-level module test plan as well as an outline for a single module test plan. The outline serves as a top-level or master plan for testing groups of modules and is then made specific to individual modules in the group of modules being tested.

Sections 1, 2, and 4 are self-descriptive. Section 3 provides a brief description of modules covered by the plan and test objectives. Section 5 discusses the pass/fail criteria in general terms for each module. In particular, this section may contain an overview of test cases and expected results for each module and a reference to test case documents or folders where test cases can be found. Section 6 describes the general approach that will be taken in performing the tests. The approach should include an overview of operator timelines or scripts that will be used, identify who will attend/witness tests, identify the test conductor and his or her authority, and describe what will happen when discrepancies are encountered during testing. Section 7 provides a general description of procedures and criteria for deciding when to halt testing and under what conditions tests may be resumed. Implicit in these decisions are general ground rules regarding regression tests at the module level. Section 8 provides detailed de-

■ TABLE 11.2   **Module Test Plan Outline**

1. Module Test Plan Identification
2. Introduction
3. Module Test Approach Description and Objectives
4. References
5. Criteria for Pass/Fail
6. Approach
7. Criteria for Halting/Continuing Testing
8. Tasks To Be Performed
9. Schedule
10. Test Products (documents)
    10.1. Test Design Specification Document
          10.1.1. Module Test Identifier
          10.1.2. Module Features To Be Tested
          10.1.3. Testing Approach To Be Employed
          10.1.4. Test Case List
          10.1.5. Module Pass/Fail Criteria
    10.2. Module Test Case Specification Document (including expected results)
          10.2.1. Identifier
          10.2.2. Unit Description
          10.2.3. Input
          10.2.4. Output
          10.2.5. Environment
          10.2.6. Special Procedures
          10.2.7. Precedence and Dependencies
          10.2.8. References
    10.3. Module Test Case Procedures Document (including operator and test director scripts)
          10.3.1. Identifier
          10.3.2. Purpose
          10.3.3. Special Requirements
          10.3.4. Procedure
    10.4. Module Test Log Document
          10.4.1. Identifier
          10.4.2. Test Environment
          10.4.3. Tests Results
          10.4.4. References
    10.5. Module Anomaly Document
          10.5.1. Test Incident Identifier
          10.5.2. Summary of the Incident
          10.5.3. Incident Description
          10.5.4. Impact of the Incident on the Project
    10.6. Module Test Summary Document
          10.6.1. Test Summary Report Identifier
          10.6.2. Summary and Conclusions
          10.6.3. Variances
          10.6.4. Comprehensive Assessment
          10.6.5. Summary of Results
          10.6.6. Evaluation
          10.6.7. Summary of Activities
          10.6.8. Approvals
11. Test Environment Description
12. Responsibilities, Staffing, Training
13. Risk Assessment and Containment

scriptions of tasks to be performed. Section 9 gives the schedule for performing the tasks discussed in section 8.

Section 10 describes the required contents of each of the six test documents associated with each module being tested. The table of contents for the six documents listed has strong similarity to the table of contents for the same six documents discussed in chapter 10, section 10.6 (Table 10.2). The contents of each document are similar to the contents of the six documents described in section 10.6. The only difference is that topics apply to modules rather than Builds.

Section 11 contains a description of the test environment including test beds, if required, test tools, and related information regarding the environment established to effect module testing. Section 12 describes responsibilities, staffing, and training requirements unique to module testing. Section 13 contains a risk analysis and a containment plan as they apply to module testing.

For each module, sections 1 through 9 of the module test plan are made specific to the individual module. The documents of section 10, whose contents are described in the top-level module test plan, are developed on a module-specific basis. The first three documents are prepared before module test execution, the next two during module test execution, and the last at the end of a module test. It is good practice to maintain a module test portfolio or folder for each module.

11.3   STATIC TESTING ■

The term *static testing* refers to testing the SRS, SDS and other nonexecutable items through requirement analysis, audits, desk checks, inspections, walk-throughs, etc. Static testing is employed to verify the correctness of requirements, designs, and code before execution of test cases. Static testing will also audit newly developed or reused code for adherence to established standards.

A successful static test of a software module depends upon several things going right: a correct allocation of requirements to the software components; a correct partitioning and suballocation of software requirements to the module; a successful (correct) module design; and a successful translation of the intermediate code (pseudocode, PDL, etc.) into programming language statements. However, truly representative test cases must be successfully executed before a software module is certified by the test and integration team. Usually this step is not, usually, a part of static testing.

11.3.1   Static Testing Functions

Static test tools and processes focus primarily on requirements specifications, design specifications, and on the architectural aspects of the software module or component. These tools analyze software module or component characteristics as viewed from available information without regard to program execution.

Functions performed in static testing are as follows: code auditing, consistency checking, cross referencing, interface analysis, input/output specification analysis, data flow analysis, error checking, type analysis, units analysis inspections, walk-throughs, and cleanroom correctness verification. There are automated tools to help software engineers to perform any or all of these functions. Often such tools carry the name of the function they perform. For example, we may hear of tools called Automated Code Auditors, Automated Consistency Checking, etc.

Code Auditing Code auditing refers to examination of source code to determine whether or not specified programming practices and procedures have been followed. Typical rules and practices include adherence to structured design and coding or use of standard coding rules. Tools that implement such functions are called code auditors or standards enforcers.

Consistency Checking A consistency check determines whether or not units of program text are internally consistent in the sense that they implement a uniform notation or terminology and are consistent with the specification. Such tools are usually used to check adherence to design ground rules or specifications and are called consistency checkers.

Cross-Referencing Cross-references are dictionaries relating entities by logical name. Cross-referencing tools are frequently features of high-level language compilers, although they also appear in debugging tools.

Interface Analysis Interface analysis checks the interfaces between program elements for consistency and adherence to predefined rules or axioms. Typical interface checks may include checks on parameters passed to subprograms and the scope of identifiers. These tools are called interface checkers.

I/O Specification Analysis The goal of input and output specification analysis is the generation of input and output data by analysis of specifications.

Data Flow Analysis Data flow analysis originated in compiler optimization studies. It consists of the graphic analysis of collections of (sequential) data definition and reference patterns to determine constraints that can be placed on data values at various points of execution of the source program. Tools that perform such functions are called data flow analyzers.

Error Checking Error checkers determine discrepancies, their importance, and causes within the module.

Type Analysis Type analysis involves the determination of correct use of named data items and operations. Usually, type analysis is used to determine whether or not the domain of values attributed to an entity are correct and consistent. The compiler for some programming languages performs a strong type checking. In such cases it may be redundant to do a separate type analysis.

Units Analysis Units analysis determines whether or not the units or physical dimensions attributed to an entity are correctly defined and consistently used. Unit analysis also includes reviews, audits, and walk-throughs of specifications, and especially examination of test-related documentation.

Walk-throughs A walk-through is a type of design review in which several participants, each with a particular area of experience or expertise, review a work product. The objective of a walk-through is to uncover errors in the product.

Inspections An inspection is a software quality assurance tool that goes a little deeper than a walkthrough. The inspection is conducted in five steps: overview, prepare, inspect, rework, and follow-up. The inspection can be a highly structured review of a product.

Cleanroom Correctness Verification Certain mathematical PDL's have incorporated correctness verification software that can automatically perform correctness tests on the program requirements. Two examples of such PDLs are ''Spec'' [1] and ''Z'' [6]. Cleanroom correctness verification, in the absence of any automated tool, can and should be performed manually.

11.4 DYNAMIC TESTING ■

Dynamic testing as used here is a term that describes the development of test cases and test procedures, the execution of test cases, and the structure and use of test logs and anomaly or incident reports. There are two popular ways to perform dynamic testing, namely, black box testing and white (glass) box testing. Either of these two methods requires a set of well-developed and well-structured test cases.

Dynamic testing cannot prove the absolute correctness of a software product unless it is performed in an exhaustive manner. An exhaustive test requires a set of test cases that guarantees the following: explicitly exercises every possible module path and every possible combination of paths with every possible module input and every possible combination of module inputs.

It is because of this requirement that exhaustive testing of a software product, even a small one, is not practical. For example, suppose one is required to test an integer addition algorithm by employing an exhaustive testing approach. An exhaustive test case would include approximately 2^{64} test executions (assuming integers are stored in 32 bits). For a computer that performs 2^{24} operations per second, it will take 2^{40} seconds or approximately 35,000 years to complete an exhaustive test of the addition algorithm. Clearly, exhaustive testing, as described here is not a viable testing approach.

11.4.1 Black Box or Functional Testing

At the module test level, there are a number of test techniques that can be applied to effect testing. One technique is called black box testing because the module is treated simply as a transfer function. The tester (from the test and integration team) is not interested in the interior makeup of the box, but just its functional performance as it converts input to output. Some modules can be effectively tested using the black box approach. The philosophy is that if the module accepts all test case inputs and produces correct (in function, timing, and performance) results, we do not care how it does it. This approach places the burden on test design, test cases, and procedures to provide enough conditions and inputs to span all possible operational eventualities. Many of the thread tests that are performed on various Builds are of the black box test type.

The challenge in black box testing is to cause failures in the module by designing test cases that, with an appropriate input and controlled external (to the module) conditions, can produce an output that will clearly indicate a module failure. The objective is to search for interface errors, function or process errors, performance shortcomings, start-up/shutdown errors, and errors in local (module) databases by selecting appropriate inputs and external conditions and monitoring outputs.

In treating interface test design, the software engineer will be concerned with the following interface types:

■ Interrupt interfaces
■ Human-to-computer interfaces
■ Intermodule interfaces
■ Other external electronic interfaces

In each case the principal issues are the response of the module to specified interfaces in terms of the following:

- Rates
- Units
- Volumes
- Precedence
- Formats
- Values and combinations of values
- Calibration
- Data types
- Exceptions

Simply stated, test case inputs are crafted to expose instances where module response does not meet specified requirements.

Required module functions such as function controls, algorithms, and database access form the basis for test cases designed to expose module functional faults. Concerns regarding input precedence dependence, external (software-related) conditions, algorithm accuracy, function completeness, performance, data typing, units conversions, and input calibrations will lead to test cases that will expose requirement errors, design errors, and coding errors in a module.

Local (module resident) databases are subject to the same errors as a large database manager software product. Data structures, access protocols, file locking, the file update process and its potential ripple effect and deadlocks are examples of error sources that can be used to establish test cases. Start-up, shutdown, and error recovery procedures that are part of a module's requirements lead to concerns regarding external conditions needed for correct start-up or shutdown, error messages, operator's role, failure criteria conditions, and checkpoint definition.

The general approach to black box test case development is to use requirements specifications and fully explore, in a systematic way, the range of possible errors that could occur. Test cases can then be developed to expose these potential faults.

By examining the input types that the module is required to handle, the software engineer can partition all permitted input types into equivalence classes. Each equivalence class contains a specific input type and a description of a valid and invalid input for that input type. For example, if an input type has a specific format, then two equivalence classes would be an input conforming to the format and one that does not conform to the format. Or if an input type had a specified range, then an equivalence class would be an input within the range, one at or above the upper bound of the range, and one at or below the lower bound of the range.

Equivalence classes of input for test data consist of the entire test data input divided into n disjoint sets. Each disjoint set of input data is designed to verify a particular software product requirement.

An analysis of a module directed at identification of all possible errors can be used as the basis for test case design. The approach requires a thoughtful consideration of likely errors of omission and commission based on experience. This approach works well when performed as a group enterprise or in a brainstorming session.

If a particular path or equivalence class is to be exercised, an approach that has some merit is to automatically, under driver or scaffold control, cycle through an input "list." The list can be deterministic or random. For example, if an input is specified in terms of its range, a sequence of inputs can be generated in the appropriate format and used as test case input. The output can often be automatically evaluated for correctness. This approach, in addition to testing the software, puts additional CPU execution time on the test item. Experience has shown that the more CPU execution time on the software, the more likely a latent error will produce a failure.

Construction of test cases should begin with tests designed to exercise input handling capabilities of the module at input limits and just beyond. The rationale for testing at input boundaries is to search for failures that occur when inputs reach maximum and minimum specification values and go just beyond. Experience has taught us that failures often surface along the input boundaries. By exceeding these boundaries by a small amount, any failures in error handling designed into the software to deal with these cases will be exposed.

Similarly, testing at specification limits and a little beyond in other processing steps or functions can often expose failures in algorithm design or failures in error handling specification and design. Some common errors that are exposed by boundary tests are the following:

1. Unintelligible error messages
2. Wrong messages
3. Interference with system-level intervention
4. Error handling triggered by correct situation
5. No bridge to appropriate references or clues to find a source of error

Although programming languages like Ada and structured design tend to reduce module-to-module interfacing failures, it is imperative that module interfaces be exercised thoroughly at the module level. This approach often requires the use of drivers.

Module testing often requires test drivers to provide test inputs, to model absent module interfaces, and to capture outputs from the module for data reduction or further analysis. Part of the test case design activity includes definition of test drivers (and scaffolds if necessary) to support module testing. It is important to recognize that the quality of test driver software should be comparable to that of the module being tested.

The overall objectives of module testing should include the following:

1. Design test case to expose faults and weaknesses.
2. Select test cases that have a high probability of surfacing faults due to errors of omission and commission.
3. Cover the full spectrum of module input conditions and module environment under combinations that tend to uncover hidden faults.
4. Use stress tests and overload the module in ways that will force failures.

Cause-and-effect graphing techniques also attempt to bring a systematic approach to design of module tests by examining the module in terms of causes (inputs) and effects (outputs). By developing a cause-and-effect graph using a special notation [5] or by simply developing a decision table for the module, the software engineer can enlarge the pool of applicable black box test cases.

It should be remembered that black box testing is noninvasive. Module failure information is based solely on probing with inputs and observing responses. A black box test, may overlook a latent fault that will manifest itself when an untested combination of events in input space, processing space, and time occur.

Example 11.4.1 Black Box Testing

The ABC project identified a need for a software product to support employee training. Training for the ABC system is to include courses that use programmed instruction, video-taped lectures, satellite-delivered courses, and conventional classroom instruction. An analysis of the SRS and some preliminary design work revealed that a test scoring module would be needed in the employee education support software segment.

The module would accept raw test data from an internal file, an external file, or the keyboard. A variety of reports were required as output. The following paragraphs are extracted from the SRS as design inputs for the test scoring module:

The software shall accept the following inputs:

1. Authorized instructor input (to be read once):
   a. Number of questions in the test ($0 < N < 250$).
   b. Correct answers, one letter ('A' to 'E') per each question.
   c. Points for each question (a one-digit number).
   d. Instructor's name (20 characters, last name, middle initial, and first name).
   e. Course department (4 letters).
   f. Course number (6 characters).
   g. Course title (25 characters).
   h. Number of students taking the test.
2. Authorized student inputs (to be provided by each student):
   a. Student's ID (9 digits).
   b. Student's name (20 characters, last name, middle initial, first name).
   c. Student's answers (one letter per question).

Output shall be provided to instructors and students. Reports shall be presented in hard copy and in soft copy. Each student shall be provided with the following report:

STUDENT ID
STUDENT NAME
COURSE ID AND DESCRIPTION

1. CORRECT ANSWERS (maximum of 50 answers per line).
2. STUDENT ANSWERS (to be vertically aligned with the correct answers).
3. QUESTION POINTS (vertically aligned with correct answers).

STUDENT	RAW SCORE _____	% SCORE _____
AVERAGE	RAW SCORE _____	% SCORE _____
HIGHEST	RAW SCORE _____	% SCORE _____
LOWEST	RAW SCORE _____	% SCORE _____
STUDENT SCORE IN PERCENTILE PLACEMENT _____		

The software shall provide the instructor with several reports for each test. The first report shall have the following form:

INSTRUCTOR NAME
COURSE ID AND DESCRIPTION

NUMBER OF STUDENTS TAKING THE TEST _____
NUMBER OF QUESTIONS ON THE TEST _____
HIGHEST SCORE (raw and percentage) ON THE TEST _____
LOWEST SCORE (raw and percentage) ON THE TEST _____
AVERAGE SCORE (raw and percentage) ON THE TEST _____
MEDIAN SCORE (raw and percentage) ON THE TEST _____
NUMBER OF A GRADES _____
NUMBER OF B GRADES _____
NUMBER OF C GRADES _____
NUMBER OF D GRADES _____
NUMBER OF F GRADES _____

The second report shall be ten columns wide. Each question number shall be listed. The percent of students who failed to answer the question correctly shall be entered next to the question and on the same line. A sample output for this page is shown as design guidance.

INSTRUCTOR NAME
COURSE ID AND DESCRIPTION

Questions with Percent Wrong Answers

Q NO	% W R O N G	Q NO	% W R O N G	Q NO	% W R O N G	Q NO	% W R O N G	Q NO	% W R O N G	Q NO	% W R O N G	Q NO	% W R O N G	Q NO	% W R O N G	Q NO	% W R O N G	Q NO	% W R O N G
1	22	2	15	3	15	4	12	5	13	6	10	7	12	8	14	9	8	10	12
11	23	12	17	13	10	14	10	15	25	16	11	17	12	18	9	19	10	20	8

The third report shall contain two separate lists of students who took the test. The first list shall be ordered by raw scores in descending order. The second list shall be ordered alphabetically by student's last name. An example of this report is provided for design guidance.

of Students Taking the Test Ordered by Raw Scores

INSTRUCTOR NAME
COURSE ID AND DESCRIPTION

STUDENT ID	STUDENT NAME	RAW SCORE	% SCORE	GRADE
222113333	Zoulu B. Brain	161	92	A
111223333	Almesri A. John	135	76	C

Continued on the following page.

Alphabetic List of Students Taking the Test

<table>
<tr><td colspan="5" align="center">INSTRUCTOR NAME
COURSE ID AND DESCRIPTION</td></tr>
<tr><th>STUDENT ID</th><th>STUDENT NAME</th><th>RAW SCORE</th><th>% SCORE</th><th>GRADE</th></tr>
<tr><td>111223333</td><td>Almesri A. John</td><td>135</td><td>76</td><td>C</td></tr>
<tr><td>222113333</td><td>Zoulu B. Brain</td><td>161</td><td>92</td><td>A</td></tr>
</table>

Additional requirements thought to be applicable to the test scoring module were also extracted from the SRS and are presented here along with pertinent information obtained from other sources. All of this accumulated information will eventually become part of the design database.

a. If the number of questions provided as input data is 999, then the correct number of questions is equal to the correct answers provided as input data. Otherwise, number of questions and number of correct answers provided must match. If there is a mismatch between the two, an error message indicating the condition shall be generated.

b. If the number of students taking the test differs from the number of student answer sheets, the test shall not be corrected. An error message shall be generated.

c. Blank answers shall be counted as wrong answers.

d. If there are more than 250 questions in a given test, the test shall not be corrected. The condition shall be reported via error message.

e. Grading policy shall be on percentage basis. The default break points are 90% for A, 80% for B, 70% for C, and 60% for D. Any score less than 60% should be assigned a grade of F. Break points shall be adjustable by an authorized instructor.

f. The software shall provide the capability for the instructor to delete questions from the test. There shall be two options for deleting questions from the test:

1. By indicating the question numbers.

2. By limiting the percent of wrong answers to that question. For example, instructor may want to exclude all questions that have been answered wrong by more than 30% of students taking the test.

g. Excluded questions shall be reported to both student and instructor.

h. An incorrect instructor's name shall be identified. A file within the software product database contains the names and identification numbers of all authorized instructors.

i. Incorrect course identification (department code, course number, and course section) shall be identified. A file within the software product database contains correct identification for all courses. The primary key to access records in this file is course identification.

j. Student's name and identification number shall be verified using class roster. A database contains all class rosters. Each class roster is identified by course identification. A class roster includes instructor's name, course identification, course description, and name and identification of all students enrolled in the course.

Through several design meetings, discussions with potential users/operators, and the static testing process, it was observed that there are some omissions and inconsistencies in the SRS. These are as follows:

a. Class roster is identified by course identification, which is a string combining three data elements: department code, course number, and section number. The first two data elements are provided as input. However, course section number is not provided.

Recommendation   Since for a given course we need only have the course identification, it is recommended that instead of having three data elements (department, course number, and section number), there be one data item called course identification, which contains department, course number, and section number.

b. The access key to the instructor file is not specified. Either the file is a sequential file or there is information missing regarding access to an instructor's record. Also, because there may be two instructors with the same name, we should identify each instructor by a unique identification, such as social security number, and use this identification as the primary key to access the instructor file. Assuming the database is using such an identification number, the SRS has not made mention of this fact.

Recommendation   When item b was discussed with the SRS authors, it became clear that there is no need to access the instructor file for checking instructor's name. The course roster includes the correct instructor name. Therefore, it is recommended that the instructor's name be checked while the course identification is being checked.

c. An incorrect course identification must be detected. On the other hand, the key to access the file containing course identifications and descriptions is the course identification itself. Is this going to cause any problem?

Answer   At first this situation presents a puzzle. However, whenever a course identification is incorrect, the access to the file containing the course identifications and descriptions will be denied. It is enough to say that the course identification is incorrect.

d. One of the reports being generated requires that a list be sorted on student's last name. However, no provision has been made in the input definition as to how to separate the last name from the rest of the name.

Recommendation   Students's name should be divided into three (or at least two) pieces: last name (12 characters), middle initial (1 character), and first name (10 characters).

e. There is a need to know the structure of the records in the following files:

Roster Master File   This file contains the roster for each course.

Roster File   This file contains the roster information, instructor, department, course number, section number, course description, names, and IDs of students enrolled in the course, etc.

Recommendation   Consult the document describing the complete database used at the ABC company. There should be a description for each file included in the database. If because of security such a document is unavailable, the system manager should be able to provide the specific file description needed for this module.

f. Within the SRS/SDS it is required that the instructor name be verified against the personnel file containing the instructor record. Since the roster includes instructor name, it is more efficient to check instructor's name with the name in the roster.

Discussion   It is possible that the original instructor assigned to a course will be changed. The change will not be posted in the database until the class roster is final. If a test is given in this period, there is a chance that the instructor's name on the roster will be incorrect. Therefore, it is safer to check the instructor name against the personnel file. It is understood that you need to have the instructor's social security to access the personnel file. The input section of the SRS will be modified to include instructor's social security as input data.

When these comments and problems have been resolved, the design completed, the SRS revised, the SDS published, the module completely coded, and static testing completed, it is time to apply a black box testing procedure. Recall that while the SRS and the SDS were being developed, reviewed, and analyzed, acceptance criteria and test cases were being developed concurrently. We have, of course, glossed over the details of SRS and SDS preparation and the development of test requirement matrix.

A black box test procedure must develop and use test cases that cover all possible cases of input, including boundary values for the variables and a little beyond boundary values. For each input variable we must develop a set of test data that includes expected, lower bound, upper bound, below lower bound, and above upper bound values for that variable. For example, one of the variables used in this software module is the number of questions in the test. The expected range for this variable is any number between 1 and 250, inclusive. The lower bound value is 1, the upper bound value is 250, below lower bound is any number less than 1 (in particular, we should test for 0 and a negative number), and beyond the upper bound any number greater than 250 will make a good test case. The software should reject, with an appropriate error message, any value that is not in the expected boundary of 1 and 250, inclusive.

Note that there are some input variables whose values cannot be so easily tested at the boundary. For example, student's name, department, course number, and section number may have an incorrect number of characters. Most software designs simply truncate any character type data that goes beyond its limit. For example, if 20 spaces for student's name are provided, any number of characters beyond 20 will be truncated and any number of characters short of 20 may be augmented by blank spaces.

To create test cases we first define the set of values for each variable that the test cases should cover. Each variable will be followed by a set of values and a short description or justification for the set of values selected.

Number of Questions   The set of input values for this variable should include the following: −5, 0, 1, 100, 121, 250, 270, and 999. Although both 100 and 121 are valid inputs, it is advisable to test with two valid numbers, one being a multiple of 50 and one not a multiple of 50. This approach will test to see if a report that contains 50 questions/answers/points per every 3 lines is forthcoming. As stated in the SRS, 999 is the default value that forces the program to use the number of answers in the test key as the number of questions included in the test.

Test Key or Correct Answers   The set of inputs for this variable includes the following: (1) a set of correct values matching the exact number of questions, (2) same as in (1) but more answers than the number of questions specified, (3) same as in (1) but fewer answers than the number of questions specified, and (4) a set of answers that includes characters other than those identified in the test.

Points for each Question The set of inputs for this variable includes the following: (1) a set of correct values for points that matches the exact number of questions, (2) same as in (1) but more values for points than there are questions, (3) same as in (1) but fewer values for points than there are questions, and (4) a set of values that includes characters other than digits 0 to 9.

Instructor Name It is sufficient to test for a valid name and an invalid one. Note that an invalid name is a name that does not exist in the personnel file.

Instructor Social Security Number It is sufficient to test for a valid SSN and an invalid one. An invalid SSN is an integer less than 9 digits or larger than 9 digits or a number with leading zeroes.

Number of Students Taking the Test The set of input for this variable includes the following: (1) a negative number, say -5; (2) zero to test the computation of average and other values when there are no data available; (3) a number that matches the number of students turning in the answer sheet for the test; and (4) a number that is different from the number of answer sheets turned in.

Student's Identification Number It is sufficient to test for a valid case and an invalid case. An invalid student identification number is one that is outside the range of valid ID numbers. Also, if a valid ID number has a name other than the one stated by the student, it should be considered an invalid ID number.

Student's Name It is sufficient to test for a valid case and an invalid case. Note that this variable is divided into three fields to specify last name, middle initial, and first name. An invalid student name is one that does not correctly match its ID number.

Student's Answers No verification is needed. Anything marked on the answer sheet is considered correct input (but not necessarily a correct answer).

All the test cases described above should be exercised, and we should verify the following:

a. All test cases are successfully completed (valid test case results compare correctly with precomputed results). Computation checks include several realistic test cases, all computations are performed by hand, and compare correctly with the results produced by the module.
b. When one or more data items are incorrect, a logical and meaningful error message is produced by the program.
c. Under no circumstances does a module terminate execution without issuing an error message. Test cases are prepared to check for possible run-time errors. For example, the inclusion of a test case with zero students taking the test can be used to check run-time computation errors caused by division by zero.

d. All hardware and software module interfaces function correctly assuring that there are no interface errors. In the event that some software interfaces are not yet available, the module has been checked using simulated interfaces.

All test case results are recorded in the test log. When a test case does not produce the expected results, a more comprehensive record is required. The complete test case and module output for that test case should be entered in the test log document. In addition, all of the circumstances surrounding test case execution should be documented in a separate anomaly or test incident report. This information is extremely useful in the debugging effort described in chapter 12.

When all test cases have successfully executed, the module is regarded as being certified. From this point on the legal owner of the module is the test and integration team organization, and officially (from the software development team's point of view at least) the module has entered its maintenance phase. At this point the module is placed under formal configuration control. When the module is included in a Build and tested, it is very likely that some failures will be experienced. As previously noted, on average there will be one fault for every 200 or 300 lines of executable code when the module is delivered to the test and integration team. That is, a module that has been certified for test and integration has a good chance of failing during later testing.

11.4.2 White Box Testing

White box testing and glass box testing are synonymous with structural testing. White box testing is described in IEEE Standard 610.12-1990 as follows: All three (white box, glass box, and structured testing) refer to testing that takes into account the internal mechanism of a system or component. Types of testing include branch testing, path testing, and statement testing, in contrast with black box or functional testing where only module inputs and outputs are of interest to the tester.

It has been shown that exhaustive white box testing even for simple software modules is, practically speaking, impossible. We might ask the question: Is there a way we can be assured that at least every logical choice and every independent program path has been exercised at least once? The answer is yes. Moreover, once these independent paths have been identified, black box testing techniques that we have already discussed can be applied to each independent path.

McCabe and Butler [4] were instrumental in developing a method called *basis path testing*, which helps a software engineer to find a minimum set of paths through a module that is guaranteed to execute every statement in the module including logical choices at least once. The method is based on flow graph theory. This test approach makes use of a software attribute called *cyclomatic complexity*. *Cyclomatic complexity* is a value assigned to a program segment or a module based on the number of branches or predicate nodes in the module. The implied assumption is that more predicate nodes means more complexity. Cyclomatic complexity is a direct measure of the number of independent paths through a module. The derivation of the cyclomatic complexity measure requires some basic understanding of flow graphs and their properties.

The following develops the necessary background and defines a few important terms regarding flow graphs and their applications.

Definition 11.4.1 A directed graph G is defined as a set of nodes, $N(G)$, and a set of directed lines (called *edges* or *arcs*) connecting the nodes. The set of edges, $E(G)$, may be

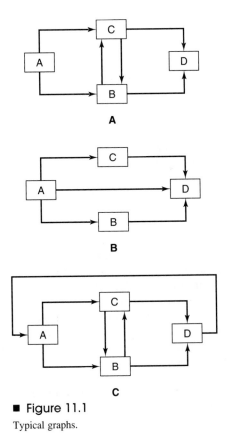

■ Figure 11.1

Typical graphs.

represented by a set of ordered pairs of nodes, each pair representing an edge initiating at the first node of the pair and ending at the second node of the pair.

Figure 11.1 presents several samples of directed graphs. Figure 11.1(**A**) represents a graph of four nodes and six edges. The sets of nodes, $N(G)$, and edges, $E(G)$, are as follows:

$$N(G) = \{A,B,C,D\}$$

$$E(G) = \{(A,C),(A,B),(C,B),(B,C),(C,D),(B,D)\}$$

Since in this chapter only directed graphs are discussed, the word *directed* as a prefix of graph will be omitted for simplicity. Hence, wherever the word *graph* is used it means *directed graph*.

Definition 11.4.2   A path through a graph G is a sequence of nodes that can be traversed by following the edges in the proper direction, that is, the direction of the arrows or the order of nodes given in $E(G)$.

Definition 11.4.3   A path is called a *cycle* if the start and end nodes along the path are the same. A cycle is called a *simple cycle* if it is not part of another cycle.

Definition 11.4.4   A set of nodes is called a *cutset* for a graph if the removal of that set of nodes (and their incident edge) breaks the graph into two separate pieces, G_1 and G_2, so that there are no paths from nodes in G_1 to nodes in G_2.

Definition 11.4.5 A graph is strongly connected if for every two nodes, X and Y, there are paths leading from X to Y and from Y to X.

Considering graph **A** in Figure 11.1, (A,B,C,D) is a path but (D,B,C,B,D) is not a path. Notice that neither graph **A** nor **B** in Figure 11.1 is strongly connected. However, graph **C** is a strongly connected graph.

Definition 11.4.6 If a graph has a unique node, h (called the *header node*), so that every other node in the graph can be reached from h and a unique node, f (called the *final node*), so that there is a path from every node in the graph to f, then the graph is called a flow graph.

A flow graph may be used as an abstract representation of a program control structure. The nodes of such a graph correspond to program statements, and the edges correspond to control paths.

Definition 11.4.7 A program path is any path through the associated flow graph (i.e., from header node, h, to final node, f). A branch is any path from decision point to decision point. In other words, $(X_1 \ldots X_n)$ is a branch if X_1 is a decision node and none of the remaining nodes $X_2 \ldots X_{n-1}$ are decision nodes.

Definition 11.4.8 In a program segment, a set of consecutive sequential statements is called a *basic block*. In a basic block the statements are executed in sequence from the first one to the last one. The last statement of a basic block is either an End statement or a jump (exclusive such as conditional or unconditional jumps; inclusive such as in While-do, Repeat-until, and Case structures) to another basic block. The basic block containing the first executable statement of the program is called the *initial basic block*, and the basic block containing the End statement is called the *final basic block* of the program.

Figure 11.2 shows the basic block decomposition for each control structure. There are two forms of If statements. In form 1, shown in Figure 11.2(**A**), the last statement in basic block A is the conditional jump, block B contains the statements in If_block, and the first statement of block C is the statement immediately following the End_if statement. In the second format block, C contains statements in the Else_block and is executed when the condition is false.

In the While condition do structure, block A contains the inclusive conditional jump to block C if the condition is false and to block B if it is true. The last statement of block B is the inclusive unconditional jump to block A. The For_loop is implemented in a manner similar to the While_loop, except the condition always checks the index of the loop against its final value.

In the Repeat_until structure, block A contains statements in the Repeat_block. Block B contains an inclusive conditional jump statement, which jumps to block A if the condition is false and to block C if it is true.

For a Case structure, block A contains an m-way inclusive conditional statement. If condition Tag = Label1 is true then block B is executed, else the next condition which is Tag = Label2 is checked. This process continues until one of the conditions becomes true. Blocks B, C, . . . , L all as their last statements have an inclusive unconditional jump to block X immediately after the End_case statement. Note that almost all of the implementation of the Case structure requires that at least one of the conditions be true. That is, Tag must be equal to one of the labels Label1, Label2, Label3, . . . or the case must have an Else option. From the basic block decomposition point of view, there is no difference between Case structures with an Else option and those without an Else option.

To compute the cyclomatic complexity measure for a module, the pseudocode or the program representing the module must be transformed into a flow graph. The following algorithm will help to achieve this transformation:

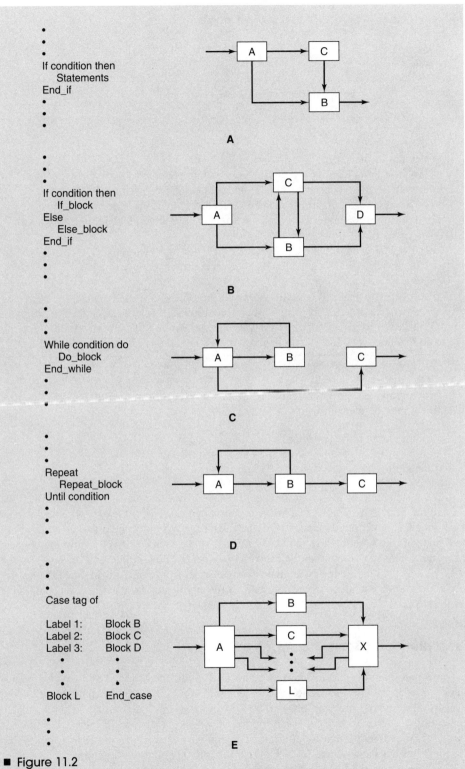

■ **Figure 11.2**

Basic block decomposition corresponding to control structures. **A**, If_then statement; **B**, If_then_else statement; **C**, While condition do statement; **D**, Repeat_until structure; **E**, Case structure.

Algorithm:

Input: A program segment (or a pseudocode segment).

Output: A flow graph representing the abstract structure of the input program.

Note: In this algorithm each function, procedure, or subprogram is considered a separate program.

Method:

1. Decompose the entire program into basic blocks.
2. The basic block containing the first executable statement of the program is called the initial basic block or the header node for the flow graph.
3. The basic block containing the last executable statement of the program (usually an End or Return statement) is called the final block or the final node for the flow graph.
4. The edges of the flow graph are as follows:
   a. A branch from block B_i to block B_j
   b. In the absence of any branch, there will be an edge from block B_i to block B_{i+1}.
5. Each call statement to a subprogram will be placed in a basic block by itself and there will be an edge from this block to the initial basic block of the subprogram. There will also be an edge from the final basic block of the subprogram to the basic block immediately following the basic block containing the invoke statement.

In a flow graph of a program segment, if there is an edge from the final node to the header node, there may be the following:

a. An infinite loop in the program,
b. A portion of the program that cannot be reached, or
c. Both a and b.

If every statement of the program can be reached from the starting statement, then every node in the flow graph can be reached from any other node with the exception of the header node, which should not be reached from the final node. We may add a dashed edge from the final node of the flow graph to its header node to make the flow graph a strongly connected flow graph. This new flow graph is called an augmented flow graph.

To be able to compute the cyclomatic complexity of a program, the augmented flow graph of that program must be strongly connected. If the augmented flow graph of a program is not strongly connected, its cyclomatic complexity is always infinity.

Example 11.4.2 Basic Blocks

The subprogram (in pseudocode) in Table 11.3 is intended to read a line of text, skip all blank spaces in the line, change lower case letters to upper case, store each nonblank character in array Command_Line, and place a "$" as the last character in array Command_Line. Table 11.4 shows the same program divided into basic blocks, and Figure 11.3 shows the flow graph representing this subprogram. The double-line arrow from the final block (block 13) to the header block (block 1) in Figure 11.3 is to augment the flow graph.

Block 1 is the initial block of the subprogram, and the arrow into block 1 comes from the block calling this subprogram. Block 13 is the final block of the subprogram, and the arrow

■ TABLE 11.3

```
/* Read_Command_Line (Command_Length);

  This procedure reads a full line of command, eliminates all of the blank spaces, converts
  lower case letters into upper case letters, and stores the command line in array
  Command_Line. It also identifies the end of command line by placing a "$" as the last
  character in array Command_Line. The argument Command_Length will return a 1 if
  the command is in short form. If the command is in long form, this argument returns the
  length of the command. A value other than 1 means the command is in long form.
  Regardless of the length of the command entered (short or long), the first 8 positions in
  array Command_Line are set aside to store the command word.

*/
Local Declarations
     Define I as integer
     Define Ch as character
     Define Is_Command as Boolean
Begin Read_Command_Line
     Set I to 0 /* character count */
     Set Is_Command to True
     Set Command_Line to a Black line
     While leading character is blank
        Read(Ch)
     End-while
     While I < 80 and more characters on the line
         Read(Ch);
         If Ch is lower case then
            Change it to upper case
         End-if
         If Ch is blank and Is_Command is True then
            Set Command_Length to I
            Set Is_Command to False
            Set I to 8 /* the longest command */
         End-if
         If Ch is not blank then
            Increment I
            Set Command_Line [I] to Ch;
         End-if
     End-while
     If less than 8 characters on the line then
         Set I to 8
     End-if
     Set Command_Line[I+1] to '$'
     Finish the current line
End Read_Com_Line
```

■ TABLE 11.4   **Subprogram Read_Command_Line (Command_Length) Basic Block**

```
        Begin Read_Command_Line
              Set I to 0
BB1           Set Is_Command to True
              Set Command_Line to a Blank line
BB2           While leading character is blank do
BB3               Read(Ch)
              End-while
BB4           While I < 80 and more characters on the line do
BB5           Read(Ch);
              If Ch is lower case then
BB6               Change it to upper case
              End-if
BB7           If Ch is blank and Is_Command is True then
                  Set Command_Length to I
BB8               Set Is_Command to False
                  Set I to 8
              End-if
BB9           If Ch is not blank then
                  Increment I
BB10              Set Command_Line [I] to Ch;
              End-if
              End-while
BB11          If I < 8 then
BB12              Set I to 8
              End-if
              Set Command_Line[I+1] to '$'
BB13          Finish the current line
        End Read_Com_Line
```

....

All Comments and nonexecutable statements are removed.
BBn = Basic Block n

out of this block represents the return from the subprogram. This arrow goes to the block immediately following the block containing the statement calling this subprogram.

Computing Cyclomatic Complexity

Corresponding to every augmented flow graph, we may define the following integer value variables:

N = The number of nodes (basic blocks) in the flow graph.

E = The number of edges (program flow lines between nodes) in the flow graph. This number should include the dashed edge from the final node to the header node.

S = The number of splitting nodes (nodes with more than one edge coming out of them) in the flow graph. Note that a node with n branches coming out of it will contribute n-1 to the count of S.

All Begins and Ends are removed for simplicity.

Enter the procedure here

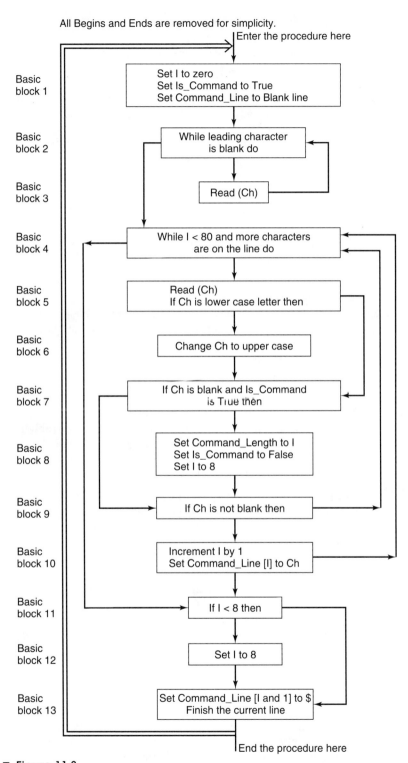

Basic block 1 — Set I to zero / Set Is_Command to True / Set Command_Line to Blank line

Basic block 2 — While leading character is blank do

Basic block 3 — Read (Ch)

Basic block 4 — While I < 80 and more characters are on the line do

Basic block 5 — Read (Ch) / If Ch is lower case letter then

Basic block 6 — Change Ch to upper case

Basic block 7 — If Ch is blank and Is_Command is True then

Basic block 8 — Set Command_Length to I / Set Is_Command to False / Set I to 8

Basic block 9 — If Ch is not blank then

Basic block 10 — Increment I by 1 / Set Command_Line [I] to Ch

Basic block 11 — If I < 8 then

Basic block 12 — Set I to 8

Basic block 13 — Set Command_Line [I and 1] to $ / Finish the current line

End the procedure here

■ Figure 11.3

Procedure Read_Command_Line (Command_Length) flow graph.

347

R = The number of regions (areas bounded by edges with no edges crossing) in the flow graph.

A value for cyclomatic complexity, C, is a measure of the structural complexity of a coded module. C can be computed using any of the following three formulas.

$$C = E - N + 1$$

or

$$C = S + 1$$

or

$$C = R$$

The cyclomatic complexity of the subprogram in Table 11.3 is 7, which is computed from the augmented flow graph of Figure 11.3. There are nineteen edges (including the double-line edge), thirteen nodes or basic blocks, six split nodes (2,4,5,7,9,11) and seven regions in the augmented flow graph in Figure 11.3.

The cyclomatic complexity, C, defines the minimum number of independent paths that must be executed to ensure that every statement will be executed at least once and every predicate node or logical choice will be exercised for both branches. For example, in Figure 11.3 the seven basis paths are as follows:

1,2,4,11,12,13	skipping blocks 3,5,6,7,8,9,10
1,(2,3)$^+$,2,4,11,12,13	skipping blocks 5,6,7,8,9,10
1,(2,3)*,2,(4,5,7,9,10)$^+$,4,11,13	skipping blocks 6,8,12 and possibly 3
1,(2,3)*,2,(4,5,6,8,9)$^+$,4,10,11,12	skipping block 7 and possibly 3
1,(2,3)*,2,(4,5,6,7,9,10)$^+$,4,11,12,13	skipping block 8 and possibly 3
1,(2,3)*,2,(4,5,6,7,8,9)$^+$,4,11,12,13	skipping block 10 and possibly 3
1,(2,3)*,2,(4,5,6,7,8,9,10)$^+$,4,11,12,13	skipping no blocks and possibly 3

Note that (2,3)* means go through the loop consisting of blocks 2 and 3 zero or more times, and (2,3)$^+$ means go through the loop consisting of blocks 2 and 3 one or more times. The same definition applies to (4,5,7,9,10)$^+$, (4,5,6,8,9)$^+$, (4,5,6,7,9,10)$^+$ and (4,5,6,7,8,9,10)$^+$.

The cyclomatic complexity metric can also be used as an indicator of how complex a module design is. For high values of C, say greater than 10, a redesign or remodularization should be considered. Note that cyclomatic complexity does not account for algorithmic complexity within sequential module statements. It is primarily a measure of structure complexity. Cyclomatic complexity values can be computed for higher level structures such as Builds or complete software products [4].

Having established the minimum number of independent paths and selected a basic path set, to exercise each logical choice and each module path at least once, the software engineer can begin to think of ways to test each independent path. That is, each path can now be viewed as a black box, and black box testing techniques as well as other techniques can be applied on a path-by-path basis.

The concept of using the cyclomatic complexity metric to assess the complexity of a design at the architectural/structural level and to infer certain integration-level test needs is a logical extension of the method applied at the module level. In principle the method would determine the number of basis paths through an architectural structure for a given set of operational timelines. This set of basis paths can then be used to structure a sequence of integration tests, define Builds, and design Build test cases. Reference [4] describes the process in more detail.

11.4.3 Dynamic Test Functions/Tools

A wide range of tools and procedures may be used to assist in testing and evaluating software products. For example, during early stages of developing and testing, drivers are often needed to simulate the external environment and to invoke the module or a part of the module. As modules are assembled into Builds for Thread testing, more sophisticated drivers may be required along with scaffolding to support the Build. Many software testing tools are not generic; in fact, they are usually unique to a specific development activity.

There are a number of module testing tasks that are very labor intensive. Execution of many test cases, logging results, post test reduction of results, comparisons with expected results, test file accumulation, logs, and other related testing information are some examples. It would be helpful if tasks could be supported by automated testing tools. A testing tool is a piece of software which automates one or more of the test functions described here. It may be possible to find a generic testing tool that can be employed to assist in performing certain testing tasks [2].

Dynamic analysis tools support testing by directly executing the program under test. In general, dynamic analysis involves the collection and reduction of information from modules or components undergoing execution of test cases. Functions performed by dynamic test tools include the following:

Coverage analysis	Symbolic execution
Tracing	Assertion checking
Simulation	Constraint evaluation
Timing	Automatic test case generators
Resource utilization	Correctness verification

Coverage Analysis   Coverage analysis means determining and assessing measures associated with the invocation of program structural elements to determine the adequacy of a test run. A tool for this function is called a coverage analyzer.

Tracing   This term means following the instruction-by-instruction progress of a program. Tracing can be further divided to path flow tracing, breakpoint control, logic flow tracing, and data flow tracing. A tool for this function is called a tracer.

Simulation   Simulation means representing certain features of the behavior of a physical or abstract system by means of operations performed by a computer.

Timing   Timing means reporting actual CPU utilization times associated with a program or its parts.

Resource Utilization   This term means analyzing the resource utilization associated with system hardware or software.

Symbolic Execution   This term means reconstructing logic and computations along a program path by executing the path with symbolic rather than actual values of data. A tool for this function is called a symbolic evaluator.

Assertion Checking   This term means checking user-embedded statements that assert relationships between elements of a program. An assertion is a logical expression that specifies a condition or relation among the program variables. Checking may be performed with symbolic or run-time data. A tool that performs this function is called a dynamic assertion processor or an assertion checker.

Constraint Evaluation   This term means generating and/or solving path input or output constraints for determining test input or for proving programs correct. This function is generally part of the symbolic evaluator and test data generators.

Automatic Test Case Generators   A number of software tools added to the CASE tools automatically generate test data for a portion of a software product as specified by program input, program structures, and program flow diagrams.

Correctness Verification   For certain PDLs there exist automated correctness verification software. Such software will verify consistency in program logic as well as correctness of mathematically defined logic. However, the programmer is required to program using the mathematical tools and specifications provided by the PDL environment.

11.4   TEST CASE EXECUTION   ■

It is not likely that module testing will proceed without a failure now and then. In fact, we should expect many of the possible failures to occur during testing. For example, for a module of 5000 SLOC, it is expected that perhaps 40 failures would be experienced, on average, during the testing process. The following presents a list of the categories of errors or faults that frequently cause the failures.

Logic Errors   Logic errors are the most common error type. Most testing is pointed toward exposing logic errors. For the most part, logic errors are repeatable and cause solid failures. That is, when a test case is run several times under the same conditions, it will produce the same failure each time.

Documentation Errors   Some documentation errors can result in failures as serious as any other error. This situation is rare, however.

Overload Errors   Errors of this type surface when algorithms, tables, buffers, queues, or storage areas are driven to capacity by legitimate test cases. These errors are particularly important in on-line systems and real-time systems.

Timing Errors   Timing errors are especially important in real-time systems. With timing errors, the added dimension (time) often results in nonrepeatable logic errors. The errors that arise are often the result of coincidental conditions in time, memory space, and program conditions.

Throughput Errors   These faults are performance errors. The software product may, even though it produces the correct output, use an exorbitant amount of primary memory, secondary memory, CPU, input/output channels, etc.

Human-to-Computer Interface Errors   In many cases the first computer-to-operator interface tests occur in the test environment. All too frequently, oversights in both operational timelines and operator-to-computer interfaces surface during module and incremental Build testing.

Error Detection and Recovery Errors   These faults are errors that arise as a result of the software not responding correctly to restart commands after a system failure or not responding correctly to protective measures designed into the software.

Hardware and System Software Errors   These faults are errors that the software engineer may feel are the ''other fellow's'' responsibility. It should be clear that the client or customer will not care who specifically is at fault if the system fails. All parties should be concerned by a failure and not be satisfied until it is found and fixed.

Standards Errors   Errors due to not following standards such as comment to executable ratios, modularity, structured programming, documentation, etc., while usually not directly related to acceptance criteria, are especially important to the maintenance phase.

Test Case Errors   These errors arise as a result of errors in the test cases or the test case results.

During test case execution, three documents are prepared: the test log, test anomaly or test incident report, and the test summary report. A short description of these three documents as they relate to Build testing is given in chapter 10, section 10.6. Here the contents of these three documents are described as they relate to individual module testing. The tables of contents for these three documents are as described in Table 11.2.

11.4.1   Test Log Document

During the actual test performance, the test log is an extremely important document. The test log provides an hour-by-hour, day-by-day account of the relevant details of a module test. In addition to identifiers and references, there is a description paragraph that characterizes the module in terms of revision or version level and references. The paragraph identifies attributes of the test environment such as CPU model number, amount of memory used, other hardware or simulated hardware being used, system software being used, and other pertinent data or information that serves to describe the character of the test environment.

Entries in the test log are associated with the test execution and the occurrence of anomalous events (failures). For each test procedure execution, its identifier is recorded in the test log along with attending personnel (director, observers, witnesses, operators, and testers) and their role. Pertinent references are added when appropriate.

The results of each test execution should be recorded. This report may include visual results (error messages, aborts, requests for operator intervention, physical effects on hardware actuators, etc.) and/or test results files (including physical location of files). The success or failure of the test execution is, of course, reported in this segment of the test log. The test log records any test environment conditions specific to the test execution not mentioned elsewhere. If an unexpected event occurs (usually a failure to meet a test case output), it is important to log the circumstances that surrounded the failure occurrence, collect the evidence, and assign a unique identifier to each anomaly. The occurrence of a failure is deemed important enough to warrant a separate report.

11.4.2   Test Anomaly or Test Incident Document

The test incident report describes the incident in detail. This report will be used as the starting point for the incident investigation. The test incident report contains the following sections: test identification, summary of the incident, incident description, and impact of the incident on the project.

The unit test log contains most of the information required for the first two sections. Frequently, copies of the appropriate pages of the test log provide a good summary of the incident. The incident description should include inputs to the module being tested, expected results, actual results, date and time incident occurred, description of the environment at the time of the incident, what happened when attempts were made to repeat the test, the names of personnel involved, and any related observations or evidence that might help investigators find the source of the failure incident. Also, the impact of this incident on the module test itself and on other test schedules should be estimated and reported in the incident report.

11.4.3 Test Summary Document

The test summary report summarizes the results of the unit testing activity and provides an evaluation based on these results. The outline for the test summary report from Table 11.2 includes the following sections:

1. Test Summary Report Identifier
2. Summary and Conclusions
3. Variances
4. Comprehensive Assessment
5. Summary of Results
6. Evaluation
7. Summary of Activities
8. Approvals

Section 1 identifies the summary report. Section 2 identifies the module being tested in terms of revision or version level, indicates the environment, and gives unit test references. Section 3 examines variances from any of the unit design or test specifications. Section 4 identifies specific areas or features that were not adequately tested and provides an explanation why testing has not been adequate. Section 5 summarizes results of the testing. All resolved incidents are summarized along with a brief description of the resolution. All unresolved incidents are listed and referenced. Section 6 provides an overall evaluation of unit performance including any limitations based on its behavior in test executions and on pass/fail criteria. The question, "Should this module be certified for inclusion in a Build?" will be resolved in this section. Section 7 summarizes the test activity and records the hours required to perform the tests, resources used (CPU, memory), and CPU hours actually executed. Section 8 describes the approval procedure and process.

These descriptions may suggest that enormous amounts of documentation and bureaucracy are associated with testing. First, for large systems and large software components this seems to be the only effective way. Second, the bureaucracy and documentation is not as bad as it reads. Most of the documentation is driven by prepared forms and templates. Much of the information is by reference or a stepwise refinement of what is already documented, and there are many ways to automate production of test documentation. Third, nearly 50% of the total dollars spent on developing a software product goes to testing, that is, nearly twice what is spent on designing and coding.

11.5 FORMAL TESTING ■

Since the 1970s, ongoing research has been directed at finding ways to automate the programming process. Although some progress has been made, there is much more to do. Formal testing is one of the steps in automating programming. In recent years DOD, NASA, and others have been more concerned about the correctness of programs being developed. More research has been devoted to formal software testing and verification. This section introduces the reader to the basics of correctness proofs and formal testing.

Formal testing can be performed on detailed SDS as well as on a program developed from the SDS. In formal testing, theoretically, there is no need to run the program to see if it works. Testing is performed purely on logical definitions of requirements and their implementation. Formal testing is truly a bottom-up testing process, in which testing begins at the single statement, construct, or expression level.

In formal testing, each statement has two predicates associated with it. These are called precondition, and postcondition predicates. The precondition predicate must be True before the execution of the statement, and the postcondition must become True after the execution of the statement. Similarly, a block of statements, $S = \{S_1, S_2, \ldots, S_n\}$, has also a precondition P and a postcondition Q. Predicate P is True before statement S_1 is executed, and predicate Q is True immediately after statement S_n is executed. Therefore, the correctness of $S = \{S_1, S_2, \ldots, S_n\}$ is shown as follows:

$$P\{S_1, S_2, \ldots, S_n\}Q$$

Note that statement S_i has its own precondition, P_i, and post condition, Q_i. A program is only a collection of blocks of statements. Therefore, the idea of formal testing begins with a single statement and extends to a complete program. We first present a few simple examples and then discuss the correctness of different forms of statements. A very important point is that this definition of correctness is silent regarding the case where P is False. That is, when the precondition is False, the results of the program cannot and should not be verified.

In the following examples, symbols used for relational operators, arithmetic operators, and assignment operators are the same as those used in algebra with the exception of :=, which means assign to. As the first example, consider the following program segment and its pre-conditions and postconditions.

$$\text{True } \{x := 0; \; y := x + 1;\} \; y > x$$

In this example we note that there is no precondition. The absence of a precondition is shown by the predicate True. The postcondition is that y must be greater than x after the execution of the program segment. Since the value of y after the program is executed is one more than the value of x, we conclude that

$$y := x + 1 \rightarrow y > x.$$

As the second example consider the following:

$$P = (x > 0 \text{ and } x + y > 0)$$

$$\{$$

read(z);

If $z < 0$ then $y := x - z$

else $y := x + y + z;$

$$\}$$

$$Q = (y > 0)$$

Assume that x, y, and z are integer variables. We want to show that if $x > 0$ and $x + y > 0$, then after the execution of the program segment, the value of y is positive, regardless of the value of z. Variable z may have a positive value, a negative value, or a value of zero. A zero value for z results in no change in the value of y. Since $x + y$ is positive, y must be positive. A positive value for z results in a value of $x + y + z$ for y. Since both $(x + y)$ and z are positive, y must be positive. A negative value for z results in a value of $x + (-z)$ for y. Since both x and $(-z)$ are positive, y must be positive.

As the third example consider the following:

$$P = (\text{Sum} = 0 \text{ and } x > 0 \text{ and } x \text{ is an integer value})$$

$$\{$$

while Sum $< x$ do

Sum := Sum + 1;

$$\}$$

$$Q = (\text{Sum} = x)$$

In the first example there was only one execution path. In the second example there were two paths through which the program could be executed, namely $\{\text{read}(z); \ y = x - z;\}$ and $\{\text{read}(z); \ y := x + y + z;\}$. In the third program segment there are many paths through which the program segment can be executed. Later we will discuss an induction method to deal with these kinds of problems. However, at this point we can argue that each time the program segment is executed, the value of Sum gets one unit closer to the value of x. Therefore, exactly x times after the program is executed, it will terminate and the value of Sum will be exactly equal to x.

It should be noted that the discussion presented for each of the previous examples must be in the form of predicates and formulas such that the entire correctness process can be expressed by a single predicate as $P\{S\}Q$.

Definition 11.5.1   An expression e is called a side-effect-free expression if its evaluation does not cause any side effect; that is, its evaluation does not alter the value of a variable in an indirect fashion.

Examples of expressions with side effect include any form of assignment to a pointer variable, and subprogram call that redefines its reference arguments or modifies any of the global variables. For simplicity, assume that all of the expressions and subprogram calls discussed in this section are side-effect-free expressions and subprogram calls.

Definition 11.5.2   A program $S = \{S_1, S_2, \ldots, S_n\}$ is said to be completely correct if and only if

a. Its postcondition, Q, is True independent of the path through the program, and
b. The program terminates in a finite time.

Condition (a) guarantees that all possible paths through the program must produce correct results. Condition (b) guarantees finite execution time for the program. It should be recognized that in computer applications the term *finite* is not defined as it is in mathematics. Instead, it means that the program must terminate, producing correct results, in a relatively short time. For example, chess is a deterministic game and the consequence of every move can be evaluated in advance. However, the program that computes such results may take many years to produce the correct results and terminate. From the point of view of mathematics, even several million years of CPU time is just a small finite number, but for all practical purposes these kinds of computations are infinite.

Definition 11.5.3 A partially correct program is a program for which condition (b) cannot be guaranteed. That is, it cannot be guaranteed that the program will terminate in finite time while producing the correct results.

For example, consider the following three program segments:

(1)	(2)	(3)
$x := 0$	read(x)	$x := \text{random}(1)$
while $x \geq 0$ do	while $x \geq 0$ do	while $x > 0.1$ do
$x := x + 1$	read (x)	$x := \text{random}(1)$

The first example is definitely an infinite loop; that is, it won't terminate no matter how long it runs. It is definitely a wrong program segment. For the second example there is no guarantee that it will terminate, but the code logic provides for its termination condition. Therefore, the correctness of this program depends on the correctness of its input value for x. The precondition for this program should be set as P = (there exists an x such that $x < 0$). This precondition implies that the input set for x must include a negative value, which in turn means that the program will terminate. Example 3 is similar to example 2 except in one way. In example 3 input is provided through a random number generator function, random(x). Assume random(x) gives a number between 0 and 1 exclusively. The probability that this program terminates is given by a binomial distribution with $p = 0.1$ and $q = 0.9$, where p is the probability that random(x) returns a value less than 0.1. Suppose Y is the number of times that the loop in the third example executes before it terminates. Variable Y is a discrete random variable, and the probability of Y being less than N is defined as

$$P(Y < N) = 0.1 + 0.1 \times 0.9 + 0.1 \times 0.9^2 + \cdots + 0.1 \times 0.9^{N-1}$$

$$= 0.1(1 + 0.9 + 0.9^2 + \cdots + 0.9^{N-1}) = 0.1 \times (1 - 0.9^N)/(1 - 0.9)$$

Therefore,

$$P(X < N) = 1 - 0.9^N$$

As can be seen, the limit of $P(X < N)$ when N is large enough is 1. For example, for $N = 20$, $P(X < 20) = 0.8784$ and for $N = 40$, $P(X < N) = 0.9973$.

Thus, for example 3 we can say, statistically speaking, the program segment will terminate. In other words, the chance that this program segment runs more than 100 times is less than 0.0000001.

As is shown by these examples, a program termination decision is something that must be dealt with one case at a time. In fact, there is a theorem in computation theory that states that "the halting problem is undecidable." That is, there exists no general algorithm that accepts as its input a given program and can decide if the program will terminate.

11.6.1 Correctness of Program Structures

There are three forms of program structures: sequential, selection, and iteration. Sequential structures are program statements that do not alter the sequential execution order of program statements. Selection structures provide two or more execution paths. Iteration structures provide for repeated execution of a block of program statements. A correctness proof method for each of these program structures follows.

Sequential Structure   Suppose S is a sequential statement and the correctness of S is represented by P{S}Q. When P is True it must be shown that after S is executed, Q is also True. For more than one sequential statement we have

$$P_1\{S_1\}Q_1, P_2\{S_2\}Q_2, \qquad P_i\{S_i\}Q_i, \ldots, P_n\{S_n\}Q_n$$

where S_i is always a simple sequential statement. In general, the postcondition of statement S_i becomes the precondition of statement S_{i+1}.

Example 11.6.1   Show the correctness of the following program segment:

$(x < n$ and $p = 2^x)$

$$\{$$
$$x := x + 1$$
$$p := p \times 2$$
$$\}$$

$(x <= n$ and $p = 2^x)$

From the precondition, $x < n$ and program statement $x := x + 1$. We conclude

$$(x < n \text{ and } x := x + 1) \rightarrow (x <= n)$$

and from the preconditon $p = 2^x$ and program statement $p := 2 \times p$. We conclude:

$$(p = 2^x \text{ and } p := 2 \times p) \rightarrow p = 2^{x+1}$$

On the other hand, $x + 1$ is the new value of x. Therefore, $p = 2^x$ after the complete execution of the program.

Selection Structure   Suppose S_1 and S_2 are two sets of sequential statements; S_2 may be empty. The structure

$$\text{if } b \text{ then } S_1 \text{ else } S_2$$

where b is a Boolean expression, is called a two-way selection structure or just a selection structure. The correctness of this structure is shown as

$$P\{\text{if } b \text{ then } S_1 \text{ else } S_2\}Q$$

This predicate may be written as

$$((P \text{ and } b) \{S_1\}Q) \text{ and } ((P \text{ and not } b) \{S_2\}Q)$$

As can be seen, the correctness of a selection structure can be reduced to the correctness of two sequential structures.

Example 11.6.2   Show the correctness of the following program segment assuming x is an integer value:

$$x <> 0 \{\text{if } x < 0 \text{ then } x := -x \text{ else } x := x + 1\} x >= 1$$

From the precondition, $x <> 0$, we can conclude one of the following cases

$$x <> 0 \text{ and } x < 0 \text{ and } x := -x \rightarrow x > 0$$
$$x > 0 \text{ and } x \text{ integer} \rightarrow x >= 1.$$

From here we have:

$$x <> 0 \text{ and } x > 0 \text{ and } x := x + 1 \rightarrow x > 1.$$

Since $x > 1$ is a subset of $x >= 1$, the program segment is correct.

Correctness of Iteration Structure Suppose b is a Boolean expression and S is a sequence of statements; then the correctness of an iteration structure is shown as

$$P\{\text{while } b \text{ do S}\}Q.$$

Depending on the values involved in evaluation of condition b, there may be many different paths through this program. Therefore, the method used to prove the correctness of a two-way selection structure is not practical for this structure. Even for a counter-controlled iteration in which the number of paths is known in advance, this number is usually too high for use of the path breakdown method discussed for the selection structure.

Definition 11.6.1 A predicate that meets the following conditions is called a loop invariant:

1. is True before evaluating the loop condition,
2. is True at the start of the initial iteration of the loop,
3. if the loop invariant and the loop condition are True at the start of any iteration, then the invariant is True at the end of that iteration, and
4. conjunction of the loop invariant and the negation of the loop condition implies Q.

It is not guaranteed that there is a loop invariant for every iteration structure nor is it necessary that the loop invariant of a loop be unique. Hence, whenever there is a loop invariant for an iteration structure, the correctness of the structure can be shown using some form of induction. To start the induction process, a hypothesis is needed. One such hypothesis may be the loop invariant.

Definition 11.6.2 If a predicate is found that satisfies the four properties of the loop invariant predicate, then the iteration structure is called a *partially correct iteration*. If it can be shown that the iteration will always terminate, then the iteration structure is called a *totally correct iteration*.

Example 11.6.3 Consider the following program and its preconditions and postconditions.

Precondition is: $P = (\text{Sum} = 0 \text{ and } I = 0 \text{ and } N >= 1)$

Program is: {while $I < N$ do

    begin

        $I := I + 1$;

        $\text{Sum} := \text{Sum} + I$;

    end;}

Postcondition is: $Q = (\text{Sum} = 1 + 2 + 3 + \cdots + N)$

To prove that this program segment is correct, the first step is to find a loop invariant. For any given I let the loop invariant be

$$\text{Inv} = (\text{Sum} = 1 + 2 + 3 + \cdots + I)$$

Before the condition of the loop is evaluated and at the start of the loop, variables I and Sum are zero; therefore conditions 1 and 2 for the loop invariant hold. Since the invariant, Sum = 1, is True at the end of the first iteration, condition 3 holds. To show condition 4 holds, it must be shown that Sum = $1 + 2 + 3 + \cdots + I$ and $I >= N$ (Aegation of the loop conditon) implies Sum = $1 + 2 + 3 + \cdots + N$. Using induction on Sum, for $I = K - 1$ assume we have Sum = $1 + 2 + 3 + \cdots + K$. For $I = K$, we have either Sum = $1 + 2 + 3 + \cdots + K + 1$ or K is equal to N and I cannot be $N + 1$.

11.6.2   Iteration Termination

In order to show that a loop will terminate, we need to define a decrementing function associated with the loop structure and show that in each iteration the decrementing function decreases. A decrementing function is mapped into a set of descending positive integers ending with zero.

In Example 11.6.4 function $f(N,I) = N - I$ could serve as a decrementing function for the loop. Each time the loop is executed, I is increased by 1; hence $f(N,I)$ is decreased by 1. Eventually, when I reaches N then $f(N,I)$ will be zero and that is when the loop will terminate.

Example 11.6.4   The following program segment is used to compute the average of a set of positive integers ending with a zero value. Discuss the correctness of this program.

```
(within the program input there exists an x such
that x = 0 and Sum = 0 and Count = 0)
{
Read(x);
while x > 0 do
begin
    Count := Count + 1;
    Sum := Sum + x;
        Read(x);
end;
Average := Sum/Count
}
(Average > 0 and Average = sum of x values divided
by the count of x values)
```

A loop invariant may be Sum as defined within the loop. It is easy to see that the first three properties of the loop invariant hold for Sum. We use induction to show the fourth property.

$$\text{Count} = 0 \rightarrow \text{Sum} = 0$$

$$\text{Count} = 1 \rightarrow \text{Sum} = x_1$$

$$\text{Count} = 2 \rightarrow \text{Sum} = x_1 + x_2$$

Suppose for Count = n we have Sum = $x_1 + x_2 + \cdots + x_n$; when Count becomes $n + 1$, the value of Sum becomes Sum + x_{n+1}.

$$\text{Sum} = \text{Sum} + x_{n+1} = x_1 + x_2 + \cdots + x_n + x_{n+1}$$

Therefore, when the loop terminates the value of Sum is equal to the number of x's read and average is computed correctly. All x's are greater than zero, which implies that the average is greater than zero. However, the average is computed correctly only if Count is greater than zero. Based on the program precondition, a set of positive integers containing zero may consist of only the element zero. In this case both Count and Sum are zero and Sum/Count is undefined. This error can be corrected by adding a restriction to the precondition predicate to guarantee that the set of positive integers has at least one positive integer in addition to the zero element. Or the program line that computes the average can be changed to the following:

if Count > 0 then Average := Sum/Count else Average is undefined

and change the postcondition to accept undefined as a correct answer.

In general, there is no guarantee that for every iteration structure there is a decrementing function. However, for all terminating iteration structures the iteration may be written such that a decrementing function can be found. For instance, in Example 11.6.4 we didn't seek a decrementing function because the conditions on the set of numbers guaranteed the termination of the iteration.

For those iterations that are controlled by a counter, such as a for-loop, it is easy to find a decrementing function. Consider the general case of a counter-controlled loop. There are four variables involved:

Index_Value: This is a loop index, which changes value each time the loop is executed.

Initial_Value: The value of the loop index will be initialized to the value of this variable before the loop is executed.

Step_Value: The value of Index_Value, loop index, is incremented (decremented) by the value of this variable. The default value for this variable is 1.

Final_Value: The value of the loop index must be less than or equal to (greater than or equal to) the value of this variable before the loop can be executed. That is, when the value of the loop index becomes more than (less than) the value of Final_Value, the loop will terminate.

The iteration counter, IC, for this kind of loop is defined as follows:

$$IC = \frac{Final\_Value - Initial\_Value}{Step\_Value} + 1$$

The decrementing function, then, is defined as follows:

$$f = IC - Index\_Value/Step\_Value$$

Note that the division in both IC and f are integer divisions. That is, only the integer part of the quotient is taken as the final answer.

For example, for the following for-loop

$$\text{for } I := K \text{ to } N \text{ do}$$

$$\text{begin}$$

$$\text{Statement;}$$

$$\text{end;}$$

We have $IC = N - K + 1$ and $f = N - K + 1 - I$.

As another example, consider the following program segment:

$$I := 0;$$

$$X := 2;$$

$$\text{While } I <= 100 \text{ do}$$

$$\text{begin}$$

$$\text{Statements;}$$

$$I := I + X;$$

$$\text{end;}$$

For this example, $IC = (100 - 0)/2 + 1 = 51$ and $f = 51 - I/2$.

To compute the decrementing function f directly, one may substitute for IC in the formula and obtain the following:

$$f = \frac{\text{Final\_Value} - \text{Initial\_Value} - \text{Index\_Value}}{\text{Step\_Value}} + 1$$

11.6.3 Correctness of Subprogram Calls

A subprogram (a procedure or a function) is itself a program entity. Therefore, it has its own precondition and postcondition predicates. However, since it is connected to another portion of the program, it must fit properly into the rest of the program. This proper fit with the rest of the program brings an additional constraint on the subprogram. In this section only those subprograms that are side-effect-free are discussed. That is, they do not alter the values of any global variables. If there is a value to be returned by a subprogram, it is assumed that a return statement will return the value. We don't distinguish between procedures and functions, assuming that they both return their value(s) through a return statement. For some languages (Pascal, for example) the return statement is embedded in the semantics of the language; for other languages the return statement is present in the procedure code, such as in the C language.

If the executable part of a subprogram is called *body*, then the correctness of the subprogram as an independent program is written as follows:

$$P'\{Body\}Q'$$

where P' and Q' are precondition and postcondition predicates, respectively. For each value of argument x we should conjunct predicate $x_0 = x$, where x_0 is the initial value of the argument x, to P'. Next define predicate $\sigma_0 = \sigma$ where σ is the current mapping of all variables (objects) to their values. The σ_0 saves the original mapping, where σ may include a new mapping for local variables (objects). Conjunct predicate $\sigma_0 = \sigma$ to P'. The precondition for the subprogram is P = (P' and $x_0 = x$ and $\sigma_0 = \sigma$). The postcondition for the subprogram is Q = (Q' and $\sigma_0 <= \sigma$).

Example 11.6.5 Define the precondition and postcondition for the following subprogram. Note that the statement Return(Ans) returns the computed value to the calling program. Prove the correctness of the subprogram.

```
Subprogram Fact (N:integer);
      Ans: integer;
begin
      Ans := 1;
      While N > 1 do
      begin
            Ans := Ans × N;
            N := N - 1;
      end;
      Return(Ans);
end;
```

We have P' = ($N >= 0$), Q' = (Ans := $N!$). From here we compute P and Q,

$$P = (N >= 0 \text{ and } N_0 = N \text{ and } \sigma_0 = \sigma)$$

and

$$Q = (\text{Ans} = N! \text{ and } \sigma_0 <= \sigma).$$

Consider the loop invariant $(\text{Ans} = N_0!/N!)$ and the decrementing function $f = N$. Each time through the loop, N is decremented by one. Therefore, the decrement function will reach 0 and the loop will terminate. Next we need to show that the four conditions for loop invariant holds.

1. Invariant holds before the loop entry: Before the loop starts, Ans is set to 1 and the precondition guarantees that N_0 is equal to N. Therefore, $\text{Ans} = 1 = N_0!/N!$ is True.
2. Invariant is true at the entry to the loop: Computation of the loop condition, $N > 0$, has no effect on the invariant. Therefore, it holds at this point as well.
3. Invariant is True at the end of the loop: The original value of N is N_0. The first time through the loop Ans is $N_0!/(N_0 - 1)! = N_0$.
4. $\text{Ans} = N!/N!$ and $N <= 1 \to \text{Ans} = N_0!/1! = N_0! = N!$.

Note that the introduction of σ_0 was just to guarantee that this procedure won't alter any global variable.

In this as well as other examples, we have shown correctness through English statements. Automatic theorem provers change the general correctness predicate, $P\{S\}Q$, to logic expressions and evaluate the expression step-by-step until it is reduced to True or False. For instance, to show that the loop invariant in Example 11.6.5 is True before the start of the loop, we must show that

$$(N >= 0 \text{ and } N_0 = N \text{ and } \sigma_0 = \sigma) \; \{\text{Ans} := 1\} \; (\text{Ans} = N_0!/N!$$

$$\text{and } N >= 0 \text{ and } \sigma_0 <= \sigma) \to \text{True}$$

using a mathematical proof similar to the following:

$$(N >= 0 \text{ and } N_0 = N \text{ and } \sigma_0 = \sigma \to 1 = N_0!/N! \text{ and } N >= 0 \text{ and } \sigma_0 <= \sigma).$$

Since $N >= 0$ and $\sigma_0 <= \sigma$ is in both sides, we can reduce the above predicate to $N >= 0$ and $N_0 = N \to (1 = N_0!/N!)$. Since $N_0 = N$ we have $1 = N!/N! \to$ True.

11.6.4   Remarks on Formal Testing

In general, there are a few reasons that formal program development and testing has not enjoyed great success in software development and software engineering. To better understand these reasons, let us examine what software engineers must do and what is expected of development tools. System analysts and software engineers must do the following:

1. Produce a verifiable SRS for the software product being built.
2. Produce a formally verifiable SDS document.
3. Produce a loop invariant and a decrementing function for each loop in a module and in the entire software system.
4. Produce a representation-independent data abstraction for each subprogram and program.

Most schools do not provide students with experience in performing formal testing tasks, and most development environments are not prepared to perform these tasks. Even better-prepared software engineers, when joining a development team, must follow the process in use. Three reasons why many new and different methods and tools have not delivered the expected improvement in the software development process are that (1) there is a lack of training the practical application of formal methods, (2) current development environments do not support the technology, and (3) there is a lack of adequate tools to support the methodology.

On the other hand, those development tools that are available have certain shortcomings. For example:

1. In many cases the correctness of the program is application dependent. When such dependency is not incorporated into the SRS or cannot be incorporated into the SDS document, the current automated theorem-proving tools may not be effective.
2. The subprograms and modules satisfy the specification, but internal interfaces have not been verified or are not verifiable.
3. The specification is wrong, and a correct program based on a wrong specification will be a wrong program. There is no automated tool for completely verifying the SRS.
4. A correct program may be identified as being incorrect because the software engineer/system analyst defined incorrect preconditions, loop invariant, or decrementing functions for the program. Today's automated tools are not able to distinguish between correct and incorrect preconditions, postconditions, and loop invariant.
5. The automated theorem-prover tool may reach a state where it cannot deduce a valid predicate as a theorem (lemma) so it can use it in the remaining proof. Someone familiar with the process used by the theorem prover may be able to augment the theorem prover with the kind of lemma needed. However, this task is difficult and is not for the average software engineer to perform.

Although a lot of work has been done to develop effective tools to automate program development, there are many unfinished tasks that must be completed and loose ends to be tied down.

11.7 PERSPECTIVES ON MODULE TESTING ■

As a closing section we repeat guidelines that have been discussed in chapter 10, to emphasize their importance and applicability to module testing. These guidelines are as follows:

1. Minimize dependence on correct functioning of predecessor tests. That is, try to design module tests so that failure to pass one test case will not preclude moving to the next test case while the problem surfaced in the first test case is being solved.
2. Test modules at their performance limits and beyond and under stressful loads and conditions. Tests of this sort will expose instances where the system will fail catastrophically under combinations of extreme but legitimate (from a specification standpoint) loads and operating conditions.
3. For each module, performance characteristics should be measured. Throughput accuracy, input and output capacities, and timing should be noted. It is far better to identify potential

failures to meet performance requirements early in the test process than when the system is ready for acceptance test.

4. Maintain an accurate and complete log book in the test environment. The log book often provides clues to help in debugging a failure. The intermittent problem that occurred a few times during a test two weeks ago and written up in the log book may provide information that will lead to uncovering an elusive fault.

5. Do not try to solve all problems simultaneously. Follow the one-unknown-at-a-time principle. Several unrelated symptoms of a problem may occur during a test run. It is tempting to postulate an explanation or solution that will make all symptoms disappear. The best approach is to isolate one symptom and design a debugging procedure that finds the source for this one discrepancy or failure. A sure sign of an undisciplined test environment and poor testing is to begin making changes to components and timelines to see if it can be made to work. Each symptom or failure should be isolated and thoroughly understood before any attempt is made to fix it.

6. Lastly, an audit and critique should be conducted after each module is tested. The main objective of such an audit should be a careful consideration of questions such as: ''What went right?,'' ''What went wrong?'' and ''How can we do it better the next time?'' More detailed questions might arise as to the adequacy of the physical test environment and personnel, system maintenance, quality of the product, test cases, and operators.

Module tests may require the presence of operators and a test director. Module tests are usually conducted by following a test script that simulates operational timelines. Most module tests involve substantially more than the testing of the module. It is important to realize that failures that occur may be the result of subtle combinations of failures in other system components such as hardware, operators, documentation, test configuration, and the software environment.

11.8 CHAPTER SUMMARY ■

A major point that has been emphasized throughout this chapter is that software testing involves much more than running the software to see if it works. Software is almost always tested in an environment that includes hardware, operators, and other software not delivered as part of the software being tested. Planning, discipline, control, and documentation are very important ingredients to a successful software testing process. The chapter has also pointed out the conceptual similarity between software module testing and system-level integration and testing. Black box testing and white box testing were discussed in some detail.

There are six documents associated with the module testing process: test design specification, module test case specification, module test case procedure, module test log, module anomaly test report, and module test summary. A knowledge of the contents of these documents will give the reader an insight as to the tasks that must be performed to complete the documents and thereby the module test.

Software testing in general (and module testing in particular) is without doubt the most important phase of the software development life cycle. Preparation and planning for the test phase should begin early in the development cycle and be a constant concern throughout the development process.

Flow graphs and their application in finding the cyclomatic complexity and basis paths of a program module were discussed in this chapter. The application of flow graphs in developing appropriate test cases, determining distinct and independent paths through a program module, finding the minimum set of distinct and independent paths which together guarantee the execution of every line in the program, and performing black box testing on each path were also discussed in this chapter. The use of flow graphs was illustrated through an extensive example.

Furthermore, it was shown that flow graphs can be created from both the detailed design and the program code. Creating and analyzing the flow graph of a detailed design may show ways to simplify a design, if necessary. The flow graph method can also be applied at higher structural levels to accomplish the same results.

It was emphasized that in testing a program module, one must test for functional validity as well as functional performance of the module. When a program module is being tested, it is important to test for all required internal and external interfaces. When appropriate, human-to-computer interfaces should be exercised with actual operators. When testing an embedded piece of software, the hardware components and the operation environment must be duplicated to assure the performance of the software in its operational environment.

11.9 EXERCISES ■

1. Consider a software system developed to automate university registration. The system allows students to register in person, by mail, by phone, or by computer (indirect access to the university computer system).
   a. Suggest any software testing tool that may be useful in testing this software.
   b. Is there a need for building a simulator for testing this software? Why?
   c. Give a comprehensive set of test data to perform black box testing of this software.
2. A dynamic analyzer is a program that counts the number of times a program statement is executed.
   a. Describe how a dynamic analyzer may be used to test a program module.
   b. Can a dynamic analyzer replace the need for a flow graph in a testing environment? Why?
   c. Explain the relative advantages of a dynamic analyzer.
   d. Explain any other automated testing tools that you have used or are familiar with that can facilitate program module testing.
3. Test data generators are programs designed to generate test cases for a program module.
   a. Describe how a test data generator may be useful in the software testing process.
   b. Describe how a flow graph can be used along with a test data generator to generate test cases to test a program module.
   c. Would you trust a program that had been tested only using test cases generated by test data generators? Why?
4. Describe why a real-time software system that has been tested in a simulated environment is not always reliable.
5. Describe the use of a dynamic analyzer in the white box testing approach.
6. A program development team, after fully testing a large program module, introduced N failure-causing software errors to the module before placing the program module for test and integration process. The idea was to see how many of these intentional built-in failures will be discovered during test and integration. The test and integration team

discovered M failures from which K were of the known failures. Observing this experiment, the development team decided that there are

$$(M - K) \times (N/K - 1)$$

failure-causing software errors remaining in the software module.
 a. Discuss the validity of this deduction.
 b. Under what conditions could the deduction by the development team be viable?
 7. Discuss the differences between black box (functional) and white box (structural) testing models.
 8. Design and develop a program module, using a programming language of your choice, to accept as input a program written in a high-level language and output a flow graph representation of that program.
 9. Develop a complete set of test cases for the program module in exercise 8.
10. Use the program written in exercise 8 as an input for itself and compute the cyclomatic complexity of the program.
12. Discuss how the two testing methods, white box and black box, may be used together to test a program module.
13. Use a programming language of your choice to write a subprogram for each of the following tasks:
 a. To sort an array of integers.
 b. To read a line of text and count the number of words in the line.
 c. To search a sorted linked list for a special element.
 d. To count the number of leaves in a binary search tree.
 e. To find the greatest common divisor of an array of N positive integers.
 f. To find a minimum cost spanning tree for a weighted graph.
 g. To find the smallest sequence of consecutive elements of an array of positive integers that add up to M, for any given positive integer M.
14. Compute the cyclomatic complexity of each of the subprograms in exercise 13.
15. Develop a set of test cases for each of the subprograms of exercise 13 in order to perform a black box testing.
16. Write a procedure that swaps the value of its two arguments and returns the swapped values through statement Return(Y,X). Prove the correctness of your answer.
17. Find a loop invariant and a decrementing function for each of the following loops:
 a. { read(x)
        while $x > 0$ do
              $x := x - 1$}
 b. { $x := 25$
      repeat
          $x := x - 2$
          if $x < 10$ then $x := 8$
      until $x = 0$}
 c. { $a[n] := a[1]$
        for $I := 1$ to $N - 1$ do
          $a[I] := a[I+1]$}
18. Formalize the specification of the following function subprograms:
 a. Sqrt(x): to compute and return the square root of its argument.
 b. Sqr(x): to compute and return the square of its argument.
 c. Min_or_zero(a,b): to return zero if either a or b is negative and return the minimum of a and b otherwise.

19. Write the formal specification for the following subprograms:
    a. PosElement(a,i): to return the number of positive elements in array a. Argument i is used to return the value.
    b. Largest(a,x): to return the largest value of array a in x.
20. Suppose the postcondition for each of the following programlike segments is the same as is $Q = (x > y > 0$ and $w * x < 0)$. Give a proper precondition for each segment.
    a. $x := y$
    b. $x := y - w$
    c. $x := 2 \times y; w := 1 - x$
    d. $x := -y$
    e. if $x > y$ then $w := 5$ else $w := -5$
21. Find precondition P for the following:
    a. P$\{x := 2 \times x\}$ $(0 < x < 20)$
    b. P$\{x := x + y\}$ $(x = -1$ and $y = 1)$
    c. P$\{$if $y <> 1$ then $y := 1$ else $y := -x\}$ $(x < 0)$
    d. P$\{x := 1 - x;$ if $x > 0$ then $y := 1 - x\}$ $(0 <= x <= 1$ and $y >= 0)$
22. Compute the truth value of the following predicate:
    True
    { if $a < b$ then begin
        $t := a$
        $a := b$
        $b := t$
    end
    if $b < c$ then begin
        $t := b$
        $b := c$
        $c := t$
    end
    if $c < a$ then begin
        $t := c$
        $c := a$
        $a := t$
    end }
    $a >= b >= c$
23. Verify the following program segments:
    a. $y > 0$
        { $z := x$
        $n := y$
        while $n > 1$ do
        begin
            $z := z + x$
            $n := n - 1$
        end }
        $z = x \times y$
    b. $n > 0$ and $x > 0$
        {$p := x$
        $k := 0$
        while $k < n$ do

begin
$$p := p \times x$$
$$k := k + 1$$
end }
$$p = x^n$$

c. $n > m$ and $n > 0$ and $m > 0$
{ $R := n - m$
while $R >= m$ do
$$R := R - m$$ }
$R = n \bmod m$

d. $n > m$ and $n > 0$ and $m > 0$
{ $R := n - m$
$q := 1$
while $R >= m$ do
begin
$$q := q + 1$$
$$R := R - m$$
end }
$R = n \operatorname{div} m$

24. Investigate the correctness of the following program segment:
$(x > 0)$
{ if $(x \operatorname{div} 2) + 2 = x$ then $x := x/2$ else $x := x \times x$ }
(x is even)

25. Write a nonrecursive program using a for-loop to compute the following function:

$$F(n) = \begin{cases} 1 & \text{if } 0 <= n <= 1 \\ F(n-1) + F(n-2) & \text{if } n > 1. \end{cases}$$

Prove the correctness of your program.

References

1. V. Berzins, Luqi, *Software Engineering with Abstraction*, Addison-Wesley, Reading, Mass., 1991.
2. R. A. DeMillo, W. M. McCracken, R. J. Martin, J. F. Passafiume, *Software Testing and Evaluation*, Benjamin-Cummings, Redwood City, Calif., 1987.
3. IEEE, *Standards Collections on Software Engineering*, IEEE Press, New York, 1994.
4. T. J. McCabe and C. W. Butler, "Design Complexity Measurement and Testing," Comm. ACM 32(12):1415–1425, (1989).
5. R. S. Pressman, *Software Engineering, A Practitioner's Approach*, Ed. 3, McGraw-Hill, New York, 1992.
6. J. B. Wordsworth, *Software Development with Z: A Practical Approach to Formal Methods in Software Engineering*, Addison-Wesley, Reading, Mass., 1995.

Debugging

12.0 OBJECTIVES ■

The principal objective of this chapter is to present a structured approach to the investigation of an apparent software failure, determine its source (the fault), and effect a change to the software to eliminate the fault that caused the failure. A second objective of this chapter is to emphasize that the source of a failure does not always lie with the software. Although a large number of failures are due to software faults, other elements may directly or indirectly contribute to the cause of a failure. Computer hardware, system software, operating environment, operators, internal interfaces, external interfaces, and data communication lines are examples of elements that may contribute to the cause of a failure.

12.1 INTRODUCTION ■

Bug is a name given to errors that are found in a software product, and *debugging* is the name of the process that locates and removes a bug from a software product. The story behind calling an error, or fault, in the software a bug has many versions. One version is that during the early years of computers, when programs were written in machine code or assembly language, a programmer, the late Grace Hopper, encountered a particularly difficult error in one of her programs. Finally, after literally checking every bit of her program without finding the error, she decided to check the hardware. Computer hardware of that era consisted of chassis containing relays, vacuum tubes, and discrete components. She found a dead moth caught between the contacts of one of the relays. The body of the dead bug had prevented the relay contacts from closing. The dead bug was removed and the program worked. Since then programmers have called an error in their programs a bug.

12.2 PROGRAM ERRORS (BUGS)   ■

Several kinds of errors are associated with the programming process. These errors are referred to as syntax, run-time, logic, inherited, and external errors.

Syntax Errors

As the name implies, syntax errors are caused by improper use of the programming language syntax. Syntax errors, sometimes called *typos*, are usually identified by the compiler and are easy to remove.

Run-Time Errors

When all syntax errors are removed, an error-free object code will be produced by the compiler. While the object code is being executed, it may reach a state from which it cannot continue execution. When in this state, it is said that a run-time error has occurred. Common sources of run-time errors are as follows:

Improper Operation   Division by zero, arithmetic operations on character type data, and certain binary operations on mismatched operands (adding logical data to numeric data, subtracting a number from a set data type, etc.) are examples of run-time errors caused by improper operation. Some programming languages are strongly typed and their compiler is able to check for mismatched operands caused by mismatched data types during compile time. Other languages provide for internal type conversion. Commercial compilers have a number of options to deal with run-time errors in general and improper operations in particular. Some of these options will be discussed shortly.

Access Violations   Writing to a file that is opened for output, accessing an invalid file, referencing an invalid memory location, having improper clearance to access certain data, and opening a file with inconsistent parameters are examples of run-time errors caused by access violation.

Improper Linkage   Calling a nonexistent or unlinked module, procedure, function, or library; unauthorized use of system utilities; and faulty database linkages are examples of run-time errors caused by improper linkage.

The classification and identification of run-time errors varies from one run-time environment to another. Most compilers and operating systems developed for commercial application environments include a run-time error manual. This manual identifies each error by a code. The cause of the error is explained in the manual, and often suggestions are provided as to how to fix the error. When a run-time error occurs, the code in error along with a message will be displayed on the console; the execution of the program may be halted permanently or until the operator provides a command for continuing the execution. The operator sees the code causing the error and can either stop execution and fix the error or continue the execution from the next statement. If the operator decides to continue, he or she gives the computer a command to continue program execution. At other times the run-time error is critical to continued operation and execution must be terminated. Under these conditions the operator will terminate execution of the program.

Logic Errors

The program executes with no run-time error, but the output it produces does not satisfy requirement specifications. In such cases it is said that the program has a logic error. Common causes of logic errors are the following: incorrect inputs, incorrect algorithms, improper linkage, improper interfaces, errors in system software, faulty interpretation of the SRS, and faulty SRS. Logic errors are the main faults we deal with during the debugging process.

Inherited Errors

Errors are inherited from reused code, faults in system software, and faults in communication lines. Inherited errors may be logic errors or errors originating in peripheral devices or software other than the software under test. The reason for placing these errors in a separate category is that the current development team was not directly responsible for creating them. However, the development team is responsible for identifying and removing them.

External Errors

Any error whose cause cannot be identified anywhere within the software system is called an external error. Examples of external errors are faults in the hardware that executes the software, changes in the operating environment, and any other errors that are outside the software system.

12.3   DEBUGGING PROCESS ■

A debugging process is initiated when a failure occurs in the execution of an operational timeline or a test case. *Debugging* is a term applied to a process whereby failure symptoms are examined, the human error or software fault that caused the failure is uncovered, and the mechanics of the failure to fault link is confirmed and documented. If there were no faults, no debugging would be necessary. Testing and debugging are different activities with different objectives. The primary objective of testing is to produce failures caused by latent faults resident in the software. Therefore, the main objective of the test team is to find legitimate ways to make the software fail. On the other hand, the primary objective of debugging is to locate and remove an identified and localized fault in the program module.

The debugging process consists of six steps: information gathering, fault isolation, confirmation, documentation, fault removal, and retesting. All of the pertinent data and information associated with the failure event should be collected and organized. The fault must be localized to within a small segment of the software, such as a function, a procedure, or a small block of code. It must then be confirmed that the fault uncovered is indeed the fault that caused the failure. The debugging process and all remedial actions taken must be documented. The error(s) must be isolated, verified, and corrected. The corrected software must be thoroughly retested (regression tested) by the development team. When the development team is satisfied with software performance, it should be returned either to module testing or to the test and integration team.

12.3.1   Information Gathering

When embarking on a debugging mission, the software engineer investigating a failure needs as much evidence as possible. The test log, test anomaly reports, test summary report, hearsay, and eyewitness accounts are possible sources for additional evidence. The quality and value of the test log and anomaly reports become apparent during the debugging process. Frequently, feedback from debugging efforts can improve the quality of the test logs and anomaly reports. One of the main purposes of the test log and anomaly reports is to support the debugging activity.

The first stages of testing and debugging a large software system is a learning process for everyone. If the testing and debugging process is approached with that philosophy in mind, the entire process will flow much more smoothly.

Debugging should proceed just as any other scientific investigation does. The software engineer should review and organize all the available direct evidence and associated external conditions. For example, it will be of interest to know what else was going on in the test environment at the time the failure occurred. Who was involved in the actual test? Is an operator involved in any way? Have other components of the test system been eliminated as potential fault sources? The object is to understand fully the failure in every possible dimension and every possible context.

12.3.2 Fault Isolation

The next step is to isolate the failure to a specific statement, a block of statements, a control structure, an implementation logic, etc. To isolate the failure, the software engineer can resort to several different approaches. The first approach is binary partition by which an attempt is made to bracket the statements or control structures that are the source of the failure. The second approach is the structured question and answer approach wherein a set of questions is posed and answered (usually by the development team). The third approach is based upon drawing other people into the failure analysis. The fourth approach relies on the development of new test cases specifically designed to isolate the known fault.

Binary Partition Approach

Isolation of the failure within a module or within an incremental Build follows the time-tested binary partitioning or bracketing approach. By observing that the correct input for a test case produces an incorrect (from requirements specifications standpoint) output from the item under test, the software engineer can determine that the failure must have occurred somewhere between module (or test item) input and its output. The next debugging step is to find a point about midway through the module code path and determine what the correct result should be at this point if the output is to be correct. A trace, a debug run, or a few output statements added to the code at this point will tell if the module code is functioning correctly at the midway point. If it is correct to that point, then the fault must lie in the last half of the module code path. The last half of the module code path can now be cut in the middle and the correct result computed for the new point (about three-quarters of the way through the module). By proceeding in this systematic fashion the fault can often be bracketed and finally revealed.

For instance, to apply the binary partition method on the program of Example 11.4.1 (the test scoring problem), the module may be divided into Read input data and Process and report. If the error seems to be in the second segment, we divide this segment into computing and reporting segments. This process is continued until a small segment of the module is identified as containing the faulty program code.

Structured Question and Answer Approach

This approach is recommended for failures that are especially difficult to locate. In this approach a series of structured questions is posed and answered in sequence. The questions may include the following:

1. What would have happened if everything went as it should?
2. What requirements were met and what requirements were not met?
3. What external conditions prevailed during the test event?
4. What changes or differences were noticed during the test and events surrounding the test?
5. What could explain what we have experienced?

These questions are answered in specific detail without regard for any other aspect of the problem. The test cases are a good source of information for answering these questions.

This structured question and answer process usually leads to several alternative hypotheses or explanations for the failure experienced. Additional tests can then be designed to eliminate or confirm the hypothesis. The method is especially effective if conducted in a group setting.

The most difficult debugging problems arise in testing real-time systems. The added complexity of a time dimension to requirements satisfaction can lead to unusual and misleading failure symptoms. The worst real-time system failure types are those that are intermittent. That is, failures occur in some test case executions and not in others or failures appear and disappear in a seemingly random pattern. Occasionally a failure will occur once and never be observed again in the test environment.

For those failures that are test case peculiar, the test cases should be carefully examined for differences using the question/answer approach. Test event conditions should also be included in the analysis. The more organized, detailed, and accurate is the available information and evidence surrounding the event, the better is the chance for successful debugging.

Similarly in intermittent failures, a systematic application of the question and answer method can frequently be employed to reduce an intermittent failure to a solid or repeatable failure. In particular, identifying the complete set of relevant internal and external conditions that exist during a failure and do not exist in the absence of a failure can lead to forcing a solid failure so that the binary partition approach can then be used more effectively. In one interesting case, what seemed to be an intermittent software failure occurred only in the operational environment. The error was forced to be a solid error only after the operational environment was simulated in every detail. The software error turned out to be an intermittent hardware failure that triggered a software failure. Both hardware and software required corrective actions.

Involving Others Approach

In this approach new people are brought into the debugging process. It is preferable that these new people were not involved in the software development process and that they become familiar with module requirements by reading those parts of the SRS and SDS document that relate to the module being tested. The new people then can use the binary partition method, if necessary with new test cases, to localize the error(s). The approach relies on obtaining a fresh, unbiased point of view.

New Test Case Approach

When it is difficult to locate the faults that have caused the failure based on the test data reported in the test log and test anomaly documents, it is advisable to design new test cases based on the characteristics of the failure. These new test cases must be fundamentally different from the test cases used previously; otherwise, no new information will be revealed concerning the fault. The new test cases should be designed to exercise the software around the point(s) where the failure manifested itself.

Often in practice, several of these approaches are combined in order to locate failure causes more quickly. A carefully designed hybrid of these approaches may prove to be more effective than any individual approach. The important point is that such combinations must be highly structured.

12.3.3   Fault Confirmation

The fault isolation process, if successfully done, identifies a function, a procedure, a control structure, a block of statements, or a single statement as being at fault. The error must now be confirmed. Through additional specialized testing, desk checking, reviews, walk-throughs, and other methods, the cause of failure must be fully verified. The fault must be confirmed as the sole cause of failure. Without such confirmation, it is not advisable to begin to take remedial action.

Example 12.3.1

Suppose an error has been identified in a control statement that transfers execution of a program to a wrong location. The first step would be to examine the data used in the evaluation of the condition in the control statement carefully, looking for truncation errors, rounding errors, improper expressions, incorrect relational operators, and other possible ways that control could be transferred to an incorrect location. As an example, consider the following program segment:

$$Y := Y \times 1000$$
If Y is not equal 1000.00 then
    statements
Else
    statements

For a particular program state, it is expected that the value of Y computed in the program segment before the If Statement will be 1, so the statements on the Else path of the program segment should be executed. If error isolation has brought us to this control statement and indicates that the Else part of the control structure is not being executed under the program condition, the first step would be to add two write statements to this program segment to check the value of Y being used in the If Statement and then trace the path.

$$Y := Y \times 1000$$
If Y is not equal 1000.00 then
    Write(the value of Y is)
    statements
Else begin
    Write(the value of Y is)
    statements

The output indicates that Y is 1000. Therefore, statements in the Else path should be executed. The programmer maintains that the code is correct and the problem lies elsewhere. The skeptical software engineer is not so easily convinced that the Write statement placed in the Else path could have produced that output. To satisfy the software engineer, the programmer modifies the program segment to look like the following:

$$Y := Y \times 1000;$$
If $Y <> 1000.00$ then
    Write (''the value of Y from If part is'', Y)
    statements
Else
    Write (''the value of Y from Else part is'', Y)
    statements

and runs the program again. The output produced surprised the programmer. The output is

The value of Y from the If part is 1000.00

The software engineer's degree of confidence in the debugging made her doubt the first output. She explained to the programmer that all of the logically oriented testing and the confirmation process directed her to this segment of the code and she was not going to change her mind based on a single output line.

For a software engineer involved in testing, how it happens is not as important as why it happens. In this case someone familiar with how a computer performs arithmetic operation explained ''how it happens'' and showed how to make the appropriate correction.*

This simple example is used to show the importance of the complete confirmation of an error, its location, and its nature. The confidence in the location and the nature of the fault must be so compelling that the software engineer seldom thinks of looking elsewhere for a possible cause of failure. In our example the debugging process was kept on track by the confidence exhibited by the software engineer in the steps that led her to the faulty control structure.

12.3.4 Documentation

Every correction, modification and addition to the module must be carefully documented. New test cases must be documented, and any abnormal behavior of the program under the new test cases must be recorded. A structured documentation of the debugging process can

----

* The actual error was that the value of the original Y, although printed as 1000.00, was computed and stored in the computer memory as a number slightly less than 1. Therefore, $Y \times 1000$ was not exactly equal to 1000.00.

help the overall testing process a great deal. It is important to include not only the new test results in the documentation, but also a description of the test environment and the testers. In some cases it may be beneficial to record the physical state of the test environment such as temperature and humidity. This information can be helpful, particularly in debugging embedded software where there is suspicion that intermittent hardware errors are manifesting themselves as software failures.

In large and complicated software systems, it is not uncommon to have programs run perfectly at the test site and not run correctly at the operational site. Embedded software is often blamed for problems that originate with hardware. In many instances system engineers, software engineers, hardware engineers, and testers must work cooperatively to locate and correct faults in a system. Just as a system uses synergism to accomplish its assigned functions, a system can also use synergism to conceal the location of system faults.

12.3.5 Fixing the Fault

When the presence of a fault in a program module, procedure, function, or program segment is proved beyond any doubt and the exact nature of the fault and its exact location have been identified and confirmed, remedial action may be initiated. It is in the nature of software that a change in one part of a program can easily influence other parts of the program. The effect may have no bearing on the ability of the software to satisfy its requirements; or the change correcting the fault may introduce additional faults that will either cause failures during retest or remain latent until certain conditions prevail In the operational environment. Therefore, when a correction is designed, its effect on the entire software product must be carefully evaluated. This procedure is best accomplished by rerunning a selected subset of acceptance tests (regression tests) as well as new tests whose design is based on the knowledge gained in the debugging process.

In many instances there is more than one way to correct a given error in a program. The method chosen for correcting an error must be as follows:

1. Weak in coupling; that is, it should create minimum effect on the other parts of the program.
2. Strong in reliability; that is, the fix should not change the reliability of the software system as a whole.
3. Quick in turnaround; that is, the module should be corrected, retested, and put back into the test cycle in as short a time as possible.
4. Sound and permanent in nature; that is, short-term repairs and patching are not acceptable.

In order to find the most appropriate correction for an error, there is a need to examine the SRS and SDS documents carefully. Often an error is not caused by the design and implementation process; it is instead an error of omission or commission in the SRS. That is, the SRS is incomplete, inconsistent, or imprecise and that is the cause of the failure. According to many informal studies, errors in the SRS are the cause of approximately 50% of software failures. Reference to the SRS and SDS documents is essential to finding an appropriate correction for an error. The SRS and SDS should also be corrected when an error in one or both of these documents led to fault insertion.

The origin of most test cases is found in the SRS, SDS documents, and acceptance criteria. Inconsistency or lack of information in the source documents may be directly related to the failure experienced. Reference to the SRS and SDS documents and acceptance criteria should be an intrinsic part of any debugging process.

12.3.6   New Testing after Each Correction

Imagine a complex network of glass pipes that are connected together at different points. Suppose that there is water running through these pipes and you inject some red dye into one of the pipes. After a short period you will probably see red fluid throughout the network. All of the pipes that have red fluid in them are connected with each other. A software system consisting of many modules and subprograms is very much like this network of pipes. Changing or correcting one segment of a module is like placing red dye in one of the pipes. In the pipe example, we could see the dye. In the case of software it is unfortunately not easy to see the effect of a change on other parts of the software. Instead, logical evaluation and physical testing must be used to assure that the change in one segment of the software has not created an unwanted effect on other parts of the software.

After each modification, change, or correction in a module, it is necessary to reexamine the entire software component, not just the point where the correction was implemented. This step is required mainly because of the "red dye" effect that exists in a module. Suppose, as in Example 12.3.1, the error caused by the control statement does not correctly transfer control. The test and integration team would have no idea as to correctness of the unexecuted statements. Now that the program is corrected to execute the statements in the Else section, the process is equivalent to testing a new module. An inexperienced software engineer may simply correct the code, show that the Else path of the control structure is executed, and regard the program as corrected. A more experienced software engineer knows that there may be new variables, data elements, files, and records exercised because of the now correct execution of the control statement. These new evaluations may affect the entire software product and may lead to additional failures and reveal new faults.

When a segment of a module is modified it is possible using a flow graph (discussed in chapter 11) to ascertain specific paths that are influenced by the change. This information could then be used to structure new test cases or modify existing test cases such that the code in the affected areas is fully executed. Only when all these test cases are executed and no additional failures are experienced can it be said that the error has been corrected.

12.4   PERSPECTIVES ON DEBUGGING   ■

The "best and the brightest" are often tempted, especially when there are several faults evident in a single test execution, to assess the failure quickly, make several changes to the software, and rerun the test cases again, hoping that all the failures will disappear. This approach may work occasionally, but there are several things wrong. The problem, which may be deep seated and have tentacles that can reach into other modules, is never really understood and documented; and the failure evidence is lost. Quick fixes may actually compound problems and perhaps compromise configuration control. The best approach is one failure at a time, thoroughly investigated, located, confirmed, documented, corrected, and tested.

It is often tempting to dump memory, run traces, insert output statements, and use debugging tools in an attempt to overwhelm the problem. It may be necessary to do this at some point. However, this "overwhelm them with raw data generation" technique should be reserved until the failure evidence has been carefully and thoughtfully examined and the debugging approach thought through.

Once the fault has been clearly understood, precisely located, and positively confirmed and a repair is designed, reviewed, and tested, documentation changes must be made (perhaps even to system-level documents) wherever necessary. The entire package must be assembled and presented to the configuration control board for approval and inclusion into system and software configurations.

12.5   DEBUGGING TOOLS   ■

Debuggers are software tools that are usually embedded within the compiler and are used to help the programmer locate logical errors within the program. The effectiveness of a debugger is directly related to expertise of its user. The debugger won't be very helpful to a programmer who cannot perform an effective desk checking of his or her program. Debuggers are actually intended to facilitate a structured walk-through of the program being executed.

Different debuggers provide different facilities and levels of sophistication. Some debuggers simply show the value of the marked variables in the program at different stages of execution. Other debuggers may be as sophisticated as providing a visual trace of the execution of the program on the screen. These debuggers will place the control of the execution of the program in the hands of the programmer. The programmer will be able to see every statement of the program being executed. The effect of execution, direct or indirect, becomes available to the programmer immediately after each statement is executed.

An experienced and mature programmer can use debuggers to reduce debugging time. Debuggers are especially helpful in isolating the source of a reported failure. The debugger, like any other CASE tool, may prove to be a problem for immature and inexperienced programmers.

12.6   AN EXAMPLE   ■

The following example illustrates how faults are handled after being identified during test execution. Most of the failures/faults have their origin in the SRS or SDS. Most of the faults have to do with human-to-computer interface. In this regard the example is typical. This particular example does not include any failures that would require application of the fault isolation techniques described in section 12.3.2.

Consider the example discussed in section 9.4 of chapter 9. When the programming team is satisfied with the module (have completed their own testing), the complete program is placed with the test and integration team to be certified and accepted. The test and integration team has returned the module along with all relative test documentation as described in chapter 11. In the next section we summarize the failures detected during the test process.

12.6.1 Test Case and Results

There have been a total of forty-seven test cases to assure that every path has been thoroughly tested. The test and integration team has informed the development team of eleven major failures experienced during the test process. In this section we provide a summary of what the test and integration team has included in the test documents, especially in the test anomaly document. The eleven failed test cases reported in the test anomaly document are as follows:

Case 1   Testing has shown that while the line-editor module is in the Edit mode the user may issue another EDIT command. The program will accept the command without producing an error message. The requirement states that only one file may be open for editing. The program either violates this requirement or ignores the second EDIT command without informing the user.

Case 2   Testing has shown that it is not possible to insert a line as the first line of the text file. Attempts to move to line zero and then insert the line also failed to insert a line at the top of the text.

Case 3   The test process has shown that when command line "E xit" is entered, it produces two error messages that are inconsistent. One message says "EDIT and INSERT have no argument," which is at best confusing to the user. The second message is "too many arguments," which indicates that the user has done something wrong. This form of user interface is unacceptable.

Case 4   The test process has shown that when command "P rint" is entered, the program generates the message "too many arguments" and then prints the current line. When the command is incorrect, the program should reject it. Partial processing of an incorrect command is unacceptable.

Case 5   Testing has shown that when command "D 2,4" is entered, the program reports "too many arguments" and the current line is deleted, which is very confusing to the user. When a user sees an error message, the assumption is that the command has been ignored. However, this program produces an error message and performs a different interpretation of the command. This problem must be corrected.

Case 6   Testing has shown that when the command "Delete 100" is entered, even if the text has only ten lines, the last line of the text will be deleted without any indication that line 100 doesn't exit. This problem is again a source of confusion for the user. Suppose a text has only ten lines in it and the user issues command "Delete 12". How would the user know that line 10 is deleted and not line 12, which does not exist?

Case 7   Testing has shown that when commands are entered in their short form and not followed by at least one blank space, the short command will not be accepted. For example, command "P" will be treated as an incorrect command. However, if the short command is followed by at least one blank space, then it will be accepted. Requiring a blank space after the short version of a command word has never been addressed as a requirement.

Case 8   Testing has shown that when command "PRINT 2-4*" is entered the program output is: "too many arguments" followed by lines 2 to 4. Suppose the user wanted to print lines 2 to 48, and the * sign was mistyped for the digit 8. Just as in other cases, an incorrect command line must not be processed.

Case 9   Testing has shown that the program doesn't allow for the name of the temporary file to be entered from the keyboard. The temporary file is always Batch.tmp. The requirement specifies that the user may enter the name of the file or accept the default name, Batch.com. However, since the temporary file name is hidden from the user and is active only when the original file is in the editing process, we feel that there is no need for the user to provide the temporary file name. This problem must be resolved at the requirement specification level.

Case 10   Testing has shown that the program will halt if the name of the file being edited is incorrect. The SRS has explicitly stated that the program should not halt when the name of the file to be edited is incorrect. The software must provide a message to the effect that the file doesn't exist and ask the user to enter the correct file name.

Case 11   If during editing the entire file is deleted (by mistake or intentionally), the program does not allow the user to enter any command except INSERT. We feel that this procedure is illogical and confusing. First suppose the user, by mistake, deleted the entire file. To prevent any adverse consequences, the user enters the QUIT command so the changes made by mistake won't affect the original copy of the file. However, the program forces the user to enter INSERT, which makes no sense to the user. Second, suppose the user intentionally deletes all the records and does not want to submit any file for execution. At this point the user should give a CLOSE command so that no file (an empty file) is submitted for execution. The program as written will not allow the user to delete the entire file and finish editing.

This is a summary of the errors found by the test and integration team. In addition to the failures explained here, the test and integration team has made several observations as stated in the paragraphs that follow.

Errors of Omission Found   The intent of the SRS is that the operator can only delete lines from the original text, add lines to the original text, and browse the text. The SRS did not expect the system operator to change any line of the text file, which is why the editor provides for no CHANGE or SUBSTITUTE command. However, using the present program, the operator can change a line in the text by deleting it and then inserting a new line in its place. The client wants to make sure that, if the operator tries to change the content of a line by deleting and inserting a line in its place, the system audit process will be able to detect the operation. The client assured us that operational procedures will be written so that no Batch.Exe will be submitted for execution until the operator Journal is audited.

Modification Action   To make sure that the audit process is able to detect any wrongful entry by the system operator, we recommend that every editing command issued by the operator be written into a Journal file, which is open only to the system auditor. The client was consulted with regard to this modification, and the decision was that we need to write into the Journal file only those lines that are deleted and those that are inserted. The client's system auditor will be able to detect any wrongful entry from such a Journal. As expected, the client was not ready to discuss specifically how the auditor would be able to identify wrongful operator entries simply by looking at the Journal.

12.6.2   Correcting Program Faults

In this section the cause of each failure reported by the test and integration team will be identified and proper action will be described to correct the fault. Since the source code for this program is not included in the book, we will not discuss the actual corrective actions needed to remove the errors discovered. However, we will discuss the probable cause of each failure, and we will isolate the error causing the failure.

Case 1 Solution   The program as designed will ignore all EDIT commands after the first one. In order to inform the user of such action, we will add the following statement at the end of the group of statements that check the commands for processing.

> If Command = EDIT then
>   write(Since a file is already open,
>   EDIT is not a proper command.)

Case 2 Solution   The original SRS does not allow the current line to be a nonexistent line (line 0). The INSERT requirement means insert one or more lines after the current line. However, if it is necessary to insert lines at the beginning of a file, we will modify the software to ask the user whether she wants to insert lines at the beginning of a file or not. In the case of an affirmative answer, the program will insert lines at the beginning of the file.

Case 3 Solution   Procedure Read_Command checks for three types of improper input lines. The last error message (too many arguments) is issued when there are characters remaining at the end of a command line. However, for EDIT and INSERT commands, since they should have no arguments the program provides two forms of error message, one because EDIT and INSERT should not have any argument and one because whatever argument is provided is considered an extra argument. In order to write only one error message, the last statement of procedure Read_Command should be slightly modified.

Cases 4, 5, and 8 Solution   Variable Error is a local variable in subprogram Read_Command. Therefore, when a command line is read, as long as the command word is correct, the program calls the proper procedures to perform the command. However, if it is desired to perform the command issued only when the entire command line is verified, then variable Error must be a global variable and be set and reset in the Read_Command subprogram. Then in the main program only when Error is False, will the input command be processed.

Case 6 Solution   The implementation is as required in the SRS document. The SRS document explicitly indicates that when arguments M or N are less than 1, set them equal to 1; and when they are greater than the number of lines in the file, set them to the total number of lines in the file. Therefore, when there are only ten lines and the user asks to delete line 12, the program will delete line 10. The only modification that can be made without modifying the SRS document is to alert the user that arguments M or N are outside their legal range and have been reset to a correct value.

Case 7 Solution   In subprogram Read_Command_Line, parameter Command_Length plays an important role in identifying the short commands. As the program is written, when a command is not followed by a blank space, variable Command_Length is not set to the length of the command. Therefore, at the end of this subprogram if Command_Length is zero, it should be set back to 1 to indicate that a short command word may have been entered.

Case 9 Solution   There is no need for the user to enter the name of the temporary file. In fact, since the user knows nothing about the use of a temporary file, it would be a mistake to ask the user to give a name to such a file.

Case 10 Solution   The answer to this problem is somewhat environment (compiler and operating system) dependent. The programming team is aware of this problem, and it will be corrected when the operational environment is finalized.

Case 11 Solution   The only commands that should be allowed while the file is empty are QUIT and CLOSE commands. Therefore, we modify the command processing part of the program to allow for QUIT and CLOSE to be processed, even when the file is empty.

12.6.3   New Testing

When the recommended changes are completed, the development team tests the corrected/ modified program using the forty-seven test cases provided by the test and integration team plus some new test cases to check changes and modifications. Any new errors discovered are corrected before the program is resubmitted for test and integration.

12.7   CHAPTER SUMMARY   ■

This chapter emphasized the separation between testing and debugging and described the major steps in the debugging process. These steps are as follows: (1) investigate failures thoroughly to isolate the failure-causing fault using the four fault isolation approaches discussed in the chapter; (2) confirm identified faults, perhaps by additional test cases, and document all essential failure- and fault-related information; (3) correct faults with the same degree of discipline and control used in the original development process; and (4) perform regression testing on the software product in its operational environment to assure that the fault has been fully corrected and that there are no undesirable side effects. This step may require development of additional test cases.

12.8   EXERCISES   ■

1. Select a newly written medium size program (1000 to 2000 lines of code) and perform the following steps:
   a. Identify any fault in the program.
   b. Isolate the cause of each fault using a desktop checking process or a debugger or both.
   c. Remove/modify all the known failure-causing codes in the program.
   d. While isolating the causes of each known fault, you may discover new failure-causing errors in the program. Report any such error found.
   e. Create new test cases for checking the success of the debugging process.
2. While performing the tasks specified in problem 1, collect appropriate data with regard to the following:
   a. Number of faults.
   b. Number of errors.
   c. Number of failure-causing errors discovered during the debugging process.
   d. Density of faults per 100 lines of code.
   e. Total time spent debugging the program.
3. Write the functional specification for an ideal debugger for an object-oriented programming language.
4. Are the functional requirements of a debugger environment dependent? If yes, divide the functional requirements of a debugger into two categories: environment dependent and general. Describe the functional requirements for each category.

Software Maintenance and Maintainability

13.0 OBJECTIVES ■

The objectives of this chapter are as follows: (1) to identify those software development tasks, products, and activities that contribute directly to a maintainable software product; (2) to describe the software maintenance process; (3) to identify factors that influence software maintenance resource estimation; and (4) to justify some of the design guidelines introduced earlier in terms of their contributions to building a maintainable software product.

13.1 INTRODUCTION ■

Software maintenance is defined as the process of modifying a software product, component, or system subsequent to delivery and installation that corrects faults, improves product performance or other product attributes, or adapts the product to a changed operational environment. Software maintainability is a software attribute defined as the relative ease with which a given software product, component, or system can be modified to (1) correct faults, (2) improve performance or other attributes, or (3) adapt to a changed environment. Software maintainability is sometimes quantified in terms of an average time required to effect a revision to the software to eliminate a fault. It is of significance to note that a software product will spend upwards of 65% of its life cycle in an operational mode in a maintenance state [4].

In addition to the three categories of maintenance just defined, a fourth category may be added. This category is the application of reverse engineering and restructuring to an existing software product for the purpose of recovering or salvaging a useful software product by bringing its documentation to a level consistent with a desired maintainability [1].

Frequently, the first time that software product support issues arise is during the test phases. Software product failures, debugging, repair, and regression testing during test and integration surfaces many of the problems that users will confront during operation. At issue are such questions as How good (accurate and complete) is the documentation? How readable is the code? How logical and clear are the architecture and detail design? How easy is it to change and regression test the product? How easy is it to update the documentation? Answers to these and related questions often reveal just how much thought has gone into an appreciation for operational phase problems.

Many software products remain in productive operation for 20 to 30 years. Some COBOL programs (perhaps a trillion lines worldwide) written during the 1960s and 1970s are still being used effectively. For these software products maintenance and maintainability are critical software engineering concerns. It is the maintenance of these expensive 25+-year-old software products that has introduced the concept of reengineering and reverse engineering.

The term reverse (or back) engineering refers to a practice that originated in the hardware world. It was (and is) common practice to purchase a competitor's product and systematically work backward from the finished product through the manufacturing process, material selection, and design to recover design, material, and production information. If these drawings, specifications, and production procedures were available, it would not be necessary to reverse engineer. Reverse engineering enables a manufacturer to capture the documentation that was used to design and build the product. This process enables the manufacturer to reproduce a competitor's product (a knockoff) without expending development resources or to improve on the original product with their own version of the product. Reverse software engineering is what a software engineer must often do to maintain "alien code" (code written by someone else).

The major difference between software reverse engineering and hardware reverse engineering is that the original developers of the software product are usually not trying to protect their development data. It just does not exist. The problem of reverse software engineering is to recover from the existing code and comment statements and whatever else in the way of evidence is available—an architecture, a design, and a requirements specification that match the current configuration.

The term *reengineering* is not well defined. It has been used to describe the renovation or reclamation of everything from a corporate organization to a consumer product. As applied to software products, reengineering means using the results of reverse software engineering to enhance, extend, restructure, and redeploy a software product or system to meet new function, performance, environmental, and operational requirements.

13.2 SOFTWARE MAINTENANCE ■

It is safe to say that from the day that a large software product goes into service, functional, performance, operator, and environmental requirements will undergo changes. Moreover, the delivered software product will contain some latent defects that were not detected during testing. Some authors regard software maintenance as being divided into corrective actions to fix latent defects, adaptive actions to deal with changing environments, and perfective actions to accommodate new requirements. We will make that same distinction in this chapter.

One way to look at the maintenance process is that it is a microcosm of the software development process. The fix or improvement must be analyzed (and requirements written), designed, coded, tested, and integrated, and finally, regression tests must be executed. However, some additional constraints must be considered. These constraints are as follows: (1) the new code must interface correctly to the existing software, (2) the new code must not change the performance of the existing software except as specified in the modification documentation, and (3) all documentation must be updated to reflect the change in software configuration.

To conduct an effective maintenance action successfully, software configuration control, good quality documentation, and a sound architectural design are extremely helpful. Maintenance activities test the quality of the software configuration management process, the ability of the configuration management process to track the product through its changes, the quality of the SRS and SDS, and the ability of an architecture to accommodate growth and functional additions or changes.

Unfortunately, the following may represent a more likely situation, especially with respect to software products developed during the past three decades.

1. Currently, operating software bears no resemblance to the configuration documentation. That is, modules in the software are not found anywhere in the documentation or requirements in the SRS are not implemented in the software.
2. It is virtually impossible to read the code and understand what the original designer/coder intended or what a module or group of modules was supposed to do.
3. Comment statements are sparse, misleading, incomprehensible, or entirely absent.
4. None of the original development team members are available to answer questions.
5. The development tools and environment have deteriorated or have been removed so that development and test of changes are much more difficult.
6. Changes, even simple ones, tend to have a ripple effect and impact many other modules and features. Many of these effects are subtle and frequently not immediately visible.
7. No evidence of the application of any configuration control or software quality assurance exists.
8. Operational timelines have, over time, become oral tradition rather than well-documented scenarios with supporting rationale.
9. Customized interfaces and functions usually provided by system software are present within the software product.

In order to stop developing software products that have these nine characteristics, the software development industry in general and the software engineer in particular must find ways to achieve the following goals while designing and developing software products.

1. Make both clients and developers more deeply aware of the importance of maintenance and maintainability as a quantifiable software product requirement. Such requirements should be included in the SRS and should be part of the acceptance test.
2. Establish a documentation process that guarantees the development of the basic documentation required for effective maintenance and maintainability.

3. Determine what software design attributes contribute positively to the development of a maintainable software product. Quantify such attributes and include them as part of the Software Quality Assurance (SQA) plan.
4. Establish an architecture and a design that preserves the integrity of the unaffected parts of the software product when another part of the product is being corrected or modified.
5. Develop a maintenance process and develop or acquire effective maintenance tools to support the process.
6. Develop an approach to maintaining software products that, unfortunately, are described by any or all of the nine ills identified previously.

The last challenge (item 6) leads to the idea of maintaining alien code, reverse (or back) engineering, and reengineering of software products. Alien code refers to code written by someone other than the individual or organization charged with the responsibility for software product maintenance. The term *alien code* has also come to mean a software product that was ''hacked out'' and has inadequate documentation and very poor software configuration management. The maintenance of these software products is the software engineer's challenge of the future.

13.2.1 Maintenance Support Documents/Tools

Ideally, we would like to enter the maintenance phase of a software product's life cycle with the following supporting documentation and information:

A. Function and Performance Requirements
   1. Operational Scenarios/Timelines
   2. Specifications
   3. Acceptance Test Criteria
   4. Review Documentation
B. Design
   1. Architecture Specification
   2. Detail Design Specifications
   3. Methodology Description Documentation
   4. Review Documentation
C. Configuration Control and Management
   1. Structure and Procedures
   2. Change Records and Change History
   3. Complete Traceability from Top-Level Requirements to Implementation and Test
D. Code
   1. Pseudocode or Equivalent
   2. Assembly/Source
   3. Comments
E. Test
   1. Plans and Procedures
   2. Test Cases/Results (Module to System-Level)
   3. Test Anomaly Reports
   4. Test Summary Reports

F. Tools
   1. Compilers/Assemblers/Debuggers
   2. User Manuals
   3. CASE Tools
   4. Standards, Practices, Policies
   5. Development Environment (if applicable)
G. Trace
   1. From Requirements to Design
   2. From Design to Implementation in Code
   3. From Requirements to Tests and Integration
   4. From Requirements to Acceptance Test

What we have listed here are most of the software product's development instruments found in a modern, professionally run software development process. The quality of the maintenance activity is directly related to the quality of the instruments just listed and especially to the assigned personnel.

Maintenance also deals with software products that are not accompanied by the foregoing complement of documents. In these cases the existing documentation must be augmented as an intrinsic part of a maintenance action or originated as part of a maintenance action so that over time the software product can be brought under some form of configuration control. If a software product with poor supporting instruments is to enjoy a long and productive life cycle, some improvement to the supporting documentation must be provided as part of the maintenance process. Of course, the utility of the software product must be worth the investment required to maintain the product.

13.2.2 Using Support Documentation

For corrective, adaptive, or perfective maintenance, it is important that the maintainer gain a thorough understanding of how the current software operates. In addition, for corrective maintenance actions, a full and accurate description of all the circumstances that existed when the failure occurred must be collected as well.

The first step in effective use of the supporting documentation is to understand thoroughly how the software functions. A full appreciation of the operational environment and operational timelines is needed for effective maintenance. When operational timelines or scenarios are not already documented, it will be necessary to observe operations, interview operators, and construct operational timelines. These documented timelines should then become part of a formal maintenance documentation file. From operational timelines, it is often possible to develop a high-level abstraction of the functions being implemented by the software product. Operational timelines or operators often use unique terminology or jargon that will also appear in comment statements or even within the executable code. Collecting and recording these definitions is often useful in reading and understanding the code.

The next step involves finding in the documentation (requirements, design, code, and test) the appropriate modules involved in the implementation of the selected operational scenarios. If the documentation exists, the task may be easy. However, even with good documentation, some additional research, study, and preparation of adjunct documentation to clarify or expand on the existing documentation may be required.

In the case of no useful documentation, it may be necessary to begin with the existing source code and construct pseudocode, flow graphs, or structure charts at a higher level of abstraction. This process is made relatively easy if the original source code followed the tenets of structured design. Automated tools exist that can provide higher-level abstractions from existing source code (such tools are at this point still at the research level). To complete this step successfully, it may be necessary to design and execute special test cases and actually trace test case executions to confirm understanding. The task is complete when implementation of the specific operational scenarios is completely understood and documented. This process is sometimes referred to as manual reverse engineering.

A worst-case situation is no existing documentation, unstructured design, and hard-to-understand code. Problems of this nature are a challenge. In these cases to understand the operational scenario to implementation link fully usually requires a great investment of resources. A cost-benefit analysis may be worthwhile to decide if it is more cost-effective to start over. If the decision is to maintain the product, it usually makes good sense to capitalize on this investment by reengineering the entire software product once the operational scenario to implementation link is thoroughly understood. Reengineering might involve developing a separate module or group of modules, perhaps in a different language, to implement each revised operational scenario independently. Continued application of this approach will result in an architecture structured around operational scenarios.

13.3 SOFTWARE MAINTENANCE PROCESS ■

The software maintenance process, for large software products or systems, is in essence the same as for any maintained software product. The organizational approach to handling maintenance actions may vary considerably, however. We shall describe the maintenance process, recognizing the variety of organizational possibilities for implementing the process. Figure 13.1 illustrates a general flow of maintenance activities. Change requests can originate with a customer or contractor as a response to a failure occurrence (corrective) or as a response to requests for adaptive or perfective maintenance. A screening process that prioritizes changes and makes estimates of cost, schedule, and system downtime is used to filter change requests. For large software products this part of the process is often highly formalized with prepared forms and well-defined criteria for requesting a change. The review and approval (or rejection) of a change request is accomplished by a configuration control board or equivalent. Several different change actions are often packaged together into a single block change by the control board for efficiency and convenience of implementation.

For small software products the process is often more informal. However, implementing a software change is a significant event. It requires resources, it involves a capital investment, it affects system operation, etc. Moving forward on a change will require a commitment of resources. Management authorization in some form is required.

The procedure for a properly conducted maintenance action should include the following steps:

1. Research the change request:
    Why the change?
    Who wants the change?
    What will be changed?
    What problem will be solved by the change?
    Can it be bundled with other changes?

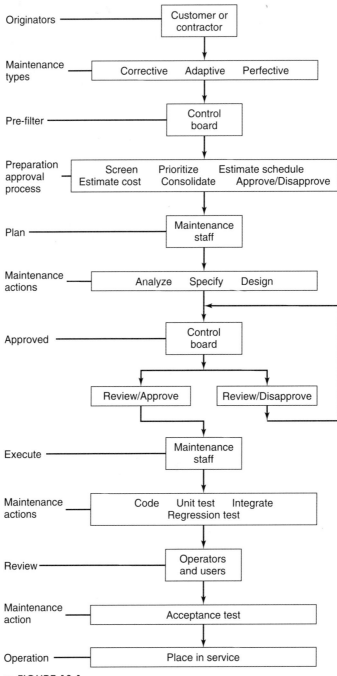

■ FIGURE 13.1

Flow of maintenance activities.

2. Estimate size, cost, and schedule for implementing change.
3. Estimate what document changes will be required.
4. Estimate changes to operational timelines required.
5. Estimate potential impact of change on other software and system components.

Completing these five steps is prologue to deciding on the disposition of the change request. If authority to proceed is granted, the five steps just described are stepwise refined by the software maintenance team.

The change implementation is thoroughly analyzed and a detail design is prepared. All affected documentation is revised. All affected operational timelines are revised. The change is implemented either on the operational system during off hours (when the system is not being used) or on a system that has been provided as part of a maintenance environment. A series of new tests are performed to assure that the change has been correctly implemented, and a series of regression tests is executed to assure that the change has not unwittingly caused any undesirable effects on the system or its operation. Finally, after a formal acceptance test, the new software configuration is placed in service.

There are several important documents that, if prepared properly, help to make maintenance action flow smoothly. These documents may be stand-alone documentation volumes or included in other documents. In either case the maintenance team needs to reference them extensively.

1. Software Functional and Performance Requirements Specification (especially sections tracing software requirements to system requirements)
2. Operational Scenario or Timeline Documentation
3. Software Design Specification (especially the section containing a trace of each line or block of pseudocode to a specific function and performance requirements)
4. All Test Documentation (especially test cases, test results, anomaly reports, etc.)
5. Adjunct System Documentation Library (including software development tools)
6. Configuration Description Documentation (including change trail)

Throughout the change implementation process reviews, audits and walk-throughs should be scheduled as quality gates. The change control board (in some instances referred to as the management committee or maintenance supervisor) is usually responsible for overseeing the review process. Changes to documentation should also be scrutinized carefully during reviews. Change documentation showing a trace from the original software product configuration (listing) to the current configuration is important to future change activity. This documentation should also be a prime consideration during the change review process. Many maintenance organizations have a well-defined procedure for documenting changes.

In summary, then, each change or block of changes to the software configuration should go through a minisoftware development life cycle. No change should be made to the software product configuration unless the change has been processed as shown in Figure 13.1 and all updates to the documentation have been completed. The criteria for success in software maintenance are the same as for developing the original software product. Quality assurance measures should be applied to any changes made to the software configuration.

Inadvertent changes that occur as a result of change actions can have devastating effects. Changes introduced to repair, add, or delete functions can result in unintentional and unwanted changes. Examples of such changes are (1) deleting or changing a module that is used by another function; (2) changing identifiers used elsewhere in the software product; (3) changing logical conditions, flags, semaphores, etc; (4) changing variable ranges; and (5) changing execution rates, which in turn upsets time dependencies.

Unanticipated effects on the database also occur when changes are introduced into a software product. These include inadvertent changes to local/global constants, formats of records/files, size of records/files, global data, initialization parameters, and subprogram parameters.

Documentation is also exposed to inadvertent errors. Errors of omission and commission can hamper subsequent maintenance actions. Attention to documentation during development of the original software product and a continued dedication to keeping all software documentation synchronized with the software product configuration are essential to reducing the occurrence of unintentionally introduced errors into code and data. The software quality as evidenced in its documentation is very influential in the reduction of maintenance costs and the continuing utility of the software product or system.

13.4 MAINTENANCE RESOURCE ESTIMATION ■

It is important to estimate accurately the resources required to support a software product effectively in the field. The developers of commonly used software products such as simulators, compilers, etc., need to know how to staff their help desk and how many developers will be needed to deal with corrective, adaptive, and perfective maintenance actions. There are also questions regarding the need for a separate development environment, training, and maintenance tools. For any major software system installation, these same questions will arise.

There is a general feeling that the productivity associated with performance of corrective, adaptive, and perfective software maintenance is far lower than the productivity associated with specifying, designing, coding, and testing an original software product. Productivity as measured in source lines of code per labor month or function points per labor month, it is claimed, is lower by a significant amount than is productivity associated with originating a software product from scratch. Maintenance productivity is influenced by the quality of the following:

- Architecture (modularity)
- Detail design (adherence to methodology)
- Documentation
- Configuration control
- Comment statements
- Adherence to standards and practices
- Maintenance personnel and their training
- Degree of complexity in the product

The software development cost estimation algorithms described in chapter 15 are, in general, not directly applicable to costs associated with maintaining software. The reason is that the number of source lines of code in a maintenance action is usually small in proportion to the maintenance effort involved. Moreover, The COCOMO* algorithms do not reflect experience with very small programs. The algorithms do, however, provide a starting point for maintenance resource estimation purposes once the approximate size of the change is known.

COCOMO resource estimation algorithms, discussed in chapter 15, can be calibrated for

....
* COnstructive COst MOdel

use in estimating software corrective maintenance cost during the test phase of a software development. This process requires collecting some information on each failure that occurs during the test and integration phase. The information to be collected includes all resources that were employed to (1) identify a problem source, (2) perform problem analysis, (3) prepare the change package, (4) conduct reviews and obtain authorization to proceed, (5) effect implementation at the module level, (6) complete test and integration/regression tests, and (7) install, train, and place the new version in service.

The calendar time required to effect a complete corrective maintenance action should be averaged and used along with failure rate data to predict software product availability. The attribute, the average time to effect a corrective maintenance action, is called *mean time to repair (MTTR)*.

The data collected during the test phase provides a good basis for calibrating the COCOMO model for use in corrective maintenance resource estimation. By carefully categorizing failures and using the reliability model discussed in chapter 17, the number of corrective maintenance actions expected can be estimated in terms of the expected number of failures per year. The number of failures can be multiplied by the average time and resources required to effect a corrective maintenance action. This information will be of value for maintenance planning.

Suppose it is determined from data collected during testing that the average corrective maintenance action required 8 working days, and productivity is computed at an average of 30 source lines of code per labor month. It is also found that changes averaged out to cost 2.8 labor months per change. From software reliability modeling (chapter 17) it is estimated that over the next three years we could expect to encounter 86 failures; thus we could estimate resources required to effect corrective maintenance to be approximately 240 labor months (86 expected failures times resources expended per failure) over the three-year period. This estimate would lead us to predict that for corrective maintenance eight people could be kept busy for three years. In terms of calendar time, we would recognize that on average there would be two maintenance actions in progress at any given time.

To estimate resources required to effect adaptive and perfective maintenance for a software product, one needs to look at historic data obtained from experience with large software systems. A large software system will experience a steady rate of adaptive and perfective maintenance actions during the lifetime of the system. Databases will also increase steadily in size at about 5% per year [2]. By making assumptions regarding expected annual change activity and using the average time and resources that were required to effect a change during test and integration, it is possible to estimate the size of the maintenance team required to support a software product in the field. For example, if the software system to be maintained contained 800,000 executable source lines of code, and if projected adaptive and perfective maintenance actions were expected to be 5% of the original product, then we can expect 40,000 (5% of 800,000) source lines of code to be revised/rewritten/replaced per year.

For perfective and adaptive maintenance our arithmetic would indicate that a 111-person staff is required (40,000 SLOC/[30 SLOC per month $\times$ 12] = 111). However, if the software product is well structured, designed, and documented and the configuration has been reasonably well maintained during development, the productivity rate can be assumed initially to be at least as high as the productivity rate for development. Let us assume, for our example, that we experienced an average productivity rate of 90 source lines of code for each labor month charged to software development. Our support or maintenance staff for perfective and adaptive maintenance of the software product would then be sized at 34 people. For planning purposes we would need 42 full-time people (34 for perfective and adaptive maintenance plus 8 for corrective maintenance) to maintain this 800,000 SLOC software product.

Typically, these forty-two people would be employed in running help desks (providing consulting services to users) and in performing corrective, adaptive, and perfective maintenance, tuning the system for optimal performance and collecting and evaluating performance data.

If, on the other hand, we found that the software product was not well supported or in spite of our best efforts our productivity was closer to our experience in the test environment, we might use the 111 person years/year as our estimate. The result would be $111 + 8 = 119$ person years/year to maintain this particular product.

Some authors have stated that productivity in the maintenance phase, in terms of SLOC produced per labor month, can be twenty to thirty times lower than it was in producing the original software. This reduction more than likely applies to software products that by our current standards would be regarded as being "hacked out"—poorly designed and poorly documented. The foregoing discussion and examples give an indication of the wide range of possible costs associated with maintaining a software product. Maintenance cost can, of course, be driven down by providing the appropriate supporting documentation and following a disciplined software development process as described in this book. If it is too late for this action, then the cost of maintaining the product will increase in inverse proportion to the quality of the support material available and in direct proportion to the complexity of the software itself.

A few observations regarding the maintenance cost estimate are in order: (1) in 15 years at a 5% per year change activity, the maintenance team will write 800,000 SLOC or an amount equivalent to the original product; (2) each change to the existing software product has the potential for introducing additional faults into the product; (3) the maintenance team will go through several generations during the software products lifetime, so a good training program will be essential; (4) the maintenance team will not be able to respond to all adaptive and perfective maintenance requests; (5) corrective maintenance resources will be undersized; and (6) the maintenance team must continue to manage and control the configuration.

13.5 DIRECTLY SPECIFIED MAINTENANCE ATTRIBUTES ■

Whenever a corporation or company makes a capital investment, there is an expected useful lifetime for that plant or equipment. A software product acquired by a company is almost always a capital investment. There should be an expected useful lifetime for a software product as a capital investment. Moreover, justification for making a capital investment usually turns on expected payback period or return on investment (Appendix B), both of which involve expected lifetime and operational (maintenance) costs. Under these circumstances it seems obvious that the SRS would contain specific maintenance-related requirements, for example, a software product requirement specifying a useful operational lifetime for the product or specifying yearly operational cost limits. Such requirements would be difficult to test directly before product delivery. However, some testable requirements have direct influence on the maintainability of a software product. Many of these can form a testable maintenance requirement structure.

Software reliability specifications provide a testable requirement that can influence the number of corrective maintenance actions per year. Chapter 17 describes a software reliability model and a means for controlling (approximately) the number of faults in a released software product.

By anticipating the growth in function, performance, and data, a requirement for growth provision in the software product can influence a software product's ability to handle perfective maintenance actions. The burden for preparing growth projections falls on the customer, system engineers, and system analysts. If software engineers and designers have a knowledge of expected growth, then designs can be developed to accommodate expected increases in function, performance, and data. A side benefit is an improvement in the maintainability of the software product.

The difficulty in making growth projections lies not in the actual mechanics of the analysis, but in deciding to make growth requirements an intrinsic part of the SRS. This decision requires a recognition that a system should be designed for the future, or the delivered system will be obsolete at acceptance. The specific growth requirements should be testable. For example, data growth projections in terms of field size, record size, file size, etc., can be tested; or the capability for accommodating additional functions, input types, protocols, rates, etc., can be tested. Accurate growth projections require a knowledge of the application area. While the software engineer is not expected to develop growth requirements, he or she should ask penetrating questions regarding growth provisions during requirement reviews.

Provision for adaptive maintenance is usually connected with portability and user interfaces. Requirements can be shaped so as to recognize that a long lifetime for a software product is associated with how easily a product can accept an upgrade in the operational environment to either hardware or software. User interface changes usually move in the direction of additional automation. Designs that can accommodate more independence from users (increased automation) or an increase in the data reduction performed on displayed information lead to a more maintainable product. Simply recognizing that the operational environment will change over time and making the design as independent as possible of the environment will probably be the best that can be done.

Low maintenance costs are associated with the resources required to effect changes. A testable software product requirement is a specification for mean time to repair (MTTR). The smaller the mean time to repair, the lower the cost of corrective maintenance and perhaps all maintenance. It would seem reasonable to specify MTTR in the SRS as a design requirement or design goal.

13.6 REVERSE ENGINEERING   ■

We can exert some control over the maintainability of software products under development; we cannot control the maintainability of those already in service. We must accept what is available in terms of support documentation and move forward from there. Rewriting an existing software product is often too large a capital investment for an enterprise to undertake. The objective of reverse or back engineering is finding cost-effective solutions to maintaining software products that are poorly supported by virtue of being poorly designed for maintainability and having inadequate documentation.

Reverse engineering or back engineering, as it is sometimes known, is useful in maintaining any software product. Even the best-supported software products are prone to lapses in their documentation, comment statements, design and test of modules, etc. In those products that are poorly supported (not easily maintained), reverse engineering is an essential and continuing process [3].

Unfortunately for the practitioner there are currently only crude tools available to support reverse engineering. There is, however, some guidance for performing reverse engineering, some of which Yourdon [5] presented as suggestions for maintaining alien code.

There has been much focus recently on the problem of reverse engineering and reengineering and tools for automating the process. Many CASE tools now provide reverse engineering capabilities as an intrinsic feature of the product. Some guidelines for reverse engineering a software product follow [5]:

1. Study the software product before problems begin to surface. Collect and organize a library of reference documents and background information. Evaluate the quality of the existing documentation.
2. Become familiar with the overall control flow. Don't worry about details. Examine the top-level structure. If none is available, draw up a control structure, a structure chart, pseudocode, etc. Document what you learn.
3. Run test cases to enhance product understanding. Use existing test cases or design new ones that help to answer questions or clarify understanding.
4. Exercise operational timelines if possible. Otherwise observe operators.
5. Use compiler and assembler features to gain more insight via listings, debugger, symbol tables, traces, etc.
6. Document any new information uncovered as a result of these studies.
7. Add comment statements to the source code to expand on explanations or make explanations more relevant. Indicate on the listing which comments were added to the original software configuration.
8. Relate the software product's current function and performance to the top-level software requirements and thence to system requirements. Normally documentation not only contains the function and performance requirements but also traces back to system-level requirements and traces forward to implementation of the requirements in code. If these documents do not provide this information, the best alternate source is operational timelines. Typically, operational timelines implement major system functions and will provide insight into the software requirements. This is a good place to start in reconstructing the function, performance requirements, and control structure that spawned the original code.
9. Don't make changes to the executable code unless driven by corrective, adaptive, or perfective maintenance actions. If changes are made, then changed lines of code should be identified directly on the listing. Don't eliminate or delete code that apparently is not used until its origin and history have been fully researched.

13.7   REENGINEERING SOFTWARE PRODUCTS   ■

Just as the designer of a software product needs good function and performance specifications, so does the software engineer about to embark on a reengineering task. There are three key inputs to reengineering a software product: (1) knowledge of the existing solution (timelines and software); (2) understanding of the function and performance requirements; and (3) appreciation of the application area, usually through a knowledge of operational scenarios or timelines.

There is always a temptation to start from scratch. However, the most cost-effective solutions are often found in introducing changes that minimize changes to naming conventions, interfaces, data, and the control structure of the existing product. For example, it is sometimes better to implement a function change by adding a separate module as a replacement module or as an adjunct module while retaining all other product features. Each change will present unique and challenging problems.

One of the methods that has been effective in maintaining a software product that is marked for reengineering is as follows:

1. Develop an operational timeline for the current software product that describes in detail how the function is currently being handled by operators.
2. Develop (or reconstruct) a data flow diagram (DFD)* and control structure describing how the current system supports the operational timeline.
3. Identify modules, segments, routines, etc., associated with the data flow and control structures. Ideally, this step should be conducted at source code or assembly code level.
4. When steps 1 through 3 are complete and reviewed, modify the operational timeline and the data flow diagram to reflect changes required to implement the new functional requirements. The goal, of course, is to minimize changes to existing external interfaces, data flow lines, functions, and data storage. The ideal solution is to be able to add bubbles, lines, and storage without perturbing the original DFD.
5. The changes to the DFD are implemented by modifying the source code listing as appropriate. This step is the most critical one because it is not always clear precisely what the original set of source statements did. At this juncture it is often necessary for the software engineer to execute test cases and run traces to confirm understanding of the original code.
6. The new functional requirements are tested (module level and product level) using new test cases and then by rerunning old test cases (regression tests) to confirm that no damage has been done to other timelines and functions.
7. An acceptance test should be performed before putting the new version of the product in service.
8. The complete change package with all standard change documentation and related cost, schedule, and size data are assembled, edited, and made part of the maintenance file. In particular, the package should include the following: (1) requirements specification with rationale for change; (2) data flow diagrams with rational for change; (3) operational scenarios with rationale for change; (4) source listings with rationale for change; (5) test cases and results anomalies reports, etc; (6) regression test results, etc; and (7) estimates and actuals for cost, schedule, size, number of faults, MTTR, etc.

Over the course of several maintenance actions there will be developed within the maintenance team a much better understanding of the application area and the software product. If this information is captured in maintenance documentation, it can be used to support future changes.

There are four axioms that should always be remembered in a reengineering process. These axioms are (1) if it isn't broken, don't fix it; (2) let sleeping dogs lie; (3) if you fool with something long enough, you will break it; and (4) best is the enemy of better.

---

* The use of data flow diagrams in the discussion is for convenience only. Any of the many techniques available can be used to describe the design. However, it is often easier to use flow diagrams and DFDs because they were most probably used in the development of the original software product.

13.8   CHAPTER SUMMARY ■

Maintainability should be specified, and the design of the software should provide for the highest level of flexibility and ease of maintenance. These attributes should be major design goals, because (1) the maintenance of a software product is a costly enterprise, (2) a software product or parts of it may spend 65% of its operational life cycle in the maintenance phase, and (3) the benefits of designing for ease of maintenance far outweigh the cost of including maintainability as a software design requirement. Some important factors that influence software maintainability are growth provisions, reliability, availability, documentation, complexity, configuration control, and architecture.

The unit testing and test and integration phase of a software product are an excellent laboratory for the study of potential corrective maintenance problems. A great deal may be learned about both the technical difficulties and the cost associated with maintaining a particular software product by collecting test data associated with cost, labor, schedule, and testing. Instruments required to support the maintenance activity and effective use of such instruments to drive down maintenance costs were also discussed.

The importance of reverse engineering and reengineering for software engineers was discussed, and it was noted that a substantial fraction of all practicing software engineers will be involved in reverse engineering and reengineering of deployed software products during the next ten to fifteen years.

13.9   EXERCISES ■

1. Pick up a program and its documentation from a classmate. Without contact with the classmate, exercise the program by designing and running several test cases. Could you maintain this program? If not, what additional information would you need to maintain it?
2. Could you envision a career for yourself in software maintenance? Describe this career path.
3. If maintainability requirements were factored into the SRS, what would they be? How would they be stated? How would they be tested? Would software engineers then be more aware of the problems confronted by maintainers?
4. If a software product or part of it spends 65% of its operational life cycle in maintenance, why do you suppose so little attention is paid to maintainability during the design phase?
5. Explain how the test phase might be described as a microcosm of the maintenance phase. What lessons can be learned in the test phase that can be applied to the maintenance phase?
6. Develop a means to quantify and measure the maintainability attribute of a software product.
7. Is it practical to specify maintainability in the SRS? How would you specify it? Would it be a testable requirement?
8. What is the appropriate set of tools and documents required to maintain a large software product?

References

1. V. R. Basili, ''Viewing Maintenance as Reuse Oriented Software Development,'' *IEEE Software* Vol. 7 No. 1:19–25, (1990).
2. W. B. Boehm, *Software Engineering Economics*, Prentice-Hall, Upper Saddle River, N.J., 1981.
3. E. J. Chikofsky and J. H. Cross, ''Reverse Engineering and Design Recovery: A Taxonomy,'' *IEEE Software* Vol. 7 No. 1:13–17, (1990).
4. S. R. Schach, *Practical Software Engineering*, Irwin-Aksen, Homewood, Ill., 1992.
5. E. Yourdon, *Techniques of Program Structure and Design*, Prentice-Hall, Upper Saddle River, N.J., 1975.

4

Software Metrics or Attributes

Unit 4 is devoted to a discussion of the measurement of software attributes or more commonly called, software metrics. Every manufactured product is specified or described by standard attributes such as dimensions, weight, volume, failure rate, constituents, finish, etc. Software for many reasons does not yet lend itself to measurement in terms of universally accepted quantifiable attributes. Software engineers are often required to define and measure software attributes in order to control and manage the software development process.

Chapter 14 categorizes and describes a number of software attributes and offers suggestions as to how they might be quantified and measured. Unfortunately there is no National Institute of Standards and Technology to whom we may appeal for the precise definition of key terms used in estimating and evaluating software attributes. Examples of such key terms are source line of code (SLOC) and function or feature point. Software engineers must establish the ground rules by which such key parameters are defined and measured. The central theme of chapter 14 is best described by the Chinese proverb, "It is better to light a single candle than to curse the darkness a thousand times."

Chapter 15 suggests that perhaps the reason that many software products have taken so much longer and have cost so much more than originally estimated is not entirely due to poor control and management of the software development process but rather, due at least in part to inability to estimate accurately software product size and forecast resources and time required to develop the software product. Chapter 15 provides a simple procedure for estimating the resources and time required to develop a complete software product. The method is a simple extension of the COCOMO. Chapter 15 offers guidance in modulating and tuning the extended COCOMO as an estimating tool. Chapter 15 also encourages the software engineer to build a project resource estimation database that will collect relevant experience during each development to calibrate the estimating model. Such an approach will make the model an even more effective estimating tool.

Chapter 16 describes a flexible methodology for estimating software development risk and establishing a risk containment plan. A major component of the risk containment plan is the periodic measurement and evaluation of certain software attributes. The generic term for this process is technical performance measurement. Technical performance measurements are the means by which certain software attributes are used as indicators to recognize impending development problems. Many clients and managers require that all software development risks be identified and quantified and that a contingency plan or risk containment plan be prepared. Moreover, they also require that a means be implemented to recognize development problems early enough that corrective action may be taken. Software that is associated with systems that involve public safety or whose failure will result in substantial financial loss are usually subjected to risk analysis or safety analysis. As software becomes more deeply embedded in system functions, it is expected that software risk analysis and risk containment planning will become a regular component of a software engineer's duties.

It is paradoxical that within the same system development, so much concern is expressed regarding hardware reliability (the probability of failure occurrence in a given operational period under specified operating conditions) and yet similar concerns for software reliability are rarely mentioned. For example, an incorrect sign in an algorithm that somehow escaped detection during tests could cause the flight path of a launched rocket to head inland rather than out over the Atlantic Ocean as desired. An incorrect range for an algorithm could, under certain conditions, result in an error in a real-time clock, causing events based on time to be incorrectly triggered by the software. An error in program logic could result in the transfer of software control to the wrong procedure. Each of these software faults would, if not discovered, result in loss of life or devastating financial and credibility loss.

Chapter 17 is devoted to the discussion of software reliability and availability. A software reliability model chosen from among many available ones is described in this chapter. It has been shown that reliability models can be used effectively in testing and maintainability planning, performance evaluation, and, in conjunction with hardware reliability, in estimating the overall system reliability for a given operating period. Design rules that, if followed, will lead to more reliable software products are discussed in this chapter.

Chapter 18 is devoted to software quality and quality assurance. It has been clearly established that software quality assurance measures, when properly carried out, significantly increase software quality. Software quality assurance is implemented by subjecting the software product and the processes and tools used to develop the product to a series of audits, inspection, walk-throughs, and reviews. One of the software quality attributes is the number of faults per source line of code that lead to failures experienced over a specified time interval. This attribute is found to be improved in direct proportion to the number and quality of the reviews.

14

Software Attributes (Metrics) and Their Estimation

14.0 OBJECTIVES ■

The principle objectives of this chapter are as follows: (1) to develop an awareness of the value of recognizing, defining, and estimating software attributes that can directly or indirectly characterize a software product, its development environment, and its operational environment; (2) to suggest ways in which many of the attributes may be defined and quantified; (3) to describe ways in which estimated attributes may be used to improve the software development process; (4) to define a candidate list of direct and indirect software attributes for a data collection effort before, during, and after a software development process; (5) to outline, in general terms, how a data collection effort can be initiated; and (6) to identify practical uses for certain estimated software attributes in planning and carrying out a software development process.

14.1 INTRODUCTION ■

In chapter 3 we mentioned the need to characterize the software product in terms of quantifiable attributes. This chapter is devoted to defining, measuring, and using some of these attributes. Measurement of specific attributes associated with a product, its environments, and its means of production is fundamental to any engineering effort. Over 100 years ago Lord Kelvin made the following statement:

> When you can measure what you are speaking about and express it in numbers, you know something about it; but when you cannot measure, when you cannot express it in numbers, your knowledge is of a meager and unsatisfactory kind: it may be the beginning of knowledge, but you have scarcely, in your thoughts advanced to the stage of science.

This quote is particularly apropos when taken in the context of software engineering.

In the past ten to fifteen years, the software development community has begun to show a strong inclination toward developing programs to define, collect, analyze, and, in particular, use software attributes in the software development process. This practice prepares the software development team for the following:

1. To understand the product better by developing descriptive measurements that distinguish between types of software and software application environments and the means of producing software (people and tools).
2. To establish measurable software attributes that can be used to quantify software product requirements and confirm that product requirements have been met.
3. To establish a means for categorizing software product quality levels and correlating them with product, application, and environment attributes.
4. To establish a means for evaluating the productivity of the people and the process employed to develop the software product.
5. To estimate development resources and calendar time required to develop and test a software product based on some of the software attributes.
6. To measure any positive (or negative) effect of the use of new development tools and methods.
7. To measure new system and software performance against the old.

In addition, many of the attributes described herein are effective tools that can be used by management to control a software development process. Questions intrinsic to the technical management of a software development process include the following:

- Is the project on schedule?
- Will function and performance requirements be met?
- What is the predicted error density (number of errors per SLOC) of the product?
- How good is the product relative to the need?
- Are computer resources adequate to support our product?
- How much will this software product cost?

Prompt and accurate response to such questions implies defining numerical values for certain software attributes such as failure rate in the test phase, software size in SLOC, software size in function points, etc.

Software attributes are often categorized as direct and indirect attributes. This distinction is based on the ease and directness with which the attribute can be objectively measured. Others separate software attributes into those associated with productivity, those related to quality, and those related to the product itself. The remainder of this chapter is devoted to a discussion of attributes as related to the following categories:

1. Identification
2. Size
3. Requirements/Design
4. Quality
5. Complexity
6. Execution time
7. Testing
8. Documentation
9. Performance
10. Labor
11. Operating Environment

It is only fair to point out that many attributes in use today are not entirely satisfactory for many software engineering applications. However, in the absence of better attributes or metrics we must continue to collect and analyze what attribute data we have and make effective use of it. By objectively and thoughtfully defining attributes and calibrating models with actual data, we have managed to limp along using experience mixed with a modicum of common sense to plan and manage many successful software development efforts.

14.2   IDENTIFICATION-RELATED ATTRIBUTES   ■

A software product, component, or module should be thoroughly and accurately identified. Table 14.1 is a template for identifying a software product and placing it in an appropriate framework.

■ TABLE 14.1   **Software Identification Template**

SOFTWARE PRODUCT NAME: _____

PRODUCT RELEASE AND VERSION: _____

DEVELOPMENT ORGANIZATION: _____

DATE (CURRENT): _____

NAME OF COLLECTOR: _____

NARRATIVE: _____

PRODUCT PARTITION STRUCTURE: _____
(Diagram may be needed)

SUBFUNCTION/MODULE/UNIT NAME: _____

LANGUAGE EMPLOYED: _____

REFERENCES: (Specifications and related system documentation)
_____

Software product name refers to the data dictionary names of the product and its components. The release date, version number, and the development organization identifiers are entered on the next two lines. The date of origination followed by a sequence of dates, each associated with subsequent revisions, is entered next. The name of the person collecting the data is entered. A brief description of the functions implemented in the product or module is described in the narrative. A simple top-level diagram showing a hierarchical product decomposition is provided next with the subject unit marked. The name of the subfunction, module, or unit as it is identified in the data dictionary is provided along with the programming language being employed. References to specifications are an important parameter in identifying the product. If appropriate, a paragraph-level reference should be made. Other sources that will help to identify the product or module and assist in establishing the setting in which the product will operate can also be included in the references.

14.3 SIZE-RELATED ATTRIBUTES ■

An extremely important software attribute that is often encountered at the inception of a software development effort is software size. Size can refer to the memory space occupied by executable code or to the number of lines of source code. The size attribute is of paramount importance to the software development planning process. What is usually sought at inception of a software development process is an accurate estimate of the size of the finished product. The size estimate is derived from the requirements that must be implemented in the software.

Source lines of code can be counted in two ways: logical and physical [5]. A logical source line of code is a single source statement in the source language. The physical source line of code is a count of the number of physical lines taken up by the source statements. In this definition a physical line of code would contain one or more logical source statements.

Logical source statements can be categorized as executable statements, data declaration statements, compiler directive statements, and comment statements. Executable source statements direct the actions of the computer at run time. Data declaration statements reserve or initialize memory at compilation time, direct the compiler to constrain or check data, or define data structure at run time. Compiler directive statements define macros, create labels, or direct the compiler to insert external source statements or units. Comment source statements are the internal documentation statements provided to assist reviewers and maintainers in reading and understanding the code.

Source statements, both logical and physical, are categorized as developed and nondeveloped source statements. Developed source statements include those statements added to or modified specifically for the software product under development. Nondeveloped source statements include deleted source statements and reused source statements. Deleted source statements may include those removed or modified from an earlier version of the software product. Reused source statements are unmodified source statements obtained from another product for the product being developed.

The following algorithm [5] provides a simple way to count source statements (SS):

1. Number of new SS   = Number of added SS +
                             Number of modified SS
2. Number of deleted SS = Number of modified SS +
                             Number of removed SS

3. Number of reused SS = Number of original SS −
                              Number of modified SS −
                              Number of removed SS

In this book we will use only logical source statements; we will use source lines of code and source statements interchangeably.

The general approach to software sizing is the divide-and-conquer method. In this method the analyst partitions requirements into small, recognizable requirement parcels. The functional partitioning or decomposition process should follow the normal top-down approach observing the concepts and criteria of modularity, cohesion, and coupling. Each parcel of requirements can then be more easily understood and estimated. A large, complex software product when viewed in small fragments is much easier to understand and size. For example, a file management function is easier to estimate if it is partitioned into subfunctions—create files, display files, edit files, read files, write files, etc.—and each subfunction studied and estimated independently.

The function or feature point method also requires a partitioning of requirements into small parcels and application of a method that counts or sizes functionality. Functional requirements must be well understood in order to apply function or feature point methodology effectively. A set of two templates, a questionnaire, and a formula are tools intrinsic to the method. These tools also serve to document the rationale that led to the sizing result. In any sizing exercise, counts should be kept on a module basis, and modules should be fully identified as described in Table 14.1.

14.3.1   Function Point Attribute Estimation

The main task is to estimate the size of the completed software product from software function and performance requirements. Most resource (labor, development time, and means of production) estimation models rely on the size attribute, SLOC, as input. The size attribute was for a long time measured by SLOC. Recently interest has been shown in two other size attributes called function points and feature points. Function points measure the functional content of a software product. The function point method was originally designed for use on MIS-oriented software products. The feature point method was designed to extend coverage to a wider range of software products including embedded and real-time software. Product size, when estimated in function points or feature points, can be converted into an equivalent number of source lines of code for use in SLOC based resource estimation algorithms.

To obtain a function point estimate for a software product, we follow an approach similar to the one developed by Albrecht in 1979 [1] and revised in 1983 [3] and 1984 [2]. This approach requires a detailed understanding of the software product's functional requirements. Nonetheless a detailed understanding must be developed from a study of the stated and implied requirements, operational time lines and the operational environment.

The first step in function point estimation is partitioning the software product requirements into relatively small units and, for each unit, describing the implementation of the functional requirements in terms of the following function point attributes:

a. User inputs
b. User outputs
c. User inquiries
d. Files
e. External interfaces

Clearly, such decomposition of the functional requirements of a software product would require a good understanding of the requirements and at least a general sense of the software architecture and design approach being considered. The first step in the process is to complete the template shown in Table 14.2 for each module/unit that will implement software product requirements.

The complexity values shown in Table 14.2 are empirical values derived from studying a large sample of completed software products [1]. The development team or software engineer ranks the complexity of a unit or module's function point attributes as low, average, or high based on experience. Then the table in Table 14.2 associates a complexity value with this attribute. Note that when there are N cases of a given function point attribute and not all N have the same complexity, the N attributes may be divided into two or more groups based on their complexity. The attributes in Table 14.2 are defined as follows:

Number of User Inputs   Each user input that provides distinct application-oriented data to the software is counted. Inputs should be distinguished from inquiries, which are counted separately.

Number of User Outputs   Each user output that provides application-oriented information to the user is counted. In this context, output refers to reports, screens, error messages, etc. Individual data items within a report are not counted separately.

Number of User Inquiries   An inquiry is defined as an on-line input that results in the generation of some immediate software response in the form of an on-line output. Each distinct inquiry is counted.

Number of Files   Each logical master file, i.e., a logical grouping of data that may be one part of a large database or a separate file, is counted.

■ TABLE 14.2   **Template for Counting Unit/Module Function Points**

UNIT/MODULE NAME _____
DATE _____ REVISED DATA _____
DEVELOPMENT GROUP _____
NAME OF RESPONSIBLE PERSON _____

Unit/Module Function Point Attributes	Count	COMPLEXITY RANK			Function Points
		Low	Average	High	
USER INPUTS	–	(3)	(4)	(6)	–
USER OUTPUTS	–	(4)	(5)	(7)	–
USER INQUIRIES	–	(3)	(4)	(6)	–
FILES	–	(7)	(10)	(15)	–
EXTERNAL INTERFACES	–	(5)	(7)	(10)	–
TOTAL UNIT/MODULE FUNCTION POINTS (TFP)					

Number of External Interfaces All machine-readable interfaces (e.g., data files on tape or disk) that are used to transmit information to another system are counted.

Once counts have been determined for each attribute and a complexity rank selected for each individual count, a complexity value is assigned (Table 14.2) via association with complexity rank (low, average, high) to the corresponding function point attribute. Organizations that use the function point method usually develop their own criteria for determining whether the complexity of a particular function point attribute is low, average, or high. Counts are then multiplied by the complexity value to obtain function points, for each attribute. Function points are summed to obtain total module/unit function points.

The second step in function point estimation is to adjust raw function point counts to account for factors that will influence the size of the final software product. Fourteen adjunct factors associated with software product requirements are used to modify a function or feature point size estimate. These fourteen factors are as follows:

1. Back-up and recovery
2. Data communication
3. Distributed processing
4. Critical performance
5. Heavily used configuration
6. On-line data entry
7. Transaction complexity
8. On-line master file update
9. Complex external processing
10. Complex internal processing
11. Reusability
12. Installation factor
13. Multiple sites
14. Change facilitation

To each of these factors we may assign a complexity adjustment value of 0, 1, 2, 3, 4, or 5. A value of zero means the factor has no effect on the product. A value of 1 means the effect of the factor is very minor. A value of 2 indicates the factor has a moderate effect, and a value of 3 indicates that it has an average effect on the software product. A value of 4 means that the effect of the factor is significant and the software design will be strongly influenced by this factor. A value of 5 means that it is essential for the software product to accommodate this factor in the product design.

The first factor considers the effect of back-up and recovery requirements. If no hard requirement is specified for back-up capabilities, we would select a value of zero for this factor. On the other hand, if the SRS indicates that back-up and recovery are an essential part of the software product, we assign a value of 5 to this factor. The second factor relates to the degree that requirements for data communication are part of the requirements associated with the unit being sized. The third factor relates to the degree to which distributed processing is required. The fourth factor assesses the degree to which certain critical performance criteria (speed, time, memory, accuracy, etc.) are embodied in the SRS. The fifth factor accounts for the kind of use that the software product will experience in its operational environment and the nature of the operational environment.

The sixth and seventh factors assess the on-line data entry requirements. The eighth factor considers certain processing requirements associated with on-line update of master files. The ninth factor weights inputs, outputs, files, and inquiries in terms of complexity. The tenth factor evaluates the complexity of the internal processing. The eleventh factor considers reusability requirements. The twelfth factor examines the extent to which installation and conversion are part of the requirements and are expected to affect designs. The thirteenth factor deals with requirements for multiple installations and multiple users. Finally, the fourteenth factor considers the extent to which maintainability is part of the software product requirements.

This set of fourteen factors associated with the nature of the requirements, along with a subjective assessment of each based on an assignment of a weighting of 0 to 5, is used to adjust the estimate of requirement complexity. This estimate in turn contributes to an estimate of the size of the software product as measured in function points.

To incorporate the effect of these fourteen adjunct factors on the estimation of the total function points (TFP), we compute function points for each unit; then we use the following empirical relationship:

$$AFP = TFP \times \left[0.65 + 0.01 \times \sum_{i=1}^{i=14} (F_i) \right] \tag{14.1}$$

where AFP is the adjusted total function points, adjusted for the fourteen complexity factors and ΣF_i is the corresponding complexity adjustment value for each of the fourteen adjustment factors. The constant value (0.65) and the weighting factor (0.01) in equation 14.1 were determined empirically [2].

Example: 14.3.1 (Order-Entry Problem)

Suppose the requirement specification for the order-entry module of the ABC project has been studied and the following results have been determined. There is a need for 7 inputs, 10 outputs, 6 inquiries, 17 files, and 4 external interfaces. Also, assume input and external interface function point attributes are of average complexity and all other function point attributes are of low complexity. Table 14.3 shows the estimated total function points required for the order-entry module.

To obtain function points for each function point attribute we multiply its corresponding count and complexity rank. The total unit/module function points, 233, is the sum of the function points in the last column.

Next we compute the AFP using the fourteen complexity adjustment factors. The complexity adjustment value for factor 1 is set to 4 because the SRS requires that the software product have a reliable back-up; factor 2 is set to 5 because the SRS emphasizes the need

---

■ TABLE 14.3   **Completed Template for Order Entry Module**

UNIT/MODULE NAME: Order Entry
DATE: April 10, 1996   REVISED DATA: December 15, 1996
DEVELOPMENT GROUP: Team 2: Behforooz/Hudson
NAME OF RESPONSIBLE PERSON: F. Hudson

| Unit/Module Function Point Attributes | Count | COMPLEXITY RANKS | | | Function Points |
		Low	Average	High	
USER INPUTS	7		(4)		28
USER OUTPUTS	10	(4)			40
USER INQUIRIES	6	(3)			18
FILES	17	(7)			119
EXTERNAL INTERFACES	4		(7)		28
TOTAL UNIT/MODULE FUNCTION POINTS					233

for reliability in data communication; factor 5 is set to 4 because the order-entry module is heavily used; factors 6 and 8 are set to 5 because the module is always on-line; all other factors are set to 1 because their effect is minimal. Thus we have the following:

$$F_1 + F_2 + \cdots + F_{14} = 4 + 5 + 1 + 1 + 4 + 5$$
$$+ 1 + 5 + 1 + 1 + 1 + 1 + 1 + 1 = 32$$

Substituting this value in equation (14.1), we obtain the following:

$$AFP = 233 \ (0.65 + 0.01 \times 32)$$
$$AFP = 233 \times (0.97) = 226.01 \text{ or } 226$$

Alternative Approach to Function Point Counting

A slightly different approach to function point counting was developed by Jones [7,8]. Jones' approach simplified Albrecht's method by employing only one complexity weighting rather than the choice of low, average, and high, as follows:

Number of inputs	× 4
Number of outputs	× 5
Number of inquiries	× 4
Number of files	× 10
Number of interfaces	× 7

where the complexity values are: 4 for inputs, 5 for outputs, 4 for inquiries, 10 for files and 7 for interfaces.

Albrecht's fourteen complexity factors and equation (14.1) are replaced in Jones' method by a complexity assessment based on logical, code, and data complexity. Only logical and data complexity are assessed for estimating the size for code to be created. Code complexity assessments are used to relate function points to existing software products. A value for logical, code, and data complexity is assigned to each based on answering the following questions.

Logical Complexity Value (LCV)   This value is 1, 2, 3, 4, or 5 depending on which of the following five cases best describes the algorithmic and computational complexity status of the software.

LCV	LOGICAL COMPLEXITY STATUS
1	Simple algorithms and simple calculations
2	Majority of simple algorithms and calculations
3	Algorithms and calculations of average complexity
4	Some difficult or complex algorithms and calculations
5	Many difficult algorithms and complex calculations

Code Complexity Value (CCV)   This value is 1, 2, 3, 4, or 5 depending on which of the following five cases best describes the code complexity status of the software.

CCV	CODE COMPLEXITY STATUS
1	Nonprocedural
2	Well structured with reusable modules
3	Well structured (small modules, simple paths)
4	Fair structure (some complex modules and paths)
5	Poor structure (large modules and complex paths)

Data Complexity Value (DCV)   This value is 1, 2, 3, 4, or 5 depending on which of the following five cases best states the data complexity status of the software.

DCV	DATA COMPLEXITY STATUS
1	Simple data with few variables and low complexity
2	Numerous variables but simple data relationships
3	Multiple files, fields, and data interactions
4	Complex file structures and data interactions
5	Very complex file structures and data interactions

The adjustment factor for total function points is obtained by assigning the most applicable value to LCV and DCV by determining the appropriate complexity status of the software with regard to logical and data complexity. Then Table 14.4 is consulted to obtain the appropriate adjustment multiplier. The adjustment multiplier is multiplied by the function point count to obtain the adjusted function point count.

Note that Table 14.4 is used only when logic and data complexity are involved. Not enough data have been collected to help us determine the value of the multiplier when code complexity is involved.

■ TABLE 14.4   **Adjustment Multiplier Value**

LCV + DCV	ADJUSTMENT MULTIPLIER
2	0.6
3	0.7
4	0.8
5	0.9
6	1.0
7	1.1
8	1.2
9	1.3
10	1.4

Example 14.3.2

In this example we apply Jones' method to Example 14.3.1.

Unit/Module Function Points	Count	Complexity Rate	Function Points
USER INPUTS	7	(4)	28
USER OUTPUTS	10	(5)	50
USER INQUIRIES	6	(4)	24
FILES	17	(10)	170
EXTERNAL INTERFACES	4	(7)	28
TOTAL UNIT/MODULE FUNCTION POINTS			300

The logic complexity value for this software is determined to be 1 and the data complexity is determined to be 2. Therefore we have LCV + DCV = 3. The adjustment multiplier is, then, 0.7. The adjusted function point is computed to be as follows:

$$AFP = 300 \times 0.7 = 210$$

The module size estimate, in function points, obtained from Jones' method is still (7%) lower than the one obtained from Albrecht's method.

14.3.2   Feature Point Estimation

The function point measure as originally designed by Albrecht was developed for business information systems. However, certain extensions called feature points, originally proposed by Jones [8], extend this size measure to include scientific and engineering-oriented software products. Feature points are based on a variation of Albrecht's method for function point calculation developed by Jones and described previously.

Table 14.5 presents a template for modules and units that are to be estimated in feature points. In this table the complexity attribute values are the same as for function points except for (1) a sixth entry added to account for the number of algorithms implemented in the module and (2) changes in weighting. An algorithm is a bounded computational problem included in a module or unit requirement specification. Examples of algorithms are the computation of the earth's gravitational field, a Runge Kutta integrator or digital filter. The total feature points column value is equal to the count multiplied by the weight. The total feature points for the module is the sum of the values in the total feature points column. A complexity adjustment factor is used to modify the calculated featured point total.

The feature point complexity adjustment factor is determined using Jones' method. It should be noted that both feature points and function points represent the same thing, an estimate of the functions provided by the software product.

■ TABLE 14.5   **Template for Counting Unit/Module Feature Points**

UNIT/MODULE NAME _____
DATE _____ REVISED DATA _____
DEVELOPMENT GROUP _____
NAME OF RESPONSIBLE PERSON _____

Point Attributes	Count	Weight	Feature Points
USER INPUTS	—	(4)	
USER OUTPUTS	—	(5)	
USER INQUIRIES	—	(4)	
FILES	—	(4)	
EXTERNAL INTERFACES	—	(7)	
ALGORITHMS	—	(3)	
TOTAL UNIT/MODULE FEATURE POINTS			_____
COMPLEXITY ADJUSTMENT (from Table 14.4)			_____
TOTAL ADJUSTED FUNCTION POINTS			_____

Example 14.3.3 (Display Function)

As an illustration of the two methods, consider a simple module whose requirements include accepting an operator entry of a key field, thereby calling up a file record for display on a screen and providing an editing capability for the operator to edit the record, print both new and original records, and revise the file. Estimate the function points for this module. For a second example assume that the module implements two algorithms that are used to revise certain fields in file records. These algorithms are of average complexity. Estimate the feature points for this case.

Function point estimation by Albrecht's method is as follows

	Counts	Low	Average	High	Function Points
user inputs	2	(3)			6
user outputs	1	(4)			4
user inquiries	1	(3)			3
files	2	(7)			14
external interfaces	2	(5)			10
Total Function Points					37

The F_i is to be determined as follows:

1. Significant back-up and recovery
2. No communication
3. No distributed processing function

4. No performance critical requirements
5. Significant   4
6. Significant   4
7. No
8. Yes essential   5
9. No incidental   1
10. No
11. No
12. Yes average   3
13. Yes average   3
14. Yes significant   4

Total F_i 28

Applying Equation (14.1) to the total FP and total F_is, we obtain

$$\text{AFP} = 37 \times (0.65 + 0.01 \times 28) = 34.41$$

function points.

Feature point estimation for the case is as follows:

	Counts	Weight	Total FP
user inputs	2	(4)	8
user outputs	1	(5)	5
user inquiries	1	(4)	4
files	2	(4)	8
external interfaces	2	(7)	14
algorithms	2	(3)	6
Total Feature Points			45

For logical complexity we select 2 as the most descriptive phrase for the module. For data complexity we select 3 as the most descriptive phrase. The sum 5 yields a value of 0.9 for the complexity adjustment factor. Applying the complexity adjustment of 0.9 to the TFP, we obtain the following:

$$\text{AFP} = 45 \times 0.9 = 40.5$$

The calculation of the complexity adjustment factor is conceptually similar to Jones' method and is described in more detail in references [8] and [7].

14.3.3   Converting Function Point Estimation to SLOC

Most of the formulas for estimating cost and schedule use the product size measured in SLOC. To transform function point or feature point estimates to SLOC, the values presented in Table 14.6 can be used. This table is the result of an analysis conducted by Albrecht [1] and Jones [7,8]. This table should be used with the knowledge that these conversion factors are only

■ TABLE 14.6   **Conversion of Function Points or Feature Points to Source Lines of Code**

LANGUAGE	SLOC/FP RATIO (AVERAGE)
Assembly (Basic)	300
Assembly (Macro)	210
C	120
COBOL	100
Fortran	100
Pascal	90
Modula-2	80
Ada	70*
Prolog, Lisp, Forth	65*
Object-Oriented Languages	30*
Fourth Generation Languages	20*
Code Generators	15*
Spreadsheet Languages	6*

....

* Not yet validated.

crude approximations. If more accurate conversion ratios are needed, then project or development team–unique ratios should be developed that reflect local experience.

Using the conversion data in Table 14.6, the function point estimation method would estimate the size of this module in Ada SLOC to be 2409 lines of Ada code, whereas the feature point estimation method would estimate the size of this module to be 2835 source lines of Ada code.

No matter what the approach—SLOC, Albrecht's function point method, Jones' function and feature point method, or some other—practical experience, a dedication to continuing objective data collection, evaluation, and model calibration is essential to establishing an effective size metric.

14.3.4   Direct Source Lines of Code Estimation

To estimate source lines of code directly, the software engineer can often estimate size by comparing each requirement parcel with an already implemented unit, module, or product. For example, the size of a real-time interrupt handling requirement can be estimated by comparison with the size of an interrupt handler in an existing operating system. If the requirement partitioning step can be taken to a level of detail where the numbers of screen generations, file operations, specific algorithms, etc., are apparent, then project sizing standards (if they exist) or personal experience can be applied. The method is to identify equivalent or similar functions already implemented in the same language, if possible, as basis for the estimation. Features may be added or deleted and estimates scaled up or down as appropriate.

Care must be exercised to assure that estimates for management, communication, and control overhead required to fully integrate the collection of parcels are taken into account. It is important to review, revise, and document the rationale for how the estimate was made for project files.

Source lines of code for a unit or module can be subdivided into lines of code that are executable, those associated with data or compiler declarations, and those associated with comment statements (internal documentation). Other software that is required by the development process are test drivers and scaffolds to support test configurations. This software, as you might imagine, should be at least as good quality as the deliverable software. Table 14.7 gives a template for recording the size estimate for each module/unit.

Reused software will usually require some effort to resurrect requirement specifications and modify them to the new application. Interfaces, at minimum, will have to be renamed. Some regression testing will probably be performed at the unit or module level to confirm the validity of reusing this software for this application and, finally, the software to be reused will have to be tested in the new application or environment. The point is that reused software has cost associated with its use, and the number of source lines of code should be identified and recorded as part of the software product sizing activity. Practical experience has shown that the cost of a line of reused code to be implemented in a new project ranges from 20% to 80% of the cost of a newly written line of code.

Occasionally the size of a module, unit, or function to be used for comparison purposes or as reused code is given as number of bytes. Dividing this number of bytes by a factor whose value is hardware dependent should yield an approximation to the number of assembly language instructions required to implement the desired module or function. Then Table 14.6 or its equivalent can be used to convert an assembly language SLOC estimate to a high-level language SLOC estimate.

If requirements are well understood and can be partitioned to a more detailed level of function such as file creation, generation of display panels, or computation of familiar algo-

---

■ TABLE 14.7   **Template for Recording Unit/Module SLOC Estimates**

```
UNIT/MODULE NAME _____
ESTIMATION DATE _____ REVISED DATA _____
DEVELOPMENT GROUP _____
NAME OF RESPONSIBLE PERSON _____
SOURCE LINES OF CODE _____
REFERENCE FOR JUSTIFICATION _____
     EXECUTABLE _____
     DATA DECLARATIONS _____
     COMPILER DECLARATIONS _____
     COMMENTS _____
NONDELIVERED SLOC _____
     DRIVERS/SCAFFOLDS _____
     OTHER _____
REUSED SLOC _____
MODIFIED SLOC _____
```

■ TABLE 14.8   **Template To Be Used for Bounded Estimation Approach (Completed for a Hypothetical Example)**

Requirements	Estimated KSLOC	RANGE			Comments and Rationale
		Best	Average	Worst	
Function 1	(3.2)	2.8	3.2	3.6	Prior project
Function 2	(1.5)	1.1	1.5	1.8	Prior project
Function 3	(2.5)	1.9	2.5	3.0	Trial PDL
Function 4	(5.5)	5.2	5.5	5.7	Prior experience
Function 5	(4.2)	3.9	4.2	4.5	Existing software
Function 6	(3.0)	2.6	3.0	3.1	See document xxx

rithms, SLOC estimates can be relatively accurate even when prepared by a relatively inexperienced individual. Table 14.8 shows a six-unit decomposition of a hypothetical software product's requirements and an estimated number of SLOC for each. The estimate is bounded to show worst case and best case. This bounded estimation approach offers several advantages. It quantifies and bounds uncertainty, enables decision makers to quantify risk, and it provides an expected range that reflects a measure of the understanding of the requirements. The smaller the range, the better the understanding and the more confidence evidenced in the estimate. The six functions can be further partitioned into smaller packets and reestimated to confirm results.

The numbers in parentheses in Table 14.8 are the estimated source lines of code required to implement each subfunction. The rationale for each subfunction estimate is documented and appended to Table 14.8. These results should be reviewed, revised as required, and made part of the project documentation. This estimation process should be repeated periodically and a history of the changes along with a rationale for each change should be kept for future reference.

Example 14.3.4 (Display Function Revisited)

As an illustration, we estimate the size of the problem of Example 14.3.3 using the divide-and-conquer approach and compare the results. The same module functions of example 14.3.3 might be partitioned and estimated as shown in Table 14.9. In both examples we have assumed Ada to be the language of implementation. The result, 2100 SLOC, compares favorably with the result obtained by function point counting, 2409 SLOC.

Many development organizations use a standard figure or rule of thumb for the number of lines of code required to implement one screen of soft copy, access a database, or perform other relatively standard functions. Estimates can be pieced together from this database. The results of the analysis leading up to the estimate should as a minimum be documented in summary form as shown in Table 14.9.

■ TABLE 14.9   **SLOC Estimate Using Divide-and-Conquer Approach For Display Function of Example 14.3.4**

UNIT/MODULE NAME: Display Function
DATE: April 15, 1996   REVISED DATA: June 10, 1996
DEVELOPMENT GROUP: Behforooz/Hudson
NAME OF RESPONSIBLE PERSON: Behforooz

Subfunction	Estimated SLOC	Reference/Source
Opening menu	125	Prior projects
First menu/prompt	100	Prior projects
User ID	50	Trial PDL
Record ID	50	Trial PDL
Recall record	75	Trial PDL
Display record 3 scr	450	Three screens
Edit record	850	DOS/estimate
Print record	75	Trial PDL
Save new record	75	Trial PDL
Record transaction	125	Trial PDL
Back up file	125	Trial PDL
Total estimated Ada.SLOC =	2100	

Example 14.3.5 (Special-Purpose Operating System)

As another specific example, we find that the XYZ project has decided to use special-purpose processors to implement some control functions at remote locations on the network. A new operating system was required for the new processor. The following functional description was prepared from the requirements and an analysis of the operational environment. The functional requirements derived from the operating system functional specification were matched with implementations found in other operating systems. The results are shown below in Table 14.10.

The approach taken in the analysis was to expand each major function into meaningful (to the software engineer) subfunctions, develop an estimate based on identifying implementations of similar or related functions in other software products, and count the source statements or source lines of code. All of these estimates are based upon equivalent functions found in other operating systems except for security and utilities. The estimates for these two functions were obtained from comparisons with other similar functions implemented for other software products. Source lines of code are estimated in Ada.

14.4 DESIGN AND DEVELOPMENT ATTRIBUTES   ■

Design and development attributes are those that define the characteristics of the software product and its operational and development environment. These attributes can be divided

■ TABLE 14.10   **Estimated SLOC for Special-Purpose Operating System (Only New and Reused SLOC Are Estimated)**

Program (Task) Management
    Scheduling, starting, stopping, and resuming a program
    Schedule for future execution based on:
        1. time delay
        2. event
        3. cyclical execution rate
    Schedule for immediate execution

Total Estimated 3.3 KSLOC* (new = 3.3, reused = 0)

I/O Management
    Read from a device (can be performed for multiple devices with one request)
    Write to a device
    Read device status (sense)
    Send device control signals
    Support access via global naming convention
    User-defined device add-on capability

Total Estimated 19.7 KSLOC (new = 3.2, reused = 16.5)

File Management (for application files)
    Read
    Write
    Update (read and write without intervening close)
    Delete

Total Estimated 19.7 KSLOC (new = 17.0, reused = 2.7)

Time Management
    Read time standard
    Update time standard
    TAI time—international atomic time provided to satisfy engineering's need for an accurate time
        standard
    Conversions between TAI and other common systems (UTC1, UTC2) 1 millisecond accuracy required

Total Estimated 6.4 KSLOC (new = 2.2, reused = 4.2)

Security and Data Integrity
    Partition subsystem processing for data integrity
    Don't allow data to be comprised by unauthorized users
    Validate user identity

Total Estimated 2.5 KSLOC (new = 2.5, reused = 0)

Real-time operation
    Internal/external interrupts
    Event management (set an event, reset an event, wait on an event)
    Responses to requests

Total Estimated 2.3 KSLOC (new = 2.3, reused = 0)

Memory Management
    Allocate processor memory space
    Set access privileges (data privacy)
    Prevent memory fragmentation

Total Estimated 5.4 KSLOC (new = 1.9, reused = 3.5)

Continued on the following page.

■ TABLE 14.10 **Estimated SLOC for Special-Purpose Operating System (Only New and Reused SLOC Are Estimated)** (*Continued*)

Initialization
  File
  Device
  Table
  Other

Total Estimated 5.2 KSLOC (new = 2.7, reused = 2.5)

Utilities
  Console
  Library
  Accounting
  Security
  Other

Total Estimated 6.4 KSLOC (new = 2.0, reused = 4.4)

Grand Total = 70.9 SLOC (new = 37.1, reused = 33.8)

• •

* KSLOC = 1000 SLOC

into product-related attributes, operational attributes, and attributes associated with the development environment itself, as follows:

1. Product-related attributes
  Reliability requirements
  Database characteristics and requirements
  Complexity
2. Operational attributes
  CPU limitations manifested as design constraints on execution time
  Memory constraints or physical limits
  Experience in the application area associated with the software product under development
3. Development attributes
  Stability of the virtual machine environment
  Capability and experience of system engineer or system analyst
  Software engineer's capability and experience
  Access to computing and development resources
  Experience with the development environment
  Experience in using the programming language and design language if applicable.
  Experience in using tools designated for use in the project
  Experience in using software engineering methods or equivalent
  Development schedule pressure

Boehm [4] in his 1981 book, *Software Engineering Economics*, introduced a set of cost and schedule estimation models, which have been widely used. These empirical models were based on carefully analyzed data obtained from sixty-three completed software development projects. We will consider these cost and schedule estimation models in chapter 15. In this section we will discuss the attributes that Boehm used in his multivariate cost and schedule estimation model.

Boehm considered fifteen design and development attributes, which were used to fine-tune his estimation models. He called these attributes cost driver attributes. Boehm's cost driver attributes with short descriptions follow:

Product Attributes:
RELY: Quantifies the effect on software development cost and schedule of the required software reliability.
DATA: Quantifies the effect of product database size.
CPLX: Quantifies the effect of software product complexity.
Computer System Attributes:
TIME: Quantifies the effect of execution time constraints.
STOR: Quantifies the effect of main storage constraints.
VIRT: Quantifies the effect of virtual machine volatility. (For a given software product the underlying virtual machine consists of the hardware and system software—operating system, editor, library, DBMS, etc.—it uses to perform its tasks.)
TURN: Quantifies the effect of the computer turnaround time (access to virtual machine).
Project Personnel Attributes:
ACAP: Quantifies the effect of analyst(s) capabilities.
AEXP: Quantifies the effect of the team's experience in the application software being developed.
PCAP: Quantifies the effect of programmer's capabilities.
VEXP: Quantifies the experience of the programming team with the host virtual machine.
LEXP: Quantifies the effect of programmer's experience with the programming language being used.
Project Attributes:
MODP: Quantifies the effect of the use of modern programming practice by the team.
TOOL: Quantifies the effect of the use of the advanced software development tools.
SCED: Quantifies the effect of the schedule constraints.

Each of these attributes may be classified as very low, low, nominal, high, very high, and extra high. Boehm also provided three tables to assist the software engineer to arrive at these classifications for a software product. Tables 14.11, 14.12, and 14.13 are reprints of Boehm's tables. A software engineer can use these tables for guidance and consult other members of the development team to decide the ranking for each of these fifteen attributes listed in Table 14.11.

Table 14.12 assists the software engineer in establishing a reliability attribute classification, and Table 14.13 assists in assigning a complexity attribute classification to the software product. Quantification of all cost driver attributes listed in Table 14.11 is presented in Table 15.2.

■ TABLE 14.11   **Rating Cost Driver Attributes**

			RATINGS			
Cost Driver	**Very Low**	**Low**	**Nominal**	**High**	**Very High**	**Extra High**
Product attributes						
RELY Table 14.12	Effect: slight inconvenience	Low, easily recoverable losses	Moderate, recoverable losses	High financial loss	Risk to human life	
DATA		$\dfrac{DB\ bytes}{Prog.\ DSI} < 10$	$10 \leq \dfrac{D}{P} < 100$	$100 \leq \dfrac{D}{P} < 1000$	$\dfrac{D}{P} \geq 1000$	
CPLX	Table 14.13					$\longrightarrow$
Computer attributes						
TIME			≤50% use of available execution time	70%	85%	95%
STOR			≤50% use of available storage	70%	85%	95%
VIRT		Major change every 12 months Minor: 1 month	Major: 6 months Minor: 2 weeks	Major: 2 months Minor: 1 week	Major: 2 weeks Minor: 2 days	
TURN		Interactive	Average turnaround <4 hours	4–12 hours	>12 hours	
Personnel attributes						
ACAP	15th percentile[a]	35th percentile	55th percentile	75th percentile	90th percentile	
AEXP	≤4 months experience	1 year	3 years	6 years	12 years	
PCAP	15th percentile[a]	35th percentile	55th percentile	75th percentile	90th percentile	
VEXP	≤1 month experience	4 months	1 year	3 years		
LEXP	≤1 month experience	4 months	1 year	3 years		
Project attributes						
MODP	No use	Beginning use	Some use	General use	Routine use	
TOOL	Basic microprocessor tools	Basic mini tools	Basic midi/maxi tools	Strong maxi programming, test tools	Add requirements, design, management, documentation tools	
SCED	75% of nominal	85%	100%	130%	160%	

[a] Team rating criteria: analysis (programming) ability, efficiency, ability to communicate and cooperate.
Source: W. B. Boehm, *Software Engineering Economics*, Prentice-Hall, Upper Saddle River, N.J., 1981, p. 119.

■ TABLE 14.12   Rating The Reliability Driver Attribute (Module Reliability vs. Project Activity)

Rating	Rqts. and Product Design	Detailed Design	Code and Unit Test	Integration and Test
Very low	Little detail Many TBDs Little verification Minimal QA, CM, draft user manual, test plans Minimal PDR	Basic design information Minimal QA, CM, draft user manual, test plans Informal design inspections	No test procedures Minimal path test, standards check Minimal QA, CM Minimal I/O and off-nominal tests Minimal user manual	No test procedures Many requirements untested Minimal QA, CM Minimal stress, off-nominal tests Minimal as-built documentation
Low	Basic information, verification Frequent TBDs Basic QA, CM, standards, draft user manual, test plans Nominal project V & V	Moderate detail Basic QA, CM, draft user manual, test plans	Minimal test procedures Partial path test, standards check Basic QA, CM, user manual Partial I/O and off-nominal tests	Minimal test procedures Frequent requirements untested Basic QA, CM, user manual Partial stress, off-nominal tests
Nominal				
High	Detailed verification, QA, CM, standards, PDR, documentation Detailed test plans, procedures	Detailed verification, QA, CM, standards, CDR, documentation Detailed test plans, procedures	Detailed test procedures, QA, CM, documentation Extensive off-nominal tests	Detailed test procedures, QA, CM, documentation Extensive stress, off-nominal tests
Very high	Detailed verification, QA, CM, standards, PDR, documentation IV & V interface Very detailed test plans, procedures	Detailed verification, QA, CM, standards, CDR, documentation Very thorough design inspections Very detailed test plans, procedures IV & V interface	Detailed test procedures, QA, CM, documentation Very thorough code inspections Very extensive off-nominal tests IV & V interface	Very detailed test procedures, QA, CM, documentation Very extensive stress, off-nominal tests IV & V interface

Source: W. B. Boehm, *Software Engineering Economics*, Prentice-Hall, Upper Saddle River, N.J., 1981, p. 123.

421

■ TABLE 14.13   Rating The Complexity Driver Attribute (Module Complexity vs. Type of Module)

Rating	Control Operations	Computational Operations	Device-dependent Operations	Data Management Operations
Very low	Straightline code with a few nonnested SP[a] operators: DOs, CASEs, IFTHENELSEs. Simple predicates	Evaluation of simple expressions: e.g., $A = B + C \times (D - E)$	Simple read, write statements with simple formats	Simple arrays in main memory
Low	Straightforward nesting of SP operators. Mostly simple predicates	Evaluation of moderate-level expressions, e.g., $D = SQRT (B\times2-4.\times A\times C)$	No cognizance needed of particular processor or I/O device characteristics. I/O done at GET/PUT level. No cognizance of overlap	Single file subsetting with no data structure changes, no edits, no intermediate files
Nominal	Mostly simple nesting. Some intermodule control. Decision tables	Use of standard math and statistical routines. Basic matrix/vector operations	I/O processing includes device selection, status checking and error processing	Multi-file input and single file output. Simple structural changes, simple edits
High	Highly nested SP operators with many compound predicates. Queue and stack control. Considerable intermodule control.	Basic numerical analysis: multivariate interpolation, ordinary differential equations. Basic truncation, roundoff concerns	Operations at physical I/O level (physical storage address translations; seeks, reads, etc). Optimized I/O overlap	Special purpose subroutines activated by data stream contents. Complex data restructuring at record level
Very high	Reentrant and recursive coding. Fixed-priority interrupt handling	Difficult but structured N.A.: near-singular matrix equations, partial differential equations	Routines for interrupt diagnosis, servicing, masking. Communication line handling	A generalized, parameter-driven file structuring routine. File building, command processing, search optimization
Extra high	Multiple resource scheduling with dynamically changing priorities. Microcode-level control	Difficult and unstructured N.A.: highly accurate analysis of noisy, stochastic data	Device timing-dependent coding, micro-programmed operations	Highly coupled, dynamic relational structures. Natural language data management

[a] SP = Structured programming.

Source: W. B. Boehm, *Software Engineering Economics*, Prentice-Hall, Upper Saddle River, N.J., 1981, p. 122.

For example, to quantify the attribute CPLX, complexity, the software engineer can use the matrix shown in Table 14.11 to assign a value to each module. The approach to using this table is to decide which factor best fits the module in terms of control, algorithmic processes, input/output, and data or file management. For instance, an embedded real-time, single-loop control system software product with cyclic process might rate very high in control operations and device-dependent operations, but low in computational operations and nominal in its data management operations. The reason for this conclusion is based on the fact that software to effect a control system function typically involves interrupts, direct interface with external devices, hard computational deadlines, and relatively simple algorithms. The value assigned to CPLX would then be the average of the complexity values assigned to each of the subfunctions of the module.

To quantify the attribute TIME, a reasonable time interval must be first determined. The CPU utilization is averaged over this time interval.

$$\text{Time} = \frac{\text{CPU ''ON''-time}}{\text{Time interval}}$$

The attribute STOR, memory use, reflects use of primary memory or virtual memory in percent of the total available. The attribute VIRT refers to the development environment stability and is measured in terms of the expected number of changes to the configuration per unit time. Experience and common sense would suggest that a development environment that has not been thoroughly tested and debugged will be more difficult to work with than one that has been in place long enough for the development team to have passed the knee of the learning curve.

The attribute TURN refers to development team access to the development environment resources and is measured in terms of turnaround time or number of opportunities or submissions per day available. For an interactive development environment with enough resources to support the development team, TURN attribute would be classified as Low. Many development environments are not interactive, especially those used for embedded systems. In these cases the developers may have to share the development facilities with others. Under these circumstances the software engineer will have to consider estimating the average number of opportunities available per day and select the appropriate value for attribute TURN.

Personnel attributes for the development team can, of course, influence the quality and reliability of the product as well as the time it takes to develop the product and the amount of rework required to complete the product. The general approach to assigning values to these attributes is to take the average experience of software engineers, system analysts, and other team members assigned to the project.

ACAP quantifies the capability of system engineers or analysts assigned to the development in terms of a subjective evaluation based on percentile. For example if, on average, our analysts or system engineers rank in the 90th percentile, we can classify the ACAP attribute as very high. On the other hand, if our analysts or system engineers, on average, are in the 15th percentile we would classify the ACAP attribute as very low.

For AEXP, average experience is used to quantify analysts' and system engineers' collective experience in the application area. An average of three years' experience for analysts or system engineers is regarded as nominal. Other ratings can be made using Tables 14.11, 14.12, and 14.13. In like manner average capability exhibited by software engineers and programmers (ACAP), average experience with the computer system, associated peripheral devices and support software (VEXP) and the average experience using the language selected for the development (LEXP) can be assigned a rating of very low, low, nominal, high or very high.

The MODP attribute categorizes the team's experience in the use of modern software development practices (structured development, DOD, NASA, IEEE, CASE tools, etc.). For example, if the development team routinely follows specification standards, top-down design, walk-throughs, quality reviews, standard design practices, etc., then the MODP attribute can be categorized as very high.

The attribute SCED refers to the schedule. The scheduled development time provided by any of the estimation models discussed in chapter 15 is regarded as nominal. If the schedule is compressed or stretched, the rate assigned to the attribute SCED is adjusted accordingly.

14.5 SOFTWARE QUALITY ATTRIBUTES ■

Software quality is a general software attribute measuring how well the software product meets stated function and performance requirements. To be effective, a quality assurance activity must have some quantifiable attributes as indicators of how closely the software product will meet its requirements. Moreover, these attributes must have predictive properties because we expect that attribute measurements made early in the development process can indicate postdelivery product quality. Chapter 18 is devoted to a discussion of the software quality assurance process. In this section we attempt to define several attributes that are used in the software quality assurance process.

Experience has shown that the use of audits, reviews, and walk-throughs has a measurable positive effect on software quality [11]. Experience has also shown that software quality improves substantially when the development team follows the development plan closely and follows internal procedures and standards rigorously. Those responsible for product quality assurance are keepers of the project conscience in this regard.

There are two general avenues of approach to enforcing quality control on the entire process and on the product itself. The first involves quantifying and measuring certain software product attributes that are strongly related to quality, then using these attributes as feedback to drive the development process toward a better product. The second approach is to apply quality criteria to the process itself, that is, to define, quantify, and measure attributes directly associated with the development process. These attributes can be used as predictors of product quality and indicators of personnel and process problems. A good quality assurance approach will employ a blend of both.

Errors, faults, defects, and failures are quantifiable attributes used in defining and measuring software reliability and software quality attributes. The standard definitions of these attributes are as follows [6]:

Error: Any human mistake that results in incorrect software; errors include omission of a critical requirement in a software specification, a developer's misinterpretation of the requirement, or an incorrect translation from design to code.

Fault: An error manifestation in software that causes a functional unit of the software system to fail in performing its required function; sometimes called a bug, a fault is a part of the code that needs to be fixed.

Defect: An anomaly in any intermediate or final software product resulting from an error or fault, ranging from an incorrectly specified set of test data to an incorrect entry in user documentation.

Failure: Inability of a functional unit of the system depending on the software to perform its required function or to perform the function within required limits.

If the word *software* is extended to include documentation and tools, then quality measures of supporting software documentation and tools can be employed to give a more general quality measure when given in terms of error, faults, defects, and failures. Table 14.14 lists product quality attributes that can be indicators of overall software quality and also identify potential problem sources. Some of these attributes can be predicted early in the development cycle.

The quality attributes listed on Table 14.14 are usually not measurable until the product is in its late stages of development or during the operational phase. In large product developments where elements of the product are scheduled to be developed sequentially, it is possible to use early testing results to improve the quality of subsequently developed product elements. In these cases many of the attributes listed in Table 14.12 are of significant value.

A second window on product quality is available through observations made on the quality of the process. By examining certain features of the process (reviews, audits, walk-throughs, key meetings, and certain other scheduled events), an implicit measure of product quality can be obtained. The advantage of this approach is that it can be applied early in the development cycle and can exert a positive influence on the quality of the product when it counts the most,

---

■ TABLE 14.14   **Software Quality Attributes**

Failures/Faults/Defects/Errors
   Per unit of CPU operating time
   (uncovered during testing and operational phase)
   Per unit of SLOC or function point

Faults/Defects/Errors
   Allocated to SDLC Phase
   Allocated to User Interface
   Allocated to Organization
   Allocated to Documentation
   Allocated to Unit or Module

Maintainability
   Number of maintenance actions per unit of CPU operating time
   MTTR = Mean time to debug, find, and fix errors (including regression testing)
   Mean time to update system (including procedures and documents)

Ratio of Failures to Faults

Availability
   (discussed in Chapter 17)

Reliability
   (discussed in Chapter 17)

■ TABLE 14.15   **Project Quality Evaluation Template**

REVIEW MEETING CONDUCT
  START ON TIME   YES _____   NO _____
  ALL MEMBERS PRESENT   YES _____   NO _____
  FINISH ON TIME   YES _____   NO _____
  MEETING CONDUCT OVERALL RATING   1   2   3   4   5   (circle one)*
  ACTIONS ASSIGNED
    (list action assignees)
    (list actions on an attached form)
    (list action closed)
  NEXT MEETING SCHEDULED   YES _____   NO _____
  COMMENTS
    (attach any comments)

DOCUMENTATION REVIEW
  ON-TIME DELIVERY OF DOCUMENT TO BE REVIEWED   YES _____   NO _____

  NUMBER OF TYPOGRAPHICAL ERRORS _____

  FIGURE QUALITY   1   2   3   4   5   (circle one)*
  READABILITY   1   2   3   4   5   (circle one)*

  ERRORS PER PAGE (all types) _____

  COMMENTS
    (any comments will be attached here)
    (any problem identified will be described here)
  ERROR CLOSURES

TEST PLAN AND TESTING REVIEW
  TEST ENVIRONMENT QUALITY   1   2   3   4   5   (circle one)*

  PROCESS   1   2   3   4   5   (circle one)*
    TRACKING   1   2   3   4   5   (circle one)*
    CONTROLS   1   2   3   4   5   (circle one)*
    CLOSURE   1   2   3   4   5   (circle one)*

  DEBUGGING   1   2   3   4   5   (circle one)*
    PROCESS   1   2   3   4   5   (circle one)*
    CONTROLS   1   2   3   4   5   (circle one)*
    CLOSURE   1   2   3   4   5   (circle one)*

ERROR SOURCE BREAKOUT SPEC/DESIGN/CODE/TEST

COMMENTS
  (attach any comments)

_____   _____   _____
      Signature   Title   Date

....
* The ranking is such that 1 = excellent and 5 = unacceptable.

early in the life cycle. Slipshod reviews and cavalier attitudes toward the development process can be identified and fixed immediately if quality assurance methods are rigorously applied.

A quality evaluation template that can be used or adapted to reviews, audits, walk-throughs, and key meetings including software development plan reviews is suggested in Table 14.15.

14.6 COMPLEXITY-RELATED ATTRIBUTES   ■

Software complexity attributes are often associated with quality, reliability, cost, and schedule. In general, the more complex the requirements, the more likely the implementation will take longer and cost more and the delivered software will contain more lines of code and more latent faults, which, of course, affects product reliability and quality.

Software complexity refers to quantification of software structure in terms of such attributes as the following: control operations, computation operations, device-dependent operations, data management operations, algorithmic structures, data structures, etc. Assigning a value to each of these attributes (this is not an exhaustive attribute list) is not an easy task and requires certain touchstones. To help communicate that experience, Boehm [4] has provided a software complexity rating chart, Table 14.13. By consulting this chart, a relatively inexperienced practitioner can quantify a software product or module in terms of its complexity as defined by Boehm and used in his cost and schedule prediction models. If complexity becomes a very useful attribute to the development team, Boehm's complexity chart can be particularized to the specific development project.

Another attempt at characterizing software requirement complexity is summarized in Table 14.16. The software module or product is classified by type and class. For example, a new application would be classified qualitatively as hard. Associated with each type and class is a complexity rank of 1, 2, or 3. The rank values can be used to compare one software product with another and can also be used as guidance in making personnel assignments, indicating areas of potential risk, and influencing scheduling.

■ TABLE 14.16   **Classification of Software for Complexity Assignment**

COMPLEXITY RANK	CLASS	SOFTWARE TYPE
1	Hard	New application
2	Not hard	Previously solved in another form
3	Static	Batchlike applications
1	Dynamic	Real-time elements
3	Sequential	In-series functions
1	Parallel	Concurrent transactions
3	Data-oriented	Data are main concern
1	Control-oriented	Control is main concern
2	Algorithm-oriented	Process is main concern
2	Deterministic	Predictable output for given input
1	Nondeterministic	Not always predictable (expert systems)

If a software module or product has reached its detail design level, another complexity attribute, cyclomatic complexity [9,10], can be measured.

Assessing each software module in terms of complexity and assigning a relative complexity number can help in staffing and personnel assignment decisions and can serve as a guide in deciding which modules to watch carefully, especially during development and test. The effort spent on estimating software complexity helps the development team better understand the overall product. In short, the project is better off as a result of having performed the effort to define and document a complexity number. In addition to assigning a complexity number to each module, a rationale for how the number was established is substantially more important than the number itself.

14.7 EXECUTION TIME–RELATED ATTRIBUTES ■

Two important elements in defining and measuring execution time attributes are real-time and concurrency constraints imposed on the software being executed. Concurrency parameters include coupling, database update dependencies, and potential for deadlock. Some additional attributes that can be employed to characterize software products with concurrent processing include intertask communication timing requirements, exceptions, precedence relationships, time slicing, task management, overhead, and intertask security. Chapter 19 provides a more detailed look at software products with real-time and concurrency requirements.

14.8 TEST-RELATED ATTRIBUTES ■

Chapters 10, 11, and 12 discussed in detail the software test and integration process. Based on the discussions in these chapters, the most important test related attributes are number of expected failures/faults, number of actual failures/faults, and CPU time as well as wall clock time spent in identifying the failures and fixing the faults.

A test environment will begin to collect data that will either confirm the predicted failure rate or permit a calibration of model parameters using actual data. By recording faults, failures, errors, and defects along with time of occurrence, actual CPU time spent in executing the software product, and time required to debug and effect a change to eliminate the fault and the source of the fault, a great deal can be learned about the potential performance of the software in its operational environment. Table 14.17 summarizes some of the data that can be collected in the test environment. These data can be used to predict such operational attributes as reliability, availability, mean time to repair, mean time to next failure, and total number of intrinsic faults in the software product.

14.9 DOCUMENTATION-RELATED ATTRIBUTES ■

Software products are usually accompanied by an abundant quantity of hard copy documents that must be produced. Specifications, listings, program description, test plans, operational

■ TABLE 14.17   **Data To Be Collected in the Test Environment**

Fault ID: _____

Wall Clock Time when Failure Identified: _____

CPU Time Elapsed since Last Failure Occurrence: _____

Symptoms Recognized:
   1. _____
   2. _____
    .
    .
   N. _____

Source of Fault:
   Development phase where fault originated: _____
   Organizational responsibility: _____
   Module location in component or product: _____

Debug Time:
   Labor hours required to locate fault: _____
   Wall clock time: _____
   CPU time required to debug: _____

Fix Description:
   Labor hours required to effect fix and document _____
   Wall clock time _____
   CPU time to design code and test fix _____

Regression Testing:
   Labor hours: _____
   Wall clock time: _____
   CPU time: _____

Number of Tests Required: _____
Comments: _____
Data Collector:
   Name: _____
   Title: _____
   Date: _____
Signature: _____

procedures, test cases, test results, and user manuals are but a few. Describing each document in terms of purpose and whether delivered or not and recording page counts provides an important attribute that describes yet another aspect of a software product. Some attributes associated with documentation are the following: (1) name and type of the document, (2) purpose of the document, (3) page counts, (4) figure counts, (5) revision schedule, (6) labor cost, and (7) printing cost. The value of this information is in its use for estimating the effort or resources required to produce, publish, control, and update project documentation and its utility in maintaining the delivered product.

14.10 PERFORMANCE-RELATED ATTRIBUTES ■

Performance attributes include those measures of software associated with the use of CPU, memory (both primary and secondary), input/output channel resources, and the use of absolute time in meeting software requirements. In many applications requirements must be met regarding computer resources and system response times. Moreover, growth provisions for both resources and CPU capacity should be considered. The application of quality assurance to this facet must include some way to determine at each stage of development how well the project team is doing in meeting these requirements. Quantifiable attributes must be defined and used to track progress in meeting these requirements. In particular, risk assessments and risk containment plans require that specific performance attributes, used as a trouble indicator, be watched carefully. Table 14.18 lists a few of these attributes. Keeping a record of all performance attributes as a project goes from concept to product can be useful to future projects, when records are accurate and reflect a complete story. For example, a sudden increase in CPU utilization could arise from a number of possible circumstances. The reasons for changes in attribute values are an essential part of the attribute tracking process and should be well documented.

Initially, of course, the actual values in Table 14.18 are estimated. As progress is made, the estimates become more accurate and eventually are replaced by true actuals.

Table 14.18 shows a format for reporting on performance attributes. CPU utilization is usually given in terms of percent of time the CPU is busy over a specific time interval. The selection of the time interval is important. For example, if it is known that a software product will be required to support 600 transactions per hour at delivery and there is an expectation that the workload will double during the lifetime of the system, then the software, working in conjunction with the system, should use less than 50% of the CPU resource at delivery. The time interval selected for averaging might be one hour. This example of establishing requirements on CPU utilization is vastly oversimplified. Only the essence of the issue has been presented. When CPU utilization reaches 85%, the CPU is effectively fully loaded. If

■ TABLE 14.18　**Performance Parameters**

	ACTUAL	REQUIRED
CPU Utilization	36%	50%
Memory Utilization		
Primary	21%	50%
Secondary	30%	50%
Real Time/Response Time		
Loop 1	80 ms	80 ms
Loop 2	40 ms	40 ms
(Substantial margin [15%] available for additional loop content)		
I/O Channel Capacity	1.1	
Terminals Supported	100	
External Device Use	N/A	N/A
Comments _____		

an acceptable provision is made to buffer transactions during peak periods, it may be possible to use 8 hours as the time interval over which the load is averaged.

Memory utilization includes both primary and secondary storage and should include both programs and data files. Usually requirement specifications include growth of data files over system lifetimes. There are frequently requirements on archiving data files off-line and on capturing and preserving certain data files for use in disaster recovery. Oftentimes the software engineer will need to identify particular modes of operation that impose the greatest load on memory resources and then size memory use based on the worst case conditions.

Input/output channel capacity can be determined by examining worst-case modes and estimating worst-case traffic. As the development progresses, estimates will be replaced by measurements that will either confirm estimates or alter predictions. Use of external devices such as printers, encryption devices, etc., should also be estimated and revisited periodically to assure that resources are adequate to the need. In keeping with the view that software development is part of a system development, it is important to prepare an estimate of the computer resources used by the software and to monitor actual utilization as software functional and performance requirements are realized in software.

14.11 LABOR-RELATED ATTRIBUTES   ■

A valuable parameter for any manager or software engineer is the amount of effort required to perform a specific task or a set of tasks. Table 14.19 lists a few labor-related attributes. The first use of these attributes is in preparing cost estimates and sizing the work force needed to perform particular tasks.

■ TABLE 14.19   **Labor-Related Attributes**

1. SLOC produced per labor month by:
   SWDLC phase
   Software type or class
2. Labor month per page of documentation by:
   SWDLC phases
   Individual document
3. Labor month per walk-through, audit, or review
4. Support labor month per SLOC by:
   SWDLC phase
   Software type or class
   (includes secretarial, clerical, management, external services, and consultants)
5. Labor month per SLOC for maintenance by:
   SWDLC phase
   Software type or class
6. Labor month per reused SLOC by:
   SWDLC phase
   Software type or class
   Module/unit

A second use for labor attributes is the performance evaluation of development team members. This task is typically assigned to senior software engineers. Having an understanding of the effort required to perform certain tasks makes it possible for a software manager to make reasonable personnel assignments and make more accurate assessments of individual performance. It is incumbent on lead technical team members and management to recognize the good, the bad, and the average performers and reward them accordingly. Team members know who the best performers are, and if leadership fails to recognize and reward them appropriately, management credibility suffers and team morale can be affected. A team's confidence in its leadership at all levels is essential to a successful development.

Some labor attributes depend on the characteristics of the software product, others depend on the characteristics of the development environment, and some depend on both. It is a highly experienced development organization that knows the required effort to perform specific tasks and produce specific items associated with developing and maintaining a software product. We will see in chapter 15 that the grassroots or bottom-up cost estimates produced by such a group are usually reliable and well supported with substantiating rationale.

14.12   OPERATING ENVIRONMENT ATTRIBUTES   ■

During operation users will expect a certain quality of performance from the software product. Some components of this behavior can frequently be quantified and measured. There are also qualitative descriptions of software product performance that are often cited in conjunction with quality evaluations. Table 14.20 lists operational behavior categorized by performance, design, and adaptation. Performance-related attributes include efficiency, integrity, reliability, and usability. The efficiency attribute needs to be more precisely defined before any consideration of measurement can be explored. *Efficiency* can refer to use of computer system resources, time (wall clock or CPU), operator interventions, testing, etc. Each situation presents a unique interpretation and definition as well as a unique way to measure efficiency. The major use of the efficiency attribute is in comparing one product with another. Absolute efficiency is difficult if not impossible to establish.

Integrity refers to the continuing accuracy of the data in the software product's files and the ability of the product to withstand attempts by unauthorized users to penetrate the software product. To fully appreciate and evaluate a system's integrity, the threats to the system must be fully characterized and security measures designed to block the threat must be described in detail. There have been attempts to quantify integrity in terms of occurrence of a specific threat and the probability that the threat will be deflected.

A number of easily quantified attributes relate to reliability. Some of these attributes are mean time to failure, availability, mean time to repair, faults, and failures. These attributes are all discussed in chapter 17.

Usability refers to the relationship between operator and system. Since the operator interface to the system is through the software (which implements operational modes and timelines), it is really a software attribute. There are some ways in which this nebulous attribute can be quantified. For example, the training and experience required to develop a competent operator and the prerequisite for qualifying as an operator trainee can be quantified. Productivity increases attributed to the new system can be quantified. Other secondary indicators of operator reaction to or acceptance of the system are found in absenteeism, requests for transfer, and lower morale.

■ TABLE 14.20   **Operating Environment Attributes**

ATTRIBUTE	ATTRIBUTE MEASURES
Performance-Related	
Efficiency	Algorithmic Analysis
Integrity	
Reliability	Mean Time to Failure
Usability	
Design-Related	
Correctness	Faults and Failures
Maintainability	Mean Time to Repair
Verifiability	Cyclomatic Complexity
Adaptation-Related	
Expandability	
Flexibility	
Interoperability	
Portability	
Reusability	
Application-Related Quality Parameters	
Safety	Integrity
	Reliability
	Correctness
	Verifiability
	Survivability
Long lifetime (A)	Maintainability
	Expandability
	Efficiency
High-level change activity (B)	Flexibility
	Expandability
Combination of A and B	Flexibility
	Reusability
	Expandability
Real-time application	Efficiency
	Reliability
	Correctness
	Functions
	Performance
	Timing

Adaptability-related attributes include expandability, flexibility, interoperability, and reusability. Your first reaction may be that quantifying these attributes is impossible and knowing the value of these attributes, if they could be quantified, would be of little practical use. However, as for other seemingly vague attributes, the adaptation-related attributes can be defined narrowly for specific applications and used for comparing one implementation with another or a new system with its replacement.

Other application-related attributes of the delivered software product include safety, lifetime, and degree of change activity. Since software has become embedded in many systems that serve the public in such areas as transportation, communication, health care, power generation, and distribution, etc., the issue of safety has become a major software concern. A fault in an embedded software product can jeopardize public safety. Attributes that can be used to specify or measure the safety of a software product are also listed in Table 14.20.

Many software products are part of systems that have twenty- to thirty-year lifetimes. Long lifetimes mean extensive change activity. A software product's ability to endure is linked to its ability to accommodate change without major revision to its architecture. In short, some attributes of a software product enhance its capability to cope with change.

Real-time application software products have their own particular characteristics and concerns. Chapter 19 is devoted to the discussion of these characteristics.

14.13   DATA COLLECTION   ■

The 1994 edition of the IEEE *Standards Collection for Software Engineering* [6] offers some attribute definitions and suggests a format for a data collection activity covering product, productivity, and quality parameters. This chapter presents a similar collection of software attributes and parameters from which a data collection template may be derived. A carefully selected subset of these parameters, unique to the development team, is recommended as a starting point in development of a software attribute database. A software development organization that intends to stay in business should maintain a database reflecting their own development experience in terms of quantified software attributes and their history. For example, the estimated size of the software product will vary throughout the development cycle as requirement understanding matures until the product is completed. A history of these variations and why they occurred can lead to an improved attribute estimation process and, at the same time, offer insights not otherwise available into the dynamics of the development process itself. Those who ignore history are doomed to repeat it.

There is a cost for maintaining such a database, of course, but once established the collection process can be automated and made intrinsic to the development process. The authors strongly advocate the establishment of a comprehensive data collection and evaluation effort within the software development organization.

The recommended approach is to begin the collection of software parameters as early as possible in the process, which means starting with attribute estimates early in the development cycle. In fact, the effort required to define the attributes, collect (estimate) attribute values, review, and document results can act as a driving force leading ultimately to a better understanding of the software product and perhaps better estimates.

14.13.1   Establishing a Data Collection Program

To establish an effective data collection function for a software data collection organization, a clear idea of the use of the database is essential. A set of objectives for a data collection task is assembled in Table 14.21.

The data that are collected must be analyzed and evaluated and the conclusions used to influence the development process with the objective of improving overall development effectiveness. Although there is a time lag associated with collecting, evaluating, and using the

■ TABLE 14.21   **Objectives for Data Collection Task**

1. Define the set of attributes to be employed clearly and unambiguously with strong guidance as to how to quantify each parameter.
2. Develop a template that can be used to collect data required to effect initial resource and schedule estimates.
3. Characterize each subsequent software product partition in terms of quantifiable attribute using the definitions of 1. above.
4. Link the cost accounting process to the data collection process to allocate cost automatically to specific products such as documents, major software product subsystems, reviews, audits, quality assurance, etc.
5. Account for all software product–related cost by identifying cost of support from other organizations such as human factors, management, reliability engineering, system engineering, etc., automatically through the cost accounting process.
6. Automate the data collection process.
7. Protect the integrity and security of the data and information derived therefrom.
8. Account for the cost of maintaining the software development database in the development cost.

data, a well-planned data collection process can have a profound effect on the development process. For large product developments with staggered deliveries of software components, the results of earlier development efforts can be used to improve development of those components whose development comes later in the development cycle.

The collected data are of no value unless they are used effectively in some way to improve the development process, improve resource and schedule predictions, or contribute to developers' personal growth and technical management skills. The feedback intrinsic in the evaluation of the collected data should enable a development team to grow in capability and improve its performance.

We have presented an extensive list of parameters, many of which are quantifiable, to choose from; collection, analysis, and documentation is a major task. It is not essential that every attribute on the list be collected. In most cases the list of attributes can be trimmed to suit individual development team needs. Moreover, an initial expenditure of effort to select attributes, establish the database, and design an automated collection method will substantially reduce the long-term cost of assembling essential data for reduction to useful information.

14.14   CHAPTER SUMMARY   ■

Examination or estimation of certain software attributes throughout the software development cycle can provide valuable insights into the product, process, and development team. Continuing the process of prediction, measurement, and refinement of models and prediction mechanics can provide a great many benefits. In particular, these benefits include the following: (1) a better technical description and categorization of the software product; (2) development of measurable software product attributes that can be made intrinsic to the function and performance specification and the design specification; (3) a means to relate quality attributes to specific process attributes or steps; (4) a means to improve objective evaluations of personnel and organization performance; (5) a means to predict size and estimate resource and schedule requirements more accurately; and (6) a way to evaluate objectively the effect of new methods and tools on quality and productivity.

This chapter has focused strongly on sizing because of its importance in developing cost and schedule estimates for planning purposes and its utility in characterizing other attributes such as failures per source lines of code or labor months per source lines of code. The fifteen COCOMO attributes were treated together in Section 14.4 because we have used the CO-COMO model in chapter 15 in our cost and schedule estimation examples.

We have emphasized the need for each development team to establish a data collection effort as part of the development process. In each instance attributes must be clearly defined, a standard means must be developed for measurement, and a formal process must be implemented for collecting and documenting attribute data and evaluating the data for use in improving product process and team performance.

In many cases we have provided a definition of the attribute and a means to measure the attribute. In others we have only offered suggestions because the attribute must be defined and measured in the context of a specific application. The attributes covered in this chapter make a long list but not an exhaustive one.

An estimate of the software product size attribute is an important input to cost and schedule prediction and software development planning. Poor size estimates (function points or source lines of code) often reflect a poor understanding of the requirements and the application. The inability to develop a good estimate of product size may be a signal that we don't understand the problem. It may be better to take more time to understand the problem at the beginning rather than wait until changes and revisions to function are very expensive in time and resources.

14.15 EXERCISES ■

1. List five attributes that you would use to evaluate and grade student-written programs.
2. Can you think of any software size attributes other than SLOC, function points, or feature points? Explain how you would estimate such an attribute.
3. Suppose you are responsible for managing a software development team. State the attributes you will use to track progress and measure your team's performance. Give a description of how each of the selected attributes will help you measure the team performance and progress.
4. Describe the features of an ideal software attribute.
5. How would you go about defining a quantitative attribute for user friendliness?
6. How can the efficiency attribute be quantified?
7. Compute the estimated size of the order-entry module of the ABC project of chapter 2 using the function point estimation method. Assume three methods of order entry: phone call with operator, mark sensor sheet, and automated data entry using phone lines.
8. Do problem 7 using Jones' feature point estimation method. Compare the results of the two estimation methods and justify any unexpected differences.
9. Compute the estimated size of the heating/cooling control system for the XYZ project of chapter 2 in function points. Assume the implementation language is the 486 assembly language and convert the estimated size into KSLOC.
10. Consider an automated teller machine with the following banking capabilities: deposit, withdraw, payment for credit card, mortgage payment, and transfer of funds. Estimate

the function points needed for implementation of such an automated teller machine. What is the number of feature points for the automated teller machine?

11. List 3 major attributes that apply to an object-oriented software development environment. Explain each attribute and its corresponding estimation method.

12. Can any of the size estimation methods discussed in this chapter be used for a software product that is to be developed using object-oriented methodology and an object-oriented programing language.

13. Which of the 15 cost driven attributes discussed in Table 14.11 won't be applicable in an object-oriented environment?

14. Modify Table 14.6 to include visual languages. Do the numbers in Table 14.6 comply with your experience? If no, explain why and in what way they differ from your experience.

References

1. A. J. Albrecht, ''Measuring Application Development Productivity,'' *Proceedings of the IBM Application Development Symposium*, Monterey, Calif., October 1979.

2. ———, ''AD/M Productivity Measurement and Estimate Validation,'' *IBM Corp. Inf. Sys.* May, (1984).

3. A. J. Albrecht and J. E. Gaffney, Jr., *Software Function, Source Lines of Code and Development Effort Prediction: A Software Science Validation, IEEE Trans. Software Engrg.* Vol. 9. No. 6:639–648, (1983).

4. W. B. Boehm, *Software Engineering Economics*, Prentice-Hall, Upper Saddle River, N.J., 1981.

5. IEEE, Standard #1045-1992, *Standards for Software Productivity Metrics*, IEEE Press, New York, 1992.

6. IEEE, *Standards Collection for Software Engineering*, IEEE Press, New York, 1994.

7. C. Jones, *Programming Productivity*, McGraw-Hill, New York, 1986.

8. C. Jones, *A Short History of Function Points and Feature Points*, Software Productivity Research, Burlington, Mass. 1988.

9. T. McCabe, *A Software Complexity Measure, IEEE Trans. Software Engrg.* Vol. 2, No. 4, pages 308–314, 1976.

10. T. McCabe and C. W. Butler, ''Design Complexity Measurement and Testing,'' *Comm. ACM* 32(12): pages 1415–1425, (1989).

11. R. S. Pressman, *Software Engineering: A Practitioner's Approach*, Ed. 3, McGraw-Hill, New York, 1992.

15

Software Development Resource Estimation

15.0 OBJECTIVES ■

The main objectives of this chapter are as follows: (1) to make the reader aware that the total resources required to develop a software product include far more than the labor needed to design, code, and test the software; (2) to present a complete picture of the various resources needed to develop a software product; (3) to suggest that surprise cost and schedule overruns are often the result of a poor cost and schedule estimation process at the inception of the project; (4) to emphasize that effective software development planning depends on the accuracy of the initial cost and schedule estimates, which in turn depend upon accurate software size estimates; (5) to make clear that, although software development cost and schedule estimates are sometimes dictated by a top-down edict (design to cost or price to win, for example), the software engineer still must make as accurate an estimate as possible based on the best available product sizing and the best estimate of product attributes; (6) to describe a widely used cost and schedule estimation model; (7) to emphasize that software product sizing and cost and schedule estimation are important software engineering responsibilities; and (8) to show that, in spite of a great deal of cynicism, a software cost and schedule estimation process is an important component in developing effective software development plans, identifying and quantifying risk, and evaluating overall project and product performance.

15.1 INTRODUCTION ■

In this chapter we consider the problem of estimating the number of labor months and single-shift calendar time in months required to develop a software product, given certain characteristics and attributes desired of the product, the conditions under which the software product is to be developed, and the amount of code required to implement software product requirements. The algorithms presented in this chapter do not make a distinction among programming languages. The implied assumption, when developing a relatively large software product, is that the cost of specifying, designing, coding, testing, and managing a line of executable code is independent of the programming language being used.

Although a number of claims have been made that certain new methodologies, approaches, tools, and languages would significantly reduce software development cost and schedule, most of these claims have not materialized. For some of the more recent claims, real supporting evidence is not yet available. There has, however, been a steady improvement in software development productivity over the last 25 to 30 years. Reference [1] estimates this productivity improvement at approximately 50%.

The resources required to develop a software product include labor, development time, and means of production (hardware and software). Labor includes the efforts of software engineers, programmers, system engineers, system analysts, librarians, clerks, data entry personnel, computer operators, verification and validation personnel, configuration management personnel, managers, secretaries, reliability analysts, publication personnel, quality assurance personnel, safety engineers, etc. In short, labor includes the efforts of all those whose activities contribute directly or indirectly to the delivered software product. Labor costs for software development are often referred to in terms of productivity and are measured in source lines of code per labor month or function or feature points per labor month. Software development time is the time interval between the initiation of the SRS and the delivery of the software product.

Means of production is sometimes referred to as the development environment. In particular, means of production refers to computer systems, models of the operational environment used for software testing, office space, furniture, compilers, assemblers, software development tools (CASE tools), scaffolds (software employed to support delivered software during development), test drivers (software employed to exercise individual units and modules during the unit test phase).

Labor resource estimates are often referred to as cost estimates, and development time estimates are called schedule estimates. Schedule estimates are based on calendar months, and labor costs are usually expressed in labor months (approximately 160 labor hours per labor month). This approach is useful because labor rates may change with time and may be different among different organizations while labor months are more consistent. To convert labor months to dollars, one multiplies labor months times average labor cost per month. Labor cost includes salary as well as overhead expense. Overhead expense pays for some of the means of production. The identification and estimation of all the relevant labor resources and schedule estimates are essential to the development of an effective SDP.

One may argue that we can decrease the development time of a project by increasing resources applied to development tasks. However, experience has shown that adding more resources to effect a substantial reduction does not seem to work [3]. The amount of additional coordination, control, communication, etc., required to make effective use of additional resources beyond those estimated by the development time estimation algorithm, as well as the sequential nature of some of the phases of the SWDLC, precludes reduction in development time beyond some optimum productivity point. It is important to planners that they have some guidance as to the length of this optimum development time interval. The initial estimates of software development time assume single 8-hour shifts.

Costs associated with means of production fall into two categories, dedicated and general. Special development tools, special hardware or software unique to a given development and unusable for other projects are considered dedicated costs and are usually charged directly to the project. On the other hand, cost of standard software/hardware tools used in all software developments are considered as general expense and are usually paid for by the overhead portion of the cost per labor month.

Jones in reference [4], section 5.2, makes some very important observations regarding the history of software development cost/productivity.

1. Average productivity, as measured in delivered source lines of code (SLOC) per labor month, has increased about 50% in the last 25 years. The authors' experience would put the improvement at closer to 40%.
2. The impact of programming language (on productivity in source lines of code per labor month) is small, typically less than 10%.
3. Software development is labor intensive. Methodologies and tools help but do not have a significant impact on cost.
4. Customers/clients are now beginning to ask developers to assume a significant part of the cost risk in the development of a software product. That is, there is now more emphasis on fixed price contracts.

These points are in line with the authors' experience and are germane to the subject of cost and schedule estimation we are about to explore.

Improvements in software development productivity will come from improvements in the process and especially by the strict conformance, on the part of the development team, to process and procedure. We may argue that we can't afford to follow all procedures or we don't have enough slack in the schedule to do all the steps in the process. The old saw, ''There is never enough time or money to do it right, but always enough time and money to do it over'' is directly applicable.

15.2 SOFTWARE PRODUCT COST AND SCHEDULE ESTIMATION ■

It is often difficult to convince students and inexperienced programmers (those who have not had the experience of participating in the development of a large software product in a professionally run software development environment) that software development cost can easily exceed $100 per delivered source line of code. Most software developed in an academic environment includes only a limited amount of design, coding, and testing. The effort that is usually *not* part of most academic software development experience includes the following:

■ Client meetings and discussions
■ Formal development reviews and formal publication of the SRS
■ Communication interfaces with other team members working on other components of the software product

- Management and secretarial support
- Tool maintenance (compilers, debuggers, etc.)
- Support to training and product documentation
- Test case development and documentation
- System integration support
- Human interface design (consulting)
- Configuration management
- Quality assurance
- Travel expense
- Development, review, and publication of SDS
- Code walk-through, review, audits

The time and money spent for these efforts can account for more that 80 percent of the total cost and schedule of some software products.

One frequently encounters accurate but incomplete software development productivity figures, incomplete because they reflect only a part of the software development cost. For clarity, software productivity figures should always be cited in terms of product attributes, development environment, application environment, and quality assurance descriptors. Moreover, it should be made very clear to what phase or phases of the software development process these productivity figures apply. The use of incomplete productivity figures for software development cost and schedule estimates leads to predictions for resource requirements and calendar time that are often grossly in error.

An instructive analogy to software cost and schedule estimation can be found in the estimation of resources and time required to paint a house. If the first estimate is based solely on the number of square feet to be covered, the resource and time estimate is then based on number of gallons required to cover the given area and the number of square feet an average painter can be expected to cover in a given time period. From these data the number of painters required, the schedule, and the number of gallons of paint can be estimated. This first estimate fails to account for preparation of the surface; scraping and burning off old paint, possibly pretreatment of the surface for mold and making minor repairs to the surface; application of a primer coat; decision by the customer to use another color for trim; the fact that painting at the ground level goes faster and costs less than painting at levels requiring scaffolds and ladders; the cost of cleanup at job completion; and travel time. Too often software cost and schedule estimates stick at the first estimate. The first estimate is the one that looks the best to the client and to management. This approach is often what leads to surprises at the magnitude of cost and schedule overruns. Finding ways to increase the number of square feet a painter can cover in an hour (analogous to improving coding productivity) does not address the real problem.

The average distribution of software development costs (as derived from data collected over the years) for most deliverable software products by software development phase is as shown in Table 15.1. Software cost estimation models have often neglected the engineering cost of the software system (the development of the SRS document) and have underestimated the cost of design and system test. In fact, even the well-used cost and schedule estimation algorithms developed by Boehm [2] neglect a significant part of the software product engineering costs as well as some administrative support costs. This oversight can account for as much as 20% of the total software development cost. These additional costs, as we shall see, must be factored into estimates.

We may summarize our initial discussion of software development cost and schedule estimation by stating the following points:

■ TABLE 15.1   **Software Development Cost Distribution**

PERCENT	PHASE	ACTIVITY AND FINAL PRODUCT
20%	Engineering	Planning, specification of function and performances, etc. Final product is the SRS document.
20%	Design	Specification of design. Final product is the SDS document.
17%	Code and Unit or Module Test	Conversion of SDS to computer programs. Final product is a set of program modules accepted by the test and integration team.
43%	System Test and Integration	Full system involvement hardware, software, operators, etc. Final product is a system ready for acceptance test.

1. Software cost and schedule estimates are an extremely important input to the initial software development planning effort and should be conducted in a serious, thoroughly professional manner. The quality of the SDP depends on the quality of these estimates.
2. Software cost and schedule estimates should be prepared by two groups working independently and using two different methods.
3. A critical software attribute, size, drives virtually all estimation methods. Every effort should be made to develop an accurate estimate of source lines of code or function (feature) points before initiating cost estimation activity.
4. A systematic estimation methodology and technique, carefully applied and well documented, that exposes for review the process followed and the rationale applied to obtain the estimates is essential.
5. Estimation results should be changed only when it is shown that the supporting rationale is in error. Software engineers should recognize the difference between estimation and negotiation and leave cost and schedule negotiation to others if possible. If not possible, then postpone negotiation until the best estimate is complete.
6. Use the supporting rationale as guidance in identifying risk areas, reducing costs, and in improving chances of development success.
7. Cost and schedule estimation should not be one-time procedures. The estimation of resources and the time required to complete the development cycle should be reviewed and revised on a periodic basis. This information is essential to effective management of the development process and improvement of the estimation process.
8. The software engineer should play a strong, active role in developing the original estimates and keeping them current.

It is true that, more often than we expect, software development cost and schedule are sometimes handed down from management or from the client. In these cases, either (1) management has decided that, in order to win a competition, a particular cost and schedule target must be met (price to win), or (2) only a given amount of resources have been allocated to develop the software (system). In either of these situations the software engineer is not absolved of responsibility for understanding and helping to produce the best possible cost and schedule estimate consistent with the available data. The need for cost and schedule estimates in these cases is to provide an understanding of the magnitude of the risk being undertaken or to determine how much software the available resources will buy.

Some experienced software engineers and project managers recommend that software resource estimation is best accomplished by a knowledgeable consultant from an organization outside the development team, with cooperation from development team software engineers and project managers [5]. The reason is the desire to produce a resource estimate that is not influenced by the competitive environment, parochial interests of the development team, and the development team's inexperience. However, this approach does not mean that a software engineer should not be familiar with the resource estimation process. On the contrary, it is the software engineer who will often, after the first resource estimation, be asked to revise the estimations or respond to questions regarding the estimations.

15.3   COST AND SCHEDULE ESTIMATION MODELS   ■

By far the most significant element of cost in software development is cost of labor. Cost estimation algorithms in general provide estimates of the number of labor months required to produce a given amount of code. The algorithms or estimation models are based on empirical, historic data obtained from completed projects. While these models are open to criticism based on the age of the data and the statistical methods employed to derive the models, the models continue to be useful. In the words of the Chinese proverb, ''Better to light a single candle than to curse the darkness a thousand times.''

It is said that there are more than 150 resource estimation algorithms or models currently available [1]. Bernard Londeix [5] provides a brief description of some of these cost and schedule estimation models. There are several models that have been widely used. Among those are COCOMO, developed by Boehm [2], and SLIM, developed by Putnam [8,9,10]. All of the over 150 estimation models may be placed in one of two categories: static or dynamic.

In a static model, project size in source lines of code, SLOC, is the basic variable used in the estimating the project cost component expressed in terms of labor months. When SLOC is the only variable used in the model, the static model is called a single-variable model. A multivariable static model, in addition to SLOC, uses other secondary attributes that characterize the product, its development, and operational environment. The general equation used to compute the labor month cost component for the single-variable static model is as follows:

$$LM = a \times (KSLOC)^b \tag{15.1}$$

where *LM* is in labor months, *KSLOC* is in thousands of source lines of code *a* and *b* are constants whose values are derived from analysis of completed projects. A number of these static models use the value of *LM* computed in Equation (15.1) to estimate the development time (schedule) for the product development. In these models the general formula used to compute development time is as follows:

$$DT = c \times (LM)^d \tag{15.2}$$

where *c* and *d* are constant values derived from the same database used to determine *a* and *b*, Equation (15.1).

In a dynamic model, cost and schedule are estimated from a set of variables that are interdependent. Pioneers in the development of dynamic models include Putnam [8,9,10], Parr [7], and Norden [6]. The Putnam model was put into an automated software product called SLIM (Software Life Cycle Management) by Quantitative Software Management, Incorporated. Since then the Putnam model has been known as SLIM. In this book we will focus our discussion on COCOMO (COnstructive COst MOdel), which is a static model.

As previously stated, in all the static models, especially COCOMO, the important point to remember is that correct sizing of the software product is essential to good quality cost and schedule estimates. In addition to estimating newly created source lines of code, reused source lines of code must be estimated and factored into equivalent new source lines of code.

It has been recognized through much practical experience that the cost of incorporating a line of reused code into a software product can range from 20 to 80 percent of the cost of a newly created line of code. The reason is that a reused segment of code needs to be examined and understood by software engineers and needs to be tested in the new operating environment; new documentation may be needed, and some modification to interfaces may be required. Very rarely can one reuse a segment of code without incurring some cost. The software development resources required to deal with the one thousand lines of reused code will be distributed differently over the development cycle than would a thousand lines of newly created code. This fact must be taken into account during SDP preparation, especially if reused code is a significant fraction of the total software product. For example, if it is known or estimated that a reused source line of code will cost only about 60 percent of a newly created source line of code, then 1000 reused SLOC will be equivalent to approximately 600 newly created SLOC.

It has also been recognized through practical experience that the cost of creating, reviewing, controlling, and documenting a line of comment can range from 10 to 20 percent of the cost associated with a newly created line of executable code. A review of a number of existing programs [2] reveals that the ratio of comment lines to executable lines is, on the average, from 0.1 to 0.2. The main reason for this wide range is due to individual company standards with regard to internal comment statements. For example, if a project size is estimated to be 100,000 executable SLOC and the company standard calls for one line of comment for each five executable statements, there will be 20,000 lines of comment. Assuming that a comment line will cost one fifth of an executable statement, the SLOC estimate should be increased by an additional 4000 (equivalent) executable SLOC to cover the cost of comment lines that must be produced for internal documentation.

15.3.1   COnstructive COst MOdels (COCOMO)

COCOMO was developed by B. W. Boehm and was originally described in his book, *Software Engineering Economics* [2]. He developed his cost estimation system by carefully studying the data related to sixty-three completed software projects. The size of the projects he studied ranged from very small (5000 SLOC) to very large (over 1,000,000 SLOC). The programs were written in assembly language and high-level languages. The complexity of the projects he studied range from simple, routine software developments to complex real-time command and control projects. Therefore, the constant values used in the equations to estimate labor months (*LM*) and development time (*DT*) may be applied to a variety of different software products and development environments. COCOMO consists of three levels of model precision referred to as basic, intermediate, and detailed. In this chapter we will discuss only the basic and the intermediate precision models. The basic COCOMO is a single variable static model, and the intermediate COCOMO is a multivariable static model.

Basic COCOMO Model

The basic COCOMO distinguishes three software development modes: organic, semidetached, and embedded. Each mode represents a different type of development environment. In the first mode, the organic mode, the development team consists of a small number of experienced developers who are familiar with both the application area and the development environment. The product size ranges from small to medium. In this mode project cost (labor months, LM) is computed from Equation (15.3) and project schedule (development time, DT) is computed from Equation (15.4).

$$LM = 2.4 \times (KSLOC)^{1.05} \qquad \text{(15.3)}$$

and

$$DT = 2.5 \times (LM)^{0.38} \qquad \text{(15.4)}$$

where LM is the estimated labor months (estimated cost), $KSLOC$ is the estimated size of the project measured in thousands of source lines of equivalent executable new code, and DT is the estimated development time (schedule).

The embedded mode demands the most resources of the three modes. In this mode the product has stringent requirements on reliability, performance, schedule, external (to the software) interfaces, and timing as well as a tightly controlled development environment, frequent reviews, and rigid test requirements. The problem being solved is usually unique in some way and frequently complex. Often the development team cannot rely on its prior experience. The product itself ranges in size from medium to very large. Examples of a highly embedded mode are a real-time command and control product and aircraft control system software. For the embedded mode software development, LM and DT are estimated from the following equations:

$$LM = 3.6 \times (KSLOC)^{1.20} \qquad \text{(15.5)}$$

and

$$DT = 2.5 \times (LM)^{0.32} \qquad \text{(15.6)}$$

where LM, $KSLOC$, and DT are as described for the organic mode.

The semidetached mode lies midway between the organic and the embedded mode. In this mode it is assumed that the software development team consists of a mix of experienced and inexperienced personnel with a minimum of experience in working together. The size of the product in this mode may vary from medium to very large with an average complexity factor. For the semidetached software development mode, LM and DT are estimated from the following equations:

$$LM = 3.0 \times (KSLOC)^{1.12} \qquad \text{(15.7)}$$

and

$$DT = 2.5 \times (LM)^{0.35} \qquad \text{(15.8)}$$

where LM, $KSLOC$, and DT are as described in the organic mode.

The basic COCOMO is very simple to use and gives a quick ballpark cost and schedule estimate. In this model, cost increases rapidly with the complexity of product requirements and limited team experience. The multiplier factor ranges from 2.4 for the organic mode to 3.6 for the embedded mode, and the exponent value ranges from 1.05 for the organic mode to 1.20 for the embedded mode.

Intermediate COCOMO Model

The intermediate COCOMO is a multivariable static model allowing for fifteen additional variables to bring the impact of product, development, and operational environment attributes into the cost estimation equations. These fifteen variables are referred to as the cost driver attributes. The cost driver attributes allow us to incorporate the attributes of the software product, the computer that runs the software, and the personnel involved in the product development and the project. COCOMO cost driver attributes are the following:

Product attributes
 RELY: Quantifies the effect of the required software reliability.
 DATA: Quantifies the effect of the size of the database used by the system.
 CPLX: Quantifies the effect of the complexity of the software product.
Computer system attributes
 TIME: Quantifies the effect of the execution time constraints.
 STOR: Quantifies the effect of the main storage constraints.
 VIRT: Quantifies the effect of the virtual machine volatility.
        (For a given software product the underlying virtual machine consists of the
            hardware and system software (operating system, editor, library, DBMS, etc.)
            it uses to perform its tasks.)
 TURN: Quantifies the effect of the computer turnaround time.
Project personnel attributes
 ACAP: Quantifies the effect of analyst(s) capabilities.
 AEXP: Quantifies the effect of the team's experience in the application software being
            developed.
 PCAP: Quantifies the effect of programmer's capabilities.
 VEXP: Quantifies the experience of the programming team with the host virtual ma-
            chine.
 LEXP: Quantifies the effect of programmer's experience with the programming lan-
            guage being used.
Project attributes
 MODP: Quantifies the effect of the use of modern programming practice by the team.
 TOOL: Quantifies the effect of the use of the advanced software development tools.
 SCED: Quantifies the effect of the schedule constraints.

Each of the cost driver attributes may be categorized as very low, low, nominal, high, very high, and extra high. Boehm [2] has provided a numeric value, Table 15.2, for each of these attributes in each of the categories just listed. The software engineer or the consultant who performs the estimation should, based on the product and its development environment, select the most applicable value for each of these fifteen variables, $C_1, C_2, \ldots, C_{15}$. Table 14.11 is a table from Boehm [2] designed to provide guidelines in rating each of the fifteen cost driver attributes with the exception of RELY and CPLX. Table 14.12 provides guidelines for rating the reliability (RELY) of each module. Table 14.13 provides guidelines for rating the complexity (CPLX) of each module.

■ TABLE 15.2   **Values for Cost Driver Attributes Based on Ratings**

	RATINGS					
Attributes	**Very Low**	**Low**	**Nominal**	**High**	**Very High**	**Extra High**
Product Related						
RELY = C_1	0.75	0.88	1.00	1.15	1.40	
DATA = C_2		0.94	1.00	1.08	1.16	
CPLX = C_3	0.70	0.85	1.00	1.15	1.30	1.65
Computer Related						
TIME = C_4			1.00	1.11	1.30	1.66
STOR = C_5			1.00	1.06	1.21	1.56
VIRT = C_6		0.87	1.00	1.15	1.30	
TURN = C_7		0.87	1.00	1.07	1.15	
Personnel Related						
ACAP = C_8	1.46	1.19	1.00	0.86	0.71	
AEXP = C_9	1.29	1.13	1.00	0.91	0.82	
PCAP = C_{10}	1.42	1.17	1.00	0.86	0.70	
VEXP = C_{11}	1.21	1.10	1.00	0.90		
LEXP = C_{12}	1.14	1.07	1.00	0.95		
Project related						
MODP = C_{13}	1.24	1.10	1.00	0.91	0.82	
TOOL = C_{14}	1.24	1.10	1.00	0.91	0.83	
SCED = C_{15}	1.23	1.08	1.00	1.04	1.10	

Source: W. B. Boehm, *Software Engineering Economics*, Prentice-Hall, Upper Saddle River, N.J., p. 118. With written permission.

The overall effect of cost driver attributes is computed as the product of the values of each of the fifteen cost driven attributes. That is,

$$C = C_1 \times C_2 \times \ldots \times C_{15}$$

where C_i is the value of the ith cost driver attribute.

For the intermediate COCOMO, the equations to compute LM and DT for each of the three modes are slightly different from those for the basic COCOMO. They are as follows:

Organic mode:

$$LM = 3.2 \times (KSLOC)^{1.05} \times C \qquad\qquad \textbf{(15.9)}$$

and

$$DT = 2.5 \times (LM)^{0.38} \qquad\qquad \textbf{(15.10)}$$

Semidetached mode:

$$LM = 3.0 \times (KSLOC)^{1.12} \times C \qquad\qquad \textbf{(15.11)}$$

and

$$DT = 2.5 \times (LM)^{0.35} \qquad\qquad \textbf{(15.12)}$$

Embedded mode:

$$LM = 2.8 \times (KSLOC)^{1.20} \times C \qquad \qquad (15.13)$$

and

$$DT = 2.5 \times (LM)^{0.32} \qquad \qquad (15.14)$$

As shown, in the intermediate COCOMO the cost estimation value is a function of the estimated size of the software product and fifteen cost driver attributes. The value of C may be as large as 9.42 or as small as 0.09. That is, C may increase labor months and schedule by a factor of 10 or decrease labor months and schedule by a factor of 10. Therefore, in computing C, we must pay careful attention to the product and its development and operational environment attributes and select the relevant value for each cost driver attribute, C_i.

It is often difficult to decide on a value for C_i. One can select a likely range for C_i and then use the average of the range as the value for C_i in computing C. For example, suppose for a software product the reliability attribute is estimated to be somewhere between high (1.15) and very high (1.40). In this case the average value, $(1.40 + 1.15)/2 = 1.28$, would be a good selection for C_1.

Cost estimating, using both the basic and the intermediate COCOMO, accounts for the following activities related to the software development process:

Development management:
   Project planning
   Cost, schedule, and performance management
   Contract management
   Subcontract management
   Customer/client interface management
   Reviews/audits, etc.
Software engineering:
   Development technical plans
   Requirements analysis
   Software design specification (including database)
   Software design reviews and audits
   Configuration management
   Quality assurance
   Acceptance test plans
   Reliability analysis
   Risk analysis
   Support library
   Design tools
Programming:
   Detailed design
   Code and unit test
   Integration support
   Debugging and repair
   Program librarians
Verification and validation:
   Software product test (all aspects)
   Software acceptance test (performance)
   Software test support (tools, test beds, data)

Documentation:
  Specifications
  Manuals
  Deliverable project documentation

Items not covered by the COCOMO include the following: the system and software engineering effort required to produce the software requirements specification; support to system-level planning; user training; installation and conversion; secretaries; postdelivery maintenance; administration of the operational database; and computer center operators. Therefore, estimated labor months must be adjusted, on the average, by 20 percent to account for these COCOMO oversights (with the exception of user training and postdelivery maintenance). Although the adjustment in labor months does automatically adjust the schedule estimates, the authors' experience and the experience of many others have shown that it is more realistic to make a 10% adjustment to the schedule. Many of the tasks not covered by COCOMO do not influence the schedule directly. The engineering of requirements, however, does have a significant effect. Therefore, in practice we will compute LM and DT using the standard COCOMO equations and then compute an adjusted LM and DT as follows:

$$ALM = LM \times 1.20$$

and

$$ADT = DT \times 1.10$$

The COCOMO has been used successfully by the authors and is presented as one of many that can produce consistently good results given the following conditions:

1. Results are based on a sound SLOC estimate.
2. Cost driver attributes (C_i) and model are continuously calibrated with new data unique to project experience.
3. A second independent estimate (preferably with an independent method and independent personnel) is performed as a cross-check.
4. The entire estimation process is well documented, reviewed, and then revised as required by reviewer comments.
5. The process (steps 1–4) is repeated periodically during the development process to confirm or revise estimates.

Other algorithms can be just as effective if the five steps given here are followed.

15.3.2 Estimation Process

The person responsible for the estimation will need to select the model and mode that best describes the product and development environment. The following descriptions provide some guidance in making the mode selection.

Organic Mode Characteristics

1. Small product size (less than 50,000 SLOC)
2. Small, in-house development team

3. Development team experienced in application area
4. Relaxed (negotiable, informal) specifications on function and performance requirements, acceptance tests, and interfaces
5. Minimal communication overhead
6. Stable development environment
7. Minimal schedule pressure
8. Existing, proven technology used

Some typical examples of software products characterized as organic mode are data reduction systems; engineering, scientific and business modeling systems; simple inventory control systems; and simple production control systems.

Semidetached Mode Characteristics

1. Size may range up to 300,000 SLOC.
2. Development team personnel is mix of experienced and inexperienced in the application area and development environment.
3. Mix of relaxed and rigid specification on function and performance requirements, interfaces, and product acceptance criteria.
4. Lies midway between the organic mode and the embedded mode.
5. Moderate schedule pressure.

Some typical examples of software products categorized as semidetached mode are simple transaction processing systems, database management systems, simple command and control systems, and simple firmware.

Embedded Mode Characteristics

1. Size may range from 20,000 to over 1,000,000 SLOC.
2. Rigorous specification of function, performance, etc.
3. Product must operate within time constraints on internal and external interface service, processing, and interrupt service.
4. Product must meet rigid, formal quality standards.
5. Close coupling among hardware, software, and operators required to meet function and performance requirements.
6. Extensive testing required.
7. Leading edge technology employed.
8. Other system components developed concurrently with software.
9. Strong schedule pressure.

Some typical examples of software products that may be characterized as embedded mode software are avionics software systems, FAA software systems, complex command and control systems, operating systems, large and complex transaction processing systems, real-time systems, and complex firmware systems.

Example 15.3.1

The best way to describe the software cost and schedule estimation process is to work through a typical scenario. Let us assume that we have been asked to provide an estimate of the resources (in labor months) and the length of the development cycle (in calendar months) required to produce an operating system for the new computer that will be used in the XYZ project. The software product and its size estimation were discussed in chapter 14. Table 15.3 summarizes the estimated source lines of code for the operating system that is to be developed.

All of these estimates are based upon approximately equivalent functions found in the other operating system except for security and time management. The estimates for these two functions were obtained from comparisons with other similar functions implemented in other software products. Source lines of code were estimated in Ada. The reused KSLOC include its appropriate comment lines. The new estimated KSLOC must be adjusted for comment lines.

Our approach will be to make an initial ballpark estimate using the static single variable model (basic COCOMO) as a point of departure. We will use the embedded mode because it is the best match for our situation. We will next refine our initial estimate using the static multivariable model (intermediate COCOMO). Choice of the intermediate COCOMO is based on the level of our understanding of the requirements and development environment. That is, we feel that we know the requirements and environment (operational and development) well enough to estimate the fifteen COCOMO attributes. The COCOMO method has been used frequently by our team and we have experienced success using it

An important first step is to revisit the size estimation results to assure that we have the most current information and that there is a consensus that the size figures given are reasonable estimates. These estimates are the basis upon which our subsequent work is built. If not already documented, then arrangements should be made for sizing results and supporting rationale to be formally documented and placed in the project file.

■ TABLE 15.3   **Operating System Functions for XYZ Project**

ESTIMATED KSLOC	REUSED KSLOC	NEW KSLOC	FUNCTION/MODULE NAME
3.3		3.3	Program (Task) Management
19.7	16.5	3.2	Input/Output Management
19.7	2.7	17.0	Application File Management
6.4	4.2	2.2	Time Management
2.5		2.5	KSLOC Security and Data Integrity
2.3		2.3	Real Time Operation
5.4	3.5	1.9	Memory Management
5.2	2.5	2.7	Initialization
6.4	4.4	2.0	Utilities
70.9	33.8	37.1	Total Project in Ada

The next step is to estimate the number of comment lines that will be written for the newly developed code and convert them to their equivalent executable SLOC. Also, we must convert the cost of reused code to the equivalent new SLOC. Let us assume that the development organization's standards require that there be, on the average, one comment line for each five executable lines. Further, suppose it is known through experience that the total cost of producing a comment statement is approximately 20 percent of the cost of an executable statement. Moreover, a careful study of the available reused code indicates that the average cost of incorporating a line of reused code into the project is 50 percent of the cost of developing a new line of code. Table 15.3 calls for 37,100 new SLOC and 33,800 reused SLOC. Therefore, we have

$$37,100 \times \frac{1}{5} = 7420 \text{ estimated comment lines}$$

$$7420 \times 20\% = 1484 \text{ estimated comment lines converted to the equivalent executable SLOC}$$

$$33,800 \times 50\% = 16,900 \text{ reused lines of code converted to the equivalent executable SLOC}$$

$$SLOC = 37,100 + 1484 + 16,900 = 55,484 \text{ rounded to 56 KSLOC}$$

The next step is to determine the mode of the software development. For this example, there should be no question that the mode is embedded. Although some might argue that a portion of the software may better be described as semidetached, at this point we shall consider the entire software product as being embedded mode software.

The next step is to use KSLOC in Equation (15.5) to obtain the estimated labor months.

$$LM = 3.6 \times 56^{1.2} = 451 \text{ labor months}$$

and use this value in Equation (15.6) to obtain the estimated development time.

$$DT = 2.5 \times 451^{0.32} = 18 \text{ calendar months}$$

Earlier it was mentioned that labor months and calendar months estimated with the CO-COMO must be adjusted to account for the labor and schedule impact of adding the missing 20% of the direct software development cost. This adjustment accounts for activities that are not covered by the COCOMO estimates. Therefore, by increasing labor months (LM) by 20%, the labor is fully accounted for. A similar adjustmen to DT extends the schedule to cover software requirements development.

$$ALM = LM \times 1.20 = 541 \text{ adjusted labor months}$$

$$ADT = DT \times 1.20 = 21 \text{ adjusted calendar months}$$

This result gives us a general estimate of cost and schedule for this product. (Note that the rounded ADT of 21, not 22, resulted from using the original DT value before rounding to 18.)

We next apply the intermediate COCOMO to refine our estimated cost and schedule for the software development. In order to use the intermediate COCOMO, we need Tables 15.2, 14.11, 14.12, and 14.13 to estimate the value for each of the fifteen cost driver attributes that are used to characterize the software product, the operating environment, and the development environment. The rating assigned to each cost driver attribute should be based on an objective rationale. The guidance supplied by Tables 14.11, 14.12, and 14.13 is derived from a large database of experience and, when blended with enlightened current experience, can produce estimates that are well supported by an objective rationale. If this rationale is made visible to other experienced developers, a constructive critique can be effected that can lead to an improved (more accurate) result.

By looking at Table 14.11 and the reliability attribute, RELY, we can select a rating that most nearly describes our software product. By asking, we determine that system designers have taken steps in the system architecture to assure that computer and software failures will not have a serious impact on system operation. Operating system designers are confident that recovery from failures will be effected quickly and with little or no serious loss of data and control. We can then feel confident that a rating of normal with an attendant numerical value of 1.00 (from Table 15.2) is reasonable. The details of how we arrived at this particular value should be documented carefully, completely, and briefly.

The DATA attribute can be determined directly from Table 14.11. The ratio of database bytes to deliverable source instructions for this product is less than 10 and therefore a value of 0.94 was assigned. As with RELY the rationale for the rating of DATA should be documented carefully and completely.

Complexity, the attribute CPLX in Table 14.11, is further described in Table 14.13. We find after much discussion and debate that three of the four paragraphs in the very high category best describe this particular software product. Again the rationale is carefully and completely documented. A value of 1.30 from Table 15.2 is selected for the attribute CPLX.

For the attributes TIME and STOR we have discovered that CPU and memory have been sized so that the computer system (CPU memory and I/O) is expected to be less than 50 percent loaded at system delivery. Therefore, the associated values for these two attributes are estimated to be 1.0.

The attribute VIRT refers to the stability of the computer system. Because of the nearly parallel development of hardware and operating system software, we are expecting to see a major change every few months and some minor changes two or three times a month. Thus we select a rating of very high and a value of 1.30 for this attribute.

The rating for attribute TURN is selected as low because we have an interactive development environment employing both hardware and interpretive emulators. The value associated with the low rating is 0.87.

For the analyst capability attribute, ACAP, we anticipate that our system and software engineers are for the most part good performers and there are some strong people with good leadership qualities. The main shortcoming is in experience. The somewhat subjective assessment is that we will credit our analysts as being in the 55th percentile range for the ACAP attribute, but will recognize the analysts' lack of experience by selecting low or one year for the analyst experience attribute, AEXP. The values associated with these ratings are 1.0 and 1.13 respectively.

Similarly, we can rate our programmers (designers, coders, testers) as being nominal in both operating system capability and experience with software, the computer, and the development environment. This yields a value of 1.0 for both the PCAP and VEXP attributes.

The language attribute LEXP is another matter. This will be our first major project in which the language we use is Ada. Although we do have some people with limited experience, the projectwide average experience is less than four months. We therefore call this attribute very low and assign a value of 1.14 to the attribute LEXP.

The use of modern programming practices, attribute MODP, is evaluated as high. Our organization has a well-established set of standards and practices. Our team has been singled

out as being one of the more disciplined development groups in adhering to modern programming practices. There is an obvious feeling of pride and a strong sense of confidence in
the project team. The leadership seems to feel that we know how to develop software. We
have a history of successes that seems to justify our confidence. Moreover, we feel that we
have been selected for this job because we are the only team that can pull it off. The evaluation
is highly subjective, but tends to support a rating of high for MODP. The value for a high
MODP is 0.91.

The TOOL attribute is regarded as nominal. Ada tools are relatively new to the team, but
other tools have been used effectively on past projects and the leadership has shown an
appreciation for the effectiveness of tool use on productivity. The value for the TOOL attribute
selected is 1.0. We will not know what the schedule will be until we complete the cost and
schedule analysis work. For the present we will assume a nominal value of 1.00. We have
heard that the master schedule calls for delivery of release one with full capability eighteen
months after project initiation. In summary we have the following:

Cost Drive Attribute	Value	Cost Drive Attribute	Value
RELY	1.00	AEXP	1.13
DATA	0.94	PCAP	1.00
CPLX	1.30	VEXP	1.00
TIME	1.00	LEXP	1.14
STOR	1.00	MODP	0.91
VIRT	1.30	TOOL	1.00
TURN	0.87	SCED	1.00
ACAP	1.00		

From these values we can compute the value of C.

$$C = 1.00 \times 0.94 \times 1.30 \times 1.00 \times 1.00 \times 1.30 \times$$

$$0.87 \times 1.00 \times 1.13 \times 1.00 \times 1.00 \times 1.14 \times 0.91 \times 1.00 \times 1.00 = 1.62$$

Using Equations (15.13 and 15.14) for the intermediate COCOMO in embedded mode we
have the following:

$$LM = 2.8 \times 56^{1.2} \times 1.62 = 568$$

$$DT = 2.5 \times 568^{0.32} = 19$$

As previously noted the COCOMO algorithm neglects about 20 percent of the legitimate
software development labor. It is therefore necessary to adjust this result to account for the
oversight. Therefore,

$$ALM = 568 \times 1.20 = 682$$

$$ADT = 19 \times 1.20 = 23$$

This result will be input to the software development planning activity.

The entire results of this study, especially the rationale for the fifteen cost driver attributes (C_i), should be documented and distributed for review and presentation to qualified individuals for critique and constructive criticism. Both the documentation process and the criticism may lead to revisions and a stronger, more objective rationale.

If the software product is large enough and enough is known about the requirements, a more accurate estimate may be made by partitioning the product into distinguishable components that can then be estimated independently using different COCOMO models, modes, and C_is. For instance, in our example it might make better sense, based on our analysis of requirements, to consider utilities and application file management modules separately and convince ourselves that the static single-variable model in semidetached mode is a better match for these particular components. This choice is left for the reader as an exercise. It is probably a good idea *not* to use the COCOMO for software components smaller than 5000 SLOC.

15.3.3 Comments

A great deal of flexibility exists in applying the COCOMO algorithms, including calibrating model parameters and the cost driver attributes that determine the C_is with recently gathered data. However, the results obtained from the algorithms can be no better than the sizing information and the C_i estimates. We must keep in mind that ± 20 percent accuracy for first estimates is probably pretty good. The estimation process is normally repeated, and accuracy improves as development proceeds.

Frequently a completed, well-developed, and carefully documented estimate will be met with hostility and a request that the estimate be arbitrarily reduced to meet a number established without a realistic consideration for the tasks to be accomplished. If the estimate has been developed based on an objective rationale, justifiable ways to reduce the estimates can be found in the rationale itself.

For example, in our estimation procedure we rated language experience, LEXP, as very low and assigned it a value of 1.14. If a reduction in the estimated cost is desired, one place to look is in the attribute LEXP. If additional training in the language is provided to the development team or some Ada-experienced developers are hired or transferred to the development team, a reduction in LEXP might be justified. Or we may change the implementation language from Ada to a language in which the team has more experience to reduce the LEXP value. If a strong case can be made that selection of the embedded mode was inappropriate or prior project experience indicated that some other rationale was incorrect, then and only then should documented changes be made to the estimate.

The point is that the software engineer should not arbitrarily change a cost and schedule estimate that has been thoughtfully prepared without an equally well-thought-out rationale. If changes are made to the cost estimates, original estimates should be maintained in project files for future reference, as part of the collective learning process and as a basis for risk assessments.

In the next section we will discuss grassroots resource and schedule estimation to provide a comparison base. It is useful to compare algorithmically derived results with the results of the grassroots analysis. If results of the two independent analyses are consistent (within 10 percent of each other) then either one of the two could be used as a basis for the planning effort. Otherwise differences must be resolved to reach a common ground.

15.4   GRASSROOTS RESOURCE AND SCHEDULE ESTIMATION   ■

Grassroots is a term applied to the act of obtaining cost and schedule estimates from development team members on a module-by module-basis and building a bottom-up estimate of development cost and schedule from these grassroots inputs. A good grassroots cost and schedule estimate also depends on having a good understanding of the software product requirements and a good sizing estimate as input. Software product requirements are first broken down into small packages or modules. It is much easier to estimate cost and schedule requirements for a small module than for an entire software product. The estimator can more easily visualize what has to be done and how long it will take if the product requirement size is close to recent experience. A student who has recently written a small program to perform fundamental matrix operations can more easily extrapolate that experience to the task of preparing a small program that returns results from trigonometric functions than to the task of designing, developing, testing, and documenting a complete math function package.

Likewise the grassroots estimation process can proceed by taking the best functional partition of the software product and estimating the required effort by software develop phase. To assure uniformity of results, a project template should be constructed and a procedure written describing how the template should be used. A rationale for the quantification of effort should be provided to support each of the estimates. When results of the grass roots estimates are compared with the algorithmically based estimates, the rationale for each of these quantifications will be needed to resolve any discrepancies in the two approaches. If these two estimation processes are conducted independently and are well documented, particularly the rationale for each quantification, usually a far better estimate will be forthcoming. If both of the independent estimates are subjected to thoughtful reviews before comparisons, an even better estimate will result. Typically, the grassroots estimates neglect some of the cost and schedule factors that are not visible to the grassroots estimator. These discrepancies can be identified when the results of the two approaches are compared.

Each subfunction should be scheduled by the estimator as an independent development entity and dependencies on other subfunctions or events noted. A product-level scheduling effort will need this information to establish a master schedule for software development planning and as a cross-check on the development time predicted by the algorithmic approach. The scheduling effort can often identify errors of both commission and omission in resource estimates. A companion estimate for expected software development facility usage is frequently prepared at this point.

Example 15.4.1 (Resource Estimation)

As an example of grassroots resource and schedule estimation, consider the application file management module of Example 15.3.1. This function is treated as a separate software subsystem. We also assume that all of the 19.7 KSLOC must be newly created code. The subfunctions associated with this function are read (5 KSLOC), write (5 KSLOC), update (5 KSLOC), and delete (4.7 KSLOC). Table 15.4 shows the cost allocated to each of these subfunctions broken down by development phases.

The size estimates shown in Table 15.4 are obtained from prior experience with similar requirements or by examining, in detail, the functions associated with each major com-

■ TABLE 15.4   **Labor Months per Phases per Subfunctions**

Software subsystem: Application file management
Software subsystem Estimated Size: 19.7 new KSLOC

Subfunctions (Components)	PHASES			
	Engineering*	Design	Code and Unit Test	System Test and Integration
Read (5 (KSLOC)	8	10	7	13
Write (5 KSLOC)	8	7	5	12
Update (5 KSLOC)	8	8	7	15
Delete (4.7 KSLOC)	7	8	8	13
TOTAL	31	33	27	53

Software subsystem total cost = 144 labor months

••••••••••••••••••••••••••
* Engineering phase includes activities leading to the production of the SRS and SDP documents and activities related to the analysis of the SRS document.

ponent of the application file management module. For example, for the read component several displays or screens must be generated, an access security check made, accesses performed, memory space allocated in both primary and secondary storage, interface interpreted, etc.

The effort, which includes every labor hour required to complete the software development, is then estimated by SWDLC phase as shown in Table 15.4. Effort includes documentation, reviews, management, and travel. A good test to determine if a particular task is software related is to ask the question: Would we have to do this if there were no software? If the answer is no, we should include the effort as part of the total effort allocated to the software product.

When the two independent estimation processes (COCOMO and grassroots) are complete, the two estimates should be reconciled by examining the rationale behind each of the estimates and attempting to resolve the source of discrepancy. If no agreement can be reached, one of the two estimates can be selected or perhaps the average of the two can be used. In any event, the rationale for how the final value was selected should be documented and made part of the project record.

In our example, the grassroots approach estimates the labor cost to be 144 labor months, whereas the basic COCOMO estimates the labor cost for the same function to be 180 months. We could say that the two estimates are so close that reaching a reconciliation will not be difficult. It should be clear by now that the COCOMO results will usually be higher than the results produced by the grassroots approach, simply because those who make the grassroots

■ TABLE 15.5   **Total Labor Month Breakdown by Development Phase**

Development Phases	Total Labor Months	Planned Labor Months	Contingency
Engineering	100	90	10
Design	110	100	10
Code and Unit Test	110	100	10
System Test	221	200	21
TOTAL	541	490	51

Note: Costs associated with building the development environment, if any, are not included in the COCOMO estimates.

estimate will often overlook certain tasks and activities. The total effort is developed from these module-by-module estimates.

A wise planner would probably withhold a small fraction, 10 to 15 percent, of the resources allocated to each function for contingency. Software product attributes can be used as a guide in making these allocations. Table 15.5 presents a resource allocation for the example discussed in section 15.3.3 using the cost estimation algorithm derived from the basic COCOMO (541 labor months).

The next step is to refine the software development plan by allocating time and resources to individual subfunctions and then allocating resources to each step in the development cycle. This process can usually be accomplished by partitioning the software product into pieces that can be treated as independently developed units.

Example 15.4.2 (Schedule Estimation)

Continuing with our planning example, we see that the schedule result obtained from the COCOMO algorithm represents only a starting point for the scheduling process. For example, the 541 labor months estimated for the development of the software system discussed in Example 15.4.1 are initially distributed as shown in Table 15.5. The main schedule for the software system, based on the estimated 21 calendar months, is shown in Table 15.6. A second tier of schedules would be prepared showing a schedule for each of the major components of the software system. Resources and time can be allocated based either on a ratio of software component size to the product size or perhaps using an experience base derived from prior developments. Tasks that appear on the schedule chart should exhibit a one-to-one correspondence to tasks in the work breakdown structure (Section 3.2.4).

Table 15.7 (**A**) shows the allocation of COCOMO-estimated resources to one of the components (application file management) of the software system. Table 15.7 (**B**) shows the allocation of estimated resources to the read module of the application file management component of the software system. Table 15.8 (**A**) shows a schedule for the engineering

■ TABLE 15.6   **Development Schedule for the Software System of Section 15.3.2**

DEVELOPMENT PHASES	CALENDAR MONTHS
	0 1 2 3 4 5 6 7 8 9 10 11 12 13 14 15 16 17 18 19 20 21
Engineering Planning	SDP
Requirements	SRS
Design	SDS
Code and Unit Test	
System Test and Integration	
Acceptance test	

■ TABLE 15.7   **Resource Allocation by Development Phase**

A. Application File Management

Component: Application file management

Estimated size in new KSLOC: 18.3 (17.0 new and 2.7 reused → 18.3)

Estimated cost: 180 labor months

Allocated cost: 150 labor months

Phase	Labor Months Allocated
Engineering	30
Design	30
Code and Unit Test	28
System Test and Integration	62

B. Read Module of Application File Management

Module: Read module

Estimated size in new KSLOC: 5

Allocated cost: 35 labor months

Estimated cost: 39 labor months

Phase	Labor Months Allocated
Engineering	7
Design	7
Code and Unit Test	6
System Test and Integration	15

■ TABLE 15.8   **Development Schedule for Engineering Phase**

A. Application File Management

CALENDAR MONTHS

Tasks	0	1	2	3	4	5	6	7	8	9	1 0	1 1	1 2	1 3	1 4	1 5	1 6	1 7	1 8	1 9	2 0	2 1

Management
Planning
Requirements Analysis
Input Definition
Process Definition
Output Definition
Interface Definition
Review/Audit
SRS Document
Design Support
Test Support

B. Read Module of Application File Management

CALENDAR MONTHS

Tasks	0	1	2	3	4	5	6	7	8	9	1 0	1 1	1 2	1 3	1 4	1 5	1 6	1 7	1 8	1 9	2 0	2 1

Requirement Analysis
Input Definition
Process Definition
Output Definition
Interface Definition
SRS Development

– – – Represents intermittent activities.

efforts associated with the application file management component of the software system. Table 15.8 (**B**) shows a schedule for engineering efforts associated with the read module of the application file management component of the software system.

To produce a good estimate for resources and schedule requires several iterations of the dual independent estimation process. An independent algorithmic approach and an independent grassroots approach with a formal reconciliation of differences is the first step. An exposure of the resource and schedule estimation to as many knowledgeable people as possible to take advantage of all their available experience is the next step. Sizing and resource and schedule estimation are the foundation of software development planning. Often cost and schedule overrun problems are built into a software development plan initially by poor estimation and failure to track and revise the original estimate as better information becomes available.

15.5   CLOSING COMMENTS   ■

A good cost and schedule estimation process as described herein and subsequent planning based on these estimates are characteristic of most successful software development projects. The methods and techniques for estimating software product size, development cost, and schedule may vary. The main estimation effort is directed toward understanding those features of the product that drive cost, applying the scientific (engineering) method to the estimation process in a professional way, taking the entire process seriously, and following up by reestimating and revising cost estimates and schedules as more information becomes available.

Just as independent resource and schedule estimates can lead to better overall estimates of cost and schedule, independent sizing estimates can frequently result in better overall size estimates. A good way to approach sizing, cost, and schedule estimation is to consider a range of possible results. The range might include pessimistic, most probable, and optimistic estimates. Then use a weighted average, shown below, to compute the average value to be used in the estimation and planning efforts.

$$AV = \frac{PV + (4 \times MPV) + OV}{6}$$

where AV represents average value, *PV* represents pessimistic value, *MPV* represents most probable value, and *OV* represents optimistic value.

As an adjunct to a cost estimation, any unique expenditures required to carry out the development project should be made part of the collected cost data. Training, capital investments, and test beds or simulators whose procurement can be attributed to the software product should be identified and recorded along with their cost.

Resources other than direct labor estimated by the COCOMO algorithms include dedicated—that is, unique to this specific development—hardware and software. These elements can be treated as follows. Dedicated hardware required for the development environment can be sized and estimated in the conventional manner. The hardware may be off-the-shelf equipment or special-purpose hardware designed and built for the application. Unique support software can be sized and estimated in the same manner as the delivered software. Development support software also falls into two categories, off-the-shelf and special purpose. Special-purpose software should be treated with the same care as the delivered software. Off-the-shelf software should be specified in function and performance as though it were going to be developed by the development team. Cost estimates should include estimates for the effort required to specify, test, and maintain these unique hardware and software means of production.

Unique hardware items might include computers, real or simulated hardware interfaces and responses, sensors, actuators, person-machine interfaces, and other peripheral devices. Unique software items would include CASE tools, compilers, assemblers, debuggers, emulators, and firmware. Those items that are unique to the specific development and cannot be used for any other product development must be considered as part of the software development cost.

The schedule for acquiring new or additional development environment capabilities must be factored into product development schedules. Often hidden dependencies must be identified, resolved, and worked into the software development plan.

Software development costs have remained relatively stable, which perhaps is one explanation for why software development cost and schedule estimation models developed in the 1970s and early 1980s remain effective in predicting software development resource requirements.

In summary: (1) the estimation process is iterative in nature and should be repeated at periodic intervals throughout the development process; (2) the rationale and critical assumptions leading to the estimates should be documented each time an estimate is made; (3) the estimation process should be exposed for critique to as many qualified people as possible; (4) the resource estimation process can lead directly to formulation of task descriptions, and (5) the level of software product requirements understanding should be consistent with the level at which partitioning for estimation purposes stops.

15.6 CHAPTER SUMMARY ■

A summary of our discussion of software development cost and schedule estimation can be made by stating the following points: (1) software cost and schedule estimates are extremely important input for preparation of the SDP document; (2) software cost and schedule estimates should be prepared by two independent groups, one of which is preferably consultants; (3) software size estimation is the most critical element in cost and schedule estimation; (4) it is essential to employ a systematic estimation methodology to use in the estimation process; (5) it it essential to document the process followed and the rationale applied to obtain the estimate; (6) estimation results should be changed only when it is shown that supporting rationale is in error; (7) supporting rationale should be used to identify risk areas in the cost and development schedule; (8) cost and schedule estimation should not be one-time activities; and (9) the software engineer should play a strong, active role in development of the original estimates and keeping them current.

Next we discussed the COCOMO estimation model. The different equations involved in basic and intermediate COCOMO are as follows:

Basic organic mode:

$$LM = 2.4 \times (KSLOC)^{1.05}$$

and

$$DT = 2.5 \times (LM)^{0.38}$$

Basic semidetached mode:

$$LM = 3.0 \times (KSLOC)^{1.12}$$

and

$$DT = 2.5 \times (LM)^{0.35}$$

Basic embedded mode:

$$LM = 3.6 \times (KSLOC)^{1.20}$$

and

$$DT = 2.5 \times (LM)^{0.32}$$

where *LM* is the estimated labor months (estimated cost), *KSLOC* is the estimated size of the project measured in thousands of equivalent executable new code, and *DT* is the estimated development time in calendar months.

Intermediate organic mode:

$$LM = 3.2 \times (KSLOC)^{1.05} \times C$$

and

$$DT = 2.5 \times (LM)^{0.38}$$

Intermediate semidetached mode:

$$LM = 3.0 \times (KSLOC)^{1.12} \times C$$

and

$$DT = 2.5 \times (LM)^{0.35}$$

Intermediate embedded mode:

$$LM = 2.8 \times (KSLOC)^{1.20} \times C$$

and

$$DT = 2.5 \times (LM)^{0.32}$$

where C is the product of fifteen cost driver attributes and LM, DT, and $KSLOC$ are as defined for the basic COCOMO.

15.7 EXERCISES ■

1. Estimate the cost and the schedule for Example 15.3.1 considering utilities and application file management modules as a separate software subsystem. Assume this subsystem is semidetached mode software and use basic COCOMO for its cost and schedule estimation. Then use the method described in sections 15.3.1, 15.3.2 to arrive at the estimate for the rest of the software system. Compare your results with those of section 15.3.2.

2. Assume that you have been asked to reduce the estimated cost of the operating system product discussed in Example 15.3.1 by 20 to 25 percent. Explain how would you achieve this reduction and document your suggestions with sound rationale. Give an estimate of any exposure or risk introduced by your suggestions.

3. The following table represents data collected at Mountain Ore Software Company with respect to their last five completed software development projects.

Project Estimates	Project 1	Project 2	Project 3	Project 4	Project 5
Size (KSLOC)	40	35	20	30	45
Cost (labor months)	260	220	105	180	285
Schedule (calendar months)	21	15	12	15	23

a. Compare the actual data for project 1 to the results obtained from the basic COCOMO in all three software development modes (organic, semidetached, and embedded) and decide which set of estimated values is closer to the actual values.

b. Assume project 5 is characterized as an embedded mode software development. Use intermediate COCOMO to estimate the cost and schedule for this software development project. Using logical arguments, change your cost driver attributes to get as close to the actual values as possible.

4. a. Use the basic COCOMO to develop three tables (one for each mode) of cost and schedule estimates for the five projects given in exercise 3.

b. Compute the percent differences between the actual values and the estimated values in each table.

c. Does basic COCOMO provide a reasonable cost and schedule for the software developed by this company?

d. Based on your judgment, should this company use a different estimation model? Note that if an estimation model provides estimated values that are within 20 percent of the actual values over 65 percent of the time, such a model is considered to be a good estimation model.

5. Consider Example 15.3.1. Compute a set of values for the cost driver attributes based on the following:

a. Optimistic approach
b. Pessimistic approach
c. Most probable approach.

6. A software development production ratio is defined as:

$$Pr = \frac{\text{delivered software size}}{\text{total labor months}}$$

Express Pr as a function of *KSLOC* for each of the three modes of the basic COCOMO.

7. The following is a simple formula to compute development time based on labor months:

$$DT = 2.5 \sqrt[3]{LM}$$

Compare estimates from this formula with the actual results in exercise 3. Use the semidetached mode for basic COCOMO to estimate *LM*.

8. The least-square curve-fitting algorithm attempts to fit a curve of the form $y = f(x)$ to a set of n pairs of (x_i, y_i) values such that the sum of the squares of the differences between the y and y_is is minimum. That is, we must minimize the difference as follows:

$$\delta^2 = \sum_{i=1}^{i=n} (y - y_i)^2$$

a. Use the least-square curve-fitting algorithm to fit an exponential curve of the form

$$LM = a \times (KSLOC)^b$$

to the actual cost data given in exercise 3. For simplicity, you may rewrite this equation as follows:

$$\ln(LM = \ln(a) + b \times \ln(KSLOC)$$

If we assume $Y = \ln(LM)$, $A = \ln(a)$, and $X = \ln(KSLOC)$, we have

$$Y = A + b \times X \tag{15.16}$$

which is a linear function. Applying the least-square algorithm to this linear function results in the following values for A and b:

$$b = \frac{\sum\limits_{i=1}^{i=n} (X_i - \bar{X})(Y_i - \bar{Y})}{\sum\limits_{i=1}^{i=n} (X_i - \bar{X})^2}$$

$$A = \bar{Y} - b \times \bar{X}$$

where

$$\bar{X} = \sum\limits_{i=1}^{i=n} X_i \quad \bar{Y} = \sum\limits_{i=1}^{i=n} Y_i$$

Replacing the values of $a = e^A$ and b in Equation (15.16) results in the exponential function

$$LM = e^A \times (KSLOC)^b$$

b. Use the same algorithm as in (a) to find values for c and d such that the exponential curve

$$DT = c \times (LM)^d$$

fits the schedule data in exercise 3.

c. Use the equations obtained in (a) and (b) to estimate the cost and the schedule for all five projects in exercise 3.

d. Compare the data obtained in (c) with the actual data to decide whether the equations in (a) and (b) provide a viable estimation model for the Mountain Ore Software Company.

9. Plot labor months versus calendar time for all three static single-value COCOMO development modes for software products varying in size from 10 to 1000 KSLOC. Explain the underlying message.

10. Plot labor months versus KSLOC for the semidetached multivariable mode for best-case values for the fifteen COCOMO attributes and for worst-case values. What can you say about this result?

11. Estimate the cost in labor months of developing a complete computer program that will be used by mechanical engineers to model thermal effects on engine parts. The program will replace an older version. The new software will have a strong graphics component and permit an increase in the number of nodes in the finite element model that is the central algorithm in the product. An initial estimate of the number of source lines of code has been provided, as follows:

20,000   Executable SLOC
1000   Comment lines

The language to be used is Fortran because there is a wealth of experience with the language and the development environment. The users are also familiar with Fortran and it is believed that they will assist in testing and debugging. Provide a complete description of your approach including assumptions and rationale and explain exactly how you arrived at your solution. Use both COCOMO models. Estimate development time.

12. For exercise 3 prepare a list of the ten most important questions you would ask to improve the quality of your estimates. Rank them in order of importance.

13. The SRS for the order-entry component of the ABC software project is given to you (developed as an example in chapter 5).

    a. Prepare a cost and schedule estimate for this software component. Justify your choice of the software attribute values, software development mode, values for cost driver attributes (if used), and COCOMO (basic, intermediate, embedded) selected for estimation.

    b. Partition this component into several modules and prepare a schedule for the order-entry component as well as for its individual modules.

References

1. C. Anderson, and M. Dorfman, "Aerospace Software Engineering," Vol. 136, *Progress in Astronautics and Aeronautics*, AIAA, Washington, D.C., 1991.
2. W. B. Boehm, *Software Engineering Economics*, Prentice-Hall, Upper Saddle River, N.J., 1981.
3. F. P. Brooks Jr., *The Mythical Man-Month: Essays on Software Engineering*, Addison-Wesley, Reading, Mass., 1982.
4. C. Jones, *Programming Productivity*, McGraw-Hill, New York, 1986.
5. B. Londeix, *Cost Estimation for Software Development*, International Computer Science Series, Addison-Wesley, Reading, Mass., 1987
6. P. V. Norden, "Useful Tools for Project Management," in *The Management of Production*, Starr (ed.), Penguin, New York, 1970.
7. F. W. Parr, "An Alternative to the Rayleigh Curve Model for Software Development Effort," *IEEE Trans. Software Engrg.* Vol. **6**, No. 3 291–296 (1980).
8. L. H. Putnam, "Macro-Estimating Methodology for Software Development," proceedings *IEEE COMPCON 76*, September 1976, 138–143.
9. L. H. Putnam, "A General Empirical Solution to the Macro Software Sizing and Estimation Problem," *IEEE Trans Software Engrg.* Vol. 4, No. 4, 345–361, (1978).
10. L. H. Putnam, "The Real Economics of Software Development," in *The Economics of Information Processing*, Vol. 2, Wiley, New York, 1982.

16

Software Development Risk Assessment and Containment

16.0 OBJECTIVES ■

The main objectives of this chapter are as follows: (1) to define software development risk, (2) to acquaint the reader with the concept of software development risk analysis and risk management, (3) to show how a software engineer is directly involved in the process of identifying potential areas of risk in a software development environment, (4) to show how to analyze risk areas, (5) to show how to quantify and prioritizes risks, and (6) to discuss ways to reduce or contain risks. Within the software development process there are many areas of risk. Software engineers must develop ways and means to assure that the occurrence of an undesirable event will be anticipated early enough to exercise a corrective action plan so that disastrous consequences can be avoided.

16.1 INTRODUCTION ■

We live in a world that contains an element of risk at every turn in both professional and personal environments. To survive, we learn to contend with risk and control it. A risk-free life would indeed be dull, and without some perceptible risk in system or software development, it is doubtful that we would ever make much progress. No risk, no gain, as it were.

The spiral software development life cycle includes a risk analysis following each process step [1]. This chapter provides a simple approach to performing these risk assessments and developing risk containment plans.

Software development risk can be defined in general terms as the potential (probability of) occurrence of an event that would be detrimental to the software development process, plans, or products. The risk attribute is measured as the combined effect of the likelihood of the undesirable event occurring and the likelihood that a particular quantified, measured, or assessed consequence will result given the occurrence of the undesirable event.

Risk management is simply an organized means of identifying each risk area, quantifying the risk, developing ways to predict the occurrence of the undesirable event from attribute measurements, tracking the measurement on a continuing basis, and developing planned alternatives or corrective actions in case the undesirable event does occur. Several methods or approaches are available to assist the software engineer in prioritizing technical risks, recognizing the warning signals, and initiating corrective action as necessary.

Most audits of failed system (and software) developments, when studied carefully, reveal an inadequate appreciation of risk on the part of system or software developers. Consequently, no plan for managing or controlling risk has been included in the product planning efforts. In these situations, when a probable risk becomes a reality, no one is prepared to deal with it.

One reason for performing risk analysis and developing plans for controlling or containing risk is that senior management frequently demands it and for just cause. Even though management may have accepted the risks associated with the software development process they are reluctant to leave risk entirely to the fickle goddess of chance. A second reason for performing risk analysis is to alert management to potential trouble spots very early in the development cycle. The analysis of risk in the software development process and the development of a risk containment plan is often the software engineer's responsibility.

In this chapter we will discuss some of the most common risk areas, present a simple risk model to help to quantify some of the risks associated with the software development process and present a discussion of management and containment of software development risks using Technical Performance Measurements.

16.2 SOFTWARE DEVELOPMENT RISK AREAS ■

Some of the areas where software development risk might lurk and some general risk management techniques that might be applied are presented in Table 16.1. This table does not provide an exhaustive list of software development–related risk areas. There are, of course, other risk areas, many of which are unique to a given development. Performing a software development risk analysis can be a very challenging assignment for a software engineer. A major challenge in risk analysis and management is finding the most important risk areas,

■ TABLE 16.1   **Top Ten Software Risk Items and Suggested Risk Management Techniques**

1. Personnel Shortfall

Risk Management Techniques: Staffing with appropriate personnel, job matching, team building, securing key personnel agreements, cross-training, rescheduling key people, subcontracting

2. Unrealistic Schedule and Budget

Risk Management Techniques: Detailed multisource cost and schedule estimation, designing to cost, incremental development, software reuse, requirement scrubbing, renegotiation with client

3. Developing the Wrong Software Functions

Risk Management Techniques: Organization analysis, mission analysis, ops-concept formulation, user surveys, prototyping, early user manual development, development of and agreement to acceptance criteria

4. Developing the Wrong User Interface

Risk Management Techniques: Prototyping, operational scenarios, task analysis, user characterization (functionality, style, workload)

5. Gold Plating

Risk Management Techniques: Requirement scrubbing, prototyping, cost benefit analysis, designing to cost

6. Continuing Stream of Requirement Changes

Risk Management Techniques: High change threshold, information hiding, incremental development, deferral of changes to later increment, tight change control, agreement to acceptance criteria

7. Shortfalls in Externally Furnished Components (Procured Software)

Risk Management Techniques: Benchmarking, inspection, reference checking, compatibility analysis, acceptance testing

8. Shortfalls in Externally Performed Tasks (Subcontractors)

Risk Management Techniques: Reference checking, preaward audits, award-fee contracts, competitive design or prototyping, team building

9. Real-Time Performance Shortfalls

Risk Management Techniques: Simulation, benchmarking, modeling, prototyping, instrumentation tuning analysis

10. Straining Computer Science Capabilities

Risk Management Techniques: Technical analysis, cost-benefit analysis, prototyping, reference checking, performance analysis, sizing analysis

Source: W. B. Boehm, ''Software Risk Management: Principles and Practices,'' *IEEE Software*, Vol. 8, No. 1, (1991)

evaluating each identified risk, quantifying and prioritizing the risk, and finding a suitable risk management technique. For example, if it is thought that item 6 of Table 16.1 may be a significant risk area, the risk analyst can examine the functional and performance requirements allocated to the software product (through the SRS) for telltale signs of a potentially high software development risk. These signs include the following: (1) many unresolved requirement issues, (2) inadequate interface definition (important details lacking), (3) vague and inconsistent requirement statements, (4) untestable requirements in the SRS, (5) ambiguous requirement statements, (6) lack of a test definition for each requirement, (7) imprecise or missing performance requirements, (8) poor use of specification language, (9) generally poor quality documentation, and (10) inadequate customer definition of needs or desires.

If it is found upon investigation that any of these ten conditions prevail, the likelihood of encountering serious problems in schedule delays, cost increases, and poor performance of the product (failure to meet client expectations) in the field is quite high or, perhaps, inevitable.

It remains for the software engineer to quantify the risk, compare this risk with other development risks, and find a way to either remove or control the risks.

16.3   A RISK MODEL ■

Risk can be modeled as the interaction of two variables: probability of failure, P_F, and the effect or consequence of that failure, C_F. Consequences can be measured in terms of impact on cost, schedule, and technical performance of the delivered software product. This simple model can be used to focus attention on areas where the probability of failure (P_F) is high and the consequences of failure (C_F) are, relatively speaking, not severe, as well as areas where the probability of failure is low but the consequences of a failure are very high. The model can also indicate relative risk by quantifying each identified risk area and comparing with other risk areas. The model expresses the risk factor, R_F, as follows:

$$R_F = P_F + C_F - P_F \times C_F$$

As we shall see, assignment of values to P_F and C_F is highly subjective. The model is simple and if correctly applied, consistent and almost self-documenting. Therefore the model can be reviewed by others, consequently removing some of the subjectivity from the risk analysis process.

The general approach to risk analysis consists of three steps. The first step is to identify areas of potential risk. The second step is to partition each specific risk area into critical factors. The third step is to examine the consequences of a failure. When areas of potential risk are identified, the software engineer is encouraged to solicit help from experienced colleagues and other expert opinion to partition each specific risk area into critical factors. Once these factors are identified, each one is further reduced to a set of possible outcomes with a probability of occurrence assigned to each possible outcome. The range of possible outcomes or situations should go from mildly unfavorable to a worst-case situation. From this step a most likely or expected outcome can be selected and the associated value for the probability of failure selected for use in the risk model. Each factor can be weighted. A composite probability of failure can be determined by assigning a weighting to each factor (sum of the weights is equal to one) or by a simple averaging of the probability of failure associated with each factor. The remainder of this section is devoted to carrying out these three steps with regard to risk area number 6 in Table 16.1 When a high level of requirement changes late in the development process is regarded as a definite risk, the software engineer should look for factors that could influence the occurrence of this highly undesirable event. The most logical place to look is in the SRS. Some change activity will, of course, be inevitable, but if the SRS is incomplete or of poor quality, there is good reason for concern. If no effort is being made to address these SRS problems, concerns should escalate.

Concerns about risk of a high level of change activity in the latter phases of the development cycle could result in finding three factors that, in this instance, would strongly influence the occurrence of the undesirable event. The first might be related to the overall quality of the SRS, the second factor might be the methods in place for controlling change activity, and the third factor might be the degree to which the client or customer is committed to the requirements specification. The software engineer would lay out these three factors as shown in Table 16.2.

■ TABLE 16.2.   **Three Factors Affecting Risk 6**

VALUE	SRS QUALITY	CHANGE CONTROL	CLIENT CONCURRENCE
0.1	Minor corrections required	Hierarchy of control boards. Strong discipline	Has agreed to acceptance criteria
0.3	Some SRS problems need significant work to resolve. Issues being addressed. Plan in place	Control boards in place. Tendency to a relaxed discipline	Understands need to establish acceptance criteria. Working to close out agreements
0.5	Significant problems remain. Some ongoing activity to address major issues	Change activity not following established procedures. Informal procedures are working	Operators often change operational timelines and surface new requirements
0.7	Very significant SRS problems. Insufficient resources to address and fix	Informal procedures not working well. Formal procedures ignored	Operators unconcerned about cost and schedule
0.9	Major problems in SRS. No plan to fix	No formal change control process in place	Client lacks will to control user/ operator change requests

The software engineer would then, in conjunction with others, attempt to establish the expected outcome for each factor. As seen from Table 16.2, the rationale for the assignment of a value to the outcome is contained in the model. The risk attribute can be obtained either by averaging the three assigned values for the three factors as follows:

$$P_F = \frac{\text{sum of values assigned to each factor}}{\text{number of factors}}$$

or by weighting each factor as follows:

$$P_F = (0.5 \times \text{value for factor 1}) + (0.3 \times \text{value for factor 2})$$
$$+ (0.2 \times \text{value for factor 3})$$

Arriving at a value for each factor requires a comprehensive analysis of the factor and a solid experience base.

If the ranges of possible outcomes reflect likely occurrences and the assignment of values are well documented, a review by experienced consultants or team members can reduce the subjectivity implicit in the model. The software engineer has great flexibility in performing risk analysis. There is no standard model or specific approach. Creativity, common sense, and analytic skills are required to get good results. In many system developments, risk analysis and subsequent follow-up are formal review items and on the agenda at each major review.

The last step in the process is to examine the consequences of a failure in terms of its impact on cost, schedule, and technical performance. There may be other consequences, but these three are usually of greatest concern; the treatment is the same for any other consequence factor. In this step consequences of failure factors are modeled in terms of a range of

■ TABLE 16.3.   **Factors Related to Consequences of Failure in Risk 6**

VALUE	COST	SCHEDULE	PERFORMANCE
0.1	Within budgets	Within plan	Minimum consequences, manageable
0.3	1–5% increase	Minor slip: 1 month	Small reduction in product, performance, and function
0.5	5–20% increase	1–3 month slip	Some reduction in product, performance, and function
0.7	20–40% increase	Greater than 3 months	Significant reduction in product, performance, and function
0.9	Greater than 40%	Greater than 6 months	Product is unusable, rejected by client

possible outcomes. The value for consequences of failure, C_F, associated with minimal impact on cost schedule and technical performance is 0.1. Values for consequences of failure increase as the severity of the consequences increase. The value for each consequence factor can also be weighted or averaged. The consequence of a failure, C_F, is most often modeled with three factors—cost, schedule and performance—as shown in Table 16.3.

The consequences of failure model can be better standardized than the probability of failure model since the consequences of failure factors are usually cost, schedule, and product performance in the field. The consequences of failure value C_F is computed either by

$$C_F = \frac{\text{sum of values for consequences of failure factors}}{\text{number of factors}}$$

or by weighting

$$C_F = (0.6 \times \text{value for cost factor}) + (0.2 \times \text{value for schedule factor})$$
$$+ (0.2 \times \text{value for product field performance})$$

Again, note that the assignment of weight to each factor is highly subjective and should be analyzed carefully. The risk factor is then computed based on C_F and P_F as follows:

$$R_F = P_F + C_F - P_F \times C_F$$

Figure 16.1 can be consulted to determine the severity of the risk. In this figure minimum, moderate, and high risk areas are shown based on the value of C_F and P_F. Values less than 0.3 are considered minimal, between 0.3 and 0.7 are considered moderate, and higher than 0.7 are considered high-risk values.

The risk factor expression is developed from considering the occurrence of a failure, P_F, and the occurrence of a specific consequence, C_F, as not being mutually exclusive events. There is, admittedly, some criticism that could be directed at this highly subjective approach to analyzing and quantifying software development risk. What may be to one person an unacceptable risk may be to another an irresistible challenge. Hence, polling many experienced people and averaging their replies will result in a more objective quantification of risk.

Risk Factor

$$R_F = P_F + C_F - P_F \times C_F$$

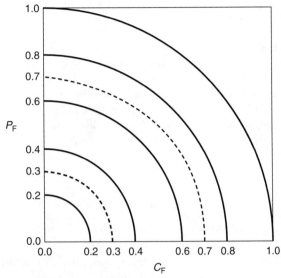

■ **FIGURE 16.1**

Risk factor.

16.4 RISK CONTAINMENT AND RISK MANAGEMENT   ■

Once an understanding of a risk area has been gained from analysis and its relative magnitude with respect to other risk areas has been determined, there are several ways in which risk may be managed. These are as follows:

1. Avoidance
2. Prevention (control)
3. Assumption
4. Transfer
5. Knowlege and research

To avoid risk is to avoid the failure consequence. If the risk is too great, a contractor may decline to bid on or accept a job, a customer may choose another option to satisfy a need, etc. However, it may not always be possible to avoid every risk.

Prevention or control implies that key development indicators are continuously sensed and alternative approaches and contingency plans are formulated to keep tight control over the risk areas that have been identified and analyzed. The best sensors in this regard are cost and schedule monitoring. Cost and schedule monitoring periodically asks the following questions.

Are the schedules for intermediate milestones being effectively met? Are related cost targets (sometimes called cost performance measurements) being met? and are certain risk parameter measurements (defined as technical performance measurements, TPM) following the plan? An example of a TPM application is monitoring the closure schedule for open software requirement specification issues.

Assuming risk consists of acknowledging the existence of a risk by accepting the consequences of a failure if it occurs. Assuming risk may include increasing cost and lengthening the schedule to cover at least part of the risk. In some cases it may be possible to estimate the cost of risk by computing the expected cost associated with a given probability of failure. For example, suppose an untried compiler is to be used in a software development, and the probability of a compiler failure caused by a serious flaw in the compiler design is 0.2. If it is estimated that the impact will be a 2-month slip in the code and unit test phase (costing approximatley $0.6 million), the expected loss due to compiler failure is $120,000. It might be prudent to increase estimated cost by this amount and extend the schedule 0.4 months. It might be even more prudent to use a more mature compiler, if possible.

$$\text{expected value} = 0.2 \times \$0.6 \text{ million} = \$120,000$$

$$\text{expected value} = 0.2 \times 2 \text{ months} = 0.4 \text{ month}$$

The transfer of risk can sometimes be effected by insurance. For example, we transfer risk of a collision with another automobile from ourselves to another party by auto insurance. We can hire a subcontractor to perform certain high-risk tasks because he or she has the appropriate skills and protection from the risk. For example, a construction contractor will hire a subcontractor to do the blasting because the subcontractor has the skills, the experience, the equipment, and the appropriate insurance. From a contractual standpoint, risk may be transferred from contractor to customer and vice versa by means of product warranties; cost, schedule, and technical performance incentives; fixed price contracts; and cost plus award fee or fixed fee contracts.

Knowledge through research as a method for dealing with risk includes the following: reducing schedule risk by initiating certain critical or high-risk tasks early in the development cycle, prototyping performance-critical software subsystems or software functions, developing simulations to confirm certain critical performance requirements, and parallel development of critical software functions.

In practice, if the computed risk attribute is less than 0.3, the risk is usually regarded as minimal. The normal development plan monitoring and technical reviews are sufficient to deal with this kind of risk. If the risk factor is greater than 0.3 but less than 0.7, risk is regarded as moderate. In this case a risk report should be generated fully documenting the analysis, and a risk containment/risk management plan should be formulated identifying specific technical performance measurements that will be used to monitor progress and provide an early warning of an impending failure event. If the risk factor exceeds 0.7, in addition to the risk analysis report and risk containment plan, the risk issue should be made visible to the appropriate senior management levels. Senior management may wish to assign a special review team, take up the issue with the customer, make corporate resources available to assist, or decide against the development. In any event, senior management should be made aware of the existence of this risk and its magnitude.

As shown in Figure 16.1, a high risk factor can be caused by (1) a high consequence of failure and a low probability of failure, (2) a low consequence of failure and a high probability of failure, or (3) a moderate consequence of failure and a moderate probability of failure.

16.5 TECHNICAL PERFORMANCE MEASUREMENTS   ■

The most frequently used risk management tools include schedule and cost monitoring and technical performance measurements. By carefully matching actual development team expenditures with planned expenditures, it is possible to identify early signs of a development problem. Similarly, carefully comparing actual schedule milestones with planned milestones in terms of accomplishments is also a good barometer of development status. A third tool is the technical performance measurement (TPM).

A TPM is defined as the continuing measurement of a quantifiable attribute of the software product, subproduct, or development process that can be used to forecast critical attributes of the delivered software product. A TPM is used to measure differences at specified intervals between achieved values of the attribute and the planned value for the attribute. The main goals of TPMs are as follows: (1) to provide a measure of the actual versus planned value of an attribute, (2) to provide early detection or prediction of problems which require technical or administrative attention, and (3) to serve as indicators of the effect of changes on the software product.

For example, if CPU use is a TPM for a particular development, then at program inception we might estimate 20% utilization over an appropriate time interval. Based on experience we might expect use to grow linearly over 18 months to 35% utilization and over the following 12 months to 40% utilization at delivery.

The demonstrated value of the TPM is the value estimated, computed, or measured at any specific time. In the CPU example the demonstrated value would be an estimated value initially and ultimately a measured value in the test environment. Figure 16.2 shows two different scenarios for the CPU utilization example; the curve marked by Xs represents TPM

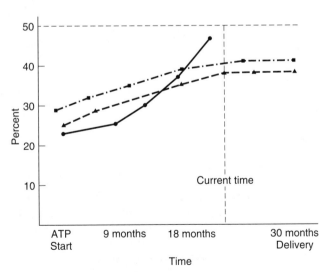

- Planned or predicted
- Actual for programs heading for trouble
- Actual for programs under control

■ **FIGURE 16.2**

CPU utilization TPM.

that closely tracks the planned value. The curve marked with circles represents a trend that might lead to a failure to meet the 50% performance requirement.

In many software development environments technical performance measurements are reported to the client at regular intervals. The responsibility of the software engineer is to develop the process by which the measurement is defined, formulate a measurement method, define a planned value, collect and analyze measurement data, and prepare a report for presentation.

In some software developments, particularly those associated with DOD, NASA, and aerospace projects and embedded systems, technical performance measurement tasks are often used as incentives to the development contractor. That is, how closely these TPMs are followed is a factor in determination of profit.

Some typical software-related technical performance measurements are the following: (1) throughput, (2) CPU and memory utilization, (3) command allocations, (4) I/O capacity, (5) operator/maintenance personnel required, (6) reliability/availability/maintainability, (7) response time, (8) staff, (9) cost and schedule, (10) test case completions, (11) resolution of requirement issues, (12) task execution times, etc.

16.6 EXAMPLES TO ILLUSTRATE SOFTWARE DEVELOPMENT RISK ANALYSIS ■

One way to appreciate what risk analysis and management are all about is to work through a simple but realistic example. In this section we present two realistic examples. The first example concentrates on risks associated with the SRS, and the second example concentrates on risks associated with project staffing.

Example 16.6.1

Ray Luciani's boss, Fred Shepherd, the lead software engineer for one of the XYZ critical application products, asked Ray to report to his office at 8:30 A.M. on Tuesday to discuss a problem. Fred began by giving Ray a brief summary of what had transpired during the last few days. Fred mentioned that he had been approached by several of his more experienced people assigned to help in the preparation and review of the SRS, who expressed concern that the SRS currently being prepared was inadequate in several areas.

The first concern was that there were far too many unresolved TBD (to be determined) requirements, the project's jargon for functional and performance requirements that were left blank in the specification. The overall quality of the specification was very poor, and very little progress was being made to respond to documented deficiencies. Many of the interfacing requirements were vague and incomplete. It was common knowledge that some of the functional and performance requirements were part of a contract squabble between client and contractor. The customer's operators and users were openly and vocally concerned about their needs and wants being overlooked in the software requirements specification. They claimed that there was much that the system and software engineers did not understand about the application area and how operators did their work. Many in the software development community felt that the specification should be redone and reissued with an attendant slip in the software schedule.

Fred asked Ray to look at the software development risk associated with using this specification and to suggest some viable solutions. Fred gave Ray two documents (references [3] and [4]) to help him get started. Ray spent the remainder of the day reading Fred's reference material, checking the library for additional reference material, talking with colleagues about the assignment, and looking for people who had worked on similar problems.

Following a general approach suggested in reference [3], Ray identified five specific risk factors that he felt would be directly associated with the occurrence of an undesirable event, namely failure of the software requirements specification to accomplish its intended purpose (which is to define accurately and completely the function and performance requirements to which the software must be designed). A failure of the SRS would certainly lead to a significant impact on cost, schedule, and performance. In particular, Ray established that unless the specification improved significantly and quickly in these five areas, significant negative consequences would be inevitable. The five critical factors that he thought would most influence the usefulness of the specification are as follows:

TBD closure (completion of requirement definition)
Operator concerns addressed
Improved detail (especially in input/output)
Improved document quality
Resolution of requirement-related contract issues

Specific negative consequences associated with these factors include the following:

Late start in software design
High level of change activity
Late (in the SWDLC) changes to the requirements
Compromises in function and performance of the product

For each of these individual risk components, Ray constructed a range of possible occurrences. The range extended from a best-case situation to a worse-case situation. Ray decided, with the help of colleagues, that a best case would be that all TBDs are satisfactorily closed out in one month, operator issues are satisfactorily settled early, the specification is reissued with substantial improvement in detail and quality, and contract issues are successfully resolved. The reissue of the specification, while not as important from a purely technical standpoint, was judged to be important from a morale standpoint. Ray had realized that by reissuing the specification, project management formally recognized that the specification was inadequate and that the concerns expressed by the development team were justified. The worst-case condition is that virtually nothing is done to address the five factors.

For the next step in the process, Ray estimated the probability of failure associated with each of the possible outcomes. For example, if all TBDs can be settled in one month, operators satisfied, specification quality improved, and contract issues resolved, the probability of a development failure (in terms of cost, schedule, and performance) is approximately 0.1. If no action is taken, the probability of failure is 0.9. The remainder of the model can be filled in using similar rationale. It now remains for Ray to estimate the most likely or expected occurrence for each factor.

The first risk factor on Ray's list was the unresolved TBDs. To quantify the likelihood that these TBDs would be closed out, Ray contacted the system engineering manager to find out who was assigned to the closure of the TBDs and their schedule for resolving and closing the TBDs. He quietly made an assessment of the degree of concern and commitment exhibited by the system engineering manager to closing the TBDs. He was supplied with a complete list of the TBDs from the system engineering manager. The list identified all of the known TBDs plus a few new ones and included the individual assigned to each one along with a schedule for closure of each TBD. Ray reviewed this information with some of the more experienced members of the software development team. The resulting discussions left Ray with a strong feeling that, given the reputation of the people assigned, the nature of the technical problems being addressed, and the degree of commitment he sensed in his discussions with the system engineering manager, there was a good chance that the TBDs would be closed out in a timely manner (in time to be included in the currently scheduled preliminary design activity). However, he wanted to quantify "good chance" more objectively.

To summarize the results of his assessment, Ray grouped the set of outcomes into the following five events ordered from most favorable to worst case.

Event	Probability of Failure
1. All TBDs are closed out in one month	0.1
2. 75% of TBDs are closed out in 6 weeks	0.3
3. Half of the TBDs are closed out in 3 months	0.5
4. 25% of TBDs are closed out in 4 months	0.7
5. Few TBDs are satisfactorily closed out in 6–9 months	0.9

That is, if all open TBDs are satisfactorily closed within 1 month, the probability of a software development failure that could be attributed to the currently open TBDs is 0.1. The longer it takes to fix the specification problems, the greater the probability of failure. If no actions are taken, the probability of a software development failure of major proportions is 0.9.

Ray documented his rationale for selection of factors, the range of possible outcomes for each factor, and the assignment of a probability of failure in his software engineering notebook. His next step was to determine the likely outcome for each factor.

Based on his reading of the system engineering manager's commitment to completing the task, the quality and experience of the people assigned to the task, and the confidence exhibited by his own organization and the client, Ray thought that despite all the assurances from the system engineering manager and the degree of commitment, he perceived that a more likley case will be 75% complete in one and one-half months. Associated with this conclusion is a failure probability of 0.3, which Ray thought would be a conservative estimate. The rationale for selecting 0.3 was based on the fact that, although the specification correction task was a top priority with the system engineering manager and appropriate resources were committed, there was still doubt in Ray's mind that all TBDs could be closed out in one month simply because there were so many. In looking at the schedule for closure, there was no margin for error. Each TBD would have to be resolved on time, and there was little time for resolution, review and rework in the schedule.

In a similar fashion, Ray examined, in turn, operator's satisfaction, improvement in the level of detail, improvement in the quality of the specification, and the resolution of contractual issues that affected the specification. The effort required Ray to spend much time with other specialists and functions including the financial, legal, contract, and client organizations. Ray constructed Table 16.4 as a summary of his findings.

Ray felt that there was only a 50% chance that operators would be satisfied with the specification unless they were directly involved in its development. Based on his discussions with some of the operators, Ray was convinced that the user community would be a hard sell. The system engineering organization publicly acknowledged that the specification was in need of substantial improvement in level of detail and consistency and had assigned people to the task. Ray saw this action as very positive and assigned 0.3 as the probability (likelihood) of failure. He felt the probability of failure due to the overall quality of the specification was in the 50% (0.5 range). Contractual issues, he discovered, were virtually resolved and a likely failure event probability would be 0.1.

The next step was to review the chart and the assigned probability of failure with some of the more senior and more experienced members of the development team and with people not on the development team who had been recommended by Fred. The final step was to document the process and Table 16.4 in a memorandum and pass it along to Fred.

Meanwhile, Ray began to look at the consequences of failure to bring the specification to an acceptable level. The major consequences are, of course, cost overruns, schedule overruns, and delivery of a software product that does not satisfy the customer's needs.

Following guidance he found in the references provided by Fred, he developed Table 16.5. Ray again with the help of more experienced people developed a range of possible outcomes or consequences of failure for each of the three factors—cost, schedule, and performance. To each he assigned a probability or magnitude.

Again the research that led to producing the table took him to other organizations and to other more experienced team members as well as to people recommended by Fred who were not members of the development team.

Ray's best estimate of the likely consequences associated with a failure were as follows:

■ TABLE 16.4.   **Probability of Failure Model**

	FACTORS				
P_F	TBDs Closed	Operators Satisfied	Detail Improved	Quality Improved	Open Contract Issues Resolved
0.1	All in 1 month	Mostly satisfied	Reissue specification	Yes	Yes
0.3	3/4 in 1.5 months	3/4 satisfied	Significant improvement	75%	75%
0.5	1/2 in 3 months	1/2 satisfied	Some improvement	50%	50%
0.7	1/4 in 4 months	1/4 satisfied	Little change	25%	25%
0.9	Few in 6–9 months	Still unhappy	No change	No	No

$$P_F = \frac{0.3 + 0.5 + 0.3 + 0.5 + 0.1}{5} = 0.34$$

■ TABLE 16.5   **Consequences of Failure Model**

C_F	FACTORS		
	Cost	**Schedule**	**Performance**
0.1	Minimal Impact	Minimal	Minor concern
0.3	5% increase	1 month slip	Small reduction in performance
0.5	10% increase	Slip of 1–3 months	Some reduction in performance
0.7	25% increase	3-month slip	Significant reduction in performance
0.9	50% increase	Slip greater than 3 months	Unsatisfactory performance

$$C_F = \frac{0.5 + 0.7 + 0.3}{3} = 0.5$$

a 10% increase in cost, 0.5; a 3-month slip in product delivery, 0.7; and a small reduction in software performance, 0.3. Once again Ray reviewed his conclusions with a wide range of people whose experience was varied, whose judgment was established and respected, and who recognized the importance of risk analysis and were willing to devote time to a careful review of Ray's material. From the risk factor formula, Ray computed a risk factor as follows:

$$R_F = P_F + C_F - P_F \times C_F$$
$$= 0.34 + 0.50 - 0.34 \times 0.50$$
$$= 0.67$$

A risk factor value of 0.67 is moderate but close to the 0.7 limit for a moderate risk and although acceptable cannot be ignored. Fred arranged for a meeting with project management and their technical staff where Ray presented his results followed by a recommendation that a risk containment plan be developed. After a brief discussion, Ray was directed to establish a formal risk containment plan. The meeting gave Ray an opportunity to be seen by some of the senior members of the technical and management staff. He was surprised at how much interest his results generated. He was also impressed at how quickly his presentation was digested and at the quality of the suggestions he received to improve his results, get additional help, and find answers to some of the questions he had not fully answered during the question and answer session.

Ray had already worked out several ideas for a containment plan and had recorded them in his software engineering notebook. In addition, from the people who had reviewed his analysis material, he had heard many ideas and realistic examples of ways to improve chances of avoiding specification problems. Ray's list of ideas included the following:

1. Assign a few of the better software engineers with application area experience to assist system engineers in closing out TBDs.

2. Involve experienced, mature operators in requirements and preliminary design work.
3. Encourage the system engineering manager to reissue the specification. Encourage a positive response by providing additional resources from the contingency fund.
4. Assign a technical writer experienced in specification development to the specification rework.
5. Encourage the contracts organization to press the client for faster resolution of contract issues and assign a software or system engineer to monitor the negotiations.
6. Notify the customer of the potential problem and what is being done to correct the situation.
7. Negotiate a change to the contract schedule.
8. Assign more experienced people to the specification development.
9. Break the specification into two separate modules and produce them sequentially.
10. Expedite the development of the acceptance criteria document and its sign-off by the client.

Ray asked Fred to help in implementing his list of corrective actions. Although Ray knew what had to be done, he felt that at least some of those who would have to implement corrective action would need to hear it from a more senior person. Having direction from project management to implement corrective action gave Fred more authority to implement Ray's suggestions.

Several other ideas were subsequently added to the list. Ray was impressed with Fred's approach to fixing the problem without fixing the blame. In each case when another organization was involved, Fred found a way to provide additional support to help in carrying out suggestions. Fred was able to create a positive environment in which specification problems could be addressed and solved without stirring up emotions and producing a lot of finger pointing.

Fred asked Ray to think of ways in which progress toward fixing the specification problem could be measured. Again Ray had already picked up several ideas in his discussions. He suggested the following. Keep track of the closure of all TBDs and any other specification problems that arise. That is, maintain a formal list of TBDs or open questions, the individual assigned to resolve the issue, dates committed for closure, disposition of each issue, and the closure date. Maintaining this list and reporting progress on a twice-weekly basis would provide a simple measure of how well the specification problem was being handled. Issues not settled on the given schedule would be a warning of impending failure.

Ray was assigned to implement a tracking procedure on all open issues related to the SRS and make a formal report twice a week until further notice. The list of open SRS issues and TBDs and their status relative to closure were declared a TPM and placed on the agenda of all relevant reviews.

The method we followed in Example 16.6.1 attempts to introduce objectivity and a wide range of relevant experience into the analysis and quantification process. The method also permits the software engineer to design a simple risk model or template to suit his or her unique purposes. The basis of this method is as follows: (1) to identify critical risk areas for a specific development; (2) to determine key factors that influence the occurrence of the undesirable event; (3) to prepare two charts or templates, one for treatment of the probability of occurrence and the other for consequences of the occurrence of the undesired event; and (4) to establish a means to identify as early as possible the occurrence of events that warn of impending problems.

Example 16.6.2

For this example, we assume that there is a major concern regarding staffing for the development of the control/security software for the XYZ project. Several projects are starting up at the same time, and there is much contention for the best software engineers and developers. Because Ray did so well on the specification risk problem, Fred asked him to look at the staffing problem.

Every project will have staffing risks. A common question is, Are we able to recruit, transplant, or transfer the proper skills when we need them for this development? However, there will be instances where staffing carries an exceptional risk. It will take some experience to judge whether staffing risk for a given software development is more than just the norm for a new development or if certain factors make staffing risk different on this project. Lack of immediate access to particular skills coupled with a tight delivery schedule allowing little or no time for training or recruiting is not a normal staffing risk. The main point here is that some thought and some experience is required to identify specific areas of risk for further analysis. Since risk planning is an iterative process, risk analysis will be revisited periodically.

Ray now feels confident in his use of the templates and the approach he used in Example 16.6.1 and begins immediately to reshape the templates into probability of failure due to a failure to solve the staffing problem effectively. He has already set up a meeting with the personnel department's Betty Rogers, who has the responsibility for helping in staffing the development team. Ray's first cut is:

Staffing Problems—Probability of Failure Assignment
0.1   Easy to find skills in time available
0.3   Average recruiting problem
0.5   Hard to find skills in time allocated
0.7   Very hard to find these skills
0.9   Almost impossible to locate these skills in time

However, not much useful information is contained in this form. Therefore, Ray decides to develop tables similar to those developed for Example 16.6.1. Table 16.6 summarizes

■ TABLE 16.6   **Factors Contributing to Probability of Failure**

P_F	Approval P1	Skills P2	Dependency P3
0.1	Sign-off local	Entry level	Within project control
0.3	Minimum staffing for hiring approval	Can be found but are committed to other projects	Outside project significant control
0.5	Full range of staff approvals	Significant interviewing	Outside project adequate control
0.7	Hiring freeze. Need additional approval and justification	Limited supply but can be found with time	Less than adequate control
0.9	Very difficult to hire outside	Unusual skills, hard to locate	Very little control

■ TABLE 16.7   **Factors Contributing to Consequences of Failure**

C_F	Technical C1	Cost C2	Schedule C3
0.1	Minimum consequence	Within budget	Chance of minuscule slip
0.3	Small reduction in performance	1–5% increase	Minor slip 1 month or less
0.5	Some reduction in performance	5–20% increase	Small slip of 1–3 months
0.7	Significant degradation	20–50% increase	Slip in excess of 3 months
0.9	Can't meet specifications	Greater than 50% increase	Significant. Can impact all delivery schedules

factors contributing to the probability of failure, and Table 16.7 summarizes factors contributing to the consequences of failure.

Table 16.6 contains more specific guidance on how to estimate the probability of success and therefore how to arrive at a rationale for assigning a probability that we will fail in staffing our development with the right people at the right time. Designing a separate template to prompt those whose experience you want to employ will focus on the specific factors that contribute to success or failure. Asking each respondent to provide a rationale for choices forces more objective thinking into the risk analysis process. Table 16.7 provides a means to quantify consequences of failure. Having our personnel department helping to fill these positions requires that we consult them to find out whether this task will be difficult for them or something they have done routinely in the past. The personnel organization will need to ascertain the availability of these skills in the job market. How much interviewing must be done, length of time to get a new employee productive, etc., are questions or assessment that must be factored into the analysis. After much debate and discussion, the following values are assigned to each probability of failure factor (Table 16.6):

$P1 = 0.3$ There may be some minor problems with approvals to hire.
$P2 = 0.5$ We expect a lot of interviewing to find the right people.
$P3 = 0.5$ We are depending on another organization with other priorities and agendas to solve our problem.

Examining Table 16.7, we might with appropriate supporting arguments select the following values for C1, C2, and C3 as the most likely occurrence.

$C1 = 0.1$ Minor adjustments
$C2 = 0.3$ 2% increase in cost due to overtime and training
$C3 = 0.7$ 3-month impact due to domino effect

Ray circulated the templates he had prepared to several of the people he had talked to and to those suggested by Fred. After a few days had passed Ray collected all the templates, looked for major divergences in opinions, resolved the major differences, and produced a composite value for each risk factor. The resulting risk attribute he calculated from the composite risk factors using the risk formulas. The probability of failure calculation is as follows:

$$P_F = \frac{0.3 + 0.5 + 0.5}{3} = 0.43$$

The consequence of failure is

$$C_F = \frac{0.1 + 0.3 + 0.7}{3} = 0.37$$

The risk attribute is

$$\begin{aligned} R_F &= P_F + C_F - P_F \times C_F \\ &= 0.43 + 0.37 - 0.43 \times 0.37 \\ &= 0.64 \end{aligned}$$

A risk attribute of 0.64 is a moderate risk. Ray documented the rationale associated with the analysis and got it reviewed by as many experienced people as possible before incorporating results in his report. If after review the risk attribute remains 0.64, senior management will be made aware of this risk so that they can take steps to help in staffing or at least understand the details. The next step is to establish a means for following up on recruiting efforts to assure that appropriate urgency is communicated. More important, if it becomes clear this staffing problem is not getting solved, we must go to ''Plan B.'' Plan B is a contingency plan that we would develop as a result of recognizing the risk. Plan B could involve subcontracting the work that required the subject skills or revising schedules and order of delivery, etc. The value of this approach to risk analysis is that templates can be tailored to fit specific risk areas; the process is repeatable; it is easy to automate, modify, and disseminate; it is almost self-documenting; it makes use of organizational experience; and it is highly visible.

16.7 CHAPTER SUMMARY ■

The spiral software development model proposed by Boehm [1] and others as a characterization of (or a desirable approach to) the software development process inserts a risk analysis step at each cycle of the spiral. This chapter describes one way that such risk analyses might be performed. In most successful software developments, risk is implicitly or explicitly well understood and managed. Chapter 16 provides a simple, structured, and disciplined approach to risk analysis and risk containment. Many sources provide guidance in the location of risk areas and the identification of risk factors—failure modes and effects analysis, reliability analysis, cost and schedule estimates, fault tree analysis, software sizing estimates, software development plans, etc. The resource investment required to analyze risk factors, quantify risk attributes, and define a technical performance measurement process will pay great dividends.

The risk analysis and management process is straightforward. A risk analysis associated with an area of potential risk identifies the possible occurrence of undesirable events and determines those critical factors that give rise to the occurrence of the undesirable event. If a risk analysis reveals that a significant risk exists or that an undesirable event will occur, a decision is made whether to either simply accept the risk or to take corrective and/or contingency action. The most important points made in chapter 16 are as follows: (1) accept the fact that risk is intrinsic to all software developments, (2) have a structured methodology for dealing with the analysis and management of risk, and (3) confront problems and issues early on that will, if not dealt with, cause the occurrence of an undesirable event.

16.8   EXERCISES ■

1. Assume you are a software engineer working on a complex system to be developed for a large hospital chain. The system requirements include integrating hospital records of all patients, providing a means of digitizing and storing physicians reports, acquiring and displaying digital images from equipment provided by another manufacturer, and providing a local area network interconnecting physician's offices with each other and with a central file server. The hardware/software/operator system is required to allow a physician to call up an enhanced radiographic image from the central file server, evaluate the image, and dictate the report to a microphone attached to his display. The system will be required to store the report, distribute the report to the referring physician, and add the fee to the patient's bill.

   Further assume that you have been assigned to a team that is performing a system risk analysis. Recognizing that many of the requirements will be implemented in software, your participation has been requested. The first task is to identify and prioritize the areas of greatest technical risk. Provide a rationale for your results.
2. Develop a set of risk factors for the case in which it is felt that there is a risk that budgets and schedule for software development are inadequate. Software size estimates, software development plans, and other software attributes are good sources for risk factors. Develop a probability of failure model. Prepare to discuss your results in class.
3. Identify technical performance measurements that might be used to keep track of the risk attribute associated with inadequate budget and schedule.
4. Develop a risk assessment table for the SRS developed in Example 4.4.1 in Section 4.4 of Chapter 4. Give a list of containment suggestions. Follow the procedure developed in Example 16.6.1.
5. Do problem 4 for the SRS developed for Example 4.4.2.
6. Assess the risk factors involved in staffing the project described in Example 4.4.1
7. Identify risk factors, risk consequence and the risk probability associated with staffing for the XYZ project described in chapter 2. You must give adequate reasons for any subjective decision made in the process.
8. Do problem 7 for the ABC project.
9. Consider the SRS developed for the problem of Example 11.4.1 in section 11.4 of chapter 11. One of the risk areas associated with this example is security. Develop the risk factor table, risk consequence table and the highest, the lowest, and the expected probabilty of risk associated with any form of security.

10. Consider a university registration system. The system is to handle student registration, transcript, grade recording, add/drop and other functions associated with registration. Identify the risk areas associated with such a software system. Develop the risk factor table for and the risk consequence table associated with security issues.

References

1. B. W. Boehm, ''A Spiral Model of Software Development and Enhancement,'' *IEEE Comp.*, Vol. 21, No. 5, 61–72, (1988).
2. ———, ''Software Risk Management: Principles and Practices,'' *IEEE Software*, Vol. 8, No. 1, 32–41, (1991).
3. DOD, *System Engineering Management Guide*, Ed. 2, Defense System Management College, Washington, D. C., 1986.
4. E. J. Henley and H. Kumamoto, *Probabilistic Risk Assessment*, IEEE Press, New York, 1992.

Reliability

17.0 OBJECTIVES ▪

The main goals we have set for this chapter are (1) to emphasize the importance of formal reliability attributes in the development of software products, especially those software products that are directly or indirectly associated with public safety; and (2) to introduce the reader to standard models used in reliability prediction and the application of these models to software product reliability. We have also set the following secondary objectives for this chapter: (1) to provide a sound definition for terms such as hazard function, reliability, quality, and availability as they relate to software; (2) to identify and describe the important properties of good reliability models for software reliability measurement; (3) to develop a software reliability model and illustrate its utility not only in predicting software reliability but in test planning and test completeness decisions; (4) to show how reliability experience accumulated in testing and in the field can be used in establishing software design guidelines that can lead to more reliable software product designs; and (5) to discuss redundancy and fault tolerance in terms of requirements imposed on software products.

17.1 INTRODUCTION ▪

Reliability research originated in the early 1950s with concerns about vacuum tube failure rates in military and commercial airline communication equipment as well as early computer systems. Continuing research sponsored by government and industry has stimulated and supported the development of hardware reliability as an engineering discipline. The field has grown to embrace a wide variety of elements and has developed a sophisticated technology. Many of the ideas and approaches have a direct analogue in software reliability.

It has always been a paradox that so much effort is expended on hardware reliability for safety-critical systems while software reliability is largely ignored, particularly when a software failure could cause as much or more damage as a hardware failure. We have, therefore devoted a few pages to a brief discussion of reliability from the system and hardware point of view to orient the reader.

Figure 17.1 shows the hardware failure phenomenon, the "bathtub curve," as initially observed in certain hardware components. The initial period, called infant mortality, refers to initially high failure rates due to those components that are weak by virtue of damage in shipping, hidden defects in materials, manufacturing processes, etc. The so-called infant mortality period is followed by a service period in which the failure rate is observed to be relatively constant. During this period failures will continue to occur randomly due to hidden flaws in materials, undetected deficiencies in the manufacturing process, and unintentional or accidental overloading of a component. Changes in device properties over time and inappropriate selection and use of components also contribute to these random failures. The last phase is dominated by wear-out failures. Components fail at an increasing rate due to age, chemical reactions, corrosion, and other changes in material composition. The operating or service period is relatively long for most electronic parts. By way of comparison, software failures can include the following: hidden flaws introduced in specifications, design, and coding and overlooked in reviews and testing; accidental input overloads or stress; unanticipated combinations of codes and numbers within the CPU and memory in space and time that result in a failure; and operator-induced errors.

By collecting and analyzing hardware field data and supporting analysis with laboratory tests and parts analysis, hardware failure phenomena have been, to some degree, confirmed and the observation model validated (to some extent). It is important to note that reliability models apply to the service period portion of the bathtub curve where failures are not due to wear out. This fact is frequently misunderstood by software engineers.

Failure rates have been tabulated for many commonly used electronic and electromechanical devices and published in handbooks. A frequently used handbook is MIL HBDK 217E [3]. Designers of electronic equipment routinely use these handbooks to select parts for a design. Reliability analysts predict mean time to failure based on handbook data. For example, a black box requiring the successful operation of 1000 devices, each of which has a failure

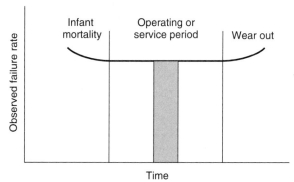

Confirmed by: Testing many devices in controlled environment; field data collection/editing

■ **FIGURE 17.1**

Bathtub curve.

rate of 0.000047 per hour, would itself have a failure rate of 0.047 failures per hour. Failure rates are additive for a common operating time. Such handbooks make it possible for a designer to predict accurately the performance of a black box subsystem before construction. Unfortunately, no such standard handbook for software products is currently available.

Reliability predictions based on handbook data are generally conservative. One of the consequences of too conservative a reliability prediction is an oversized maintenance work force and an oversized spare parts inventory. The mis-estimates associated with ultraconservative reliability predictions are subsequently corrected at substantial expense.

Hardware reliability is improved by maintaining programs that collect and analyze field data and feed results back into component design. This process helps to create more reliable components. The identification of specific failure modes and failure phenomena enables parts manufacturers to improve fabrication techniques, tighten inspection processes, and take other steps to improve overall reliability and performance of electronic parts.

More aggressive approaches to intrinsic hardware reliability improvement require expenditure of substantial resources and therefore must be justified based on a cost-benefit analysis. Such aggressive approaches include the following: (1) the measurement of individual part parameters to screen out or select only those components that conform exactly to specification; (2) a burn-in of components at elevated conditions (for example, running the device in a controlled environment at temperatures in excess of specification) to force failures of weak components; (3) application of demanding quality assurance procedures at each step of the design and development process; and (4) building several units exclusively for destructive reliability testing. These and other approaches to improving intrinsic reliability of parts or components of hardware subsystems have generally proved effective. The major applications of these aggressive methods to improve intrinsic component reliability are found in NASA, in aircraft design, and in certain military products. Work continues in this field and improvement in component reliability continues.

When intrinsic component reliability cannot meet reliability design requirements or the cost of screening, burn-in, and other quality assurance steps is excessive (a screened part can cost ten to fifteen times more than the same part unscreened), then the designer may resort to using redundant systems or fault-tolerant designs. Implementation of redundant and fault-tolerant systems frequently includes software that recognizes failure conditions and effects a switchover and recovery process, thus placing software directly in the critical path of system reliability requirement satisfaction. Section 17.10 discusses this approach to meeting reliability requirements.

The major goal of reliability and quality assurance is to identify all possible influences on failure rates and take appropriate steps to reduce or eliminate those influences. Government and industry work jointly through professional groups and sponsored research to spur improvements in component and system reliability.

This chapter begins with a brief overview of reliability concepts and a few application examples to provide the reader with an appropriate frame of reference. To define reliability attributes in a formal way, we need to be familiar with introductory probability theory. Therefore, a summary of probability theory is presented as a refresher for readers and to make what follows stand independent of references. Reliability is defined in terms of a model parameter called the hazard function. Some models for the software hazard function are described. Desirable features for models in general and reliability models in particular are discussed. The process by which system level reliability requirements are established and allocated among constituent subsystems is presented. The development of failure rate requirements from both mission and operating times and operating environments is considered. The iterative nature of reliability studies and analyses for a specific product is pointed out. System availability as a function of reliability and maintainability (mean time to effect a system repair) is defined.

A specific software reliability model (hazard function) is defined and used as the basis for predicting mean time to failure (MTTF) and the number of test hours required to achieve a particular MTTF. These models can also be used to estimate the number of intrinsic faults in a software product.

To achieve high reliability and availability, system designers frequently resort to redundancy and fault tolerance. The chapter includes a brief discussion of fault tolerant systems and redundant systems. The critically important role of software in implementing redundant systems and fault tolerant systems is discussed. The chapter also looks briefly at failure modes, effects analysis, and fault tree analysis as applied to safety and reliability concerns.

17.2 OVERVIEW ■

We often apply the word *reliability* to describe our confidence in a person or thing being able to perform a specific function or duty. ''I want a reliable vehicle for transportation'' or ''He/she can always be relied upon to meet schedules.'' There is an implied assumption that the vehicle or person will not fail to carry out the assigned function or duty adequately. The field of reliability engineering concerns itself with defining reliability quantitatively, developing models to predict this quantitative reliability attribute, confirming models through data collection and evaluation, and inferring design and development rules that can improve product reliability.

Performing adequately implies a definitive knowledge of what constitutes adequate performance. If reliability is to be employed as a formal parameter in specifying performance criteria, then what constitutes adequate performance must also be specified clearly and completely. For example, if adequate performance of a four-engine aircraft is specified as taking off, traveling to a destination 1000 miles away, and landing successfully, then a failure of one engine during flight may not be inadequate performance of the aircraft. If the aircraft has been designed to fly on less than four engines and if the overall performance of the aircraft does not deteriorate enough to prevent completion of the take off, the 1000-mile flight, and the safe landing, then the aircraft has met its reliability specification. If, on the other hand, the aircraft could not complete its flight or adequate performance was clearly specified as all four engines operational throughout the flight, we would say the aircraft failed to meet its reliability requirement specification. The point is that, to evaluate performance against a required reliability value, one must also have a well-defined definition or criteria of precisely what constitutes adequate performance.

The importance of reliability to system and software design has many facets. More and more the loss of business revenue, credibility, and customer goodwill is being identified with reliability of information systems. Eight hours of downtime for a major segment of the telephone system (which includes a significant software component), for example, can cost in excess of $100 million in lost revenues and sales for the telephone company and its customers. Some software products can, through failures, cause major financial loss, physical damage, and perhaps even loss of life.

Use of computer software in critical aircraft applications such as a computerized flight control system is a good example of a case where a software failure may place public safety at risk. Design and implementation of such systems requires deep concern for reliability. The more we come to depend on automation and the more we depend on successful operation of complex systems, the more reliability, and indirectly safety and quality, becomes a major design requirement concern.

The importance of reliability as a design attribute can be illustrated by considering a relatively mundane example. A manufacturer of a household appliance would like to guarantee the product for a specified period against defects in workmanship and parts and maintain the product effectively in the field. The following questions arise: (1) How can the company quantify and predict the reliability of the product? (2) What price must be set on each unit to cover replacement of failed units during the first year? (3) How large a repair team must be maintained? (4) What spares inventory must be maintained? (5) How can the reliability of the product be improved during design, test, and deployment phases? (6) How can parts suppliers be encouraged to be concerned with reliability and quality? (7) If the company sells maintenance insurance to cover failures after the guarantee expires, at what rate should the insurance premium be set? (8) How should the guarantee be phrased to assure that the appliance will be used properly? (9) How should failures be reviewed for legitimacy? (10) How should user manuals be written to improve the chances of units surviving the first year? Good answers to all of these questions are important to the success of a business engaged in producing a competitive, marketable product. A key piece of information is the answer to question 1, how to quantify and predict reliability.

In most large development environments, reliability analyses and predictions are carried out by reliability specialists. Detail reliability modeling for very complex systems and critical applications requires more background than is provided here. However, it is important for a software engineer to have a full appreciation for reliability concepts and the application of models, techniques, and tools that enable designers to meet specific reliability requirements and for testers to make fundamental judgments regarding a product's readiness for release and for planning purposes.

The developer of a software product for any application involving a larger user community and the potential for a substantial loss to users, in the event of product failure, must consider software reliability. Reliability considerations both implicitly and explicitly include quality assurance and safety issues. Reliability and quality assurance both require an appreciation of a few fundamental ideas from probability and statistics.

17.3   REVIEW OF PROBABILITY THEORY   ■

This review is not intended to be adequate for the reader encountering the subject for the first time. For a complete treatment the reader is directed to one of the many excellent texts on the subject [2,9]. A strong background in probability and statistics is important in the study of advanced reliability and quality assurance topics. However, for the purposes of this chapter, we have given a brief review of the fundamental rules of probability and their application to reliability theory.

There are two fundamental approaches to the treatment of probability: the frequency approach and the axiomatic approach. The frequency approach deals with experimentally derived results that are viewed as approximations to the underlying truth. The axiomatic approach derives results from a set of axioms. We will develop the theory from the axiomatic standpoint with the understanding that the frequency approach, when sample sizes are sufficient, approximates results obtained from the axiomatic development.

17.3.1 Axiomatic Probability

Basic set theory forms the foundation for the axiomatic definition of probability. We define Ω to be the set of all possible outcomes of an experiment. Any subset of Ω is called an event. Therefore, any event A is an element of the power set* of Ω. We define the following operations on the set of events:

1. Complement: $\sim A$ (not A) represents the complement of event, $\sim A$ meaning all events except A.
2. Union: $A \cup B$ is the event that events A or B occur.
3. Intersection: $A \cap B$ is the event that events A and B both occur.
4. Inclusion: $A \subset B$ means that event A occurring implies event B occurs.

The set of all events is closed under the operations complement, union, intersection, and inclusion. Thus if A and B are events, then $A \subset B$, $A \cup B$, $A \cap B$, and $\sim A$ are also events.

Example 17.3.1.

In a toss of a die, the set of all outcomes is

$$\Omega = \{1,2,3,4,5,6\}$$

and $A_1 = \{1,2\}$, $A_2 = \{1,2,3\}$, $A_3 = \{2,3\}$, and $A_4 = \{3,4,5,6\}$ are four events. The complement of A_1 is A_4, the intersection of A_1 and A_3 is $\{2\}$, the union of A_1 and A_3 is A_2, and $A_3 \subset A_2$.

Definition: Two events A and B are called *disjoint events* if and only if the intersection of A and B is an empty set.

Defintion: Let $P(A)$ denote the probability that an event A occurs. Then $P(A)$ is called the *probability function* for event A.

Axioms of Probability:

1. For any event $A \subset \Omega$, we have $0 \leq P(A) \leq 1$.
2. For Ω, the set of all possible experimental outcomes, also called the sample space, we have $P(\Omega) = 1$.
3. If $A_1, A_2, A_3, \ldots$, such that $A_i \cap A_j = \varnothing$ for $i \neq j$ then we have

$$P\left(\bigcup_{i=1}^{\infty} A_i\right) = \sum_{i=1}^{\infty} P(A_i)$$

All of the properties of the probability theory may be derived from these three axioms. A partial list of these properties is as follows:

1. $P(A) \leq 1$ for any event A;
2. $P(\sim A) = 1 - P(A)$, where $\sim A$ denotes the complement of A.

....

* Power set of a set is the set of all subsets of that set, including the null set and the set itself.

3. $P(A \cup B) = P(A) + P(B) - P(A \cap B)$, for arbitrary events A and B.
4. If A and B are disjoint events, then

$$P(A \cap B) = P(\emptyset) = 0$$

5. $A \subset B \Rightarrow P(A) < P(B)$.

Note that $\emptyset$ means null set and $\Rightarrow$ means "implies."

17.3.2 Conditional Probability

The idea of the probability of an event can be extended to establish relationships between two events. The conditional probability of event A conditioned on event B, $P(B) > 0$, is defined as follows:

$$P(A|B) = \frac{P(A \cap B)}{P(B)}$$

The term $P(A|B)$ is the probability that event A occurs conditioned on occurrence of event B. The events A and B are said to be independent if $P(A \cap B) = P(A)P(B)$. Therefore, if A and B are independent, then

$$P(A|B) = P(A)$$

meaning that the occurrence of event B has no bearing on the probability of the occurrence of event A.

Bayes Rule

A set of events $A_1, A_2, \ldots, A_n$ is said to partition the probability space, Ω, if and only if we have

$$\bigcup_{i=1}^{i=n} A_i = \Omega$$

and

$$A_i \cap A_j = \emptyset \quad \forall i \neq j$$

Any event B can be expressed in terms of the disjoint events $A_1, A_2, \ldots, A_n$ as

$$B = \bigcup_{i=1}^{i=n} (A_i \cap B)$$

and from axiom 3 we have

$$P(B) = \sum_{i=1}^{i=n} P(A_i \cap B)$$

This is called the law of total probability. The application of this law to the conditional probability $P(A_i|B)$ results in the following formula, known as Bayes rule.

$$P(A_i|B) = \frac{P(A_i)P(B|A_i)}{\displaystyle\sum_{i=1}^{i=n} P(A_i)P(B|A_i)}$$

17.3.3 Random Variables, Probability Distributions, and Density Functions

A random variable is a function on the set of experimental outcomes mapping the experimental outcomes onto the real line. Discrete random variables are mapped onto a countable set of points on the real line, possibly infinite. Continuous random variables are mapped into an interval on the real line. Continuous random variables may be characterized by their probability distribution functions, which are defined as

$$F_X(x) = P(X < x)$$

Thus the probability distribution function evaluated at x is the probability of a set of experimental outcomes that map into the interval $(-\infty, x)$. When the association of F_x with the continuous variable X is understood, we may omit the subscript X from F_X and just write $F(x) = P(X < x)$. Note that X represents a random variable and x is one of the values of that random variable.

From the basic axioms of probability, the following properties for the probability distribution function may be shown:

$$F(-\infty) = 0$$

$$F(+\infty) = 1$$

$$x_1 < x_2 \Rightarrow F(x_1) < F(x_2)$$

From the probability distribution function one could calculate the probability of an event lying in an interval

$$P(x_1 < X < x_2) = F(x_2) - F(x_1)$$

For a discrete random variable X we define

$$f(x) = P(X = x)$$

and call $f(x)$ the density function of the discrete random variable X. The probability $P(X = x)$ is defined as follows:

$$P(X = x) = F(x) - F(x^-)$$

where

$$x^- = \lim_{\varepsilon \to 0} x - \varepsilon, \ \varepsilon > 0$$

The probability distribution function $F(x)$ for discrete variable X is a step function as shown in Figure 17.2. The height of each step is the probability of the random variable assuming a particular value associated with that step.

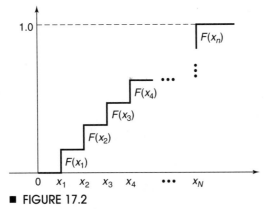

■ **FIGURE 17.2**
Probability distribution function: discrete random variables.

Suppose x_i, $i = 1, 2, \ldots, n$ are possible values for a discrete random variable X. From the axioms of probability we conclude the following:

1. $P(X = x_i) > 0$, for $i = 1, 2, \ldots, n$
2. If $A = \{y_1, y_2, \ldots, y_k\}$ is an event consisting of k outcomes, $y_1, y_2, \ldots, y_k$, then we have

$$P(A) = \sum_{j=1}^{j=k} P(X = y_j) = \sum_{j=1}^{j=k} f(y_j)$$

3. If $\Omega = \{x_1, x_2, \ldots, x_n\}$, then

$$P(\Omega) = \sum_{i=1}^{i=n} P(X = x_i) = \sum_{i=1}^{i=n} f(x_i) = 1$$

17.3.4 Distribution Functions

The distribution function for a discrete random variable X is defined as:

$$P(X \leq x) \equiv F(x) = \sum_{X \leq x} f(x)$$

As can be seen, the distribution function of X is a cumulative probability; sometimes it is called the cumulative distribution function. For example, $F(x) = x/6$, $1 \leq x \leq 6$, is the distribution function for the experiment of tossing a single die.

Binomial Distribution

There are many discrete distribution functions used in real-world problems. However, the two most commonly used functions are the binomial distribution and the Poisson distribution. The binomial distribution applies to situations in which an experiment has two possible outcomes, success and failure. The probability of success is p and the probability of failure is

$q = 1 - p$. In n successive trials of such an experiment, the probability of r successes and $n - r$ failures is defined as follows:

$$B(r,n,p) = \binom{n}{r} p^r (1 - p)^{n-r}$$

where

$$\binom{n}{r} = \frac{n!}{r!(n - r)!}$$

Example 17.3.2:

In tossing a coin 10 times, compute the probability of obtaining 4 heads. Note that 4 heads out of 10 trials is different from 4 consecutive heads out of 10 trials.

$$B(4;10,1/2) = (10 \times 9 \times 8 \times 7)/(4 \times 3 \times 2 \times 1)(1/2)^{10}$$

$$= \frac{210}{1024} = 0.205$$

Poisson Distribution

Another commonly used discrete distribution function is called Poisson distribution. Poisson distribution is the limit of a binomial distribution when n is very large and p is very small. Let $\mu = np$. When n goes to infinity and p goes to zero, the binomial distribution approaches a limit, which is called Poisson distribution as follows:

$$f(r;\mu) = \frac{\mu^r e^{-\mu}}{r!}$$

When we are interested in events that are a function of time, we may assume the average rate of occurrence per unit time is the constant λ. With this assumption we have $\mu = \lambda t$ and the Poisson distribution becomes

$$f(r;\lambda t) = \frac{(\lambda t)^r e^{-\lambda t}}{r!}$$

where $\mu = \lambda t > 0$ is the mean or the expected value of the random variable with Poisson distribution. In general, if X is a discrete random variable with probability distribution

$$P(X = r) = \frac{\mu^r e^{-\mu}}{r!}$$

then X is said to have Poisson distribution. For example, the number of detected errors in a software program over a period of time is assumed to have a Poisson distribution.

Continuous Random Variables

For a continuous random variable, X, the probability distribution function, $F(x)$, is a continuous monotonically nondecreasing function. The probability density function, $f(x)$, is defined as follows:

$$f(x) = \frac{dF(x)}{dx}$$

or

$$F(x) = P(X < x) = \int_{-\infty}^{x} f(u) \, du$$

From the axioms of the probability we can conclude that for a continuous random variable X with density function $f(x)$, we have

$$P(\Omega) = P(x < \infty) = \int_{-\infty}^{+\infty} f(x) \, dx = 1$$

and

$$P(X = x) = \int_{x}^{x} f(x) \, dx = 0$$

Normal Distribution

Suppose X is a continuous random variable with a mean value of μ and a standard deviation of σ. If the density function of X is defined as

$$f(x) = \frac{1}{\sigma\sqrt{2\pi}} e^{-(x-\mu)^2/2\sigma^2}$$

then X is said to have a normal distribution with a mean of μ and standard deviation of σ. The distribution function of X is defined as follows:

$$F(x) = P(X < x) = \frac{1}{\sigma\sqrt{2\pi}} \int_{-\infty}^{x} e^{-(z-\mu)^2/2\sigma^2} \, dz$$

where z is a dummy variable of integration. If the mean of X is zero and its standard deviation is 1, then X is said to have a standard normal distribution function. The density function of a standard normal distribution is shown as

$$f(x) = \frac{1}{\sqrt{2\pi}} e^{-x^2/2} \quad -\infty < x < \infty$$

and the standard normal distribution function is shown as

$$F(x) = \frac{1}{\sqrt{2\pi}} \int_{-\infty}^{x} e^{-z^2/2} \, dz$$

where z is a dummy variable of integration.

Exponential Distribution

The exponential density function of a continuous random variable X is defined as follows:

$$f(x) = \lambda e^{-\lambda x} \quad 0 < x \le \infty$$

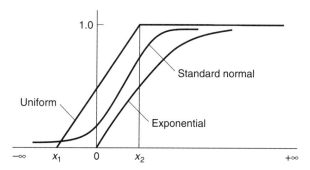

■ FIGURE 17.3

Probability distribution functions: continuous random variables.

where λ is a parameter. For example, the distribution of the probability of failure for a number of electronic devices is exponential. For such devices λ is a constant called the failure rate.

The probability distribution function for an exponential density function is defined as follows:

$$F(x) = P(X < x) = \int_0^x \lambda e^{-\lambda u} \, du$$

Uniform Distribution

A continuous random variable X is said to have uniform distribution over the interval (x_1, x_2) if its density function is defined as

$$f(x) = \begin{cases} \dfrac{1}{(x_2 - x_1)} & x_1 < x < x_2 \\ 0 & \text{otherwise} \end{cases}$$

The probability distribution function for a uniform distribution is defined as

$$F(x) = P(X < x) = \int_{x_1}^x \frac{dz}{x_2 - x_1}$$

Figure 17.3 shows the standard normal distribution as well as uniform and exponential distributions.

17.3.5 Joint Distribution of Random Variables

In this section we consider relations between two or more random variables. We define the joint probability distribution function of two random variables X and Y as follows:

$$F(x,y) = P(X < x, Y < y) \quad -\infty < x,y < \infty$$

where x and y are real numbers. The random variables may represent different mapping onto the real line from the same space of experimental outcomes. The properties of the joint distribution function are as follows:

$$F(-\infty,-\infty) = 0$$

$$F(+\infty,+\infty) = 1$$

$$x_1 < x_2 \Rightarrow F(x_1,y) < F(x_2,y)$$

$$y_1 < y_2 \Rightarrow F(x,y_1) < F(x,y_2)$$

The joint probability density function of the random variables X and Y is defined as follows:

$$f(x,y) = \frac{d}{dx}\left(\frac{dF(x,y)}{dy}\right)$$

In analogy with the single variable density functions, we have the following properties for the joint density function:

$$f(x,y) > 0 \qquad \text{for} \qquad -\infty < x < \infty \text{ and } -\infty < y < \infty$$

$$\int_{-\infty}^{\infty}\int_{-\infty}^{\infty} f(x,y)\,dydx = 1$$

The marginal distribution and density functions, when they exist, may be calculated from the joint functions. We have

$$F(x) = P(X < x, Y < \infty) = \int_{-\infty}^{x} dz \int_{-\infty}^{\infty} f(z,y)\,dy$$

$$F(y) = P(X < \infty, Y < y) = \int_{-\infty}^{y} dz \int_{-\infty}^{\infty} f(x,z)\,dx$$

$$f(x) = \int_{-\infty}^{\infty} f(x,y)\,dy$$

$$f(y) = \int_{-\infty}^{\infty} f(x,y)\,dx$$

Two random variables are said to be independent if and only if

$$F(x,y) = F(x)F(y)$$

or equivalently in terms of probability density functions

$$f(x,y) = f(x)f(y)$$

For random variables that are not independent, the concepts of conditional distribution and density functions come into play. We define the conditional distribution function

$$F(x|y) = \frac{P(X < x, Y < y)}{P(Y < y)} = \frac{F(x,y)}{F(y)}$$

or in terms of density functions we have

$$F(x|y) = \frac{F(x,y)}{F(y)} = \frac{\int_{-\infty}^{x} du \int_{-\infty}^{y} f(u,v)\,dv}{\int_{-\infty}^{y} dv \int_{-\infty}^{\infty} f(x,v)\,dx}$$

This equation gives the probability that $\{X < x\}$ given that $Y < y$. We may also define the conditional density of the random variable X as

$$f(x|y) = \frac{f(x,y)}{f(y)}$$

This is the probability density of $X < x$ conditioned on the event that Y is less than y.

We have discussed joint density functions, joint distribution functions, and independence in connection with only two random variables. The same concepts apply in a straightforward way to three or more random variables.

17.3.6   Expectation of Random Variables—Moments

Associated with a random variable X we define a number, $E(X)$, which is called the expectation or the mean value of the random variable. The mean value of a discrete random variable X is defined as

$$E(X) = \sum_{x_i's} x_i P(X = x_i)$$

and the mean value for the continuous random variable X with density function $f(x)$ is defined as

$$E(X) = \int_{-\infty}^{\infty} xf(x) \ dx$$

The expectation of a random variable, Y, which can be expressed as a function of another random variable, X, can be found from the distribution function of the random variable X. Suppose random variable Y is defined as $Y = g(X)$. If X and Y are discrete random variables we have

$$E(Y) = E(g(X)) = \sum_{x_i's} g(x_i)P(X = x_i)$$

and if X and Y are continuous random variables, we have

$$E(Y) = E(g(X)) = \int_{-\infty}^{\infty} g(x)f(x) \ dx$$

Two of the most useful functions, in terms of characterizing random variables, are of the form $Y = X^k$ and $Z = (X - E(X))^k$. The mean of Y is called the kth moment of the random variable X, and the mean of Z is called the kth central moment of the random variable X. The variance of a random variable, X, is the second central moment of X.

$$\mathrm{Var}(X) = E((X - E(X))^2) = E(X^2 - 2XE(X) + E(X)E(X))$$
$$= E(X^2) - 2E(X)E(X) + E(X)E(X)$$
$$= E(X^2) - (E(X))^2$$

If the joint probabilities of two random variables are known, joint moments may be calculated. In the case of discrete random variables we have

$$E(X,Y) = \sum_{x_i s} x_i \sum_{y_j s} y_j P(X = x_i, Y = y_j)$$

and in the case of continuous random variables we have

$$E(X,Y) = \int_{-\infty}^{\infty} x dx \int_{-\infty}^{\infty} f(x,y) y dy$$

The joint first moment of random variables X and Y is called the correlation or the autocorrelation of the random variables X and Y. The joint first central moment of the random variables X and Y is called the covariance or the autocovariance of the variables X and Y. If X and Y are discrete variables, we have

$$\text{cov}(X,Y) = E(X - E(X))(Y - E(Y)) = \sum_{x_i s} (x_i - E(X)) \sum_{y_j s} (y_j - E(Y)P(X = x_i, Y = y_j))$$

and if X and Y are continuous variables we have

$$\text{cov}(X,Y) = \int_{-\infty}^{\infty} \int_{-\infty}^{\infty} (x - E(X))(y - E(Y))f(x,y)\ dxdy$$

Two random variables, X and Y, are said to be uncorrelated if

$$E(X,Y) = E(X)E(Y) \text{ or } \text{cov}(X,Y) = 0.$$

When random variables are independent, they are of necessity uncorrelated. However, it is only for Gaussian random variables that uncorrelatedness implies independence.

Since taking the expectation of a random variable is a linear operation, the expected value of the sum of two random variables is simply the sum of the expected values, as follows:

$$E(X_1 + X_2) = E(X_1) + E(X_2)$$

This equivalence holds even if the random variables are not independent. When two random variables are uncorrelated, the variance of the sum is equal to the sum of the variance, as follows:

$$\text{Var}(X_1 + X_2) = \text{Var}(X_1) + \text{Var}(X_2)$$

17.3.7 Markov Process

An important class of processes is known as the Markov chain or Markov process. There are many useful applications of Markov processes in physics, astronomy, biology, and social science. Many interesting reliability and availability problems can be solved by application of the Markov process.

A stochastic process is a sequence of trials of an experiment defined in a probabilistic sense. A Markov process is a stochastic process in which the outcome of any individual trial is dependent only on the outcome of a preceding trial. A conditional probability is associated with every pair of outcomes. The concept of state and time must be introduced in the treatment. The possible states must be defined, and the transition from one state to another must be characterized over a series of trials. For example, the state of a machine might be operating or not operating, and the transition from operating to nonoperating might be characterized by its probability of failure and from nonoperating to operating by its probability of repair.

Classes of systems that can be described by Markov processes include the following:

a. Time and state discrete
b. Time continuous and state discrete
c. Time discrete and state continuous
d. Time and state continuous

There are many interesting reliability and availability problems that fall into classes c and d. For our current purposes, however, we will examine class a.

If a system has N unique states that are equivalent to the outcomes of an experiment governed by chance, we can represent the outcome X as a $1 \times N$ matrix.

$$X = (X_1, X_2, X_3, \ldots, X_N)$$

The system can occupy any one of the N states at any point in time and may move to another state or remain in its current state over time. The probability that the system will move from one state to another or remain in its current state in the next increment of time depends only on the two states, current and transition states. That is, the move from state X_i to state X_j in the next time increment $(t + 1)$ depends on the probability of transition from state X_i to state X_j; and it is independent of how the system arrived at state X_i. It should be noted that the system's "memory" extends back only to the previous state. The dynamics of transition can be represented by a matrix of the form

$$P = \begin{bmatrix} P_{11} & P_{12} & P_{13} & \cdots & P_{1N} \\ P_{21} & P_{22} & P_{23} & \cdots & P_{2N} \\ P_{31} & P_{32} & P_{33} & \cdots & P_{3N} \\ \vdots & \vdots & \vdots & \cdots & \vdots \\ P_{N1} & P_{N2} & P_{N3} & \cdots & P_{NN} \end{bmatrix}$$

The rows of matrix P must sum to unity since the system must be in one of the N states at any given time. Matrix P is stochastic and is known as the stochastic transitional probability matrix for a discrete stationary Markov process. We will simply call P a transition matrix. The entities of matrix P are the following conditional probabilities:

$$P_{ij} = P(X_j|X_i)$$

That is, P_{ij} is the probability that the system moves to state X_j assuming that it is at state X_i. In general, the transition matrix, P, is time dependent. That is, for any time interval $(t_n - t_{n-1})$, we may have a different transition matrix, P_n. However, for reliability applications we can assume that the transition matrix P remains the same over the life of the system.

Let p_i be the probability that the system is at state X_i. Define Π as a $1 \times N$ matrix whose elements are p_i, for $i = 1, 2, \ldots, N$ as

$$\Pi = [p_1\, p_2\, p_3 \cdots p_N]$$

Then $\Pi(n)$ is the collective probability matrix corresponding to the N states of the system at time $t = n$. Note that the sum of the N elements of Π must always be 1. Matrix $\Pi(0)$ represents the initial configuration of the system. All but one of the elements of $\Pi(0)$ are zero. The only nonzero element of $\Pi(0)$ is a 1 and corresponds to the initial state of the system. The relationship between $\Pi(n)$ and $\Pi(n + 1)$ is defined as follows:

$$\Pi(n + 1) = \Pi(n) \times P$$

where P is the transition matrix of the system. Using this relation we have

$$\Pi(1) = \Pi(0) \times P$$
$$\Pi(2) = \Pi(1) \times P$$
$$\Pi(3) = \Pi(2) \times P$$
$$\cdot \qquad \cdot \quad \cdot$$
$$\cdot \qquad \cdot \quad \cdot$$
$$\cdot \qquad \cdot \quad \cdot$$
$$\Pi(n) = \Pi(n-1) \times P$$

From here we can conclude that

$$\Pi(k) = \Pi(0) \times P^k$$

It is possible that the process will converge in the long term to a steady state wherein transitions are unaffected by previous system performance so that over time the system will occupy a state with constant probability. That is,

$$\Pi = \Pi \times P$$

Example 17.3.3

Suppose we have the following transition matrix corresponding to a system with two states:

$$P = \begin{bmatrix} 0.6 & 0.4 \\ 0.2 & 0.8 \end{bmatrix}$$

Assume that initially the system is at state 1 with probability 1 and at state 2 with probability 0. Therefore, $\Pi(0) = [1 \quad 0]$.

$$\Pi(1) = \Pi(0) \times P = [0.600 \quad 0.400]$$
$$\Pi(2) = \Pi(1) \times P = [0.440 \quad 0.560]$$
$$\Pi(3) = \Pi(2) \times P = [0.376 \quad 0.624]$$
$$\Pi(4) = \Pi(3) \times P = [0.350 \quad 0.650]$$
$$\Pi(5) = \Pi(4) \times P = [0.340 \quad 0.660]$$
$$\Pi(6) = \Pi(5) \times P = [0.336 \quad 0.664]$$

The reader is encouraged to confirm these values by performing the indicated operations. As we can see, $\Pi(n)$ and $\Pi(n + 1)$ appear to converge to a limit. That is, Π is approaching its limit. Let us assume when we approach the steady state of the system, p is the probability of the system going to state X_1 and q is the probability of the system going to state X_2. With these assumptions, we have

$$[p \quad q] = [p \quad q] \times \begin{bmatrix} 0.6 & 0.4 \\ 0.2 & 0.8 \end{bmatrix}$$

or

$$[p \quad q] = [0.6p + 0.2q \quad 0.4p + 0.8q]$$

or

$$p = 0.6p + 0.2q \text{ and } q = 0.4p + 0.8q$$

The last 2 equations are not independent and they reduce to the single equation $q = 2p$. From this equation and the fact that $p + q$ must always be 1 we conclude that $p = 1/3$ and $q = 2/3$. As we can see, $\Pi(6)$ is very close to the steady state of the system.

17.4   RELIABILITY DEFINITIONS   ■

Failures in systems that include both hardware and software have been observed to occur randomly in time and be independent of each other. There is more evidence to support this observation in the hardware domain than in the software domain. However, most if not all software reliability models are based on these two assumptions.

A formal definition of reliability originally provided by the Electronics Industries Association [4] and still valid is as follows: *"Reliability is the probability of a device performing its purpose adequately for the period of time intended under operating conditions encountered."* In one form or another this definition is accepted as standard. It can be applied to systems and hardware or software subsystems. There are four important elements to this definition: probability, adequate performance, operating time, and operating conditions.

The probability element is best described by an example. If the reliability of a system, subsystem, or device is 0.95 for a 100-hour operating period, the device will operate successfully for 100 hours with probability 0.95; or in slightly different terms, in an experiment employing 100 such devices, at the end of 100 hours it is expected that 5 of the 100 devices will have experienced a failure. We sometimes say that the device has a 95 percent chance of surviving 100 hours of operation. Reliability is a quantifiable, probabilistic parameter used to describe or specify one aspect of system or component performance.

Adequate performance is defined by function and performance requirements specifications. As long as the performance of the product is within the range defined in the requirements specification, we say the product is performing adequately. A good descriptive example (the four-engine aircraft) of adequate performance is given in section 17.2.

Operating time represents the duration over which adequate performance of the device or system is to be maintained. Operating time requirements are derived from a knowledge of overall system needs. As an example, consider the manufacturer of refrigerators who offers a one-year unconditional guarantee on his product. It will be very important for him to know how his refrigerators will perform (how many will fail) over the one-year operating time. Clearly operating time is a critical element of a reliability specification.

Lastly, operating conditions (operating environment) are important in establishing a reliability specification. The operating environment of a system specifying temperature, dust, vibration, shock, and humidity in the case of physical components and operators and computer system characteristics in the case of software components is also an important element of a reliability requirement specification. In summary, any meaningful specification of a reliability attribute should include a clear description or specification of what is meant by adequate performance, applicable operating time, and applicable operating environment.

Quality is usually defined as follows: ''The degree of conformance of a device to applicable specifications and workmanship standards.'' Specifications and workmanship standards refer to function and performance specifications, various industry and company standards and procedures, or to specific reviews or tests required to confirm that a device or system is capable of performance within certain limits without reference to time. Good quality is clearly an important ingredient in producing highly reliable products.

As previously noted, reliability, $R(t)$, is defined as the probability that a device, component, unit, module, or system will function correctly (meet specifications) for a specified period of time in a specified operating environment. If T is a continuous random variable representing the specified failure-free service life, then reliability as a function of the length of any operating time t is defined by

$$R(t) = P(T > t)$$

The probability that the successful operating time will be greater than the specified service life, T, is often referred to as the probability of failure-free operation or the probability of survival. The function $R(t)$ is a monotonically decreasing function of time and

$$0 < R(t) < 1$$

$$R(0) = 1 \text{ and } R(\infty) = 0$$

The unreliability or probability of failure, $F(t)$, is obtained simply as follows:

$$F(t) = 1 - R(t) = P(T < t)$$

$F(t)$ is a monotonically increasing function of time and is often referred to as the cumulative distribution function of the service life, T. The derivative of $F(t)$ with respect to t

$$f(t) = \frac{dF(t)}{dt}$$

is the probability density function of the continuous random variable T, service life.

An important parameter in reliability work is the instantaneous failure rate. A failure is defined as an event in which the component fails to meet the specified performance. A failure rate is the rate at which these failures occur. To develop an analytic expression for the instantaneous failure rate, consider a device that has successfully survived for an operating period t. The conditional probability of failure in the next time increment dt is as follows:

$$P(t < T < t + dt | T > t) = \frac{P(t < T < t + dt)}{P(T > t)}$$

To show this recall that the conditional probability of two events A and B is given by

$$P(A|B) = \frac{P(A \cap B)}{P(B)}$$

Then if

$$A = \{t < T < t + dt\}$$

$$B = \{T > t\}$$

and

$$A \cap B = \{\{t < T < t + dt\} = A$$

we conclude that

$$P(t < T < t + dt \mid T > t) = \frac{P(t < T < t + dt)}{P(T > t)}$$

Recognizing that

$$P(t < T < t + dt) = F(t + dt) - F(t)$$

and that

$$P(T > t) = R(t)$$

we conclude that

$$P(t < T < t + dt \mid T > t) = \frac{[F(t + dt) - F(t)]}{R(t)}$$

The instantaneous failure rate, $Z(t)$, is then determined by dividing both sides of the expression for the probability of a failure occurrence in the interval t to $t + dt$, given that the device is operating at t, by dt and allowing dt to approach zero.

$$Z(t) = \lim_{dt \to 0} \frac{F(t + dt) - F(t)}{dt} \times \frac{1}{R(t)}$$

Therefore,

$$Z(t) = \frac{dF(t)}{dt} \times \frac{1}{R(t)} = \frac{F'(t)}{R(t)} = \frac{f(t)}{R(t)} \tag{17.4.1}$$

If we replace $R(t)$ with $[1 - F(t)]$ in $Z(t)$, we have

$$Z(t) = \frac{f(t)}{1 - F(t)}$$

We often refer to $Z(t)$, especially when it is written in this form, as the hazard function.

The reliability function, $R(t)$, and the probability density function, $f(t)$, can be expressed explicitly in terms of the hazard function $Z(t)$. Differentiating $F(t) = 1 - R(t)$ with respect to t yields

$$\frac{dF(t)}{dt} = \frac{-dR(t)}{dt}$$

or

$$F'(t) = -R'(t)$$

On the other hand, we had $Z(t) = F'(t)/R(t)$. Substituting for $F'(t)$ we get

$$Z(t) = \frac{-R'(t)}{R(t)}$$

Integrating this equation with respect to t we obtain

$$\int Z(t) \, dt = -\int \frac{R'(t)}{R(t)} \, dt = -\ln R(t)$$

and from this we have:

$$R(t) = e^{-\int_0^t Z(u)\ du} \qquad\qquad (17.4.2)$$

and

$$f(t) = Z(t)R(t) = Z(t)e^{-\int_0^t Z(u)\ du} \qquad\qquad (17.4.3)$$

As previously noted, $Z(t)$ for hardware failures can be closely approximated by a constant failure rate.

The following are five models for the hazard function:

1. Constant $Z(t) = \lambda$
2. Exponential decay $Z(t) = A \cdot e^{-Bt}$
3. Linear increasing $Z(t) = Kt$
4. Weibull $Z(t) = Kt^M$ for $M > -1$
5. Logarithmic $Z(t) = A/A\Theta + 1$

The first model, a constant failure rate model, has been used quite successfully in system and subsystem reliability work, including computer hardware reliability. Substituting in Equation (17.4.2) for $Z(t)$ the constant λ, we have

$$R(t) = e^{-\int_0^t \lambda\ du}$$

Since

$$\int_0^t \lambda du = \lambda t$$

we conclude that

$$R(t) = e^{-\lambda t}$$

and substituting for $Z(t)$ in Equation (17.4.3), we have

$$f(t) = \lambda e^{-\lambda t}$$

where λ is the mean failure rate.

The second model, an exponentially decreasing failure rate, has been used with various values for A and B, in software reliability work. The third model is a linearly increasing hazard function. This model, as well as the Weibull model has been proposed as a better approximation to certain observed software failure rate data. The fifth model, a logarithmic model, has also been proposed as an approximation to certain observed software failure rate data. Data collection and evaluation can be employed to confirm models or perhaps indicate applications where each of these models are best suited.

17.5 RELIABILITY MODELS ■

The ability to predict future behavior of a system accurately requires a model. A model is a representation of reality through a mathematical expression involving one or more measurable variables and parameters. The model is usually configured iteratively as a result of observations followed by analysis of the observation data and synthesis of a model. Subsequently, the model is used to predict future behavior. The model is either confirmed or modified to better match reality as a result of comparisons of predicted performance with actual observed performance. Some desirable model characteristics include the following:

Simplicity: Easy to understand and explain in terms of measurable and observable parameters. Only parameters that are important to performance are included in the model.

Completeness: All parameters that are important to performance are identified and included in the model. Model constraints and limitations are clearly stated and observed.

Accuracy: Matches real world in performance to the accuracy level desired.

Utility: Used to predict future behavior accurately. Provides better understanding of reality. Can replace reality for experiment purposes.

Validity: Model performance confirmed through exhaustive testing and constraints carefully defined to limit model application to regions where the model is valid.

Reliability models are structured based on observations and subsequently on controlled tests that provide confirmation of model efficacy. The value of the model, if the model is an accurate replication of the real world, is that we can control real-world performance by modulating or controlling certain parameters identified in the model. Hardware reliability models have led to improved design methods, better testing, better products, and ultimately to better models. The intention is for software reliability as a discipline to catch up with hardware reliability. There is much to be learned about software reliability by examining results in system and hardware reliability in some detail.

While hardware reliability models have been predicated on an observed constant failure rate, software reliability or hazard models have been based more on a logically or analytically derived failure rate. Figure 17.4 shows one rationale for cumulative software failure rates. The figure shows that initially, when a software product is introduced to the system test environment, reported failure rates are low because testers are not familiar with the product and have difficulty separating failures from test operator errors, errors in test cases, and

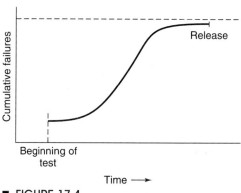

■ FIGURE 17.4

Cumulative software failure rate.

sources other than the test object. This period is followed by a test period in which failure rates are initially high but decline as testing continues and faults are removed. The failure rate declines until the software product is released. At this point the failure rate increases (sometimes dramatically) again, followed by a decline in failure rate until the next product release.

The explanation given for this failure rate behavior is that there is a learning curve for testers. Once testers become familiar with the product, the resident faults in the software product are more easily detected. Since software faults, once corrected, are unlikely to cause other failures, the rate at which faults are found declines as faults are eliminated. Software products are released when failure rates reach some established threshold. Shortly after release there is usually an increase in failure rates due to more users (more execution time), different environments, and different test cases. This scenario is followed by a declining failure rate as faults are removed. Each subsequent release follows essentially the same failure rate pattern. This pattern has been observed frequently in software development and in operational use.

The following equation

$$R(t) = e^{-\int_0^t Z(u)du}$$

represents a family of software reliability models, in which $Z(u)$ is the hazard function. $Z(u)$ may be represented by 5 different models (see page 507), each of which will give us a software reliability model. The simplest $Z(u)$ is when $Z(u)$ is a constant value equal to an average software failure rate. This will result in a reliability model represented by the following equation:

$$R(t) = e^{-\lambda t}$$

17.6 SOFTWARE FAULTS   ■

A software fault (defined as an intrinsic error in the software) can stem from a wide variety of possible sources. Table 17.1 lists possible sources for software faults. One might argue that an error in a test driver that masks a software failure and fault or an error in a compiler that introduces a subtle software fault is not a true software product fault. In terms of a software failure, its effect is the same as a design or coding error. In particular, the software product fails to meet stated function and performance requirements while operating in the design environment.

From the preceding discussion it would seem clear that the constant failure rate model employed for hardware failure rates does not adequately describe software failure rates. On the other hand, for mature software products, assuming a constant failure rate over relatively short time intervals might yield a conservative reliability prediction. A number of software reliability models are based on a fault-proportional failure rate. That is, failure rates are proportional to the faults remaining in the software product.

A data collection and analysis task was undertaken by the Rome Air Development Center (RADC) in 1987 [7] with the objective of producing a software reliability handbook equivalent to the hardware reliability handbooks. Table 17.2 is a three-part table derived from an analytical standpoint, A and C, compared with results from the RADC work, B.

As in other aspects of software development, particularizing failure rate studies to the

■ TABLE 17.1 **Source of Faults in Software**

Errors in requirement statements
Errors in requirement interpretation
Errors in design
Errors in coding
Errors in test plans and procedures
Poor quality reviews/audits/walk-throughs
Errors in documentation
Errors in compilers/assemblers/tools/libraries
Errors in test drivers and simulators
Intermittent hardware failures including single-event upsets in hardware
Operator errors
Host system software errors

development team and to the specific product or class of products is essential. Software development projects will find it useful to collect and categorize information on all failures and faults encountered in development of software products. A well-run testing environment will routinely document all relevant information regarding a failure/fault. The development of a data collection process for all failures experienced during software product development followed by an analysis of fault sources can identify areas for subsequent improvement of the entire development process. It is important to note that software testing is more than simply a test of the software product; it is also a test of the development team and the development process.

■ TABLE 17.2 **Results of Failure Rate Studies**

A. Typical Initial Fault Densities at Initiation of System Test (Composite)

2–5	Faults per 100 assembly instructions Quality level 1 (no Q & A)
0.2–0.5	Faults per 100 assembly instructions Quality level 2 (Moderate Q & A)
0.02–0.5	Faults per 100 assembly instructions Quality level 3 (Extensive Q & A)

B. From RADC Data (Keyed to COCOMO Model) (at Initiation of System Test)

0.8–1	Faults per 100 SLOC; organic mode
0.55–0.65	Faults per 100 SLOC; semidetached mode
0.1–0.3	Faults per 100 SLOC; embedded mode

C. Derived from 1 Error per 100 SLOC Baseline (at Initiation of System Test)

1	Fault per 100 SLOC at inception of system test; no formal reviews or quality control measures applied
0.5	Faults per 100 SLOC; modest reviews and some quality control applied [5]
0.25	Faults per 100 SLOC; a highly disciplined review structure and strong quality control measures applied [5]

For example, finding many design errors or faults that should have been recognized during the review/audit/walk-through process should lead to a careful evaluation of the quality of the review/audit/walk-through process and perhaps to a change in personnel and procedures. The importance of following each software fault to its source cannot be overstated. For projects of significant size with a long development cycle, early evaluation of software faults (even during unit test) can be fed back to the development process to improve the development process in real time, the argument that we don't have time or we can't spare the resources notwithstanding. Table 17.3 shows an example of a fault/failure data collection form. Forms such as these should be personalized to the project and product to be fully effective.

Failures encountered in software or system test frequently exhibit an elusiveness in terms of locating the fault that caused the failure. Either the failure cannot be repeated or there is no apparent reason for the failure. It is failures of this type that emphasize the need for close communication of all development team members. The most difficult faults to locate are those

■ TABLE 17.3   **Fault/Failure Data Collection Form**

CASE number (ID) _____   Date initiated _____

How detected

☐ Hand calculation   ☐ Personnel communication
☐ Infinite loop   ☐ Interrupt error
☐ Incorrect output   ☐ Missing output
☐ Other (Please explain) _____   _____

Hours spent on diagnosis _____

Number of executions required to locate the error _____

Software change required (reason)	Nature of change	Software change not required
☐ Mission	☐ Documentation	☐ H/W problem
☐ Engineering model	☐ Instruction	☐ Support S/W
☐ S/W implementation	☐ Constants	☐ Test error
☐ Hardware	☐ Structural	☐ Not reportable
☐ Other (explain)	☐ Algorithmic	☐ No error
	☐ Other (explain)	☐ Other (explain)

Correction	Correction implementation
☐ Spec. error	☐ Number of executions
☐ Incomplete spec.	☐ CPU time
☐ Program error	☐ Labor hours
☐ I/O software	
☐ Support software	
☐ Software interface	
☐ Hardware interface	
☐ Other (explain)	

Other information

Program type	Program complexity
☐ Database control	☐ Simple
☐ Algorithm	☐ Moderate
☐ Hybrid	☐ High
	☐ Very high

that involve errors of omission in documentation of hardware and system software that result in incorrect use of either hardware or system software features in software design or coding. These are difficult to find for two reasons: (1) there is a reluctance to accept responsibility for finding the fault if it is not clear whose subsystem has caused the failure; and (2) these faults usually cause failures only when a unique combination of events in space and time occur. These failure conditions are often difficult to replicate in the test environment.

Intermittent hardware failures can manifest themselves as software failures. One common intermittent hardware failure that has been identified as a potential source for software failure symptoms is the single-event upset of a single bit in a microcircuit. The effect is caused by the impact of a high-energy particle on a critical junction in a microcircuit that changes the state of one bit. Most computer memories are protected by error correction and detection logic, but there is a suspicion that some elusive apparent software failures could actually be triggered by a single-event upset or some other similar intermittent hardware failure. These events are virtually impossible to replicate.

Modeling software failure rates is difficult for the following reasons: (1) data collection, editing, and evaluation are usually not well standardized; (2) raw failure data is suspect because of innocent errors of omission and commission; (3) software products vary widely in characteristics, use, and quality; (4) there is a built-in resistance to employing models to predict software reliability. Eventually ongoing research efforts, user pressures, and the use of computers and software to automate sensitive functions involving loss of substantial resources and human life will result in handbooks, models, and development guidelines.

17.7   DESIGN RULES ■

We can point to ten specific steps that will lead to a reduction in software failure rates or at least accelerate the rate at which faults are discovered. Most of these rules emerged from the study of system and software reliability models and evaluation of the results obtained from such models. One should keep in mind that several studies have shown that a human being will make one or two mistakes for every one hundred operations performed. Software developers are not immune to human errors.

1. Design for simplicity.
   - Makes it easier to locate problems during reviews.
   - Complexity and cleverness frequently conceal flaws in logic or reasoning and obscure potential error sources.
2. Avoid overstressing memory and CPU.
   - CPU and memory-constrained software designs are potential sources of error.
3. Apply quality assurance rigorously to all aspects of the development process, even to the quality assurance process and procedure itself.
   - Apply to all products, tools, subproducts, and reviews.
   - Apply to quality assurance process.
   - Enforce all procedures and standards to the letter.
   - Attention to what some might regard as trivial details can sometimes lead to exposure of deeper problems.
4. Establish a projectwide reputation for tough, objective, no-nonsense technical reviews.
   - Make each review an effort to prove that it won't work.
   - Avoid skipping any steps in the review process.

- Motivate reviewers to find the flaws.
- Force thorough preparation for each review.
5. Understand the requirements.
    - Take the time to understand thoroughly the application area and the user.
    - Assume a direct responsibility for ensuring the completeness and correctness of the SRS.
6. Control change activity.
    - Maintain formal records of all changes (configuration control).
    - Recognize that changes will affect cost and schedule and factor into planning.
    - Keep client and management aware of change activity and potential impact.
7. Follow good engineering practices during testing.
    - Document all test cases, test results, and anomalies. Test to expose weakness.
    - Run every failure and anomaly to its source, including intermittent and transient failure occurrences.
    - Document all failures and anomalies fully, even those faults not found.
    - Document all corrections.
    - Control full configuration.
8. Recognize that errors or faults in tools, system software, test drivers, and other subsystems can sometimes manifest themselves as software failures in the object product.
    - Recognize that software results can be used to locate faults in other subsystems.
9. Burn in software.
    - Many versions running in different environments for many hours with different operators will expose more faults and hasten the reduction in intrinsic faults.
    - Exercising configuration control over all versions of the software product is essential.
10. Failure modes and effects analysis (FMEA) and fault tree analysis (FTA), discussed in section 17.11, when selectively applied to specific software functions can also result in exposure of certain software faults.

17.8 SYSTEM RELIABILITY AND AVAILABILITY REQUIREMENTS ■

Reliability requirements for given system functions are usually determined as part of the system requirements analysis effort. Some of the driving factors include the following: safety concerns; cost or impact of a failure; ability to work around a given failure (manual intervention, for example); realizable reliability performance of hardware, software, and operators; mission timelines; and probabilities associated with failure of subsystem components. Figure 17.5 is a schematic describing an approach to developing system reliability requirements. In this example, mission requirements analyses identify specific modules (hardware, software, and operators) needed to implement a given system requirement or function. The mission duration and the mission environment are also established, along with a clear specification of success criteria for the function. In the case of software, execution time is more important than mission duration. For hardware, operating time is more important than mission duration. Combining environment, mission duration, and operating time with estimates of hardware failure rates derived from handbooks (for example, MIL HDBK 217E [3]) provides an initial estimate of hardware reliability (or failure probability).

In similar fashion software reliability could be estimated. Unfortunately there are at present no accepted standard handbooks for software reliability available. If there were, hardware

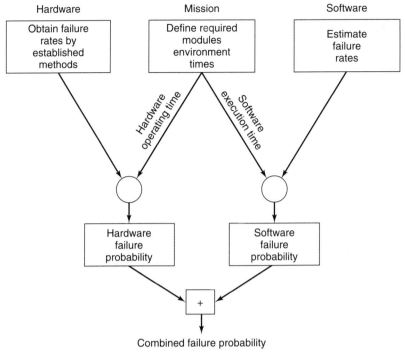

■ **FIGURE 17.5**

Developing system reliability requirements.

and software estimates could then be combined to produce an estimate of probability of successful completion of the system function over the required period of time in the specified environment. If the results of this process fail to meet reliability requirements, the process can be repeated using different allocations, different hardware components, redundancy, or any other plausible method to achieve the reliability requirement. Difficulty in meeting reliability needs of a system usually means there is a significant risk associated with the development. This risk should be addressed during risk analysis.

Example 17.8.1:

As a simple example, consider a system function that controls the operation of a manufacturing process. The process involves a computer, two sensors, an actuator, a portion of an operating system, and an application software product. Figure 17.6 shows a block diagram of the implementation. For this example we might find that the sensors, electronic devices, are operational 100% of the time. The computer and operating system, which are also employed to perform other system functions, are found to be operational 60% of the time. The application software product is executed ten times per second but for only 1/100 of a second each time. The actuator, an electromechanical device powered from the computer, executes ten times per second but on average is active for only about 1/50 of a second each time.

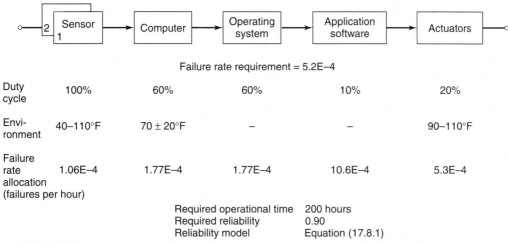

Failure rate requirement = 5.2E–4

	Sensor 2 1	Computer	Operating system	Application software	Actuators
Duty cycle	100%	60%	60%	10%	20%
Environment	40–110°F	70 ± 20°F	–	–	90–110°F
Failure rate allocation (failures per hour)	1.06E–4	1.77E–4	1.77E–4	10.6E–4	5.3E–4

Required operational time   200 hours
Required reliability   0.90
Reliability model   Equation (17.8.1)

■ **FIGURE 17.6**

Operation of manufacturing process.

Having characterized operating time for each subsystem, the next step is to obtain estimates for achievable hardware and software reliability, that is, to determine what constitutes reasonable reliability allocations. By examining specific hardware components, a reliability analyst can predict the reliability of the hardware elements that lie in the function path. Many manufacturers have reliability estimates for their products already available. For new designs estimates can be obtained by synthesis from handbook information. Software estimates are not so easily obtained. From such an analysis, allocations can be made for each component and designers can begin to go about meeting the requirements. In this example, for simplicity, we allocated on equal reliability requirement to each of the 5 system components.

Assuming the system is required to work 200 hours with a required reliability of 0.90, the objective of this example is to compute the mean failure rate for each of the 5 components of the system as well as the system itself.

We use the reliability model

$$R(t) = e^{-\lambda t}$$
(17.8.1)

where λ = mean failure rate and t = operating time, to compute the mean failure rate. The results of our computations are tabulated as follows:

Component	Required Operating Time in Hours	Failure Rate Allocation/Hour	Reliability Allocation
Sensors	200	1.06E-4	0.979
Computer	120	1.77E-4	0.979
Operating System	120	1.77E-4	0.979
Application Product	20	10.6E-4	0.979
Actuators	40	5.3E-4	0.979
Overall System	200	5.3E-4	0.90

The probability allocated to each component of the system was driven by the fact that

$$R(t) = R_1(t) \times R_2(t) \times R_3(t) \times R_4(t) \times R_5(t).$$

Where $R(t)$ is the reliability required of the entire system, and $R_i(t)$ is the reliability allocated to the ith component. Since we allocated the same reliability to each component we obtained:

$$R(t) = (R_i(t))^5$$

or

$$0.90 = (R_i(t))^5$$

from here the value of 0.979 was obtained for $R_i(t)$.

17.8.1   Availability

Another parameter related to reliability is called availability. Availability is often a more meaningful system performance parameter. Availability takes into account the ability to repair a system and restore it to operating condition. The definition of *availability* is the probability that a system (subsystem or module) is fit for operation at a time t. Availability can also be stated in terms of the amount of expected downtime over a specified time interval. To take a specific example, the telephone switching system might have a 2 minute per year specification for expected downtime. Clearly then, availability depends on the probability that a repair is required at time t as well as the length of time required to effect the repair. The probability that a repair is needed depends, of course, on the reliability of the system. To develop an expression for availability requires definition of two terms, mean time to failure (MTTF) and mean time to repair (MTTR). If $R(t)$ is the reliability function for the system, then

$$\text{MTTF} = \int_0^\infty R(t)\, dt$$

Or if it is known that there have been n failures occuring at times $t_1, t_2, \ldots, t_n$, then we have

$$\text{MTTF} = \frac{1}{n} \sum_{i=1}^{i=n} t_i$$

The reciprocal of MTTF is called the hazard function. For example, if $R(t)$ is as shown in Equation (17.8.1), then MTTF is $1/\lambda = 1/Z$.

Mean time to repair is defined as the average time required to effect a maintenance action. Its reciprocal, $r(t)$, is called the repair hazard. Therefore,

$$\text{MTTF} = \frac{1}{Z(t)}$$

and

$$\text{MTTR} = \frac{1}{r(t)}$$

One can employ a Markov process to derive an expression for availability.

A schematic of the process is shown in Figure 17.7. Briefly, the probability that the system will change from state X_1 to state X_2 in the time interval dt is $Z(t)\, dt$, and the probability that the system will be restored to state X_1 is $r(t)\, dt$. $Z(t)$ is the mean failure rate and $r(t)$ is the reciprocal of the average maintenance or repair cycle. Modeling the behavior of this two-state system as a Markov process produces a set of linear differential equations by the following process:

$$[p(t + dt)\ q(t + dt)] = [p(t)\ q(t)] \times \begin{bmatrix} a & b \\ c & d \end{bmatrix}$$

where

$$a = 1 - Z(t)\, dt \qquad b = Z(t)\, dt$$
$$c = r(t)\, dt \qquad d = 1 - r(t)\, dt$$

which upon substitution yields

$$p(t + dt) = p(t)[1 - Z(t)\, dt] + q(t)r(t)\, dt$$
$$q(t + dt) = p(t)Z(t)\, dt + q(t)[1 - r(t)\, dt]$$

or

$$\frac{p(t + dt) - p(t)}{dt} = q(t)r(t) - p(t)Z(t)$$

$$\frac{q(t + dt) - q(t)}{dt} = p(t)Z(t) - q(t)r(t)$$

or

$$\frac{d[p(t)]}{dt} + p(t)Z(t) = q(t)r(t)$$

$$\frac{d[q(t)]}{dt} + q(t)r(t) = p(t)Z(t)$$

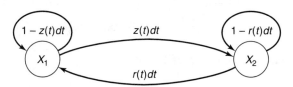

$r(t)$ = Repair hazard
$z(t)$ = Failure hazard

■ FIGURE 17.7

Two-state Markov process.

With initial conditions $p(0) = 1$ and $q(0) = 0$, we find the solutions for these differential equations as follows:

$$P(t) = \frac{r(t)}{r(t) + Z(t)} + \frac{Z(t)}{r(t) + Z(t)} e^{-(r(t)+Z(t))t}$$

$$q(t) = \frac{Z(t)}{r(t) + Z(t)} - \frac{Z(t)}{r(t) + Z(t)} e^{-(r(t)+Z(t))t}$$

The probability that the system is operational, $p(t)$, is the desired availability expression. Note that as t increases, the first term dominates and eventually a steady state availability is reached; at which point

$$p(t) = \frac{r(t)}{Z(t) + r(t)}$$

or in terms of MTTF and MTTR, we have

$$p(t) = A = \frac{\text{MTTF}}{\text{MTTF} + \text{MTTR}}$$

where A is the availability, the probability that the system is in service.

Example 17.8.2

To see how one can respond to a combined reliability and availability specification, assume that an availability of .999 per year (2000 hours of operation) in system service is acceptable, which translates into an availability

$$A = \frac{r}{Z + r} = 0.999$$

or

$$r = 999 \times Z$$

There are many combinations of failure rate and repair hazard that can meet this requirement. However, if a reasonable system reliability for one year, 2000 hours of operation, is set to be 0.9, and the hazard function is considered to be a constant failure rate, λ, then a failure rate of 5.3E-5 is obtained from Equation (17.4.1).

$$R(t) = e^{-\lambda t}$$
$$0.9 = e^{-\lambda 2000}$$
$$\lambda = \frac{-ln0.9}{2000} = 0.000053 = 5.3E\text{-}5$$

We can then compute r from $r = 999 \times Z$.

$$r = 999 \times 5.3E\text{-}5$$

$$r = 5.3E\text{-}2 = 0.053$$

Therefore, MTTR is approximately 19 hours (18.81). Mean time to repair and mean time to failure values can be traded to achieve realistic design goals for both system equipment (and software) and maintenance hardware and software requirements. The availability based on the combination of a mean time to repair of 19 hours and a reliability for one year of 0.9 yields a probability of the system being in service of 99.9%.

Example 17.8.3

A requirement for a 0.975 probability of no interruption of service greater than 10 seconds might be imposed on certain air traffic control functions. To meet this requirement with state-of-the-art hardware/software reliability of say 0.37 for a one-year period of continuous operation (8766 hours) implies an availability of 0.999999842 and a mean time to repair of approximately 5 seconds. The 5-second MTTR is needed to assure that 97.5% of the interruptions will not exceed 10 seconds. The following computations confirm these numbers.

$$R(t) = e^{-\lambda t}$$
$$R(t) = 0.37$$
$$t = 8766$$
$$0.37 = e^{-\lambda 8766}$$
$$Z(t) = d = 0.000113421$$
$$\text{MTTF} = \frac{1}{Z(t)} = 8816.676002 \text{ Hours}$$
$$A = \frac{\text{MTTF}}{\text{MTTF} + \text{MTTR}}$$

Since the probability of no service interruption over a full year of continuous service is 0.975, we must have an MTTR of 5 to 6 seconds to guarantee that 97.5% of the time the repair takes less than 10 seconds. With this assumption we have

$$A = \frac{8816.676002}{8816.676002 + \dfrac{5}{3600}} = 0.999999842$$

Requirements such as these lead to the need for redundant systems and fault-tolerant systems. As we shall see, redundancy offers a way to improve both reliability and availability. In the air traffic control case, the need to make repairs in less than 5 seconds implies automatic error detection and correction schemes for both hardware and software failures.

17.9 APPLICATION OF A SOFTWARE RELIABILITY MODEL ■

Several reliability models have been developed for software. For reasons already discussed, the problem of confirming a software reliability model is difficult. Nevertheless, several of the available models, if appropriately tailored to the application and environment, can produce useful results. The most useful applications are in testing the software product. Reliability models can be effective in predicting the mean time to failure of a software product; in estimating the number of faults remaining in a given software product, estimating the number of failures that will have to occur and faults located and repaired in order to reach a particular mean time to failure; and estimating the number of hours of CPU execution time required to force a given number of failures. Estimates of these software-related reliability attributes are valuable in making decisions regarding test duration, test resources, and product release.

There is an intuitive connection between cost and the requirement for a software product with high reliability. The increased cost comes from the application of formal quality assurance, additional reviews, more formal documentation, and extended formal testing. It will require extensive data gathering and thoughtful analysis for a development team to establish an accurate, quantifiable link between reliability and specific quality assurance measures.

Of the many existing models for software reliability, we have selected for discussion the model developed by Musa [6]. It is very similar to a model developed by Shooman [10]. Most software reliability models are similar in structure. The Musa model assumes that the rate at which software failures occur is proportional to the number of faults, MO, remaining in the software. Moreover, the assumptions for Musa's model do not require that every software failure result in a reduction by one of the resident faults. The hazard function for Musa's model is an exponentially decreasing function of time. Musa assumes that the number of faults are related to the occurrence of failures, NO, by

$$MO = B \times NO$$

where MO = total number of latent faults resident in the software product at delivery to the system test phase and NO = total number of failures that must be experienced to locate and correct MO. Parameter B is a measure of the effectiveness of the fault location and correction process. A number of factors can influence B. Most of these factors are dependent on product, development team, and the development environment.

The initial failure rate, LO, is assumed to be related to the total number of faults, MO, through the rate at which instructions are executed and a variable of proportionality, K. That is,

$$LO = KfMO$$

where f, the frequency at which instructions are executed, is determined by taking the ratio of average instruction execution rate to the total number of assembly language instructions in the software product.

$$f = \frac{\text{Average instruction execution rate}}{\text{Total number of instructions to be executed}}$$

The parameter K accounts for the variety of different execution paths that may be taken through a software product, the operational timeline, and other product-dependent factors that influence the rate at which instructions pass through the CPU. The variable K is also sensitive to the software product, development team, development environment, and operational environment.

Parameters B and K can be estimated from a development team's prior experience base or obtained from the literature [2,6]. An acceptable range for B is [0.8 0.95] and for K is [1.3E-7 3.2E-7]

A software reliability model can also be derived directly from the following assumptions: (1) software failures occur randomly in time, (2) software failures are independent in the short term (that is, they do not appear to depend on past history), and (3) software fails only when it is being executed. In order not to confuse the system operation time, t, with software execution time, we denote the latter by ξ. Given these assumptions, a Poisson distribution may be used as follows to compute the number of failures in the software being executed. The following equation, then, will compute the number of failures:

$$P(N(\xi) = n) = \frac{u(\xi)}{n!} = e^{-u(\xi)}$$

where

$$N(\xi) = \text{failures as a function of CPU time}$$

$$n = \text{number of failures}$$

$$u(\xi) = \text{number of failures expected to occur in execution time } \xi$$

As can be seen, the probability that n failures will have occurred in ξ CPU time units is a function of the number of software failures, $u(\xi)$, expected to occur in execution time ξ.

Our main interest lies in the zero failure case, that is, the probability that we will encounter no failures in a given time interval. We are interested in

$$P(N(\xi) = 0) = e^{-u(\xi)}$$

The exponent, $u(\xi)$, can be interpreted as the number of failures expected to occur in a given CPU execution time interval, ξ. The expression $u(\xi)$ plays the same role as $Z(t)$ in the previous development. As we have already noted, the hardware reliability model employs

$$u(\xi) = \frac{1}{\text{MTTF}} \times \text{operating time}$$

or

$$u(\xi) = \text{failure rate} \times \text{operating time}$$

as a model for expected failures in a given operating or service time interval. For hardware the failure rate is assumed to be a constant. A similar model could be assumed for failures in mature software. The fact that every failure does not result in a fault removal (fault removal attempts may in fact inject new faults) and that many software failures are due, at least in part, to randomly occurring events in hardware and operator actions is a strong argument in favor of assuming a constant failure rate for mature software. Such an assumption would probably result in software reliability estimates that are somewhat conservative. Another representation or model for software failure rate is one in which the failure rate declines exponentially as faults are removed. In this representation, the cumulative failures $N(\xi)$ could be modeled as a function of time [1,6,10], as follows

$$N(\xi) = MO(1 - e^{\frac{LO}{MO} \xi})$$

Then $u(\xi)$ is obtained by assuming that the rate of failure occurrence is proportional to the number of faults remaining in the software product rather than a constant. That is, if the remaining number of faults, $M(\xi)$, is given by

$$M(\xi) = MO - MR(\xi)$$

where $MR(\xi)$ = faults removed as a function of CPU execution time, we then have

$$\frac{dN(\xi)}{d\xi} = K' \times (MO - MR(\xi))$$

where K' is a constant of proportionality ($K = LO/MO$).

If every failure, N, experienced results in removal of BM faults, then from $N = BM$ we can write

$$\frac{dN(\xi)}{d\xi} = K' \times [MO - N(\xi)]$$

and

$$\frac{dN(\xi)}{d\xi} + K' \times N(\xi) = K' \times MO$$

which has the solution

$$N(\xi) = MO - MO \times e^{-K'\xi}$$

From initial conditions K' is found to be LO/MO and failure rate changes are obtained by differentiating $N(\xi)$ and noting that $k' = LO/MO$. The rate of failure occurrence per CPU time is determined as follows:

$$L(\xi) = LOe -\frac{LO}{MO}\xi$$

Since we now have a description of the remaining faults at any point in time and the instantaneous rate at which faults will manifest themselves as failures, we can project the

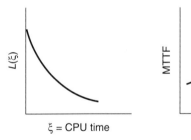

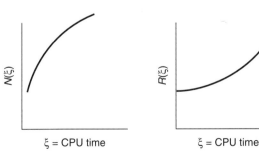

■ FIGURE 17.8

Typical behavior of model parameters.

CPU time, ξ, required to eliminate a given number of faults and the number of failures, u, that must be experienced to reach a target software failure rate, as follows:

$$\xi = \frac{MO}{LO} \times \ln\left(\frac{LO}{LD}\right)$$

and

$$u = \frac{MO}{LO} \times (LO - LD)$$

where LD is the desired failure rate set by the reliability requirement and LO is the initial failure rate. An important piece of information is the initial failure rate and the number of resident faults in the software product at inception of testing. Figure 17.8 illustrates the behavior of model parameters during testing and provides a means for better understanding model behavior.

Example 17.9.1

To illustrate an application of these tools in a test environment consider the following. One of the XYZ project's software products, consisting of 100,000 assembly language instructions, is delivered to system test. If previous experience or reference to available literature suggests a value for B of 0.9 and by a similar process we assume a value of 2.0E-7 for K, we can proceed to define other model parameters. If prior experience with software of this type developed by similar processes and procedures by teams of similar personnel indicates that initially we can expect three to four faults per thousand assembly language instructions, we might assign 3.5 faults per thousand instructions as the initial value for resident faults (see Table 17.2). From our knowledge of the instruction processing rate associated with the computer hardware, we can determine an average value for f. Assume, for the purposes of our example, that the instruction processing rate is 1.5E6, which yields an average value of 15 for f.

$$f = \frac{1.5E6}{100,000} = 15 \text{ execution cycles per second}$$

or

$$f = 5.41E4 \text{ execution cycles per hour}$$

$MO = 3.5$ faults per thousand assembly language instructions $\times 100,000 = 350$

The number of failures that must be experienced to eliminate all resident faults is computed as follows. Recalling that

$$MO = B \times NO$$

we obtain

$$NO = \frac{MO}{B} = \frac{350}{0.90} = 389$$

Continued on the following page.

Note that we have assumed $B = 0.90$ for our example. Substituting for K (assumed to be 2.0E-7), f, and MO in

$$LO = K \times f \times MO$$

we can expect

$$LO = (2.0\text{E-7})(5.41\text{E4})(350)$$

$$= 3.78 \text{ failures per CPU hour}$$

Armed with this basic information, associated with software product attributes and the general environment, we can now look to the reliability requirements allocated to the product. Recall that the specification for the reliability (probability of successful operation) of this product (the application software component of the previous example) was 0.980 for an operational period of two hundred hours. The duty cycle or CPU time during this 200 hour period was 10% or 20 hours. Strictly speaking, neither hardware nor software can fail when it is Off. Our objective in testing is to assure that a failure rate of approximately 1.0E-3 is achieved. We want to compute required CPU time and total number of faults that we must experience during testing time to achieve the required failure rate at delivery. From the reliability model

$$R(t) = e^{-\lambda t}$$

we compute λ.

$$0.98 = e^{-\lambda \times 20}$$

$$\ln 0.98 = -\lambda 20$$

$$\lambda = -\ln \frac{0.98}{20} = 0.001$$

The required CPU time is:

$$\xi = \frac{MO}{LO} \times \ln\left(\frac{LO}{LD}\right)$$

$$\xi = \frac{350}{3.78} \times \ln\left(\frac{3.78}{0.001}\right)$$

$$= 763 \text{ hours}$$

The expected number of faults within the required CPU time is:

$$u = \frac{MO}{LO} \times (LO - LD)$$

$$u = \frac{350}{3.78} \times (3.78 - 0.001)$$

$$= 349 \text{ faults}$$

The model gives us essential data that may now be used in technical planning. We have an estimate of the CPU time required to test the product to assure that reliability requirements will be met. We also have an estimate of the number of failures (and faults) we should encounter during this period. From this information, planning for the testing phase can proceed. The number of shifts required, the number of test runs, test cases, personnel requirements, calendar time, and debug and repair effort can also be estimated.

As you may have realized, this model depends heavily on the estimate of initial values for *MO* and *LO*. Also, the model depends to a lesser degree on the values for *B* and *K*. There is a good possibility that we have not made an accurate estimate of these attributes. By carefully monitoring cumulative failures, failure rates, and indirectly the two parameters *B* and *K*, a subsequent curve fit can improve estimates of remaining faults and failure rates. Just as in cost and schedule modeling, reliability model parameters must be tailored to applications, application development environments, and operational environments.

One advantage of this model is the fact that only CPU or execution time is used, eliminating model concerns about the ratio of test time to operational time. Another very useful feature of the Musa software reliability model is that it can be directly combined with hardware reliability models to compute overall system reliability.

Returning to our example, suppose subsequent testing experience during the first 50 CPU hours revealed the data in Table 17.4; then a comparison between the actual data and the estimated data in each column indicates that the initial values selected for the model have been most appropriate. However, if we experience an unacceptable difference between actual and estimated data early in the test process, we may fit a curve to

$$L(\xi) = LO(e - \frac{LO}{MO} \xi)$$

to give us better estimates for *LO* and *MO* and new estimates for testing time and failures.

An exponential curve fit to the actual data from the previous table can provide a new estimate of the number of resident faults and a new projection for test time in CPU hours and required number of failures that must be experienced to achieve desired mean time to failure. As a result of curve fitting we get new estimates: *MO* = 3.52 and *LO* = 325. These values are not appreciably different from the original estimates, so we would expect little or no change to our test plans. However, if the actual data were as shown in Table 17.5, then revised values for *MO* and *LO* from the curve fitting process would be *LO* = 2.95 and *MO* = 167. These values for *LO* and *MO* will in turn lead to new values for required CPU time and expected number of failures to achieve the required software failure rate. These new values would require a revision of our test plans.

The software engineer will need to work with system engineers and reliability analysts to understand reliability requirements and translate reliability requirements to requirements

---

■ TABLE 17.4   **Laboratory Testing Data (Edited)**

CPU TIME (HOURS)	FAILURES		AVERAGE FAILURE RATE		CUMULATIVE FAILURES	
	Actual	Estimate	Actual	Estimate	Actual	Estimate
0–10	32	34	3.2	3.4	32	34
10–20	31	30	3.1	3.0	63	64
20–30	28	27	2.8	2.7	91	91
30–40	23	25	2.3	2.5	114	116
40–50	21	22	2.1	2.2	135	138

■ TABLE 17.5 **Alternative Data Set**

CPU TIME (HOURS)	FAILURES		AVERAGE FAILURE RATE		CUMULATIVE FAILURES	
	Actual	Estimate	Actual	Estimate	Actual	Estimate
0–10	26	34	2.6	3.4	26	34
10–20	24	30	2.4	3.0	40	64
20–30	20	27	2.0	2.7	60	91
30–40	15	25	1.5	2.5	75	116
40–50	13	22	1.3	2.2	88	138

analysis, design, and test actions to assure that delivered software meets reliability requirements.

17.10 REDUNDANCY AND FAULT TOLERANCE ■

The term *redundancy* refers to a parallel or alternate path in a system architecture to meet system requirements in two or more independent ways. The purpose of a redundant system is to improve reliability. There are two general approaches to redundancy implementation, system redundancy and component redundancy. System redundancy involves the connection of two identical systems in parallel between system inputs and system outputs. In the event of a failure of the active system, the inactive or backup system can be switched on to replace the failed system. A variation of system redundancy is the use of a hot backup system. In this approach both prime and backup systems are in the On state. There are manual and automatic approaches to recognizing system failures and effecting a switchover from the failed system to the backup system. Figure 17.9 shows a practical example of a redundant system with automatic means for detecting failures and initiating a switchover and restart action. This configuration employs built-in tests (0.ww in the figure), a watchdog timer and a small, separate memory device to implement redundancy. The figure also shows each of the systems with redundant inputs *A* and *B*. The figure shows a range of typical values for the probability of successful failure detection and switchover. These values must be included in the system reliability calculation.

Software and firmware play a dominant role in the implementation of redundant systems. Many of the built-in tests are in software or embedded in firmware. Setting and resetting the watchdog timer and updating the checkpoint restart memory are software functions. Switchover and restart are also software functions.

The concept of component redundancy suggests making only those subsystems or components that are relatively unreliable redundant. In many cases, by making a few critical components in a system redundant, one can provide enough improvement in overall reliability to meet system reliability requirements. For example, in a redundant automobile braking

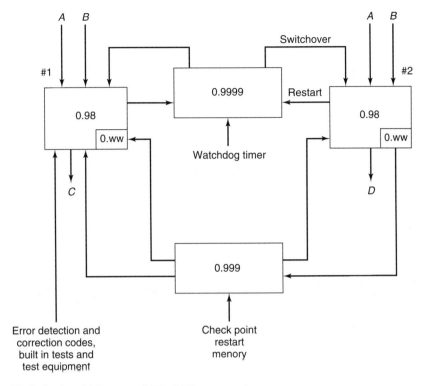

Typical values for 0.ww are 0.95 – 0.97.

■ **FIGURE 17.9**

Dual Redundancy.

system the brake pedal and linkage are not redundant (simplex) while the master brake cylinder is redundant. The same concerns in system redundancy implementation regarding failure detection and switchover are also found in component redundancy implementation. In the braking system just described, a failure of one master cylinder results in degraded braking performance. This system might be better described as fault tolerant.

The cost of a redundant system or a system with redundant components is, of course, greater than the cost of a simplex system. In the short term, it is definitely more expensive to use a redundant system. Therefore, the additional cost must be justified by a cost benefit analysis (Appendix B).

Reliability modeling for redundant systems is a straightforward application of probability theory. The total reliability of a string of *n* subsystems or components connected in a series configuration, Figure 17.10 (A), such that a failure in any one subsystem results in loss of the entire system's capability is determined by the product of the *n* individual subsystem reliabilities. The rule for serial connection is as follows:

$$R(t) = \prod_{i=1}^{i=n} R_i(t)$$

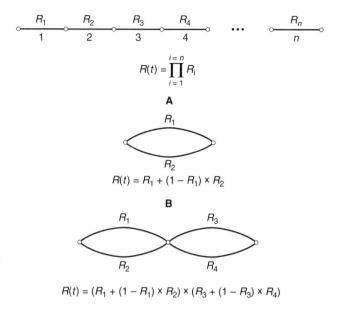

■ FIGURE 17.10

Serial, parallel, and combined system connections. **A**, Serial system connection; **B**, Parallel system connection; **C**, Combined system connection.

Two subsystems connected in parallel, as shown in Figure 17.10 (B), with the indicated reliabilities will have a total reliability of

$$R(t) = R_1 + (1 - R_1) \times R_2$$

The event representing system success is the union of R_1 and R_2.

The third configuration, shown in Figure 17.10 (C), illustrates the method for dealing with complex configurations. The configuration shows two parallel configurations connected in series. The total reliability of this configuration is given by

$$R(t) = (R_1 + (1 - R_1) \times R_2) \times (R_3 + (1 - R_3) \times R_4)$$

Systematic application of elementary series and parallel results can be used to reduce complex configurations and obtain a single reliability value for the entire configuration.

The implementation of redundancy and fault tolerance in most systems relies heavily on software. The software is frequently called upon to interpret sensor inputs from internal hardware checks such as built-in test equipment (BITE) and built-in tests (BIT), which often contain test firmware and other failure-sensing hardware and software. A commonly used method for detecting system failures is the watchdog timer. This method entails adding a simple timer that can be set and reset by a computer command and a separate memory element that can be accessed by both primary and backup systems. Initially, at the beginning of an operational period, the timer is set for, let us say one second. The application software is designed to include a module that transfers restart data at a particular rate to the separate memory location and resets the timer to zero before one second has elapsed. If the watchdog timer is not reset within one second, it generates a hardware interrupt that triggers a sequence of events that includes shutdown of one system and transfer of restart data to initialize the backup system. Some considerations associated with implementing a watchdog timer include the following:

1. Conditions under which the reset command will be issued
2. Specific data that must be saved in the separate memory location to initialize the backup system and the rate at which data must be saved.
3. Details of how the shutdown, start-up, and transfer of control will be effected and how the system will recover

In some circumstances the watchdog timer module will be designed to check on external error detection devices as well as internal BITE and BIT before deciding to issue the reset command. The selection of initialization data items is usually straightforward. The rate at which initialization data must be stored is usually a joint software/system consideration. The point at which the software restarts is sometimes referred to as the checkpoint. Developing a logical design for system restart and recovery of operational status that minimizes use of possibly contaminated data without introducing errors in time-based algorithms or missing important transactions is yet another design consideration requiring a joint effort among users, system engineers, and software engineers. How, precisely, power and control will be transferred and the sequence of restoration events must also be addressed jointly. Close communication among hardware, software, and system engineers is essential to developing a design approach that assures a smooth transition to the backup system.

There are several important points to be made regarding redundancy and redundancy management. First, software is frequently part of redundancy management and must itself be highly reliable. Second, design and implementation of redundant systems requires a blend of skills from several disciplines, all of which have a full appreciation of the general problem. Third, the modeling and analysis of redundant systems (and fault-tolerant systems) becomes very complex as the number of system states becomes larger. Fourth, testing redundant and fault-tolerant systems is a challenging assignment for a software engineer.

Thus far we have only scratched the surface of redundant systems and redundancy management issues. Some system designs have active backup units whereas others have inactive backup units. some systems have software developed by two independent development teams designed from two independently developed software requirements specifications to effect a software redundancy.

One must also be aware that adding redundancy to a system reduces intrinsic reliability simply because more components have been added. Even inactive backup systems have a finite probability that they will fail when turned on. Effective management of redundancy is a very challenging design problem for both the software and the system engineer.

Fault-tolerant systems are an extension to the idea embodied in employing redundant systems to improve reliability and availability. In principle, systems that are able to continue to perform their required functions in the face of the occurrence of faults are called fault-tolerant systems. That is, "a fault tolerant system will continue to produce correct results or actions even in the presence of faults or other anomalous or unexpected conditions" [8]. Redundancy is one way to improve the fault tolerance of a system. Other approaches include fault masking, fault containment, and automatic fault isolation and recovery.

A good example of a fault-tolerant module or component is the primary memory of many large computers. The memory unit contains special circuits that append a few parity bits to each word as it is stored in memory. When the same word is read from memory, any single bit error in the word can be detected and corrected by decoding the appended parity bits. Multiple failures are detected but not corrected. Each time a single-bit failure is detected, it is recorded so that a record of memory failures is maintained. Habitually failing memory units can be replaced at convenient times. Report of a multiple-bit failure in a word can be acted upon by removing that block of memory addresses or locations from use. Software or firmware is required to implement many fault-tolerant strategies. To appreciate fully how memory error detection and correction schemes improve reliability and availability of a computer system's memory, consider the following example.

Example 17.10.1

A typical eight-megabyte memory unit has an intrinsic failure rate of 1.28E-4 based on an intrinsic memory chip failure rate of 1.0E-6 per hour. Adding ten additional chips to implement error detection and correction logic and parity bits increases the memory unit failure rate to 1.38E-4. Figure 17.11 illustrates the example. Memory unit reliability for 1000 hours of continuous operation can be determined from

$$R(t) = e^{-\lambda t} = e^{-(1.38E\text{-}4)1000} = e^{-0.138} = 0.871$$

If error identification and memory switching takes 100 microseconds (MTTR = 3.0E-8 hours), the availability of this memory unit is very nearly unity.

$$A = \frac{MTTF}{MTTF + MTTR}$$

and

$$MTTF = \frac{1}{Z} = \frac{1}{1.38E\text{-}4} = 7246$$

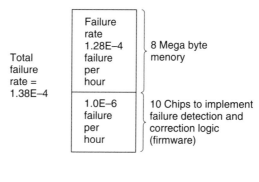

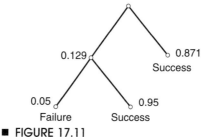

■ **FIGURE 17.11**

Redundant components.

Therefore,

$$A = \frac{7246}{(7246 + 0.00000003)} \simeq 1$$

which is approximately 100 percent.

A new reliability for a 1000-hour operating interval can be computed from the following:

$$R(t)_{\text{new}} = RI + PR \times PF$$

where RI is memory unit intrinsic reliability, PR is probability of the restoration of service given a fault occurrence, and PF is the probability of fault occurrence ($1 - RI$). Typical values for PR are 0.95 to 0.97. These values reflect software or firmware probability of successful error detection and correction.

$$R(t)_{\text{new}} = 0.871 + 0.95(1 - 0.871) = 0.9936$$

The models cited in this section are relatively simple and results are easily computed. To model redundancy and fault tolerance at more detailed levels usually requires application of Markov process analysis to models involving many system states. This process results in systems of homogeneous differential equations requiring computer solutions to obtain estimates for reliability and availability. However, simple models can often provide enough insight to answer reliability and availability questions.

17.11 FAILURE MODES AND EFFECTS AND OTHER ANALYSIS TOOLS ■

Other steps that are often taken to improve reliability and safety are failure modes and effects analysis (FMEA) and fault tree analysis (FTA) [4]. FMEA is an analytic approach based on inductive reasoning, often initiated to verify the safety features of a design. The procedure attempts to identify all failure modes and the effects of each identified failure mode on system safety and performance. This systematic procedure identifies the ways in which each subsystem or component might fail. For example, an interruption of power to a unit might be one of many unit failure modes. The analyst determines the failure mechanisms that lead to an interruption of power to the unit and then determines the overall effect on the system of loss of power to the unit in question. In general, this analysis is very labor intensive and expensive if applied exhaustively. The potential benefits in terms of improving reliability and safety of a design must be weighed against the cost of performing an FMEA before embarking on the FMEA effort. Products that involve public safety or where there is a high cost associated with failure are good candidates for a FMEA.

It is not unreasonable to expect that a failure modes and effects analysis would be directed at software components in a system. The analyst would list all the modules or units and for each identify all possible failure modes and the cause of the failure including operator error. Symptoms, method of detection or recognition, effects upon the system, compensating provisions, and any other observations would be recorded. Forms are often provided to assist in the analysis to assure uniformity of treatment.

A simple example might be a failure mode in which a protective system does not recognize a faulty sensor. The software associated with the protective system, shown in Figure 17.12, is required to read the sensor at a given rate to determine if the sensor value is within absolute

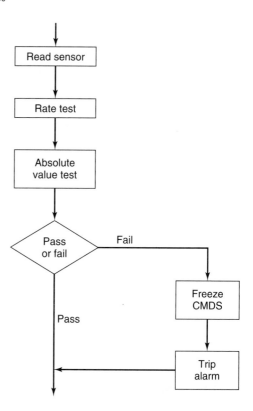

■ **FIGURE 17.12**

Software associated with protective system.

bounds and if the change in sensor value from reading to reading is within a predetermined range. If the sensor reading fails either of these tests, then the software must issue an alarm and freeze output commands at their last command values.

The FMEA would examine each potential failure mode for this module beginning with incorrect algorithms for the tests, incorrect settings for constants in the algorithms, etc. The effect of not issuing an alarm or not freezing the output commands would be thought through and recorded. The symptoms of the failure and any compensating provisions, such as the action of another protective device in another part of the system, would be recorded. An analysis such as this can surface latent errors in requirements interpretation and implementation and suggest tests that can increase confidence in module correctness.

Fault tree analysis is related to FMEA but is deductive rather than inductive in approach. The fault tree analysis produces a graphic view of a failure structure. Initially a particular undesired event is established. A tree of subevents that could lead to this undesired event is developed until a series of individual component failure probabilities can be related to the occurrence of the undesired event. The probability of occurrence can be estimated by assigning values to each subevent. As a simple example, consider the undesired event to be the inability to stop an aircraft while taxiing or landing. A second level of events (subevents) would include dual failures of the redundant hydraulic subsystem, brake lining contamination, and failure of the antilock braking subsystem.

The third level would examine each of these subevents in detail. The hydraulic system could fail because of a sequence of events that jammed valves, ruptured hydraulic lines, failed both hydraulic pumps, or failed electronic controls, or by a pilot error perhaps. The next step would involve finding out how a hydraulic valve could fail. Hydraulic valves can be jammed by contaminants in the oil or by electrical problems in the circuits in the electromechanical first stage. This process continues until a point is reached where a tree of faults has been established, each path of which could lead to loss of braking capability. A probability is computed or estimated for each subevent. This value is frequently obtained from handbook reliability data.

The fault tree built from this analysis is then the basis for further studies. Probability of occurrence is assigned to each event and a probability of occurrence of the original undesired event is calculated. Reliability data are frequently used to assign these probabilities. If the resulting probability of occurrence is unacceptable, a redesign takes place. The fault tree gets broader as we go deeper. Exhaustive application of this analysis is labor intensive and very expensive. Justification for expending resources on these analyses also lies in questions regarding public safety and cost of failure.

The principle value of fault tree analysis is its ability to do the following:

1. Guide the analyst to find hidden failure paths
2. Point out aspects of system, mechanism, or operation critical to the failure event being analyzed
3. Provide a graphic view of the sequence of events leading to an undesirable situation
4. Focus attention on safety and operationally critical components for reliability studies
5. Isolate analysis to one specific failure event at a time
6. Provide another viewpoint from which to evaluate system performance and improve understanding

The reason for including this overview of fault tree analysis can be found by examination of the simple fault tree in Figure 17.13. The undesired event, an explosion in a test chamber, can be caused by the occurrence of a failure in a computer-controlled protection system and a failure in a mechanical protection device. A failure in the computer-controlled protection system could arise from hardware failures in computer components, sensors, or actuators or in the software that implements the protection function. A software failure is an event that could, in conjunction with a failed relief valve, cause the undesired event. The reliability of the software is therefore an important concern in this instance.

Targeting these two techniques to very specific failure modes or to only specific parts of a system can achieve desired improvements in a cost-effective way. Employment of more effective FMEA or FTA techniques in the design of the THERAC-25 software [5] might have resulted in a safer, more reliable system.

17.12 CHAPTER SUMMARY ■

The intent of this chapter has been to make the software engineer acutely aware of the importance of reliability to the system (and especially to software). As software-dependent systems that directly serve the public become more prevalent and as software-dependent systems become more deeply embedded in our transportation, communication, justice, political, security, military, financial, research, health care, and mass media infrastructure, the focus on software reliability will most certainly increase.

Chapter 17 defines and discusses several important reliability-related terms and develops

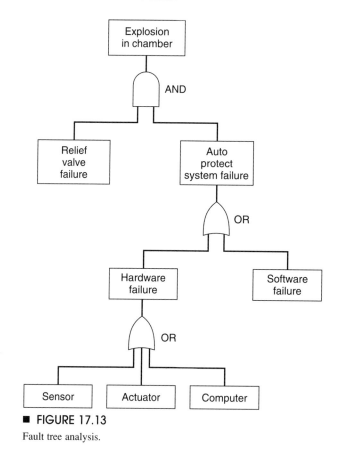

■ **FIGURE 17.13**

Fault tree analysis.

a software reliability model that can be used in conjunction with system and hardware reliability models. A suggested approach to data collection and evaluation to correct, confirm, or calibrate reliability models is also discussed in this chapter. An example of how a software reliability model could be used in a test environment for planning purposes is presented. Several sources of software errors are listed as well as some simple design guidelines for producing reliable software designs.

The chapter also introduces some ideas regarding redundancy as a means to improve reliability. A key point is made pursuant to justifying the added expense (especially for redundant software) of introducing redundancy to satisfy stringent reliability, availability, or safety requirements.

Failure modes and effects analysis and fault tree analysis are introduced briefly as a systematic examination of a system and software design for potential failure paths. These two techniques have been used frequently in safety analysis and can be applied selectively to specific components to identify potential faults.

Although a software engineer will frequently rely on reliability specialists for technical support, it is important that the software engineer understand the principles and concepts of reliability. A brief review of probability, as it relates to reliability, is provided in this chapter. A sound background in probability and statistics is essential to a fuller understanding of reliability and availability concepts.

17.13 EXERCISES   ■

1. Ten units are placed in a test environment. Failures and failure times are recorded. The results are as follows:

Failure number	Operating time
1	8
2	20
3	34
4	46
5	63
6	86
7	111
8	141
9	186
10	266

Using this table as raw data, plot failure density and hazard rate as a function of time. Also plot failure distribution and reliability as a function of time.

2. A four-hour computation process involving a computer, operating system, and an application software product must run from initialization to completion with a very low probability of error. Describe in detail the process you would follow to allocate failure rates to individual subsystems. List the questions you would ask and the issues that would need resolution in order to complete the allocation process. Where would you expect to get your answers?

3. Determine the required mean time to repair for a system with an availability requirement of 99.9% and a mean time to failure of 5000 hours. What observation would you make?

4. Compute the end-to-end reliability (*A* to *B*) for the configuration below. Assume probability of failure detection, switchover, and recovery is unity.

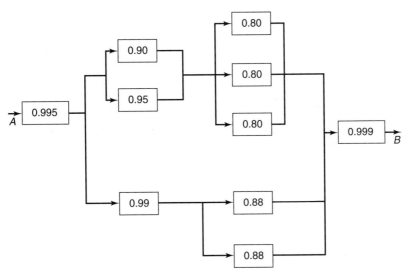

5. It is known that the failure rate of a particular item is, after a burn-in of 50 hours, approximately constant thereafter and has a value of 1.25E-4. What is the reliability of this unit for a service time of 2000 hours? If 20,000 units are sold each year, how many failed units can we expect to see in the first year? The second year?

6. List all of the errors you have uncovered in your own work in software development. How could these have been avoided or detected early in the process?

7. Estimate the resident faults and initial failure rate for a software product delivered to system test. The product contains 70,000 SLOC (assembly language) to be run on an object machine of 3 MIP CPU capacity.

8. Research the THERAC-25 incident (reference 5) and report your findings in terms of the need for standards imposed on software used for systems where public safety is at stake.

References

1. C. Anderson and M. Dorfman, *Aerospace Software Engineering,* AIAA, Washington D.C., 1991.
2. S. Ghahramani, *Fundamentals of Probability*, Prentice-Hall, Upper Saddle River, 1996.
3. *Mil HDBK 217E,* Government Printing Office, Washington D.C., 1989.
4. E. J. Henley and H. Kumamoto, *Probabilistic Risk Assessment,* IEEE Press, New York, 1992.
5. N. G. Leveson and C. S. Turner, ''An Investigation of the Therac-25 Accidents,'' *IEEE Comp.* Vol. 26 No. 7: 18–41, (1993).
6. D. Musa, A. Iannino, and K. Okumoto, *Software Reliability: Measurement, Prediction, Application,* McGraw-Hill, New York, 1987.
7. SAIC, *RADC-87-171 Methodology for Software Reliability Prediction,* Rome Air Development Center, Rome, New York, 1987.
8. A. D. Singh and S. Murugesan, Guest Editors, *Fault-Tolerant Systems,* IEEE Computer, Vol. 23, No. 7. A collection of papers, pages 19–83, July 1990.
9. M. L. Shooman, *Probabilistic Reliability: An Engineering Approach,* McGraw-Hill, New York, 1968.
10. M. L. Shooman, *Software Engineering,* McGraw-Hill, New York, 1983.

18

Software Quality and Quality Assurance

18.0 OBJECTIVES

The major objectives of this chapter are as follows: (1) to define and describe software quality and software quality assurance; (2) to discuss the relevance of software quality assurance to software engineering and to the software engineer; (3) to describe a formal software quality assurance plan and its benefits; (4) to show where the software engineer fits into the software quality assurance picture; (5) to provide guidelines and checklists that will enable the software engineer to work more effectively with the software quality assurance organization; and (6) to emphasize that software quality is a natural by-product of a strongly disciplined software development process which is followed to the letter.

18.1 INTRODUCTION

Every day we hear, read, and see the word *quality* in conjunction with advertisements for consumer products. Those of us who are engaged in product development and manufacture are also exposed to the word in connection with quality assurance programs such as ''Quality is job #1,'' zero defects, and quality circles designed to instill the notion of quality in all employees and to focus their attention on quality issues. Just what is this quality we hear so much about?

Quality is the degree to which a finished product conforms to explicitly stated function and performance requirements. Quality is also the degree to which the development and manufacture of the product conforms to all explicitly stated policies, standards, and practices. It is also the degree to which the product possesses certain implicit properties and characteristics normally perceived by the consumer as being of high quality. A more succinct definition is, "Quality is whatever the customer or client says it is."

Conformance of a software product to its specification of function, timing, and performance is easy to understand and measure. The degree to which the SRS reflects the actual needs, the SDS responds to these needs, and the tested software and adjunct products meet the customer or client expectations are implicit quality measures.

The software development cycle has as its backbone a collection of rules and regulations (usually documented) governing how the software product is to be developed. These rules could be drawn from DOD, IEEE, ANSI, company, or team development standards, practices, and policies. A major element in the definition of quality refers to how well or closely the development process, its documentation, and its reviews conform to these standards, practices, and policies.

The last part of the quality definition is often the most troublesome because it is so often difficult to quantify expectations or to anticipate reaction to the physical realization of the abstraction we call a design. Nevertheless, over the long term, even these highly subjective elements of quality can be quantified.

Philip Crosby [1] defines quality in terms of what it is not. Following his lead, we affirm that quality is not reliability, although reliability is one of many quality attributes. Quality is not a measure of worth among different items of the same genre. Quality is not an intangible and unmeasurable attribute. Quality is not an indicator of cost, meaning that the better the quality, the higher the cost. Quality is not the province of any one individual or area and is not the responsibility of one person or one group. The control or assurance responsibility for quality may be assigned to a group or an organization, but achieving the desired level of quality is the responsibility of everyone involved in the process. Quality can be influenced positively or negatively by anyone who is associated in any way with the design, development, test, and manufacture of a product.

It is important to understand the meaning of quality as it applies to software development. For example, from a quality standpoint, a Rolls-Royce is not necessarily a better-quality car than a GEO. A Rolls-Royce is more prestigious, more impressive, more expensive, larger, and made of better materials, but it may not be of better quality. As long as the GEO is correctly built to its specifications and built by correctly following production standards and practices, it can be of the same quality level or an even higher level than the Rolls-Royce. From a quality assurance standpoint, the use of the word *quality* in the statement, "The Rolls-Royce is a higher-quality car than the GEO" is not necessarily correct.

By way of contrast, the Second College Edition of the *New World Dictionary of the American Language,* Collins Ward, 1974, defines quality as follows:

> 1. any of the features that make something what it is; characteristic element; attribute 2. basic nature; character; kind 3. degree of excellence which a thing possesses 4. excellence; superiority

Normal use of the word *quality* is different from that used in the world of quality assurance. We need to be careful about how we use the word to avoid confusion. Software quality assurance is defined by IEEE [5] as follows:

1. the planned and systematic pattern of all actions necessary to provide adequate confidence that an item or product conforms to established technical requirements 2. a set of activities designed to evaluate the process by which products are developed or manufactured.

Software Quality Assurance (SQA) can be thought of as having two major components. The first component consists of the formal and informal measures taken to assure that the software product delivered at the end of the development cycle conforms to actual system needs according to specific, well-defined agreements between customer and developer. The contents of this agreement include derived acceptance test criteria, contractual agreements, budgets, schedules, and intangible perceptions and expectations.

The second component alludes to the formal and informal steps taken to assure that the software product has been developed in strict accordance with applicable standards and practices. The contents of this agreement include the following:

a. Identification and allocation of software requirements and documentation
b. Specification of software requirements and documentation
c. Specification of design at multiple levels and documentation
d. Tools and training
e. Coding process and documentation
f. Testing and testing documentation
g. Delivery (installation, operator training)
h. Postdelivery support and evaluation
i. Maintenance

Historically, quality assurance was the responsibility of the senior shop craftsman. It was the responsibility of the senior craftsman to establish and enforce the quality standards for shop journeymen and apprentices. The first formal quality assurance program is thought to have been introduced in 1916 by the Bell Technical Laboratory.

Software quality control is not yet well defined. That is, there is no standard, commonly accepted definition in software engineering. Likely candidate definitions include the following: (1) a set of activities designed to evaluate the quality of developed or manufactured products and (2) the process of verifying one's own work or that of a coworker. The term is also used as a synonym for quality assurance.

A quality metric is (1) a quantitative measure of the degree to which an item possesses a given quality attribute or (2) a function whose inputs are software data and whose output is a single numerical value that can be interpreted as the degree to which the software possesses a given quality attribute. These numerical values are often referred to as quality factors.

It has been demonstrated both analytically and in practice that an aggressively implemented SQA program can detect and remove upwards of 80% of all potential defects in a delivered software product during the software development process [2]. Frequently, however, management and senior technical personnel give only lip service to SQA. Whenever schedule, performance, or cost pressures increase, SQA is the first to be neglected. In many cases SQA is more a marketing strategy or tactic than an actual corporate commitment to the spirit of SQA. SQA is often regarded as being not nearly as important as most other activities in the software development process.

A good development team attitude is to recognize that the SQA is a kind of independent verification and validation of the product and the development process. The SQA organization should be treated as an essential and important contributor to the successful development of a software product.

In this chapter, software quality assurance, SQA, planning is discussed first; next a generic

SQA plan is described. Quality factors and attributes are listed and quality metrics for each are described and discussed, followed by a discussion of a general procedure for collecting and using these attributes and their values to improve product and development process quality. The discussion will be centered on the software engineer's role in software quality assurance.

18.2   SOFTWARE QUALITY ASSURANCE PLANNING   ■

The general contents of an SQA plan should include, as a minimum, a list of required tasks, a schedule for performance of the tasks, identification of task responsibilities, and the applicable rules of conduct (standards, practices, policies, etc.) employed in carrying out the tasks. The following is a list of fundamental tasks that must be included in an SQA plan:

1. *Selection and modification of quality assurance practices:* Identification of specific tools, techniques, and requirements for software development quality monitoring. Shaping each tool, technique, and practice to fit the unique aspects of the development.
2. *Software project planning evaluation:* The evaluation of the software development planning process and plan parameters is one of the most important reviews and often the most difficult to conduct.
3. *Acceptance requirements evaluation:* Early agreement, in detail, as to what constitutes an acceptable (to the customer) product is essential to the perceived quality of the delivered product.
4. *Specification (requirements and design) evaluation:* Poorly defined requirements will ultimately impact every aspect of a software development process including cost, schedule, and technical integrity.
5. *Design process evaluation:* If software design processes follow a planned methodology, are firmly based on requirements, and are rigorously managed and controlled, quality of the end product is assured.
6. *Coding practices evaluation:* Poor coding practice can negate good requirements specifications and good design.
7. *Test and integration process evaluation:* The adequacy of test plans and the integrity of the entire test program, especially the test and integration phase, is the surest indicator of a product's quality.
8. *Management and project control process evaluation:* Project management and controls are essential ingredients for software development success. Continued monitoring and evaluation is required.
9. *Configuration management practice evaluation:* Maintaining tight control of the software configuration during the dynamic development process is an important feature of a product's ultimate quality. Loss of control impacts cost, schedule, and technical performance.
10. *Tailoring quality assurance procedures:* Although quality assurance discipline follows a consistent structure, the techniques must be tailored to the specific software development.

18.2.1   Reviews as Quality Gates

At key points in the software development process, a set of quality gates is integrated into the development process to monitor the quality and integrity of interim products before they are used as the basis for the next development step. Through these gates quality assurance, configuration management, technical integrity evaluations, and control disciplines are blended into the development process. These gates are the basic quality assurance filters and form the backbone of the SQA plan.

The quality gates are formal and informal reviews involving customers, management, peers, consultants, etc. The objective of these quality filters is to provide a means to evaluate the process being used to develop the software, conformance of the software product to the needs of the customer, and response to technical requirements, goals, and objectives of the system into which the software will eventually be integrated. These quality gates are planned as regularly scheduled events and are conducted according to a standard procedure. Formal reviews include SRR (software requirements reviews), SSR (software specification reviews), SPDR (software preliminary design reviews), SCDR (software critical design reviews), and various configuration audits and test reviews. These reviews mark major milestones in a software development process. These reviews are attended by the customer and are often go/ no go quality gates. That is, unless certain conditions are met the review is not held, and unless all work has been satisfactorily completed and approved by the reviewers, further development on the item being reviewed is halted until the work is completed to the satisfaction of the review team.

There are also many informal quality gates. These include walkthroughs, internal audits, peer reviews, inspections, etc. These informal quality gates or filters are applied, often in a formal environment, on lower-level products or partial products. The distinction between formal and informal reviews is often blurred.

18.2.2   Generic Software Quality Assurance Plan

One can find among various standards (IEEE, ANSI, DOD, NASA, etc.) outlines and content descriptions for SQA plans. What we have described here is a general description of the SQA planning process.

The main tool for implementing SQA is the quality gate, the review. The SQA tasks are then preparation for reviews, attendance at reviews (or review of the item's documentation), and the filing of a postreview report. For each review the preparation includes the following: (1) development of checklists and questions based on general knowledge and experience that can be applied to the item being reviewed; (2) identification of review-related quality attributes and factors along with their appropriate quality metrics, and the collection and analysis of the values associated with each quality attribute; and (3) development of a general background in the application area, the software product, and the system, and of any background that the development team may have acquired as a result of participation in similar related developments.

Preparation of quality standards for the development process is helped in many instances by the fact that detail descriptions of the review items are implicit in the software development methodology. Quality-oriented checklists are relatively straightforward derivations from these descriptions. For example, SRS, SDS, and software configuration management plan content are often well defined in development methodologies. The task of SQA is to confirm that the item is prepared to the prescribed development standards. Therefore, the SQA task involves checklists and analyses to assure that process standards are being met.

The plan will also identify the basic standards that are applicable to this particular development, including any negotiated waivers and additions. These standards apply to documen-

■ TABLE 18.1 **Software Quality Assurance Plan Outline**

1. Purpose of the SQA Plan
2. References (Related Documents)
3. SQA Management (Organization, Tasks, Responsibilities)
4. Documentation (Schedule, Description of Contents, Etc.)
5. Standards Practices, Conventions, and Measurements (Metrics)
6. Reviews, Walk-throughs, and Audits (Schedules, Purpose, Responsibilities, Entrance and Exit Requirements, SQA Role)
7. Test (Unique to SQA)
8. Problem Reporting and Corrective Action
9. Tools and Methodologies
10. Code Control Description
11. Media Control Description
12. Supplier Control Description
13. Records Collection, Maintenance, and Retention
14. Training
15. Risk Management

tation, logic structure, coding, commentary, testing, and other practices associated with the development process.

The plan will also describe the so-called statistical quality assurance component of the SQA. The software quality attributes and attribute values will be defined, and the collection process details, rates, tools, and reporting frequency will be specified. Table 18.1 presents the outline of a typical software quality assurance plan.

18.3 SOFTWARE QUALITY ASSURANCE PROCESS ■

SQA should begin at project inception, and every member of the software development team should be dedicated to SQA. The SQA process begins by performing an in-depth review of the software development process, its standards, documentation, reviews, conventions, practices, and policies for verifying the following:

a. Completeness: Software development plan should cover all aspects of the development process.
b. Applicability: The software development plan should be tailored to the specific development needs.
c. Team Commitment: The development team should understand, accept, and be committed to following the chosen discipline.
d. Training Needs: Training needs should be identified, and plans should be in place for required training.
e. Roles and Responsibilities: The role of the SQA team should be defined and clearly communicated to the development team.
f. Management: The management team should be in place and functioning.

g. Staffing: The key personnel should be in place and a plan should have been developed for satisfying further personnel needs.

h. Documentation: Key documentation should have been reviewed and in place (generally top level plans, charters, responsibility allocations, etc.)

i. Self-review: The SQA plan should have been reviewed, accepted, and in place.

A thorough review of the software development process conducted by the SQA group can be very beneficial at this point in the development cycle. The partial checklist just presented indicates that SQA reviewers should be senior level, knowledgeable in both technical and management issues, and familiar with the development organization. Those performing this review function do not have to be members of an SQA group. Anyone with the appropriate background can perform these reviews. In reviewing documents it is important to conduct a clerical review to assure that the document is complete. Applying SQA to the correctness of the software product entails the following preparation:

Full Understanding of Contractual Requirements: Specifically what is required by the contract and statement of work? A careful reading of contract and statement of work or equivalent is the only way to obtain the required understanding.

Assessment of Training Needs: An identification of deficiencies in software engineering, design, testing, tools, etc., and institution of a training program or equivalent to overcome the recognized deficiencies.

Understanding of Acceptance Test Criteria: The development of a negotiated acceptance test criteria incorporated into the contract is a crucial point to be reviewed by the SQA team.

Definition of Formal and Informal Reviews: The quality gates with explicit entrance and exit requirements and a well-thought-out checklist should be defined. Section 18.5 presents checklists for some of the major formal reviews and a general checklist for an informal review. These SQA checklists are only the starting point. Each checklist item should be expanded and detail developed based on the specific review item. The checklist should be incorporated into the review entrance and exit criteria.

Assessment of Development Tools: Tools can be contributors to software product quality assurance. A quality check of all tools for completeness, certification, documentation, maintenance or support arrangements, maturity, and training in their use is an important quality assurance responsibility. In fact, the entire software development environment should receive the attention of the quality assurance group. The quality of the development environment should meet or exceed the expected quality of the software product.

Assessment of Traceability: A formal process should be described for tracing defects in products, process, or procedure to source. The most significant SQA contributions are those that eliminate defect or fault sources.

The next step in the process is to establish a set of quality attributes that will serve as indicators of software quality during the development cycle. In many instances the software attributes selected for quality assurance monitoring will be the same as those selected by development managers to manage risk and monitor cost, schedule, and potential technical performance. It is important that the definition of these attributes and the measurement process itself be clearly understood.

The last step is attendance at all reviews and application of prepared checklists to the item under review. A formal quality assurance assessment should be part of every review.

The SQA process is relatively straightforward. The development team (software engineers) should know all the expected SQA questions (checklists) and prepare answers. The entire team should be open-minded and dedicated to reviewing the product to assure that quality is intrinsic. Whenever there is doubt, return to the definition of quality. The SQA questions are the same as those asked in verification and validation. Simply stated, Is this the correct product? Was it developed correctly?

18.4   SOFTWARE QUALITY ATTRIBUTES   ■

A number of software attributes that could be used to quantify certain aspects of the software product were listed and described in chapter 14. Many of these attributes can also be used to quantify software quality. For example, the number and type of errors found in an SRS during a review is a useful measure of that specification's quality and perhaps a measure of the quality of the SRS review process itself. The number and type of defects uncovered in testing and field operation of a software product that traces back to the specification is also a measure of the specification quality. Table 18.2 lists many of the currently recognized software quality attributes often cited as measures of a software product's quality.

The categorization, analysis, trace to source, and finally and most important, elimination of the *root cause* of each defect found in the software product or in development process steps and products is the essence of quality assurance. Simply removing the product defect is not enough. Often it is possible to uncover persistent problems in the software development process by tracing defects to the source and understanding the mechanics of how they got into the software. The problem may be specific people, a process step, a subcontractor, train-

---

■ TABLE 18.2   **Software Quality Attributes**

1. Correctness:	Meets specifications.	
2. Reliability:	Meets reliability requirements.	
3. Efficiency:	Meets utilization of resources in development and operation.	
4. Integrity:	Meets accuracy, stability, and security of databases and robustness of process as specified in SRS.	
5. Usability:	Operators can understand and operate the system.	
6. Maintainability:	Readability of specifications, code, and other documentation and ease with which changes can be implemented.	
7. Flexibility:	Meets the abilit to accommodate growth and change.	
8. Testability:	Every requirement testable and entire system capable of being tested in environment equivalent to operational environment and with operational scenarios.	
9. Portability:	If required, ease of movement to another host environment.	
10. Reusability:	Ability to integrate into the suprasystem.	
11. Availability:	Meets availability requirements.	
12. Complexity:	As defined by cyclomatic complexity.	

ing, tools, management, review structure, checklists, etc. Understanding the root cause of the defect and taking appropriate measures to correct it is the main goal of quality assurance.

The IEEE standard [5] on software quality assurance, in the section Software Quality Indices, presents a more complete list of quality attributes as they relate to a software product. Also, Hallstead [3] in *Elements of Software Science* devotes a great deal of discussion to quality as it relates to software products.

Strictly speaking, with the exception of correctness, which is directly measured in terms of the number of defects or deviations from the specification detected during software test and integration (module or system), and acceptance test, all other quality attributes should be spelled out in the SRS. If, for example, there is no specific requirement to accommodate growth and change (flexibility), attempting to provide for growth and change in the design is, in fact, a deviation from the specification. The point is that with exceptions noted, quality attributes should be quantified and spelled out in the SRS. For example, when the SRS contains a requirement for a particular reliability value, this value becomes a quality attribute that can be quantified, measured, and followed through the development process. On the other hand, an attribute such as efficiency is meaningless unless it is framed as a quantifiable attribute and appears in the SRS as a requirement.

18.4.1   Statistical Software Quality Assurance

Statistical software quality assurance refers to the use of systematic methods to investigate and expose faults in software development products and processes. The purpose of statistical software quality assurance is to analyze a development process or its product so as to take appropriate action to achieve and maintain a desired quality for the software product and to generally improve the overall capability of the process. A number of tools and techniques have been used rather successfully in performing statistical quality assurance in system development. It is widely accepted that the same tools and techniques are effective in statistical software quality assurance. Some of these tools and techniques are briefly described here.

Pareto Chart: A Pareto chart is a special form of a vertical bar graph that could be used, for example, to determine which of several problem areas or defects should be attacked first. A Pareto chart can (Figure 18.1) show fault sources identified in a software product during test and the number of faults traced to each of those sources.

Cause and Effect Diagram: This diagram (sometimes called a fishbone diagram) represents the relationship between some effect and all possible causes that could exert an influence on the occurrence of that effect. Figure 18.2 shows a cause and effect diagram used to analyze a situation in which the effect is a larger than expected number of compiler runs required to get source modules successfully compiled. In this example the effect is too many compiling runs required for removal of errors from source modules being compiled. It is expected that the causes for this effect may be personnel, process, tools, and/or schedules.

Under personnel, level of training, experience, motivation, and morale of the design and development team may have a direct influence. Under process, quality of audits, reviews, design, and PDL may also have direct bearing on this effect. The tools being used, especially the compiler, debugger, and system library, may have an adverse influence. Finally, the

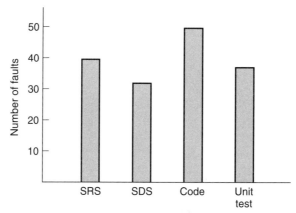

■ FIGURE 18.1

Pareto chart.

tightness of the schedule may have directly influenced the quality of reviews, thereby, having an indirect influence on the effect. Developing a cause can structure the approach to identifying the source of a particular problem.

Collection and analysis of data during the compilation and test process can be used to confirm conjectures based on the cause and effect diagram. Results may be used to support any of the following conclusions:

a. All four mentioned causes equally influence the effect.
b. One (or more) causes influence the effect much more than the other causes.

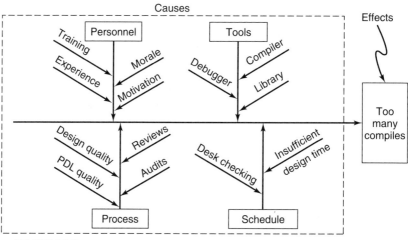

■ FIGURE 18.2

Cause and effect diagram.

c. The data collected points to other cause(s) involved. For example, a hardware problem may cause the module to be compiled too many times.

When a cause is established, the analysis of collected data may point to a single source within the cause that is the major source of the problem.

Run Chart: A run chart is a graph that shows long-range trends in a particular attribute, for example, the variation of estimates of execution time for a task (Figure 18.3). The figure also shows an upper bound on execution time for the task. Run charts are often used to track technical performance measurements.

Histogram: A histogram displays an approximation to the distribution of an attribute or measurement. Typically, histograms reveal the intrinsic variation in a given product or process.

Scatter Diagram: A scatter diagram can be used to examine the possible relationship (correlation) between one variable and another.

The application of statistical SQA methods can often lead to a deeper understanding of the dynamics of the development process. By sampling methods, collection, analysis, and categorization of defects and quantification of software attributes, the software engineer can frequently pinpoint potential problem areas and identify underlying causes of errors and failures in both product and process. Consider an actual case in which a software product in its last stages of test continued to experience failures at a constant rate. A careful categorization of each failure followed by an in-depth analysis revealed that one individual and one process step was involved in virtually every defect. This employee's responsibility was to make the changes approved by the configuration control board and produce a new version of the product. His lack of training and understanding of the application area and his overconfidence in his own ability, coupled with his carelessness, resulted in the introduction of one or more new faults into the product every time a fault was corrected and a new version of the product was created. The employee was moved to another job and the revision process itself was improved to prevent a recurrence of the same problem.

As an example of the Pareto chart method, assume that each defect found in testing is carefully charted as to its origin first by phase, Figure 18.4 (**A**), then by source, Figure 18.4 (**B**). For example, the requirements development phase is expanded to allocation, SRR, partitioning, and SRS. The largest source of defects, the SRS, is attacked first. The next step is

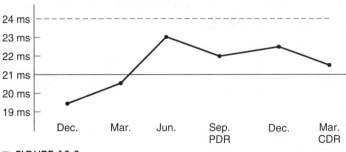

■ FIGURE 18.3

Estimate of execution time for specific task.

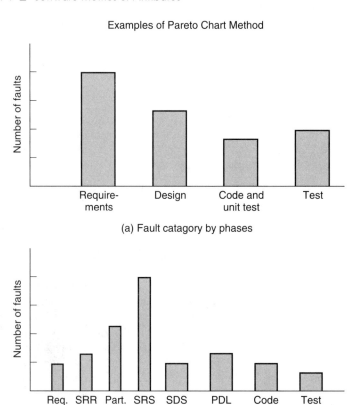

Examples of Pareto Chart Method

(a) Fault catagory by phases

(b) Fault catagory by source

■ **FIGURE 18.4**

Example of Pareto chart method. **A**, Fault category by phase; **B**, Fault category by source.

to look deeper into the mechanics of fault insertion. For example, in looking at SRS fault categories (Figure 18.5), there are many possible sources for faults. In our example, human-to-computer interface is seen to be the most significant error source. The next step is to delve more deeply into the reasons for fault insertion in this area. This effort may lead to another fault categorization and perhaps identification and elimination of a process, procedure, personnel, or organizational deficiency or weakness. Finally we should ask why these faults were not detected by the related quality gates. Answering that question can lead to more effective quality gates.

For the SQA team, being able to pinpoint the precise cause of an effect makes it possible to eliminate the root cause of the defect as well as the defect itself. Although each software product has a unique set of defect categories, the following are typical defect categories:

1. Software requirements allocations
2. Partitioning, analysis, SRS
3. PDR and other reviews
4. SDS
5. CDR and other reviews

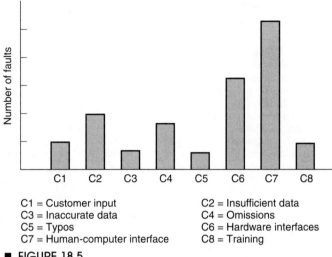

C1 = Customer input   C2 = Insufficient data
C3 = Inaccurate data   C4 = Omissions
C5 = Typos   C6 = Hardware interfaces
C7 = Human-computer interface   C8 = Training

■ **FIGURE 18.5**

SRS fault categories.

6. Test specifications
7. Test cases
8. Debugging
9. External interface
10. User/Operator interface
11. Standards and practices
12. Related documents
13. Coding

Each of these categories can be further partitioned to provide better visibility. For example, SRS defects can include the following: incorrect or missing inputs, outputs, or function specifications; incorrect performance figures; incorrect references; poorly conducted reviews; ambiguous requirements; contradictory requirements; and HCI requirements.

18.5 GUIDELINES AND CHECKLISTS ■

Many of the SQA tasks are clerical. For example, checking a document against a standard to confirm that all required sections are included, are complete, and appear to have adequate coverage would be considered a clerical task. On the other hand, a technical assessment of some sections of the document to determine if contents are correct, adequate, meet standards, etc., often requires the capability of an experienced software engineer. A well-run SQA group will employ software engineers to deal with the technical assessments and assign entry-level people to the more mundane SQA tasks. Tables 18.3 through 18.11 provide SQA checklists for various formal and informal reviews throughout the SWDLC. Although these checklists

■ TABLE 18.3   **Software Development Plan Checklist**

1. Is scope clearly defined and bounded?
2. Are terminology and jargon defined?
3. Are resources reasonable? Are they available?
4. Is risk assessment complete? Is risk containment plan in place?
5. Are tasks defined, scheduled, allocated?
6. Are cost estimates and schedule estimates reasonable? (Were two independent methods used?)
7. Do cost and schedule estimates relate to historical data?
8. Does software development schedule match with related schedules?
9. Is there a documentation standard being applied?
10. How will SDP document be used and controlled?
11. How well was the review conducted?
12. Is a software development environment needed?

are not exhaustive and are not detailed enough to be applied directly, they cover most of the SQA concerns.

18.5.1 Using Checklists

There are four steps in using a checklist. The first step is to collect and review all standards, procedures, and practices that are applicable to the item under SQA review. The second step is to identify any quality attributes that are directly or indirectly related to the item being reviewed. The third step is to assemble the information and review it carefully for understanding. The fourth step is to tailor the checklist by adding or deleting items and expanding each item in the checklist into specific actions. For example, if the software development schedule has no dependencies, then item 8 of Table 18.3 may be dropped from the checklist. Likewise, if the software development environment is a major concern, a separate checklist for the software development environment plan can be derived from the software development plan checklist.

The tailoring process for each item involves expanding each checklist item in more detail. For example, item 4 of Table 18.3 could be expanded to include the following questions:

1. Have risk areas been identified?
2. Has risk analysis been adequately reviewed?
3. Has it met internal or external standards?
4. Was review of analysis results thorough?
5. Does risk analysis documentation meet standards?
6. Are there any open risk issues? If yes, is a plan in place to close them?
7. Is a risk containment plan in place?
8. Are technical performance measures defined?
9. Is there a commitment to implement the plan?
10. Have alternatives been defined in the event that failure occurs?
11. Is the reporting frequency appropriate?

■ TABLE 18.4   **Software Requirements Checklist**

1. Are all functions clearly defined and described, bounded, and unambiguous?
2. For every functional requirement, is a performance requirement stated and the functional requirement testable?
3. Are all inputs and outputs defined in terms of ranges, protocols, rates, etc., to the satisfaction of the software designer?
4. Is test and integration plan in place? Were acceptance test criteria negotiated with customer?
5. Is feasibility study complete?
6. Were trade-off studies reviewed and accepted?
7. Is risk analysis initiated/complete?
8. Is there a documentation standard being applied?

■ TABLE 18.5   **Software Requirements Specification Checklist**

1. Are any requirement issues open? If yes, are plans in place to close them out?
2. Is first level partitioning complete and rationale documented?
3. Are all internal and external hardware and software interfaces adequately defined in terms of protocols, ranges, rates, structure, encryption, etc.?
4. Is data model completely and accurately defined in terms of attributes, relationships, etc.?
5. Is trace of lower level software requirements to higher software levels and system level complete and accurate?
6. Can performance requirements be met?
7. Are timing requirements clearly stated and achievable?
8. Are all requirements testable?
9. Does every stated requirement have a test defined to confirm correct implementation?
10. Are sizing and software development cost and schedule estimates consistent with allocated resources and project schedules?
11. Are available hardware resources, CPU, IO, memory, etc., adequate to meet software needs?
12. To what standard is SRS being written?
13. Are any SQA standards being applied to the SRS?

■ TABLE 18.6   **Software Design Specification Checklist**

1. Is software architecture consistent with overall architecture?
2. Are all requirements accounted for in the structure?
3. Does partitioning meet modularity criteria (coupling, cohesion)?
4. Are module-to-module interfaces adequately defined?
5. Is data structure design consistent with data requirements?
6. Are maintainability, growth, potential change action factored into design?
7. What quality attributes apply?
8. Were documentation standards met?
9. Were pseudocode, structure chart, etc., standards applied? Have they been met?
10. How well was the review conducted?

■ TABLE 18.7   **Informal Gates Checklist**

1. Are there entrance and exit requirements for this gate? Have they been met?
2. Does the design accurately implement the given function?
3. Are logic, algorithms, etc., correct?
4. Are all interfaces (both sides) consistent with standards?
5. Is complexity reasonable? Does it meet standards?
6. Have quality attributes been addressed?
7. Are error and exception handling covered adequately?
8. Are local data structures adequately defined and compatible with other items?
9. Have all standards been followed throughout?
10. Has testing and maintenance been considered?
11. How well was the review conducted?
12. Does associated documentation meet standards?

■ TABLE 18.8   **Coding Checklist**

1. Has pseudocode or structure chart, etc., been correctly realized in code? Have agreed-to standards been met?
2. Have documentation standards been met?
3. Have comment statements met standards? Are they correct and unambiguous?
4. Are data types and data declarations correct (do they meet standards)?
5. Are data correct (program and physical constants, for example)?
6. Have quality attributes been addressed?
7. Is there full compliance with all coding standards?

■ TABLE 18.9   **Testing Checklist**

1. Have acceptance test criteria been defined, negotiated, and accepted? Were revisions made as required?
2. Were test plans prepared and reviewed for quality and technical content?
3. Was testing adequately addressed during other development phases?
4. Are test environment (tools and resources) adequately defined, sized, and available when needed?
5. Is traceability from raw requirements to confirmation tests completed and correct?
6. Are major functions confirmed early in testing phase?
7. Have standards for conducting tests been defined and accepted and have testers been trained?
8. Have test cases been given the proper emphasis? Have comparison data been prepared? Have drivers, scaffolds, stubs, etc., been identified and will they be ready in time?
9. Have limit tests and stress tests been defined?
10. Is testing comprehensive (black box and white box combined)?
11. Have all independent paths been confirmed?
12. Have error and exception handling been tested?
13. Do test case expected results contain tolerances?

■ TABLE 18.10   **Configuration Management/Control Checklist**

1. Was configuration management plan reviewed? How good was the review?
2. Is there a change control board functioning? Is it effective?
3. Are lines of authority and responsibility for the board clearly defined?
4. Is there a clearly defined procedure for handling change? Is it understood and followed?
5. Are there formal, documented procedures for requesting change, disseminating change information, and accepting, documenting, and effecting change?

■ TABLE 18.11   **Checklist for Review Evaluation**

1. Is material complete (does it meet standards)?
2. Was material distributed on time?
3. Are applicable standards referenced and available?
4. Were attendees prepared to contribute?
5. Did evaluation start on time?
6. Were number of defects identified?
7. Was review conducted per standard protocols?
8. Were entrance criteria met?
9. Were exit criteria met?
10. Are all issues scheduled for resolution?
11. Are interface issues coordinated?
12. Is disposition of all defects complete?
13. Were HCI, testing, maintenance, tools considered?
14. Were quality attributes reported?
15. Has trace of defects been initiated?

Most of the checklist items in Tables 18.3 through 18.11 are listed in the form of a question; however, the answer to many of these questions may not be a simple yes or no. In fact, many of these questions are subjective and have answers other than a simple yes or no. For example, if 20 quality attributes must be checked in a given review and 19 of these attributes are satisfactorily reported, what is an appropriate answer to the question, "Were quality attributes reported?" It is easy to see that a simple yes would be inaccurate and a simple no would not be accurate either. In this case a value of 19 out of 20 would be reported.

Implementation of a quality gate involves examination of documentation, interviews, and attendance at formal and informal reviews in an effort to answer the checklist questions satisfactorily. Since these and other similar questions will be posed by the SQA group, it is important that the software engineer have answers for these questions. To be forewarned is to be forearmed. If the software engineer has already anticipated what questions will be asked, he or she can prepare by having a satisfactory (to the SQA group) answer for each anticipated question.

Software quality attributes associated with documentation and reviews are an indirect measure of the quality of the product. For example, the number of defects found in a document or module is a rough indication of the potential quality of the delivered software product. The vastly more important value of these defect data is uncovering persistent problems in process, procedure, personnel, and organization that are contributing to poor quality. Knowing what these problems are can lead to improvements or changes that will permanently improve product quality. For example, a group in the development organization that has more difficulty than other groups in getting through walk-throughs or reviews without a great deal of rework and friction may need more help or better leadership. On the other hand, perhaps this group should be the norm because those groups not experiencing a great deal of rework and contention during reviews are not getting into the real issues that must be resolved. At any rate this situation should be identified and escalated to the appropriate level so that steps can be taken to improve quality. Finally, when the SQA group has completed its tasks, it is important that the quality of the performance of each SQA task itself be assessed.

A key item in any software development process is the manner in which the software configuration is controlled. The SQA group can make an important contribution by policing the software configuration control process throughout the project.

18.6   SOFTWARE SAFETY   ■

As long as software quality (reliability and availability attributes in particular) remains suspect, there will be a reluctance to use software in safety-critical applications involving a high cost of failure. However, there is also strong pressure from other quarters to use software in critical applications because of cost and technical advantages; this pressure drives software developers to find ways to produce software with a high reliability.

Safety considerations are also the domain of quality assurance. Some of the tools employed in software safety analyses include failure modes and effects analysis (FMEA), fault tree analysis, event tree analysis, hazard analysis [4], and Petri nets (chapter 5). Usually these analyses include comprehensive models of hardware, software, and operator performance.

The objective of FMEA is to analyze an information system's components systematically to determine how a component might fail and evaluate the effect of such a failure on system performance under a variety of operational conditions. The objective is to identify ways in which combinations of external events, operator reactions, and hardware/software failures can lead to serious failure consequences. Some analytical approaches (fault tree analysis or event tree analysis, for example) begin by assuming the occurrence of a catastrophic failure and working backwards to find out what logical sequence of events would result in such a failure.

Software designed to operate in safety-critical environments will be subjected to safety analysis. Software engineers can expect to be involved in this activity.

18.7   CHAPTER SUMMARY   ■

Strictly speaking, every step in the software development process is part of a quality assurance effort. The purpose of SQA is to act as the development team's conscience in matters impacting quality. A quality software product meets its requirements as formally stated in documents visible to both developer and customer. Its development has unequivocally conformed to standards and practices visible to both customer and developer, and its appearance as manifested to the user conforms to an acceptable level of quality as perceived by users and operators. This chapter makes the following points:

1. The software engineer should know what SQA means and what will be expected, from an SQA standpoint, of product and process in reviews and audits. This information should enable the software engineer to prepare the appropriate answers beforehand. The SQA checklists included in the chapter are clues to potential review and audit questions.
2. In terms of software quality assurance, simply fixing a software fault is not enough. The origin or source of the fault should be found and confirmed and the underlying cause removed. This simple idea is at the heart of the software quality assurance process.
3. The so called software quality attributes, to be of any significant value to the practicing software engineer and SQA, must be quantified and imposed as requirements in the SRS.
4. Software quality assurance should extend to software development environments and tools. The software quality assurance process itself should be subjected to review and audit to assure its continued cost-effectiveness and quality.
5. Application of SQA methods that are associated with the collection, categorization, and analysis of quantifiable software attributes can have a significant benefit to software development.

The clean room software engineering concept discussed briefly in chapter 1 has as its objective a quantum step forward in software product quality improvement. The approach employs statistical quality assurance methodology and formal testing techniques to produce high-quality software.

18.8   EXERCISES

1. Explain how reliability, availability, and safety relate to quality.
2. If a software quality attribute is not specified in the SRS, can a software developer be held accountable if the software product is judged to be deficient in that quality attribute?
3. Software quality assurance has been described as structured nagging. Explain what this means. Is it fair? Is it accurate?
4. List the ways in which you can improve the quality of your in-class performance. Use the definition of quality given in this chapter.
5. Is it possible to have a good-quality software product that is unreliable and unsafe?
6. Is it possible for a correct program be of poor quality? How?
7. Use Table 18.9 to perform a quality evaluation of a program that you have recently tested. What changes would you make to improve the quality of the testing you did?
8. Describe how you would go about quantifying flexibility as a quality factor.
9. Prepare an argument for dedicating one software engineer to collecting, categorizing, and investigating all defects uncovered by quality gates.

References

1. P. B. Crosby, *Quality Is Free,* McGraw-Hill, New York, 1979.
2. M. Fagan, Advances in Software Inspection, IEEE Transactions on Software Engineering, Vol. 12, No. 7, July 1986, pages 744–751.
3. H. Hallstead, *Elements of Software Science,* Elsevier, North-Holland, New York, 1977.
4. E. Henley and H. Kumamota, *Probabilistic Risk Assessment,* IEEE Press, New York, 1991.
5. IEEE, *IEEE Standard For Software Quality Assurance Plans, STD 730.1-1989,* IEEE Press, New York, 1989.

Standards Related to Software Quality and Quality Assurance

6. IEEE Standard For A Software Quality Metrics Methodology,'' Draft, May 1, 1992, in *IEEE Standards Collection, Software Engineering,* IEEE Press, New York, 1994.
7. ''IEEE Standard Software Quality Management System,'' STD 1298-1992 (Adopted from Standards Australia) in *IEEE Standards Collection, Software Engineering,* IEEE Press, New York, 1994.
8. *IEEE Standard For Software Configuration Management Plans, IEEE STD 828-1990,* IEEE Press, New York, 1990.
9. *IEEE Standard Guide To Software Configuration Management, STD 1042-1990,* IEEE Press, New York, 1990.
10. *Software Engineering,* DOD-STD-2167A.
11. *Software Quality Evaluation,* DOD-STD-268.
12. Software Quality Assurance Standard for FAA, FAA-STD-018.
13. Standard For Software Quality Assurance Plans, IEEE STD-730-1984.
14. SQA Planning, IEEE STD-983-1986.
15. Standard For Software Reviews and Audits, IEEE STD-1028-1988.

Special Topics

Unit 5 addresses two topics that are of increasing concern in software engineering, (1) real-time software design and (2) human-to computer-interfacing. Four appendices are also included in Unit 5. The four appendices address communication skills, cost-benefit analysis, decisions and trade-offs, and reviews. Each appendix treats an important area of software engineering that is usually not thought of as being germane to the discipline.

Chapter 19 identifies a key concern in the development of real-time software, the schedulability of tasks. In software products designed to meet real-time requirements, tasks must be scheduled to execute within specific time windows. Scheduling, of course, implies that task execution times are known. Chapter 19 also offers some guidance on how to estimate task execution times.

In the past, real-time software was designed using manually constructed task timelines or simulated task timelines using estimated execution times for each task. There was always uncertainty as to whether, eventually, accumulated time shifts from various sources such as different execution paths through tasks, clock drifts, aperiodic tasks, interrupts, etc., would cause a critical task to miss a deadline (not execute within its assigned window). Within the last few years a set of scheduling algorithms and associated theorems has been developed that removes much of this uncertainty. These algorithms and theorems are discussed in chapter 19, and some examples are worked to demonstrate the approach.

Chapter 19 also offers the software engineer some idea of how real-time software requirements are stated and what should be provided as minimum input to the designer. The chapter lists some important questions that a software engineer should ask when requirements for real-time software are involved. General design guidelines for real-time software products are presented. The chapter also provides some insights on how real-time software can be effectively tested. As software becomes intrinsic to applications involving controllers, the need for an understanding of unique real-time software requirements among software engineers will increase.

Chapter 20 discusses human factors in software engineering. The chapter first provides some background as prelude to discussion of the human-computer interface (HCI). Throughout the book there has been an emphasis on the fact that the operator is an important component of any system. The fact that nearly half of the source lines of code in a typical software product are devoted to the human-to-computer interface certainly bears that out.

Often, especially in large systems, human factors specialists are employed to establish certain display standards and design guidelines for interfacing the computer to its human operators. In smaller systems the HCI design is frequently left to the software engineer. In either case it is important for the software engineer to have an appreciation for the principles of HCI requirement specification and HCI design. This information is provided in chapter 20. Some supplemental approaches to the development of operational timelines and operator task analysis are presented along with guidelines for design and for HCI-unique testing.

Inability to communicate effectively will severely compromise anyone's ability to perform his or her job effectively, particularly the software engineer who must be facilitator, persuader, coordinator, presenter, and writer. The software engineer is expected to communicate effectively with management, clients, operators, programmers/ coders, system engineers, etc. Fortunately, one can learn to be an effective communicator. Appendix A offers some suggestions for becoming better at making presentations and writing.

Appendix A emphasizes planning as a critical step in improving one's communication skills. A useful planning tool, the storyboard, is described. Some hints for making better oral presentations are provided. Effectiveness in participating in or conducting meetings is discussed. The importance and utility of maintaining a software engineer's notebook is considered. Participating in design reviews, often a major activity in a software engineer's career, is discussed. Finally, listening skills are discussed and it is emphasized that listening is part of the communication process.

Many important decisions in a software development turn on cost-benefit analyses. Appendix B provides a brief overview of how a cost-benefit analysis is conducted. An example is provided to convey the important points.

It is felt that all important technical decisions in a software development should be made using a standardized decision-making process. Appendix C describes a simple trade-off study-approach whose main value lies in its simplicity and its self documenting features. The central theme in Appendix C is that every important decision should be made using an objective decision-making procedure and the rationale for the decision reached should be documented.

Software engineers spend a great deal of their time participating in reviews of one type or another. They may be reviewing the work of others or their work may be undergoing review. Appendix D describes the variety of reviews that are conducted during a software development and describes the roles of the participants.

Real-Time Software

19.0 OBJECTIVES ■

Real-time software development is a broad topic with its own unique characteristics. The overall objective of this chapter is simply to acquaint the reader with the main issues and problems encountered during the design and development of real-time software. Other objectives of this chapter are as follows: (1) to define what is meant by real-time software; (2) to explain how real-time requirements are expressed in software requirements specifications; (3) to describe unique design issues related to real-time software; (4) to discuss techniques and tools for designing real-time software; (5) to identify unique testing requirements and problems associated with development of real-time software; and (6) to discuss real-time scheduling issues.

19.1 INTRODUCTION ■

Finding an adequate formal definition for real-time software is difficult because all software has of necessity certain real-time properties. It is the degree to which the software product exhibits these real-time properties that is important. The *Oxford Dictionary of Computing* provides the following informal definition of real-time systems:

> Any system [software] in which the time at which output is produced is significant. This is usually because the input corresponds to some movement in the physical world and the output has to relate to the same movement. The lag from input time to output time must be sufficiently small for acceptable timelines.

This initial definition should help to provide some intuition about real-time software and its intrinsic properties.

Software products can be grouped into two general categories, those products in which time is not regarded as a critical resource and those products in which time is a critical resource. The latter is called real-time software. The design of real-time software requires effective management of the processing resource, time. Some authors further separate real-time software into hard real-time software and soft real-time software. The distinction lies in the impact of a failure. Hard real-time software refers to software whose failure to meet a computational deadline or to respond to an interrupt within a specified time can result in death, injury, or substantial property loss. Soft real-time software products, on the other hand, are those in which failure to meet timing requirements will not result in catastrophic consequences.

Real-time software (especially hard real-time software) is among the most challenging of all software to develop. The software engineer must first have a clear idea of all of the specific timing requirements imposed by the software requirements specification. Moreover, the software engineer must understand the relative importance of each time-based requirement, which often requires working closely with system engineers and control engineers during the formulation of requirements.

There is a continuing need to estimate execution time accurately for all real-time tasks (modules that have an intrinsic timing requirement) before and during the preliminary design phases. The software engineer will frequently be called upon to perform these pivotal estimates.

The software engineer designing a real-time software system should have an in-depth understanding of system hardware components, especially in relation to processing functions. There is usually a need to use modeling and simulation to design and test real-time software. Confirming designs for real-time software often requires that critical hardware timing characteristics and certain critical software characteristics be modeled and simulated in detail. These models are often upgraded and used again in the test environment.

Because of the added time dimension, testing, an already challenging problem, is further complicated by requiring the software product not only to be functionally correct and performance correct but also to be correct in its timing. The main problem is assuring that the software product satisfies all requirements for worst-case task execution times. That is, the software meets all of its task deadlines (executes its tasks within a defined time window), satisfies all other time-related requirements (absolute time, time intervals, relative time), and meets all of its functional and performance requirements.

The timing source for real-time applications is frequently derived from an external clock. In most computer systems, system time measurements are only a minor concern. Scheduling soft deadline resource allocations with resolutions at perhaps 10 milliseconds is the major application concern. In real-time computer systems, on the other hand, timing problems are compounded by the need for stable, accurate clocks for both absolute time and relative time. These clocks are to have low drift rates and high resolution (10s of microseconds). It is safe to say that the timing source will be a design concern in virtually every real-time application.

There are many examples of real-time software. One of the most common is the real-time component of an operating system employed in servicing user terminals for an on-line system. Other examples are control software for aircraft system controllers, data communication software, video games, electronic toys, automobile engine controllers, appliances, network control software, etc. It is expected that we will see even more applications for real-time software emerging in the future.

A number of real-time software applications execute in a dedicated operational environment. Embedded software systems are good examples. In these instances the software engineer has more design latitude and greater control over hardware resources. In real-time applications, control of computing system resources is often allocated to an executive program that has as its principal requirements the support of task dispatching or scheduling and unencumbered access to shared resources.

19.2   REAL-TIME REQUIREMENTS SPECIFICATION   ■

As in all software functional and performance requirements, software real-time requirements are rooted in the application area. Real-time requirements arise when elapsed time is a key module or task performance parameter. The source of the most critical real-time performance parameters is when the computer (including software) is a component of a controller. In these cases, the controller task implemented by the software is executed periodically at a fixed rate. Failure to maintain this fixed rate can cause the controller to fail catastrophically.

Some of the terminology used in real-time requirements specification is as follows: execution time, task period, task execution rate, jitter, transport lag, and task deadline.

Task Execution Time   This term refers to the CPU time required to execute a module or task.

Task Period   This term refers to the time interval between task initiations. To say that task τ has a period of 100 milliseconds means that every 100 milliseconds, task τ must be initiated and completed.

Task Deadline   Task τ may have a period of T but a completion requirement of D, where $D \le T$. Such a completion requirement is called a task deadline. The default value for task deadline is task period.

Task Rate   Task rate is the reciprocal of task period. In a fixed time interval t, the task execution rate is t/T where T is the task period.

Jitter   Jitter is the time interval in which a task execution may begin at any point and complete before its deadline. Therefore, task deadline is task execution (or task completion) time plus allowable jitter.

Transport Lag   Transport lag is a term borrowed from control system terminology meaning the elapsed time between the actual occurrence of a sensor measurement and the receipt at the actuator of the output (actuator input) command. Transport lag is important to controller stability and accuracy.

Real-time software specifications often contain specific values with tolerances for each of the parameters defined above. Figure 19.1 shows these parameters. Time interval $[t_i, t_{i+1}]$ is the period of task τ_n. The task deadline is shown by point F on the timeline. Thus the task must complete its execution on or before point F. Time interval $[A, E]$ is the jitter associated with the ith execution of task τ_n. The sensor initiates measurement at point B and the actuator receives the computation result at point C. Therefore, time interval $[B, C]$ is the transport lag. The ith execution begins somewhere in the interval $[A, E]$ and ends somewhere before point F. Time interval $[A, G]$ represents the period of task τ_n.

Other terminology used in scheduling a real-time module or task includes the following:

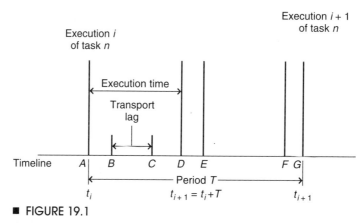

■ **FIGURE 19.1**

The *i*th execution of task *n*.

application time line, static priority, blocking, priority inversion, and preemption. A short definition for each and an illustrative example follows.

Application Timeline This term describes a time interval during which every computation task is initiated and completed through one complete cycle.

Priority Priority is some form of level of importance assigned to a task. Static priority assignment is the level of importance assigned to a task before the software executes. An example of static task priority is the rate of execution of the task. Dynamic priority assignment assigns a priority to a task during the execution of the software product. That is, task importance varies during the course of software product execution. Semantic priority assignment refers to absolute importance in terms of task criticality to successful operation of the system.

Preempt When a task of higher priority must be scheduled during the time that a task of lower priority is using CPU resources, the task with higher priority will preempt the execution of the task of lower priority and the execution of the high-priority task will start immediately. Synonyms for the word *preempt* are interrupt and displace. In this chapter preempt will mean interruption or displacement of one task by another.

Blocking When task *B* needs to utilize a server or utility that is being used by a task of lower priority, it is said that task *B* is being blocked. Therefore, being blocked means delay in execution by a lower-priority task.

Priority Inversion A priority inversion occurs when a lower-priority task blocks a higher priority task from a resource.

Priority Inheritance This term means raising the priority of a task that has created a block to the highest level of priority of tasks being blocked. Therefore, priority inheritance will change block to a preempt.

In a real-time software design there is, of necessity, a priority scheme developed to assure that the most critical tasks are given resources when needed. In some instances, requirements to recognize the occurrence of an event in time (within a specific tolerance) is a specified requirement. In some cases, specified timing accuracy requires taking into account interrupt latency. Often, a timed sequence of output commands keyed to the occurrence of an event is a specified requirement. The software engineer must probe the requirements carefully to ferret out all of the timing-related requirements.

Since real-time requirements will probably drive software architecture design, it is important for the software engineer to understand the real-time requirements thoroughly. In real-time parlance a task usually refers to a function or group of functions with similar timing requirements.

There are three general types of real-time tasks: periodic, aperiodic, and server. The periodic task is executed at fixed intervals. Task execution time is given in terms of CPU utilization (ratio of computation time to period). Aperiodic tasks are characterized by random arrival rates, typically expressed in terms of minimum interarrival rates or average arrival rates. A server is used to encapsulate and protect common resources. Servers are also used for task synchronization and handling aperiodic tasks. Periodic task requirements are described in terms of period or rate, priority, transport lag, jitter, nominal execution time, deadline, and exceptions. Periodic tasks are time critical in the sense that the system cannot function unless they are completed on time.

Aperiodic tasks are specified in terms of activation conditions, response time or deadline, execution time, priority, relative timing constraints, and execution conditions. An example of an aperiodic task is the action taken upon detection of a failure condition in a redundant system where a task is initiated that locates the failed component, switches it out of service, switches a replacement component into the system, and restarts the system.

Servers are normally tasks performed for any other task that needs them. An example of a server is a table, in memory, used by several tasks to maintain and use results of keeping track of the exact location of an aircraft or ship.

Task deadlines, if not explicitly defined, are assumed to be the same as task period. In real-time software products, they are often classified as hard, firm, or soft. Not meeting a hard deadline can result in catastrophic failure. Typically, control system–related periodic tasks have hard deadlines. A deadline is said to be firm if task results cease to be useful as soon as the deadline expires. However, the consequences are not catastrophic. An example might be updating a database. The soft deadline describes the situation in which deadlines are neither hard nor firm but results are less useful as time elapses.

Time-dependent tasks have other unique requirements. These requirements include the following: (1) input/output resource acquisition and use; (2) internal and external task communication; (3) database access, locking, and updating; (4) process constraints; and (5) dependability/performance constraints.

The desirable attributes of a real-time software product include predictability and schedulability. Complete predictability is often difficult to achieve through design. Schedulability, however, is the key to successful real-time software design. The design challenge is to schedule tasks whose execution time behavior may be somewhat unpredictable so that all of the requirements can be met under normal circumstances and the critical requirements can be met in overload conditions.

Example 19.2.1

An example of a real-time software requirement is shown in Figure 19.2. In this figure, there are three periodic tasks, two server tasks, and two aperiodic tasks that must be executed. Task 1 has a period of 100 milliseconds (it must be executed at least once every 100 milliseconds) and requires 20 milliseconds to execute its worst-case path. Task 2 has

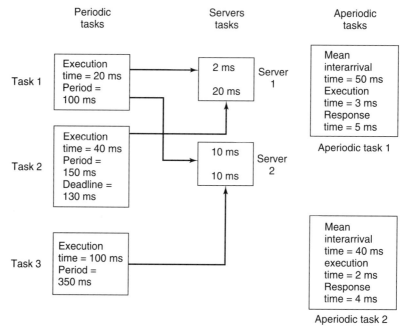

Periodic tasks

Task 1
Execution time = 20 ms
Period = 100 ms

Task 2
Execution time = 40 ms
Period = 150 ms
Deadline = 130 ms

Task 3
Execution time = 100 ms
Period = 350 ms

Servers tasks

2 ms
20 ms
Server 1

10 ms
10 ms
Server 2

Aperiodic tasks

Mean interarrival time = 50 ms
Execution time = 3 ms
Response time = 5 ms

Aperiodic task 1

Mean interarrival time = 40 ms
execution time = 2 ms
Response time = 4 ms

Aperiodic task 2

■ **FIGURE 19.2**

Periodic, aperiodic, and server tasks.

a period of 150 milliseconds and requires 40 milliseconds to execute its worst-case path. Task 2 also has a deadline of 130 milliseconds that must be met. Task 3 has a period of 350 milliseconds and requires 100 milliseconds to execute its worst-case path. Tasks 1 and 3 must complete execution in the time windows provided. That is, absolute task deadlines are the beginning of the next time window or period.

Server task 1 is a results table accessed by periodic tasks 1 and 2. The second server task is another common resource accessed by periodic tasks 1 and 3. Task 1 utilizes server 1 for 2 milliseconds and server 2 for 10 milliseconds. Task 2 utilizes server 1 for 20 milliseconds. Task 3 utilizes server 2 for 10 milliseconds. Server task execution time is included in the periodic tasks that access the server.

The first aperiodic task is specified in terms of a minimum interarrival time of 50 milliseconds. That is, the arrival time of this task is a discrete random variable with Poisson distribution. The task executes in 3 milliseconds and must complete its execution 5 milliseconds after receipt of its interrupt. The second aperiodic task is specified in terms of a mean interarrival time of 40 milliseconds. That is, the arrival time of this task is a random variable with a uniform distribution with a mean of 40 milliseconds. Task execution time is 2 milliseconds and desired response time (to its interrupt) is 4 milliseconds.

19.2.1 Execution Time Estimation

The software engineer is frequently required to provide execution time estimates for a software module or task when only a sketchy description of the function is available. Task

■ TABLE 19.1   **Interrupt Timing**

TIME INTERVAL		DESCRIPTION
t_0	—	Occurrence of interrupt
t_0–t_1	—	Save state of current task
t_1–t_2	—	Decode interrupt
t_2–t_3	—	Initiate action and run to complete
t_3–t_4	—	Save state of interrupt action
t_4–t_5	—	Restore interrupt task state
t_5–t_6	—	Begin execution of interrupted task

execution times are used to develop predictable scheduling for tasks and to establish execution time requirements for designs. The following information facilitates an accurate estimate of execution time: (1) the average instruction execution time of the host computer, (2) the interrupt latency of the host computer, (3) the best available description of the functions to be performed, and (4) the time required to execute a single input/outout instruction.

Technical information regarding computer hardware performance is readily available from hardware documentation. Often, benchmark data with a variety of instruction mixes can be used to obtain average instruction execution times. However, the software engineer must be familiar with hardware performance and the terminology used in discussing hardware performance.

An example of the need for a software engineer to understand hardware performance characteristics is found in incorporating interrupt handling in estimating a task execution time. In order to estimate a task execution time accurately, interrupt latency (the time required to process an interrupt) must be known. Table 19.1 shows the sequence of events in handling an interrupt. It should be noted that many of the delays experienced in processing an interrupt are due to hardware. The time required to halt an executing task and assign the CPU to another task is often referred to as context switching time.

The time interval t_0 to t_2 is regarded as part of the task execution time and must be known by the software engineer. The time interval t_2 to t_3 is the actual execution time of the subject task. Interrupts may be based on the occurrence of internal events, external events, or time. For many periodic tasks an external timer is employed to generate the interrupt at regular intervals.

Fortunately, many real-time tasks are strongly algorithmic in nature so that estimates of the number of source lines of code required to implement task functions are relatively easily obtained. These estimates are frequently imposed as design requirements or design constraints. For the purposes of estimating execution time, the longest path through the task or module should be used.

Example 19.2.2

As an example, consider a periodic real-time task that has a rate of twenty executions per second. The number of high-level language SLOC required to execute the longest path through the task is estimated to be 3600. Prior experience has shown that there is a 5:1 expansion of the high-level language SLOC to assembly instructions for these algorithms. The task will be initiated by a timed interrupt. Average interrupt latency has been determined from documentation and analysis to be 0.02 milliseconds. There are six inputs from external sources required to initiate computations. The average time required to obtain these inputs is estimated from hardware documentation to be 0.55 milliseconds. Average instruction execution time is estimated for this task at 225 nanoseconds. The estimated execution time for the task is then computed as follows:

$$5 \times 3{,}600 = 18{,}000 \text{ assembly instructions}$$

Time to execute an instruction is

$$\frac{225}{1{,}000{,}000} = 0.000225 \text{ ms}$$

Total time to execute instructions is

$$18{,}000 \times 0.000225 = 4.05 \text{ ms}$$

Total execution time is

$$4.05 + 0.55 + 0.02 = 4.62 \text{ ms}$$

This task will require $4.62 \times 20 = 92.4$ milliseconds out of each second for execution. The prudent software engineer would add a cushion of perhaps 20% to the estimate to cover oversights. This simple example outlines the general approach to estimating task execution times.

19.3 DESIGN GUIDELINES FOR REAL-TIME SOFTWARE ■

Real-time software architecture is most often structured around a resource manager, a scheduling algorithm, and a set of standard input/output services all packaged in an ''executive.'' The remainder of the software is divided into procedures or tasks, each with known execution times. These tasks are scheduled according to an application timeline.

Three design guidelines can be identified with regard to real-time software products. The first guideline is to partition the design based on periodic and aperiodic tasks tempered by priority considerations. For example, since hard deadline tasks are the most critical, they should have the highest priority and be protected from overload conditions. In developing the architecture, then, it is important that hard deadline task execution form the backbone of the architecture.

The second design guideline is to assure that each task is independent as well as being self-contained (low coupling and high cohesion). By minimizing task coupling, we may reduce or eliminate task dependencies and minimize synchronization requirements. Thus it becomes possible to reduce scheduling complexity and eliminate intertask communication. The simpler the software architecture and the more independent each of the periodic and aperiodic tasks are, the better the design will be. The design that is easier to understand, build, and test is always a better design. The rationale for decoupling resource scheduling is to reduce the complexity of schedulability analysis. This approach has special advantages when many resources such as networks, processors, memory banks, etc., are being scheduled or the development team is geographically distributed.

The third design guideline is to recognize that changes to function and performance requirements can drive task timing and schedulability as well as timing requirement changes. It is highly desirable to make the design as impervious to changing requirements (robust) as possible. This goal can be accomplished in part by (1) decoupling resource scheduling requirements from function and performance requirements; (2) providing standard, application-independent input/output services for all shared sensors, actuators, and other special devices; and (3) separating timing control structures from the code that is employed to provide computational functionality.

Separation of the software structure used to manage concurrency and timing from the code used to perform functions is based on the fact that timing behavior depends upon such factors as the speed of the hardware, protocols and structure of the run-time system (or executive), and compiler behavior—especially optimization, tasking control structures, etc. The task functions, on the other hand, are largely independent of these factors. Therefore it makes sense to partition requirements along these lines.

Following these three guidelines facilitates use of certain scheduling approaches like the rate monotonic scheduling (RMS) algorithm. The advantage of RMS is that a collection of useful, practical analytical tools support the RMS approach to real-time software development.

Based on the three guidelines just discussed, the first step in designing a top-level architecture is to group functional requirements based upon their execution rate requirements. The second step is to reduce the number of different execution rates to the minimum. This step should be taken with caution. It is probably acceptable to execute a function at a rate greater than required but not acceptable to execute it at a lower rate. All rate requirements should be justified, but especially those high task rates that will stress the CPU. There is a tendency on the part of system and control engineers to specify (out of conservativeness) execution rates for functions that are much higher than can be supported by real system needs. The software engineer should challenge any rates that appear to be higher than needed. It is important that software engineers work closely with those who formulate the requirements. This policy is always a good one, especially in developing real-time software. The third step is to partition those functional requirements with common execution time requirements into modules (tasks), using coupling and cohesion as criteria. Each task is then estimated for its worst-case execution time, usually the longest path through its code. Figure 19.3 depicts this top-level design procedure.

The software architecture is then structured on allocating resources to each task at its required execution time. Individual tasks can be designed, coded, and tested to meet allocated function and performance requirements and execution time requirements derived from analysis of the SRS requirements. Designers have one additional requirement to meet beyond logical and algorithmic requirements. A task or module must be designed to meet a worst-case execution time requirement. Failure to meet the execution time requirement can result in a failure of the entire software product to meet acceptance tests.

Meeting task execution times is always an area of risk in a development with real-time requirements. It is common practice to use task execution times as a technical performance measurement (TPM). This TPM would be reviewed frequently during design and development to assure that execution time budgets were being met and to take appropriate action if they are not being met. In real-time software products the correctness of a module or task result depends not only upon the result itself but also the time at which outputs are generated.

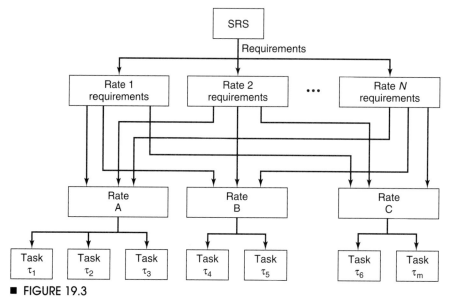

■ **FIGURE 19.3**

Real-time architecture design process.

19.4 SCHEDULABILITY CONCERNS   ■

The key to design of real-time software architecture lies in scheduling periodic, aperiodic, and server tasks so that all deadlines are always met. A second design goal is to provide for dealing with predictable and unpredictable transient overloads. In this section we consider the scheduling problem of a set of n independent periodic tasks with their specific deadlines, periods, and worst-case execution time estimates. A set of n tasks is called independent if their execution need not be synchronized. For instance, tasks that share certain services are not considered independent.

An important concept to understand with regard to scheduling independent real-time tasks is the application timeline. The application timeline refers to a period of time during which all tasks can be completed at least once. Figure 19.4 is an example of a application timeline. Each task is scheduled according to its timing requirements, and then the timeline is examined for schedulability. The scheduling in Figure 19.4 is based on the rate monotonic scheduling algorithm. That is, priority is based on task rates. The higher rate task is assigned the highest priority. Therefore, task 1 has the highest priority, task 2 has the next highest priority and task 3 has the lowest priority. The period for each of the three tasks begins at time zero. However, the highest priority task, task 1, is scheduled and other tasks must wait. Task 2 is scheduled at time 20 for the first time. Task 3 is scheduled for the first time at time 60. Task 3 utilizes CPU resources for 40 ms, then task 1 is scheduled again. Hence, task 3 is preempted by the scheduling of task 1, which has a higher priority. After 20 ms, task 3 will recapture CPU resources until task 2 preempts it. Task 3 completes its 100 ms execution time with three preemptions.

The RMS algorithm schedules the highest rate, hard deadline, periodic task first and assigns the highest priority to that task. Assume tasks τ_1, τ_2, τ_3, . . . , τ_n are n independent periodic tasks with worst-case execution times e_1, e_2, e_3, . . . , e_n and period T_1, T_2, T_3, . . . , T_n.

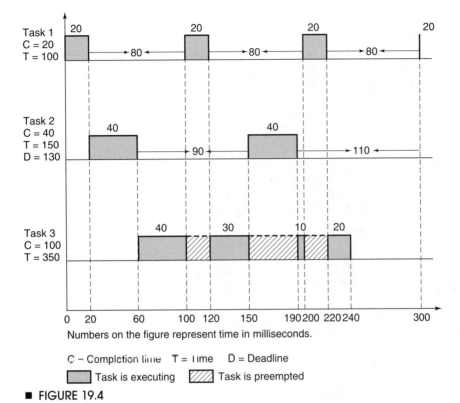

■ FIGURE 19.4

Application timeline example.

Furthermore, assume that the deadline for each task is the end of its respective period. The priority assigned to each task is based on the task rate. Tasks with higher rates have higher priorities. Also, assume S_i is the scheduling overhead (the time to move from one task to another one) for task τ_i. The completion time for task τ_i is shown as

$$C_i = e_i + S_i$$

Then

$$\frac{C_i}{T_i}$$

where C_i is the worst-case completion time required by task τ_i, is called the CPU utilization of task τ_i.

Theorem 1   Suppose n independent periodic tasks (aperiodic tasks are considered as periodic with a period equal to the mean arrival time) $\tau_1, \tau_2, \ldots, \tau_n$ with worst-case completion times $C_1, C_2, \ldots, C_n$ and periods $T_1, T_2, \ldots, T_n$ are scheduled using the RMS algorithm. If

$$\frac{C_1}{T_1} + \frac{C_2}{T_2} + \cdots + \frac{C_n}{T_n} = \sum_{i=1}^{i=n} \frac{C_i}{T_i} \leq U(n) = n(2^{\frac{1}{n}} - 1) \tag{19.1}$$

then all n tasks will always meet their deadlines at any time during product execution.

The value of $U(n)$ in equation (19.1) is the CPU utilization of all n tasks. The following are values of $U(n)$:

$U(1) = 1.0$	$U(4) = 0.756$	$U(7) = 0.728$
$U(2) = 0.828$	$U(5) = 0.743$	$U(8) = 0.724$
$U(3) = 0.779$	$U(6) = 0.734$	$U(9) = 0.72$

As n gets larger $U(n)$ approaches the value of $\ln 2 = 0.69$.

The rate monotonic scheduling algorithm and related theorems are based on work done by Sha [5, 6], Liu and Layland [4], and Leung and Whitehead [3]. They showed that it is optimum to schedule tasks so that those with the highest rates (or narrower windows in time) are given the highest priorities.

Example 19.4.1.

Suppose there are four tasks, τ_1, τ_2, τ_3 and τ_4, to be scheduled. Tasks τ_1, τ_2, and τ_3 are assumed to be high-rate, periodic, hard-deadline tasks. Task τ_4, a large task, would not normally be regarded as having a real-time requirement. The requirements state that if task τ_4 completes execution in less than 2 seconds, there is no real concern. Even if it exceeds 2 seconds, while not desirable, it is not a serious concern since all time dependencies have either been removed or accommodated within its algorithms.

Using the RMS design approach, tasks τ_1, τ_2, and τ_3 are scheduled and prioritized with the highest-rate task being given the highest priority. Let us assume the completion times of the four tasks are estimated to be $C_1 = 40$, $C_2 = 30$, $C_3 = 20$ and $C_4 = 200$ milliseconds. Also, assume Task τ_1 must be executed 10 times every second and tasks τ_2 and τ_3 must each be executed 5 times every second. We can then conclude $T_1 = 100$, $T_2 = 200$ and $T_3 = 200$ milliseconds. We would first like to see whether we can schedule these four tasks within a 1000 millisecond timeline or window. The maximum CPU utilization of these four tasks, based on Equation (19.1) is:

$$\frac{40}{100} + \frac{30}{200} + \frac{20}{200} + \frac{200}{1000} = 0.85$$

This value is larger than $U(4) = 0.756$. Therefore, theorem 1 cannot guarantee that these tasks will always meet their deadlines when scheduled in a 1000 millisecond window. However, there is no driving requirement to schedule these tasks within a 1000 millisecond (1 second) window. The soft deadline for task τ_4 is 2000 milliseconds. If we were to assume the period for task 4 is 2 seconds and use equation 19.1 again, then

$$\frac{40}{100} + \frac{30}{200} + \frac{20}{200} + \frac{200}{2000} = 0.75$$

This value is less than $U(4) = 0.756$. That is, we can schedule these four tasks within a 2000 millisecond window if we assume that task τ_4's period is 2000 milliseconds. Theorem 1 guarantees that no task will miss its deadline in all subsequent task executions.

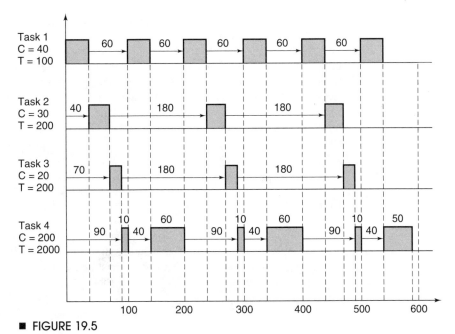

■ **FIGURE 19.5**

Scheduling of four tasks of Example 19.4.1.

Theorem 1 provides a very pessimistic CPU utilization bound. On the average, 88% of a CPU resource can be effectively scheduled [2]. Also, theorem 1 assumes that a task deadline is the same as task period. Whenever conditions for theorem 1 do not hold for a set of independent tasks or there is a need for higher CPU utilization, we can turn to the exact schedulability test based on another theorem called the critical zone theorem.

Theorem 2 (the Critical Zone Theorem): For a set of independent periodic tasks, if a task with period T_i meets its first deadline, $D_i \leq T_i$, when all higher priority tasks are started at the same time, then it meets all its future deadlines with any other task start times.

This theorem provides assurance that when it is possible to successfully schedule one complete cycle of all tasks without missing a deadline, then no deadline will be missed in the subsequent executions of these tasks. Theorem 2 applies to any static priority assignment, not just rate monotonic priority assignment. Theorem 2 explains why real-time software products designed, using manually developed timelines, were successful.

For example, using this theorem we can show that the four tasks in Example 19.4.1 may be scheduled in a time interval much smaller than 2 seconds. Figure 19.5 shows the scheduling of the four tasks of Example 19.4.1 in 600 milliseconds. A careful examination of Figure 19.5 reveals that these four tasks could actually be scheduled in 590 milliseconds.

To determine if n independent tasks can meet their first deadlines, consider the fact that in any time interval, t, the cumulative demand on CPU resources by n independent tasks may be expressed as

$$W_n(t) = C_1 \left\lceil \frac{t}{T_1} \right\rceil + C_2 \left\lceil \frac{t}{T_2} \right\rceil + \cdots + C_n \left\lceil \frac{t}{T_n} \right\rceil \tag{19.2}$$

where C_i is the worst-case completion time for task τ_i and t/T_i represents the number of times that task τ_i must be scheduled in time interval t.

Application of theorem 2 is sometimes referred to as the *completion time test*. If we can show that there exists a finite time interval during which all tasks are completed before their respective deadlines, then the set of tasks is schedulable. That is, during the entire product execution time, these n tasks will always be completed before their corresponding deadlines.

Time t in Equation (19.2) is the value that must be computed. The following algorithm provides a method to compute the minimum time interval, t, needed to schedule n independent periodic tasks at least once.

19.4.1   Algorithm to Compute $W_n(t)$

Let t_i represent the value of t in the ith iteration of the following algorithm and let $N_{i,j}$ be the number of times task j must be scheduled and completed during the time interval $[0, t_i]$. Hence, $N_{i,j} - N_{i-1,j}$ is the number of additional times that task τ_j must be completed in time interval $[t_{i-1}], t_i$. Also, assume we have organized the n tasks such that

$$T_1 \leq T_2 \leq T_3 \leq \ldots \leq T_n$$

We define

$$t_0 = C_1 + C_2 + C_3 + \cdots + C_n$$

and

$$N_{0,1} = N_{0,2} = N_{0,3} = \cdots = N_{0,n} = 1$$

which means the minimum value of t, t_0, is equal to the total time needed to complete each of the n tasks once.

Algorithm to Compute_$W_n(t)$

1.0 Set $i = 0$ and $t_0 = C_1 + C_2 + C_3 + \cdots C_n$
2.0 If $T_j > t_0$ for $j = 1, 2, 3, \ldots, n$ then
   2.1 Set $W_n(t) = t_0$ and terminate the process
       {all n tasks meet their deadline}
3.0 If there is at least one task τ_j for which T_j is less than or equal to t_0 then perform the following:
4.0 Repeat
   4.1 Set $i = i + 1$
   4.2 Set $t_i = t_{i-1}$
   4.3 For $j = 1$ to n do
       4.3.1 If $T_j \times N_{i-1} \leq t_i$ then
           4.3.1.1 Set $N_{i,j} = N_{i-1,j}, + \left\lceil \dfrac{t_i - T_j \times N_{i-1,j}}{T_j} \right\rceil$
           4.3.1.2 Set $t_i = t_i + (N_{i,j} - N_{i-1,j})C_j$
       4.3.2 Else
           4.3.2.1 Set $N_{i,j} = N_{i-1,j}$
   4.4 End_for
5.0 Until $t_i = t_{i-1}$
6.0 Set $W_n(t) = t_i$
7.0 Terminate the algorithm

Note that there is no guarantee that this algorithm will terminate. In fact, a very large t should be regarded as a sign that the tasks are not schedulable.

Example 19.4.2

For the four tasks of example 19.4.1 we have

Tasks	C	T	D
1	40	100	100
2	30	200	200
3	20	200	200
4	200	2000	2000

Times are all in milliseconds. We want to compute the minimum value of a time interval t during which all four tasks can be scheduled and completed at least once, assuring that the conditions of theorem 2 apply. Using the procedure described in this section we have

$$t_0 = 40 + 30 + 20 + 200 = 290$$

$T_1 = 100 < 290$ implies that we must schedule task τ_1 more than once in this time period. The number of times task τ_1 must be scheduled and completed in the time interval $[0, 290]$ is computed as

$$N_{1,1} = N_{0,1} + \left\lceil \frac{t_1 - T_1 \times N_{0,1}}{T_1} \right\rceil$$

$$N_{1,1} = 1 + \left\lceil \frac{290 - 100 \times 1}{100} \right\rceil = 3$$

therefore, the value of t_1 must be revised as

$$t_1 = t_1 + (N_{1,1} - N_{0,1})C_1 = 290 + 80 = 370$$

Similarly, the number of times that task τ_2 must be completed in interval $[0, 370]$ is

$$N_{1,2} = N_{0,2} + \left\lceil \frac{t_1 - T_2 \times N_{0,2}}{T_2} \right\rceil$$

$$N_{1,2} = 1 + \left\lceil \frac{370 - 200}{200} \right\rceil = 2$$

from here

$$t_1 = t_1 + (N_{1,2} - N_{0,2})C_2 = 370 + 30 = 400$$

Similarly, the number of times that task τ_3 must be completed in interval $[0, 400]$ is

$$N_{1,3} = N_{0,3} + \left\lceil \frac{t_1 - T_3 \times N_{0,3}}{T_3} \right\rceil$$

$$N_{1,3} = 1 + \left\lceil \frac{400 - 200}{200} \right\rceil = 2$$

$$t_1 = t_1 + (N_{1,3} - N_{0,3})C_3 = 400 + 20 = 420$$

Since $T_4 \times N_{0,4} > t_1$ we don't need to reschedule task 4. Therefore,

$$N_{1,4} = N_{0,4} = 1$$

Since t_1 is not equal to t_0, the algorithm must perform at least one more iteration.

At the start of the second iteration of the repeat loop, we have $t_2 = 420$. With this new value for t_2 we have

$$N_{2,1} = N_{1,1} + \left\lceil \frac{t_2 - T_1 \times N_{1,1}}{T_1} \right\rceil$$

$$N_{2,1} = 3 + \left\lceil \frac{420 - 100 \times 3}{100} \right\rceil = 5$$

therefore, the value of t_2 must be revised as

$$t_2 = t_2 + (N_{2,1} - N_{1,1})C_1 = 420 + 80 = 500$$

$$N_{2,3} = N_{1,2} + \left\lceil \frac{t_2 - T_2 \times N_{1,2}}{T_2} \right\rceil$$

$$N_{2,2} = 2 + \left\lceil \frac{500 - 200 \times 2}{200} \right\rceil = 3$$

$$t_2 = t_2 + (N_{2,2} - N_{1,2})C_2 = 500 + 30 = 530$$

$$N_{2,3} = N_{1,3} + \left\lceil \frac{t_2 - T_3 \times N_{1,3}}{T_3} \right\rceil$$

$$N_{2,3} = 2 + \left\lceil \frac{530 - 200 \times 2}{200} \right\rceil = 3$$

$$t_2 = t_2 + (N_{2,3} - N_{1,3})C_3 = 530 + 20 = 550$$

Since $T_4 \times N_{1,4} > t_2$, we don't need to reschedule task 4. Therefore,

$$N_{2,4} = N_{1,4} = 1$$

The third iteration through the repeat loop starts with $t_3 = 550$. With this new value for t_3 we have

$$N_{3,1} = N_{2,1} + \lceil (t_3 - T_1 \times N_{2,1})/T_1 \rceil$$
$$N_{3,1} = 5 + \lceil (550 - 100 \times 5)/100 \rceil = 6$$

Therefore, the value of t_3 must be revised as

$$t_3 = t_3 + (N_{3,1} - N_{2,1})C_1 = 550 + 40 = 590$$

Since $T_2 \times N_{2,2} > t_3$, we have

$$N_{3,2} = N_{2,2} = 3$$

Since $T_3 \times N_{2,3} > t_3$ we have

$$N_{3,3} = N_{2,3} = 3$$

Since $T_4 \times N_{2,4} > t_3$ we have

$$N_{3,4} = N_{2,4} = 1$$

The fourth time through the repeat loop the value of t_4 will be 590. A quick look at the algorithm shows that there will be no change in the value of t_4. Hence, the algorithm will terminate at step 7.

19.4.2 Task Synchronization

Theorem 1 of the previous section applies only to independent periodic tasks with deadlines the same as their periods. Theorem 2 of the previous section can accommodate independent periodic tasks with deadlines shorter than their periods. In this section we discuss periodic tasks that may share resources and have deadlines shorter than their periods.

Suppose B_i is the period during which task τ_i is blocked. Also, assume $E_i = T_i - D_i$ represents the difference between the period and the deadline of task τ_i. If task τ_i is the last task to be completed, the effect of blocking on task τ_i is the same as if its completion time is increased by B_i. That is, the completion time of task τ_i becomes $C_i + B_i$. Similarly, the effect of the shorter deadline can be accommodated by assuming an increase of E_i in the completion time of task τ_i. Therefore, when task τ_i has a block delay of B_i and a deadline occurring earlier by an amount, E_i, its completion time will be

$$C_i + B_i + E_i$$

where C_i is the worst-case estimated execution time of task τ_i. With this new completion time, theorem 1 for n periodic tasks may be restated as follows:

Theorem 3   A set of n periodic tasks is schedulable by the RMS algorithms if

$$\forall i, 1 \le i \le n, \frac{C_1}{T_1} + \frac{C_2}{T_2} + \cdots + \frac{(C_i + B_i + E_i)}{T_i} \le i(2^{\frac{1}{i}} - 1) \tag{19.3}$$

The meaning of this theorem is that for every task τ_i that has a chance to be blocked (dependent tasks) or has a deadline shorter than its period or both, the schedulability of tasks $\tau_1, \tau_2, \ldots, t_i$ must be confirmed using theorem 3.

Example 19.4.3

Check the schedulability of the following four tasks given

Tasks	C	T	D	E	B
1	40	100	97	3	2
2	30	200	200	0	0
3	20	200	195	5	5
4	200	1000	1000	0	0

Using theorem 3 we find that task 1 is schedulable because

$$\frac{40 + 3 + 2}{100} = 0.45 \le U(1) = 1$$

Tasks 1 and 2 are schedulable because

$$\frac{40}{100} + \frac{30}{200} = 0.55 \leq U(2) = 0.828$$

Tasks 1, 2, and 3 are schedulable because

$$\frac{40}{100} + \frac{30}{200} + \frac{20 + 5 + 5}{200} = 0.70 \leq U(3) = 0.779$$

Tasks 1, 2, 3, and 4 are not guaranteed by theorem 3 to be schedulable because

$$\frac{40}{100} + \frac{30}{200} + \frac{20}{200} + \frac{200}{1000} = 0.85 > U(4) = 0.756$$

Whenever theorem 3 cannot guarantee the schedulability of a task, we must resort to the completion time test to verify whether the task is schedulable or not. The application of the completion time test (theorem 2) to dependent periodic tasks is the same as for the independent periodic tasks except that the blocking time of the task being tested for schedulability must be added to its execution time. This change is formalized by theorem 4.

Theorem 4   Let $\tau_1, \tau_2, \ldots, \tau_n$ be n dependent periodic tasks with periods $T_1, T_2, \ldots, T_n$, deadlines $D_1, D_2, \ldots, D_n$, and worst-case execution times $C_1, C_2, \ldots, C_n$. Task τ_i meets its completion deadline time D_i if

$$W_i(t) = C_1 \left\lceil \frac{t}{T_1} \right\rceil + C_2 \left\lceil \frac{t}{T_2} \right\rceil + \cdots + (C_i + E_i + B_i) \left\lceil \frac{t}{T_i} \right\rceil \leq D_i \qquad \textbf{(19.4)}$$

The same algorithm as described for theorem 2 may be used to compute $W_i(t)$.

Example 19.4.4

Consider the following table presenting the information about three tasks. The objective is to verify schedulability of these tasks using either theorem 3 or theorem 4.

Tasks	C	T	D	E	B
1	30	100	100	0	0
2	70	200	200	0	30
3	30	200	150	50	6

Since $30/100 = 0.30 < U(1) = 1$, task 1 is schedulable. Since $(30/100) + (70 + 30)/200 = 0.80 < U(2) = 0.828$, tasks 1 and 2 are schedulable. Since $(30/100) + (70/200) + (30 + 50 + 6)/200 > U(3) = 0.779$, tasks 1, 2, and 3 are not schedulable using theorem 3. At this point we resort to theorem 4. The initial value for $W_3(t) = t_0 = 30 + 70 + 30 + 6 = 136$ ms. In the interval [0, 136] task 1 arrives for the second time and must be scheduled. The completion time for task 1 is 30 ms. Therefore, $t_1 = 136 + 30 = 166$ ms. The completion time of task 3 goes beyond its deadline of 150. Hence tasks 1, 2, and 3 are not schedulable.

However, if the priority order of tasks 2 and 3 is exchanged, we can schedule tasks 1, 2, and 3 in the order 1, 3, and 2 because the deadline of task 2 is 200 ms and is larger than $30 + 30 + 70 + 30 = 160$ ms.

Priority Inversion

Priority inversion occurs when a high-priority task is blocked from execution by a task with lower priority. The following example should illustrate the circumstance in which priority inversion occurs.

Assume that tasks A and C both require access to a common server but task B does not have such a requirement. Furthermore, assume task A has the highest priority, task B has the next highest priority, and task C has the lowest priority. The following sequence illustrates how priority inversion could occur.

1. Task C is being executed and the common resource is locked by task C.
2. At this time, task A is ready to execute and preempts task C because of its higher priority. Task A attempts to access the common resource and finds that it is locked (task C locked it). Task A now is placed in a queue waiting for the availability of the common resource. This is a forced interrupt of A by the system. Now the CPU is ready to accept the next task.
3. Task B is now ready to run and since its priority is higher than the priority of task C, it preempts task C, leaving task A still waiting in the queue for the common resource. Remember, task B does not use the common resource, so it executes to completion before task A, which is a higher-priority task.

Thus a lower priority task (task B) executes before a higher priority task (task A). This effect is called a priority inversion.

There are several solutions to the priority inversion problem. The one we describe here is called the *priority ceiling protocol*. The priority ceiling protocol also prevents mutual deadlock between tasks. In addition, under priority ceiling protocol, a task can be blocked by lower priority tasks at most only once. The priority ceiling protocol has the following three rules:

1. *Preemption Rule:* A task with a higher execution priority always preempts tasks with lower execution priorities in capturing the CPU resource.
2. *Inheritance Rule:* A lower priority task (task C) that blocks a higher priority task (task A) inherits the priority of that task (task A). That is, any task (task B) whose priority lies between the executing task and the blocked task (task A) will not be allowed to execute.
3. *Priority Ceiling Rule:* A task cannot enter its critical section (access to the shared resource) unless its priority is higher than the ceilings of semaphores locked by other tasks.

The priority ceiling of a shared resource such as a server task or semaphore* is the priority of the highest priority task that may lock that resource.

The priority ceiling protocol process is as follows. We define the priority ceiling of a binary

---

* A shared variable used to synchronize a concurrent process by indicating whether an action has been completed or an event has occurred. IEEE Std 610.12-1990.

semaphore, S, (a resource shared by two tasks) to be the highest priority of all tasks that may lock S. When a task A attempts to execute one of its critical sections, it will be suspended unless its priority is higher than the priority ceilings of all semaphores currently locked by tasks other than A. If task A is unable to enter its critical section (access to the server) for this reason, the task that holds the lock on the semaphore with the highest priority ceiling is said to be blocking task A and hence inherits the priority of task A. As long as task A is not attempting to enter one of its critical sections, it will preempt every task that has a lower priority. Therefore, the key to solving the priority inversion problem is the manner in which the lock is placed on the shared resource.

We now have the tools necessary to confirm schedulability of periodic task requirements with deadlines not equal to their period and tasks with synchronization requirements. We also have a design approach for avoiding priority inversion and deadlock.

The phrase *high priority* may be used in the SRS to indicate the urgency of a task. Any use of the word *priority* in the SRS should not be confused with reference to priority in scheduling. Therefore, priority as used in the SRS is called semantic priority. The priority used for rate monotonic scheduling is a numeric value derived from the characteristics of the task being scheduled. It is, therefore, possible to find a task that is given the highest semantic priority in the SRS but not the highest priority as assigned by the RMS algorithm. There are three ways to deal with this problem:

1. Increase the task execution rate requirement of a semantically high priority task so that the task becomes the highest rate task. If this increase is not possible because CPU resources cannot support the load, then resort to the next solution.
2. Partition the task into two sections, A and B, such that the two sections become a single task run at twice the original rate. There will be some minor overhead associated with task execution control to execute section A of the task on the first call and section B on the second call. This method preserves the RMS priority structure and the semantic based priority will equate with the priority used by the RMS algorithm. Again as before, if this solution creates any problem, resort to the third solution.
3. Use a different static priority measure that directly corresponds with the semantic priority. In doing so make sure priority assignment accounts for task blocking.

19.5 TESTING REAL-TIME SOFTWARE ■

In developing real-time software, the goal of the design process is to separate time-based requirements from requirements based on function and performance. The software architecture has as its central kernel a task execution scheduling structure. Tools, already discussed, are available to confirm schedulability of tasks for certain task execution protocols. Task or module software can be tested for function and performance correctness as in conventional module testing. Execution time tests can confirm assumed execution times used to determine task schedulability. Integration and test of the entire real-time system almost always requires some form of dynamic simulation of the operational environment's timing features [7].

In general, there are three primary integration and test strategies that can be followed to test the time-based requirements of real-time software products. The first strategy uses stored timelines to drive the system through a comprehensive set of test scenarios. Test results are recorded during execution of test scenarios (test cases). After test execution is completed, results are analyzed to determine test success or failure. The only process running in real-time is the software under test. The test scenario consists of input data generated before test execution. Stored input data and expected results can be recorded operational and environmental data or they can be derived from simulations by an adjunct test scenario generator. The following are some disadvantages associated with this strategy:

a. A large number of test scenarios must be generated to span all possible environmental, functional, performance, and timing situations that may occur in the operational environment.
b. Test success or failure is unknown until the analysis of test results is complete.
c. There is usually no way to change test scenarios dynamically during the test to react to ongoing events. What is learned in testing can be applied, but only with a relatively long delay.
d. If problems are encountered during test, it may be necessary to develop completely new sets of test scenarios. This process could result in long delays in testing progress while new scenarios are developed.

In spite of these disadvantages, strategy 1 may be the only approach possible to testing a particular system (or part of a system) in a particular environment. Because of time constraints it may be necessary to perform strategy 1 tests in a scaled time environment. That is, one second of real time is equal to n seconds of test scenario time.

The second strategy involves simulating the important features of the external environment in real time. In this approach test scenarios modeling the operational environment are produced in real time. Test scenarios drive the system under test through a variety of tests spanning the full range of expected operational conditions. Generally, there is a real-time, two-way exchange between simulator and software; that is, sensor inputs (in real time) are accepted and processed by the software, and software outputs (also in real time) to actuators in turn drive the simulator. The test results are recorded and analyzed after test completion. The principal advantage of this test configuration is the ability to create new test scenarios quickly and easily by simply altering simulation parameters. Strategy 2 may also be carried out in scaled time. There are two major disadvantages associated with this strategy:

a. Identification and modeling those critical features of the operational environment that must be accurately simulated is often more difficult and more expensive than developing the real-time software product.
b. The lag between test execution and results analysis can slow test progress, particularly if problems are encountered during test.

The third strategy is approximately the same as strategy 2. Simulations may require a more comprehensive system model and perhaps include actual hardware components as part of the model. The principal difference is that strategy 3 permits a real-time analysis of test results, which can often be accomplished by performing data reduction concurrently with test case execution. This approach eliminates data reduction delays in factoring test results into development of additional test scenarios.

Regardless of the method used, the following actions are critical to a successful real-time test process:

1. Accurately matching simulator time, software time, and wall clock time is nontrivial. Errors tend to occur in clock drifts, in algorithms involving integration, and in round-off and truncation in all time-based algorithms. A major problem is usually found in modeling

a continuous environment by means of a discrete model. Therefore, the clock used to synchronize simulator and software is a key consideration.

2. Establishing an accurate model of only those elements and details of the operational environment that are meaningful to system operation requires sound technical judgment. If the model becomes too complex, it will be difficult to execute in real time. If the model is too simple, it may not characterize a performance-critical operational feature.

3. Developing a comprehensive set of test scenarios (test cases that depict all operating conditions, especially timing, that the system will see in its operational environment) is very important. A wide variety of event combinations in time and in operating conditions will naturally occur in the operational environment. Capturing a set that will maximize chances that errors will be caught is a challenge to both system and software engineer.

4. Accumulation of as much operating time as possible by as many different parties as possible in the simulator is highly desirable. The likelihood of encountering a problem and exposing a fault increases with operating time.

19.6   CHAPTER SUMMARY ■

A real-time software product is software that has components that are strongly time dependent. The major concerns in developing real-time software are as follows:

1. The specification of time-dependent features of the software product must be correct, accurate, and complete. The SRS for time-dependent components must clearly define time dependency among a variety of tasks and their interaction with shared software resources. For each task, the SRS must indicate whether the task is periodic or aperiodic and describe its period and deadline including the nature of the deadline (hard or soft).

2. The design of the time-dependent components of real-time software requires particular attention. For each periodic or aperiodic task, the SDS must include an accurate estimate of task execution time (under a worst-case scenario) and task completion time (task execution plus overhead time plus possible block time). The SDS must present an account of task dependency among all tasks. The SDS must estimate the execution time for each shared service used in the system. These estimations cannot be overly conservative because a collection of very conservative estimates makes it difficult or even impossible to schedule tasks. These estimates will become design requirements imposed on detailed design and coding.

3. The scheduling of independent and dependent periodic and aperiodic tasks is another major problem that must be addressed in the SDS. Four theorems were presented in this chapter that can provide help in establishing a schedule for independent as well as dependent periodic tasks.

4. Real-time software requires special attention in the test and integration phase. Many real-time requirements should be tested in the operation environment. However, for many real-time software products, testing in the operational environment is either too costly or too dangerous. The other alternative is to use a simulated operational environment to test the software. Hence, many real-time development environments must have access to very accurate simulation software for testing purposes.

There are many more scheduling and testing concerns that have not been addressed in this chapter. For a full account of the schedulability of real-time software, the reader needs to refer to periodicals and journal publications dedicated to the discussion of real-time software problems.

19.7 EXERCISES ■

1. Discuss the following questions, using a formal method (trade-off matrix, cost-benefit analysis, decision table, etc.) to arrive at an answer.
   a. How does the testing of real-time software differ from the testing of other software?
   b. Is assembly language the most appropriate coding language for real-time software?
   c. Is it feasible to solve the deadlock and blocking problems by duplicating resources?
   d. What are the major characteristics of real-time software? Does real-time software mean faster software?
   e. In your view, are the characteristics of embedded software the same as the characteristics of real-time software?
   f. What are the real-time components of a typical multiuser, multiprogram operating system?
   g. What are the real-time components of a database management system?
   h. Can the deadline of a periodic task exceed its period? What will happen if the deadline of a task is larger than its period?
2. Suppose you are to design a software system to run an automobile in which the driver commands the steering wheel and provides vision. Write the SRS for such a system. Specify the real-time components of this system. Note that the driver may choose to control the gas and/or brake pedals or leave it to the software to control either one or both.
3. Develop a schedule timeline, if possible, using the RMS algorithm for the following independent periodic tasks. If the tasks are not schedulable, indicate the reason. When there is more than one timeline for task schedules, find the shortest timeline. Note that task 4 in (a) is a periodic task with a soft deadline. As long as it is completed within 100 to 200 milliseconds of its arrival, there will be no problem.

a.

Task 1	Task 2	Task 3	Task 4
$C = 25$	$C = 20$	$C = 10$	$C = 50$
$T = 100$	$T = 120$	$T = 80$	$T = 100\text{–}200$

b.

Task 1	Task 2	Task 3	Task 4
$C = 20$	$C = 20$	$C = 40$	$C = 5$
$T = 100$	$T = 60$	$T = 100$	$T = 25$

c.

Task 1	Task 2	Task 3	Task 4
$C = 10$	$C = 20$	$C = 20$	$C = 25$
$T = 100$	$T = 100$	$T = 80$	$T = 125$
$D = 80$	$D = 60$	$D = 80$	$D = 100$

4. Develop a schedule timeline, if possible, using the RMS algorithm for the following periodic tasks. If the tasks are not schedulable, indicate the reason. When there is more than one schedule timeline, find the shortest. There are three servers (S_1, S_2, and S_3) that may be utilized by these tasks. Note that $S_i = 0$ in a task column means the corresponding task is not using server S_i. On the other hand, $S_i = n$ in a task column means the corresponding task is utilizing server S_i for n milliseconds.

a.

Task 1	Task 2	Task 3	Task 4
$C = 25$	$C = 20$	$C = 10$	$C = 10$
$T = 100$	$T = 120$	$T = 80$	$T = 100$
$S_1 = 0$	$S_1 = 2$	$S_1 = 3$	$S_1 = 0$
$S_2 = 1$	$S_2 = 0$	$S_2 = 4$	$S_2 = 0$
$S_3 = 2$	$S_3 = 3$	$S_3 = 0$	$S_3 = 0$

b.

Task 1	Task 2	Task 3	Task 4
$C = 20$	$C = 20$	$C = 20$	$C = 5$
$T = 100$	$T = 60$	$T = 100$	$T = 125$
$S_1 = 0$	$S_1 = 2$	$S_1 = 3$	$S_1 = 1$
$S_2 = 0$	$S_2 = 1$	$S_2 = 0$	$S_2 = 0$
$S_3 = 0$	$S_3 = 3$	$S_3 = 0$	$S_3 = 1$

In the following, the value 0-2 for task 2 means that task 2 uses server S_1 on even number of times scheduled. That is, on the first frame (a timeline on which all tasks are scheduled and completed at least once) task 2 won't use S_1, on the second frame it will use S_1 for 2 milliseconds, on the third frame it won't use S_1, and so on.

c.

Task 1	Task 2	Task 3	Task 4
$C = 10$	$C = 20$	$C = 20$	$C = 25$
$T = 100$	$T = 100$	$T = 80$	$T = 125$
$D = 80$	$D = 60$	$D = 80$	$D = 100$
$S_1 = 0$	$S_1 = 0\text{-}2$	$S_1 = 3$	$S_1 = 1$
$S_2 = 3$	$S_2 = 1$	$S_2 = 2$	$S_2 = 0$
$S_3 = 0$	$S_3 = 2$	$S_3 = 0$	$S_3 = 1$

5. If there was a case in problem 3 where there was no scheduling timeline possible (tasks were unscheduable), use the reciprocal of the task deadline as its priority and try to schedule tasks using this new priority assignment.

6. For any case in problem 4 where a deadlock or priority inversion has occurred, use the priority ceiling protocol to remove the deadlock and the priority inversion.

7. Create an example of independent tasks that cannot be scheduled, using the RMS algorithm.

8. Create an example of three tasks and two servers that frees both deadlock and priority inversion during the first round of scheduling.

9. Schedule the tasks of problem 3 using task completion time as priority of the task.

10. Schedule the tasks in problem 3 using the reciprocal of the completion time as the priority of each task.

11. Schedule the tasks in problem 4 using the reciprocal of task deadline as the priority of the task.

12. Four static priorities are schedule rate, schedule deadline, schedule completion time, and the reciprocal of task completion time. Discuss the advantages and the disadvantages of each of these static priorities.

13. One dynamic priority measure could be the number of output signals produced by a task in its previous execution. Is there a situation in which this dynamic priority would be helpful in rescheduling tasks?

14. Define preset timelines to test the tasks in problem 3.

15. In testing real-time software, the lag between test execution and results analysis can slow down the process and even jeopardize the accuracy of the results. Discuss this problem in more detail and devise a solution.

References

1. R. Kurki-Suonio, "Real-Time: Further Misconceptions (or Half Truths)," *IEEE Comp.* Vol. 27, No. 6 pages 71–76 (1994).

2. J. P. Lehoczky, L. Sha, and Y. Ding, "The Rate Monotonic Scheduling Algorithm—Exact Characterization and Behavior," in *IEEE Real-Time System Symposium*, IEEE, New York, 1989.

3. J. Leung and J. Whitehead, "On the Complexity of Fixed Priority Scheduling of Periodic, Real-Time Tasks," *Perf. Eval.* Vol. 2, No. 4. (4):237–250, (1982).

4. C. Liu and J. Layland, "Scheduling Algorithms for Multi-programming in a Hard Real-Time Environment," *J. ACM* **20**(1):46–61, (1973).

5. L. Sha, R. Rajkumar, S. H. Son and C. H. Chang, "A Real-Time Locking Protocol," *IEEE Trans. Comp.* **40**(7):793–798, (1991).

6. L. Sha, R. Rajkumar, and S. Sathaye, "Generalized Rate-Monotonic Scheduling Theory: A Framework for Developing Real-Time Systems," *Proceedings of the IEEE, Special Issue on Real-Time Systems*, **82**(1):68–82, (1994).

7. K. D. Shere and R. A. Carlson, "A Methodology for Design, Test and Evaluation of Real-Time Systems," *IEEE Comp.*, Vol. 27, No. 2, pages 35–48 (1994).

Additional Reading

8. S. H. Son, ed., *Advances in Real-Time Systems*, Prentice-Hall, Upper Saddle River, N.J., 1995. (This book contains a collection of 41 recent research papers related to problems concerning real-time systems.)

20

Human Factors in Software Engineering

20.0 OBJECTIVES ■

The primary objective of this chapter is to call attention to the fact that the integrated efforts of both the machine (information system) and its operators are required to accomplish mission or system goals. The second objective is to outline, in general terms, a process whereby the operator/user is treated as a major component of the information system and his or her interaction with the system is elevated to the same status as any other component interface to the information system. The third objective is to make the software engineer aware that human-to-computer interface design is a broad technical field with many areas of specialization.

20.1 INTRODUCTION ■

Typically, fifty percent of a software product's code is associated with effecting an interface between the operator/user and the information system [1]. Neglect of human factors or human-computer interfaces has often been cited as a major contributor to the "software crisis" and information system problems in general. Often a poorly designed operator-to-information system interface has been at least partially responsible for tragic accidents such as the

THERAC-25 incidents [4], the unfortunate attack on the Iranian airliner (flight 655) by the SS *Vincennes*, and the 1979 Three Mile Island (TMI) incident. An excerpt from a critique of the TMI incident reads as follows:

> The disregard for human factors in the control room was appalling. In some cases the distribution of displays and controls seemed almost haphazard. It was as if someone had taken a box of dials and switches, turned his back, thrown the whole thing at the board and attached things wherever they landed. For instance, sometimes 10 to 15 feet separated controls from displays that had to be monitored while controls were being operated. Also at times no displays were provided to present critical information to the operators.
>
> There were many instances where information was displayed in a manner that was not usable by the operators or else was misleading to them. A textbook example of what can go wrong in a man-machine system when people in the system have not been taken into account. There were also failures of automatic equipment that had nothing to do with disregard for human engineering so you cannot make the flat statement that the incident could have been prevented if human factors had been taken into account, but the probability of its happening would have been much lower.

The Association for Computing Machinery Special Interest Group on Human Computer Interface (ACM-SIGHCI) offers the following definition of human computer interactions [1]: ''Human-Computer interaction is a discipline concerned with the design, evaluation, and implementation of interactive computing systems for human use and with the study of major phenomena surrounding them.'' We will find this definition useful if we broaden computing systems to include the more general information systems.

There are many large information systems that are connected to hundreds or thousands of operator workstations where routine operator tasks are performed hundreds of times per day. Operator performance enhancements that arise as a result of a more efficient human-computer interface (HCI) can produce significant savings in operating costs. For example, a savings of 10 to 15 seconds in 80% of the customer transactions for a health insurance company were estimated to produce an overall savings of nearly $40,000 per month [2]. In many instances savings in operating cost are realized through the following: (1) reduced interaction time with each customer, (2) reduced telephone connect time, (3) reduced training time required for new employees, (4) reduced number of errors requiring additional interaction, (5) improved customer relations, and (6) better operator morale.

Other information systems are connected to a few operators' stations, performing critical tasks and making decisions that involve public safety or the operation of major parts of the power generation or communication infrastructure. Improved HCI can also reduce the likelihood of occurrence of undesirable incidents that are associated with public safety (FAA air traffic control system, for example) and the power and communication networks. These improvements can be obtained by (1) minimizing the complexity of operator tasks, (2) reducing display clutter, (3) protecting the system from operator error, and (4) simplifying HCI designs. The net effect is a reduction in operator stress and an improvement in operator morale, both of which lead to better performance.

A negative reaction on the part of operators and users of software products, although often expressed as a dissatisfaction with the system, is frequently only a reaction to a poorly designed human-computer interface. The software engineer should be sensitive to all operator comments to gain a better appreciation of operator reaction to the HCI design.

It should be made clear that reading a few pages in a software engineering text is not adequate preparation for designing human-to-computer interfaces. However, this chapter does provide an overview and a few fundamental principles for guidance in human-to-computer interface design. For systems that will be widely used by many operators or system designs that allocate mission-critical functions to operators, a specialist in HCI should be consulted.

20.2   HUMAN FACTORS HISTORY   ■

Human factors as a recognized discipline grew out of the field of operations research and analysis before and during World War II. Human factors studies were stimulated by the need to design systems that included humans as a critical operational element. Designers were forced to consider the human in terms of machinelike or control system performance attributes. Attributes such as cognitive abilities, ability to process sensor inputs, and motor skills were measured and used as design parameters. For example, a major concern was the ability of the human operator to recognize the presence of a signal in a noisy background, to make critical decisions, and to control an actuator by responding to a signal observed on a display. The end objective of human factors was (and is) to design sensors, displays, and controls that will result in an operationally successful integrated human/machine system.

One definition of *human factors* that has appeared frequently in the literature is the following: a discipline that discovers through study and measurements information about human abilities, limitations, and other physical and mental characteristics; and applies this knowledge to the design of tools, machines, systems, tasks, jobs, and environments for safe, comfortable, and effective human use [3]. A wealth of information has been accumulated on human performance over the years. Most of this material is in the domain of human factors specialists.

Ergonomics is a more recently coined term and covers both human factors and industrial engineering. Ergonomics is the study of anthropometric and physiological characteristics of people and their relationship to work space and environmental parameters. The goal of ergonomics is to develop the appropriate work environment (physical and emotional) so that human resources may be applied in the most effective way.

We view the HCI discipline as a blend of human factors, industrial engineering, and ergonomics applied to computer information systems. Other fields that are related to the study of human factors in general and HCI in particular are the following: applied experimental psychology, bioastronautics, biomechanics, engineering psychology, human engineering, human factors engineering, human performance evaluation, life sciences engineering, life support system design, man-machine design, personnel, subsystem design, and software psychology.

20.3   HCI REQUIREMENTS AND DESIGN PROCESS   ■

While the obvious focus of HCI is on how the operator/user routinely interfaces with the computer information system, there are some not-so-obvious aspects of HCI such as error messages, documentation, maintenance issues, and training that deserve attention. In the THERAC-25 system [4], an important error message was routinely ignored by operators because they did not understand its meaning. Error messages were given in terms of a number that referenced a highly technical explanation of the problem. Operators quickly learned how to circumvent all error messages and continue to use the system. In several instances the ambiguous ''malfunction 54'' error message was warning of an unsafe operating condition. Circumventing the error message and proceeding with the operation of the system in the face of this error message resulted in killing and maiming several human patients [4]. Documentation is another form of human-computer interface. Who of us has not been frustrated by poorly written, ambiguous, misleading, and inadequate documentation? Another interface issue, maintenance of a system, is often not thought about until the system is nearly complete and in its final test phases. Maintainers need to have their interface to the system considered during design. Who of us has not experienced the frustration of trying to make a routine replacement of a failed component only to find that the item must be completely disassembled in order to replace the component? Those involved in training new users or maintainers also interface with the system. Their needs are an important consideration in the design of the HCI.

We consider five major steps in the design of a successful HCI. Step 1 is to allocate system functions to the three system components—software, hardware, and operators/users. Step 2 is to develop operator functions as a family of operational scenarios or timelines. Step 3 is to analyze operational tasks derived from these timelines. Step 4 is to develop the HCI design. Step 5 is to construct a prototype of the HCI design to test operational timelines, operator satisfaction, operator task execution, etc. This design process is depicted in Figure 20.1.

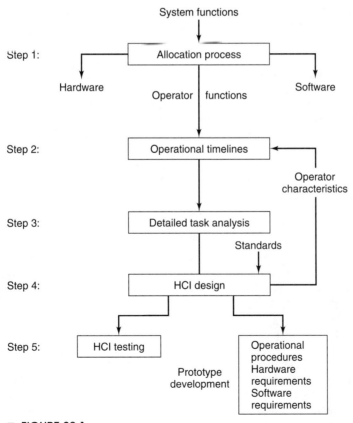

■ FIGURE 20.1

HCI design process.

20.3.1 System Function Allocation (Step 1)

Even though we have postponed discussion of HCI until this chapter of the book, consideration of the HCI should begin early in the development cycle. In fact, as functions are being allocated to hardware and software components, functions are either explicitly or implicitly being allocated to operators and users. The architecture of both system and software often have significant implications regarding interfaces to the system by operators, users, maintainers, and trainers. At this point in system and software development, HCI considerations can have high leverage influence.

In some system and software development processes, there is an explicit step in which allocation of system functional requirements to operators is accomplished. In these processes the role of the operator is defined early in the development cycle and made an intrinsic part of the design process. Unfortunately, this explicit function allocation step is often not addressed early enough in the development cycle.

20.3.2 Operational Timelines (Step 2)

An operational timeline is a graphic depiction of system operational modes showing, step-by-step, the dynamics of integrated system operation. Operational timelines are used to describe system operations where time is an important factor. Operational scenarios are used to describe system operations where time is not a critical factor. We shall use operational timelines to refer to both. Operational timelines are the basis for operator/user manuals, training materials, position description handbooks, etc. Frequently, the development of detailed operational timelines will uncover system requirements that were not recognized during initial studies and analyses.

The development of operational timelines requires a knowledge of system operational requirements and operator characteristics as well as the functions allocated to operators. An important ingredient in the HCI design process is a well-defined description of operator characteristics. In order to match the operator to the system it is essential to have a clear understanding of the capabilities of the operator community. Having developed timelines for each operational mode including those associated with off-nominal situations (failures, unusual operational circumstances, rare events, etc.), the software engineer develops (in conjunction with operators) a set of detailed operator task descriptions for each workstation and each mode. These operator task descriptions are written in the input/process/output format. Operator task descriptions enable the software engineer to identify what specific information the operator needs from the system and what the system needs from the operator. In establishing the HCI design, the software engineer may draw upon certain existing policies, guidelines, and standards.

Figure 20.2 shows a simple example of one form of operational timeline. The function of each system component is shown as it relates to performance of a specific system function. The operator keys a six-character customer ID to initiate the transaction. The HCI uses this input as a command to download the customer file. A second keystroke initiates a credit card approval and an accounting check. In the meantime the operator is verbally confirming with the customer what the customer file reads as a balance. The next step is to download a specific decision matrix, a script and operator prompt function based on the nature of the customer's

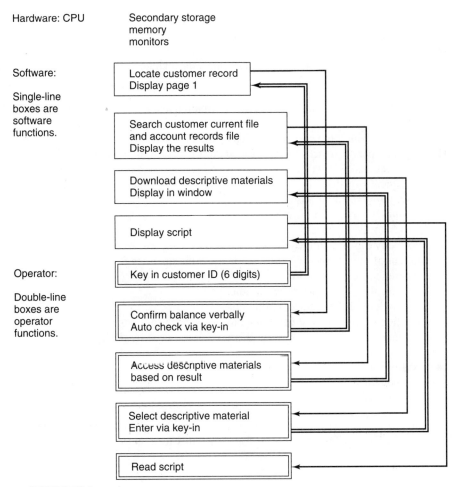

Hardware: CPU   Secondary storage
                       memory
                       monitors

Software:

Single-line
boxes are
software
functions.

Operator:

Double-line
boxes are
operator
functions.

■ FIGURE 20.2

Typical Operational timeline.

business. The involvement of operators, users, and customers in establishing these timelines is the means by which the customer maintains contact with the software development cycle, expresses satisfaction (or dissatisfaction) with development progress, and becomes acquainted with a major component of the acceptance criteria.

20.3.3   Operational Task Analysis (Step 3)

Task analysis includes developing a comprehensive description or specification of the required tasks in sufficient detail to permit a determination of the number of operators required, skills and knowledge required of each operator, and training requirements. To perform a task analysis, a preliminary or conceptual version of the information system must be available. In addition, operational timelines must have been developed. As in many other information system development activities, the process is iterative with a stepwise refinement of the detail as more insight is developed.

The data collected during operational task analysis include, but are not limited to, the following:

1. Information required by the operator and information available to the operator to perform the task
2. The manner in which the operator evaluates the information
3. The way the operator reaches a decision about the action to be taken and:
     Specific actions to be taken
     The frequency of the actions
     Precisely how the action is effected
     How quickly the action must be taken
     Feedback to the operator
4. Operator body movements required by the action being performed
5. The amount of physical work space available to the operator for the action
6. Other operators involved in the action
7. The exact location of the work environment
8. The exact nature of the work environment
9. A description of the working conditions to include the following:
     Additional tools, equipment, data, information required by the operator
     Special hazards involved
10. The level of training and/or experience required of operators
11. General operator interactions
12. A staffing description and limitation

The results of a task analysis can be entered on a predefined form described in MIL-H-46855, section 3.2.1.3.2. The compressed format for this form is as follows:

0. Heading identifying the specific task
1. Start time
2. Task or step name
3. Description
4. Start cue
5. Information provided to operator
6. Evaluations and decisions
7. Operator actions
8. Feedback to operator
9. Duration and frequency
10. Communication and coordination
11. Concurrent tasks
12. Other pertinent data

20.3.4   HCI Design (Step 4)

In this section some of the most common concerns in the HCI design process are discussed and some guidelines to help in developing the most effective HCI design are presented. The common concerns in the HCI design are system failures, help packages, response times, operator characteristics, and external environment.

System Failures

The most critical time in an operational system is when anomalies are experienced. That is, the system fails outright or unusual performance situations are encountered that are outside the design envelope. Systems are designed to respond to these situations by issuing error messages to operators, automatically shutting down the system, making the system safe, etc. Oftentimes, the software is relied upon to implement fail-safe procedures and notify operators of actions they should take or explain actions already taken automatically. The following are some general design guidelines with regard to a system failure situation:

1. Error messages should convey a clear description to the operator of what has happened. The message should be designed to be understandable by the operator. If the problem requires the attention of someone other than the operator, the error message should identify that person.
2. If a failure has occurred, the error message should describe the recovery path in terms understandable to the operator.
3. The error message should provide a reference source for further information.
4. The error message should indicate any consequences that the operator must either correct or avoid given the failure occurrence.
5. Other indications that will confirm the failure source should be made part of the error message.

Help Packages

On-line help is often part of the delivered software product. Reference manuals, operator guides, position description handbooks, etc., are other sources for help. The best approach to on-line help is to keep it brief, focused, and direct and provide references for further information. Support documentation is difficult to write; it requires writing skills that are usually in short supply and must address an audience with varied background. However, an experienced software engineer with good writing skills can produce a set of useful supporting documents.

Response Times

There are two response times associated with the HCI design, system response time and operator response time. System response time is the time the system takes to react to the operator input. System response time must be consistent, and there should be an absolute response time specified by the HCI designer in advance. Normally, a one-second absolute response time is both practical and acceptable. It is understood that there are tasks that may take only a few milliseconds to complete and there are tasks that may take 5 to 15 seconds to complete. When tasks take longer than the specified response time, the HCI design must require the software to communicate with the user by a message such as "This task will take a bit longer than a normal task," "Your task will be completed in a few seconds," or "We are still working on your task."

Operator response time is the time taken by the operator to issue a new command. The HCI design must take into account the fact that operators may possess a wide range of physical capabilities, and the software side of the HCI must also recognize this fact and account for it in designs. For example, a design that reverts to a default option without giving the operator ample time to absorb information and make a decision could place many operators in a stressful situation and result in errors.

Operator Characteristics

Operator characteristics are important inputs to the design process. The designer needs to have a clear picture of those who will operate the system. There is an amusing story about a classroom software product designed for use by preschool children that had very complex on-screen written instructions to the children explaining how to use the software. Probably the most important concern regarding operator characteristics is the operator's workload. The operator task descriptions offer an indication of the expected workload for each operator. Some additional analysis may be required to obtain peak, average, and low workload levels.

External Environment

Another significant parameter in the HCI design activity is the expected external environment. Additional probing may be needed to ascertain the full range of physical environment and emotional conditions under which the operator will handle his or her workload.

A great deal of effort by the Department of Defense has produced the following useful HCI references:

MIL-H-46855B	Human Engineering Requirements
AFSC-DH 1-3	Human Factors Engineering
MIL-STD-1472C	Human Engineering Design Criteria
MIL-HDBK-759A	Human Factors Engineering for Army Material

These documents are available from the Government Printing Office. Many of the HCI design rules and much of the design guidance contained in these documents are directly applicable to information systems designed for use in the private sector. The HCI design rules and design guidance are the result of a great deal of experience and research in human behavior. It would be foolish indeed to ignore this experience. The following HCI design guidelines reflect both good and bad features the reader will recognize from some popular software products. These guidelines are organized into three categories: general guidelines, display guidelines, and operator command guidelines.

General Guidelines

1. Standardize on-screen formats, menus, alarms, etc., as much as possible.
2. Keep the operator informed. Make sure each on-screen feedback message is clear and meaningful.
3. Force operators to confirm any commands that have destructive consequences.
4. Make it possible for operators to cancel commands without penalty of exiting and returning.
5. Treat the operator as having zero memory capability. Eliminate the need to retain information from screen to screen.

6. Make every effort to minimize the input required of operators in time and motion.
7. Protect the system from operator errors so that it is not necessary to exit and reenter when an entry error is made. Clear visual or audible signals should be used.
8. Structure menus and other command hierarchies in logical function groups. That is, produce some form of organization in presenting on-screen information.

Display Guidelines

1. Minimize information displayed to the operator. Focus operator attention on task-relevant information only.
2. Use graphics rather than text where appropriate to convey information.
3. Follow the idea of consistency in how and where information is displayed. Standardize on colors, sizes, abbreviations, jargon, and location of messages.
4. Make use of windows concept to keep the operator in the proper context.
5. Use standard formats for text presentation.

Operator Command Guidelines

1. Reduce operator workload to the absolute minimum consistent with carrying out functional requirements.
2. Exercise caution in allowing operators to freewheel. If possible, frequently used command sequences should be grouped and activated by a single command. These packaged commands should be fully tested to assure that there are no subtle problems.
3. Provide options (mouse and command line entry, for example) for operator entries.
4. Make it possible to specialize a workstation to a single operator's functions. For example, if an operator does only one set of tasks, that workstation (HCI) should be confined to support only those tasks (in keeping with the first display guideline).

20.3.5 HCI Testing (Step 5)

The last step in the process is to test the design. Software tools such as user interface development systems (UIDS) can assist in rapidly prototyping and evaluating HCI designs. These tools enable software engineers to synthesize and test candidate HCI designs quickly using operators as testers. There are four major reasons for performing HCI testing as early as possible:

1. Test results will have a definite bearing on other design efforts, either confirming existing designs or forcing changes to existing designs.
2. The HCI will be the basis for acceptance testing. The HCI will be the most important element during acceptance testing. These early HCI tests will be a rehearsal for acceptance tests.
3. Operational timeline development almost always produces surprises and additional function and performance requirements overlooked in the analysis phase.
4. Emphasis on HCI design early in system and software design will make the development team aware that satisfactory system performance will depend upon all components functioning in concert.

Prototypes of the HCI design can also be used to train operators, perform human factors research studies, demonstrate system operation to customers, and prepare test personnel for system integration and test.

As depicted in Figure 20.1, the HCI design process is sequential. However, in practice, the process steps are often concurrent and the process is always highly iterative.

20.4 THE HUMAN AS INFORMATION SYSTEM COMPONENT   ■

If we look at the human component in a system as shown in Figure 20.3, we can see that the human sensors are eyes, ears, and tactile sense. The processing is handled in the brain and the extremities, voice, eye, and head motion are employed as actuators. The communication between the human component and the information system component is through displays, usually visual but frequently audio, and control panels of one sort or another. One fact that is important and often overlooked is the environment in which the HCI is conducted. The human component of an information system can be influenced by heat, stress, humidity, and factors totally unrelated to the immediate environment. In short, the operator is a relatively unpredictable component in an information system (any system, for that matter). The operator does have advantages as a component that far outweigh his or her disadvantages. First, the human operator is adaptive; that is, the operator can learn and adapt to situations and then anticipate or extrapolate to similar situations by making small adjustments in performance.

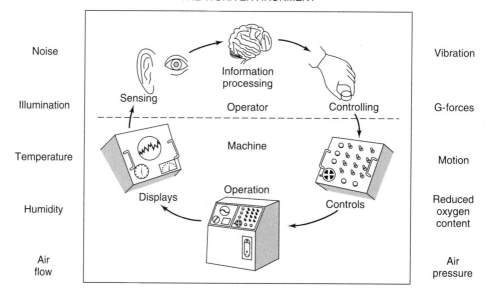

THE WORK ENVIRONMENT

■ FIGURE 20.3

Operator-machine model.

Human factors studies have confirmed this ability and quantified associated performance parameters [6]. Second, the operator can make unprogrammed decisions; that is, the operator can recognize emerging patterns and situations and make new decisions based on a dynamic development of new decision criteria.

The HCI designer has a variety of display options available. Figure 20.4 shows some of these options. For visual display size, color, contrast, illumination, format, location, shape, rates, and motion may be used to effect a useful interface. For audio ''display'' the designer can use frequency, complexity, signal-to-noise ratio, intensity, and duration to effect communication. The HCI designer can employ such parameters as shape, size, rotation, motion, location, texture, spacing, force feedback, and key travel to accept inputs from the operator.

The human component can be characterized as follows. Input devices include eyes, ears, and tactile sense. The interpretation of any input is handled by the brain. The results are stored in the brain as either long-term memory or short-term memory. Information is recalled as needed and employed to make a decision and effect some reaction. This process has been characterized mathematically in the terminology of control system dynamics [7]. It may be of some interest to explore this model in more detail.

The rate at which data can be effectively displayed is determined by the ability of the human operator to respond to information in an appropriate manner. Of the many proposed human response functions we present one:

$$G(S) = \frac{D(1 + T_1 S)e^{-DS}}{(1 + T_2 S)(1 + T_3 S)} \qquad (20.1)$$

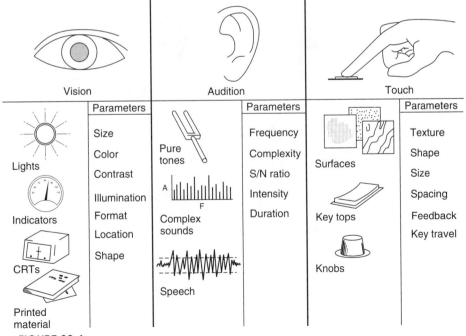

■ **FIGURE 20.4**

Display selection and design.

where

D = Operator transport lag
K = Constant
T_1 = Anticipation time constant
T_2 = Error-smoothing time constant
T_3 = Short neuromuscular delay
S = Laplace transformation variable

Human factors studies have shown that the human transfer function, $G(S)$, varies over a wide range [5,7]. The human data rate capacity is, for example, somewhere between 50 and 100 bits per second. What this means to the HCI designer is that displayed information rates must be adjusted for the human operator by retaining displayed images, filtering, extracting critical information, and producing and displaying a reduced version. Update times of 1 to 2 seconds are roughly compatible with human capabilities if more than a few bits of information are to change. In many cases 10 to 30 seconds are required to accommodate slowly changing data with large information content. The HCI designer must often match the best performance features of the human component with the best performance features of other system components.

It is difficult to model or characterize human performance because humans are adaptive and their behavior is nonlinear. Some attention has recently been directed at use of neural networks to enhance human-to-computer interfaces.

In the model represented by Equation (20.1), the average reaction delay time for the human operator is 0.14 seconds. Models such as the one shown in Equation (20.1) might be useful in the analysis and modeling of applications in which operator response is an important system design parameter.

But these are the most basic of the physical attributes of the human information system component. Other parameters also can influence the human to machine interface. These parameters are associated with background, intelligence, education, level of comfort with using an information system interface, personal attitudes, and motivation.

The HCI designer must be sure that the operator/user community characteristics are well understood since they will be part of the means for satisfying system requirements. The software engineer must also be concerned because software will be used to effect the interface. One often repeated problem has been that the HCI was designed for use by someone with the same characteristics as the designer. That is, it is implicitly assumed that operators will have the same background, motivation, and skill level as the designer. Another common problem has been the use of part of the operational timeline to fix or cover up a design oversight. For example, the development of operational timelines late in the development process uncovers omission of a design feature; for convenience, the missing design feature or function is handled by increasing operator workload and altering operational timelines rather than redesigning the information system. The negative consequences are operator complaints during system acceptance testing.

20.5 OPERATOR TASK DEVELOPMENT ■

Development of operational timelines for each operator position and each operational mode forms the basis for development of operator task descriptions. Operator involvement in constructing and reviewing operational timelines is absolutely essential. The task descriptions also form the new material for such documentation as position description handbooks and user manuals. Task descriptions also form the basis for training material development. Operational modes should include start-up, shutdown, and especially exceptions. It is difficult to see how a software design can be effected without a deep and comprehensive understanding of operational timelines. Moreover, operational timelines should be an intrinsic element of the information system design phase.

Perhaps the most effective way to start describing operator tasks is to think of the operator in terms of just another system component. Then the input/process/output approach will define requirements that need to be satisfied by operator tasks. This approach also determines the operator input and any other support needs. In general, operator tasks can be categorized as follows: recognition, interaction, decision, and control.

A recognition task involves the identification of events, situations, or circumstances that require an operator intervention of some form. Usually recognition tasks require some human judgment capability, an unprogrammable decision process, or a safety-critical event recognition. The designer's objective is to provide the operator with the best possible information presented in the most appropriate form for recognition. Frequently the event being looked for will appear in a noisy environment where uncertainty is large. False alarms are more frequent in this kind of operational situation. A good question that might be asked of a human factors consultant is, ''What is the most effective way to get the attention of an operator?''

An interaction task involves the operator in a continuing interactive dialogue with the information system. An example might be an operator fitting a curve to raw data with a time requirement for obtaining a best fit. The operator might have at his or her disposal editing tools, several curve fitting schemes, and a means to evaluate residuals for each fit. The rest of the process might be fully automated, but system designers feel that editing requires operator judgment and intervention. A design to effect this interface can be complex and require a significant amount of software to accomplish. A great deal of short-term memory is also required.

A decision task requires that the data and information needed to make a good decision be presented in a format that can be interpreted quickly and unambiguously. It is often necessary to allow the operator to query the system (database) for additional information or data. All the possible combinations of data and information that might be used should be identified and prepared beforehand.

A control task usually has an operator response time requirement with the operator placed in the control path. Oftentimes the operator is in control of the entire system and functions as an in-line component of the system. Models such as the one described in section 20.4 may prove useful for control task allocations.

In practice most systems are not 100%, newly conceived systems. They are old systems being replaced by new systems with more automation and newer technology, or perhaps they are existing systems being augmented by adjunct components to meet new requirements. Thus there is an experience base and some ideas about how operator tasks can be defined, modified, or eliminated.

20.5.1   Operator Requirements Specification

To document an operator task description (actually an operator requirement), we can follow the format we established in chapter 4 for hardware and software requirement specifications.

We can begin by identifying what is expected of the operator as a task output. The description should be stated as a requirement. For example, ''The operator shall eliminate unreasonable points in the raw data based on the following criteria . . . .'' The definition of input data, other adjunct information requirements, and operator subtasks should follow easily. Special terminology and jargon should be avoided if possible or at least clearly defined. The focus should be on what the operator is required to do, not how he or she should do it.

Some specific operator considerations include workload, expected response, input (rates, frequency, volume, error recognition, range), output (rates, defaults, errors, error recovery) as well as other avenues of control and off-nominal modes of operation. Workload involves the tasks the operator is expected to perform in a given time interval in terms of peak, average, and low arrival rates. The external environment is a critical concern since a set of tasks that are easy to perform under normal circumstances may be very difficult to perform under conditions of physical and mental stress. It is felt that the SS *Vincennes* incident was due, at least in part, to a failure to recognize the impact of stress on the performance of certain operator tasks.

The objective of characterizing operator function and performance requirements is to understand completely the operators function within the timelines and the expected environment. It has been shown that increased workload and increased environmental stress lead to increased operator error. Therefore, workload consideration is of prime concern in designing HCI.

With a comprehensive understanding of both the operator's role in the operational timeline and the range of external environment characteristics, the choice of menus, icons, windows, prompts, on-line accesses, and presentation formats can be made. The fundamental design question is how can the human and machine together accomplish the given task in the expected range of internal and external environments.

20.6 OPERATOR CHARACTERISTICS ■

As Figure 20.1 showed, operator characteristics play an important role in the HCI design, that of input to both operational timelines and the HCI design process. Operator characteristics might be categorized in one of three ways:

1. Operators possess little overall understanding of the application area and the system. They are trained as operators for only one position. They do not stay long on the job. They are trained only briefly and not highly motivated.
2. Operators do understand the application area but not the system. They are cross-trained on other positions. The best performers are moved to related supervisory positions. Many stay on for several years and become very proficient operators.
3. Operators are highly motivated, have a good knowledge of both application area and system, and are upwardly mobile. The best performers move up. The average performers stay for a few years, and poor performers are terminated or moved to other jobs.

The three categories given above are typical of most system operator communities. It is best to examine the specific user community for a given system development and then develop a composite characterization of the operator team. It may also work the other way. That is, based on revisions being made to the system, a new operator type may be needed to handle new operator tasks developed from new operational timelines. The direction is usually toward reducing the number of operators as well as skills, judgment, training, etc., required of those remaining operators, thereby reducing operating cost. Reducing the number of required operators by one can result in a $100,000 per year saving.

In summary, it is important to remember that to develop a good HCI, an accurate portrayal of operator tasks must be derived from a comprehensive set of operational timelines. In addition, the operators must be characterized in terms of their abilities, motivation, and attitude.

20.7 CHAPTER SUMMARY ■

The overall performance of an information system depends upon the integrated performance of its hardware, software, operators, and maintainers. To expect quality performance from operators and maintainers, a quality HCI design is required. We described a sequence of five steps in the HCI design process. These steps were to confirm function allocation, develop operational timelines, analyze operator task definitions, develop an HCI design, and test the HCI design.

Validation and verification of HCI is a continuing effort throughout the development cycle. There are many ways to confirm an HCI design; however, all take time and effort. The HCI design process must begin early in the development cycle so that firm answers can be obtained to questions of operability and operator satisfaction.

A major objective of the HCI design is to predict in advance what can be expected of the human operator and the combined human operator-information system performance. A major area of concern during acceptance test is to confirm the acceptability of the HCI design. The following are objectives for a successful HCI design:

a. To reduce errors
b. To increase safety
c. To improve information system performance
d. To improve reliability
e. To improve maintainability
f. To reduce training requirements
g. To reduce personnel requirements for number of operators
h. To improve operator working environment
i. To reduce fatigue and physical stress
j. To increase comfort for human operators
k. To reduce boredom and monotony
l. To increase user acceptance
m. To reduce loss of time and information system equipment
n. To increase efficiency of operation

20.8 EXERCISES ■

1. Describe an HCI that you feel is poorly designed. Explain why you think it is poorly designed.

2. Describe an HCI that you feel is exceptionally well designed. Explain why you think it is a good design.

3. Describe the HCI design considerations you would envision for an air traffic controller's workstation.

4. Develop an operational timeline and task descriptions for an on-line credit card confirmation system.

References

1. ACM-SIGHCI, *Curricula for Human Computer Interaction*, ACM, New York, 1992.
2. C. Bangert, T. Gillespie and K. Hughes *Project Callpath, Towson State University Report*, Baltimore, Maryland, 1993.
3. Engineering Data Compendium, *Humans' Perception and Performance*, Wright Patterson Air Force Base, Fairborn, Ohio, 1988.
4. N. G. Levison and C. S. Turner, "An Investigation of the Therac-25 Accident" *IEEE Comp.* Vol. 26, No. 7 pages 18–41, (1993).
5. R. E. Machol, *System Engineering Handbook*, McGraw-Hill, New York, 1962.
6. D. Meister, *Behavioral Foundations of System Development*, Wiley, New York, 1976.
7. S. Sherr, *Fundamentals of Display System Design*, Wiley, New York, 1970.

Communication Skills

A.0 OBJECTIVES ■

The primary objective of this appendix is to provide the reader with guidance in becoming a better communicator using any form of communication. In particular, guidelines and suggestions are provided to help the reader in (1) structuring more effective reports and memoranda; (2) preparing more readable and less confusing specifications; (3) preparing and giving oral presentations; (4) organizing and conducting effective meetings; and (5) being a more active and effective listener. A secondary objective is to emphasize the use and advantages of having and maintaining a software engineering notebook.

A.1 INTRODUCTION ■

Several studies have shown conclusively that successful people in any field share a common trait, good communication skills. Fortunately, communication skills can be learned. The software engineer must include among his or her arsenal of skills and capabilities the ability to communicate effectively in several media. Information is disseminated among software development participants via memoranda, specifications, reports, oral presentations with flip charts or overheads, and meetings (group meetings and one-on-one meetings). Information is communicated to users, operators, maintainers, etc., via the written report, CDs or videotapes, formal presentations, and both classroom and hands-on training sessions. How we communicate, our manner of communication, and what we communicate defines us to our peers, our subordinates, and leaders. Just as in any communication system, we need to consider the transmitter component, the media component, and the receiver component. In human communication we cannot ignore the receiver (listening component). Listening skills are also important acquisitions.

Three fundamental laws for effective technical communication apply to the transmitter or person doing the communicating: (1) the law of the sixth grader; (2) the law of responsibility; and (3) the law of the limit. The law of the sixth grader states that nothing we communicate should be so sophisticated or complicated that a grammar school sixth grader, upon hearing or seeing it for the first time, would not be able to understand it. The law of responsibility states that the person doing the communicating is completely responsible for making the material understandable to the audience. The law of the limit states that there is a limit to what can be communicated, absorbed, and digested in a given time interval. By simply attempting to satisfy these three laws, communication skills can show immediate improvement.

Often, particularly among entry-level software engineers, it is felt that the more esoteric the presentation and presentation material, the more vague the objectives and conclusions, the more ill-defined the jargon and terminology that is used, the better the presentation. In this approach, the audience either is intimidated into not asking questions of this apparently superior being, begins to think of other things, or simply throws the report away or leaves the room. The result is that no positive communication has taken place. The old saw KISS (Keep it simple, stupid) applies directly to human communication.

It is not always obvious to an entry-level software engineer that the major issues and problems confronting software engineers are relatively straightforward, simple, and mundane. Software developments fail not because of major technology issues but because of the way in which these simple issues and problems are handled (or not handled).

A.2   WRITTEN COMMUNICATIONS   ■

Most of the guidelines and suggestions given with regard to written communication apply to other forms of communication as well. Therefore, when other forms of communication are discussed in the following sections, we rely on the guidelines discussed in this section.

As we have heard over and over, a good paper, presentation, essay, etc., is the result of good planning. It has always been emphasized that a good outline is the starting point for a good paper or document. In preparing, reviewing, and using an outline, an effective plan is needed. The outline should be of a type that has proved effective in technical communication, and the planning process should go through the following steps:

Step 1. Determine the audience.
Step 2. Set goals and objectives.
Step 3. Review the results of steps 1 and 2.
Step 4. Prepare the outline and create a storyboard.
Step 5. Review and revise the outline and the storyboard.
Step 6. Expand the storyboard.

....

* Storyboards, originally used in making movies and plays, were adapted for use in technical proposals and ultimately for use in preparing technical reports, presentations, and memoranda.

A.2.1 Determine the Audience

The approach to preparing the communication will be dictated by the audience (readers). The more knowledge we have about the audience, the better prepared we will be for the communication. A technical presentation given to a nontechnical audience is not effective communication. It also makes no sense to present information to an audience for the purpose of getting a decision or approval when no one in the audience has the authority to make the decision or grant the approval.

In preparing a report or memorandum the organizational level of the audience is important in sizing the document. The executive level needs to have a summary report of one to two pages. The longer the report, the less likely it will be read by the executive. More likely, a long report will be turned over to a subordinate. "I can't boil this down to two pages; it's too complex" is often given as an excuse for an overly long report. A good response is, "Perhaps *you* don't understand it well enough to explain it in one or two pages." Similarly, middle-level executives might pay attention to a three- to five-page report while line-level supervision might read a ten- to fifteen-page report. The point is that knowing and understanding the audience is important to effective communication.

A.2.2 Set Goals and Objectives

The second step in the planning process is to decide on objectives. Specifically, what is to be accomplished with this communication? The following are some possible objectives:

a. Inform the audience, in detail, of some event, fact, design, etc.
b. Sell a change to hardware, software, or procedures.
c. Ask for resources (people, funds, etc.).
d. Sell a new idea.
e. Ask for approval of a decision (design, purchase, etc.).
f. Explain why something happened.
g. Head off criticism.
h. Confirm understanding of an issue or problem.
i. Present trade-off study results.
j. Address concerns or rumors.

A.2.3 Review Results of Steps 1 and 2

A quick review of the objectives with an experienced colleague can often save rework, embarrassment, or even the need for producing the communication in the first place. For example, an experienced colleague may know that requests for resources are not handled in the conventional manner in this particular software development culture or that the target audience does not grant the approval that is being requested. The important point is that the audience and the communication objectives are linked and should be carefully thought through and reviewed.

A.2.4   Prepare Outline and Create Storyboard

The outline should follow a standard outlining approach. Table A.1 is a sample outline used for discussion purposes.

The construction of a storyboard is often driven by a prepared template such as the one shown in Table A.2. A filled-in example expanding the outline in Table A.1 is shown in Table A.3. Table A.4 shows the storyboard for one of the subsections (3.4.1.1) subordinate to section 3.4.1. The top of the template is reserved for the section identification, hierarchical relationship, author, section objectives, and a thematic sentence. Table A.5 shows the bottom section of the template. The bottom left-hand side is used to identify headings for subordinate subsections or text describing specific points to be made in the section. The bottom right-hand side is used to describe figures or tables that will be used to support the text. The bottom of the template is used to record the estimated number of pages, tables, figures, and photographs that will appear in the section. One storyboard is filled out for each section. By posting storyboards on a wall in sequence, the reviewer can quickly assess the flow and content of the product and make constructive comments.

Clearly this approach is useful for planning and preparing memoranda, specifications, reports, books, and other documents. The basic idea is to lay out the entire document in terms of theme sentences, important points, etc., for each section, subsection, and paragraph, following the given outline. The theme sentence is followed by a few one-line facts that will be covered in the paragraph. The idea is to make it clear to the reviewer of the storyboard just what is to be covered in each paragraph. Good theme sentences convey the critical information contained in the section or paragraph. Preferably, the sentence will contain quantitative information. Theme sentences should be designed so that, if the reader sees only the theme sentence, the reader will have gotten the main message in that section or subsection. Theme sentences should also be designed to attract the reader's interest.

Some additional theme sentences for subsections of 3.4.1 for the example are given in Table A.5 along with figure or table descriptions. The reader is encouraged to develop a storyboard for each.

An entire section, chapter, or report can be assembled at the storyboard level. The review

---

■ TABLE A.1   **Sample Outline**

> •
> •
> •
>
> 3.4.1 Software Size Estimation (Two independent methods)
>   3.4.1.1 Method 1 description
>   3.4.1.2 Method 2 description
>   3.4.1.3 Comparison of results
>   3.4.1.4 Resolution of differences
>   3.4.1.5 Composite estimated range and caveats
> 3.4.2 . . .
>
> •
> •
> •

■ TABLE A.2   **Storyboard Template**

SECTION NO. _____ NAME _____ PHONE _____

SUBSECTION TITLE _____

SECTION TITLE _____

SECTION REQUIREMENT _____

_____

_____

_____

_____

THEMATIC SENTENCE _____

_____

_____

_____

HEADINGS: POINTS TO BE MADE UNDER EACH HEADING	ILLUSTRATIONS: GIVE FIG.# HEADING REFERENCES

DOUBLE-SPACE PAGES OF TEXT: _____ FIGURES: _____ TABLES: _____ PHOTOS: _____

COMMENTS, REVISIONS, ETC.

■ TABLE A.3   **Storyboard Example**

SECTION NO. 3.4.1 _____   **NAME** R. Luciani _____   **PHONE** X3955

SUBSECTION TITLE Software Size Estimation _____

SECTION TITLE Software Development Resource Estimation _____

SECTION REQUIREMENT Show that our resource estimation for software development is based on a thorough and professional study. Identify areas of risk and provide appropriate caveats. Give confidence limits and justify them.

THEMATIC SENTENCE The 61,000- SLOC sizing estimate (shown in Figure 3.4.1–1) is the result of two independent studies, one conducted by an independent consultant and the other performed by software engineers within our own organization.

HEADINGS: POINTS TO BE MADE UNDER EACH HEADING	ILLUSTRATIONS: GIVE FIG.# HEADING REFERENCES
3.4.1.1 One team used the function point method to make the initial estimates and then converted estimates to SLOC using a conversion factor obtained from our consultant.	Figure 3.4.1–1 SLOC Estimate Summary
3.4.1.2 _____	
3.4.1.3 _____	Confidence Interval dd%

Figure 3.4.1–1 SLOC Estimate Summary:

Module #	Low	Avg	High
1	xxxx	xxxx	xxxx
2	xxxx	xxxx	xxxx
3	•	•	•
4	•	•	•

DOUBLE-SPACE PAGES OF TEXT: 2 **FIGURES:** 1 **TABLES:** 0 **PHOTOS:** 0

COMMENTS, REVISIONS, ETC.

■ TABLE A.4   **Second Level Storyboard Example**

SECTION NO. 3.4.1.1	NAME F. Shepherd PHONE X3954

SUBSECTION TITLE Function Point Approach

SECTION TITLE Software Size Estimation

SECTION REQUIREMENT Justify the use of the function point to SLOC conversion factor. Support with references and rationale.

THEMATIC SENTENCE Our software engineers used our own version of the function point estimation approach which has been used successfully in 6 prior projects. The conversion factors have also been used in similar estimation studies with success by our consultant.

HEADINGS: POINTS TO BE MADE UNDER EACH HEADING	ILLUSTRATIONS: GIVE FIG # HEADING REFERENCES
1. Modification to function point method includes: 　a. 　b. 　c. 2. Results shown in figure 3.4.1.1–1 are indicative of the quality of the size estimation process	Figure 3.4.1.1–1

For the illustration section:

Figure 3.4.1.1–1

Project #	Estimation	Actual
1	eeee	aaaa
2	eeee	aaaa
n	eeee	aaaa

Notes:

DOUBLE-SPACE PAGES OF TEXT: 3 FIGURES: 1 TABLES: 0 PHOTOS: 0

COMMENTS, REVISIONS, ETC.

■ TABLE A.5　　**Detail for Bottom Sections of Template**

HEADINGS: POINTS TO BE MADE UNDER EACH HEADING	ILLUSTRATIONS:
3.4.1.2 The second team used the conventional divide-and-conquer approach to obtain 57,000 SLOC as an estimate. • Discuss table 3. • Describe touchstones used.	Table (Breakdown of estimates)
3.4.1.3 The results of the two estimates differ by 4000 source lines of code or nearly $400,000 in estimated cost. • List and describe possible reasons for difference. • Describe approach employed to resolve difference.	
3.4.1.4 The major difference was found to reside in the estimate of the size of the real-time adjunct to the operating system. • Describe process used to reestimate this function. Describe confidence limits.	Table (Final breakdown)
3.4.1.5 The estimate presented to senior management was 61,000 source lines of code with the possibility of growth to 68,000. • Explain what drives growth. • Explain how we will track the growth.	Table (Growth drivers)

process is often conducted by posting the storyboard templates on a wall in a large room in the order or sequence in which they appear in the report outline. Reviewers can walk along and review the storyboard for the following features, among others:

■ Continuity and flow
■ Organization
■ Figure significance
■ Topical sentence clarity, validity, and key points
■ Omissions
■ Errors

Reviewers of storyboards are not peers of authors. Typically, they are consultants, senior technical managers from other organizations, etc.

A.2.5　Review and Revise Outline and Storyboard

Being able to view the entire report at this level of detail and from this perspective is very useful for reviewers. Changes can be made at this level to organization, figures, topical sentences, etc., without a major rewriting effort. When the review and revise cycle is complete, those responsible for converting the storyboards into text and figures have a good plan with which to work. Expansion of storyboards to text will flow smoothly if the storyboarding step has been effective.

The storyboard review just described has many of the attributes of a structured walkthrough (discussed in Appendix D). That is, the review

- Requires established entry and exit criteria
- Requires a coordinator and a recorder
- Should not allow ego-related discussions
- Should be based on catching errors early in the development cycle
- Requires that deficiencies be identified (but not fixed) during the review
- Results in storyboard acceptance, acceptance with revision, or rejection (sending authors back to rewrite storyboards with better directions)

The reviewed and approved storyboards provide authors with a detailed plan for writing the report text and producing the figures. There is also a good estimate of the number of pages the end product will contain and the figure-to-text ratio. The value of this approach for large, important technical documents involving many authors can be easily appreciated. However, the approach is equally effective for small, one- or two-author documents and, in fact, often makes the writing process more efficient.

A.2.6   Expand Storyboard

The storyboard is now developed into a first draft by expanding theme sentences into paragraphs. A topical sentence conveys to the reviewer a clear sense of the context and content of the planned section or paragraph. A few points (one or two lines for each) supporting the topical sentence or perhaps referencing the figure on the facing page show the plan for expanding the paragraph. A few points are added to support the topical sentence. Such points may include the following:

- Explain consultant's approach, credentials, etc.
- Explain our approach and credibility.
- Contrast results and explain conclusions.

A.3   ORAL PRESENTATIONS   ■

A slightly different approach is taken in developing storyboards for oral presentations. Topical sentences (one to a chart) are used to describe the point that must be made on each chart. For example,

Chart number 10 shows the performance results obtained in acceptance test 6. Use a table or curve to show how much performance falls short of requirements.

Or

Chart number 6 lists the six unresolved issues/problems in the software requirements specification.

In software development much of the communicating is effected by oral presentations or briefings. Advantages of an oral presentation include an immediate and spontaneous impact on the audience and immediate feedback. Questions, concerns, challenges, etc., can be surfaced and dealt with without the delay associated with other communication media. The communicator can use inflection, emphasis, dramatic pauses, asides, and body language to get points across. An oral presentation makes a greater impression than a written report or memorandum. A question-and-answer discussion period allows for immediate feedback. A well-designed and well-delivered presentation results in quicker response to issues, questions, and requests. An oral presentation is often the only contact that junior personnel have with senior technical and management personnel.

A simple time distribution template for a general oral presentation is shown in Table A.6. This template is generally applicable and will fit almost any presentation objective. A planned oral presentation should not exceed an hour. Experience has shown that about 3 minutes, on the average, is spent on each chart. Therefore, a one-hour oral presentation with a 10-minute discussion period should include fifteen or sixteen charts or overheads.

It is important to emphasize that you have asked for an hour of your audience's time. They have planned to give it to you. You have one hour to make your case and get what you want. You cannot rely on the force of your own personality or the efficacy of what you are saying to hold your audience beyond the one hour you asked for.

A.3.1 Making Oral Presentation

One very useful tool in the preparation of an oral presentation is the dry run. A dry run is a rehearsal of the oral presentation before an audience that simulates the real audience. The benefits of the dry run are as follows: (1) the presenter builds confidence in the presentation

---

■ TABLE A.6   **Time Distribution Template for Oral Presentation**

1/6 of the presentation should be devoted to the problem statement and work performed to date, if any.

2/3 of the presentation should be devoted to the following:
    a. Summary of an existing system, problem, limitation, etc.
    b. Summary of proposed solutions
    c. Feasibility of proposed solution. Justification, qualification, etc.
    d. Proposed schedule for effecting solution
    e. Questions/discussion

1/6 of the presentation should be devoted to concluding remarks such as the following:
    a. Summary of proposal, request, etc.
    b. Specifically what is requested—dollar amount, schedule relief, approval, etc.

material; (2) many of the questions that are likely to arise in the actual presentation are surfaced in the dry run; (3) annoying presenter mannerisms can be identified and corrected; (4) errors of omission and commission can be corrected; (5) charts can be modified as needed; and (6) the general quality of the presentation can be improved substantially. The dry run is especially important to those who do not make oral presentations frequently or who are newcomers to the field. The dry run is equivalent to the formal review of a report.

The mechanics for developing an oral presentation are similar to those used in preparing any other communication. In particular,

- Plan the presentation flow carefully to assure that goals and objectives are met.
- Storyboard the presentation. Try to maintain a 50/50 mix of word charts and graphics.
- On word charts limit items to six per chart.
- Use stand-alone phrases on word charts. Design phrases so that they are difficult for the presenter to read to the audience during the actual presentation. The reason is to discourage the presenter from reading the chart to the audience.
- One item on each chart should be the key point you want the audience to remember. Dwell on this item and allow the audience to read the other items for themselves.

Often the objectives in oral presentations are the same as those for written reports and memoranda. These objectives include the following: (1) to clarify facts, (2) to address concerns or rumors, (3) to sell ideas, (4) to verify conclusions, (5) to sell changes, (6) to ask for approval, (7) to head off criticism, and (8) to report progress.

In conducting the presentation, it is appropriate to dress somewhat formally in suit and tie, etc., even if the dress code in the work place is informal. This attire shows a certain respect for the audience and calls attention to the fact that you view the presentation as a little more important than the normal work activity.

When making the presentation or talk, avoid using ''I'' as much as possible. Maintain eye contact with the audience. Find someone in the audience, preferably at the rear, who seems to respond positively to the presentation; that is a good person with whom to maintain eye contact.

Many people become intimidated when standing before an audience. In the theater it is called stage fright. Some of the best professional actors experience it. One trick that can help to get the presenter off to a good start is to memorize the opening remarks and what is to be said about the first one or two charts. This approach often gets the presenter into the presentation flow. Another artifice is to imagine that everyone in the room is naked except you. However, there is nothing like being thoroughly prepared, knowing what you want to say, having a couple of dry runs under your belt, and believing in what you are doing to overcome stage fright.

The presenter should exhibit confidence and, if he or she does not have the answer to a question, say so and promise to get an answer (and keep the promise). As the advertisement says, ''Never let them see you sweat.'' The presenter is often unaware that little personal mannerisms can detract from the presentation. Dry runs should reduce or eliminate most of these mannerisms. The presenter, however, should become aware of these mannerisms and over time eliminate them. The presenter should anticipate questions and prepare answers. All of us have a tendency to overlook or miss certain things in preparing reports or presentations. Dry runs and reviews help to cover these blind spots. However, it is better that we learn about them ourselves and build a personal checklist that forces us to cover these blind spots ourselves.

A.4 MEETINGS ■

Meetings consume resources. If eight or ten people spend an hour in a meeting without accomplishing anything, then eight to ten potentially productive labor hours have been lost. Overall, software development productivity can be improved greatly by improving the quality of meetings. Some of the common objectives for calling a meeting are the following:

To solve problems, clarify issues, etc.
To brainstorm solutions to problems
To resolve conflicts
To conduct reviews
To collect and merge facts and data
To report progress
To assign actions
To communicate

The first step in planning a meeting is to define clearly the expected results or outcomes of the meeting. Unless we go into the meeting with a clear idea of what we want to accomplish, it is unlikely that we will accidentally stumble onto anything of value during the course of the meeting.

Once we know the expected outcome of the meeting, the second step in planning a meeting is to find a way to eliminate the need for the meeting. This step may be accomplished by answering the following two questions:

1. Do we really need the outcome of this meeting at this moment?
2. Is there another more efficient and more effective way to accomplish what is to be accomplished by holding this meeting?

If the answer to question 1 is yes and the answer to question 2 is no, then preparation for the meeting should proceed.

The third step in planning a meeting (if it can't be avoided) is to prepare the agenda for the meeting. With a clear idea of meeting objectives in hand, an agenda can now be created. The agenda should have reasonable time allocations for each topic. The agenda should be circulated at least two days before the meeting, if possible. Two days is enough time to allow attendees to prepare for the meeting, comment on the agenda, and make schedule arrangements.

Before distributing the agenda, required meeting attendees should be identified and notified. It is important to have the right people at the meeting. The right people include those with the following:

- The appropriate information and knowledge to support meeting goals and objectives
- The authority (direct or delegated) to make decisions and commitments if required by the meeting's goals and objectives
- The inclination or power to obstruct any decisions or commitments that might be made at the meeting
- The need to understand what is going on and the rationale behind any decisions or commitments made during the meeting

The fourth step in planning a meeting is to consider meeting location. Meeting quality can be impacted by the physical environment. Room size, lighting, noise, temperature, and humidity can offer distractions. A room too small or a room too large is sometimes a distraction. A noisy meeting environment can distract meeting attendees; a noisy meeting can distract those in the vicinity of the meeting room. A room too hot and humid or too cold can be a further distraction. All of these factors can be overcome by finding a suitable location before the day of the meeting. It is very annoying to spend the first 20 minutes of a meeting correcting meeting environment problems, changing rooms, or making excuses. Similarly, it is important to have considered the need for audio or visual aids or audio and video teleconferencing and to have taken steps to assure that they are there, connected, tested, and in working order before the meeting.

When arranging or conducting a meeting, the proper attitude is always to keep in mind the dollar cost of the meeting. The dollar cost of a meeting is the number of attendees times the length of the meeting in hours times the average labor rate. It is the responsibility of the meeting organizer and conductor to assure that the money is well spent. Meeting conductors may benefit from many personal styles and approaches. Some of the most effective ones are as follows:

1. Start on time. If participants are more than a few minutes late without informing the meeting organizer, cancel the meeting and reschedule. This approach may seem extreme, but it is effective, particularly when the meeting organizer reports that the meeting was canceled and meeting objectives were not met because certain attendees did not appear on time.
2. Record and publish minutes. Emphasis in the minutes should be on decisions made, concurrences and nonconcurrences, action assignments and dates committed for completion, schedule for follow-up meeting, etc.
3. Have handouts ready for distribution at the meeting. Some presenters prefer to withhold presentation material until after the presentation, and some place the handouts on the table before the meeting starts. In any case, it is not a good practice to distribute handouts during the meeting.
4. Review the agenda, meeting goals, and objectives first. Be sure attendees understand where the meeting leader is taking them and what they must accomplish.
5. Discourage interruptions and deflections from the topic at hand. Keep the meeting focused on the agenda and on the goals and objectives. At the same time, allow for free discussion within the framework of the agenda.
6. Follow the agenda schedule as closely as possible. If, because of unforseen issues, problems, etc., it is not possible to follow the agenda schedule, then schedule another meeting to complete the agenda.
7. End the meeting on time. Some attendees may have already scheduled themselves for the time following the meeting.

This approach may seem like a harsh discipline, but to conserve resources and hold high-quality, productive meetings, it is essential. A social scientist might argue that a great deal more goes on in meetings than simply following the agenda and accomplishing meeting objectives. Crisply run disciplined meetings do not preclude normal group dynamics. Technical meetings are not social events. There are meetings whose primary objective is to air grievances, express opinions, exchange views, make announcements, discuss policy, etc. However, these kinds of meetings are not of primary concern in the software development environment. Meetings are essential but very expensive ways to conduct software development. The efficiency and quality of meetings can have a very important impact on the cost and quality of the software product.

A.4.1 Brainstorming

A very important meeting type is the brainstorming session. Often a design issue or problem seems insurmountable. No fresh ideas or thoughts have come to the fore. What is needed is some fresh thinking, some creative approaches, something new. Faced with this situation, a brainstorming session often provides the creative impulse to produce some new avenues or solutions.

The brainstorming meeting is unstructured with no apparent agenda. The objective is the production of ideas unfettered by criticism in an unconstrained environment. A moderator creates a relaxed environment conducive to freewheeling idea generation. The brainstorming session moderator is expected to enforce the following rules:

1. No criticism, challenges, evaluations, or judgments are allowed to any of the ideas generated. Only questions of clarification are permitted.
2. Quantity of ideas rather than quality is stressed. The moderator discourages any evaluations, challenges, judgments, etc., that would negate the idea.
3. For each idea generated, the moderator attempts to get the group to suggest improvements and use combinations of different ideas to synthesize additional ideas.
4. The moderator records the ideas on a blackboard, flip chart, or on blank overhead foil. In recording each idea, the moderator asks the group to assist in describing the idea. The group attempts to clarify the idea description and often, as a result, generates new ideas.

It often takes a while to get participants into the spirit of the session. A skilled moderator can often see a linkage between two different ideas that together can offer a fundamentally different and unconventional approach to a knotty problem. The duration of a brainstorming session is usually longer than the duration of a regular meeting. Therefore, the format for a brainstorming session should allow for breaks as mandated by the meeting duration.

A.5   SOFTWARE ENGINEERING NOTEBOOK ■

A good habit for a software engineer to establish is to carry a software engineering notebook. Many organizations make the notebook mandatory for software engineers. The notebook is essentially a technical diary of the software engineer's daily activities. The notebook documents the following:

1. Meetings attended, date, start and stop time, attendees, decisions, actions assigned, dates committed, etc.
2. Important results of studies performed, reviewed, or read about germane to the project or to professional growth including sizing estimates, cost and schedule estimates, new methods or techniques for performing tasks, references, etc. Often pertinent memos, tables, or graphics are stapled to the notebook pages.

3. Assignments along with any dates committed to for completion and the task schedule for carrying out the assignment.
4. The results of any technical work, the rationale behind certain decisions or designs, information collected as part of tasks and sources.
5. Hours worked on a particular task or spent in traveling or training, etc.

The purpose of the notebook, in general, is to keep a record of the technical activities of a software engineer. The notebook is a portable personal file for the software engineer. The notebook can be used when memory fails to pinpoint the when, where, why, and what of a specific meeting held in the past or the results of a study that perhaps was not documented elsewhere. Often this notebook provides a means for a software engineer to record his or her own rules of thumb for estimation factors for development tasks, etc. The greatest value of this notebook, however, is as a source of information when it comes time to prepare formal documents. It is often the only source of information for justifying an approach or solution or a study result. When it is known that the software engineer is using an engineering notebook, those with whom he or she comes into contact will be less likely to be careless with information and data; they know the information and the source are going into a notebook.

A.6   LEARNING HOW TO LISTEN   ■

Learning how to be an effective listener can also improve the efficiency of information transfer in personal communication settings. We can all remember the game we played as children in which a message is passed around a circle by initially whispering the message into the ear of the first player just once. The first player then whispers the message they thought they heard into the ear of the next player just once. The message is passed around the circle of players in this fashion until it reaches the last player. Usually there is absolutely no correspondence between the initial message and the final message. The game is an excellent illustration of the problem of verbal communication.

In one-on-one conversations we often have a dynamic in action that involves biases, preconceived notions, prejudices, personal agendas, power, etc. Focusing on the topic and its related facts can reduce or eliminate many of the subliminal effects that often impede good communication. However, even when focusing on just the facts, any or all of the following questions may transpire when a speaker makes a statement to a listener:

What did the speaker mean to say?
What did the speaker actually say?
What did the listener think the speaker said?
What did the listener actually hear the speaker say?
What did the listener think the speaker meant by what he or she said?
What did the speaker think the listener understood?

Clearly, under these circumstances we have what communication engineers would call a noisy channel.

To get the most out of what an individual is saying, one must become an active listener. The objective is to make what the speaker meant to say equivalent to what the listener thought the speaker meant to say. The following guidelines will help to define an active listener, and following these rules should help to make everyone a more active, attentive listener.

1. An active listener clears his or her mind of everything except the speaker, the topic, and what the speaker is actually saying. The objective is to try to prevent reading more into what the speaker is saying than the speaker is actually saying.
2. An active listener captures, as accurately as possible, the information that the speaker is conveying.
3. An active listener lets the speaker know by actions that he or she is interested in what is being said.
4. An active listener should help the speaker communicate by being sensitive to other communication channels being used by the speaker, such as body language and other cues that support information being communicated.
5. An active listener should ask questions as they arise to clarify points, indicate understanding, and provide feedback to the speaker.
6. An active listener should ask that central ideas, themes, and summaries be repeated to assure complete understanding.
7. An active listener should repeat what he or she understood to be the theme of the speech so that the speaker can critique the understanding of what was said and correct any misunderstandings.
8. An active listener should not attempt to formulate replies, rebuttals, or counterexamples while the speaker is talking.
9. An active listener should focus completely on understanding what the speaker is saying.
10. An active listener shouldn't draw conclusions until he or she has heard the speaker's whole story.
11. An active listener shouldn't be judgmental.
12. An active listener should encourage the speaker to be open and complete.
13. An active listener should provide a nonthreatening environment that makes both speaker and listener comfortable.
14. An active listener shouldn't be afraid to ask if there is anything that he or she hasn't been told, especially when bad news is being communicated.
15. Both parties, the active listener and the effective speaker, should appreciate that understanding is not equivalent to agreeing.

Only after the listener has a clear understanding of what was said and has confirmed that understanding with the speaker is it time for the listener to weave what was said into the fabric of what he or she knows. The objective is to decide if what has been heard is consistent with what the listener already knows and to determine how it fits into his or her existing knowledge structure. If there is a contradiction, it is important to focus on answering the following questions:

Why is there an inconsistency?
Where is the inconsistency, precisely?
When did the inconsistency emerge?
How is the inconsistency manifested?
Who is involved in the inconsistency?
Who may have caused the inconsistency?

It is important at this point to examine what was heard from different perspectives. For example, a software designer might view and interpret a set of facts in a way that is markedly different from the way an analyst might view the same set of facts. It is also important now to examine critically what was heard and, if warranted, develop rebuttles, opposing views, etc. It is also useful to extend what was heard to other situations or environments to see if what was heard still holds.

Being a good listener is a valuable asset. One can learn more efficiently, reduce rework, and become more productive in virtually everything one does by being a good listener. One's own views are better supported because of having a better understanding of the views of others. And finally, one learns how to be a better overall communicator by being a good listener.

Cost-Benefit Analysis

B.0 OBJECTIVES ■

An information system is a capital investment. Most customers view the cost of acquiring a new information system or upgrading an old one in this light. There are also instances where acquisition of software development facilities may be considered as capital investments, and the software engineer may find himself or herself directly involved in a cost-benefit analysis. Thus the principal objective of this appendix is to describe the means by which capital investments are evaluated. A second objective is to give the software engineer a full view of the setting in which he or she often works and perhaps explain the mechanics of how and why a technically sound idea is rejected on economic grounds.

B.1 INTRODUCTION ■

A cost-benefit analysis can be viewed as another form of trade-off, in which financial considerations are balanced against potential benefits for one alternative versus another. Cost-benefit results can also be just one of many decision criteria within a larger trade-off context. That is, results of a cost-benefit analysis along with other criteria form a decision criteria. A cost-benefit analysis can also evaluate the financial merit of making a capital investment in a system or software product.

Conceptually, the cost-benefit analysis attempts to quantify the cost of acquiring or upgrading an information system and maintaining it in operational condition for its estimated lifetime. These costs are then compared with the quantified benefits derived from operating the new system.

Benefits are categorized as tangible and intangible. Tangible benefits are those that are easily identified and quantified. For example, if using the new system allows us to eliminate one operator, this benefit can be easily quantified in terms of one employee's salary plus burden rate saved for every year of operation. Tangible benefits can be found in improved productivity, increased sales, decreased cost of each transaction, reduced number of required operators, etc.

Intangible benefits, although important, are usually difficult to quantify. Analysts often fail to account for intangible benefits accurately because they are so difficult to quantify. This situation is unfortunate because a potentially good capital investment could be rejected because of a failure to account adequately for all benefits.

The comparison criteria of the costs and benefits can take many forms. We will consider a few in this appendix. One criterion is the *payback period*, which is defined as the number of elapsed months of the new system's operation required for the benefits of the new system to pay back the initial investment. It is the point in time where benefits derived from the new system equal the costs of acquiring and operating the new system. Another criterion is the return on the initial investment over the projected lifetime of the system. *Return on investment* is defined as the ratio of the difference of total benefits minus total cost divided by the total cost for a given period of time, usually measured from the point at which the system is placed in service to the end of the system's lifetime. Both of these criteria are based on a year-by-year assessment of acquisition and operating costs and benefits. Alternative designs or approaches can be compared in terms of their return on investment and payback period.

One additional factor to be considered before proceeding with a detailed discussion of the cost-benefit analysis process is cost of money or net present value. The net present value factor accounts for the fact that a sum of money received or spent in the future is not equivalent to that same sum of money currently on hand. The difference is due to the fact that a given sum of money invested today at a given interest rate will be worth more in the future. For example, $1000 invested at 12% today will be worth $1120 twelve months from now, which is the same as saying that a sum of $1120 acquired twelve months from now is worth $1000 in terms of today's value. Another way to think of the net present value method is as a way to determine how much more beneficial this particular capital investment is than simply investing our money at current interest rates.

Often cost associated with multiyear projects is cited in fiscal year dollars. For example, 12.3 million in FY-1998 dollars means that the development cost has been adjusted to reflect its value in terms of a single reference year. It is, in some cases, a more accurate portrayal of costs. Present value analysis reflects cost and benefit dollars to the present year or may be used to adjust multiyear development costs to the year the system is put into operation.

B.2 COSTS ■

The following lists describe the acquisition and operating costs associated with an information system. Acquisition costs include the following direct costs:

Computing resources
    Hardware procured or developed
    Software procured or developed

Brick and mortar
  New buildings
  Real estate acquisition
  Modified buildings

Installation
Other development
Training
Testing
Conversion

Operation and maintenance costs include the following direct costs:

Staffing
  Operators
  Maintainers
  Security

Supplies
  Paper
  Disks and tapes
  Other supplies

Maintenance
  Hardware
  Software
  Facilities (heating, ventilation, air conditioning)

Utilities
  Power
  Communication

■ TABLE B.1   **Standard Annuity Table**

YEAR	9%	10%	11%
0	1.0000	1.0000	1.0000
1	0.9174	0.9091	0.9009
2	0.8417	0.8264	0.8116
3	0.7722	0.7513	0.7312
4	0.7084	0.6830	0.6587
5	0.6499	0.6209	0.5934

■ TABLE B.2   **Adjusted Costs***

	YEAR 0	YEAR 1	YEAR 2	YEAR 3	YEAR 4	YEAR 5
Cost	$10,000	$1000	$1200	$1500	$1800	$2000
Adjusted Cost	$10,000	$909	$992	$1127	$1229	$1242

....
* Using 10% discount rate.

Facilities
  Rent
  Building maintenance
  Furniture
  HVAC (heating, ventilation, and air conditioning)

Insurance
Security

   Acquisition, operating, and maintenance costs should be carefully identified, accumulated, and allocated to the year in which they occur. For multiyear system developments, all the acquisition cost should be allocated to the year the system goes into service or on-line.
   The next step is to adjust each year's operating cost to account for the cost of money. The acquisition cost is allocated to year zero; therefore, there is no adjustment required. The future operation and maintenance costs are adjusted to reflect their current value (year zero). Table B.1 shows a standard annuity value of 1.000 dollar over 5 years using a discount rate of 9%, 10%, and 11%. The local financial organization should be consulted before a discount rate is selected for use in the analysis. In fact, the financial community should be included in any cost-benefit analysis. Their experience and knowledge are very useful. Moreover, their direct involvement will lend credibility to the results. If they are not involved in the analysis, they will most certainly be involved in the review. As a result of this step (selecting 10% as the discount rate), an information system that would cost $10,000 to acquire would have a current cost and adjusted operating cost as shown in Table B.2.

B.3   BENEFITS   ■

The tangible benefits associated with a new or improved information system usually fall into one of the following categories:

Reduced operating personnel
  Operators
  Maintainers
  Trainers

Improved performance
  Fewer errors
  Reduced time per transaction

Increased functional capability
  Additional functions/services
  Improved accuracy

Increased system capacity
  More records
  More fields
  More speed

Improved response time

For each of the listed tangible benefits, the software engineer or system analyst will need to quantify the expected benefit. In many cases these quantifications are obvious and require only a little thought to put a value on the benefit. For example, improved response time or reduced transaction time can be measured and translated to a telephone connect time or labor saving associated with the improved response time. A specific example might be found in on-line operators servicing hundreds of calls per day. If it is estimated that the average time reduction for a transaction is 25 seconds, then calculating 25 seconds times the cost of telephone connect time times the average number of transactions per unit time would be one way to quantify the benefit of improved response time. Similarly, for operator labor the 25-second saving per transaction would allow an operator to handle more calls, which would offer another means for quantifying the benefit of improved response time. The analyst must be careful not to double count benefits or become too liberal in quantifying benefits. The credibility of the benefit analysis is at stake.

The class of benefits labeled intangible offers an even greater challenge to the analyst. Quantification of intangible benefits often requires some degree of creativity to get a credible value. An example of an intangible benefit is improved customer goodwill. If one benefit of the new information system is cited as improved customer goodwill, the analyst might quantify this benefit in the following way. Examining records of the previous year may reveal that there were 500 customer incidents requiring management attention and costing a given amount of labor and material to resolve each problem and satisfy the customer. An average cost for each incident could be developed from existing records, and the cost of maintaining customer goodwill could be quantified. That is, to maintain customer goodwill, each year it will cost the business 500 times the average cost to handle a customer incident. If personnel can show by reasonable arguments that the new system can reduce customer incidents by 30%, then a quantification for the intangible benefit called customer goodwill can be computed as follows:

$$\text{Goodwill} = 500 \text{ times average incident cost} \times 30\%$$

This value would determine the benefit associated with improved customer goodwill. This approach is certainly speculative but better than ignoring this benefit entirely. For a large volume mail-order house, handling 500 customer incidents could, when labor costs are considered, easily cost as much as $50,000. Thirty per cent savings would be $15,000 per year. Ignoring these savings means missing a significant benefit of a new information system.

Another approach to quantifying vague and intangible benefits, like increased sales, is to

■ TABLE B.3   **Expected Value Table for Increase in Sales**

SALES INCREASE	×	PROBABILITY	=	EXPECTED VALUE
0.0%		0.05		0.0%
5.0%		0.40		2.0%
10.0%		0.30		3.0%
15.0%		0.20		3.0%
20.0%		0.05		1.0%
		Total expected value		9.0%

construct an expected value table such as Table B.3. An expected value table is a table with three columns. Column 1 gives the expected improvement, column 2 gives the probability that the expected improvement will happen, and column 3 gives the expected improvement in sale.

As an example, consider the intangible benefit called sales increase. First, the rate of possible increase in sales is estimated and entered in column 1 of Table B.3. This step should be done in consultation with marketing and sales people. The probability associated with the occurrence of each incremental sales increase is obtained and entered in the second column of Table B.3. The third column, expected value, is the product of the first two columns. The total of column 3, 9.0%, is the total value of the expected sales increase. This benefit can then be converted to dollars.

The point is that all legitimate benefits should be quantified in some credible way in order to perform a sound cost-benefit analysis. Many intangible benefits like ''less stressful for operators to use'' and ''better human-to-computer interface design'' can be linked to better productivity, reduced absenteeism, and reduced training needs, all of which can be quantified and changed to a dollar value.

Benefits are totaled and allocated by year. The benefits must also be adjusted for the same discount rate that was used to adjust the yearly cost entries. Table B.4 shows a complete cost-benefit value for a $10,000 information system.

■ TABLE B.4   **Adjusted Costs/Benefits***

	YEAR 0	YEAR 1	YEAR 2	YEAR 3	YEAR 4	YEAR 5
Cost	$10,000	$1000	$1200	$1500	$1800	$2000
Adjusted Cost	$10,000	$909	$992	$1127	$1229	$1242
Benefit	0	$4000	$6000	$7000	$7000	$8000
Adjusted Benefit	0	$3636	$4959	$5259	$4781	$4970

....
* Adjusted for 10% discount rate.

The groundwork has now been completed. At this point it is advisable to review and/or discuss the results of the analysis with those who can offer constructive advice or critique. Sales improvement rationale can be reviewed with people in marketing, sales, or planning groups. Financial data can be reviewed with people from the financial organization. Productivity rationale can be reviewed with individuals from personnel and from line management.

There are two major advantages to these informal reviews and discussions. One is to obtain as much information from as many sources as possible. A second is to acquaint as many people as possible with the facts, rationale, and conclusions because some of these people may be called upon to review the cost-benefit analysis results. Eventually the results will be reviewed formally, and it is always best to have completed your staff work before the formal review occurs. To have answered questions, explained your position, and responded to criticism before the formal review is the professional way.

When all the values associated with costs and benefits are reviewed and verified, the cost-benefit table can be completed by adding a new row to show the accumulated adjusted benefit over the years. Table B.5 is the reproduction of Table B.4 with an accumulated adjusted benefit row added.

The results shown in Table B.5 tell us that this information system will pay for itself and begin to increase profits at the end of its third year of operation. Costs and benefits have been adjusted for cost of money using a 10% discount rate. This purchase would be regarded as a good investment in most organizations.

A competing information system design could be put through the same analysis process and the two systems compared based on payback period criteria.

A value for return on investment could also be computed from Table B.5. Assume that we wish to determine the return on our initial $10,000 investment at the end of the fifth year. To obtain return on investment, ROI, we divide the difference between total adjusted cost and total adjusted benefits by the total adjusted cost of the information system for its five-year lifetime.

$$\text{ROI} = \frac{23,605 - 15,499}{15,499} = 52.3\%$$

■ TABLE B.5   **Cost-Benefit Analysis***

	YEAR 0	YEAR 1	YEAR 2	YEAR 3	YEAR 4	YEAR 5
Cost	$10,000	$1000	$1200	$1500	$1800	$2000
Adjusted Cost	$10,000	$909	$992	$1127	$1229	$1242
Benefit	0	$4000	$6000	$7000	$7000	$8000
Adjusted Benefit	0	$3636	$4959	$5259	$4781	$4970
Accumulated Adjusted Benefit	($10,000)	($7273)	($3306)	$826	$4378	$8106

* Adjusted for 10% discount rate.

This result can be interpreted as the return on our $10,000 investment after cost of money has been accounted for.

A third comparison criterion is called present value index, PVI. Many feel that this is a more realistic criterion for comparing competing systems because it weights the magnitude of the initial investment heavily. The PVI is computed by dividing the difference between total adjusted benefits and total adjusted operating and maintenance costs by the original investment. Using the data in Table B.5, the PVI for the $10,000 information system would be computed as follows:

$$PVI = \frac{23,605 - 5499}{10,000} = 1.8106$$

Any of these measures, ROI, PVI, or the actual benefit, or combinations of them may be used for cost-benefit trade-offs.

APPENDIX C

....

_____

Decisions and Trade-Offs

C.0 OBJECTIVES ■

The primary objective of this appendix is to emphasize that the end product of the trade-off study is a rationale for the decision being made as well as the decision itself. The rationale behind a decision should be easily communicated; should obtain, for similar situations, repeatable results; must form a basis for demonstrating that software design satisfies requirements; and should provide a firm base for moving to the next software design level.

Other objectives of this appendix are as follows: (1) to emphasize the importance of making sound, objective decisions based on factual evidence and a logical rationale; (2) to describe a simple process for making these decisions; and (3) to use the results as a tool to improve the quality of the decision.

C.1 INTRODUCTION ■

Someone once said all of life is a trade-off. Perhaps this is true but we know for a fact that most of a software engineer's working hours are filled with technical decisions and trade-offs, thoughtful consideration of alternatives and consequences. In many instances important decisions must be made before all the evidence can be collected. An important tool for the software engineer is a standard method for handling technical decisions and documenting the rationale behind the decision.

This appendix describes a simple method for (1) making objective decisions in a systematic, structured fashion; (2) documenting the decision and the decision process; and (3) using the results of the process to strengthen or improve the quality of the decision. In many organizations, management will not accept a technical decision unless it is supported by a formal trade-off study.

C.2   TRADE-OFF PROCESS ■

The process that is described in this section is generally applicable and can be employed in making decisions of virtually any type. There are six steps in a general trade-off process: defining and understanding the decision problem; establishing evaluation criteria; defining alternatives; quantifying each criterion for each alternative; evaluating alternative scores based on the established criteria; and performing a sensitivity analysis. The final product of a trade-off process, as expected, should be the selection of an alternative with a sound rationale supporting the decision.

C.2.1   Define and Understand Decision Problem

A typical class of decision problems or simply decisions that are often subjects of trade-off studies includes the following:

■ Design options
■ Subcontractor selections
■ Make or buy decisions
■ Architecture options
■ Selection of a software product for purchase
■ Hardware selection
■ Implementation language selection

The first step in defining and understanding the decision problem is to review requirements related to the decision problem. The following questions should be asked and at least partially answered before a decision is made:

Why are we making this decision?
Why are we making it now?
Who is affected by this decision?
Should we wait for better data upon which to base the decision?
How long can we safely keep our options open?

Two points worth remembering are (1) don't make a decision until you have to make it, and (2) when you have to make it, use a formal trade-off method to arrive at the decision.

C.2.2   Establish Criteria

When the decision problem is understood, we must proceed to establish a set of criteria for the evaluation of alternatives. There are often several criteria for a given decision. The following are some common criteria:

- Cost (implicit in several other criteria)
- Accuracy
- Cost vs. benefit
- Schedule
- Availability
- Operability
- Security
- Response time
- Capacity
- Cost performance
- Resource utilization (memory, CPU, IO, etc.)
- Implementation difficulty
- Reliability
- Maintainability
- Environmental impact
- Installation difficulty
- Training
- HCI considerations
- Testing
- Increased productivity

Selection of a set of appropriate criteria for a decision problem is often a group endeavor. The selection of decision criteria should be thrashed out among those who will be most affected by the decision and those who must implement the decision. The objective is to get those involved in the ultimate implementation of the decision committed to the decision, whatever it is.

Each criterion selected must be numerically measurable for each alternative. Some criteria are easily measurable. Reliability, cost benefits, schedule, and resource utilization are examples of such criteria. Other criteria may require additional effort to quantify. Operability, implementation difficulty, security, and increased productivity are examples of such criteria. Quantification of the criteria that will be used in the trade-off analysis is an absolute necessity. Without such quantification, comparisons between alternatives become heavily subjective and perhaps useless.

There is no doubt that the selection criteria must be ranked in order of their importance. In any situation we will, of course, find some criteria more important than others. The ranking process for criteria is also best conducted in a group setting to reduce subjectivity. Two criteria with the same order of importance should receive identical rank value. Rank can be based on assigning N to the most important criterion, 1 to the least important criteria, and numbers between 1 and N to those criteria that lie between.

Suppose the rank values for criteria $C_1, C_2, \ldots, C_n$ are $r_1, r_2, \ldots, r_n$ respectively.

In this appendix, for simplicity of computation, we assume the largest rank value, N, is 10 and the weighting factors are equal to the rank values. That is, $w_i = r_i$.

C.2.3 Define Alternatives

At any point in the software development process, there are potential alternatives for virtually every situation. The ideal solution (without constraint) is frequently used as the reference point alternative. Often one finds solutions based on the following general types of alternatives:

1. Minimum-cost. That is, pushing or promoting an alternative based on its comparative cost.
2. Leading-edge technology. This alternative is usually presented with the assumption that the best technology will produce the best result.
3. Outside purchase (off-the-shelf solution for software products). This alternative is usually presented as being both cost- and time-efficient.
4. Upgrade what is in place. This alternative is argued as not confronting the user group with a sudden change in the entire operation.
5. Retain what is in place, but modify operational timelines or procedures. This option is normally a compromised alternative often proposed with regard to software systems.

The definition of alternatives and quantification of each alternative in terms of selection criteria requires that each alternative be fully characterized, especially in terms of selection criteria. Models are often used to characterize alternatives. Verbal descriptions based on conceptual designs structured around specifications, probabilistic models, mathematical models, state machine models, and computer simulations are all examples of ways in which alternative designs can be characterized. A by-product of trade-off performance is that it forces a deeper understanding of requirements, alternative approaches, design problems, etc.

C.2.4 Evaluate Each Alternative

Each alternative must now be measured in terms of the selection criteria chosen for this trade-off. For example, if CPU resource utilization (execution time) was chosen as one of the design selection criteria, then each design alternative would have to be fairly compared in terms of its use of the CPU resource.

When each alternative has been fully characterized in terms of selection criteria, we now have enough data to begin an evaluation of the alternatives. The evaluation of alternatives, once decision criteria have been selected and ordered based on importance to the decision, can be accomplished in many ways. We shall focus on a factor-weighting approach, an elementary approach that has proved very effective.

The general approach is to compute a trade-off score for each alternative. The trade-off score becomes the value of a particular alternative. The higher the total score or value, the better the alternative. The alternative score is computed as the sum of each quantified criterion associated with the given alternative times a weighting factor whose value is based on the importance of the criteria. Assume there are n criteria with weighting factors $w_1, w_2, \ldots, w_n$ and there are k alternatives $A_1, A_2, \ldots, A_k$. The raw value of criterion C_i for alternative A_j is denoted by $V_{i,j}$, and the total score for alternative A_j is denoted by $S(A_j)$. Thus for the unnormalized trade-off score, $S(A_j)$, we have

$$S(A_j) = \sum_{i=1}^{i=n} V_{i,j}(w_i)$$

■ TABLE C.1   **Typical Trade-Off Matrix**

CRITERIA	WEIGHTING FACTOR	ALTERNATIVE 1 RAW SCORE	ALTERNATIVE 2 RAW SCORE
Criterion 1	10	10	8
Criterion 2	9	9	10
Criterion 3	8	10	7
Criterion 4	6	12	12
Scores		333	298

The trade-off data can be displayed in a matrixlike format as shown in Table C.1. The use of an automated spreadsheet makes it possible to make changes easily and perform "what if" and sensitivity studies.

$$S(A_1) = 10(10) + 9(9) + 8(10) + 6(12) = 333$$

$$S(A_2) = 10(8) + 9(10) + 8(7) + 6(12) = 298$$

As in other software engineering processes, we will iterate and expose as many people as possible, even customers, to the rationale we are using to make the decision. There are a number of good reasons for doing this: (1) we want to take advantage of all the resident knowledge, wisdom, and experience that we can; (2) we want to keep all members of the team informed of our problems and progress; (3) we want the entire team to feel that they have participated in arriving at the decision; and (4) we want the entire team to feel that they have a commitment to make it work.

C.2.5   Quantifying Each Criterion

The main objective is to convert every decision criterion into a representative numerical value and to decide how each number is to be derived, calculated, or estimated for each alternative—in short, to establish the ground rules for a fair and honest comparison of alternatives for each selection criterion. Quantification of criteria can be made on a relative basis. Quantification should, however, be structured so that the best alternative has the highest raw score. However, there are usually two kinds of criteria, those for which a higher value means a better choice and those for which a lower value means a better choice. For example, number of transactions per second is one criterion where a higher value can mean a better choice. On the other hand, cost, response time, and number of interrupts per second are criteria for which a lower value may indicate a better choice. To better illustrate this point consider the following example.

Example C.2.1

Suppose we have two criteria, response time and number of transactions processed per second. The shorter the response time, the better the design. The higher the number of transactions that can be handled in a second, the better the design. Suppose design alternative 1 has an average response time of 3 seconds and handles an average of ten transactions per second. Design alternative 2 has an average response time of 4 seconds and handles twenty transactions per second. The weighting factor for response time is 10 and for number of transactions is 8. The trade-off matrix for this example is

Criterion	Weight	Design 1	Design 2
Response time in seconds	10	3	4
Transactions per second	8	10	20
Scores (incorrect)		110	200

Comparing 110 and 200 is meaningless. In fact, adding 10×3 and 8×10 is like adding apples and oranges. The design with the lowest response time and highest number of transactions is the more desirable. Comparing 110 and 200 won't reveal this fact.

A second problem with using raw numeric values for each criterion and each alternative is that they may lead to a bad decision because of difference in the measurement scales of different criteria. To illustrate this point we consider another example.

Example C.2.2

Suppose there are two criteria, response time and size in SLOC, with weighting factors 10 and 2, respectively. Alternative 1 provides 1-second response time and is 3000 SLOC. Alternative 2 provides a response time of 20 seconds (chosen to illustrate the point) and is 2700 SLOC. These two criteria are of the same type; that is, the smaller their value, the better the design. The trade-off matrix for this example may be shown as

Criterion	Weight	Design 1	Design 2
Response time in seconds	10	1	20
Size in SLOC	2	3000	2700
Scores		6010	5600

Trade-off values are $S(A_1) = 6010$ and $S(A_2) = 5600$. Therefore, based on these values, we would select alternative 2, which produces a lower trade-off value, even though its response time is very high.

Normalized Criterion Value

There are two objectives for normalizing criteria values. First is to eliminate the effect of differences in the measurement scale for different criteria. The second objective is to assure that, regardless of criterion type, for each criterion the best alternative will always have the highest value for that criterion. This criterion value is called a normalized value. Hence, by using normalized criteria values in the trade-off matrix, a higher trade-off score will always mean a better alternative. The following algorithm normalizes criteria values $V_{i,j}$ for alternatives $A_1, A_2, \ldots, A_k$ and criteria $C_1, C_2, \ldots, C_n$.

Normalization Algorithm

For every criterion C_i perform the following three steps to compute $N_{i,j}$, the normalized value of criterion C_i for alternative A_j, for $j = 1, 2, \ldots, k$.

1. Let $V_{i,p}$ be the best-case value for alternative p. Note that $V_{i,p}$ may be the largest (or the smallest) value of

$$V_{i,j}, \text{ for } j = 1, 2, \ldots, k$$

2. Set $V_{i,p}$ to a fixed value, say 10 or 100 or 1. We will use 100 for our normalization process. That is, we set $V_{i,p} = 100$. Note that in this case we always have $N_i, p = 100$.
3. For $j = 1, 2, \ldots k.$

If $V_{i,j} <= V_{i,p}$ then

$$\text{Compute } N_{i,j} = \frac{V_{i,j}}{V_{i,p}} \times 100$$

Else

$$\text{Compute } N_{i,j} = \frac{V_{i,p}}{V_{i,j}} \times 100$$

The normalization algorithm not only provides a normalized and meaningful criterion measure, but will take into account whether the largest or smallest criterion value is the best choice.

Example C.2.3

The normalized criteria values for Example C.2.1 are as follows:

$$V_{1,p} = V_{1,1} = 3 \text{ and } V_{2,p} = V_{2,2} = 20$$

therefore,

$$N_{1,1} = 100, N_{1,2} = \frac{3}{4} \times 100 = 75$$

and

$$N_{2,2} = 100, N_{2,1} = \frac{10}{20} \times 100 = 50$$

The normalized trade-off matrix is then

Criterion	Weight	Design 1	Design 2
Response time in seconds	10	100	75
Transactions per second	8	50	100
Scores		1400	1550

Based on the trade-off scores obtained, we conclude that design 2 is the better design and should be selected.

Example C.2.4

The normalized trade-off values for Example C.2.2 are computed as follows:

$$V_{1,p} = V_{1,1} = 1 \text{ and } V_{2,p} = V_{2,2} = 2700$$

therefore,

$$N_{1,1} = 100, N_{1,2} = \frac{1}{20} \times 100 = 5$$

and

$$N_{2,2} = 100, N_{2,1} = \frac{2700}{3000} \times 100 = 90$$

Therefore, the trade-off matrix is

Criterion	Weight	Design 1	Design 2
Response time in seconds	10	100	5
Size in SLOC	2	90	100
Scores		1180	250

For this trade-off matrix we have $S(\text{Design 1}) > S(\text{Design 2})$. Therefore, the first design is clearly superior. Note that the trade-off scores from unnormalized criteria values suggested that design 2 is a better design.

C.2.6 Sensitivity Analysis

Sensitivity analysis has two objectives. The first objective is to estimate the total differential of the score of the best choice with respect to the weighted criteria values involved in the trade-off. The second objective is to determine which of the criteria play a dominant role in the decision process. Partial derivatives can be estimated analytically if trade-off functions are simple and continuous or by numerical methods otherwise. The insight gained from examining the total differential and its sensitivity to changes in criteria quantification and to weighting is important in assessing the quality of the decision.

At the completion of the first round of a trade-off study, one of the two situations may happen: (1) the alternative selected is accepted by most people involved in the process and is acceptable to management and client or (2) the alternative selected does not appeal to intuition, and the prestudy favorite did not emerge as the best choice. In the second case a reevaluation of the process is in order. It is important to understand why the result does not seem to be a sensible one. A reevaluation beginning with the selection of decision criteria, weighting factors, and criteria quantification should be performed. It is a preferred practice that someone else perform the second round of a trade-off study to eliminate personal bias that may have crept into the process.

Before we work through an illustrative example it should be made clear that there are two wrong attitudes regarding the numbers used in performing trade-off studies. The first is that the numbers are meaningless in that quantifications, although consistently applied, are often arbitrary and the weighting factor values are of little true significance. The second is that the numbers are meaningful in the sense that there is some absolute significance to the values obtained. Both of these attitudes miss the point. The correct attitude is that these numbers, if consistently computed and applied, are good for relative comparisons of alternatives. They have no significance beyond that.

A frequently asked question is, When should a trade-off study be performed? The answer is whenever a decision must be made, extending from concept formulation to final test, delivery, and installation. Trade-offs should be used for allocation of function, decomposition of functional and performance requirements, selection of system and software architecture, decisions on design approaches, etc.

Example C.2.5

Let us assume that there are three design approaches to a real-time software product that is intended for use in an embedded system. The critical decision criteria have, after considerable discussion, been reduced to the following four:

1. Execution time
2. Number of source lines of code
3. Testing difficulty
4. Memory requirements

It is highly desirable that execution time be minimum because of the load imposed by other non-real-time functions on the CPU. The number of SLOC has cost ramifications, and there is also a strong motivation to minimize memory requirements. Testing is always a major concern in real-time software development.

To quantify these four criteria, we can estimate average execution time for CPU resource utilization, source lines of code, and dynamic memory use. For the testing criterion we can use average module-level cyclomatic complexity as a quantification.

■ TABLE C.2 $V_{i,j}$ **Values for Illustrative Example**

	ALTERNATIVE 1	ALTERNATIVE 2	ALTERNATIVE 3
Cyclomatic Complexity Average	6	5	8
Execution Time (ms)	9	8	6
SLOC	500	700	800
Memory Use (in bytes)	2100	2600	1900

In analyzing the three design alternatives in terms of the four selection criteria, we obtain the estimates summarized in Table C.2.

In our deliberations we have decided that testing is the most important criterion ($w_1 = 10$) followed by execution time ($w_2 = 9$), source lines of code ($w_3 = 6$), and memory use ($w_4 = 5$), in that order. Of course, all three design alternatives fully meet formal requirements, a necessary condition for an alternative.

To compute the normalized criteria values, we recognize that alternative 2 obtains the best value for C_1 (testing), alternative 3 obtains the best value for C_2 (execution time), alternative 1 obtains the best value for C_3 (size) and alternative 3 obtains the best value for C_4 (memory use).

Therefore, we observe that

$$N_{1,2} = 100, N_{2,3} = 100, N_{3,1} = 100, \text{ and } N_{4,3} = 100$$

■ TABLE C.3   **Normalized Trade-Off Matrix for Illustrative Example**

CRITERIA	WEIGHT	ALTERNATIVE 1	ALTERNATIVE 2	ALTERNATIVE 3
Testing	10	83.3	100.0	62.5
Execution Time (in ms)	9	66.7	75.0	100.0
SLOC	6	100.0	71.4	62.5
Memory Use (in bytes)	5	90.5	73.0	100.0
Score		2485.8	2468.4	2400

Alternative 1 is the winner by a relatively small margin. Alternatives 2 and 3 take second and third positions, respectively. The results are very close. Most tough decisions have that characteristic.

from this observation we compute

$$N_{1,1} = \frac{5}{6} \times 100 = 83.3 \qquad N_{1,3} = \frac{5}{8} \times 100 = 62.5$$

$$N_{2,1} = \frac{6}{9} \times 100 = 66.7 \qquad N_{2,2} = \frac{6}{8} \times 100 = 75$$

$$N_{3,2} = \frac{500}{700} \times 100 = 71.4 \qquad N_{3,3} = \frac{500}{800} \times 100 = 62.5$$

$$N_{4,1} = \frac{1900}{2100} \times 100 = 90.5 \qquad N_{4,2} = \frac{1900}{2600} \times 100 = 73$$

Table C.3 is the normalized trade-off matrix for this example.

Next we would revisit each step in the process to confirm our results. A review with other interested parties would also help to build confidence in our results. An examination of the sensitivity of the results to small changes in the quantification would tell us if our decision was robust. This is where an automated spreadsheet would be helpful. We might, for example, try quantifying criterion on a 10 is best, 9 is next best, 8 is next best basis to see if that would have made a difference in results. We could also change criteria weighting and observe its effect on the result. With only a few selection criteria, the relationship of selection criteria weighting and alternative quantification is easy. With eight, nine, or ten criteria the interplay is not obvious.

We could also conclude, based on these results, that any one of the three alternatives would be a successful design approach. That is, there is no dominant winner. Or we could use the results of the study to strengthen our alternative 1 design and thereby improve the quality of our decision. Table C.3 suggests that an improved (decreased) execution time would improve the score for alternative 1, as would reduced testing score (average cyclomatic complexity) and reduced memory use. Designers can reexamine these areas of the design to see if improvements to execution time, cyclomatic complexity, and memory use can be effected. These improvements, when factored into the trade-off study, may serve to make the alternative 1 score higher and the decision more robust.

The process described here is called a weighting factor approach. To make effective use of this process, the software engineer must use creativity, imagination, and common sense. Reviewing the process and results with those affected by the decision and soliciting their inputs and ideas will serve to make them feel committed to the decision and committed to making it the best decision.

Reviews

D.0 OBJECTIVES ■

The main objective of this appendix is to define and describe various forms of reviews and describe the purpose and the appropriate point in the development process to conduct each of these reviews. A second objective is to provide some guidance in preparing, conducting, or participating in reviews, audits, and walk-throughs. The major objectives of all reviews can be summarized briefly as follows: (1) to identify and expose errors and failures; (2) to acquaint/inform peers, leaders, and customers; (3) to improve overall product quality; (4) to impose an implicit collective or group standard on the item being reviewed, and (5) to force review item developers to produce a clearer and technically deeper item description.

D.1 INTRODUCTION ■

In this appendix we will regard the term *review* in its broadest context to include design reviews of the software product and all software development related products, inspections, and walk-throughs of various products at various stages of the development process. What we say here applies equally to formal and informal reviews. A formal review is one in which a signature indicating approval or acceptance by someone in authority is an implicit exit criterion. Many feel that there should be no informal reviews in a software development process.

Each review has a prescribed set of entrance criteria that the review item must meet before the review can be conducted. Our objective will be to indicate, in general terms, typical entrance criteria for each of the identified reviews. Each review has a structure, a specific set of attendees, and a degree of formality associated with it. Our objective will be to characterize briefly each review type in these terms. Each review has a finite product or expected result (exit criterion). Our objective is to describe the expected result in general terms for each identified review type.

The general purpose of software reviews is explicitly to identify and expose errors of omission or commission in the development of a software product or a related item as early in the development process as possible. In particular a review should identify and expose failures to conform to policy, quality, or design standards; failure to meet a specified performance requirement; and failure to provide a required function.

For each review item or product, there are specifications or other applicable standards to which the review item must conform. The applicable standards for comparison must be made available to reviewers before the review. It is then up to the review team, using prior personal experiences, to find deviations from applicable standards by studying and analyzing appropriate documentation, by asking questions, and by listening critically to oral presentations.

The review serves to make attendees, those involved in the preparation for the review, and those who read the review results more deeply aware of the details of issues and problems as well as the positive aspects of the item under review. Many reviews serve as a means to inform the customer and operators regarding some aspect of operation and performance as well as development progress.

By imposing the strict discipline of a formal review on an item, it has been shown that item quality can be improved substantively. Usually, a representative from a quality assurance group is present at the review to assure that quality standards have been observed. Software of high reliability (and high quality) is usually the result of a series of highly structured, strongly disciplined, formal review processes. The connection between review quality and software product quality has been widely established.

By subjecting a software product (particularly its design) to reviews, it has been found that an implicit design approach or standard is imposed on the overall product. This standard approach represents a group consensus or norm on how the product should be designed. For example, a new member of the development team is guided by peer reviews as well as by reviews by leadership to conform to a kind of ad hoc standard approach. If his or her designs are complex or esoteric, reviews will drive the designs to a simpler, readily understood solution. If the designs are too simple and clumsy, reviews will drive designs to be cleaner and more sophisticated. The review process has a leveling effect. The resulting product is usually more consistent in quality, complexity, and overall character. The ''genius'' design solutions are brought down to a more humble level, and the ''dumb'' designs are brought up to a more sophisticated level. In both cases overall product quality benefits.

In preparing for a design review presentation, the very act of preparing often surfaces questions and issues not previously recognized. The effort (including reviews) required to produce clear, easily understood communication products (presentation) is itself a driver to force better understanding and recognition of previously unrecognized patterns, consequences, relationships, and connections in the review item. In general, almost everything that happens in a review is positive. The negatives are the high cost of conducting reviews and the potential for giving the development team a bad reputation with what might, to an outsider, be termed a poor review—that is, a review that identifies and exposes many problems and issues.

D.2 FORMAL SOFTWARE-RELATED REVIEWS ■

There are four important software-related reviews: the software requirements review (SRR), the software preliminary design review (PDR), the software critical design review (CDR), and the test plan review (TPR). The SRR is conducted after system requirements have been allocated. The allocation of requirements to software, operator, and hardware is an essential step requiring concurrence and approval of customer and contractor or their equivalent. The purpose of the SRR is to solicit formal approval for the allocation of requirements to software and to solicit formal agreement from the software development team that software requirements are understood and acceptable.

The PDR is usually more a formal review and approval focused more on the software requirements specification than on the software design. Typically, the SRS is reviewed and approved and a preliminary or first-level design is reviewed and approved at the PDR. The purpose of the PDR is primarily for gaining formal approval of the software requirements specification. This formal review process marks the handoff of the design problem and design responsibility to the software development team. The entry criterion is (1) a complete specification of software requirements to the satisfaction of project quality standards and to applicable SDLC standards and (2) a preliminary design that must convince reviewers that there exists at least one design solution to the problem posed in the specification.

The purpose of the CDR is to obtain formal approval for the detail software design. The design is often manifested in the form of a program design language or detail flow charts. Many software development teams wait until successful completion (approval) at CDR before initiating coding of the design. The CDR entry criterion is completion of all detail designs including databases to the level of a program design language or detail flow charts. This review must be conducted by the software development team. It is made difficult because reviewers need a certain level of competence in software development methodology to be effective participants, and presenters must do an effective job in communicating.

The TPR is conducted when system acceptance criteria have been worked out with the customer and the plans for module testing and integration testing have been formulated. The system acceptance criteria, schedules for module delivery, the specific modules in each build, test facilities, etc., are described in this review, and an approval of the overall plan is sought. This review is conducted early in the development cycle when the focus is on design issues and therefore often does not get the attention it deserves. The critical item in the TPR is the acceptance test plan with criteria. This review is important because it involves customer and contractor concurrence on what constitutes acceptance of the final product. For software-dominant products, this agreement will be primarily a software development concern. For those systems that are not software dominant, there will be other parties involved and concerned. Since operators and operational timelines or scenarios are involved, the software development team is also involved.

The reviews described above are not peer reviews; they are formal and have clearly defined entrance and exit criteria. Preparation usually includes delivery of specifications and other supporting information in advance of the review. The actual review often involves formal, oral presentations and a formal response from the review team itemizing deficiencies and recommending changes, etc., that must be made before approval can be granted. Approvals and concurrence come from relatively high up in both contractor and customer organizations. Major elements of the contractor's development team are also involved in the approval process.

In summary, for every formal review there will be an entrance criterion that includes the following:

■ Documentation reflecting accomplishment of technical work
■ Documentation content criteria

- Documentation completion and quality criteria
- Oral presentation material completion and quality criteria
- Demonstration material completion and quality criteria

Attendees must include those empowered to grant approvals or designated by them to grant approvals as well as those qualified by experience and knowledge to assess the material provided and the presentations given and decide on the merits of the review item.

Often exit criteria are subjective and depend upon how well the presentations were delivered. But it is safe to say that well-written specifications prepared and delivered on time and a well-prepared oral presentation effectively and confidently delivered will go a long way toward obtaining the desired approvals. Exit criteria for formal reviews usually involve the number of allowable discrepancies identified and their severity. For example, the exit criteria for a given SRS may be as follows: (1) no more than ten open issues or defects are allowed and (2) an acceptable plan for closing out each issue is required before SRS approval will be granted. The approval is usually a sign-off by someone in authority indicating agreement that all acceptance criteria have been satisfied.

D.3 PEER REVIEWS (WALKTHROUGHS) ■

In the course of preparing for formal (nonpeer) reviews, it is often necessary to employ peer reviews and walkthroughs of material being prepared for the formal review. For example, the author of presentation storyboards being prepared for a PDR might seek a peer walkthrough before a review by software development leadership. It is always an excellent idea to have trusted peers or those with perhaps more experience or a higher level of responsibility sit in review of material that is being produced. The degree of formality is arbitrary. However, it is recommended that deficiencies always be noted and recorded and presenters be required to reply, in writing, to each deficiency. That is the professional way to conduct any review.

There is a formal peer walkthrough process that has been shown to be effective in software development. E. Yourdon [2] has produced an amusing and useful book describing the process. It is a worthwhile addition to the software engineer's reference library. A walkthrough is a type of review. An entry-level software engineer is most likely to encounter a walkthrough almost immediately upon joining a development team.

The term *walkthrough* usually applies to a peer group review of any item associated with a software product. However, it is not restricted to software product–related items. Some of the review items that might be the subject of a walkthrough include prototypes, specifications, design charts, listings, data flow diagrams, presentations, program design language, etc. A walkthrough may be conducted at any point in the software development cycle. The primary purpose of a walkthrough, as in any other review, is to improve the quality of the product. Walkthroughs are sometimes referred to as inspections, although some [1] would argue that inspections are more disciplined and structured than the walkthrough.

Advantages of a walkthrough are the same as for any review. A unique advantage of a walkthrough lies in the education of peers who may be assigned responsibility for the review item if the person who originally developed the review item leaves the project. Software walkthroughs are particularly valuable because the formal project reviews are spaced so far apart that the interim guidance provided by peer review is needed for continuity.

D.3.1 Types of Walkthroughs

Common forms of software walkthroughs include the following:

Specification Walkthrough: This form of walkthrough is concerned with the function and performance of the system and indirectly of the software. The objective is to identify poorly stated, vague, inadequate, ambiguous, and incorrect requirement specifications before the formal PDR.

Operational Timeline Walkthrough: Operational timeline or user interface walkthroughs are extremely useful in uncovering problems in HCI requirements and design. The purpose is to confirm understanding of how the system will operate in the field and to assess the adequacy of the procedures and interfaces provided for operators and users.

Design Walkthrough: The design walkthrough is conducted at several levels ranging from a system or architecture level to a detail procedural level. The objective is to uncover weaknesses, oversights, conceptual errors, mismatches, partitioning errors, etc., associated with the complete design (including databases) at every level.

Code Walkthrough: The code walkthrough, often referred to as code inspection, is probably the most discussed of the walkthroughs. Usually, the review items are pseudocode, design charts, or any other form of PDL and its associated program listings or source code. The purpose is to ensure that the PDL correctly interprets design requirements and that the source code correctly reflects the PDL. In cases where PDL is compiled directly, the code walkthrough is used to verify that the PDL correctly reflects the design requirements.

Test Walkthrough: The test walkthrough is also conducted at several levels ranging from the overall system test plan down to individual module test cases and procedures.

A few observations of considerable importance should be made here:

1. Walkthroughs, to be effective, must have some degree of formality. Those in attendance must have a sense of responsibility for review item quality. The formality of naming walkthrough attendees in the meeting report and requiring participant signatures for approvals, formal minutes in the project file, etc., all increase the sense of responsibility among reviewers.
2. Attendees must be selected for their ability to contribute to the quality of the review item. For example, a reviewer who understands the software requirements specifications related to the review item should attend PDL or code walkthroughs. Otherwise it will be assumed (perhaps incorrectly) that the requirements have been accurately interpreted and realized in the design. Someone who understands the basic system requirements should also be among the reviewers to assure that requirements, designs, and PDL are responsive to actual needs.
3. The use of walkthroughs must be adopted for the entire development process to be fully effective. Most development organizations that report success in the use of walkthroughs have applied them to all elements of the development process from requirements to code to testing and even to installation, maintenance, and training items.

As in any other review process, walkthroughs should have a specific entrance criterion. That is, a candidate review item must meet some minimum set of requirements before it can be the subject of a walkthrough. For example, for a code walkthrough, associated external documentation, design charts, and source code must be prepared, and the required number of copies must be ready for distribution to the review team. To check the entrance requirements for a walkthrough, in many cases a clerical check is all that is needed. However, it is unwise to permit a walkthrough to proceed without assuring that entrance requirements have been completely satisfied. Allowing a presenter to "wing it" is a serious breakdown of walkthrough discipline. Development organizations that use the walkthrough type of review usually have written standards for entrance criteria or at least guidelines for developing entrance criteria. The main reason for entrance criteria is to avoid a poor-quality walkthrough. It is important to make walkthroughs work to the benefit of the development process and the final products. The cost associated with a one hour walkthrough with ten participants can be as high as two labor weeks.

A walkthrough must always include a moderator or coordinator, a presenter, and a recorder. Other attendees should represent the following groups or interests: users, operators, maintenance, software development standards and practices, system level operational requirements, application area and specifications, architecture and design, and the presenter's peers. Some participants may fill multiple roles in a walkthrough.

The key person in the walkthrough is the coordinator or moderator. He or she is responsible for keeping the walkthrough focused on the review items and assuring that walkthrough rules (to be discussed shortly) are followed.

The recorder should have enough technical background to filter inconsequential comments or discussion items from the minutes and reduce walkthrough documentation to the key discussion facts and elements. It is especially important that the recorder review walkthrough material thoroughly before the meeting. The recorder will be busy taking notes during the review meeting.

The presenter is usually the individual responsible for the review item. Presentation preparation guidance for whatever medium is chosen can be found in Appendix A. To avoid the possibility that a presenter with a strong personality will intimidate or bluff reviewers, or vice versa, some organizations require that someone else present (defend) the review item. This approach forces the item originator to do a more thorough job of meeting entrance criteria and developing presentation material. It also serves to remove some of the defensive attitudes that often prevail in walkthroughs.

Other reviewers should be selected so that the review item can be exposed to concerns about maintainability, adherence to development standards and practices, design requirements, and operator interfaces. Still other reviewers should be selected to raise questions regarding meeting true operational, functional, and performance requirements. Clearly each walkthrough will have a unique set of needs regarding participants.

D.3.2   Rules for Conducting Walkthroughs

Some of the common rules that help ensure an effective walkthrough can be summarized and described as follows:

1. Duration of a walkthrough should be one hour as a norm. Occasionally, a two-hour walkthrough makes sense. The size of the review item will dictate the length of the walkthrough. A balance must be struck between the attention span of reviewers, other responsibilities of reviewers, and size of the review item.

2. Participants must commit not only to attendance at the actual walkthrough, but also to a review of the material and attendance at a follow-up meeting to hear the presenter's response to comments generated as a result of the walkthrough. If unable to make this kind of commitment, an invited participant should decline rather than try to fake it.

3. The presenter is responsible for preparation of all walkthrough materials on a schedule that permits time for adequate review before the actual walkthrough.

4. Coordinators must not allow the walkthrough to degenerate into a problem-solving session. Problems should be identified and concurrence obtained as to the existence of the problem. An identified problem will, of course, require some action on the part of the review item originator. This action should be carefully documented, and the presenter should have a clear understanding of the problem. It is often helpful for the walkthrough participants to help in formulating the wording of the required action to assure understanding. Often prepared forms help in standardizing actions. Response to these actions will be the basis for a follow-up walkthrough and a subsequent approval. Often actions are graded in terms of severity. Some actions may be only a suggestion that the presenter may ignore. It is customary to reply to actions of this genre. An action associated with a defect is something that cannot be ignored. This action must be addressed and closed to satisfy exit criteria. An open issue commonly refers to a situation in which more information and study are required before it is determined that some action must be taken.

5. All participants must commit to following the rules of the walkthrough. Especially, participants must agree to accept the authority delegated to the coordinator and the authority delegated to the walkthrough team in rejecting or approving the review item. The originator of the review item must treat the addressing of actions assigned as mandatory.

6. The walkthrough is designed to detect errors in the review item, not to correct them. Nor is the walkthrough designed to discipline or evaluate employees.

7. Some form of sign-off should be employed to make participants feel a sense of responsibility for the item under review.

The walkthrough team can take one of three possible courses of action after completion of a walkthrough: unqualified acceptance of the review item; conditional acceptance of the review item based on the commitment to complete certain actions; or rejection of the review item. The first and the third course of action rarely materialize in a real-world environment. Often, at the end of a walkthrough session, the second course of action is taken.

There are two possible ways that the second course of action can proceed. If actions to be completed are relatively minor, the walkthrough team may agree to let the coordinator or another member of the walkthrough team confirm that the actions have been completed successfully. In the case of more significant actions, a second walkthrough will be required to confirm that actions have been completed to the satisfaction of the walkthrough team.

Exit criteria are derived from considering completeness, integrity, correctness, and quality in relation to the review item. Completeness can often be confirmed by a clerical check of documentation—for example, confirming that data diagrams are properly labeled and there is a corresponding process specification or the data dictionary contains a definition for a term. Exit criteria associated with completeness are dictated by the characteristics of the review item.

Exit criteria associated with integrity focuses on correctly defining data elements, references, input and outputs, etc.—in other words, confirmation that all supporting documents are internally consistent.

Exit criteria associated with correctness focuses on accuracy issues. This means verification that operational needs and requirements have been accurately interpreted, designs accurately respond to requirements, and PDL and/or source code represent correct realizations of designs.

Exit criteria associated with quality usually relate to following standards and practices that have been accepted by the development team. Issues often turn on interpretations. The co-ordinator often has to arbitrate and must be careful not to let trivial issues of a standard interpretation for a pathologic case tie up a walkthrough. A representative from the quality assurance group can be a beneficial addition to the walkthrough team.

Finally, it is probably a good idea to evaluate the quality of the walkthrough itself. The results of such a quality review can be used to improve the overall walkthrough process and develop some measures of the value of the walkthrough process. It would be useful to know just how effective the reviews have been.

References

1. M. Fagan, "Advances in Software Inspections," *IEEE Trans. Software Engrg.* Vol. SE-12, No. 7, pages 744–751 (1986).
2. E. Yourdon, *Structured Walkthroughs*, Ed. 4, Yourdon Press Computing Series, Prentice-Hall, Upper Saddle River, N.J., 1989.

Index

t indicates table; *f* indicates figure